On the Cover: Fort Belvoir Travel Camp, Virginia. Photo courtesy of Fort Belvoir MWR.

TABLE OF CONTENTS

	Retail Order Form	Order online at militaryliving.com/store Call 703.531.8692 or email customerservice@militaryliving.com for Wholesale orders

Select Your Guide	Price	Qty
2020 RV, Camping & Getaways Travel Guide™ includes installation details, contact information, driving directions, GPS coordinates and maps	$42.60	
2020 Temporary Military Lodging Guide™ includes installation details, contact information, driving directions and maps	$39.95	
2020 U.S. Military Travel Guide™ includes installation details, lodging, RV & Camping and Space-A contact information by geographic region	$59.75	
2020 Overseas Travel Guide™ includes installation details lodging, RV & Camping and Space-A contact information	$19.95	
United States Military Road Map™ Paper Version (new smaller size, 39" X 26.75"folds to 4"x9")	$9.95	
Add Annual Digital Subscription to any book purchase (add on purchase only, cannot be purchased by itself)	$59.05	
Annual Digital Subscription-Standalone Purchase not to be combined with a book purchase	$81	
VA and WA Residents add applicable Sales Tax (VA 6%, WA 6.5% + your local tax rate), then Add shipping Fee—All Customers add shipping	$4.95	

Order Today and Travel on *Less per Day...The Military Way*™

Name:_____

Address:_____

Phone Number:_____

Credit Card Number: _____

Exp Date:_____ CVC:_____ MC___VISA___DISC___AMEX___

Email (Required for digital orders)_____

Important Information

Customers with a shipping address in Virginia or Washington State must add sales tax to book portion of the order. Virginia Tax Rate 7%, Washington State Tax Rate 6.5% + your local tax rate. Orders without sales tax or shipping added will either be returned unprocessed or will have a balance due upon shipping. Prices are subject to change without notice.

All Books and Maps are shipped by USPS Priority Mail or UPS Ground. Return Policy: Returns must be accompanied by the original invoice within 30 days of purchase and in original condition. Customer will pay the return shipping cost except in cases of our error. Once returned item is received, refund less shipping and handling will be issued via the original payment method. If the product was damaged in shipment, you must contact the shipping company directly to file a claim.

Form updated 8-21-2019

Travel on less per day...the Military way!™

2020 U.S. RV, Camping and Getaways Guide™

By

William "Roy" Crawford, Sr., Ph.D.
Chief Executive Officer,
Ann Cadell Crawford
Executive Vice President, Publisher
R.J. Crawford, President

Military Marketing Services, Inc.
and Military Living® Publications
333 Maple Avenue East, #3130, Vienna, VA 22180
www.militaryliving.com

Editor,
Trenna Nees

ALABAMA

Anniston Army Depot

Address: Anniston Army Depot, 7 Frankford Avenue, Bldg 94, Anniston, AL 36201-4199.
Information Line: C-256-235-7445, DSN-312-571-7445.
Main Base Police: C-256-235-6222. Emergencies dial 911.
Main Installation Website:
http://www.anad.army.mil/
Main Base Location: Nestled in the foothills of the Appalachian Mountains in northeast Alabama, Anniston Army Depot (ANAD) occupies over 25 square miles of land in the southeastern United States. ANAD is located between two major cities, Atlanta, GA, 90 miles to the east on Interstate 20 and Birmingham, AL, 60 miles west on Interstate 20. ANAD has been transformed into a state-of-the-market maintenance facility, earning its highly esteemed reputation as "The Tank Rebuild Center of the World."
Directions to Main Gate: From Birmingham Airport: Exit on Airport Highway and turn left to I-20 East/I-59 North. Take 1-285 North and take Exit 10B. Merge on I-20 East. Go approximately 55 miles. Proceed to Exit 179/Munford/Coldwater. Follow Coldwater sign and proceed to Hwy 78. Turn left onto Hwy 78 East seeing Anniston Army Depot sign on right. Turn right onto Bynum Cutoff Road and follow to stop sign. Turn left into right lane to Anniston Army Depot. Follow Road to Main Gate (Victory Drive). From Atlanta Airport: Exit on S Terminal Parkway. Take Airport Blvd/Camp Creek Parkway SW, merging onto I-20 West. Travel approximately 85 miles and take Exit 179/Munford/Coldwater. Follow directions as above from this point.
NMC: Birmingham, 53 miles west.
NMI: Dobbins ARB, 104 miles east.
Base Social Media/Facebook:
https://www.facebook.com/AnnistonArmyDepot

Base Social Media/Twitter:
https://twitter.com/AnnistonDepot
Clubs: Desoto Pastime Center, C-256-235-7160.
Places to Eat: Java Cafe, C-256-240-3526; Cafeteria, C-256-235-7643; Nichols Dining Facility, C-256-235-7127; Post Restaurant, C-256-235-4353.
Fitness Center: Physical Fitness Center, C-256-235-7170.
ITT/ITR: C-256-235-7170.
Military Museum: Museum Support Center ANAD, C-256-235-4243.
MWR: C-256-235-7170.
MWR Website:
https://anniston.armymwr.com/
Outdoor Recreation: C-256-235-6768. Offers Victory Valley Sports Complex, deer hunting, fishing, Desoto Splash Park, Desoto RV and Campground, equipment rental. Cone Reservoir, Jones Knob and White Oak Recreation Area offer a variety of outdoor recreational activities including fishing piers, boat launch, pavilions and walking trails.
Things To Do: Fishing, deer hunting, Talladega Super Speedway nearby and Cheaha State Park, Alabama's highest point.
Walking Trails: Available at outdoor recreation areas.

RV CAMPING & GETAWAYS

Desoto RV Park & Campground

Reservations: C-256-235-7549.
Recreation Security: Emergencies dial 911.
Reservations: Accepted and recommended up to one year in advance. Office hours 0700-1630 Mon-Fri. Check-in upon arrival. Maximum stay 14 days for short-term sites. Season of Operation: Year-round.
Eligibility: AD, NG, Res, Ret, DoD-Civ.
Camper/Trailer Spaces: RV Sites (8): E(30A/50A)/W/S, picnic table, grill, Wi-Fi. Rates: $16 daily, $300 monthly.
Tent Spaces: Primitive with no hookups, overflow area. Rates: $4 daily.
Support Facilities: Bathhouse, Dining Club, Equipment Rental, Exchange,

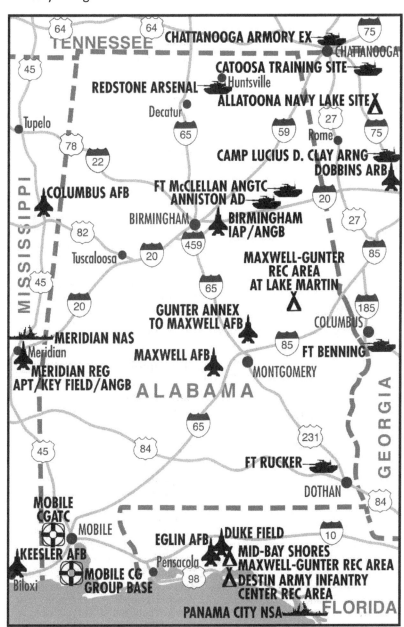

Fitness Center, Laundry, Park and Picnic Area.
Activities: Splash Park and Swimming, Lake Activities, Trails.
Credit Cards: Cash, Mastercard and Visa.

Restrictions: Pets allowed on leash. No firearms.
RV Driving Directions/Location: On Base. From Victory Drive: Turn right onto Harry M. Ayers Road (listed as Bynum Road on most online map services) directly across from the

Physical Fitness Center, Bldg 206. Proceed to the stop sign and turn right onto Beck Road. Trail runs directly into the RV Park.

Area Description: Located near Talladega Speedway and Motorsport Musuem. Area is surrounded by the Talladega National Forest and a short drive to the Cheaha State Park.

RV Campground Physical Address: Anniston Army Depot, Outdoor Recreation Office, Bldg 74, Anniston, AL 36201.

Engineer Beach RV Park & Campground

Address: Johnston Road, Fort Rucker 36362.

Information Line: C-334-225-1110, DSN-312-558-1110.

Main Base Police: C-334-255-2222.

Main Installation Website: http://www.rucker.army.mil

Main Base Location: The Army Aviation Warfighting Center, Fort Rucker, Alabama, is located in the southeast corner of Alabama. The post is located in Dale County. Fort Rucker is approximately 80 miles south of Montgomery and 20 miles northwest of Dothan. Florida's Gulf Coast lies 80 miles to the south. The communities of Enterprise, Daleville, and Ozark are west, south and east of the post, respectively and serve as our three main gates. The post covers about 64,500 acres of countryside in an area known as the "Wiregrass," named for a wild grass peculiar to the region.

Directions to Main Gate: Engineer RV Park and Campground is located at the end Johnston Road, just past the West Beach Singing Pines Cabins and minutes from the main gate.

NMC: Dothan, within city limits.

Base Social Media/Facebook: https://www.facebook.com/ftrucker

Commissary: C-334-255-6671.

Exchange Gas: Bldg 6600 Express & Pumps*, C-334-503-9338. Bldg 22305 Express & Pumps*, C-334-598-1295. Bldg 2906 Class 6, C-334-598-1137. *24-hour pumps.

Exchange: C-334-503-9044.

Places to Eat: Fort Rucker offers dining on base.

MWR: C-334-255-2100.

MWR Website: https://rucker.armymwr.com

Outdoor Recreation: Outdoor Recreation Service Center West Beach, Lake Tholocco, C-334-255-4305. Lake Tholocco recreation includes hunting, fishing outdoor equipment rental, and swimming.

Things To Do: "Dixie's Heartland" is sprinkled with fine freshwater fishing. Lake Tholocco is open for boating and summer swimming. Lifeguards on duty Memorial Day - Labor Day. Landmark Park has 60 acres of shady nature trails and boardwalks, picnic sites and historic restorations. Waterworld in Dothan is good family entertainment. Westgate Sports Complex/ Water World (3.0 MI), U.S. Army Aviation Museum, Outdoor Recreation at Lake Tholocco.

RV CAMPING & GETAWAYS

Engineer Beach RV Park & Campground

Reservations: C-334-255-4234/4035.

RV Website: https://rucker.armymwr.com/programs/lake-tholocco-lodging

GPS Coordinates: 31°24'35"N/85°42'60"W

Reservations: Accepted up to six months in advance on a first come, first serve basis. Cancellations require 48-hour notice to avoid fee. Telephone reservations only. Office hours 0730-1700 daily. Closed Thanksgiving, Christmas and New Year's Day. Discounts available to holders of Golden Age, Golden Access or America the Beautiful passports for campsites only. Check in between 1500-1700 hours at Bldg 24235, check out 1100 hours. Season of Operation: Year-round.

Eligibility: AD, NG, Res, Ret, and DoD-Civ (active and retired).

Camper/Trailer Spaces: Sites (43): Partial hookup E(110V/220/15/50A)/W, picnic table, short- and long-term sites. Rates: Short term $18 daily; long term $16 daily.

Tent Spaces: Primitive Sites (4): Rates: $10 daily.

Yurt, A Frame, Cabin, Apt, Spaces: Yurt (1): 12 foot canvas tent like structure complete with very comfortable bunk beds and linens, a dresser, lanterns and its own fire pit. Rates: $30 daily.

Support Facilities: A full range of support facilities available on base.

Activities: Enjoy the boat ramp, and a great mix of outdoor activities to include hunting, fishing, kayaking and canoeing, in addition to the breathtaking view of the scenic Lake Tholocco.

Credit Cards: Cash, Check, MasterCard and Visa.

RV Driving Directions/Location: Of Base: Located just past West Beach cabins at the end of Johnston Road.

Area Description: Located in the southeast corner of Alabama approximately 85 miles south of Montgomery and 90 miles north of the Florida Gulf Coast. The camping area is on the shores of 700-acre Lake Tholocco. Full range of support facilities available on post.

RV Campground Physical Address: Bldg 24235, Johnston Road, Fort Rucker, AL 36362.

Fort Rucker

Address: Novosel Street, Building 5700, Room 177, Fort Rucker, AL 36362.

Information Line: C-334-225-1110, DSN-312-558-1110.

Main Base Police: C-334-255-2222.

Main Installation Website: http://www.rucker.army.mil

Main Base Location: The Army Aviation Warfighting Center, Fort Rucker, Alabama, is located in the southeast corner of Alabama. The post is located in Dale County. Fort Rucker is approximately 80 miles south of Montgomery and 20 miles northwest of Dothan. Florida's Gulf Coast lies 80 miles to the south. The communities of Enterprise, Daleville, and Ozark are west, south and east of the post, respectively and serve as our three main gates. The post covers about 64,500 acres of countryside in an area

known as the "Wiregrass," named for a wild grass peculiar to the region.

Directions to Main Gate: Entry to the post is through three main gates: the Ozark Gate from the east, the Daleville Gate from the south and the Enterprise Gate from the west. Arriving from Ozark via Highway 231, turn onto Alabama 249 westbound (also known as Andrews Ave.) and continue driving until reaching the Ozark Gate. Arriving from Enterprise, take Rucker Boulevard to the Enterprise Gate. From Dothan, take Highway 84 West, turn right at the Daleville exit, continue driving on Daleville Avenue for about two miles and then enter the post at the Daleville Gate. The Faulkner and Newton Gates are only open from 4:30am-8:30pm, Mon-Fri and closed on the weekends and holidays.

NMC: Montgomery, 80 miles north.

NMI: Maxwell AFB, 94 miles northwest.

Base Social Media/Facebook: https://www.facebook.com/ftrucker

Base Social Media/Twitter: https://twitter.com/Ft_Rucker

Chapels: C-334-255-2989/3946.

Dental Clinic: C-334-255-2367.

Medical: Lyster Army Health Clinic, C-334-255-7000, DSN-312-558-7000.

Veterinary Services: C-334-255-9061.

Beauty/Barber Shop: Barber, C-334-598-4484/2498. Beauty, C-334-598-4315.

Commissary: C-334-255-6671.

Exchange Gas: Bldg 6600 Express & Pumps*, C-334-503-9338. Bldg 22305 Express & Pumps*, C-334-598-1295. Bldg 2906 Class 6, C-334-598-1137. *24-hour pumps.

Exchange: C-334-503-9044.

Financial Institutions: Armed Forces Bank, C-334-598-2402. Army Aviation Center Federal Credit Union, C-334-598-4411, C-1-800-448-4096.

Clubs: Mother Ruckers' Sports Bar, C-334-503-0396, Divot's Restaurant and Grille, C-334-255-0088, The Landing, C-334-255-0768,

Places to Eat: West Beach Snack Bar, C-334-255-4035, Larry's Real Pit BBQ, C-334-598-3772, Burger King, C-334-598-1140, Rucker Lanes Snack Bar, C-334-

255-0473. Popeyes, C-334-503-9044.
Charley's, C-334-503-9044. Subway, C-334-598-1330

Bowling: Rucker Lanes, C-334-255-9503.
Fitness Center: C-334-255-2296/3794.
Golf: Silver Wings Golf Course, C-334-255-0089.
Horse Stables: C-334-255-0021.
Hunting & Fishing Info: OTR, C-334-255-4305
ITT/ITR: C-334-255-2997/9517.
Library: Center Library, C-334-255-3885.
Outdoor Recreation: C-334-255-4305.
Military Museum: Army Aviation
Museum, C-334-598-2508.
Military Museum Website:
http://www.armyaviationmuseum.org/
MWR: C-334-255-2100.
MWR Website:
https://rucker.armymwr.com
MWR Facebook:
https://www.facebook.com/ftruckermwr
MWR Twitter:
https://twitter.com/FortRuckerMWR
Outdoor Recreation: Outdoor
Recreation Service Center West Beach,
Lake Tholocco, C-334-255-4305. Lake
Tholocco recreation includes hunting,
fishing outdoor equipment rental, and
swimming.
Swimming: SPLASH! Pool & Spray Park,
C-334-255-2096, Flynn Pool, C-334-255-1875, Lake Tholocco's West Beach
swimming area, C-334-255-9162, Indoor
Pool, C-334-255-3386. Supports PT,
instructional swim, various military
trainings and recreational activities for
adult and youth.
Theater: C-334-255-2408.
Things To Do: "Dixie's Heartland" is
sprinkled with fine freshwater fishing.
Lake Tholocco is open for boating and
summer swimming. Lifeguards on duty
Memorial Day - Labor Day. Landmark
Park has 60 acres of shady nature trails
and boardwalks, picnic sites and historic
restorations. Waterworld in Dothan is
good family entertainment. Westgate
Sports Complex/ Water World (3.0 MI),
U.S. Army Aviation Museum, Outdoor
Recreation at Lake Tholocco.
Walking Trails: Seven on-base walking
trails, Lake Tholocco walking trails,
Dothan Area Botanical Gardens.

RV CAMPING & GETAWAYS
Lake Tholocco

Reservations: C-334-255-4234/4035.
RV Website:
https://rucker.armymwr.com/programs/lake-tholocco-lodging
GPS Coordinates:
31°24'31"N/85°42'58"W
Reservations: Accepted up to six
months in advance on a first come, first
serve basis. Cancellations require 48-hour notice to avoid fee. Telephone
reservations only. Office hours 0730-1700 daily. Closed Thanksgiving,
Christmas and New Year's Day.
Discounts available to holders of Golden
Age, Golden Access or America the
Beautiful passports for campsites only.
Check in between 1500-1700 hours at
Bldg 24235, check out 1100 hours.
Cabins require two night minimum on
Fri-Sat. Must take both nights during
peak season. Short-term RV sites and
Cabins: Maximum stay 14 days.
Season of Operation: Year-round.
Eligibility: AD, NG, Res, Ret, and DoD-Civ (active and retired).
Yurt, A Frame, Cabin, Apt, Spaces: East
Beach Cottages and West Beach Cabins
(16): Two and three-bedroom, one
handicap accessible, four pet-friendly
with non-refundable deposit at West
Beach. Fully equipped kitchens,
furnished living space, SAT TV/DVD,
screened back porch with picnic table,
grill. Rates: $65-$95 daily. Note: Six new
cabins available.
Support Facilities: Auto Craft Shop,
Bath House, Beach, Boat Launch, Boat
Rental/Storage, Bowling, Cafeteria,
Chapel, Commissary, Convenience
Store, Diesel**, Equipment Rental,
Exchange, Fire Rings, Fishing Pier,
Fitness Center, Golf, Grills, Ice,
Laundry**, Marina, Mechanic/Auto
Repair, Mess Hall, Pavilion, Picnic Area,
Playground, Pool, Propane, Rec Center,
Rec Equipment, Restrooms*, Sewage
Dump, Showers, Snack Bar, Sports
Fields, Stables, Tennis Courts, Trails, *
Handicap accessible. **located off-base.
RV Storage: C-334-255-9020.

Activities: Bicycling, Fishing*, Golfing, Hiking, Hunting**, Paintball, Swimming, Waterskiing. *AL state and base permits required. **AL state permit, hunter's education card, and registration for weapons picture ID required.

Credit Cards: Cash, Check, MasterCard and Visa.

Restrictions: All personal firearms must be registered prior to bringing to gate. Pets allowed as long as they are not a nuisance or disturbance to other guests. No pets allowed in East Beach cabins. No smoking in cabins.

RV Driving Directions/Location: On Base. From the Daleville Gate: Come in Daleville Gate on 3rd Avenue and continue straight until it merges with Andrews Avenue. Take a Left on Christian Rd then a right on Johnston Rd. Follow Johnston Rd to the Outdoor Recreation Marina. Turn right and follow road to Outdoor Recreation Service Center. From the Enterprise Gate: Come in Enterprise Gate on Andrews Avenue and take a left on Lowe Field Rd. Take a right on Traffic Minder St, then a right on Christian Rd. Go left on Johnston Rd and follow to the Outdoor Recreation Marina. Turn right and follow road to Outdoor Recreation Service Center. From the Ozark Gate: Come in Ozark Gate on Andrews Avenue. Take a right on Whittaker Rd. Take a right on Christian Rd then a right on Johnston Rd. Continue ahead the Outdoor Recreation Marina. Turn right and follow road to Outdoor Recreation Service Center. Directions to East Beach: Leave Outdoor Recreation and turn left onto Johnston Rd. In .6 miles at the caution light, turn left onto Whittaker Rd. Follow Whittaker Rd for 2 miles then turn left onto Lake Rd. Cabins are on the right about a mile down Lake Rd.

Area Description: Located in the southeast corner of Alabama approximately 85 miles south of Montgomery and 90 miles north of the Florida Gulf Coast. The camping area is on the shores of 700-acre Lake Tholocco. Full range of support facilities available on post.

RV Campground Physical Address: Bldg 24235, Johnston Road, Fort Rucker, AL 36362.

Riding Stables RV Campsites

Reservations: C-334-255-0021.

RV Website: https://rucker.armymwr.com/programs/lake-tholocco-lodging

GPS Coordinates: 31°20'59"N/85°41'22.4"W

Reservations: Contact Riding Stables for reservation information.

Season of Operation: Year-round.

Eligibility: AD, NG, Res, Ret, and DoD-Civ (active and retired).

Camper/Trailer Spaces: Riding Stables RV Campsites (20): Rustic sites with water and electricity, grass. Dump station available at Engineer Beach RV Park & Campground on West Beach. Rates: $11 daily.

Support Facilities: Auto Craft Shop, Bath House, Beach, Boat Launch, Boat Rental/Storage, Bowling, Cafeteria, Chapel, Commissary, Convenience Store, Diesel**, Equipment Rental, Exchange, Fire Rings, Fishing Pier, Fitness Center, Golf, Grills, Ice, Laundry**, Marina, Mechanic/Auto Repair, Mess Hall, Pavilion, Picnic Area, Playground, Pool, Propane, Rec Center, Rec Equipment, Restrooms*, Sewage Dump, Showers, Snack Bar, Sports Fields, Stables, Tennis Courts, Trails.

Activities: Bicycling, Fishing*, Golfing, Hiking, Hunting**, Paintball, Swimming, Waterskiing. *AL state and base permits required. **AL state permit, hunter's education card, and registration for weapons picture ID required.

Credit Cards: Cash, Check, MasterCard and Visa.

RV Driving Directions/Location: Located on Hatch Road just south of the Silver Wings Golf Course.

Area Description: Located in the southeast corner of Alabama approximately 85 miles south of Montgomery and 90 miles north of the Florida Gulf Coast. The camping area is on the shores of 700-acre Lake

Tholocco. Full range of support facilities available on post.

Lake Martin Recreation Area

Address: Lake Martin Recreation Area, 350 Air Force Road, Dadeville, AL 36853.
Information Line: C-334-953-1110, DSN-312-493-1110.
Main Base Police: Emergencies dial 911.
Main Installation Website: http://www.maxwell.af.mil/
Main Base Location: Located on the beautiful Lake Martin Reservoir just one hour away from Montgomery.
NMC: Montgomery, 60 miles southwest.
NMI: Maxwell AFB, 60 miles southwest.
Exchange Gas: Commercial gas station within 3 miles.
Golf: Cypress Tree Golf Course, C-334-953-2209.
Marina: C-334-953-3509, C-256-825-6251.
MWR Website: http://www.42fss.us/index.html
Outdoor Recreation: Lake Martin/Gunter Recreation Area, C-256-825-6251. Lake Martin Recreation Area offers boating, camping, fishing, and hiking.
Swimming: Maxwell Pool, C-334-953-5956, Gunter Pool, C-334-416-7094 offers pool parties, lessons, swim teams.
Walking Trails: Hiking and jogging available.

RV CAMPING & GETAWAYS
Lake Martin Recreation
Reservations: C-334-953-3509. Rec Area Office, C-256-825-6251. Fax C-256-825-1805.
Recreation Security: C-256-825-4264
RV Website: https://www.lifeatthemax.us/lake-martin/
RV Email Address: mafbodritt@icloud.com
GPS Coordinates: 32°47'24"N/85°53'27"W

Reservations: Reservations required and accepted up to six months in advance for AD; 4 months in advance for all others. Payment due with cash or credit card at time of reservation. Telephone reservations accepted 1000-1630 Mon-Fri. Cancellations must be made 7 days prior to reservation to avoid fee. Cancellations within 48 hours of arrival forfeit one night's stay. Policy also applies to early departure. Check in 1500-1800 hours, check-out 1100 hours. RV Park: Maximum stay 30 days. Cabins, Mobile Homes, Trailers: Maximum stay 14 days.
Season of Operation: 1 Apr-30 Sep. Off season monthly rates available for RV spaces.
Eligibility: AD, NG, Res, Ret and DoD-Civ at Maxwell AFB.
Camper/Trailer Spaces: Sites (30): E(110/220V/30/50A)/S/W hookups, picnic table, grill. Rates: $25 daily, $135 weekly. Travel Trailers (4), sleeps 5, one bedroom with full bed, 1 set of bunk beds, table bed. Rates: $50-$65 daily depending on season. Park Trailers (2): Sleeps 6, one queen bed, bunk beds, pullout sofa and bathroom. Rates: $50-$75 daily depending on season.
Tent Spaces: Tent Sites (12): Water hookup, picnic table, grill. Rates: No Charge.
Yurt, A Frame, Cabin, Apt, Spaces: Mobile Homes: Three-bedroom (11), with one queen bed, two full beds, one bath, handicap accessible ramp, E(110/220V/30A)/S/W hookups, A/C, heat, TV. Linens not provided. Rates: $50-$75. Cabins (4): One-bedroom (2), sleeps 6, full bed, one set of bunk beds, loft area, one bath. Two-bedroom (2), sleeps 6, with queen size beds, one full size sleeper sofa, two baths. Trailers and cabins furnished with pillows, blankets, bedspreads, cable TV, kitchen appliances, coffee maker, grill. Must provide own sheets. Rates: $50-$85 daily depending on rank and season.
Support Facilities: Bathhouse, Beach, Boat Launch (fee), Boat Rental, Boat Storage, Fishing Pier, Gas, Golf, Grills, Ice, Laundry, Marina, Pay Phone, Picnic Area, Playground, Rec Equipment,

Restrooms*, RV Storage, Sewage Dump, Showers*, Trail. * Handicap accessible.
RV Storage: Long term RV storage available. Rates: $35/month. Limited availability. Rec area maintains a waiting list, C-256-825-6251.
Activities: Boating, Fishing*, Golfing, Hiking, Jogging, Sailing, Swimming, Volleyball, Water Skiing. *State license required for all lakes. Base permit required for Lake Maxwell.
Credit Cards: Cash, MasterCard and Visa.
Restrictions: Pets allowed in RV park but not in mobile homes or tent areas. No firearms allowed. No open fires, fireworks, BB guns, or bows and arrows.
RV Driving Directions/Location: Off Base. Located near Dadeville, southeast of Birmingham, northeast of Montgomery. From I-85 north of Montgomery: Take Exit 32/Tuskegee/Franklin exit. Turn left (north) on AL-49 to Stillwaters Road/Tallapoosa County Road 34. Proceed to the recreation area.
Area Description: Located on Lake Martin Reservoir near dam. Excellent fishing and a variety of water and woods-oriented activities. Recreation area includes areas for day picnicking and primitive camping. Voted "Outstanding Recreation Area of the Air Force". Full range of support facilities available at Maxwell AFB.
RV Campground Physical Address: 350 Air Force Rd, Dadeville, AL 36112. Mailing Address: Outdoor Recreation Reservations, 206 West Selfridge St, Maxwell AFB, AL 36112.
Maxwell Air Force Base
Address: Maxwell Air Force Base, 55 South Mitchell Street, 42 FSS/FSFR, Bldg 677, Montgomery, AL 36112.
Information Line: C-334-255-1110, DSN-312-558-1110.
Main Base Police: C-334-953-7222.
Main Installation Website: http://www.maxwell.af.mil/
Main Base Location: Maxwell AFB and Gunter Annex are located in Montgomery County, city of Montgomery, Alabama's state capitol, and in Alabama's historic River Region.

Montgomery's Tri-County area is rich in history and combines a small-town atmosphere with big city features.
Directions to Main Gate: Maxwell is located in the northwest corner of the city of Montgomery. Exits from Interstates 85 and 65 leading to the base are marked. Driving from the East: Take I-85 south and exit at Day Street/Exit 171. This leads directly to the front gate at Maxwell, 2-3 miles located on the right.
NMC: Montgomery, 1.5 miles southeast.
NMI: Fort Rucker, 94 miles southeast.
Base Social Media/Facebook: https://www.facebook.com/MaxwellAFB
Base Social Media/Twitter: https://twitter.com/MaxwellAFB
Chapels: C-334-953-2109. After Hours, C-334-953-7474.
Dental Clinic: C-334-953-7822.
Medical: Appointments, C-334-953-3368. Dental Clinic, Flight Medicine, Immunizations, Mental Health, Optometry, Pharmacy, Physical Therapy.
Veterinary Services: C-334-953-7357.
Beauty/Barber Shop: Stylique Salon, C-334-272-6785, Barber, C-334-409-0476.
Commissary: C-334-953-7175.
Exchange Gas: C-334-265-7773. *24-hour pumps.
Exchange: Mini-mall, C-334-265-7472, DSN-334-493-6681
Financial Institutions: Max Federal Credit Union, C-334-215-5472, C-334-271-7171, C-1-800-776-6776.
Clubs: Falcon's Nest Lounge, C-334-953-7820. Two Putts Bar and Grill, C-334-953-5885.
Places to Eat: Exchange Food Court, C-334-263-6044 offers Anthony's Pizza, Taco Bell, Charley's Steakery and Popeye's Chicken. Maxwell Bowling Center Snack Bar, C-334-953-5049, River Front Inn Dining Hall (active-duty only), C-334-953-5127, OTS Dining Facility, C-334-953-4723, Two Putts Bar & Grill, C-334-953-5885.
Bowling: C-334-953-5049.
Fitness Center: C-334-953-5953.
Golf: Cypress Tree Golf Course, C-334-953-2209/5885.

Horse Stables: C-334-953-7365.
ITT/ITR: C-334-953-6351.
Library: Gunter, C-334-416-3179.
Fairchild Library, C-334-953-2888
Marina: Lake Martin Recreation Area, C-334-953-5717.
Military Museum: U.S. Air Force Enlisted Heritage Hall, C-334-416-3202.
Military Museum Website: http://afehri.maxwell.af.mil/
MWR: C-334-953-7410.
MWR Website: https://www.lifeatthemax.us/
MWR Facebook: https://www.facebook.com/42dfss
Outdoor Recreation: Maxwell-Gunter Outdoor Recreation, C-334-953-6168. Offers a variety of outdoor recreation equipment as well as information regarding several local camping, boating, hiking and fishing areas. Lake Martin Recreation Area, C-334-953-5717.
Swimming: Maxwell Outdoor Pool, C-334-953-5956 offers two-flume 12-foot slides, pool side basketball goals, locker rooms and an eating area.
Things To Do: While here, be sure to visit the Civil Rights Memorial, Montgomery Zoo, W.A. Gayle Planetarium, Executive Mansion, State Capital Archives and History Museum, the first White House of the Confederacy and the Rosa Parks Museum.

RV CAMPING & GETAWAYS

Maxwell AFB FamCamp

Reservation/Contact Number Info: C-334-953-5161/6144.
RV Website: https://www.lifeatthemax.us/maxwell-famcamp/
GPS Coordinates: 2°22'9"N/86°22'10"W or 390 March Road, Maxwell AFB, AL 36112-6335.
Reservations: Accepted 90 days in advance. Office hours 0900-1700 Mon-Fri. Check in at FAMCAMP office, Bldg 1161. New laundry/bathhouse facility (3).
Season of Operation: Year-round.

Eligibility: AD, NG, Res, Ret and DoD-Civ.
Camper/Trailer Spaces: RV Sites (71): Paved with E(110/220V/15/30/50A)/S/W hookups, picnic table, grill, local and sat TV channels. Rates: $24 daily, $135 weekly, $450 monthly.
Tent Spaces: Primitive, open space, no hookups, fire pit. Rates: $5 daily.
Support Facilities: Auto Craft Shop, Bath House, Boat Launch, Boat Rental/Storage, Bowling, Chapel, Commissary, Convenience Store, Diesel**, Equipment Rental, Exchange, Fire Rings, Fishing Pier, Fitness Center, Gas, Golf, Grills, Ice, Laundry/Pay, Mechanic/Auto Repair**, Mess Hall, Pavilion, Picnic Area, Playground, Pool, Propane, Recreation Center, Restrooms*, Sewage Dump, Shoppette, Showers, Sports Fields, Stables, Tennis Courts, Wi-Fi. *Handicap accessible, **Off-Installation.
RV Storage: C-334-953-6144.
Activities: Bicycling, Boating**, Canoeing, Fishing*, Golfing, Jogging, Kayaking, Pool. *License required. **Vessel license to rent and operate motorized boats required.
Credit Cards: MasterCard and Visa.
Restrictions: Pets allowed but must be on leash at all times. Owners must clean up after pets. No firearms allowed. Quiet hours 2200-0700.
RV Driving Directions/Location: On Base. From the Maxwell Blvd Gate: Continue straight for 1.5 miles to where Maxwell Blvd changes to Kelly Street. Continue on Kelly until it ends. Turn right onto March Street and continue until seeing the FAMCAMP on the left. From the Day Street Gate: Continue through gate then turn left at first traffic light. At the next street, past the service station, turn left. Pass the BX and parking lot on the right. Go to the Yield sign and turn left onto Kelly Street. Continue for 0.25 miles and go right March Street to FAMCAMP on the left.
Area Description: Situated next to a small lake on base. Lake Martin and many other freshwater lakes and reservoirs located within 50 miles. Site

of Wright Brothers Flying School and historic airplanes which have been retired. Historic city of Montgomery has much to offer in the way of sightseeing. Full range of support facilities available on base.
RV Campground Physical Address: 1161 March Road, Maxwell AFB, AL 36112-5005.

Redstone Arsenal

Address: Redeye Road, Bldg 3338, Redstone Arsenal, AL 35898.
Information Line: C-256-876-2151, DSN-312-746-2151.
Main Base Police: C-256-876-2222.
Main Installation Website:
http://www.garrison.redstone.army.mil/
Main Base Location: Redstone Arsenal's 38,248 acres are bordered by Huntsville, Alabama, on the north and east with the Tennessee River forming Redstone's southern boundary. Huntsville is located in the northwest area of Alabama in Madison County.
Directions to Main Gate: From Birmingham travel north on I-65 for 80 miles. Turn right on I-565 and go 10 miles east toward Gate 9, Rideout Road. Turn right toward the installation gate. From Nashville: Travel 81 miles south on I-65. Take Exit 1, US-31/TN-7 toward Huntsville, Ardmore. Go Left on US-31/TN-7. TN-7 becomes TN-53. Travel 18 miles to Research Park Boulevard NW/AL 255 S. Turn right on Research Park Boulevard NW and travel 6 miles to Gate 9.
NMC: Huntsville, adjacent.
NMI: Anniston Army Depot, 105 miles southeast.
Base Social Media/Facebook:
https://www.facebook.com/teamredstone
Base Social Media/Twitter:
https://twitter.com/TeamREDSTONE
Chapels: C-256-842-2177.
Dental Clinic: C-256-876-9761
Medical: Hospital Military Treatment Facility, C-256-955-8888, C-256-876-4147, DSN-312-645-8888 ext 1152.
Veterinary Services: C-256-876-2441.

Beauty/Barber Shop: Barber, C-256-881-7409, Beauty Shop, C-256-883-1450.
Commissary: C-256-955-3517.
Exchange Gas: Bldg 3234 Express, Class 6 & Pumps, C-256-883-0367. Bldg 5215 Express, C-256-881-1521.
Exchange: C-256-883-6100, C-256-876-1064.
Military Clothing: C-256-882-1248.
Financial Institutions: Redstone Federal Credit Union, C-256-722-3740. Regions Bank, C-256-535-0196.
Clubs: Brooklyn's Sports Bar, C-256-876-6634; Firehouse Pub, C-256-842-0748; C-256-830-2582.
Places to Eat: The Overlook at Redstone, Soldatenstube, The Cliffs, Cafe Java, C-256-830-9227; C-256-842-0449; Weeden Mountain Grill, C-256-842-0012;, C-256-830-2582; Sparkman Center and Post Dining Halls, C-256-876-8741; Exchange Restaurants, C-256-881-3326; Burger King, C-256-881-0048.
Bowling: C-256-842-2695.
Fitness Center: Scott, C-256-955-6844. Sparkman, C-256-313-6091. Fox Army Health Center, C-256-955-8888.
Golf: The Links at Redstone Golf Course, C-256-842-7977.
Horse Stables: Outdoor Recreation Saddle Activity. C-256-876-4868/6854.
ITT/ITR: C-256-876-4531.
Library: C-256-876-4741.
Outdoor Recreation: C-256-876-4868.
MWR Phone Number: C-256-876-2073.
MWR Website:
http://www.redstonemwr.com/
MWR Facebook:
https://www.facebook.com/pages/Redstone-MWR/265439900161054
MWR Twitter:
https://twitter.com/redstonemwr
Outdoor Recreation: Redstone Arsenal Outdoor Recreation Services, C-256-876-4868/6854. Offers hunting, fishing, camping, skeet shooting, disc golf course, picnic areas, running trails, horse stables, car wash, storage.
Swimming: Redstone Aquatic Center, C-256-313-1201/1200, Outdoor Pool # 1, C-256-876-6605, Pool # 2, C-256-876-6758, Pool # 3, C-256-876-6713.

Things To Do: Visit the Alabama Space and Rocket Center, I-565 West of Huntsville. Huntsville, Alabama offers a wide variety of cultural activities, recreational opportunities and fine shopping. The Tennessee River, which borders Redstone Arsenal on the south, is a prime location for those who enjoy fishing, hunting, boating, water skiing, picnicking, hiking, biking, or enjoying the scenery.

Walking Trails: 1-6 mile running trails. Community trail is paved but there are also wooded areas, C-256-842-2574 for more information.

RV CAMPING & GETAWAYS

Redstone RV Park & Easter Posey Campground

Reservation/Contact Number Info: C-256-876-4868/6854, DSN-312-749-6854. Fax C-256-842-9134, DSN-312-788-9134.

Recreation Security: C-256-876-2222. Emergencies dial 911.

RV Website: http://redstone.armymwr.com/us/redstone/programs/outdoor-recreation

GPS Coordinates: Easter Posey: 34°35'16"N/86°41'01"W. Vincent Drive: 34°41'33"N/86°38'20"W

Reservations: Reservations recommended and accepted by telephone only. Office hours 0930-1730 hours daily. Check-in 1130 hours, check-out 1100 hours. Maximum stay 60 days on space available basis.

Season of Operation: Year-round.

Eligibility: AD, NG, Res, Ret, DoD-Civ.

Camper/Trailer Spaces: Easter Posey Campground: Hardstand (23), maximum 30', E(110V/20/30/50A)/W hookups, picnic table and grill. Summer Rates: $12 daily, $72 weekly. *Camping is allowed at Easter Posey only. Redstone RV Park: Paved pads (70), pull-thru, full hookups with CATV access, bathhouse, Wi-Fi. Rates: $20 daily, $120 weekly. Note: Two sites available for overnight only.

Tent Spaces: Camping allowed at Easter Posey Campground.

Support Facilities: Auto Craft Shop, Basketball Court, Bathhouse, Boat Launch, Boat Rental, Bowling, Cafeteria, Chapel, Commissary, Convenience Store, Disc Golf Course, Equipment Rental, Exchange, Fishing Pier, Fitness Center, Gas, Golf, Grills, Horseshoes Pit, Ice, Laundry/Pay, Mechanic/Auto Repair, Pavilions, Picnic Area, Playground, Pool (Memorial Day-Labor Day), Propane, Rec Center, Restrooms, RV Storage, Sewage Dump, Shoppette, Showers, Sports Fields, Tennis Courts, Trails, Volleyball Court.

RV Storage: C-256-842-7540.

Activities: Boating, Fishing*, Golfing, Hunting*, Jogging, Tennis. *See Hunting & Fishing.

Credit Cards: MasterCard and Visa.

Restrictions: Pets allowed on leash. Children must be escorted to the bathhouse. Firearms must be registered with Security.

RV Driving Directions/Location: On Base. From I-565: Take exit 14 toward Gate 9/Redstone Arsenal heading south and go 1.2 miles (clearing the gate and inspection in a right lane; then moving to the left-most lane after the gate). Turn left at the first light at Goss Road. Follow road for approximately .25 miles as it turns north and runs along the golf course. Continue on the road as it turns right. Follow Goss Road straight, heading east for 1.9 miles. Turn right onto Vincent Drive for 5 miles. Go right onto Spartan Drive for .2 miles. Take a right onto Nike Street and follow signs to RV Park. Easter Posey: Limited Gate access from Gate 10 on weekends. Guests should ask for directions and which gate to use at time of reservation.

Area Description: Situated along the Tennessee River in northern Alabama. U.S. Space and Rocket Center, Huntsville, AL near I-565. Full range of support facilities available on post.

RV Campground Physical Address: Outdoor Recreation, Bldg 5139, Sportsman Dr, Redstone Arsenal, AL 35808.

ALASKA

Birch Lake Recreation Area

Address: 354 Force Support Squadron, MWR, 354 Broadway Street, Eielson AFB, AK 99702.
Information Line: C-907-377-1110.
Main Base Police: Emergencies dial 911.
Main Installation Website:
http://www.eielson.af.mil/
Main Base Location: The camp is nestled in the wilderness on the shore of Birch Lake, about 35 miles south of Eielson AFB on Richardson Hwy/AK-2 at mile post 305.2.
NMC: Fairbanks, 55 miles north.
NMI: Eielson AFB, 35 miles northeast.
Base Social Media/Facebook:
https://www.facebook.com/EielsonAirF orceBase
Commissary: Approximately 6 miles to Eielson AFB Commissary, C-907-377-2173 ext 3009.
Exchange Gas: Self service pumps availalble 24 hours daily at Eielson gas station, C-907-372-5391.
Exchange: Approximately 6 miles to Eielson AFB Exchange facilities, C-907-372-1640.
Places to Eat: Burger King, Thai Cuisine Restaurant, The Pump House, Gambardella's Pasta Bella and more available at nearby at Eielson and Fairbanks.
Golf: Golf Driving Range, C-907-377-1232
Hunting & Fishing Info: Call Outdoor Adventure Program for more information, C-907-377-1232. Fishing license required. Birch Lake is stocked every year with RainbowTrout, land locked Salmon, Grayling and Arctic Char. Ice Fishing available in the winter season.
ITT/ITR: C-907-377-2722/2642.
MWR: C-907-377-1232
MWR Website:
http://www.eielsonforcesupport.com/
MWR Facebook:
https://www.facebook.com/pages/Eiels on-Outdoor-Recreation/1424792344435232
Outdoor Recreation: 354th Force Support Squadron MWR, C-907-377-1075. Birch Lake is stocked every year with rainbow trout, land locked salmon, grayling and Arctic Char.
Things To Do: Birch Lake Recreation Area offers the closest thing to a beach in interior Alaska offering fishing, camping, pontoon party boats, paddle boats, aqua cycles, and pavilion area for parties. The Birch Lake Lodge is a great place to cool off and play games after a long day of sunbathing. Some bait and tackle can be purchased at the Boat House. Activities include boating, canoeing, water skiing, fishing, berry picking, wading and barbecuing. Enjoy snowmobile trips, ice fishing and snowshoe walks during the winter months.
Walking Trails: The area abounds with hiking opportunities at Eielson AFB and nearby Fairbanks.

RV CAMPING & GETAWAYS
Birch Lake Recreation

Reservation/Contact Number Info: C-907-377-1317/1232.
Recreation Security: C-907-377-5130.
RV Website:
http://www.eielsonforcesupport.com/i ndex.php/recreation/odr#odr--birch-lake-
RV Email Address:
info@eielsonservices.com
GPS Coordinates:
64°19'12"N/146°39'3"W
Reservations: Accepted. Office hours 1000-1800 Thur-Mon or visit the website for information. Check-in 1300 hours, check- out 1100 hours. Call for cancellation policy. Note: Outdoor Adventure Program offers weekend cabin rental on select weekends along with ice fishing and snowmobile trips during winter season, C-907-377-1232.
Season of Operation: Memorial Day-Labor Day.
Eligibility: AD, NG, Res, Ret and DoD-Civ.

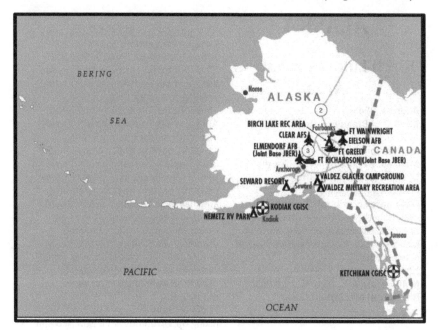

Camper/Trailer Spaces: RV Sites (36): Gravel, any size, E(110/220V/30A) hookups; picnic tables and grills available. Rates: $22 daily. No dump station on campground. Equipped for one RV's only.

Tent Spaces: Primitive (7): No hookups. Rates: $15 daily.

Yurt, A Frame, Cabin, Apt, Spaces: Cabins (23): Two Person Cabins (4), sleeps 2, two twin beds, refrigerator. Rates: $30 daily. Standard Family Cabins (16): Provide either a single room or a separate bedroom floor plan, and up to four sleeping areas, coffee pot, stove, refrigerator, picnic area, barbecue grill, fire ring. Some cabins have a screened in patio area and wood burning heaters. No indoor plumbing. Rates: $60 daily. Super Deluxe Cabins (2): One-bedroom, loft, living/dining area with a futon and fireplace, one full bath with shower, and toilet. Rates: $90 daily. Note: Limited cooking facilities. All cabins offer picnic tables and grills. Must bring cookware, linens and towels. Most cabins are dry. Drinking water is available at the lodge. A bathhouse is available on-site. Several cabins have wood-burning stoves.

Moose, eagles and beaver have been spotted in the area.

Support Facilities: Bathrooms, BBQ Grills, Beach, Boathouse, Lodge with TV/Games, Fireplaces (firewood available for purchase during summer), BBQ Grills, Picnic Tables, Snack Bar, Showers.

RV Storage: None.

Activities: Fishing*, Camping, Pontoon Party Boats, Paddle Boats, and Aqua Cycles available for rent. Pavilion area for parties. *See Hunting & Fishing.

Credit Cards: MasterCard and Visa.

Restrictions: Pets allowed on leash. No firearms permitted in sight. All firearms must be secured in vehicle. Check camper pad size when making reservations. Numerous water faucets throughout the camp supply potable water.

RV Driving Directions/Location: Off Base: Thirty-eight miles south of AFB. On southwest side of Richardson Highway (AK-2) at mile post 305.2. Travel southwest at Recreation Area sign and drive one mile to entrance. Check in at Boat House.

Area Description: The Recreation Area is 804 acres located on spring-fed Birch

Lake which is stocked with rainbow trout and silver salmon. The area provides a rustic base for enjoying the state's unlimited outdoor recreational resources. Spectacular mountain scenery and unsurpassed fishing and hunting are in the general area. A full range of support facilities is available at Eielson AFB.

Eielson Air Force Base

Address: 2631 Wabash Avenue, Eielson AFB, AK 99702-1720.
Information Line: C-907-377-1110, DSN-317-377-1110.
Main Base Police: C-907-377-5130, DSN-317-377-2036.
Main Installation Website:
http://www.eielson.af.mil/
Main Base Location: Eielson AFB is located 26 miles southeast of Fairbanks, in the interior of Alaska, about 110 miles south of the Arctic Circle.
Directions to Main Gate: Eielson is serviced by the Fairbanks International Airport. There are no shuttles or busses to Eielson. Rental cars are available at the airport but will not be reimbursed by the government. When leaving the airport proceed down Airport way to the Richardson Highway and bear right. Eielson AFB on the left approximately 25 miles down the road.
NMC: Fairbanks, 26 northwest.
NMI: Fort Wainwright, 25 miles northwest.
Base Social Media/Facebook:
https://www.facebook.com/EielsonAirForceBase
Chapels: C-907-377-2178.
Dental Clinic: C-907-377-1846.
Medical: 354 Medical Group Clinic, C-907-377-1847, DSN-317-377-1847. Veterinary Services: C-907-361-3013.
Beauty/Barber Shop: Beauty Shop, C-907-372-3265, Barber, C-907-372-2290.
Commissary: C-907-377-2173.
Exchange Gas: Bldg 3338 Express, C-907-372 1231.
Exchange: C-907-372-1640.
Clubs: Yukon Club, C-907-377-5219, Club 354 Enlisted Lounge, C-907-377-2734, MIG Alley Officer's Lounge, C-

907-377-2051. 354 Sportsbar C-907-377-2228
Places to Eat: Burger King, C-907-372-2158. Charley's, C-907-372-2155. Papa John's Pizza, C-907-372-4141. Lane 21 Snackbar/Temporary DFAC, C-907-377-5154. Subway, C-907-372-1166. Yukon Club, Bonfire Grill & Restaurant, C-907-377-5219. Sunrise Bagel & Espresso, C-907-372-1410.
Bowling: Arctic Night Lanes Bowling Center, C-907-377-1129.
Fitness Center: C-907-377-1925.
Golf: Driving Range, C-907-337-1232.
Hunting & Fishing Info: Available at Bear Lake and Birch Lake.
ITT/ITR: C-907-377-2722.
Library: C-907-377-3174.
MWR: C-907-377-1075.
MWR Website:
http://www.eielsonforcesupport.com/
MWR Facebook:
https://www.facebook.com/EielsonFSS/
MWR Twitter:
https://twitter.com/EielsonFSS
Ski Area: C-907-377-1232. Offers cross country skiing, sledding, ski lift, equipment rental available.
Outdoor Recreation: Eielson Air Force Base Outdoor Recreation Services, C-907-377-1232. Offers par course, paintball course, skeet & trap range, sled hill, skiing, camping, RV storage, equipment rental.
Skeet Range Name and Phone Number: Skeet & Trap Range, C-907-377-5338.
Swimming: C-907-377-1232, indoor pool for open swim and lap swim.
Things To Do: Enjoy Denali National Park, historical Fairbanks, hunting, fishing and skiing in season. All outdoor activities are available both on and off base.
Walking Trails: Hiking info available through Outdoor Recreation.

RV CAMPING & GETAWAYS
Bear Lake FamCamp

Reservation/Contact Number Info: C-907-377-1232/1317, DSN-907-377-1232/1317. Fax C-907-377-5275. Recreation Security: C-907-377-5130.

RV Website:
http://www.eielsonforcesupport.com/index.php/recreation/odr
RV Email Address:
eielson.odr@gmail.com
GPS Coordinates:
64°42'17"N/147°7'3"W
Reservations: Accepted for PCS in/out only. All others first come, first serve. Check in at Outdoor Recreation, Bldg 1377 between 1000-1800 hours, check-out 1100 hours. Call to confirm rates. Season of Operation: May-September.
Eligibility: AD, NG, Res, Ret and DoD-Civ.
Camper/Trailer Spaces: RV Sites: Dirt (41), pull-through, any size, E(110V/20A)/W hookups. Rates: $18 daily.
Tent Spaces: Primitive (10): Water hookups only. Rates: $13 daily.
Support Facilities: Restrooms, Showers, Dump Station, Picnic Tables, Playground. Full range of support facilities available on base, approximately two miles away.
RV Storage: C-907-377-1232.
Activities: Biking, Canoeing, Fishing, Hiking, Kayaking, Pavilion rental available.
Credit Cards: MasterCard and Visa.
Restrictions: Pets allowed on leash. No firearms permitted at camp and must be secured in vehicle. No mail delivery available.
RV Driving Directions/Location: On Base. On eastside of Richardson highway AK-2 at mile post 341. Exits to Eielson AFB clearly marked. Enter main gate and take first left onto Transmitter Road. Bear Lake is approximately one mile down on right.
Area Description: Located in the center of Alaska near the city of North Pole. Provides base for enjoying state's unlimited outdoor recreational resources. Spectacular mountain scenery; unsurpassed fishing and hunting in general area. Denali National Park approximately 130 miles southwest.
RV Campground Physical Address: Bear Lake Pavilion and FAMCAMP, Eielson Air Force Base, AK 99702-1895.

Elmendorf Air Force Base

Address: 8535 Wewak Drive, JBER, AK 99506.
Information Line: C-907-552-1110.
Main Base Police: C-907-552-3421.
Main Installation Website:
http://www.jber.af.mil/
Main Base Location: JBER AFB is located in the south-central part of Alaska. The beautiful and diverse city of Anchorage, Alaska is immediately outside the base. This part of Alaska is sometimes referred to as "The Banana Belt" of Alaska.
Directions to Main Gate: From the Airport: There are two terminals, the South (Main) terminal and the North (International) terminal. Be sure your sponsor will meet you at the airport, otherwise you will have to hire a taxi from there to the base (~$50). There is no shuttle service from the airport to the base. Get a receipt for the taxi fare for travel voucher purposes. This facility is located off Glenn Highway (AK-1) adjacent to north Anchorage. Take Boniface Parkway Exit. Take either Elmendorf Access Road or North Post Road. The base is adjacent to Fort Richardson and is now Joint Base Elmendorf-Richardson (JBER). The base is approximately 10 miles from the airport.
NMC: Anchorage, 2 miles southeast.
NMI: Fort Richardson, adjacent.
Base Social Media/Facebook:
https://www.facebook.com/JBERAK?v=wall
Base Social Media/Twitter:
https://twitter.com/JBER_Official
Chapels: C-907-552-4422.
Dental Clinic: C-907-580-6260/5010.
Medical: JBER Hospital Information, C-907-580-6260/3128, DSN-317-580-6260.
Veterinary Services: C-907-384-2865/2872.
Beauty/Barber Shop: Barber, C-907-753-1344. Beauty, C-907-753-1215.
Commissary Phone Numbers: C-907-580-4425/4863.

Exchange Gas: Bldg 3827 Class 6 & Pumps, C-907-753-0323. Bldg 5201 Class 6, C-907-753-1291/1210. Bldg 560 Class 6, C-907-428-3190. Troop Store, C-907-428-0042.
Exchange: C-907-753-4422/6275.
Financial Institutions: First National Bank of Anchorage, C-907-753-1170, Alaska USA Federal Credit Union, C-907-563-4567, C-1-800-525-9094. Bank/Currency Exchange: First National Bank; Bldg 3-850, Hours: 1000-1700, C-907-777-4362, 2-3 miles away.
Clubs: The Permafrost Pub, C-907-384-7619. Enlisted Club, C-907-753-5190, 907 Sports Bar & Grill, C-907-384-7619. Fire Pit, C-907-384-7619.
Places to Eat: Food Court, C-907-723-4123. American, C-907-723-4123. Anthony's Pizza, C-907-725-4124. Manchu Wok, C-907-723-7458. Burger King, C-907-738-6228. Popeyes, C-907-738-6228. Subway, C-907-725-7386. Taco Bell, C-907-725-7368. Baskin Robins, C-907-725-4124.
Bowling: Polar Bowl, C-907-753-7467.
Fitness Center: Buckner Fitness Center, C-907-384-1308, Elmendorf Fitness Center, C-907-552-5353.
Golf: Eagle Glen Driving Range, C-907-552-3821. Moose Run Golf Course, C-907-428-0056.
Horse Stables: C-907-552-3998.
Hunting & Fishing Info: C-907-854-1734.
ITT/ITR: C-907-753-2378
Library: C-907-384-1648.
MWR: C-907-552-2468.
MWR Website:
http://www.jberlife.com/
MWR Facebook:
https://www.facebook.com/JBERLife
Ski Area: Hillberg Ski Area, C-907-552-5026, offers tubing, alpine skiing, snowboarding, ice skating, equipment rentals, ski and snowboard lessons, dog sledding, ice fishing tournaments.
Outdoor Recreation: C-907-552-2023. Offers both winter and summer recreational items for a nominal fee. You can choose from items such as fishing gear, picnic supplies, cross-country skis, camping accessories, campers, sleds, snow blowers, and ice skates.

Swimming: BPFC Pool, C-907-384-1301 offers lap swim, pool parties, water aerobics, family swim.
Things To Do: Alaska's largest city boasts many cultural events, museums, sporting events and restaurants in a spectacular setting. There are many outdoor activities to enjoy locally. The Anchorage Bowl, which is a world class ski resort, is also nearby for the enjoyment of visitors. Warrior Zone, Lounge and Lounge games, 907-384-9006. Warrior Xtreme Paintball Course, 907-384-6245.
Walking Trails: 2-mile to 9-mile walking/running trails.

RV CAMPING & GETAWAYS
Elmendorf AFB FamCamp

Reservation/Contact Number Info: C-907-552-2023.
RV Website:
https://jberlife.com/campgrounds/
GPS Coordinates:
61°14'17"N/149°45'6"W or 5970 Zeamer Ave, Elmendorf, AK 99506.
Reservations: No advance reservations. All spaces first come, first serve. Office hours 1100-1800 Mon-Fri, 1000-1800 Sat and Sun. Closed holidays. Self-service check-in with envelopes and pay box at campground entrance at information board. Camp Host available at Space 38. Check-out 1200 hours. To pay by credit card, go to the Outdoor Recreation Office. Maximum stay 14 days. Extensions based on availability.
Season of Operation: May-Sep. Self-contained dry camping during Winter months.
Eligibility: AD, NG, Res, Ret, Dep, DoD/NAF-Civ, and Guests.
Camper/Trailer Spaces: Gravel (60), E(110V/30A)/W hookups. Peak Season Rates: $30 daily; Winter Rate: $27 daily.
Tent Spaces: Primitive (10), no hookups. Rates: $12 daily.
Support Facilities: Auto Craft Shop, Bath House, Boat Rental, Chapel, Commissary, Exchange, Fitness Center, Gas, Golf, Grills, Laundry, Playground, Rec Equipment, Restrooms, RV Storage, Sewage Dump, Shoppette, Showers,

Shuttle Bus, Snack Bar, Sports Fields, Stables, Telephones, Tennis Courts, Trails.

RV Storage: C-907-552-2023. Minimum one month.

Activities: Canoeing, Equestrian Riding, Fishing*, Golfing, Paintball, Skeet Trap, Skiing, Swimming (indoor). *State license required.

Credit Cards: Cash*, Check*, MasterCard, Visa. *Self-pay envelopes only.

Restrictions: Pets must be leashed (no longer than six feet) and not left unattended. Maximum two pets per site. Owners must clean up after pet immediately. No firearms. Quiet hours 2200-0800 hours.

RV Driving Directions/Location: On Base. North of Anchorage from Glenn Highway AK-1 east or west: Enter AFB at Boniface or Muldoon Gates. The AFB is on the northeast corner of Anchorage and is adjacent to Fort Richardson. Follow signs. The FamCamp is adjacent to hospital.

Area Description: Located near the city of Anchorage on the state's south-central coast at the head of Cook Inlet in a low-timbered area surrounded by mountains. The camp provides a good base for enjoying spectacular and varied sightseeing and outdoor recreational opportunities. Full range of support facilities available on base.

RV Campground Physical Address: JBER Elmendorf, 5970 Zeamer Ave, JBER, AK 99506.

Fort Richardson

Information Line: C-907-384-1110, DSN-317-384-1110.

Main Base Police: C-907-552-3421. Emergencies dial 911.

Main Installation Website: http://www.jber.af.mil/

Main Base Location: Joint Base Elmendorf-Richardson (JBER) is located in South-central, Alaska, amid picturesque, majestic, snow-capped mountains, lakes, rivers and glaciers. The area abounds with wildlife. Nearby is the largest city in Alaska, Anchorage, with a population of over 282,000. JBER is 2,090 miles north of Seattle, Washington, and 300 miles south of Fairbanks, Alaska.

Directions to Main Gate: Directions from Anchorage International Airport (approx. 30 min): Exit airport on International Airport Road. Left at C Street. Right onto 6th Avenue (becomes the Glenn Hwy). Exit at JBER Left at the top of the ramp. Proceed through the main gate. You'll need ID and vehicle tags/proof of insurance.

NMC: Anchorage, eight miles southwest.

NMI: Elmendorf AFB, adjacent.

Base Social Media/Facebook: https://www.facebook.com/JBERAK?v=wall

Base Social Media/Twitter: https://twitter.com/JBER_Official

Chapels: C-907-552-4422.

Dental Clinic: C-907-580-6260/5010.

Medical: C-907-580-6260/3128, DSN-317-580-6260.

Veterinary Services: C-907-384-2865/2872.

Beauty/Barber Shop: Barber, C-907-753-1344. Beauty, C-907-753-1215.

Commissary: C-907-580-4425/4863.

Exchange Gas: Bldg 3827 Class 6 & Pumps, C-907-753-0323. Bldg 5201 Class 6, C-907-753-1291/1210. Bldg 560 Class 6, C-907-428-3190. Troop Store, C-428-0042.

Exchange: C-907-428-3190

Financial Institutions: Alaska USA Federal Credit Union, C-907-563-4567, C-1-800-525-9094. First National Bank of Anchorage, C-907-753-1170.

Clubs: 907 Sports Bar & Grill, C-907-384-7619. Fire Pit, C-907-384-7619.

Places to Eat: Food Court, C-907-723-4123. American, C-907-723-4123. Anthony's Pizza, C-907-725-4124. Manchu Wok, C-907-723-7458. Burger King, C-907-738-6228. Popeyes, C-907-738-6228. Subway, C-907-725-7386. Taco Bell, C-907-725-7368. Baskin Robins, C-907-725-4124. ; Phillips International Inn, C-907-428-7606 is within driving distance. Arctic Chill Club, C-907-384-7619, Wilderness Inn, C-907-384-1704, Moose Run Snack Bar, Gold Rush Inn, C-907-384-6852, Fairways, C-

907-552-8529. T-Bar Grill located at the Hillberg Ski Area. Paradise Cafe, C-907-552-8529 and Warehouse Grill, C-907-753-3131/0777 are also on base.
Bowling: Polar Bowl, C-907-552-4108.
Fitness Center: C-907-384-1308.
Golf: Moose Run Golf Course, C-907-428-0056, Eagle Glen Driving Range at Elmendorf AFB, C-907-552-3821.
Horse Stables: C-907-552-3998.
Hunting & Fishing Info: C-907-552-2023.
ITT/ITR: C-907-753-2378, DSN-317-552-0297.
Library: C-907-384-1648.
MWR: C-907-552-2468.
MWR Website:
http://www.jberlife.com/
MWR Facebook:
https://www.facebook.com/JBERLife
Ski Area: Hillberg Ski Area, C-907-552-5026, offers tubing, alpine skiing, snowboarding, ice skating, equipment rentals, ski and snowboard lessons, dog sledding, ice fishing tournaments.
Outdoor Recreation: JBER-Richardson Outdoor Recreation, C-907-384-1475. Offers cross country skiing, expedition rentals, indoor rock climbing, dog sled trips, raft rentals, snowshoe geocaching, snow machine trips and snowboarding trips. Outdoor Adventure Program Outfitting, C-907-552-4599 offers kayaking, camping, fishing, boat rentals at Otter Lake, paintball, skeet & trap, archery ranges and a wide variety of equipment rentals.
Swimming: Swimming pool is available on base, C-907-384-1301.
Things To Do: The Earthquake Park in Anchorage commemorates those lost in the earthquake of 1964, while towering mountains, wildlife parks, the Cook Inlet and great downhill skiing welcome visitors nearby. Warrior Zone, Lounge and Lounge games, 907-384-9006. Warrior Xtreme Paintball Course, 907-384-6245.
Walking Trails: Contact Outdoor Recreation for more information.

RV CAMPING & GETAWAYS
Blue Spruce RV Campground
Reservation/Contact Number Info: C-907-552-2023 option 3.
Recreation Security: C-907-384-0820.
RV Website:
http://www.jberlife.com/fun/outdoor-recreation/famcamp/
GPS Coordinates:
61°15'36"N/149°43'27"W
Reservations: No reservations accepted. All sites are a first come, first serve basis. Prioroty given to AD on PCS orders. JBER-E daily Office hours 1100-1800 Mon-Fri, 1000-1800 Sat-Sun. Check-in with Camp Host 0900-1900 hours. If Camp host is not available, guests should check-in at JBER Richardson Outdoor Recreation, Bldg 7301, next business day.
Season of Operation: May-Sept.
Eligibility: AD, NG, Res, Ret and DoD/NAF-Civ.
Camper/Trailer Spaces: RV Sites (45): Gravel, pull-thru, any size, E(110V/30A)/S/W hookups, picnic table, bbq pit. Rates: $33 daily.
Tent Spaces: Primitive sites, no hookups. Rates: $12 daily.
Support Facilities: Bath House, Golf, Grills, Laundry, Picnic Tables, Playground, Racquetball, Rec Equipment, Restrooms, Sewage Dump, Showers, Tennis Courts.
RV Storage: Four (4) RV Storage lots operated by JBER-Elmendorf ODR, C-907-552-2438.
Activities: Archery, Fishing*, Golfing, Hunting*. *See Hunting & Fishing.
Credit Cards: MasterCard and Visa.
Restrictions: Pets allowed on leash. Firearms must be registered with military police.
RV Driving Directions/Location: On Base. From the Main Gate: Camp is located off Loop Road. Ask for directions at gate to Outdoor Recreation.
Area Description: Beautiful mountain scenery, lakes and rivers make for varied recreational opportunities and

exceptional fishing. Full range of support facilities available on post.

RV Campground Physical Address: Outdoor Rec Center, Bldg 7301 13th Street, JBER-E AFB, AK 99506-5000.

Otter Lake Recreation Area

Reservation/Contact Number Info: C-907-384-6245.

Recreation Security: C-907-384-0820.

RV Website: http://www.jberlife.com/fun/outdoor-recreation/otter-lake/

GPS Coordinates: N 61 17', W 149 44'

Reservations: Reservation accepted 30 days in advance with AD priority. Office hours 1200-1900 Mon-Sun and holidays. Check-in 1400 hours, check-out 1200 hours.

Season of Operation: May-Sept.

Eligibility: AD, NG, Res, Ret and DoD/NAF-Civ.

Camper/Trailer Spaces: RV Sites: No hookups, picnic table. Rates: $17 daily.

Tent Spaces: Tent Sites: No hookups, picnic table. Rates: $12 daily, $5 for each additional. Maximum four.

Yurt, A Frame, Cabin, Apt, Spaces: Lake Log Cabins: Rustic, sleeps 6, one full bed, bunk beds, pullout sofa sleeper, wood-burning stove, microwave, mini fridge/freezer, table/chairs, picnic table, grill, firepit. No indoor plumbing, outhouses nearby. No linens provided. Rates: $50 daily. Rustic Cabins: Rustic, sleeps 4, two sets of bunk beds without mattresses, wood-buring stove, table/chairs, picnic table, grill, firepit. No indoor plumbing, outhouses nearby. No linens provided. Rates: $25 daily. Spillway Cabins: Rustic, sleeps 4, one full bed, bunk beds with mattresses, table/chairs, picnic table, grill, firepit. No indoor plumbing, outhouses nearby. No linens provided. Rates: $35 daily. Upper Otter Lake Cabins: Rustic, sleeps 6, one full bed, bunk beds with mattresses, pullout sofa sleeper, wood-burning stove, table/chairs, picnic table, grill, firepit. No indoor plumbing, outhouses nearby. Rates: $45 daily.

Support Facilities: Boat Rental, Boathouse, BBQ Grills, General Store, Pavilion, Playground. Full range of support on base.

Activities: Canoeing, Horseshoes, Fishing*, Kayaking, Paddle Boating, Skiing/Tubing**, Volleyball. *See Hunting & Fishing. **Seasonal at Hillberg.

Credit Cards: MasterCard and Visa.

Restrictions: No pets allowed in cabins. No swimming allowed. ISportman permit required for boating, fishing, and other related activities. Available online at www.jber.isportsman.net, or at the JBER visitor center.

RV Driving Directions/Location: On Base. From the Main Gate: Remain on D Street to Otter Lake Road. Go right and continue to Otter Lake Recreation Area and boathouse.

Area Description: A National Wildlife and Loon Sanctuary, Otter Lake is a great place to relax and explore. Full base amenities available.

RV Campground Physical Address: Otter Lake Road, JBER, AK 99505. Mailing Address: JBER-R Outdoor Recreation, Bldg 794 Davis Hwy, JBER, AK 99505.

Nemetz MWR RV Park

Address: 2597 Mill Bay Road, Kodiak, AK 99615

Information Line: C-907-487-5760.

Main Base Police: C-907-487-5555. Emergencies dial 911.

Main Installation Website: https://www.dcms.uscg.mil/Our-Organization/Assistant-Commandant-for-Human-Resources-CG-1/Community-Services-Command-CSC/MWR/Coast-Guard-Lodging/

Main Base Location: Kodiak Island is situated in the Gulf of Alaska approximately 250 miles southwest of Anchorage. Travel to the mainland is available by either a one hour airplane ride or by ten to twelve hour Alaska Marine Highway ferry ride to Whittier or Homer, Alaska. Both methods of travel off island are expensive and Kodiak is a high cost of living area due to its remote location and unique environment.

NMC: Kodiak, 6 miles.

NMI: Kodiak Coast Guard ISC, 1.5 miles.
Medical: Rockmore-King Clinic, C-907-487-5757/5360.
Commissary: Approximately 10 miles to USCG Base Kodiak Commissary, C-907-487-5015.
Exchange Gas: C-907-487-5170. Commercial gas station within 7 miles.
Exchange: Approximately 10 miles to USCG Base Kodiak Exchange facilities, C-907-487-5773/5772.
Places to Eat: Tsunami Lanes Snack Bar, C-907-487-5401, Golden Anchor Sports Pub, C-907-487-5798, Bear Valley Golf Course Snack Bar, C-907-487-5323, Billiken Theater Concession Stand, C-907-487-5884, MWR Pizza Parlor, C-907-487-5988.
Fitness Center: C-907-487-5272.
Golf: Bear Valley Golf Course, C-907-487-5323 located 3 miles from base.
MWR Website:
http://www.kodiakmwr.com/
Outdoor Recreation: Kodiak CGES Recreation Services, C-907-487-5108. Offers camping and fishing. The Boat House, C-907-487-5047 offers campers, boats, and crab cookers to rent.
Swimming: Northern Lights Aquatics Facility, C-907-487-5391 offers lap and family swim, aerobics, swim lessons, pool slide, aqua tots classes.
Things To Do: Kodiak is known for its enormous bears, breathtaking, scenery and delicious seafood, including wonderful king crab and salmon. Don't miss the chance to take an afternoon whale-watching cruise while here. There is a movie theatre, a bowling alley and a beach with a gazebo within walking distance from the lodging facility.
Walking Trails: Beach strolling is available.

RV CAMPING & GETAWAYS
Nemetz RV Park

Reservation/Contact Number Info: C-907-487-5446 ext 1. Fax C-907-487-5075.
Recreation Security: OOD, C-907-539-7477.

RV Website:
http://www.kodiakmwr.com/rv_park.shtml
Other Info Website:
https://www.dcms.uscg.mil/Our-Organization/Assistant-Commandant-for-Human-Resources-CG-1/Community-Services-Command-CSC/MWR/Coast-Guard-Lodging/
GPS Coordinates:
57°45,43"N/152°30'11"W
Reservations: Accepted. Reservations by phone or fax. Credit card required to hold reservation. Office hours 0700-1500 Mon-Fri. Check-in 1200 hours, check-out 1130 hours. Maximum stay 14 days. Late cancellations or no-shows will be charged one night's stay.
Season of Operation: 1 May-1 October.
Eligibility: AD, NG, Res, Ret, DoD-Civ, Dep.
Camper/Trailer Spaces: Grass (4): Pull-through, max length 40', full hookups, picnic table, cooking grate, fire ring. Rates: $30 daily. Dry sites (4): Picnic table and fire ring. Potable water and dumping site nearby. Rates: $15 daily.
Support Facilities: Auto Hobby Shop, Basketball Court, Boat House, Bowling, Dining, Exchange, Fitness Center, Golf Course, Indoor Pool, Indoor Golf Cage, Movie Theater, Pub, Racquetball Court, Solar Therapy Room, Teen Center, Woodworking Shop.
Activities: Fishing*, Hiking, Playground, Rafting, Soccer. Full MWR facilities at ISC Kodiak 1.5 miles away. State license required.
Credit Cards: American Express, MasterCard and Visa.
Restrictions: Only recreational vehicle or hard shell trailers are permitted to use the RV Park. Fires in fire rings only. Camp stoves and grills permitted but must be properly stored for safety and to keep bears away. Pets allowed on leash and must be supervised at all times. Owners must clean up after pets.
RV Driving Directions/Location: Off Base. From Main Gate at Kodiak ISC: Turn right on Rezanof Dr. Continue approximately 1.5 miles, past Kodiak Intl. Airport across the Buskin River Bridge, turn left on Anton Larsen Rd. Go

one block and turn right on Tom Stiles Rd. Continue two blocks and turn right on Barometer. RV Park is at the end of the road.

Area Description: The MWR RV Park is situated between the majestic Barometer Mountain and Lake Louise at the edge of an open field and within walking distance to the lake.

RV Campground Physical Address: MWR RV Park, Barometer Street, Kodiak, AK 99619-5030. Mailing Address: Guest House, U.S. Coast Guard Integrated Support Command, P.O. Box 195030, Kodiak, AK 99619-5030.

Seward Resort

Address: 2305 Dimond Blvd, Seward, AK 99664.

Information Line: C-907-384-1110, DSN-317-384-1110.

Main Base Police: Emergencies dial 911.

Main Installation Website: http://www.jber.af.mil/

Main Base Location: Southern Alaska in the Last Frontier amongs spectacular glaciers and wildlife.

NMC: Anchorage, 125 miles north.

NMI: Fort Richardson, 135 miles north.

Base Social Media/Facebook: https://www.facebook.com/SewardMilitaryResort

Base Social Media/Twitter: https://twitter.com/SewardResort

Exchange Gas: Commercial gas station within 2 miles.

Financial Institutions: The First National Bank, Wells Fargo Bank, Wells Fargo ATM and Cardtronics ATM are all located within 2 miles of the resort.

Places to Eat: Freedom Fighters Bar & Grill.

Ski Area: Hillberg Ski Area, C-907-552-4838 offers tubing, dog sled rides and sledding hill. Ice fishing, C-907-552-2023. Cross country skiing, snowshoeing, and ice rink located on the far side of Hillberg Lodge.

Things To Do: Charter fishing (four large 42' fishing boats) for individuals and groups in Resurrection Bay and Prince William Sound. Wildlife Glacier Cruises (53' boat) to Holgate Glacier. Discounted tickets and tours from local operators include Fly-in fishing, Alaska SeaLife Center tickets, sea kayaking, Kenai River fishing, horseback riding. Also, see Seward Resort concierge for discount travel and tour/ticket information.

Walking Trails: Hiking and running trails available.

RV CAMPING & GETAWAYS

Seward Resort

Reservation/Contact Number Info: Seward Resort, C-907-224-5559, C-1-800-770-1858. RV Park, C-907-224-2659/2654.

Recreation Security: Emergencies dial 911.

RV Website: http://www.sewardresort.com

RV Email Address: smrops@gmail.com

GPS Coordinates: 60°7'58"N/149°25'58"W

Reservations: Reservations recommended. Office open 24 hours daily Memorial Day-Labor Day. Off Season office hours 0700-2200 daily. All reservations require cancellations to be made at least seven days prior to arrival date to avoid a one night's stay fee. A 48-hour notice is required for early checkout. A one night's stay will be charged for guests not providing a 48-hour notice of early departure. Guests must inform the front desk by 1100 hours 2 days prior to departure. Log Cabin, Townhouses and Yurts: Reservations may be made one year in advance and must be secured with a credit card. Cancellations require a 7-day notice to avoid fee. Check-in 1300 hours, check-out 1200 hours. RV Park: Reservations may be made one year in advance and must be secured with a credit card. Sites assigned upon check-in. Must check in at Resort Desk. Check in 1300 hours, check out 1200 hours. Confirmed reservations held until 1200 hours following day. Maximum stay 14 days. Tent Camping: Accepted 365 days in advance. Check-in 1300 hours, check-out 1200 hours.

Season of Operation: Year-round.

Eligibility: AD, NG, Res, Ret, DoD/NAF-Civ, Dep, 100% DAV and Guests.

Camper/Trailer Spaces: RV sites (40): Gravel, pull-through and back-in, E(110V/50A)/W hookups, dump station, CATV hookup. Rates: $26-$30 daily.

Tent Spaces: Tents Sites (3): Primitive, laundry room and shower facility nearby. Near picnic pavilion, charcoal grills, picnic tables. Rates: $13-$17 daily.

Yurt, A Frame, Cabin, Apt, Spaces: Deluxe Townhouse (2): One bedroom, sleeps six, double bed, sofa bed, loft with two twin beds, full bath, furnished, living room, kitchenette, coffee maker, fireplace, internet access, phone, CATV. Linens provided. Peak Season Rates: $192-$248 daily. Standard Townhouse (10): One bedroom, sleeps six, double bed, sofa bed, loft with two twin beds, full bath, furnished, living room, kitchenette, coffee maker, internet access, phone, CATV. Linens provided. (One townhouse is handicap accessible). Peak Season Rates: $182-$235 daily. Log Cabin (1): One bedroom, sleeps two, queen-size bed, bath with shower, furnished, kitchenette, TV, gas grill. Linens provided. Peak Season Rates: $141-$190 daily. Motel Rooms (56): Sleeps four, two double beds, full bath, small refrigerator, microwave, coffee maker, CATV, phone and linens. (Three rooms are handicap accessible). Peak Season Rates: $96-$141 daily. Yurts (6): Cabin/tent structure, twelve feet in diameter with a wooden floor, two windows, and stretched-canvas covering with a skylight and comes furnished with three cots, a table with three chairs. No bathroom, kitchen, linens or hook ups. Peak Season Rates: $25-$29 daily. Seasonal rates apply.

Support Facilities: Freedom Fighters Bar & Grill (Memorial Day-Labor Day), Conference Facilities, Fish Cleaning Facility, Fish Freezer (shipping available), Fishing Rods, Grills, Ice, Laundry Facilities, Playground, Picnic Area, Restrooms, Sewage Dump, Showers, Vending Machines, Transportation.
RV Storage: None.

Activities: Deep Sea Fishing Charters, River Fishing, Wildlife and Glacier Cruises, Scenic River Excursions, Kayaking, White Water Rafting, Horseback Riding, Scenic Airplane Flights, Helicopter and Dog Sled Tours, Glacier Treks, Zip Lining, SeaLife Center, Special Events. State licenses and permits applicable for fishing. Discounted tickets available at Front Desk. Ask for details at time of booking.

Credit Cards: American Express, Discover, MasterCard and Visa.

Restrictions: Pets are not permitted in cabins, motel units, common buildings or on boats. Pets must be kept on a short leash (6' and under) and are not to be left unattended. Owner must clean up after pets. No open fires; grills and fire rings may be used. No smoking in cabins, motel units, or common buildings. No fish cleaning in motel or cabins.

RV Driving Directions/Location: Off Base. From Anchorage: Take the Seward Highway/AK1 south to AK 9. Continue south until reaching the Seward City Limit sign. Take the first right on Hemlock. At the stop sign, turn left on Dimond. The Resort is on the right.

Area Description: There is much to do in this picturesque area. Great hiking, biking and running trails in Chugach National Forest, Caines Head State Recreational Area and Kenai Fjords National Park. Sea kayaking, guided river fishing, deep sea charter fishing, and glacier cruises available. During the summer, local dog sled tours run on dry land.

RV Campground Physical Address: Seward Resort, 2305 Dimond Blvd, Seward, AK 99664.

Valdez Glacier Campground

Address: Valdez Glacier Campground, 1200 Airport Road, Valdez, AK 99686.
Information Line: C-907-873-1110, DSN-317-873-1110.
Main Base Police: Emergencies dial 911.
Main Installation Website:
http://www.greely.army.mil/

Main Base Location: Located at the base of the Chugach Mountains.
NMC: Valdez, five miles.
NMI: Fort Greely, 260 miles north.
Base Social Media/Facebook: https://www.facebook.com/ValdezGlacierCampground
Exchange Gas: Commercial gas station within 5 miles.
Places to Eat: Nearby Valdez offers a Subway Restaurant along with a multitude of local restaurants offering steaks, seafood, breakfast, Chinese and Thai food.
MWR Website: https://greely.armymwr.com/pacific/greely

RV CAMPING & GETAWAYS
Valdez Glacier Campground

Reservation/Contact Number Info: For group reservations, C-907-873-4311. All other inquiries, C-907-873-4795. Fax C-907-873-5663.
RV Website: https://greely.armymwr.com/programs/valdez-campground
RV Email Address: valdezglaciercampground@gmail.com
GPS Coordinates: 61°08'17"N/146°12'20"W
Reservations: Reservations only for large group camping and travel trailer rentals. Tent and RV Camping & Getaways is first come, first serve. Camp host available 0800-1200 hours and 1700-2100 hours daily. Check in at Fort Greely Family and MWR, Outdoor Recreation Bldg 627.
Season of Operation: Memorial Day-Labor Day.
Eligibility: The campground is open to the public. Military, DoD Civilians, 100% DAV and Retirees rates are assessed at a lower rate. Note: Fishing trips and rental trailers are available only to Military/DoD ID Cardholders.
Camper/Trailer Spaces: RV Sites (21): E(20/30/50A), picnic table, fire ring, grill. Rates: Call for current rates. Travel Trailers (2): Kitchen with stove, refrigerator, microwave, and sink. Bathhouse and showers nearby. Must provide own bedding, linens, pillows, towels, kitchen utensils. Sleeping bags are available for check-out. Rates: Call for current rates.
Tent Spaces: Primitive (87): No hookups, picnic table, fire ring. Large group camping sites available. Rates: Call for current rates.
Support Facilities: Boat Rental, Dumpster, Equipment Rental, Pavilion, Primitive Outhouses, Sewage Dump Station, Showes, Glacier Fed Potable water is available at the shower house. Firewood is sold by the bundle during normal hours of operation. Equipment rental available through JBER MWR.
Activities: Abundant Wildlife, Fishing*, Hiking, Nature Trails. *Valid Alaska fishing licenses are required for all persons above the age of 12 participating in a fishing trip.
Restrictions: Pets are welcomed in the campground on leashes but are not allowed in the rental trailers. Owners must clean up after their pets. Limited shower time limit to 15 minutes.
RV Driving Directions/Location: Off Base. Traveling south on the Richardson Highway, the trip is approximately 260 miles from Fort Greely. About 5 miles before arriving in Valdez, a major intersection with a flashing yellow light is visible. Turn right onto Airport Road. Proceed approximately three miles to campground.
Area Description: Valdez Glacier Campground is located at the base of the Chugach Mountains beneath the famous Valdez Glacier Glacier run-off provides a beautiful waterfall that cascades into a crystal clear creek in the Large Group Camping Area. Visitors to the campground will be struck by its beauty and grandeur. Campers can watch mountain goats graze on the steep slopes overlooking the campground or a nesting pair of bald eagles in the summer months. The campground is perfect for both outdoor enthusiasts and nature photographers alike. Family and pet friendly, the Valdez Glacier Campground is the perfect place to spend an Alaskan Summer.

RV Campground Physical Address: 1200 Airport Road, Valdez, AK 99686.

Valdez Military Recreation Area

Address: Eagle's Rest R.V. Park, Military Recreation Site Office, 139 East Pioneer Drive, P.O. Box 610, Valdez, AK 99686.
Information Line: C-907-377-1110.
Main Base Police: Emergencies dial 911.
Main Installation Website:
http://www.eielson.af.mil/
Main Base Location: Located on the north shore of Port Valdez.
NMC: Valdez, adjacent.
NMI: Fort Greely, 260 miles north.
Exchange Gas: Commercial gas station within 3 miles.
Places to Eat: Nearby Valdez offers a Subway Restaurant along with a multitude of local restaurants offering steaks, seafood, breakfast, Chinese and Thai food.
MWR Website:
http://www.eielsonforcesupport.com/
MWR Facebook:
https://www.facebook.com/EielsonFSS
MWR Twitter:
https://twitter.com/EielsonFSS

RV CAMPING & GETAWAYS

Valdez Recreational Area

Reservation/Contact Number Info: C-907-377-1317/1232.
RV Website:
https://www.eielsonforcesupport.com/index.php/recreation/odr#odr--valdez-eagles-rest
Reservations: Located at Eagles Rest RV Park where a military recreation site office is located. Reservations accepted by calling Eielson ODR reservations.
Season of Operation: Memorial Day-Labor Day.
Camper/Trailer Spaces: Trailers (8): On site with full hookups, CATV. Note: RV trailers positioned right on the Prince William Sound coastline, surrounded on three sides by the Chugach Mountains. Rates: $125 daily.
Support Facilities: Dump Station, Restrooms, Showers.

Activities: Fishing, Hiking, Sightseeing.
RV Driving Directions/Location: Off Base: From A4/Richardson Hwy in Valdez: Take the exit for E Pioneer Drive. Eagle's Nest Campground will be on the right.
Area Description: Located on the north shore of Port Valdez, a deep-water fjord in Prince William Sound, Valdez offers some of the best fishing, hiking and terrific potential for whale sightings. It is the southern terminus of the trans-Alaska oil pipeline.
RV Campground Physical Address: Eagles Nest RV Park: 139 East Pioneer Drive, Valdez, AK 99686.

ARIZONA

Camp Navajo

Address: Camp Navajo Training Site, 1 Hughes Avenue, Bldg 15, Bellemont, AZ 86015.
Information Line: C-928-773-3226, DSN-312-853-3226.
Main Base Police: C-928-773-3297.
Main Installation Website:
https://dema.az.gov/army-national-guard/camp-navajo
Other Info Website:
https://dema.az.gov/army-national-guard/camp-navajo/garrison-operations
Main Base Location: Approximately 12 miles west from Flagstaff on I-40 West, exit 185. Close to Flagstaff Pulliam Airport (12 miles).
Directions to Main Gate: From Flagstaff Pulliam Airport: Travel northwest on S. Pulliam Dr toward S Liberator Lane. Turn left onto W John Wesley Powell Blvd. Merge onto I-17 then merge onto I-40 W/Purple Heart Trail via Exit 340B toward Los Angeles. Take the Transwestern Road/Exit 185 toward Bellemont. Go left back-over the over-pass and follow the road over bridge to Camp Navajo Guard Gate.
NMC: Flagstaff, 10 miles east.
NMI: Luke AFB, 156 miles south.
Chapels: Chapel on base.

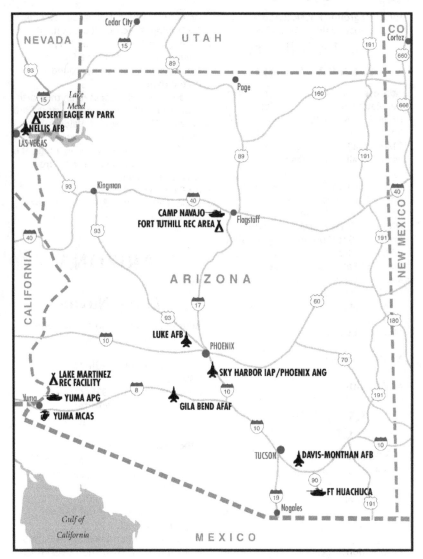

Clubs: Community Post Club, C-928-773-3289.

Places to Eat: Many restaurants within a short drive.

Hunting & Fishing Info: Hunting and Fishing Coordinator C-928-773-3124.

MWR: MWR Coordinator, C-928-928-773-3124.

Outdoor Recreation: Archery range is available.

Things To Do: There are great tourist locations within a drive from Camp Navajo including Historic Route 66, Snowbowl Ski area, Oak Creek Canyon and the Grand Canyon Railway and Resort to name a few attractions. Camp Navajo also offers wonderful hunting and fishing opportunities. The area is forested with ancient Ponderosa pines and has miles of mountain biking trails. Nearby are skiing areas. The Grand Canyon is 62 miles north. Visit Sedona, Petrified Forest and Painted Desert.

RV CAMPING & GETAWAYS
Pine View RV Park

Reservation/Contact Number Info: C-928-699-8866.
RV Website:
https://www.facebook.com/PineViewRvParkAtCampNavajo
Other Info Website:
https://dema.az.gov/army-national-guard/camp-navajo/garrison-operations/camping-and-recreational-vehicle-regulations
Reservations: No reservations accepted but priority given to those who call first. Maximum stay 28 days. May renew if other RV sites available.
Season of Operation: May-September.
Eligibility: AD, Res, Ret, DoD-Civ, 100% DAV. Camp Navajo employees with ID.
Camper/Trailer Spaces: RV Sites (16): Partial hookups with water and electric. Sewage dump available. Rates: $18 daily. Overflow: No hookups, 2-night maximum. Rates: $12 daily.
Support Facilities: Dump site available. Limited support facilities on base. RV Storage: Yes.
Activities: Bird Watching, Hiking, Nature Enjoyment.
Credit Cards: Check, Money Order.
Restrictions: Campfire permits required, no clotheslines, 2-car max per site, 6 person maximum per site or $5 extra fee. Pets must be leashed at all times. Quiet hours 2200-0600.
RV Driving Directions/Location: On Base. From the Main Gate: Ask for directions to campground.
Area Description: Located at the highest point along historic Route 66, the area boasts beautiful mountain views, dry summers and offers vast natural beauty along one of America's most iconic routes across the states.
RV Campground Physical Address: Camp Navajo, PO Box 16123, Bellemont, AZ 86015 Attn: Pine View RV/Campground.

Davis-Monthan Air Force Base

Address: 5355 E. Granite Street, Bldg 2441, Tucson, AZ 85707-3526.
Information Line: C-520-228-1110, DSN-312-228-1110.
Main Base Police: C-520-228-3200.
Main Installation Website:
http://www.dm.af.mil/
Main Base Location: Davis-Monthan Air Force Base is located in Tucson, Arizona in Pima County. The mountains and desert scenery juxtapose to provide a beautiful backdrop for this dynamic base.
Directions to Main Gate: From the east on I-10: Exit 270 north onto Kolb Road. Go north 6 miles to Golf Links Road. Turn left (west) to Craycroft Road and turn left (south) again to Main Gate. From the west on I-10: Take exit 264 north onto Alvernon Way. Turn left (north) following road to the Main Gate (Alvernon Way turns into Golf Links Road at intersection with Ajo Way).
NMC: Tuscon, within city limits.
NMI: Fort Huachuca, 73 miles southeast.
Base Social Media/Facebook:
https://www.facebook.com/DMAFB
Base Social Media/Twitter:
https://twitter.com/DMAFB
Chapels: C-520-228-5411.
Dental Clinic: C-520-228-2652.
Medical: Appointment Line, C- 520-228-2778.
Veterinary Services: C-520-228-3529.
Beauty/Barber Shop: Main Exchange Barber, C-520-571-1604; Stylique, C-520-747-1143. Bldg 4455, C-520-748-8710.
Commissary: C-520-790-4341.
Exchange Gas: C-520-790-0244/4366.
Exchange: C-520-748-7887.
Financial Institutions: Bank of America Military Bank, C-520-512-4665. Vantage West Credit Union, C-520-298-7882.
Clubs: Club Ironwood, C-520-228-3100.
Places to Eat: Club Ironwood, C-520-228-3100; Desert Inn DFAC, C-520-228-1190; Eagles Nest, C-520-228-7066 and Headpin Cafe and Sports Hub, C-520-228-3461 are on base. Exchange Food

Court offers Anthony's Pizza, Burger King, Charley's, Freshens Fresh Food Studio, Popeye's Chicken, Qdoba, Starbucks and Subway. Many restaurants within a short drive.

Bowling: Davis Monthan Lanes, C-520-228-3461.

Fitness Center: Benko FC, C-520-228-0022/0021. Haeffner FC, C-520-228-3714.

Golf: Blanchard Golf Course, C-520-228-3734.

ITT/ITR: C-520-228-3700.

Military Museum: Pima Air and Space Museum, C-520-574-0462. Military Museum Website: www.pimaair.org

MWR: C-520-228-5596.

MWR Website: http://www.dmforcesupport.com/

MWR Facebook: https://www.facebook.com/355FSS/

Outdoor Recreation: Outdoor Recreation Services, C- 520-228-3736. Offers skatepark, paintball, skeet range, Bama Park, bikes, outdoor sporting equipment and games, camping gear, campers, trailers, fishing boats, canoes, kayaks and more.

Swimming: Benko Indoor Pool, C-520-228-0015 offers lap swim, swim lessons, and recreational swim. Seasonal Outdoor Pool, C-520-228-3759/3736 offers open swim and lap swim.

Things To Do: Visit the Pima Air and Space Museum, explore the caverns, rock climbing, bird watching, shopping, many day trips, gaming, and many more family-friendly adventures.

RV CAMPING & GETAWAYS

Agave Gulch FamCamp

Reservation/Contact Number Info: C-520-747-9144.

Recreation Security: C-520-228-3332.

RV Website: http://www.dmforcesupport.com/famcamp/

GPS Coordinates: 32°10'46"N/51°37'00"W

Reservations: All sites are available on a first come, first serve basis. Check-in at Bldg 6015, check-out 1000 hours.

Maximum stay 21 days. Extensions on a space available basis.

Season of Operation: Year-round.

Eligibility: AD, NG, Res, Ret, Dep and 100% DAV, Civ Guests with accompanied military sponsor.

Camper/Trailer Spaces: Gravel (197): Full hookup sites with Wi-Fi. Rates: $22 daily. Three and six month contracts available.

Tent Spaces: Dry Camp (57): Overflow sites with no hookups. Rates: $11 daily. Tent sites also available.

Support Facilities: A-liner Rental, Auto Craft Shop, Badminton Court, Bathhouse, Bowling, Chapel, Commissary, Convenience Store, Diesel (off installation), Equipment Rental, Exchange, Fire Rings, Fitness Center, Gas, Golf, Grills, Horseshoes Pit, Ice, Laundry/Pay, Mechanic/Auto Repair, Mess Hall, Pavilion, Picnic Area, Playground, Pool (seasonal), Propane, Rec Center, Restrooms*, RV Storage, Sewage Dump, Shoppette, Showers*,Snack Bar, Sports Fields, Stables, Tennis Courts. * Handicap accessible.

RV Storage: Very limited availability. Contact Outdoor Rec: C-520-228-3736 for more information.

Activities: Bicycling, Fishing*, Footgolf, Golfing with Youth Course, Hiking, Horseback Riding, Swimming, Tennis, Tours Available. *Off-base. Necessary permit may be purchased on base.

Credit Cards: MasterCard and Visa.

Restrictions: Pets allowed, except in buildings. Owners must keep pets on leash at all times and clean up after pets immediately. Doggie Park off-leash area provided in park. Firearms must be declared at Visitor Center upon entry. No mail services. Quiet hours 2200-0600.

RV Driving Directions/Location: On Base. From the Craycroft Gate: Turn left at first traffic light onto Quijota Blvd. Agava Gulch office check-in is on right side of road at the FAMCAMP, Bldg 6015.

Area Description: Located in a wide desert valley which has beautiful weather year-round. Home of the

Colorado Rockies spring training site. Nearby attractions include Arizona-Sonora Desert Museum, Pima Air Museum, Saguaro National Monument, Old Tucson and Reid Park and Zoo. Full range of support facilities available on base.

RV Campground Physical Address: 6170 Quijota Blvd, Bldg 6015, Tucson, AZ 85707.

Fort Huachuca

Address: 50010 Smith Street, Fort Huachuca, AZ 85613-7011.

Information Line: C-520-533-2330, DSN-312-821-2330.

Main Base Police: C-520-533-3000.

Main Installation Website: https://www.huachuca.army.mil/

Main Base Location: Fort Huachuca is located in the southeastern corner of Arizona. It is surrounded by Cochise County and the local townships of Sierra Vista, Hereford, and Huachuca City. It is approximately one hour south of Tucson.

Directions to Main Gate: Directions from Tucson International Airport to Sierra Vista/Fort Huachuca: Take Tucson Boulevard to Valencia Road. Turn right at the light on Valencia Road and continue on this road until seeing a sign on the right for I-10 East/El Paso. Go east on I-10 to exit 302/Fort Huachuca/Sierra Vista exit. Continue on SR 90 until seeing the signs for Fort Huachuca, approximately 27 miles. Entrance to the Fort is at the East Gate, which is the first gate on the right. Main Gate is further down on the right-hand side.

NMC: Tucson, 75 miles northwest.

NMI: Davis Monthan AFB, 73 miles northwest.

Base Social Media/Facebook: https://www.facebook.com/u.s.armyfor thuachuca

Base Social Media/Twitter: https://twitter.com/Fort_Huachuca

Chapels Phone Numbers: Chaplain, C-520-533-4748.

Dental Clinic: Runion Dental Clinic, C-520-533-3147.

Medical Phone Numbers

CIV/DSN/FAX: Appointment Line, C-520-533-9200. Information, C-520-533-9061.

Veterinary Services: C-520-533-2767.

Beauty/Barber Shop: Main Exchange Barber, C-520-417-1304; Stylique, C-520-458-7140. Regimental Mini Mall, C-520-417-1305. Greely Hall, C-520-533-6692.

Commissary: C-520-533-5540.

Exchange Gas: Mini Mall Express, C-520-459-4022.

Exchange: C-520-458-7830.

Financial Institutions: Huachuca Federal Credit Union, C-520-458-6044. Armed Forces Bank, N.A. Fort Huachuca, C-520-452-8630.

Places to Eat: TMAC Lunch Buffet, C-520-533-7322; Greely Hall Diner, C-520-458-8358; Jeannie's Diner, C-520-533-5759 and 19th Hole Clubhouse, C-520-533-7088 are on base. Exchange Food Court offers Anthony's Pizza, Starbucks and Subway. Regimental Mini Mall offers Baker's Flor Café, Baskin Robbins, Charley's, Popeye's Chicken and Taco Bell. Burger King is also on base. Many restaurants within a short drive.

Bowling: Desert Lanes, C-520-533-2849.

Fitness Center: Barnes Field House, C-520-533-2948. Eifler Sports Center, C-520-533-4723. Family FC, C-520-533-0041.

Golf: Mountain View Golf Course, C-520-533-7088/7092.

ITT/ITR: C-520-533-2404.

Library: Christopher G. Nason Library, C-520-533-4100.

Military Museum: Fort Huachuca Museum, C-520-533-3638.

Military Museum Website: https://www.ikn.army.mil/ap ps/iknwms/home/website/forthuachuc amuseums

MWR: C-520-538-0836.

MWR Website: https://huachuca.armymwr.com/

MWR Facebook: https://www.facebook.com/FMWRFort Huachuca

MWR Twitter: https://twitter.com/mwrhuachuca

Outdoor Recreation: Outdoor Recreation and MWR Rents, C-520-533-6707. Offers camping gear, campers, mountain bikes, kayaks, sporting and outdoor equipment, bounce houses, pavilions and park rentals and more. Sportsman Center offers skeet and trap, paintball, archery and pistol range.
Swimming: Barnes Indoor Pool, C-520-533-3858 offers lap swim, open swim, water aerobics and swim lessons. Irwin Seasonal Outdoor Pool, C-520-533-3858 offers recreational swim, water slide and lap swim.
Things To Do: Enjoy boating, fishing, camping, off road riding, or visit the old mining towns of Bisbee and Tombstone or the ghost town. Spanish ruin tours and many outdoor activities available.
Walking Trails: Walking and hiking trails are on base.

RV CAMPING & GETAWAYS
Apache Flats RV Park

Reservation/Contact Number Info: C-520-533-1335. Cell, C-520-788-2985. Recreation Security: C-520-533-2181.
RV Website: https://huachuca.armymwr.com/programs/apache-flats-rv-resort
GPS Coordinates: 31°33'37"N/110°21'56"W
Reservations: Reservations accepted and may be made up to 60 days in advance. Full payment required at time of reservation. Office hours 0900-1700 Mon-Fri. Check-in 1100 hours, check-out 1100 hours. Maximum stay 90 days. Season of Operation: Year-round.
Eligibility: AD, NG, Res, Ret, DoD/NAF-Civ, Dep, 100% DAV and Guests (limit two).
Camper/Trailer Spaces: Concrete (56), extra wide, pull-thru, maximum length 60', E(110/120V/30/50A)/W/S hookups, CATV, picnic table, grill, Wi-Fi. Rates: $23 daily, $525 monthly.
Support Facilities: Auto Craft Shop, Boat Rental, Bowling, Chapel, Commissary, Conv Store, Exchange, Fitness Center, Gas, Golf, Grills, Internet Access*, Laundry, Pavilion, Pay Telephones, Picnic Area, Playground,

Pool, Propane Sales, Rec Center, Rec Equipment, Restrooms, RV Storage, Sewage Dump, Shoppette, Showers, Skeet/Trap Range, Sports Fields, Stables, Telephones*, Tennis Courts, Walking Trails. * At the Reservations Office.
RV Storage: Long term RV storage is available through MWR. Call: C-520-533-6707.
Activities: Fishing*, Golfing, Hiking, Horseback Riding, Hunting*, Tennis. *License required.
Credit Cards: MasterCard, Visa, Checks and Cash.
Restrictions: Three pet limit. Firearms must be registered. No mail service. Guests must have mail sent c/o General Delivery, Sierra Vista, AZ 85635.
RV Driving Directions/Location: On Base. From the Main Gate: Follow signs to campground. Located at the base of the Huachuca Mountains.
Area Description: Fort Huachuca (altitude of 5,000 feet) is at the base of the Huachuca Mountains. Old mining towns Bisbee and Tombstone are within short driving distance.
RV Campground Physical Address: Apache Flats RV Park, Fort Huachuca, AZ 85613-6000.

Garden Canyon RV Park

Reservation/Contact Number Info: C-520-533-7085/6707.
Recreation Security: C-520-533-3000.
RV Website: https://www.mwrhuachuca.com/facilities/sportsmans-center
GPS Coordinates: 31°31'48.1"N/110°19'49.5"W
Reservations: Contact facility for reservations. Office hours 0900-1700 Mon-Fri. Check-in 1100 hours, check-out 1100 hours.
Season of Operation: Year-round.
Eligibility: AD, NG, Res, Ret, DoD/NAF-Civ, Dep, 100% DAV
Camper/Trailer Spaces: Sites (24), partial hookup with E/W, free waste disposal weekends. Rates: Contact facility for current rates.
Support Facilities: Auto Craft Shop, Boat Rental, Bowling, Chapel, Commissary, Conv Store, Exchange,

Fitness Center, Gas, Golf, Grills, Internet Access*, Laundry, Pavilion, Picnic Area, Playground, Pool, Propane Sales, Rec Center, Rec Equipment, Restrooms, RV Storage, Sewage Dump, Shoppette, Showers, Skeet/Trap Range, Sports Fields, Stables, Tennis Courts, Walking Trails.

Activities: Archery, Golfing, Hiking, Horseback Riding, Hunting, Paintball and Tennis are just a few activities on base for guests. A full range of support facilities on base.

Credit Cards: MasterCard, Visa, Checks and Cash.

Restrictions: Firearms must be registered.

RV Driving Directions/Location: On Base. From the Winrow Ave/W Fry Blvd Gate: Travel west past the golf course to Garden Canyon Road and turn left to facility ahead on the left.

Area Description: Fort Huachuca (altitude of 5,000 feet) is at the base of the Huachuca Mountains. Old mining towns Bisbee and Tombstone are within short driving distance.

RV Campground Physical Address: Sportsman Center, Bldg 15423 Garden Canyon Rd, Ft Huachuca, AZ 85613.

Fort Tuthill Recreation Area

Address: Fort Tuthill Recreation Area, HC 39, Box 5, Flagstaff, AZ 86001. Information Line: C-623-856-7411.

Main Base Police: C-623-856-5970. Emergencies dial 911.

Main Installation Website: http://www.luke.af.mil/

Main Base Location: Located at an elevation of 7,000 feet at the base of the San Francisco Peaks near Flagstaff.

NMC: Flagstaff, three miles north.

NMI: Luke AFB, 150 miles south.

Base Social Media/Facebook: https://www.facebook.com/fort.tuthillrecreationarea

MWR Website: http://www.forttuthill.com/index.html

Ski Area: Fort Tuthill Recreation, C-928-774-8893 for more information.

Outdoor Recreation: Fort Tuthill Recreation, C-928-774-8893. Offers downhill skis, cross country skis, snowboards, bibs, snowshoes, tubes, and a variety of miscellaneous items.

Things To Do: Fort Tuthill Outdoor Adventure Program includes trips to the Grand Canyon for hiking and climbing, tubing on the tube run in the winter, paddle rafting and mountain biking.

RV CAMPING & GETAWAYS

Fort Tuthill Recreation Area

Reservation/Contact Number Info: C-928-774-8893, C-623-856-3401. Fax C-623-856-7990.

Recreation Security: Emergencies dial 911 for Coconino County Sheriff.

RV Website: https://forttuthill.com/

RV Email Address: forttuthill@lukeevents.com

GPS Coordinates: 35°8'28"N/111°41'38"W

Reservations: Accepted and can be made online or by telephone 24 hours daily. Reservations may be made up to one year in advance for AD and dependents; six months in advance for all others. 48-hour cancellation policy and early departure fees enforced. Check-in 1500 hours, check-out 1100 hours. Seasonal rates apply. Maximum stay 14 days.

Season of Operation: Lodging year-round; RV/Camping: 15 April-September.

Eligibility: AD, NG, Res, Ret, DoD-Civ (AD/Ret w/ valid ID card), Cadets, Dep w/ valid ID card and 100% DAV w/valid ID card.

Camper/Trailer Spaces: Gravel (19), pull-thru (3), maximum length 40', back-in (16), maximum length 40', E(110V/220V/30A/50A)/W hookups, picnic table, grill. Rates: $20-$25 daily for authorized users. Specific site assignments or electrical requirements not guaranteed. Due to limited availability, assigned spots based on size and need.

Tent Spaces: Primitive (15), no hook ups. Dish-washing station. Rates: $10-$15 daily for authorized users.

Yurt, A Frame, Cabin, Apt, Spaces: Multi-Family A-Frame: Three-bedroom

(1), two story, sleeps 12, two kings, four twins, one rollaway, two sleeper sofas, two bathrooms, kitchen, family room, laundry room, furnished, fire pit, deck, picnic table, wood burning stove, TV/DVD. Linens and towels provided. Spring Season Rate: $250-$285 daily. Two-night minimum stay. Early check-out fee $100. A-Frame: Two-bedroom (10), two story, sleeps six, one double, two twins, one sleeper sofa, single bathroom, moderate kitchen facilities, dishes, cookware/utensils, deck, picnic table, charcoal grill, furnished, TV/DVD. No A/C. Linens and towels provided. Peak Season Rate: $140-$160 daily. Early check-out fee $80. Cabin: One room (10), sleeps four, one queen, one sleeper sofa, bathroom, kitchenette, two burner range top, dishes, coffee maker, furnished, deck, picnic table, charcoal grill. Spring Season Rate: $80-$90 daily. Early check-out fee $45. Hotel: Double (8), sleeps four. Queen (10-2 handicap accessible), sleeps two. Kitchenette (2), sleeps two. Spring Season Rate: $70-$80 daily. Early check-out fee $45. Yurts: (5), E(110V/30A) hookup, no plumbing, sleeps four, four twin beds, wood burning stove, refrigerator, microwave, table/chairs, large deck. Linens provided but not towels. Spring Season Rate: $50-$55 daily. Early check-out fee $25.

Support Facilities: Bath House, Conference Facility (up to 20 people), Convenience Store, Equipment Rental, Fire Rings, Game Room, Grills, Laundry, Picnic Area, Playground, Rec Equipment, Restrooms, Sewage Dump, Showers, Trails.

Activities: Outdoor adventure programs include rafting, hiking and biking in and around the Grand Canyon. Bicycling, canoeing, hiking, snow shoeing, sled run, snow skiing, tubing and sightseeing. Tube run on-site.

Credit Cards: MasterCard and Visa.

Restrictions: Limited pet friendly rental units available. Pets allowed in Campground. No smoking in rental units.

RV Driving Directions/Location: Off Base. From the north: Travel via Highway 180 from Grand Canyon or Highway 89 from Cameron and to I-17 South at Flagstaff. Exit and turn right at Pulliam Airport/Exit 337. Continue straight through the stop sign toward Coconino County Fairgrounds. Follow the signs to Luke AFB Recreation area. From the south: Take I-17 North toward Flagstaff. Exit and turn left at Pulliam Airport/Exit 337, two miles south of Flagstaff. Continue straight through the stop sign toward Coconino County Fairgrounds. Follow the signs to Luke AFB Recreation area.

Area Description: Located at an elevation of 7,000 feet at the base of the San Francisco Peaks, Fort Tuthill Recreation Area was created in 1928 as a National Guard summer camp. It is the closest military lodging near the Grand Canyon, 80 miles away. Tall pines, mild summer temperatures, and skiing in the winter make this an ideal vacation spot. Many opportunities for both sports enthusiasts and tourists within a 30-mile radius.

RV Campground Physical Address: Fort Tuthill Recreation Area, HC 39, Box 5, Flagstaff, AZ 86001-8701.

Gila Bend Air Force Auxiliary Field

Address: Gila Bend AFAF, HC-OI Box 22, Gila Bend AFAF, AZ 85337.

Information Line: C-623-856-8520, DSN-312-896-8520.

Main Base Police: Emergencies dial 911.

Main Installation Website: http://www.luke.af.mil/

Main Base Location: Gila Bend AFAF is approximately 65 miles southwest of Luke AFB and is located on 1,885 acreas four miles from Gila Bend, AZ.

Directions to Main Gate: To Gila Bend AFAF: From I-10, 34 miles west of Phoenix, take exit 112/Yuma/Gila Bend. Go south on AZ-85 through Gila Bend and right (west) at Gila Bend AFAF/Ajo sign, approximately 3.5 miles to the AFAF. Also take I-8 east or west: Take exit 115 north to left (west) at Gila Bend AAF/Ajo sign and drive 3.5 miles to base.

NMC: Phoenix, 69 miles northeast.

NMI: Luke AFB, 65 miles northeast.
Dental Clinic: Luke AFB, C-623-856-2273.
Medical: Luke AFB, C-623-856-2273, DSN-312-896-2273.
Places to Eat: Many restaurants within a short drive.
ITT/ITR: Luke AFB, C-623-856-6000.
MWR: Luke AFB, C-623-856-3245.
MWR Website:
http://www.lukeevents.com/
MWR Facebook:
https://www.facebook.com/LukeEvents/
MWR Twitter:
https://twitter.com/LUKEFSS
Outdoor Recreation Unique: Luke AFB Outdoor Recreation, C-623-856-6267.
Outdoor Recreation Text: Offers camping gear, boats, trailers, sporting equipment, lawn and garden tools, park and pavilion reservations, adventure trips and more.
Things To Do: Visit the Organ Pipe National Monument and Rocky Point, Mexico while you're here. See the Phoenix State Capitol Building murals and the Desert Botanical Garden in Papago Park. Pioneer Arizona, a living history museum, and the Phoenix Zoo are also worth a visit.

RV CAMPING & GETAWAYS
Gila Bend FamCamp

Reservation/Contact Number Info: C-623-856-5211, DSN-312-896-5211.
RV Email Address:
gilabendlodging@gmail.com
GPS Coordinates:
32°52'55"N/112°43'47"W
Reservations: No advance reservations. Availability based on first come, first serve basis. Office hours 0600-2100 Mon-Fri, closed holidays. Must register at office for spot assignment. After hours arrival must sign in at front gate. Self-registration available with prepacket assignments. Limited long term sites for 90-180 days. 180-day pre-payment accepted but no refunds. Regular sites: First 30-day payment accepted in advance with no refunds; then weekly. Extensions only if no waiting list and space available. Contact office for more information.
Season of Operation: Year-round.
Eligibility: AD, NG, Res, Ret, 100% DAV and DoD-Civ.
Camper/Trailer Spaces: Gravel (44), Pull-through, any size, E(110V/15/50A)/S/W hookups. Rates: $10 daily. Dry Camp Area: No hookups. Rates: $3 daily. No restrooms or showers.
Support Facilities: Basketball Court, Laundry Room/Free, Lobby (based on availability), Picnic Area, Running Track, Sewage Dump, Tennis Courts.
Activities: Basketball, Jogging, Tennis.
Credit Cards: MasterCard, Visa, Cash or Check.
Restrictions: Pets allowed on leash. Pets must have rabies shot. Firearms must be registered in Arizona and turned in at Security while on base. One vehicle per site. No personal mail, only Fed Ex and UPS arrivals.
RV Driving Directions/Location: On Base. From I-10: Thirty-four miles west of Phoenix, take exit 112/Yuma/Gila Bend. Head south on AZ-85 through Gila Bend. Go right at Gila Bend AFAF/Ajo sign. Travel approximately 3.5 miles to the AFAF. From I-8 east or west: Take exit 115 south to the left (west) at Gila Bend AFAF/Ajo sign and travel 3.5 miles to base.
Area Description: Located between Yuma and Phoenix in an area that enjoys pleasant winter weather. Mountain areas and Mexico within easy driving distance. No support facilities available on base, full range of facilities are available at Luke AFB.
RV Campground Physical Address: Desert Hideaway Inn, HCO1 Box 14, Gila Bend AFAF, AZ 85337-5000.

Lake Martinez Recreation Area

Address: Lake Martinez Recreation Area, MCAS Yuma, Yuma, AZ 85369.
Information Line: C-928-269-2011, DSN-312-269-2011.
Main Base Police: C-928-269-2205.
Main Installation Website:
http://www.mcasyuma.marines.mil/

Main Base Location: Located on Colorado River 38 miles north of Yuma.
NMC: Yuma, 39 miles south.
NMI: Yuma Army Proving Ground, Yuma, 15 miles south.
Commissary: Approximately 36 miles to Commissary at Yuma Army Proving Grounds, C-928-328-2240.
Exchange Gas: Gas station available at Post Exchange at Yuma Proving Ground (no phone, credit card only) approximately 36 miles away. Nearest commercial gas station within 32 miles.
Exchange: Approximately 36 miles to Exchange facilities at Yuma Army Proving Grounds, C-928-343-1132.
MWR: C-928-269-2422.
MWR Website:
http://www.mccsyuma.org/
MWR Facebook:
https://www.facebook.com/mccsyuma
MWR Twitter:
https://twitter.com/mccsyuma
Outdoor Recreation: Lake Martinez Resort, C-928-269-2262, C-928-783-3422. Recreation Services/Resort is a destination to enjoy all aspects of the lake, whether it's in the summer or winter time. Enjoy all of the outdoor and indoor activities, from boating on the water, to a day at the sand bar, or a night under the stars.
Swimming: Lake Martinez.
Things To Do: Boats, canoes, paddleboats, and fishing poles are available for rent. A written test is required for all boat rentals. A river stamp is required by anyone fishing from a boat, paddleboat or any other floatable device. Fishing licenses and river stamps may be purchased at the Manager's office. If a person is coming from California and they have a fishing license, they will only have to purchase a river stamp. Other amenities include: Air-conditioned game room with pool table, television, dartboard and vending machines.

RV CAMPING & GETAWAYS
Lake Martinez Recreation Area

Reservation/Contact Number Info: C-928-269-2262, DSN-312-269-2262. Fax C-928-269-6639.
Recreation Security: C-928-783-3422.
RV Website: http://www.yuma.usmc-mccss.org/index.cfm/lodging/lake-martinez-recreation/
RV Email Address: yumadosrios@usmc-mcss.org
GPS Coordinates:
32°59'10"N/114°28'34"W
Reservations: Accepted 60 days in advance for AD; 30 days all others. Office hours 0700-2400 daily. Check in 1500 hours, check out 1200 hours. Cancellations must be made 48 hours prior to arrival. Strictly enforced.
Season of Operation: Year-round.
Eligibility: AD, NG, Res, Ret and DoD-Civ.
Camper/Trailer Spaces: Hardstand (17), Back-in, 40' max. Sites 1-6: E(110V/50A)/W hookups. Sites 7-16: E(110V/50A) with waterator. Long term sites with rotation restrictions. Ten (10) short term sites with 14 day max and (10) long term sites with 3 month max. Prim Sites (3): All with built-in BBQ, waterside setting and privacy. Prim Site 1 holds 35FT RV/Trailer; Prim Site 2 and 3 hold up to a 25FT or smaller RV/Trailer. RV Site 17 in with Prim Sites. Nearest dump station is 2.5 miles away at Fisher's Landing. Rates: $15-$17 daily, $360 monthly; holiday and peak season rates apply.
Yurt, A Frame, Cabin, Apt, Spaces: Cabins (4): Two-Bedroom, 2 sleep six, 2 sleep eight, fully furnished, kitchen, A/C. Rates: $55-$60 daily. Park Models (8): sleeps four, kitchen, A/C, fully furnished, no smoking. Rates: $45-$50 daily.
Support Facilities: Boat Rental*, Fire Rings, Fishing Licenses, General Store, Fishing Poles, Grills, Ice, Lounge, Picnic Area, Playground, Pool Table, Restrooms, Showers, Soda/Snacks, Swimming Area.

RV Storage: None.
Activities: Boating, Fishing*, Swimming, Trails.*AZ license with River stamp required.
Credit Cards: American Express, Discover, MasterCard and Visa.
Restrictions: Pets must be on leash in other areas. Pets allowed in cabins but must be on a leash and monitored at all times. Pets cannot be left outside cabins unaccompanied. Aggressive pets not allowed. No firearms allowed. No smoking allowed in mobile homes.
RV Driving Directions/Location: Off Base. Located on Colorado River 38 miles north of Yuma. From I-8 east or west: Take exit 2 north to US-95 north for approximately 15 miles. Turn left at Martinez Lake sign (Martinez Lake Road) and continue northwest for ten miles. Turn right at sign for MCAS Recreation Area (Wildlife Refuge Road) for two miles to left on Egret Road to Lake Martinez Recreation Facility.
Area Description: Located on land administered by the Bureau of Land Management. Area provides rustic semi-private fishing camp. Campground is on a barren desert peninsula extending into the lake. Full range of support facilities available at Yuma Army Proving Ground.
RV Campground Physical Address: Mailing Address: MCCS Box 99119, MCAS Yuma, AZ 85369-9119.

Yuma Army Proving Ground

Address: 301 C Street, Yuma, AZ 85365-9498.
Information Line: C-928-328-4351/2151, DSN-312-899-2151.
Main Base Police: C-928-328-2720. Emergencies dial 911.
Main Installation Website: http://www.yuma.army.mil/
Main Base Location: The U.S. Army Yuma Proving Ground is located near the Arizona-California border, adjacent to the Colorado River, approximately 24 miles north of the city of Yuma, Arizona.
Directions to Main Gate: From Yuma International Airport: Upon leaving the airport, go straight on Pacific Avenue until reaching 16th Street. Turn right on 16th Street and remain on the road for approximately 25 miles. Traveling either East or West on I-10: It is necessary to exit in Quartzsite and then travel south on Hwy 95 (about 60 miles) until seeing two large guns on the right side of the road. Turn right at that intersection and travel approximately six miles and the main entrance to YPG is visible on the right side.
NMC: Yuma, within city limits.
NMI: Luke AFB, 170 miles northeast.
Base Social Media/Facebook: https://www.facebook.com/USAYPG
Base Social Media/Twitter: https://twitter.com/ypg_az
Chapels: Chaplain, C-928-328-2894.
Medical: Appointment Line, C-928-328-2502.
Veterinary Services: C-928-328-2064.
Beauty/Barber Shop: C-928-343-1132.
Commissary: C-928-328-2240/2895.
Exchange Gas: C-928-343-1132.
Exchange: C-928-343-1132.
Military Clothing: C-928-343-1132.
Clubs: Cutaway Lounge, C-928-328-2533.
Places to Eat: Cactus Cafe, C-928-328-2333; Coyote Lanes, C-928-328-2308; KFC Roadrunner, C-928-328-7500; ROC Garden Cafe, C-928-328-6104 and Wild Horse Cafe, C-928-328-2598 are on base. Many restaurants are a moderate drive away.
Bowling: Coyote Lanes, C-928-328-2308.
Fitness Center: YPG FC, C-928-328-2400.
ITT/ITR: C-928-328-3714.
Library: YPG Post, C-928-328-2558.
Military Museum: The Heritage Center of U.S. Army Yuma Proving Ground, C-928-328-3394.
Military Museum Website: https://www.yuma.army.mil/History/Heritage-Center
MWR: C-928-328-2530.
MWR Website: http://www.yumamwr.com
MWR Facebook: https://www.facebook.com/yumamwr
MWR Twitter: https://twitter.com/ypg_fmwr

Outdoor Recreation: Outdoor Recreation Services, C-928-328-3989/2400. Offers fishing, shopping and monthly exploration trips to San Diego and Phoenix. Also offers paintball, rock climbing wall, skatepark, Kahuna Lagoon swimming pool, multi-sport court, summer movie programs and intramural sports.

Swimming: Kahuna Lagoon Swimming Pool, C-928-328-2400 offers lap swim, open swim and 75 meter sliding tube.

Things To Do: Visit the Century House Museum, Fort Yuma, the St. Thomas Mission, Yuma Territorial Prison and the Quechan Indian Museum in Old Fort Yuma to get a taste of this pre-old west town.

RV CAMPING & GETAWAYS

Desert Breeze Travel Camp

Reservation/Contact Number Info: C-928-328-3989, DSN-312-899-3989. Fax C-928-328-3580, DSN-312-899-3580. Recreation Security: C-928-328-2720.

RV Website: http://www.yumamwr.com/travelcamp.html

RV Email Address: desertbreeze@yumamwr.com

GPS Coordinates: 32°51'48"N/114°26'41"W or 301 Cedar Grove Road, Yuma, AZ 85365-9498.

Reservations: Reservations are only accepted for monthly prepay reservations. Office hours 0830-1630 Mon-Fri. Check-out 1200 hours. Camp Host available after hours and weekends. Maximum stay seven months with a two-month vacancy before returning.

Season of Operation: Year-round.

Eligibility: AD, NG, Res, Ret, 100% DAV, DoD-Civ (Active & Ret), Dep and other U.S. Govt Civ Emp.

Camper/Trailer Spaces: Concrete (104): back-in, maximum length 42', E(110/220V/15/30/50A)/S/W, (2) partial hookup sites, CATV hookups. Rates: $30 daily, $130 weekly, $375 monthly.

Support Facilities: Auto Craft Shop, Bath House, Boat Rental/Storage, Bowling, Cafeteria, Chapel, Commissary, Exchange, Fitness Center, Gas, Grills, Ice, Laundry/Pay, Pavilion, Picnic Area, Pool (closed winter), Propane, Rec Center, Restrooms, RV Storage, Sewage Dump, Shoppette, Showers, Sports Fields, Tennis Courts.

RV Storage: Covered Storage $70/month. Contact: C-928-328-3989.

Activities: Boating, Bicycling, Fishing*, Golfing (nearby), Hiking, Hunting*, Racquetball, Tennis, Volleyball. *License required.

Credit Cards: MasterCard and Visa.

Restrictions: Two-pet limit with pet immunization records verified at time of registration. All pets, including cats, must be on a leash. Owner must clean up after pet. Firearms must be registered if stay is more than 30 days. No open fires. Quiet hours 2200-0700.

RV Driving Directions/Location: On Base. From the-Main Gate: Turn left onto A Street. Travel Camp office will be on the left.

Area Description: Located near the Colorado River in a desert area near California and Mexico, 30 miles north of Yuma and 27 miles north of Yuma MCAS. The Colorado River has numerous irrigation canals and hundreds of small lakes with excellent boating, fishing, swimming and water skiing opportunities.

RV Campground Physical Address: 301 Cedar Grove Road, Yuma, AZ 85365-9498.

ARKANSAS

Camp Joseph T. Robinson

Address: Camp Joseph T. Robinson, North Little Rock, AR 72199-9600. Information Line: C-501-212-5100. Main Base Police: C-501-212-5280.

Main Installation Website: https://arkansas.nationalguard.mil/Home/Camp-Robinson-Maneuver-Training-Center/

Main Base Location: Camp Joseph T. Robinson is located almost directly in the center of the state, just 8 miles west of Little Rock AFB and one mile north of North Little Rock. It is located in the capital city of Arkansas.

Directions to Main Gate: From east or west on I-40: Take Burns Park exit 150 to Military Drive. Follow signs two miles north to camp.

NMC: North Little Rock, within city limits.

NMI: Little Rock AFB, 8 miles east.

Base Social Media/Facebook: https://www.facebook.com/arkansasnationalguard/

Chapels: C-501-212-5621.

Beauty/Barber Shop: C-501-758-8551.

Exchange: C-501-753-9017.

Financial Institutions: Arkansas Federal Credit Union, C-501-982-AFCU.

Clubs: The Rock Lounge, C-501-758-5076.

Places to Eat: The Rock Restaurant, C-501-758-8468, Minuteman Pizzeria, C-501-771-1453.

Fitness Center: Freedom Hall Fitness Center, C-501-212-4661.

Golf: Camp Robinson Golf Course, C-501-350-5301.

Military Museum: Arkansas National Guard Museum, C-501-212-5215. Military Museum Website: www.arngmuseum.com

MWR: C-888-737-2267.

MWR Website: http://mwrcomplex.com/insidethemwrcomplex.aspx

Things To Do: Plenty to see and do in the capital city. Visit Burns Rock, Wild River Country, Quapaw District, Little Rock Zoo, Arkansas Arts Center, the Governor's Mansion, Old Mill, Pinnacle Mountain, War Memorial Park, and Arkansas Travelers Baseball are all nearby. Wild River Country and Magic Springs nearby.

Walking Trails: Walking Trail around Hunter Lake on base.

RV CAMPING & GETAWAYS
Camp Robinson RV Park

Reservation/Contact Number Info: C-501-212-5274, C-1-888-366-3205. Fax C-501-212-5271.

Recreation Security: C-501-212-5280.

GPS Coordinates: 34°49'48"N/92°17'01"W

Reservations: Pre-payment required. Office hours 0700-1530 Sun-Thur, 0700-1200 Fri, 0700-1630 Sat. Check-in at Billeting, Bldg 5130 after 0800 hours, check-out 1000 hours.

Season of Operation: Year-round.

Eligibility: AD, NG, Res, Ret, Dep, DoD-Civ (AD and Ret) and Guests.

Camper/Trailer Spaces: Hardstand (16): Back-in, no hookups, picnic table. Rates: $11 daily. Razorback Getaway Camper (1): Rates: $35 daily.

Support Facilities: Chapel, Diesel**, Exchange, Fishing*, Fitness Center, Gas**, Golf, Hunting*, Laundry, Mechanic/Auto Repair, Pavilion, Picnic Area, Pool, Propane**, RV Storage**, Sewage Dump, Shoppette, Tennis Courts, Trails. *State and base permits required. **Located off base.

Activities: Golfing, Swimming, Tennis.

Credit Cards: American Express, Discover, MasterCard and Visa.

RV Driving Directions/Location: On Base. From the Main Gate: Ask for directions at gate or follow signs to billeting check-in.

Area Description: Located on a lake with a beautiful view.

RV Campground Physical Address: Bldg 5130, Camp Joseph T. Robinson, North Little Rock, AR 72199-9600.

Fort Chafee Joint Maneuver Training Center

Address: Arkansas National Guard, Fort Chaffee Joint Maneuver Training Center, Fort Chaffee Headquarters, Bldg 1370 Fort Smith Blvd, Fort Chaffee, AR 72905.

Information Line: C-479-484-2610.

Main Base Police: C-479-484-2666. Emergencies, C-479-484-2911.

Main Installation Website: https://arkansas.nationalguard.mil/Home/Ft-Chaffee-Joint-Maneuver-Training-Center/

Main Base Location: Fort Chaffee is geographically characterized by gently rolling hills in most places; however, the southeastern portion has more steeply formed ridges running in a southwesterly to northwesterly direction. Located in Fort Smith, the state's 2nd largest city.

Directions to Main Gate: From I-40: Take the I-540 exit 7 southwest in Fort Smith. Off I-540: Take exit 8 on AR-22 southeast/Rogers Avenue continuing through the town of Barling. Fort Chaffee is one mile east of Barling.

NMC: Fort Smith, 6 miles northwest.

NMI: Little Rock AFB, 173 miles southeast.

Base Social Media/Facebook: https://www.facebook.com/arkansasnationalguard/

Exchange: C-479-478-6141.

Places to Eat: Several restaurants within a short drive.

Fitness Center: C-479-484-2550.

Things To Do: Fort Chaffee is the gateway to the Ozarks. Fayetteville-University of Arkansas provides an opportunity to view sporting events. Historic Fort Smith, on the Arkansas River is 5 miles away. Wildlife management area, excellent hunting and fishing.

RV CAMPING & GETAWAYS

Chaffee RV Park

Reservation/Contact Number Info: C-479-484-2252/2917, DSN-312-962-2252/2917. Fax C-479-484-2259. Recreation Security: C-479-484-2666.

GPS Coordinates: 35°17'52"N/94°17'38"W

Reservations: Reservations preferred as Training weekends take priority. Office hours 0700-1530 hours Mon-Fri. Check-in at Billeting Office, Bldg 1317 any time after 1000 hours, check-out 1000 hours.

Late or weekend arrivals check-in with MP at gate.

Season of Operation: Year-round.

Eligibility: AD, NG, Res, Ret, Dep, 100% DAV, US Gov't Emp and Fed/State Emp.

Camper/Trailer Spaces: Hardstand, (20), pull-through (2) and back-in, any size, E(110/220V/20/30A)/S/W hookups, picnic table. Rates: $8.50 daily with a $2.40 daily surcharge.

Yurt, A Frame, Cabin, Apt, Spaces: Cabins (9): One-bedroom (7), furnished. Rates: $30-$32 daily. Two-bedroom (2), furnished. Rates: $35 daily. Cabins provide an alarm clock, CATV/TV, linens, telephone, kitchen, cookware/utensils, microwave, housekeeping service. A $2.40 daily surcharge applies to these rates.

Support Facilities: Chapel, Exchange, Fitness Center, Picnic Areas, Playground, Restrooms, Shoppette, Sewage Dump, Showers, Sports Fields, Telephones, Tennis Courts. Limited support facilities available on base.

Activities: Bicycling, Fishing*, Golfing, Hunting*. *Current AR licenses required for both hunting and fishing. Sportsman class documentation is also required for hunting.

Credit Cards: American Express, Discover, MasterCard and Visa.

Restrictions: Pets allowed on leash. Must have current vaccinations. No firearms allowed.

RV Driving Directions/Location: On Base. From the Main Gate: Continue on 4th Street for approximately .9 miles to 4-way stop sign. Turn right onto Ft Smith Blvd and proceed to stop sign. Sign for Billeting/RV Park check-in ahead, Bldg 1317. From check-in: Turn left and then turn right at the first road to the right into the camping area.

Area Description: Situated in a flat, wooded area near the Arkansas/Oklahoma state line.

RV Campground Physical Address: Bldg 1317 Ft Smith Road, Fort Chaffee, AR 72905-5000.

Little Rock Air Force Base

Address: Little Rock AFB, 1500 Vandenberg, Little Rock AFB, AR 72099-5288.
Information Line: C-501-987-1110, DSN-312-731-1110.
Main Base Police: C-501-987-6600. Emergencies dial 911.
Main Installation Website: http://www.littlerock.af.mil/
Main Base Location: Little Rock Air Force Base, Arkansas consists of more than 6,000 acres and one runway. It is located in Pulaski County next to the city of Jacksonville in central Arkansas. It is 15 miles north of Little Rock.
Directions to Main Gate: From Interstate 30 or 40: Take US Highway 67/167 exit 155 to the air base. Upon reaching Jacksonville, take the air base exit 11 to reach the main gate. Stop at the Visitor Center at the gate to get a base map and area information.
NMC: Little Rock, 18 miles southwest.
NMI: Pine Bluff Arsenal, 50 miles south.
Base Social Media/Facebook: https://www.facebook.com/LittleRockAirForceBase
Chapels: Chaplain, C-501-987-6014.
Dental Clinic: C-501-987-7304/7331.
Medical: Appointment Line, C-501-987-8811.
Veterinary Services: C-501-987-7249.
Beauty/Barber Shop: Barber, C-501-988-1160; Stylique, C-501-988-1900.
Commissary: C-501-987-6990.
Exchange Gas: Bldg 1996 Express, C-501-988-4841. Bldg 1035 Express & Class 6, C-501-988-1130, C-501-987-8092.
Exchange: C-501-988-2337.
Financial Institutions: First Arkansas Bank & Trust, C-501-985-4025.
Clubs: Hangar 1080 Club, C-501-987-5555.
Places to Eat: C-Street Cafe; Game Time Sports and Grill, C-501-987-3338; Hercules DFAC, C-501-987-3071; Hungry Herk; Victors Grille, C-501-987-6131; V.I.Pete's, C-501-987-5555 and Wally's Java, C-501-987-4133 are on base. Exchange Food Court offers Charley's, Starbucks, Subway and Taco Bell. Popeye's Chicken and Burger King are also on base. Many restaurants within a short drive.
Bowling: Strike Zone Bowling Center, C-501-987-3338.
Fitness Center: Fitness and Sports Center, C-501-987-7716. Health and Wellness Center, C-501-987-7288.
Golf: Deer Run Golf Course, C-501-987-6825.
ITT/ITR: C-501-987-5105.
Library: C-501-987-6979.
MWR: C-501-987-3231.
MWR Website: http://www.rockinattherock.com
MWR Facebook: https://www.facebook.com/19FSS/
Outdoor Recreation: Outdoor Recreation Office, C-501-987-3365. Offers equipment rentals and trips to local areas for kayaking, fishing, mountain biking, mountain climbing, canoeing, camping, inflatables, lawn and garden equipment and more.
Things To Do: Visit the Clinton Presidential Center, Old State House Museum, Big Dam Bridge, Rock town Distillery, Riverfront Park, the River Market District, the Arkansas River Trail and plenty of outdoor activity areas and parks.
Walking Trails: Nature trails are available on base.

RV CAMPING & GETAWAYS
Little Rock AFB FamCamp

Reservation/Contact Number Info: C-501-987-3365, DSN-312-987-3365. Fax C-501-987-3809, DSN-312-731-3809. Recreation Security: C-501-987-3221.
RV Website: https://www.rockinattherock.com/odr/
GPS Coordinates: 34°53'56"N/92°9'45"W
Reservations: No reservations accepted. Check-in at FAMCAMP with the Camp Host (Site 8), check-out 1400 hours. No long term camping with the exception of Military TDY orders. Maximum stay 14 days.
Season of Operation: Year-round.

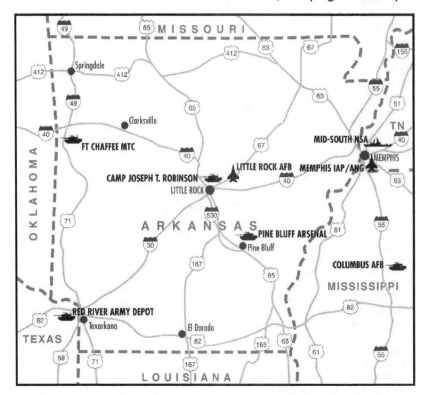

Eligibility: AD, NG, Res, Ret and DoD-Civ.

Camper/Trailer Spaces: RV Pads (24): E(110V/50A)/W/S hookups. Rates: $20 daily.

Support Facilities: Bath House, Boat Rental, Camping Equipment, Chapel, Gas, Golf, Grills, Laundry, Picnic Area, Playground, Pool, Rec Center, Rec Equipment, Restrooms, Sewage Dump, Shoppette, Sports Fields, Tennis Courts, Trailer Rental. Full range of support facilities available on base.

RV Storage: Available. Call C-501-987-3365 for more information.

Activities: Fishing*, Golfing, Hunting*, Jogging, Nature Trail, Tennis. *State and base licenses are required.

Credit Cards: MasterCard and Visa.

Restrictions: Pets allowed on leash and general clean-up rules. No open fires. No firearms allowed. Quiet hours 2200-0600. Both state and base fishing licenses are required to fish on base lake. Available at Outdoor Recreation.

RV Driving Directions/Location: On Base. From the Main Gate: Moving into the left lane, turn left onto Arnold Drive. Proceed 1.5 miles and turn right onto CMSGT Williams Drive and then make second left into the FAMCAMP.

Area Description: Located in central region of state in open terrain near lakes and wooded area.

RV Campground Physical Address: Recreation Services, 19 FSS/FSCO, 1255 Vandenberg Blvd, Little Rock, AR 72099-5013.

Pine Bluff Arsenal

Address: 10020 Kabrich Circle, Pine Bluff, AR 71602-9500.

Information Line: C-870-540-3000, DSN-312-966-3000.

Main Base Police: C-501-540-3501. Emergencies dial 911.

Main Installation Website: http://www.pba.army.mil/

Main Base Location: The Pine Bluff Arsenal is located in the Pine Bluff/White Hall area in southeast

Arkansas, 35 miles southeast of Little Rock.

Directions to Main Gate: Directions from Little Rock Airport: Depart onto Airport Road then bear right onto Annie M Bankhead Drive. Take ramp right onto I-440 West then take exit 138B. Take ramp left for I-530 South toward Pine Bluff. Take exit 32. Follow this road until the Plainview Gate is visible.

NMC: Pine Bluff, 8 miles southeast.

NMI: Little Rock AFB, 50 miles north.

Base Social Media/Facebook: https://www.facebook.com/AmericasArsenal/

Dental Clinic: Pine Bluff Arsenal Dental Clinic, C-870-540-3409.

Medical: Health Clinic, C-870-540-3409, DSN-312-966-3409.

Financial Institutions: Credit Union, C-870-540-2441.

Places to Eat: Cool Breezes Snack Bar, C-870-540-3777, Several restaurants within a short drive.

Fitness Center: C-870-540-3778.

MWR: C-870-540-3658.

MWR Website: https://pinebluff.armymwr.com/

MWR Facebook: https://www.facebook.com/PBAMWR/

Outdoor Recreation: Outdoor Recreation Services, C-870-540-3778. Offers camping equipment, inflatables, canoes, kayaks, pontoons, trailers, outdoor sports equipment, tools and equipment rental and more.

Swimming: Seasonal Outdoor Pool Complex, C-870-540-3777 offers lessons and leisure swim.

Things To Do: Visit the Arkansas Railroad Museum, Delta Rivers Nature Center, the Murals of Pine Bluff, the Pine Bluff/Jefferson County Historical Museum, Jack and Jill FunZone or enjoy a variety of outdoor parks and activities.

RV CAMPING & GETAWAYS

Cabin in the Pines

Reservation/Contact Number Info: C-870-540-3008.

RV Website: https://pinebluff.armymwr.com/programs/rec-lodging

Reservations: Reservations required.

Season of Operation: Year-round.

Eligibility: AD, NG, Res, Ret, Dep, DoD Civ.

Camper/Trailer Spaces: RV Pads Coming.

Yurt, A Frame, Cabin, Apt, Spaces: Cabin (1): One-bedroom with living area, bath, galley kitchen and loft. Fully furnished with Sat TV, outside grill. Rates: $65 daily. NEW 2016! Plans for three additional cabins.

Support Facilities: Support facilities on base.

Area Description: Located lakeside to Tulley Lake.

RV Campground Physical Address: MWR Lodging, Bldg 15-330, Pine Bluff Arsenal, AR.

CALIFORNIA

Admiral Baker Recreation Area

Address: Admiral Baker RV Park, 2400 Admiral Baker Rd, San Diego, CA 92120.

Information Line: C-619-556-1011, DSN-312-526-1011.

Main Base Police: Emergencies dial 911.

Main Installation Website: http://cnic.navy.mil/regions/cnrsw/installations/navbase_san_diego.html

Main Base Location: Nestled in the middle of the Admiral Baker Golf Course in Mission Valley, this picnic area and RV Park are surrounded by green grass and tree-lined roads. The grounds are centrally located just a few miles away from the major San Diego freeways.

NMC: San Diego, four miles southwest.

NMI: San Diego NS, 11 miles southwest.

Commissary: Approximately 9 miles to the Naval Base San Diego Commissary, C-619-556-8657 ext 3051.

Exchange Gas: Approximately 9 miles to Naval Base San Diego Exchange gas station, C-619-237-0706. Commercial gas station within 3 miles.

Exchange: Approximately 9 miles to the Naval Base San Diego Exchange facility, C-619-544-2100.

Places to Eat: San Diego offers travelers a wide variety of eating establishments.

MWR Website:
http://navylifesw.com/sandiego/

MWR Facebook:
https://www.facebook.com/navylifesw

MWR Twitter:
https://twitter.com/navylifesw

RV CAMPING & GETAWAYS

Admiral Baker RV Park

Reservation/Contact Number Info: C-1-877-NAVY-BED, C-619-487-0090.

Recreation Security: C-619-556-5555.

RV Website:
http://get.dodlodging.net/propertys/Admiral-Baker-Park

Other Info Website:
http://navylifesw.com/sandiego/recreation/parkspicnicareas/

RV Email Address:
admbakerpark@aol.com

GPS Coordinates:
32°47'32"N/117°6'11"W

Reservations: Reservations accepted 90 days in advance for AD/Res, 60 days in advance for Ret, 100% DAV; 30 days in advance for DoD-Civ. Credit Card payment for reservations accepted. Cancellation requires 14-day notice. Payment due at check-in. Office hours 0900-1700 daily. Check in 1200 hours, check out 1100 hours. Open to public on space available basis. Maximum stay 30 days. DoD max stay 14 days.

Season of Operation: Year-round.

Eligibility: AD, NG, Res, Ret and DoD-Civ of San Diego military installations only.

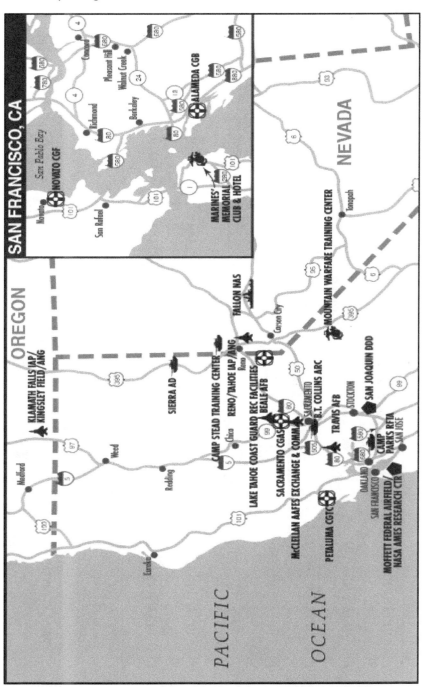

Camper/Trailer Spaces: Cement pads (47), Back-in, Max 45' in length, E(110/220V/20/30/50A)/S/W CATV hookups and free Wi-Fi. Picnic table. Rates: $30-35 daily; Civ $42 daily.

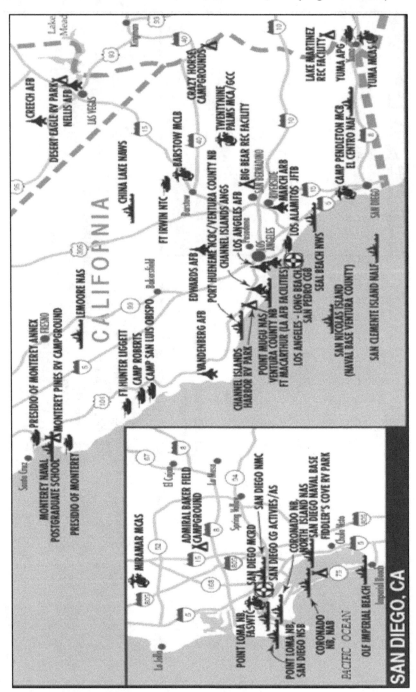

Overflow (5), no hookups. Rates: $12 daily.

Support Facilities: Bath House, Beach (7-8 miles), Chapel (1 mile), Commissary, Convenience Store (.5

mile), Diesel*, Gas*, Golf, Grills, Ice, Laundry Room, Long-term RV Storage, Mechanic/Auto Repair*, Pavilion, Picnic Area, Playground, Pool (seasonal), Propane*, Restrooms, Sewage Dump, Showers, Snack Bar (.5 mile), Sports Fields and Tennis Courts. *Located off but nearby the Naval Station.

RV Storage: C-619-487-0019 for more information.

Activities: Basketball, Dog Park, Golfing, Horseshoes, Miniature Golf, Shuffleboard, Soccer, Softball, Swimming, Volleyball. River's Edge Cafe and Admiral Baker Clubhouse on site.

Credit Cards: American Express, Discover, MasterCard and Visa.

Restrictions: Limit two pets per site, must be on leash. Owners must clean up after pets. Must keep noise down. No tent camping. No open fires. Limit one vehicle per camp.

RV Driving Directions/Location: Off Base: From Interstate 8: Take Mission Gorge Road to Friars Road and turn left. Continue on to Santo Road and turn right. Make an immediate right again onto Admiral Baker Road and follow it down the hill. At the bottom on the hill turn right into the parking lot. From Interstate 15: Exit Friars Road East. Follow Friars Road to Santo Road. At Santo Road turn left. Take an immediate right onto Admiral Baker Road and follow it down the hill. At the bottom on the hill turn right into the parking lot.

Area Description: Located just minutes from downtown San Diego and a short drive to San Diego Zoo, Qualcomm Stadium and the thriving downtown area. Waterside parks, marinas, eateries and unique shopping all close by.

RV Campground Physical Address: 2400 Admiral Baker Rd, San Diego, CA 92120.

Barstow Logistics Marine Corps Base Address: Wake Avenue & Joseph L. Boll Avenue, Bldg 129, Barstow, CA 92311.

Information Line: C-760-577-6211, DSN-312-282-6211.

Main Base Police: C-760-577-6669/6666.

Main Installation Website: http://www.mclbbarstow.marines.mil/

Main Base Location: Located halfway between Los Angeles and Las Vegas on Interstate 15. It is approximately 120 miles northeast of Los Angeles and 150 miles southwest of Las Vegas in the San Bernardino County high desert. Located along freeways I-15 and I-40, and State Highways 58 & 247.

Directions to Main Gate: Traveling from the north-east, from Las Vegas: Take the I-15 toward Barstow. Take the I-40 towards Needles and then take the Marine Corps Logistics Base off ramp. When traveling from the east: Take the I-40 to the Marine Corps Logistics Base off ramp.

NMC: Los Angeles, 120 miles southwest.

NMI: Fort Irwin NTC, 40 miles northeast.

Base Social Media/Facebook: https://www.facebook.com/pages/Marine-Corps-Logistics-Base-MCLB-Barstow/116845431679314

Base Social Media/Twitter: https://twitter.com/MCLB_Barstow

Chapels: C-760-577-6849.

Dental Clinic: C-760-830-7666.

Medical: Weed ACH Fort Irwin, C-760-380-3114/3124, DSN-312-470-3114/3124.

Veterinary Services: C-760-577-6457/6969.

Beauty/Barber Shop: C-760-577-6688.

Commissary: C-760-256-6760.

Exchange Gas: C-760-256-8974.

Exchange: MCX, C-760-256-8974, Yermo, C-760-577-7092.

Clubs: Sugar Loaf Hill Bar, C-760-577-6269.

Places to Eat: Family Restaurant, C-760-577-6429.

Bowling: Desert Lanes, C-760-577-6264.

Fitness Center: C-760-577-6817.

Golf: Tees and Trees Golf Course, C-760-577-6431.

ITT/ITR: C-760-577-6541.

Library: C-760-577-6838/6395.

MWR: C-760-577-6896.

MWR Website: http://www.mccsbarstow.com/

MWR Facebook: https://www.facebook.com/MCCSBarstow

Outdoor Recreation: Recreation, C-760-577-6896.

Things To Do: Visit Calico Ghost Town, 8 miles east. Travel to National Parks, including the Mojave National Preserve, Death Valley, Joshua Tree, Sequoia, and the Grand Canyon. Southern California and Las Vegas are within easy reach.

RV CAMPING & GETAWAYS

Oasis RV Park

Reservation/Contact Number Info: C-760-577-6418. Fax C-760-577-6947.

RV Website: http://www.mccsbarstow.com/oasistlf&rvpark.html

GPS Coordinates: 34°52'29"N/116°57'31"W

Reservations: All sites first come, first serve basis. Office hours 0800-2000 Sun-Thurs; 0800-2200 Fri-Sat. Check-in 1400 hours, check-out 1100 hours. Season of Operation: Year-round.

Eligibility: AD, NG, Res, Ret, DoD-Civ and US Gov't Civ Emp.

Camper/Trailer Spaces: Concrete Slab (36), Back-in, any size, full hookup including water, electric, and sewage. Rates: $35 daily. RV Long Term: $450 monthly.

Support Facilities: Auto Craft Shop, Bowling, Cafeteria, Chapel, Commissary, Convenience Store, Exchange, Fitness Center, Gas, Golf, Grills, Ice, Picnic Area, Playground, Pool, Rec Center, Rec Equipment, Sewage Dump, Shuttle Bus, Sports Fields, Stables, Tennis Courts.

RV Storage: Check with Exchange personnel.

Activities: Golfing, Hiking.

Credit Cards: American Express, Discover, MasterCard and Visa.

Restrictions: Pets must be kept on 6' leash at all times.

RV Driving Directions/Location: On Base. From the Main Gate: Continue on Joseph Boll Ave. Turn right on Wake Avenue then right onto Tripoli Drive. Go left at Saipan Avenue and then take a right at RV Park. Bldg 185 is on the left.

Area Description: Located near the Mojave Desert. Calico Ghost Town, Solar One and Lake Dolores are nearby. Within 2-hour drive to many great destinations including Las Vegas, Big Bear Mountain and Snow Summit ski resorts.

RV Campground Physical Address: Barstow RV Park, Bldg 185, Barstow, CA 92311.

Beale Air Force Base

Address: 17800 13th Street, Beale AFB, CA 95903.

Information Line: C-530-634-3000, DSN-312-368-3000.

Main Base Police: C- 530-634-2131, DSN-312-368-2131.

Main Installation Website: http://www.beale.af.mil

Main Base Location: Beale AFB is located in Yuba County, 13 miles from Marysville, California. It is approximately 50 miles north of Sacramento, the California state capital, and 140 miles east of the culturally rich San Francisco Bay Area.

Directions to Main Gate: From SMF: Make arrangements for sponsor to be at airport. No military shuttle to or from airport. Cabs can cost $150 or more. A Super Shuttle is available and requires reservations at www.supershuttle.com. Cost is $65 to $85. Drop off is the Gold Country Inn and no base transportation available. Car Rental at airport available but not a reimbursable expense. Driving Directions from SMF: Follow the Airport Exit to I-5 South. Take I-5 south toward Sacramento for 2.4 miles. Take the CA-70/CA-99 exit toward Marysville/Yuba City. Continue on CA-70 north at the CA-70 North/CA-99 north split. Continue on CA-70 to North Beale Rd. Follow North Beale Road for 13 miles to the Schneider Gate which is open 24 hours a day.

NMC: Sacramento, 35 miles southwest.

NMI: McClellan AFB, 50 miles south.

Base Social Media/Facebook: https://www.facebook.com/BealeAirForceBase

Base Social Media/Twitter: https://twitter.com/9thRW

Dental Clinic: C-530-634-4782.

Medical: C-530-634-4831. C-530-634-2941 (Appts Only). DSN-312-368-4831

Veterinary Services: C-530-634-2104.
Beauty/Barber Shop: C-530-634-9180.
Barber Shop, C-530-788-7527. Beauty
Shop, C-530-788-0053.
Commissary: C-530-634-2422.
Exchange Gas: C-530-788-0979.
Exchange: C-530-788-0221.
Financial Institutions: Sierra Central
Credit Union, C-1-800-222-7228, C-530-
671-4411.
Clubs: Recce Point Club, C-530-634-
4948.
Places to Eat: Consolidated Mess, C-
805-238-8237 and Snack Bar, C-805-
238-8120. Many restaurants within
driving distance in Paso Robles.
Bowling: Beale Lanes, C-530-634-2299.
Fitness Center: C-530-634-2258.
Golf: Coyote Run Golf Course, C-530-
778-0192.
ITT/ITR: C-530-634-4882.
Library: C-530-634-2314. DSN-312-368-
3434.
MWR Phone Number: C-530-634-3140.
MWR Website:
http://www.bealefss.com/index.html
MWR Facebook:
https://www.facebook.com/Beale9FSS
MWR Twitter:
https://twitter.com/beale9fss
Outdoor Recreation: C-530-634-2054.
Offers a wide selection of items
available for rent including ski
equipment, snowboards, bikes, boats,
camping equipment and more. They
also offer many trips during both the
summer and winter seasons.
Swimming: Two Community Pools,
open seasonally, C-530-634-2262.
Things To Do: National Automobile
Museum, Animal Ark, Nevada Museum
of Art, Casinos, Wild Island Family
Adventure Park, Ultimate Rush Thrill
Park, Reno-Tahoe Open, American
Century Celebrity Golf Classic, Reno Jazz
Festival, Cinco de Mayo in Reno, Reno
River Festival, Reno Rodeo, Lake Tahoe
Shakespeare Festival.

RV CAMPING & GETAWAYS
Beale AFB FamCamp

Reservation/Contact Number Info: C-
530-634-3382, DSN-312-368-3382. Fax

C-530-634-6272. Outdoor Adventure
Center, C-530-634-2054.
Recreation Security: C-530-634-2131.
RV Website:
http://www.bealefss.com/famcamp/
RV Email Address:
bafbfamcamp@comcast.net
GPS Coordinates:
39°7'47"N/121°23'2"W
Reservations: Accepted 90 days in
advance. Less than seven days notice
first come, first serve. Office hours
0900-1200 and 1300-1630 Mon-Fri.
Closed weekends and holidays. Check-in
at FamCamp Office, located at the
corner of 34th & C St. Campers are
requested to check-in prior to choosing
a site and parking vehicle. Self-
registration available 24-hours daily
next to the FamCamp Office. Must
register prior to finding a site. Check-
out 1100 hours. Late arrivals must use
self-registration or check-in with Camp
Host at site F6.
Season of Operation: Year-round.
Eligibility: AD, NG, Res, Ret, DoD-Civ,
Dep and 100% DAV.
Camper/Trailer Spaces: Hardstand (44),
back in, handicap accessible, maximum
length 60', E (110/220V/30A/50A)/S/W
hookups, free Wi-Fi, picnic tables,
Laundry facility, and Lounge with full
kitchen and cable TV. Limited overflow.
Rates: $18 daily for AD, RET, RES, &
100% DAV, $20 daily for sponsored non-
military guest and DOD-Civ.
Tent Spaces: Dry Sites: $8 daily.
Support Facilities: Auto Craft Shop,
Auto Repair, Boat Rental, Bowling,
Cafeteria, Chapel, Coin Laundry,
Commissary, Convenience Store,
Equipment Rental, Exchange, Fishing
Pier, Fitness Center, Gas, Golf, Grills, Ice,
Mess Hall, Movie Theatre, Pavilion,
Picnic Area, Pool, Propane Filling, Rec
Center, Restrooms*, RV Storage,
Sewage Dump, Shoppette, Showers,
Skeet Range, Snack Bar, Sports Fields,
Stables, Telephones, Tennis Courts,
Trails, Wi-Fi. *Handicap accessible.
RV Storage: Long-term RV storage is
available through Auto Hobby, C-530-
634-2296. Fair availability; usually has
short waiting list.

Activities: Fishing*, Golfing, Hunting**, Snow Skiing, Whitewater Rafting. *CA license/Beale permit required. **CA hunting license and weapons permit required.

Credit Cards: Cash, Check, MasterCard and Visa.

Restrictions: No firearms. Check-out 1100 hours. The maximum length stay in the FamCamp Park is 120 days per calendar year. Extensions beyond 120 days will be at the discretion of the 9FSCO Director. Extension requests for stays beyond 360 days will be directed to the 9 FSS Commander to determine eligibility. Requests must be submitted in writing to the FamCamp Manager. Guests on "Extended Stays" may be required to park in a designated area and may be asked to vacate their site if park becomes full.

RV Driving Directions/Location: On Base. From the Main Gate/North Beale Road: Continue on N Beale Road and once around the bend take a left at the first 4-way intersection (J street) follow signs for FamCamp. Make a right onto Doolittle, then left onto C street. Office is on the right. For larger rigs or if Schneider/Main Gate is closed continue on CA-70 North until it turns into CA-65. Turn left onto South Beale Rd. This is the Wheatland Gate which is open to incoming traffic 24/7

Area Description: Located in northern California in the midst of a variety of interesting recreational opportunities. Two-hour drive to Reno. Full range of support facilities on base (no emergency medical services on base). Restaurants and shopping nearby.

RV Campground Physical Address: 220 Cedar Lane, Beale AFB, CA 95903.

Big Bear Recreational Facility

Address: Big Bear Recreational Facility, 42499 Bristlecone, Big Bear Lake, CA 92315.

Information Line: C-858-577-1011, DSN-312-267-1011.

Main Base Police: Emergencies dial 911.

Main Installation Website:
http://www.miramar.marines.mil/

Main Base Location: Big Bear Recreation Facility is located in the heart of the San Bernardino Mountains. Operating installation is MCAS Miramar, but the nearest military installation is March ARB, approximately 55 miles southwest.

NMC: San Bernardino, 10 miles southwest.

NMI: March ARB, 55 miles southwest.

Base Social Media/Facebook:
https://www.facebook.com/MarineCorpsCabinBigBear

Exchange Gas: Commercial gas station within 5 miles.

Places to Eat: Alpine High Country Cafe, C-909-866-1959, Boo Bear's Den, C-909-866-2167, La Montana Restaurant, C-909-866-2602 and several fast food restaurants are within driving distance. Grizzly Manor, C-909-866-6226, Bear Belly Deli, C-909-585-4266 and several other quality restaurants are within driving distance.

Marina: Big Bear Marina, C-909-866-3965.

MWR: C-858-577-4126/4141.

MWR Website:
http://www.mccsmiramar.com/

MWR Facebook:
https://www.facebook.com/MCCSMiramar

Outdoor Recreation: Outdoor Adventure Center, C-619-556-7493. Offers volleyball, basketball, tennis, fishing, boating, hiking/biking trails, skiing and snowboarding seasonally.

Swimming: Big Bear Lake Swim Beach, Open May-Oct.

Things To Do: In Winter: Snow Summit/Bear Mountain ski resorts located within two miles of facility, snow play hills and snowshoeing. In Summer: Boating, fishing, camping, back packing, hiking, biking, off road, zip line, music/art festivals and Octoberfest.

Walking Trails: Facility trail is a one-mile loop with a 500ft elevation change. Starting at Cabin 4 and ending at Cabin 1. It is a moderate trail with views of Big Bear Lake and Snow Summit.

RV CAMPING & GETAWAYS

Big Bear Recreation Area

Reservation/Contact Number Info: C-858-271-7111 ext 5. Fax C-858-695-7371.

Recreation Security: Contact Facility Attendant at Main Lodge.

RV Website: http://www.mccsmiramar.com/big-bear-cabins/

RV Email Address: Miramar.reservations@usmc-mccs.org

GPS Coordinates: 34°14'9"N/116°52'41"W

Reservations: Reservations accepted 2 months in advance, starting the first calendar day of the month. 1st day of the month: All AD Marines and Military stationed on a Marine Corps installation; 2nd day: All Active Duty; 3rd day: AD, Ret, Res. Dep and DO. Accepted 24 hours daily by phone or online. Cancellations and changes made 14 days prior to date of stay receive full credit towards another stay or refund. Within 13 days, a $10 cancellation/change fee will be charged. Within 48 hours, no refunds.

Season of Operation: Cabins: Year-round; RV & Tent Campsites: Year-round weather permitting.

Eligibility: AD, NG, Res, Ret, DoD-Civ.

Camper/Trailer Spaces: Paved (5), Back-in, maximum 35' in length, E(110V/30A)/W, picnic table, fire ring, dump station. Rates: $25 daily. Bath house with hot water and electricity.

Tent Spaces: Primitive (5), no hookups. Rates: $20 daily.

Yurt, A Frame, Cabin, Apt, Spaces: Cabins: One-bedroom (8), sleeps six and offers a sofa, love seat, wood burning fireplace, TV/DVD/VHS player, dining room, full cooking utensils and dishes and flatware for six, downstairs bedroom with queen-size bed, dress; upstairs loft has two full-size beds and a dresser. Linens and towels provided. Charcoal grill and picnic area are provided outside each cabin. Highchairs and playpens available at Main Lodge

for checkout. Peak Season Rates: $150 daily. Seasonal rates apply.

Support Facilities: BBQ/Fire Rings, Basketball, Bath House, Bicycling, Billiards, Boats and Boating Equipment at Big Bear Marina, Local tour and Event Discounts, Firewood, Community Fire Pit, Fishing Poles and Gear, Games, Hiking Trails, Mini-Mart Out-Post with free movie selections, Picnic Area, Playground, Sleds, Snow Shoes, Tennis, Volleyball and Wi-Fi in Lodge.

RV Storage: None.

Activities: Basketball, Boating, Fishing*, Hiking Trails, Snow Shoeing, Snow Skiing, Tennis, Volleyball, Water Skiing. Many on-site recreational activities and nearby attractions. *State license required.

Credit Cards: American Express, Discover, MasterCard and Visa.

Restrictions: No pets allowed. No firearms (including air-powered and bow weapons) allowed. No fireworks. Campfires permitted in fire rings only. Quiet hours 2200-0800 hours. Sponsor must be present.

RV Driving Directions/Location: Off Base. Located at Big Bear Lake. From I-10 at Redlands: Take CA-30 north to CA-330. Go north on CA-330 to CA-18 at Running Springs. Take CA-18 east to Big Bear Lake. At the Big Bear Dam, turn right. This is still CA-18, but it is also called Big Bear Blvd. Take Big Bear Blvd past the village and turn right on Moonridge Rd. Turn right on Elm St, then right onto Switzerland Dr and then take an immediate left. Facility is approximately .25 miles down the dirt road. Note: Do not be tempted to take a shortcut through Snow Summit Ski Area as the road is gated during winter month.

Area Description: Centrally located 7,000 feet above sea level between Snow Summit and Bear Mountain ski resorts in the San Bernardino National Forest, about three hours northeast of San Diego. Area offers excellent fishing, boating, hiking and skiing. Full range of support facilities available in town.

RV Campground Physical Address: MCCS Big Bear Recreational Facility,

42499 Bristlecone, Big Bear Lake, CA 92315.

Camp Pendleton Marine Corps Base

Address: 14th & C Street, Camp Pendleton Marine Corps Base, CA 92055.

Information Line: C-760-725-4111, DSN-312-365-4111.

Main Base Police: C-760-725-0911, Emergencies dial 911. Desk Sergeant Non-Emergencies, C-760-725-3888.

Main Installation Website: http://www.pendleton.marines.mil/

Main Base Location: Camp Pendleton is located about 42 miles north of the San Diego airport, Lindberg Field and about 88 miles south of the Los Angeles International Airport, LAX. Driving direction to Camp Pendleton is fairly easy due to the base being located off of Interstate 5 which runs up and down the entire west coast.

Directions to Main Gate: From North County San Diego area via Interstate 1-5: Travel I-5 north to exit 54B for Camp Pendleton. Follow signs to main gate. NOTE: during inclement weather, the main gate may close due to flooding. In such cases, from I-5 north, please exit at #71 for Basilone Road Gate.

NMC: Los Angeles, 80 miles northwest.

NMI: March Air Reserve Base, 70 miles north.

Base Social Media/Facebook: https://www.facebook.com/pages/Camp-Pendleton-Scout/244860127876?v=wall

Base Social Media/Twitter: https://twitter.com/mciwpendletonca

Dental Clinic: C-760-725-1200/3929.

Medical: C-760-725-1288/1289, DSN-312-365-1288.

Veterinary Services: C-760-725-3439.

Beauty/Barber Shop: C-760-763-3118.

Commissary: C-760-725-4012. San Onofre, C-760-725-7136.

Exchange Gas: 13 Area, C-760-725-6387. 20 Area, C-760-763-3840. 21 Area, C-760-725-2391. 33 Area, C-760-725-4684. 43 Area, C-760-725-1789. 51 Area, C-760-725-7792. 62 Area, C-760-725-7321.

Exchange: C-760-725-6979.

Financial Institutions: Pacific Marine Credit Union, C-760-725-4491, C-1-800-829-7676, Express Line, C-1-800-736-4500.

Clubs The "O" Officers' Sports Bar, Iron Mike's SNCO Club, Sharky's All Ranks Lounge, Eagle's Landing Bar, C-760-725-2231, Officers' Pub 1795, C-760-763-7888, The Tern Snacks & Beverages, C-760-725-5331.

Places to Eat: Coco's Bakery and Restaurant, C-760-430-5049, Johnny Rockets, C-760-829-1258 and Pacific Views Event Center, C-760-763-3200 offers a variety of restaurants. Sharky's Lounge, C-760-725-2231, Mainside MCX offers Wok and Roll, Wendy's, Dominos, Roberto's Very Mexican food and Subway.

Bowling: Stars & Strikes Bowl & Grill, C-760-725-5945.

Fitness Center: 14 Area, C-760-725-5941. 21 Area, C-760-725-2951. 21 Area, C-760-763-9117. 22 Area, C-760-725-3163. 24 Area, C-760-763-1353. 31 Area, C-760-725-2678. 33 Area, C-760-725-8737. 41 Area, C-760-725-2033. Area, C-760-725-3468. 52 Area, C-760-725-7262. 53 Area, C-760-725-7404. 53 Area, C-760-725-7075. 62 Area, C-760-725-7421.

Golf: Marine Memorial Golf Course, C-760-725-4653.

ITT/ITR: C-760-725-5864/2218/7094.

Library: C-760-725-5669/2032/7325.

Marina: C-760-725-7245.

Military Museum: The Marine Corp Mechanized Museum, C-760-725-5758. Military Museum Website: http://www.themech.org/

MWR: C-760-725-5355/6287. C-1-888-375-6227

MWR Website: http://www.mccscp.com/

MWR Facebook: https://www.facebook.com/mccsCP

MWR Twitter: https://twitter.com/mccscp

Outdoor Recreation: San Luis Rey Rec Checkout, C-760-725-5296. San Onofre Rec Checkout, C-760-725-7519.

Offers trailers, gas grills, tables/chairs, camping gear, boat rentals and jump houses.

Swimming: 13 Area Pool SEP, C-760-725-4344 offers lap swim and lessons. The Scuba Center SEP, C-760-725-5910.

Things To Do: A variety of activities for all. Enjoy Legoland, professional sports teams, beautiful beaches, Disneyland, guided fishing trips, the San Diego Zoo or Safari Park, the Living Coast Discovery Center, Maritime Museum, SeaWorld and Lake O'Neill.

RV CAMPING & GETAWAYS
Del Mar Beach Resort

Reservation/Contact Number Info: C-760-725-2134/2313

RV Website: http://www.mccscp.com/delmarbchresort

RV Email Address: delmarbeach@usmc-mccs.org

Reservations: Reservations accepted 3 months in advance with following guidelines to reflect the soonest each group may make reservations: 1st Day of the Month – Active Duty; 2nd Day of the Month – Reservists and Retired Military'; 3rd Day of the Month – DOD Patrons; 4th Day of the Month – ALL Eligible Patrons and Group Bookings. After the 4th day, reservations accepted as received. Del Mar Beach Resort Guest Services, Bldg 210841. Del Mar Resort Guest Services open 24/7. Season of Operation: Year-round.

Eligibility: AD, NG, Res, Ret, DoD and MCCS.

Camper/Trailer Spaces: RV Site Beachfront: $43-$55 daily depending on season. RV Site, 2nd-5th rows: $35-$45 daily depending on season. Additional fees may apply.

Yurt, A Frame, Cabin, Apt, Spaces: One Bedroom Beachfront Cottage: $132-$152 daily. Kitchen with full-size refrigerator, microwave, stove, pots/pans, coffee maker, table for four. Bedroom with queen-size bed and closet. Living room with leather seating and flat screen TV. Bathroom with walk-in shower. Outdoor patio with seating on the beach and BBQ grill. One Bedroom Marina View Cottages: $107-$127 daily. Kitchen features a full-size refrigerator, microwave, stove, pots/pans, coffee maker, table for four. Bedroom with queen-size bed with cozy linens and closet. Living room with comfortable seating and flat screen TV. Fully appointed bathroom. Patio furniture. Two Bedroom Marina View Cottages: Queen Beds, fully furnished with kitchen appliances and utensils. Towels and linens are supplied daily. Rates: $191-$211 daily. Summer rates listed.

Support Facilities: Dump Station, Restrooms, Showers, Playground, Lifeguard station, Vending. Activities: Swimming.

Credit Cards: MasterCard and Visa.

Restrictions: Dogs must be on a leash at all time and are not allowed on the beach. Call Guest Services and Reservations for specific information, restrictions and quiet hours.

RV Driving Directions/Location: On Base. Del Mar Resort: From San Diego International Airport (SAN): Take I-5 North toward Los Angeles. Exit Camp Pendleton, Oceanside. Turn left on A St. Turn left on 12th Street and proceed until Del Mar Beach Guest Services visible the right. From Los Angeles Area: Take I-5 South toward San Diego. Exit Camp Pendleton, Oceanside. Turn left on A St. Turn left on 12th St and proceed until Del Mar Beach Guest Services visible on the right.

Area Description: Camp Pendleton contains the largest undeveloped portion of coastline in Southern California. The ecosystem includes beaches, bluffs, mesas, canyons, mountains and Southern California's only free-flowing river. There are more than 1,000 species of plants, fish and animals, some of which are either threatened or endangered.

Lake O'Neill Campground

Reservation/Contact Number Info: Recreation office: C-760-725-5611. Fax C-760-725-5135. Campground Office C-7760-4241.

RV Website: http://www.mccscp.com

Reservations: Lake O'Neill RV/Camping, Bldg 276024T. Recreation Office open daily, Apr-Oct 8am - 5pm; Nov-Mar 8am - 4pm. Check in 1300, check out 1200. Reservations accepted 3 months in advance with following guidelines to reflect the soonest each group may make reservations: 1st Day of the Month – Active Duty; 2nd Day of the Month – Reservists and Retired Military; 3rd Day of the Month – DOD Patrons; 4th Day of the Month – ALL Eligible Patrons and Group Bookings. After the 4th day, reservations accepted as received.

Season of Operation: Year-round.

Eligibility: AD, NG, Res, Ret, DoD and MCCS.

Camper/Trailer Spaces: RV Spaces: Full hookup $35-$40 daily; partial hookup $30-$35 daily. Additional fees may apply.

Tent Spaces: Dry Sites $20-$25 daily. Additional feels may apply.

Support Facilities: Dump Station, Fishing Pier, Restrooms. Full range of support activities available on base.

Activities: Fishing, hiking, watercrafts, rowboats, RV and tent camping, cabanas, playgrounds (includes ADA playground), basketball, softball, and ADA miniature golf.

Credit Cards: MasterCard and Visa.

Restrictions: Call Guest Services and Reservations for each location for specific information, restrictions and quiet hours.

RV Driving Directions/Location: Ask for directions at the gate.

Area Description: Camp Pendleton contains the largest undeveloped portion of coastline in Southern California. The ecosystem includes beaches, bluffs, mesas, canyons, mountains and Southern California's only free-flowing river. There are more than 1,000 species of plants, fish and animals, some of which are either threatened or endangered.

San Onofre Beach

Reservation/Contact Number Info: C-760-763-SAND (7263), C-763-SURF (7873).

RV Website:
http://www.mccscp.com/sanocampground

Other Info Website:
http://www.mccscp.com/sanocot

RV Email Address:
sanonofrebeach@usmc-mccs.org

Reservations: Reservations accepted 3 months in advance with following guidelines to reflect the soonest each group may make reservations: 1st Day of the Month – Active Duty; 2nd Day of the Month – Reservists and Retired Military; 3rd Day of the Month – DOD Patrons; 4th Day of the Month – ALL Eligible Patrons and Group Bookings. After the 4th day, reservations accepted as received. San Onofre Beach Guest Services, Bldg 51811. Office Hours: 0800-2000 daily. Reservations 0800-1700 daily.

Season of Operation: Year-round.

Eligibility: AD, NG, Res, Ret, DoD and MCCS.

Camper/Trailer Spaces: RV Sites: Full hookups. Rates: $45 daily; partial hookup. Rates: $40 daily. Water hookup only. Rates: $35 daily. Additional fees may apply.

Tent Spaces: Group Camping: Contact facility directly for details and rates.

Yurt, A Frame, Cabin, Apt, Spaces: 1, 2- and 3-bedroom cottages located on a bluff overlooking the ocean just a short walk from the beach. Rates: 1 bedroom $93-$113 daily; 2 bedroom $103-$123 daily; 3-bedroom call for availability and rates.

Support Facilities: Dump Station, Restrooms, Showers, Picnic areas, Playground, Ballfields, Lifeguard station, Laundry, and Beach club.

Activities: Recreation Area offers fishing, hiking, watercrafts, rowboats, cabanas, playgrounds (includes ADA playground), basketball, softball, ADA miniature golf and a peninsula for group activities.

Credit Cards: Mastercard and Visa.

Restrictions: Dogs must be on leash at all times. No dogs allowed on beach. Call Guest Services and Reservations for specific information, restrictions and quiet hours.

RV Driving Directions/Location: From Interstate 5 exit #71 for Basilone Rd. Head NE on Basilone Rd through the gate straight to the first stoplight. Turn right onto Beach Club Rd. Continue to straight to San Onofre Beach. Turn left at the stop sign to reach guest services.

Area Description: Camp Pendleton contains the largest undeveloped portion of coastline in Southern California. The ecosystem includes beaches, bluffs, mesas, canyons, mountains and Southern California's only free-flowing river. There are more than 1,000 species of plants, fish and animals, some of which are either threatened or endangered.

Camp Roberts

Address: CANG Maneuver & Training Center HQ, Camp Roberts, Bldg 109, Camp Roberts, CA 93451-5000.
Information Line: C-916-854-3000, DSN-312-949-8210.
Main Base Police: C-805-238-8647, DSN-312-949-8647.
Main Installation Website: http://www.calguard.ca.gov/CR
Main Base Location: Camp Roberts is approximately 9 miles north of Paso Robles on Hwy 101.
Directions to Main Gate: From US 101 go north 13 miles toward Paso Robles. Take exit 24 toward east Garrison.
NMC: Paso Robles, 13 miles north.
NMI: Fort Hunter Liggett, 25 miles northwest.
Base Social Media/Facebook: https://www.facebook.com/pages/HHC-MTC-Camp-Roberts/241093112651304
Exchange: C-805-238-8195.
Places to Eat: Cafes, pizza and diners and more are within driving distance.
Military Museum: Camp Roberts Historical Museum and Museum Annex, C-805-238-8288; Curator, C-805-237-8471.
Military Museum Website: http://www.militarymuseum.org/CampRobertsMuseum.html
MWR: C-805-238-8397.
MWR Website: http://www.calguard.ca.gov/CR/Pages/Personnel--Resource-Management.aspx

MWR Facebook: https://www.facebook.com/CampRobertsInstallationServices/info

RV CAMPING & GETAWAYS

Camp Roberts RV Park

Reservation/Contact Number Info: C-805-238-8312, DSN-312-949-8312. Fax C-805-238-8384.
RV Website: https://calguard.ca.gov/cr/
GPS Coordinates: 35°46'38"N/120°43'9"W
Reservations: Reservations must be secured with credit card. Cancellations must be received prior to 1200 hours on arrival day to avoid charge. No-shows charged one night's stay. Office hours 0800-1630 daily. Closed holidays. Check in at Billeting, Bldg 6037.
Season of Operation: Year-round.
Eligibility: AD, NG, Res, Ret , Dod-Civ and Guests.
Camper/Trailer Spaces: Camper Spaces: Hardstand (22), E(110V/30A)/S/W hookups. Rates: $10 daily.
Support Facilities: Chapel, Exchange, Gym.
RV Storage: Available through MWR.
Activities: Fishing*. *State license required.
Credit Cards: American Express, Discover, MasterCard and Visa.
Restrictions: Pets allowed on leash. Patrons must always carry ID. All firearms must be registered with Provost Marshal upon entering installation. No swimming or tubing. No campfires.
RV Driving Directions/Location: On Base. Located on US-101 halfway between Los Angeles and San Francisco, 13 miles north of Paso Robles. Take Camp Roberts exit 244 to Main Gate. Follow gate road then turn left at TSC sign. Follow signs to FAMCAMP.
Area Description: Camp Roberts is located north of historic Mission San Miguel de Archangel. Hwy 101 follows the old Mission Trail, making this a recommended scenic drive for history buffs.

RV Campground Physical Address:
Billeting, Bldg 6037, Camp Roberts, CA 93451-5000.

Camp San Luis Obispo

Address: CANG Western Mobilization & Training Complex, 10 Sonoma Ave, Bldg 738, San Luis Obispo, CA 93405.
Information Line: C-805-594-6510, DSN-312-630-6510.
Main Base Police: C-805-594-6605/6571, Emergencies dial 911.
Main Installation Website:
http://www.calguard.ca.gov/CSLO
Main Base Location: Located along the coast halfway between Los Angeles and San Francisco.
Directions to Main Gate: From US 101 north or south: Take to San Luis Obispo then northwest on CA-1/Pacific Northwest Highway for about five miles toward Morro Bay to Camp San Luis Obispo on southwest side of CA-Hwy1.
NMC: San Luis Obispo, five miles southeast.
NMI: Camp Roberts, 48 miles south.
Base Social Media/Facebook:
https://www.facebook.com/CAGUARD
Base Social Media/Twitter:
https://twitter.com/theCaGuard
Beauty/Barber Shop: C-805-594-6412.
Exchange: C-805-541-3284.
Clubs: Officers' Club, 805-541-6168.
Places to Eat: Nearby San Luis Obispo offers a wide variety of dining opportunities including Indian food, Creole food, Japanese food, fast food and much more.
Fitness Center: C-805-594-6630
MWR: C-805-594-6500.

RV CAMPING & GETAWAYS

Camp San Luis Obispo RV Park

Reservation/Contact Number Info: C-805-594-6500, DSN-312-630-6500. Fax C-805-594-6524, DSN-312-630-6500.
Recreation Security: C-805-594-6571.
RV Website:
https://calguard.ca.gov/CSLO/
GPS Coordinates:
35°19'24"N/120°44'15"W

Reservations: Reservations may be made up to 30 days in advance. Maximum stay is 30 days per calendar year. Office hours 0800-1630 daily. Closed holidays. Check-in 1400 hours at Billeting Office, Bldg 738; check-out 1200 hours. After hours arrival must use Overflow.
Season of Operation: Year-round.
Eligibility: AD, NG, Res, Ret and Fed/State Emp.
Camper/Trailer Spaces: RV Sites: Gravel (12) pull-thru, E(110V/220V/20A/30A/50A)/S/W hookups, picnic table, fire ring and grill. Rates: $23 daily. Gravel (8), pull-thru, E(110V/20A)/W hookups, picnic table, grill. Rates: $16 daily. Overflow, no hookups. Rates: $5 daily. Maximum 30-day stay per year. Tents allowed in overflow only. Call to confirm current rates.
Support Facilities: Chapel (Summer Only), Exchange, Fire Rings, Grills, Mess Hall, Picnic Area, Playground, Restrooms, Sewage Dump, Showers. Limited support facilities available on post.
Activities: Baseball, Biking, Fishing, Golfing, Hiking, Jogging and Sightseeing.
Credit Cards: American Express, MasterCard and Visa.
Restrictions: Pets allowed only in RV Park. No firearms allowed. Campfires allowed only in fire rings. Maximum 30 day stay per year. Max 6 people per site.
RV Driving Directions/Location: On Base: From Main Gate: Take first left. Check in at second building on right at Bldg 738, Billeting Office. From Billeting Office, turn right on Ventura, then right on Colusa. The camp is just past the fire station on the left side.
Area Description: Located on California's Central Coast in an area offering a variety of entertainment, sports, sightseeing and tourist activities, including Mission San Luis Obispo, Hearst Castle and Morro Rock.
RV Campground Physical Address:
Camp San Luis Obispo, 10 Sonoma Ave, Bldg 738, San Luis Obispo, CA 93405.

Channel Islands Harbor RV Park

Address: Camp Coast Guard Office, Channel Islands Harbor, 4201 Victoria Avenue, Oxnard, CA 93035-8399.
Information Line: C-805-985-9822.
Main Base Police: Emergencies dial 911.
Main Base Location: Located at Channel Islands Harbor, across the street from the Coast Guard Station. Well maintained rustic atmosphere, near many community attractions.
NMC: Santa Barbara, 30 miles north.
NMI: Channel Islands Coast Guard Station.
Commissary: Approximately 4 miles to the Port Hueneme Naval Construction Battalion Center Commissary, C-805-982-2400.
Exchange Gas: Approximately 4 miles to NEX gas station at Port Hueneme, C-805-982-4770. Commercial gas station within 5 miles.
Exchange: Approximately 4 miles to the Port Hueneme Naval Construction Battalion Center Base Exchange facility, C-805-982-6801.
Places to Eat: Many restaurants are a short drive away in nearby Oxnard offering Mexican food, seafood, pizza, fast food and more.
MWR Website:
http://www.uscg.mil/mwr/lodging/District11.asp

RV CAMPING & GETAWAYS
Channel Islands RV Park

Reservation/Contact Number Info: C-805-861-0785.
Recreation Security: C-805-984-7705.
RV Website:
https://www.dcms.uscg.mil/Our-Organization/Assistant-Commandant-for-Human-Resources-CG-1/Community-Services-Command-CSC/MWR/Coast-Guard-Lodging/
GPS Coordinates:
34°09'44"N/119°13'16"W or 4202 S. Victoria Avenue, Oxnard, CA 93035.
Reservations: Reservations required by application only. Reservations should be made as early as possible, at least 21 days in advance, but no more than 50 days in advance. Office hours 0800-1630 daily. Check-out 1200 hours.
Season of Operation: Year-round.
Eligibility: AD, Res, Ret, and CG Auxiliary.
Camper/Trailer Spaces: Camper Spaces: Gravel (10), E(110V/50A)/W hookups. Rates: $14-$16 daily. Other Information: Gravel spaces being updated with cement. Seven sites have been upgraded from 30A to 50A. Call to confirm current upgrades and rates.
Support Facilities: No support facilities available. Dump Station available. RVs must be totally self-contained.
RV Storage: None.
Activities: Basketball Court, Bicycling, Boating, Fishing, Golfing, Hiking, Pavilion, Surfing, Swimming, Touring, Volleyball Court.
Credit Cards: None.
Restrictions: Pets allowed on leash only. Owners must clean up after pets. No open fires. No restrooms, self-contained RVs only. No tents allowed.
RV Driving Directions/Location: Off Base. From Los Angeles: Take Highway 1 North to the Channel Islands off ramp. Go west on Channel Islands Boulevard for 3.5 miles until reaching Victoria Avenue. Turn left on Victoria and drive one mile to Camp Coast Guard which is on the left side, next to the Coast Guard Recruiting Station. From Santa Barbara or San Francisco: Take US 101 South to Victoria Ave. Go south on Victoria Avenue 6.5 miles to Camp Coast Guard.
Area Description: Located near the southern coast of California at Channel Islands Harbor across from the Coast Guard Station. Minutes away from water sports, charter boat fishing, shopping and bicycle touring and within easy driving distance of local tourist attractions such as the Los Angeles area. Full range of support facilities available at Channel Islands Coast Guard Station.
RV Campground Physical Address: Camp Coast Guard Office, Channel Islands Harbor, 4201 Victoria Avenue, Oxnard, CA 93035-8399.

China Lake Naval Weapons Air Station

Address: Naval Air Weapons Station China Lake, 1 Administration Circle, China Lake, CA 93555-6100.
Information Line: C-760-939-9011, DSN-312-437-9011.
Main Base Police: C-805-982-3124.
Main Installation Website:
http://www.cnic.navy.mil/regions/cnrsw/installations/naws_china_lake.html
Main Base Location: China Lake is located next to the town of Ridgecrest, a thriving town of about 27,000. It lies 150 miles northeast of Los Angeles on the western edge of California's Mojave Desert. China Lake/Ridgecrest is located near three major highways: US Hwy 395 and California State Highways 14 and 178.
Directions to Main Gate: Whether flying or driving to China Lake, try to arrive during the daylight hours as the town is very isolated: Take Interstate 405 North from the airport over the Hollywood Hills and across the San Fernando Valley. Then take Interstate 5 North a short distance to State Route 14. Remain on Highway 14 through Palmdale, Lancaster, Mojave and Red Rock Canyon until the Inyokern turnoff. Take Highway 178 east through Inyokern to China Lake and Ridgecrest, approximately 160 total miles.
NMC: Los Angeles, 153 miles south.
NMI: Barstow MCLB, 90 miles southeast.
Base Social Media/Facebook:
https://www.facebook.com/NAWSChinaLake
Base Social Media/Twitter:
https://twitter.com/NAWS_CL
Chapels: C-760-939-3506.
Dental Clinic: C-760-939-8040.
Medical: Appointment Line, C-760-939-8000 option 1. Pharmacy, C-760-939-8001. C-760-939-8035
Beauty/Barber Shop: C-760-446-6210.
Commissary: C-760-939-3807/3138/0004.
Exchange Gas: C-760-446-5044.
Exchange: C-760-446-6707/3288/7474.

Financial Institutions: AltaOne Federal Credit Union, C-760-371-7000, C-1-800-433-9727.
Clubs: Paradise Bar, C-760-939-3633.
Places to Eat: Deli Cafe, C-760-446-1149, The Flying Bean Coffee House, C-760-446-4242, Mulligans Grill at the Golf Course, C-760-939-2002, Strike Zone Snack Bar, C-760-939-8665 and MaryAnne's Kitchen, C-760-939-2739 are within walking distance. Denny's, C-760-375-5572, Kentucky Fried Chicken, C-760-375-4551 and McDonald's, C-760-446-8876 are within driving distance.
Bowling: Hall Memorial Lanes, C-760-939-3471.
Fitness Center Phone Numbers: C-760-939-2334.
Golf: China Lake Golf Course, C-760-939-2990.
ITT/ITR: C-760-939-8644.
Library: C-760-384-5870.
Military Museum: China Lake Museum of Armament and Technology, C-760-939-3530.
Military Museum Website:
http://www.chinalakemuseum.org/
MWR: C-760-939-2595/4386/3440.
MWR Website:
http://navylifesw.com/chinalake/
MWR Twitter:
https://twitter.com/NAWS_CL
Outdoor Recreation: China Lake NAWS Outdoor Recreation, C-760-939-3006. Offers outdoor adventure trips and tours to all surrounding Southern/Northern California and Nevada attractions as well as recreational equipment rental for volleyballs, softballs, footballs, bats, horseshoes, mountain bikes and safety gear, camping equipment, camping trailers, generators, frisbees, BBQs and more.
Swimming: Indoor Pool, C-760-939-2334 offers lap swim and swim lessons. Oasis Outdoor Swimming Pool, C-760-939-3799 offers recreational swim and water slide.
Things To Do: Many activities to enjoy. Try land sailing or take a Black Canyon canoe trip. Visit Aquarium of the Pacific, Universal Studios Hollywood,

Disneyland, Knotts Berry Farm, and Six Flags Magic Mountain. Or experience more outdoor adventure with an 8-mountain hike, full moon night hike, a trip to Death Valley or full moon day hikes. Also enjoy Pinnacles National Monument, Red Rock Canyon State Park, Devil's Post Pile day trip or the Rademacher Hills Mountain bike trip. Wine tasting at the Souza Family Vineyard in beautiful Tehachapi is also enjoyable.

RV CAMPING & GETAWAYS

Sierra Vista RV Park

Reservation/Contact Number Info: C-760-939-3006.
RV Website:
http://navylifesw.com/chinalake/housing/navygetaways/
Other Info Website:
http://get.dodlodging.net/propertys/China-Lake-RV-Park
GPS Coordinates:
35°39'40.7"N/117°38'39.2"W
Reservations: Telephone or on-line reservations accepted. Office hours 1100-1600 Mon-Fri. Use the Main Gate located on the corner of China Lake Blvd and Inyokern Rd. Cancellations require 30-day notice.
Season of Operation: Year-round.
Eligibility: AD, DoD Civ, and other authorized users.
Camper/Trailer Spaces: RV Park (60), 25 pull through and 35 back-in 40' long sites with water, electricity and sewage. Rates: $18-$28 daily; $119-$175 weekly; $420-$710 monthly depending on eligibility status.
Support Facilities: Clubhouse with free Wi-Fi, pet walk area, coin-operated laundry, restrooms with showers. Full range of support facilities on base.
RV Storage: C-760-939-3006.
Activities: Golfing, Hiking, Tennis Courts. Parks and picnic areas available.
Credit Cards: Mastercard, Visa, Cash.
Restrictions: Pet owners must clean-up after pets and is pet friendly.
RV Driving Directions/Location: On Base. Use the Main Gate at China Lake Blvd and Inyokern Rd. Ask for specific directions to RV Park.
Area Description: Located in California's Mojave Desert, the RV Park is near mountains, deserts, canyons, caves and forests. This is an explorer's paradise.
RV Campground Physical Address: Sierra Vista RV Park, 2115 Halsey St, Ridgecrest, CA 93555.

Coronado Naval Base – North Island NAS

Address: Bldg 678, McCain Blvd, North Island NAS, CA 92135.
Information Line: C-619-545-1011, DSN-312-735-1011.
Main Base Police: C-619-524-6999.
Main Installation Website:
http://www.cnic.navy.mil/regions/cnrsw/installations/navbase_coronado.html
Main Base Location: Naval Base Coronado is located in Coronado, California, one of the most unique and beautiful beach front cities in the world. Measuring only 13.5 square miles and located just minutes from downtown San Diego, this enchanted island has it all: beaches, parks, numerous recreational activities, highly rated schools, top notch municipal services, a wonderful climate, and an ideal location. San Diego, a military town, has a higher cost of living than most cities in America but is also known as "America's Finest City."
Directions to Main Gate: From San Diego: Take I-5 north or south to CA-75 across Coronado/San Diego Bay Toll Bridge to CA-282 northwest directly to Main Gate. Or take CA-75 north from Imperial Beach to downtown Coronado. Go left (northwest) on CA-282 directly to Main Gate.
NMC: San Diego, within city limits.
NMI: Coronado NB, Pacific Naval Amphibious Base, 6 miles east.
Base Social Media/Facebook:
https://www.facebook.com/NavalBaseCoronado
Base Social Media/Twitter:
https://twitter.com/CoronadoNavy
Chapels: C-619-545-8213.
Dental Clinic: C-619-545-6395.

Medical: General Information, C-619-545-4263, DSN-312-735-4263, Active Duty, C-619-545-9473 option 2, Family Medicine, C-619-532-8225.
Veterinary Services: C-858-577-6552.
Beauty/Barber Shop: C-619-522-7222 ext. 7230.
Commissary: C-619-545-6560.
Exchange Gas: C-619-437-6761.
Exchange Main Phone Number: C-619-522-7222.
Financial Institutions: Armed Forces Bank, N.A., C-619-435-6030. North Island Federal Credit Union, C-619-656-7156, C-1-800-848-5654.
Clubs: 19th Hole, C-619-545-9660, CPO Cantina, C-619-767-1576, 10 Pin Cafe & Lounge, C-619-545-8709, World Famous I-Bar, C-619-545-9199.
Places to Eat: Bowling Center, C-619-545-7240, McDonald's, C-619-437-8911, Pizza Parlor, C-619-545-7229 and NEX Food Court with Rubio's, Panda Express, Five Guys and Subway, are within driving distance.
Bowling: Sea 'N Air Lanes, C-619-545-7240.
Fitness Center: Main Fitness Center, C-619-545-2877.
Golf: Sea 'N Air Golf Club, C-619-545-9659.
ITT/ITR: C-619-545-9576.
Marina: Fiddler's Cove Marina, C-619-522-8680. Navy Yacht Club, C-619-437-0320.
MWR Phone Number: C-619-544-9576.
MWR Website:
http://navylifesw.com/sandiego/
MWR Facebook:
https://www.facebook.com/navylifesw
MWR Twitter:
https://twitter.com/navylifesw
Outdoor Recreation: Outdoor Recreation Services, NBSD, C-619-556-7493. Offers everything from coolers to fishing boats and its shelves are stocked with information on all types of outdoor activities. Take a bike ride into the local mountains, climb some rocks in the Cleveland National Forest, or enjoy the beautiful coastal waters. Gear rental includes surfboards, wetsuits, snorkel sets, boogie boards, kayaks, canoes, and more.

Swimming: Island Club at North Island, C-619-545-7228 offers a 25 meter, 5 lane heated outdoor pool with cabanas, grass area, locker rooms, lawn furniture and kiddie pool. Outdoor Crews Pool, C-619-545-2880 offers lap swim, lessons and scuba diving classes. Breakers Beach, C-619-545-9203 offers a large beach area with swimming, surfing, grills, bathrooms, showers, cabanas & fire rings.
Things To Do: Visit Sea World, San Diego Zoo, Pacific Ocean, Disneyland, The USS Midway Museum, Big Cat and Exotic Animal Rescue, Legoland, Six Flags Magic Mountain, Knotts Berry Farm, and the Titanic Artifact Exhibition. Go deep sea fishing, take a Black Canyon canoe trip or explore Hearst Castle. Home to the San Diego Padres. Enjoy the beautiful beaches of Coronado.
Walking Trails: Beach strolling available.

RV CAMPING & GETAWAYS
North Island Cottages

Reservation/Contact Number Info: C-877-NAVY-BED, C-619-435-1227.
Recreation Security: Emergencies dial 911.
RV Website:
http://get.dodlodging.net/propertys/North-Island-Beach-Cottages
Reservations: Reservations accepted up to one year in advance for AD, all others 6 months. Cancellations require 30-day notice prior to arrival to avoid fee. Accepted via phone or online.
Season of Operation: Year-round, limited.
Eligibility: AD, NG, Res, Ret, DoD-Civ, Dep.
Yurt, A Frame, Cabin, Apt, Spaces: Cottages (20): Two-bedroom, full kitchen, flat-screen cable TVs with a Blu-ray/DVD player, Wi-Fi Internet access, linens, a private bath, patio, and BBQ. These single-story units are right on the beach with stunning views of the Pacific Ocean. Rates: Call for current rates.
Support Facilities: Commissary, Exchange, Golf Course, Gymnasium, ITT,

Officer Club, Restaurant, Swimming, Pool, and Tennis Courts.

Activities: Enjoy beach swimming, golfing, nearby Coronado eateries and events. Downtown San Diego is a short drive.

Credit Cards: AMEX, DISC, MC, VISA.

Restrictions: Contact facility for pet policy.

RV Driving Directions/Location: On Base. From the Main Gate: Ask for directions at time of reservation or at gate.

Area Description: Located on the beach with spectacular views.

RV Campground Physical Address: 1401-A Rogers Road, San Diego, CA 92135.

Edwards Air Force Base

Address: 550 South Bailey Avenue, Bldg 7020 95 MSS/DPF, Edwards AFB, CA 93524-1860.

Information Line: C-661-277-1110, DSN-312-527-1110.

Main Base Police: C-661-277-3340, DSN-312-527-3340.

Main Installation Website: http://www.edwards.af.mil/

Main Base Location: Edwards AFB, in the western portion of the Mojave Desert, is 100 miles northeast of Los Angeles and is ideally located for shopping, sightseeing and recreational activities.

Directions to Main Gate: From LAX via the 405/San Diego Fwy North: Merge to the I-5/Golden State Fwy North. Exit right to the I-14/Antelope Valley Fwy North. Proceed North on the 14 through Palmdale, Lancaster. Enter Rosamond just past Avenue "A". Exit 55 leads to Edwards AFB exit. Turn right onto Rosamond Boulevard. Proceed through two lights, across the railroad tracks and straight onto EAFB property. "Welcome to Edwards" marker visible. Proceed straight to the West Gate on Rosamond Blvd which is about a 17 mile stretch of desert. The housing area and Billeting Office are approximately 8 miles beyond the gate.

NMC: Los Angeles, 90 miles southwest.

NMI: China Lake Naval Weapons Station, 85 miles north.

Base Social Media/Facebook: https://www.facebook.com/EdwardsAirForceBase

Base Social Media/Twitter: https://twitter.com/edwardsafb

Dental Clinic: C-661-277-2872.

Medical: C-661-277-7118, DSN-312-527-7118

Veterinary Services: C-661-275-7387.

Beauty/Barber Shop: C-661-277-2946, C-661-258-5371.

Commissary: C-661-277-9175.

Exchange Gas: C-661-258-0709.

Exchange: C-661-258-1078.

Financial Institutions: Armed Forces Bank, N.A, C-661-258-0183. Telebanc/Customer Service, C-888-929-2265. Edwards Federal Credit Union, C-661-952-5945, C-661-945-6626, C-877-256-3300.

Clubs: Club Muroc, C-661-275-2582.

Places to Eat: BX Food Court, C-661-258-1078 ext 201.

Bowling: High Desert Lanes, C-661-275-BOWL.

Fitness Center: C-661-275-4961.

Golf: Muroc Lake Golf Course, C-661-275-7888.

ITT/ITR: C-661-275-8747.

Library: C-661-275-2665/7323.

Military Museum: Edwards AFB Museum, C-661-277-3517/4803/8707/3510/3511.

Military Museum Website: http://afftcmuseum.org/afft-museum/edwards-museum/

MWR: C-661-277-4240.

MWR Website: http://edwardsfss.com/wordpress/

MWR Facebook: https://www.facebook.com/EdwardsFSS

Outdoor Recreation: Edwards Air Force Base Outdoor Recreation Services, C-661-275-2267. Offers sporting goods, outdoor equipment, trailers and RVs, gardening equipment, skis and boards, party/event equipment and more.

Swimming: Oasis Center Indoor Pool and 2 outdoor pools open seasonally, C-661-275-2267.

Walking Trails: See Fitness center or Lodging for maps.

RV CAMPING & GETAWAYS

Edwards AFB FamCamp

Reservation/Contact Number Info: C-661-275-2267, DSN-312-525-2267. Recreation Security: C-661-277-3340.
RV Website: http://edwardsfss.com/wordpress/recreation/outdoor-recreation
GPS Coordinates: 34°55'6"N/117°55'31"W
Reservations: No advance reservations. Office hours 0830-1730 Mon-Fri, 0800-1400 Sat, 1000-1500 Sun. Check-in at FamCamp Space 25, Camp Host on site. Pre-payment required at check-in. Season of Operation: Year-round.
Eligibility: AD, NG, Res, Ret and DoD-Civ.
Camper/Trailer Spaces: Camper Spaces: Hardstand (36), Pull-through, Max of 50' in length, handicap accessible, E(220V/30A/50A)/S/W hookups, picnic table, grill. Rates: $30 daily. Grass/Dirt (36), Pull-through, Max of 50' in length. No hookups. Rates: $10 daily.
Tent Spaces: Tent Spaces: Grass (4), no hookups. Rates: $10 daily
Support Facilities: Auto Craft Shop, Boat Rental/Storage, Bowling Chapel, Commissary, Exchange, Fitness Center, Gas, Golf, Grills, Ice, Laundry/Pay, Museums, Pavilion, Picnic Area, Playground, Pools/Indoor, Outdoor, Propane, Racquetball, Rec Center, Rec Equipment, Restrooms, RV Storage, Sewage Dump, Shoppette, Showers, Snack Bar, Sports Fields, Telephones/Pay, Tennis Courts.
RV Storage: Contact Outdoor Recreation for more information, C-661-275-2267. Spots available for 20'-45' RV's. Rates: $15-$35 per month, minimum 6 months.
Activities: Bowling, Fishing, Golfing, Racquetball, Rod and Gun Club, Swimming, Trap & Skeet Club in town.
Credit Cards: Cash, Check, MasterCard and Visa.
Restrictions: Pets allowed in designated areas only. No firearms allowed. No open fires. No feeding of wild animals. Limit of stay: 90 consecutive days, them must leave for 14 days before being able to return. No more than 168 total days in a 12 month period.
RV Driving Directions/Location: On Base. From north or south on CA-14: Drive 11 miles north of Lancaster to Rosamond. Exit east onto Rosamond Blvd, then travel approximately 16 miles to Edwards AFB Main Gate. Follow E Rosamond Blvd northeast then turn left onto N Lancaster Blvd/Redman Road. Take a left onto Fitzgerald Blvd. Follow Fitzgerald for two blocks to Coliseum Dr. FAMCAMP is located behind the bowling alley. From east or west on CA-58: Exit at Edwards AFB exit. Enter the North Gate and follow the signs.
Area Description: Located in Mojave-Lancaster-Barstow section of California's hilly desert region northeast of Los Angeles metropolitan area. Convenient base for visiting Lake Arrowhead and other points of interest in the San Bernardino-Pasadena-Los Angeles complex. Full range of support facilities available on base.
RV Campground Physical Address: 5217 Lathrop Drive, Edwards AFB, CA 93524.

El Centro Naval Air Facility

Address: Naval Air Facility El Centro, Bennett Road, El Centro, CA 92243-5001.
Information Line: C-760-339-2519.
Main Base Police: C-760-339-2542. Emergency, C-760-339-2588.
Main Installation Website: http://www.cnic.navy.mil/regions/cnrsw/installations/naf_el_centro.html
Main Base Location: Naval Air Facility El Centro is located in the heart of Southern California's Imperial Valley. It is a two-hour drive from San Diego and Palm Springs, one hour from Yuma, AZ, and fifteen minutes from the Mexican border.
Directions to Main Gate: From Los Angeles: I-10 East to CA-86 South. CA-86 becomes Imperial Avenue. Turn right on Adams, Adams becomes Evan Hewes Highway. Turn right on Bennet Road to NAF El Centro main gate. From San Diego: I-8 East, exit on Drew Road

toward Seeley. Turn left onto Drew Road, turn right onto Evan Hewes Highway. Turn left onto Bennet Road to NAF El Centro main gate. From Yuma Arizona: I-8 West to Forrester Road. Turn right onto Forrester Road. Turn left onto Evan Hewes Highway. Turn right onto Bennet Road to NAF El Centro main gate.

NMC: El Centro, seven miles east.
NMI: Yuma MCAS, 64 miles east.
Base Social Media/Facebook:
https://www.facebook.com/NAFEC
Chapels: C-760-339-2461/2454.
Medical: C-760-339-2674. Pharmacy, C-760-339-2631.
Beauty/Barber Shop: Barber, C-760-339-2597.
Commissary: C-760-339-2558.
Exchange: C-760-339-2342.
Clubs: The Sundowner Club, C-760-339-2319.
Places to Eat: The Mirage Club, C-760-339-2319, Dining Room, C-760-339-2996, Cyber Café, C-760-339-2559, Hot Stuff Pizza, C-760-339-2918.
Bowling: Desert Lanes Bowling Center, C-760-339-2575.
Fitness Center: Fitness and Sports Center, C-760-339-2488. Family Fitness Center, C-760-339-2644.
Golf: Driving Range, C-760-339-2575.
ITT/ITR: C-760-339-2559.
MWR: C-760-339-2481.
MWR Website:
http://navylifesw.com/elcentro/
MWR Facebook:
https://www.facebook.com/navylifesw
MWR Twitter:
https://twitter.com/navylifesw
Outdoor Recreation: Offers camping equipment, sports gear, bounce houses, RV space, boats, go kart trak, bicycles and adventure programs. Equipment Rental, C-760-339-2486.
Swimming: Large Pool, C-760-339-2487, Olympic size pool offers 3 and 1 meter boards, two water slides and rock climbing wall. Family Pool, C-760-339-2627, 25 yard recreational heated pool with a separate shaded kiddie pool, in-water basketball hoop and water volleyball, carpeted cabana area, changing/restrooms and two BBQ grills.

Things To Do: MWR-sponsored trips to Mexico, San Diego, Palm Springs, and more, the "Pearl of The Desert" is the place to vacation year-round. Watch the Blue Angels during winter and early Spring at NAF El Centro practice their daring maneuvers for the air show season.

RV CAMPING & GETAWAYS
Palm Oasis RV Park

Reservation/Contact Number Info: C-760-339-2486, DSN-312-658-2486. Fax C-760-339-2326.
Recreation Security: C-760-339-2222.
RV Website:
http://navylifesw.com/elcentro/recreation/recreationallodging/
Other Info Website:
http://get.dodlodging.net/propertys/Palm-Oasis-RV-Park
GPS Coordinates:
32°49'3"N/115°40'48"W
Reservations: Reservations accepted 30 days. Office hours 0800-1630 Mon-Fri. Check in at Outdoor Adventure Center, Bldg 318. After hours check in with Camp Host, Space 43. Check-out 1200 hours. Maximum stay 30 days.
Season of Operation: Year-round.
Eligibility: AD, NG, Res, Ret, DoD-Civ (AD/Ret), Dep and 100% DAV.
Camper/Trailer Spaces: Hardstand (21), back-in, maximum length 40', E(110/220V/15/30)/S/W hookups, phone, CATV, picnic table. Gravel (70), back-in, maximum length 40', E(220V/30A)/S/W hookups, phone, CATV, picnic table. Rates: $22-$35 daily, $400-$475 monthly. Call to confirm current rates. Free Wi-Fi at each site.
Tent Spaces: Primitive sites, no hookups. Rates: Call for rates.
Support Facilities: Auto Craft Shop, Auto Repair, Bath House, Bowling, Chapel, Commissary, Convenience Store, Diesel (off-installation), Driving Range, Dump Stations, Equipment Rental, Exchange, Fitness Center, Grills, Gas, Golf*, Grills, Ice, Laundry/Pay, Library, Mechanic/Auto Repair, Mess Hall (AD only), Pavilion, Picnic Area, Playground, Pool, Propane (bottle or

fill), Rec center, Restrooms, RV Storage, Sewage Dump, Shoppette, Showers, Sports Fields. * Three nearby golf courses.

RV Storage: Offered Oct- Mar; limited availability. Rates: $25/month. Contact Auto Hobby Shop: C-760-339-2689 for information.

Activities: Bicycling, Canoe Trips, Fishing*, Golfing, Hiking, Hunting*, Off Roading, Sporting Events, Swimming, Water Skiing. Fishing and hunting licenses sold at MWR. *License required. Complimentary Family Movie Night the last Wed of each month.

Credit Cards: Mastercard and Visa.

Restrictions: Pets allowed, must be on leash at all times. Owners must clean up after pets. Pets are not allowed on the running track or football field. Firearms must be checked at Security.

RV Driving Directions/Location: On Base. From the Gate: Bear left at "Y" and left again onto First St. Continue until street name changes to D St. Go past the sign for Palm Oasis RV Park and look for a large asphalt area on the right, past the bus stop. Pull in and park there. Check-in is across the street, on the North end of Bldg 318.

Area Description: Located in the Imperial Valley of southern California. El Centro NAF is where the sun spends the winter! Climate is warm and dry with more sunshine recorded in the area than any other in the United States. Temperatures can reach 120ºF Jun through Aug. Full range of support facilities available on base.

RV Campground Physical Address: D Street, Bldg 318, Naval Air Facility, El Centro, CA 92243.

Fiddler's Cove RV Park

Address: Fiddler's Cove RV Park, 3205 Silver Strand Highway 75, Coronado, CA 92118.

Information Line: C-619-437-2011, DSN-312-577-2011.

Main Base Police: C-619-524-2030.

Main Installation Website:
http://www.cnic.navy.mil/regions/cnrsw/installations/navbase_coronado.html

Main Base Location: RV Park overlooks the glimmering waters of the San Diego Bay and offers scenic views of the bay, bridge and downtown skyline.

NMC: Coronado, within city limits.

NMI: Naval Amphibious Base Coronado, 1.5 miles north.

Base Social Media/Facebook:
https://www.facebook.com/pages/MWR-Fiddlers-Cove-Marina-and-RV-Park/126660090689236

Medical: C-619-545-8624.

Commissary: Approximately 5 miles to the North Island Navy Commissary, C-619-545-6560.

Exchange Gas: NEX gas station at North Island, approximately 5 miles away, C-619-437-1928. Commercial gas station within 10 miles.

Exchange: Approximately 5 miles to the North Island Navy Exchange, C-619-522-7222.

Places to Eat: Fast food and fine dining are within driving distance.

MWR Website:
http://navylifesw.com/sandiego/

MWR Facebook:
https://www.facebook.com/navylifesw

MWR Twitter:
https://twitter.com/navylifesw

RV CAMPING & GETAWAYS

Fiddler's Cove RV Park

Reservation/Contact Number Info: C-619-522-8680/8681, C-1-800-NAVY-BED. Fax C-619-522-7679. Recreation Security: C-619-524-2030.

RV Website:
http://navylifesw.com/sandiego/recreation/navygetaways/

Other Info Website:
http://get.dodlodging.net/propertys/Fiddlers-Cove-Marina--RV-Park

GPS Coordinates:
32°39'4"N/117°8'51"W or 3205 Silver Strand Blvd/Hwy 75, Coronado, CA 92118-5000.

Reservations: Reservations may be made one year in advance for AD; 6 months in advance for Ret/DoD. All MWR eligible customers are welcome. Maximum stay 30 days. Office hours

0800-1700 Mon-Sun. Check-out 1100 hours.

Season of Operation: Year-round.

Eligibility: AD, NG, Res, Ret, DoD-Civ, Dep and 100% DAV.

Camper/Trailer Spaces: RV Sites: Pads (59), Full hook up for all spaces with water, sewage and electric with (110V/120V/150V) availability. Three Rows: Rates for Oceanside First Row: $35/36 with ring per night for AD/Ret; $40/$41 with ring for DoD. Middle pull-thrus: $30 per night for AD/Ret; $38 per night for DoD. Third Row: $30 per night for AD/Ret; $38 per night for DoD. Call to confirm current rates.

Tent Spaces: Tent Spaces (2) with power outlet. Rates: $20 per night for AD/Ret; $25 per night DoD.

Support Facilities: Auto Craft Shop, Bathhouse, Beach, Boat Launch, Boat Rental/Storage, Boat Slip Rental, Bowling, Coin Laundry, Commissary, Convenience Store, Equipment Rental, Exchange, Fire Rings, Fitness Center, Golf (nearby), Grills, Ice, Marina, Mess Hall, Pavilion, Pay telephones, Picnic Area, Restrooms, Sewage Dump, Shoppette, Showers, Snack Bar, Trails, Wi-Fi.

RV Storage: None.

Activities: Bicycling, Boating, Fishing*, Jogging, Sailing. *State fishing license required.

Credit Cards: MasterCard and Visa.

Restrictions: Pets allowed on leash. Owner must keep noise down and clean up after pet. No open fires. All base regulations apply.

RV Driving Directions/Location: Off Base. From the north in San Diego on I-5: Take Coronado Bridge exit west. Cross bridge and go south (left) on CA-75/Orange Avenue/Silver Strand Highway. The RV park is two miles south of the Hotel Del Coronado. From the south on I-5: Take exit west to Palm Avenue which later becomes CA-75 for 10 miles traveling through Imperial Beach. The RV park is located on the east side of the highway, just past Leyte Road.

Area Description: Located on east side of Silver Strand facing east on San Diego Bay and within three miles of Coronado City Public Beach and two miles of the State Beach. Popular activities include tours of historic sites, shopping in Tijuana, and attractions in San Diego. Full range of support facilities available on base.

RV Campground Physical Address: Fiddler's Cove RV Park, 3205 Silver Strand Highway 75, Coronado, CA 92118.

Fort Hunter Liggett

Address: 238 California Avenue, Fort Hunter Liggett, CA 93928.

Information Line: C-831-386-2505.

Main Base Police: C-831-386-2513.

Main Installation

Website: http://www.liggett.army.mil/sites/local/home.php

Main Base Location: Fort Hunter Liggett is located in Monterey County, in the central coast of California, 150 miles south of San Francisco and 250 miles north of Los Angeles. The installation is bound on the north by the Salinas Valley, on the east by the foothills of the Santa Lucia Mountains, on the south by the Monterey/San Luis Obispo county line and on the west by approximately 55 miles of Los Padres National Forest.

Directions to Main Gate: The nearest airport is San Jose International Airport, which is located 134 miles from the installation. From the airport: Proceed towards the airport exit on Airport Blvd. Take a slight right to stay on Airport Blvd (signs for Departures A/Terminal C). Take a Slight right and follow signs for CA-87/US-101/Skyport Drive. Merge right onto CA-87 South/Guadalupe Pkwy toward Downtown. Take the exit toward CA-85 South. Take exit 1A on the left to merge onto CA-85 South toward Gilroy. Take exit 1A to merge onto US-101 South toward Los Angeles then take the CR-G14/Jolon Road exit toward Fort Hunter Liggett.

NMC: King City, approximately 20 miles north.

NMI: Camp Roberts, 36 miles southeast.

Base Social

Media/Facebook: https://www.facebook.com/FortHunterLiggett

Base Social Media/Twitter:
https://twitter.com/FtHunterLiggett
Chapels: Religious Support Office, C-831-386-2808.
Medical: C-831-386-2516.
Beauty/Barber Shop: C-831-386-2825.
Commissary: C-831-386-2181/2178.
Exchange: C-831-385-4585.
Clubs: Club Hacienda, C-831-386-2900.
Places to Eat: Hacienda Lounge and Lodge, C-831-386-2900. Liggett Lanes Snack Bar, C-831-386-2194.
Bowling: Liggett Lanes, C-831-386-2194.
Fitness Center: DeAnza Sports Center, C-831-386-2784.
ITT/ITR: C-831-386-2406.
Library: C-831-386-2719.
MWR: C-831-386-2400/2988.
MWR Website:
https://hunterliggett.armymwr.com/us/hunterliggett
Outdoor Recreation: C-831-386-2417. Offers a variety of indoor and outdoor equipment including bicycles, camping equipment and group trips.
Swimming: Indoor Pool, C-831-386-2784 offers a 25-meter pool and a wading pool.
Things To Do: Visit the Los Padres National Forest, enjoy hunting and fishing. The area has varied outdoor activities and natural attractions. The fort covers hundreds of acres of grassland, chaparral and oak woodland. There are several vernal pools, a rare habitat type. The entire world population of the rare Santa Lucia mint (Pogogyne clareana) occurs on Fort Hunter Liggett grounds.

RV CAMPING & GETAWAYS
FHL Primitive Camp

Reservation/Contact Number Info: C-831-386-2417.
RV Website:
https://hunterliggett.armymwr.com/programs/outdoor-recreation
Reservations: Office hours 0830-1700 Mon, Thur; 0830-1800 Fri; 0730-1600 Sat-Sun. Closed Tue-Wed.
Season of Operation: Year-round.
Eligibility: AD, NG, Res, Ret. Open to public.

Camper/Trailer Spaces: Primitive sites (27) equipped with electricity and fire pits. Full Hookup Sites 1&2: Rates: $15 daily, $250 monthly; Sites 3-23 $10 daily, $200 monthly; 24-27 Golden Age Pass Sites $10 daily, $200 monthly. Additional pet, vehicle and late fees apply.
Tent Spaces: Overflow and Group Sites: Rates: $10 daily; $200-$300 monthly.
Support Facilities: Car Wash, Commissary, Equipment Rental, Exchange, Fitness Center,
Activities: Boating, Bowling, Fishing, Hunting, Kayaking, Mountain Biking, Nature Sightseeing, Paintball, Swimming,
Restrictions: Hunters must have FHL hunting permit, valid California Department of Fishing and Wildlife hunting license, species tags and/or stamps, and photo identification. Not available on base.
Area Description: Located amidst 162,000 acres of grasslands, woodlands, and chaparral habitats in the beautiful mountains of California. A prime area for outdoor enthusiasts.
RV Campground Physical Address: Bldg 191 Javelin Ct, Fort Hunter Liggett, CA 93928.

Lake Tahoe Coast Guard Recreation Facilities

Address: USCG Station Lake Tahoe, 2500 Lake Forest Road, Tahoe City, CA 96145.
Information Line: C-530-583-4433. Mon-Fri 0800-1400.
Main Base Police: Emergencies dial 911.
Main Installation Website:
http://www.uscg.mil/d11/staLakeTahoe/
Main Base Location: Located about 30 miles southwest of Reno, NV and about 100 miles east of Sacramento, CA.
Directions to Main Gate: From I-80: Take Hwy 89 southwest/North Lake Blvd through Tahoe City and proceed north on Hwy 28 for approximately 2 miles. Turn right onto Lake Forest Blvd and proceed to the CG Station. It is well marked by signs.

NMC: Reno, 30 miles southeast.
NMI: Reno-Tahoe IAP/ANG, NV, 40 miles northeast.
Places to Eat: Many restaurants and fast food establishments in Reno and Tahoe City.
Golf: Complimentary golf passes are available for guests. Contact the lodging facility for more information.
Outdoor Recreation Text: Hiking, fishing (with state license), sailing, swimming, water sports, picnicking, mountain climbing, skiing, boating much more are available. There are no other military support facilities available but nearby businesses offer marine, boat rental and boat launch facilities.
Swimming: Lake swimming.
Things To Do: There is much to do and see in nearby Reno and Carson City. Many recreational activities are available on Lake Tahoe and surrounding Sierra Mountains.
Walking Trails: Nature trails are available.

RV CAMPING & GETAWAYS

Lake Tahoe USCG Station A-Frames

Reservation/Contact Number Info: C-530-583-4433.
Recreation Security: C-530-583-4433.
RV Website:
https://reservations.vacationrentaldesk.com/StationLakeTahoe/homepage.html
RV Email Address:
uscgaframes@uscg.mil
GPS Coordinates:
39°11'3"N/120°7'11"W
Reservations: Reservations required and accepted ONLY through web site at https://reservations.vacationrentaldesk.com/StationLakeTahoe/homepage.html . Payment through automated online system only. Preferred method of contact is email. Reservations may be made 90 days in advance for AD, 60 days in advance for all others. Check in 1600-2000 hours at the North Building, through the door located closest to the lake. Must present payment receipt and valid military ID upon arrival. Check-out

1000 hours. Maximum stay 10 days to include only one weekend.
Season of Operation: Year-round.
Eligibility: AD, NG, Res, Ret, DoD-Civ (AD and Ret), Dep, 100% DAV, CG NAF-Civ and other federal civilians.
Yurt, A Frame, Cabin, Apt, Spaces: A-Frame Cottages: Two-bedroom (2), ground floor apartment, sleeps eight, private bath, furnished, kitchen, microwave, heat, DirecTV, dishes, cooking utensils, coffee pot, hair dryer, linens, grill. Only one apartment will be rented to any applicant. Rates: $145 daily, $1,015 weekly. One-bedroom (2), second floor apartment, sleeps six, private bath, furnished, kitchen, microwave, heat, DirecTV, dishes, cooking utensils, coffee pot, hair dryer, linens, grill. Rates: $125 daily, $875 weekly. Wi-Fi provided in all cabins.
Support Facilities: Boat launch, Convenience Store, Fishing Pier, Golf, Grills, Pay Phones, Trails. No parking for boats, U-hauls, trailers or campers.
Activities: Bicycling, Boating, Fishing*, Hiking, Picnicking, Playground, Sailing, Skiing, Snowboarding, Snow Sports, Swimming, Water Skiing, Wind Surfing. *State License required.
Credit Cards: Credit Cards only through the online automated system.
Restrictions: No camping or RVs. No pets allowed. No late checkouts. No firearms. No smoking. Alcohol allowed on the decks and picnic tables between the cabins only. This unit is an operational Search and Rescue and Law Enforcement Unit. Check-in is handled by duty personnel on a not-to-interfere basis. If actively running a Search and Rescue and/or Law Enforcement Case, patrons may be asked to return at a later time to check-in.
RV Driving Directions/Location: On Base. From the Gate: Follow the directions on the intercom to speak to someone for buzzed-in entry.
Area Description: Located at Lake Tahoe Coast Guard Station on northwest shore of the beautiful lake which is on the California/Nevada border in the heart of the Sierra Nevada Mountains at 6,225 feet above sea

level. Much to do and see in nearby cities of Reno and Carson City. Many recreational activities available on Lake Tahoe and surrounding Sierra Nevada mountains.

RV Campground Physical Address: 2500 Lake Forest Road, Tahoe City, CA 96145.

Lemoore Naval Air Station

Address: NAS Lemoore, Franklin Ave & Enterprise Ave, Lemoore, CA 93245. Information Line: C-559-998-0100.

Main Base Police: C-559-998-4811/4766.

Main Installation Website: http://www.cnic.navy.mil/regions/cnrsw/installations/nas_lemoore.html

Main Base Location: Naval Air Station Lemoore, the Navy's prime West Coast Tactical Naval Air Station, is located in California's Central Valley.

Directions to Main Gate: From I-5 south: If traveling south from San Francisco/Sacramento area on I-5, take Route 198 East. Turn left at the stoplight at the Reeves Bypass intersection. Take the right hand lane to the security gate. From the Fresno Airport: Turn left onto Peach, travel one quarter of a mile, turn right onto McKinley Avenue. Take Route 41 South for 40 miles. Take Route 198 West. Follow directions above. From I-5 North: If traveling north from Los Angeles/San Diego area on I-5, take Route 41 North to Route 198 West. Turn right at the stoplight at the Reeves Bypass intersection. Follow directions above. From Route 41 South: If traveling south from the Fresno area on Route 41 South, take Route 198 West. Follow directions above. From Route 99: Take Route 198 West.

NMC: Fresno, 45 miles north.

NMI: Camp Roberts, 100 miles southwest.

Base Social Media/Facebook: https://www.facebook.com/pages/Naval-Air-Station-Lemoore/162253324084

Chapels Phone Numbers: C-559-998-4618.

Dental Clinic: C-559-998-4219/4220.

Medical: Naval Hospital Lemoore, C-559-998-4481/4228, DSN-312-949-4481. United Healthcare Military and Veterans, C-1-877-838-7532.

Veterinary Services: C-559-998-2753. Beauty/Barber Shop: C-559-998-4655.

Commissary: C-559-998-4669.

Exchange: C-559-998-4722.

Financial Institutions: Armed Forces Bank, C-559-997-0348. Navy Federal Credit Union, C-1-888-842-6328.

Clubs: Spuds Restaurant & Pub, C-559-998-2211. Tailhook Tavern, C-559-998-2246.

Places to Eat: Bowling Alley, C-559-998-4648, McDonald's, C-559-998-6850, NEX Food Court, C-559-998-4722, Zeny's Restaurant, C-559-924-4973, Vineyard Inn, C-559-924-1988, Jade Garden, C-559-925-9002 and Reynas, C-559-925-9125 all within a short drive.

Bowling: Tailhooks Bowling Center, C-559-998-4647.

Fitness Center: C-559-998-4883. Ops Fitness Center, C-559-998-3694.

Golf: Lemoore Golf Course, C-559-924-9658.

ITT/ITR: C-559-998-0837.

MWR: C-559-998-4886.

MWR Website: http://www.navymwrlemoore.com/

MWR Facebook: https://www.facebook.com/LemooreCSP

MWR Twitter: https://twitter.com/navylifesw

Outdoor Recreation: C-559-998-4352. Offers a variety of outdoor equipment including camping trailers, ski boats, tents, sleeping bags, skis, toboggans, snowboards and sleds. They also have horseshoes, barbecues and ice chests. Additional information available at OAC.

Swimming: Heated lap pool at the NAS Lemoore main-side gym.

Things To Do: Located in the San Joaquin Valley, near Sequoia and Yosemite National Parks, two hours from the coast or mountains and three hours from Los Angeles or San Francisco. The Tachi Palace Casino is located in the city of Lemoore. This base offers excellent support facilities.

RV CAMPING & GETAWAYS
Lemoore NAS RV Park

Reservation/Contact Number Info: C-1-877-NAVY-BED, C-559-998-0838/7051. Recreation Security: C-559-998-4769.
RV Website:
http://navylifesw.com/lemoore/recreation/recreationallodging/
Other Info Website:
http://get.dodlodging.net/propertys/Navy-Getaways-Lemoore-RV-Park
RV Email Address:
lemr_rv_reserve@navy.mil
GPS Coordinates:
36°15'36"N/119°53'52"W
Reservations: Accepted via phone, on-line or in person at Bldg 951. Office hours 0900-1700 Mon-Fri. Closed holidays and weekends. After hours arrival should use self check-in board at park entrance.
Season of Operation: Year-round.
Eligibility: AD, NG, Res, Ret, DoD-Civ, Dep and 100% DAV.
Camper/Trailer Spaces: Hardstand (18), Pull-thru, maximum length 55', E(110/220V/15/30/50A)/S/W, CATV hookups, Wi-Fi, picnic table, grill, dumping station. Rates: Call for current rates.
Support Facilities: Auto Craft Shop, Bathhouse, Boat Rental/Storage, Bowling, Chapel, Commissary, Convenience Store, Equipment Rental, Exchange, Fitness Center, Gas, Golf, Grills, Laundry/free, Mess Hall, Pavilion, Picnic Area, Playground, Pool, Propane, Rec Center, Restrooms, RV Storage, Sewage Dump, Showers, Sports Fields, Stables, Telephones/Pay, Tennis Courts, Wireless Internet.
RV Storage: Available. Call ahead, as space is very limited. RV park maintains waiting list. Rates: $20/month. Auto Hobby Shop: C-559-997-8983.
Activities: Bicycling, Boating, Fishing*, Gold Panning, Golfing, Hiking, Hunting*, Jet Skiing, Scuba Diving, Swimming.
Credit Cards: MasterCard and Visa.
Restrictions: Pets must be on leash at all times when outside of campers. Owner must clean up after pet. All vaccinations must be current and have valid documentation. Pets staying longer than 30 days must be micro-chipped and registered with the base.
RV Driving Directions/Location: On Base. From the Main Gate: Continue north on Enterprise to four-way stop. Turn right onto Franklin Ave. At the next four-way stop, turn right onto Hancock Ave. Make an immediate left turn into the Village Parking Lot. The RV Park entrance is located on the southeast corner of the parking lot. Check-in is located at Tickets & Tours inside Bldg 920 (The Village Complex), first door on the right.
Area Description: Located in the heart of the beautiful San Joaquin Valley.
RV Campground Physical Address: 920 Franklin Ave, Lemoore, CA 93246.

Los Alamitos Joint Forces Training Base

Address: California Army National Guard, 11200 Lexington Drive HQ Bldg 15, Los Alamitos, CA 90720-5001.
Information Line: C-562-795-2000, DSN-312-972-2000.
Main Base Police: C-562-796-2100.
Main Installation Website:
https://calguard.ca.gov/jftb_losalamitos/
Main Base Location: Los Alamitos, CA.
Directions to Main Gate: From I-405/San Diego Freeway north or south: Take exit to I-605/San Gabriel River Freeway north approximately 1.5 miles to exit east onto East Katella Avenue. Turn east 1.7 miles to right (south) on Lexington Drive and proceed to Main Gate. Clearly marked.
NMC: Los Angeles, 15 miles northwest.
NMI: Seal Beach Naval Weapons Station, 5 miles south.
Medical: C-562-796-1111.
Beauty/Barber Shop: C-562-430-3698.
Commissary: Los Angeles AFB, C-310-414-9001 ex 2999.
Exchange: C-562-430-1076, Los Angeles AFB, C-310-414-9404.
Financial Institutions: Bank of America, C-1-800-4320-1000, Sea Air Federal Credit Union, C-562-430-8066, Wells Fargo Bank, C-562-594-0975 and more are within easy reach.

Places to Eat: Fiddler's Green, C-562-795-2168 on post and a cafeteria available. Katella Deli, Fish Company and Paul's Place are off post and within walking distance. Gilders Inn, Spaghettini's and Walts of Seal Beach are within driving distance.

Fitness Center: Gym on base.

ITT/ITR: C-562-795-2126.

MWR: C-562-795-2124.

MWR Website:
https://jftbmwrbillets.com/

MWR Facebook:
https://www.facebook.com/JFTB-MWR-140035016636160/

Swimming: Outdoor Pool, C-562-795-2628 offers lap swim and lessons. Varied hours.

Things To Do: Nearby Anaheim and Orange County offer beautiful beaches and many tourist attractions, including Disneyland.

RV CAMPING & GETAWAYS

MWR RV Park

Reservation/Contact Number Info: C-562-795-2128.

Recreation Security: C-562-796-2100.

RV Website:
https://jftbmwrbillets.com/rv-park-storage/

GPS Coordinates:
33°47'41.8"N/118°02'59.0"W

Reservations: Must call for reservations. Limited availability. Office hours 0800-1700 daily. Check in at Billeting, Bldg 19. Check-in 1300 hours, check-out 1100 hours. Maximum stay 30 days.

Season of Operation: Year-round.

Eligibility: AD, NG, Res, Ret, and dependents.

Camper/Trailer Spaces: RV Sites: Full hook-ups, max 30' allowed. Rates: $23 daily.

Support Facilities: Exchange, Gym, Laundry Facilities.

Activities: Gymnasium, Swimming Pool.

Credit Cards: American Express, MasterCard, Visa.

RV Driving Directions/Location: On Base. From Main Gate: Continue on Lexington then go left onto Shiloh Way.

Go right onto Independence Drive. Go right onto Yorktown Avenue. Check in at Billeting.

Area Description: Nearby Anaheim and Orange County offer beautiful beaches and many tourist attractions, including Disneyland.

RV Campground Physical Address: 4525 Yorktown Avenue, Bldg 19, Los Alamitos, CA 90720.

March Air Reserve Base

Address: 452nd AMW Public Affairs, 895 Baucom Avenue SE, Bldg 317, March ARB, CA 92518.

Information Line: C-951-655-4137, DSN-312-447-1110.

Main Base Police: C-951-655-2981.

Main Installation Website:
http://www.march.afrc.af.mil/

Main Base Location: March Air Reserve Base is located in north west Riverside County which, along with San Bernardino County, is called the "Inland Empire" region of Southern California. Los Angeles is approximately 60 miles west.

Directions to Main Gate: From north or south on I-215/CA-215: Use March ARB exit, Cactus Street East. Continue east approximately 1.5 miles to traffic light. Main Gate on right (south) side of road.

NMC: Riverside, 9 miles northwest.

NMI: Camp Pendleton, 63 miles southwest.

Base Social Media/Facebook:
https://www.facebook.com/teammarch

Base Social Media/Twitter:
https://twitter.com/march_arb

Chapels: C-951-655-4105.

Beauty/Barber Shop: Barber, C-951-653-7814. Beauty, C-951-653-5577.

Commissary: C-951-653-2206. Bakery, 951-655-3967 ext 131.

Exchange: C-951-653-3111.

Financial Institutions: Chase Bank, C-951-776-0024; Wells Fargo Bank, C-951-653-6128 and U.S. Bank, C-951-780-5584 are within easy driving distance.

Clubs: Aces Sports Bar, C-951-653-2121.

Places to Eat: Back Street Cafe, C-951-655-3663, Toscano's Subs/Noble Roman's Pizza, C-951-653-8505.

Bowling: Sallys Alley, C-951-655-3828.
Fitness Center: C-951-655-2292/2284.
Golf: General Old Golf Course located on March ARB, C-951-697-6690.
ITT/ITR: C-951-655-4123.
Military Museum: March Field Museum, C-951-902-5949.
Military Museum Website: http://www.marchfield.org/index.html
MWR: C-312-447-4301.
MWR Website: http://marchfss.com/
MWR Facebook: https://www.facebook.com/MarchFSS/
Outdoor Recreation: C-951-655-2816. Offers plenty of recreational activities including bike rentals, kayaks, paddleboards, motocross training, snowtubing in Big Bear and team building kits.
Things To Do: Visit Getty Villa, Laguna Beach, Los Angeles, Las Vegas, National Comedy Theater, Medieval Times, Disneyland, or the Maritime Museum. Go to Malibu Creek State Park, enjoy deep sea fishing and horseback riding or skiing at Big Bear.

RV CAMPING & GETAWAYS

March ARB FamCamp

Reservation/Contact Number Info: C-951-655-3983, DSN-312-447-3983. Fax C-951-655-5221.
RV Website: http://marchfss.com/fun-recreation/outdoor-recreation/fam-camp/
GPS Coordinates: 33°53'36"N/117°15'W
Reservations: No advance reservations. All sites a first come, first serve basis. Office hours 0830-1630 Mon-Fri. Check-in anytime, check-out 1200 hours. Maximum stay 14 days. Stay may be extended space permitting.
Season of Operation: Year-round.
Eligibility: AD, NG, Res, Ret, DoD-Civ, ID Card holders and family members.
Camper/Trailer Spaces: Hardstand (40): handicap accessible (30), pull-thru (10), maximum length 60', E(120/220V/30/50A)/S/W hookups, concrete patio and patio seating grills. Rates: $17 daily; $224 bi-weekly.

Support Facilities: Boat Rental/Storage, Chapel, Commissary, Convenience Store, Exchange, Fitness Center, Golf, Grills, Ice, Laundry/Pay, Pay Phone, Picnic Area, Rec Equipment, Restrooms, RV Storage, Sewage Dump, Shoppette, Showers, Snack Bar, Sports Fields, Tennis Courts, Summer Outdoor Movie Theater. Full range of support facilities on base.
RV Storage: Long-term RV storage available. (400+ spaces). One-month minimum. Very busy, with waiting list year-round. Rates: $35/month. Contact Outdoor Recreation Office at C-909-655-2816.
Activities: Boating, Biking, Boating, Fishing, Golfing, Hiking, Skiing, Surfing, Tennis and Amusement Parks.
Credit Cards: MasterCard and Visa.
Restrictions: Pets (2) allowed on leash. No firearms. No tent camping. Quiet hours 2200-0700.
RV Driving Directions/Location: On Base. From the Main Gate: Ask for camp directions at gate.
Area Description: Located in a semi-desert area with mountains close by. 45 miles to Palm Springs and local casinos. 90 miles to San Diego and Los Angeles. One to two-hour drive to Southern California major attractions, such as Disneyland, Magic Mountain, Knott's Berry Farm, Universal Studios, San Diego Zoo, Sea World and museums.
RV Campground Physical Address: Outdoor Recreation, 1870 Graeber Street, Bldg 434, March ARB, CA 92518.

Monterey Pines RV Park

Address: 1250 Garden Road, Monterey, CA 93940.
Information Line: C-831-656-2441, DSN-312-756-4221.
Main Base Police: Emergencies dial 911.
Main Installation Website: http://www.nps.edu/
Main Base Location: Located off base, across the street from the school.
NMC: Monterey, 0.5 miles north.
NMI: Monterey Naval Postgraduate School, 1.3 miles northwest.

Commissary: Approximately 2 miles to the Monterey Naval Postgraduate School Commissary, C-831-242-7668.

Exchange Gas: Approximately 2 miles to the Monterey Naval Postgraduate School NEX Gas Station, C-831-373-7271. Commercial gas station within 3 miles.

Exchange: Approximately 2 miles to the Monterey Naval Postgraduate School Exchange facility, C-831-373-7277.

MWR Website:
http://navylifesw.com/monterey/

MWR Facebook:
https://www.facebook.com/navylifesw

MWR Twitter:
https://twitter.com/navylifesw

RV CAMPING & GETAWAYS

Monterey Pines RV Park

Reservation/Contact Number Info: C-1-877-NAVY-BED, C-831-656-7563. Fax C-831-656-7662.

Recreation Security: C-831-656-2556.

RV Website:
http://get.dodlodging.net/propertys/Monterey-Pines-RV-Campground

Other Info Website:
http://navylifesw.com/monterey/recreation/recreationallodging/

RV Email Address: cminouye@nps.mil

GPS Coordinates:
36°35'36"N/121°51'57"W or 1250 Garden Road, 93940.

Reservations: All reservations are made on a first come, first serve basis without regard to rate or rank. Reservations may be made up to 1 year in advance for AD; 6 months in advance for Ret/DoD-Civ. Cancellations must be made within 30 days to avoid fee. Office hours 0800-1700 Mon-Fri. Check-in 1300 hours at Golf Pro Shop, check-out 1200 hours. Maximum stay 30 days.

Season of Operation: Year-round.

Eligibility: AD, NG, Res, Ret, Dep, DoD-Civ, Naval Post Graduate School DoD-Civ and Sponsored Guests.

Camper/Trailer Spaces: Asphalt (38, 1 handicap accessible) Back-in, Maximum 50' RV, with (30) full hookup, (8) partial hookup and dry camp sites, E(120V/30A)/S/W hookups, picnic table,

grill. Wi-Fi available at Clubhouse and throughout most of RV Park. Rates: $26-$38 daily. Call to confirm current rates.

Support Facilities: Aquarium, Bathhouse, Beach, Boat Launch, Bowling, Cafeteria*, Chapel*, Club/Bar*, Commissary (Nearby), Convenience Store*, Dining Facilities*, Exchange*, Fitness Center*, Flying Club*, Gas*, Golf, Grills, Laundromat, Marina, Picnic Area, Rec Center*, Rec Equipment*, Restrooms, RV Storage, Sewage Dump, Showers, Snack Bar, Sports Fields, Tennis Courts*, Ticket Office*, Trails. * Located at Naval Postgraduate School.

RV Storage: Contact General Manager at the campground. Rates: Vary based on the size of the space.

Activities: Bicycling, Fishing*, Golfing, Hiking, Historic walks, Jogging, Kayaking, Sailing, Shopping, Swimming, Tourist Attractions, including whale watching. *License required.

Credit Cards: MasterCard and Visa.

Restrictions: Two pets per site, must be leashed at all times. No tents allowed. Firearms are prohibited. One extra vehicle per RV is authorized to park in designated areas.

RV Driving Directions/Location: Off Base. From the north on CA-1: In Monterey exit and turn left onto Casa Verde Way. Go straight across Fremont Blvd to the dead end and turn right onto Fairgrounds Road. At next light, turn left onto Garden Road. Make an immediate left then turn right to entrance and main gate to Monterey Pines Golf Course and RV Park. From the south on CA-1: Exit at Mark Thomas/Aguajito Road and follow to third stop light. Turn right onto Garden Road and follow directions above.

Area Description: Located in a nature sanctuary situated between the 13th hole of the golf course and picnic grounds amongst Monterey pine trees on the historic grounds of the old premier coastal resort, The Del Monte Hotel. Gated installation.

RV Campground Physical Address: Monterey Pines RV Campground, 1250 Garden Rd, Monterey, CA 93940.

Petaluma Coast Guard Training Center

Address: Coast Guard Training Center Petaluma, 599 Tomales Road, Petaluma, CA 94952.
Information Line: C-707-765-7000.
Main Base Police: Non-Emergency, C-707-765-7215. Emergency on-base dial 8-911.
Main Installation Website: https://www.forcecom.uscg.mil/Our-Organization/FORCECOM-UNITS/TraCen-Petaluma/
Main Base Location: Located 60 miles north of San Francisco, Training Center Petaluma is the west coast's largest Coast Guard's training center.
Directions to Main Gate: From north or south on US-101: Exit at Petaluma onto East Washington Street southwest through city of Petaluma. Washington Street becomes Bodega Avenue. Continue west following signs to Coast Guard Training Center approximately 11 miles. Turn left (southwest) onto Tomales Road. A flashing amber light marks the Main Gate. Between 0600-0900 hours, enter the Training Center by taking a left on Spring Hill Road. Training Center is on the right.
NMC: San Francisco, 60 miles north.
NMI: Travis AFB, 62 miles east.
Base Social Media/Facebook: https://www.facebook.com/TRACENPetaluma/
Chapels: C-707-765-7330.
Dental Clinic: C-707-765-7200 option 2.
Medical: C-707-765-7000 option 1.
Beauty/Barber Shop: C-707-765-7311.
Exchange: C-707-765-7256.
Financial Institutions: Sea West Coast Guard Credit Union, C-1-800-732-9378.
Clubs: The Penalty Box Consolidated Club and Two Rock Pizza, C-707-765-7247/7248.
Places to Eat: Two Rock Coffee, C-707-765-7340, Haley Hall Dining, C-707-765-7151/7166.
Bowling: Bowling Center, C-707-765-7351.
Fitness Center: C-707-765-7348/7349. Exercise room also available at hotel.
ITT/ITR: C-707-765-7580.

Library: C-707-765-7580.
MWR: C-707-765-7341.
MWR Website: https://www.petalumamwr.com/
Outdoor Recreation: C-707-765-7580/7341. Offers two softball fields, lake area camping and picnic grounds, a skeet and archery range and Intramural sports teams, canoes and kayaks, playgrounds, volleyball courts, canoes and kayak rentals, and horseshoes.
Swimming: Petaluma Aquatic Sports Center, C-707-765-7483 offers lap swimming, wading pool, water slide and spa.
Things To Do: The Petaluma area is saturated with historical lore and legend. Early California missions, a Russian fort (Fort Ross), Sonoma County wineries, Russian River, swimming, fishing and canoeing all draw visitors to this delightful area.
Walking Trails: Walking trails available at the lake recreation area. For more information call the outdoor recreation.

RV Camping & Getaways
Petaluma Lake Area Campsites

Reservation/Contact Number Info: C-707-765-7341.
Recreation Security: C-707-765-7215.
RV Website: https://www.petalumamwr.com/lake-recreation-area-campground
RV Email Address: MWRHub@gmail.com
GPS Coordinates: 8°14'50"N/122°47'2"W
Reservations: Application for reservation required. Accepted 90 days in advance. Check in at The Hub. Maximum 14 day stay during peak season with a 90-day cumulative stay. Season of Operation: Year-round.
Eligibility: AD, NG, Res, Ret, DoD-Civ, Dep and U.S. Govt Civ Emp.
Camper/Trailer Spaces: Hardstand (6), Back-in and pull-thru, any size, E(110V/15A)/W, CATV, Wi-Fi, picnic table, fire pit with grill. Rates: $25 daily; $50 daily for guests.

Tent Spaces: Lake Sites: Primitive lake sites. Rates: $10 daily; $20 daily for guests.

Support Facilities: Bowling, Cafeteria, Chapel, Convenience Store, Equipment Rental, Exchange, Fitness Center*, Gas, Golf, Grills, Ice, Mess Hall, Pavilion, Picnic Area, Playground, Pool, Restrooms, Sewage Dump, Showers*, Snack Bar*, Sports Fields, Tennis Courts, Volleyball (sand). * Available at gymnasium.

Activities: Basketball, Fishing, Golfing, Hiking, Horseshoes, Jogging, Racquetball, Softball, Tennis, Volleyball.

Credit Cards: Cash, Checks, MasterCard and Visa.

Restrictions: Pets allowed on leash; owner must clean up after pets daily. No open fires. No firearms allowed.

RV Driving Directions/Location: On Base. From the Main Gate. Ask for directions to campsites.

Area Description: Located in beautiful Sonoma County, campsites are near a small lake in a quiet, rustic atmosphere. Full range of support facilities on base.

RV Campground Physical Address: Commanding Officer, Petaluma Lake Reservations, Attn: Library-Bldg 250, 599 Tomales Road, Coast Guard Training Center, Petaluma, CA 94952-5000.

Point Loma Naval Base

Address: Naval Base Point Loma, 140 Sylvester Road, San Diego, CA 92106.

Information Line: C-619-553-1011, DSN-312-553-1011.

Main Base Police: Emergency Dispatch, C-619-556-6460, After Hours, C-619-524-2030/2037, DSN-312-526-6460. Emergencies dial 911.

Main Installation Website: http://www.cnic.navy.mil/regions/cnrs w/installations/navbase_point_loma.ht ml

Main Base Location: Point Loma is one of the oldest communities in San Diego, and certainly one of the finest. Surrounded by the ocean on one side and beautiful San Diego Bay on the other, Point Loma's prestigious

neighborhoods boast incredible skyline and water views.

Directions to Main Gate: From I-5 North: Exit onto Pacific Hwy and proceed to the Barnett Street Exit. Go straight on Barnett, which turns to the right and becomes Lytton Street. Stay on Lytton to the first traffic light which is Rosecrans Street. Turn left onto Rosecrans Street. Stay on Rosecrans to the Main Gate (Post 6).

NMC: San Diego, five miles southeast.

NMI: Coronado NB, North Island NAS, 13 miles east.

Base Social Media/Facebook: https://www.facebook.com/NavalBaseP ointLoma

Base Social Media/Twitter: https://twitter.com/nbplpao

Chapels: C-619-556-2658.

Dental Clinic: C-619-556-8240/7680.

Medical: C-619-524-4947, C-619-532-8225 (Hospital 24/7), DSN-312-524-0103.

Veterinary Services: C-858-577-6552.

Beauty/Barber Shop: C-619-221-1094.

Commissary: Naval Base San Diego, C-619-556-8657.

Exchange Gas: C-619-221-1095.

Exchange: Sub Base Mini-Mart, C-619-523-1214. Naval Base San Diego Main Exchange C-619-544-2100.

Financial Institutions: Armed Forces Bank, C-619-758-9345. Point Loma Credit Union, C-858-495-3400.

Clubs: The Hub, C-619-553-9138.

Places to Eat: Subway, C-619-446-7785. There are many restaurants within driving distance of the facility.

Bowling: C-619-556-7486.

Golf: Sail Ho Golf Club, C-619-222-GOLF (4653), Fax C-619-222-4656. Admiral Baker Golf Course, C-619-487-0090 at Naval Station San Diego. Sea 'N Air Golf Course, C-619-545-9659 at Naval Air Station North Island.

ITT/ITR: C-619-221-1005.

Library: C-619-524-1850.

Marina: C-619-524-6498.

MWR: C-619-556-4798.

MWR Website: http://www.navymwrsandiego.com/

Outdoor Recreation: C-619-553-9138. Adventure Center at Naval Base San

Diego, C-619-556-7493. Outdoor gear rentals available at Point Loma NMAWC Sailing Center, C-619-524-6498. Outdoor Adventure office offers watersports and camping equipment rentals. Also provides information for local outdoor adventure attractions like mountain bike riding at national forests and ocean adventures. Also on base, Admiral Baker Picnic Area, C-619-487-0090. Bainbridge Park, C-619-556-7444, Waterfront Recreation Center, C-619-556-2174 and Harborside, C-619-556-7444.

Swimming: American Red Cross Lifeguard Training, C-619-553-0934. Sharks Club, C-619-553-0931, Masters Swim Program, C-619-553-0931, Swim Lessons, C-619-553-0934. Pacific Ocean is nearby for excellent swimming and beach fun. Naval Base Point Loma Main Pool, C-619-553-0934.

Things To Do: Located on beautiful Point Loma, with a spectacular view of San Diego Harbor and the city, this facility is on the bus line to beaches, Old Town, SeaWorld, the San Diego Zoo and other attractions. Visit Disneyland, The USS Midway Museum, Big Cat and Exotic Animal Rescue, Legoland, Six Flags Magic Mountain, Knott's Berry Farm, and Titanic Artifact Exhibition. Take a Black Canyon canoe trip or explore Hearst Castle. There are plenty of activities in the San Diego Area to enjoy.

RV CAMPING & GETAWAYS
Point Loma Bay View Cottages

Reservation/Contact Number Info: C-1-877-NAVY-BED, C-619-524-5382.
Recreation Security: Emergencies dial 911.
RV Website: http://get.dodlodging.net/propertys/Point-Loma
Reservations: Reservations required and accepted up to one year in advance for AD; all others 6 months. Cancellations require 30-day notice to avoid fee. Office hours 0900-1700

hours. Check-in 1400 hours, check-out 1100 hours.
Season of Operation: Year-round.
Eligibility: AD, NG, Res, Ret, DoD-Civ, Dep.
Yurt, A Frame, Cabin, Apt, Spaces: Cottages (2): Single-story, one and two-bedroom units with fully-equipped kitchens, flat-screen cable TVs with DVD players, Wi-Fi, telephones, linens, private baths and patios. Newer facility. Rates: $100 daily.
Support Facilities: Full range of support facilities on base.
Activities: Sailing, Swimming with activities on base.
Credit Cards: American Express, Discover, MasterCard and Visa.
Restrictions: Pets are not allowed in lodging facilities.
RV Driving Directions/Location: On Base. From the Main Gate: Ask for directions at the gate or at time of reservation.
Area Description: Located along the Bay with spectacular views, close to downtown activities and nightlife.
RV Campground Physical Address: 32444 Echo Lane, Suite 100, San Diego, CA 92147-5199.

Point Mugu – Ventura County Naval Base

Address: 311 Main Road, Suite 1, Bldg 1, Point Mugu, CA 93042.
Information Line: C-805-989-7209.
Main Base Police: C-805-989-7034, DSN-312-351-7034.
Main Installation Website: http://www.cnic.navy.mil/regions/cnrsw/installations/navbase_ventura_county.html
Main Base Location: Naval Base Ventura County (NBVC) Port Hueneme/Point Mugu is located on the vast Oxnard plain, just 30 miles northwest of Los Angeles, California.
Directions to Main Gate: Traveling to Point Mugu by car from Los Angeles: Take Highway 101 or Pacific Coast Highway/PCH-1 North and exit off Las Posas Road. Driving from Northern California: Take Highway 101 South and exit at Las Posas Rd and turn right. From

the 101: Follow Las Posas Road west for about 6 miles to Las Posas Gate 3. For night arrival: Take the frontage road to the right off Las Posas Road, it runs parallel to Pacific Coast Highway 1/PCH-1. At the second stop sign turn left. Main gate entrance ahead. The Main Gate is open 24 hours.

NMC: Los Angeles, 30 miles southeast.
NMI: Port Hueneme, 8 miles northeast.
Base Social Media/Facebook: https://www.facebook.com/NavalBase VenturaCounty
Chapels: C-805-989-7967.
Dental Clinic: Port Hueneme, C-805-982-5584.
Medical: C-805-989-8815/8816, DSN-312-351-8815/8816.
Veterinary Services: Port Hueneme, C-805-982-3271.
Beauty/Barber Shop: C-805-989-7271.
Exchange Gas: C-805-986-2174.
Exchange: C-805-989-8896.
Financial Institutions: Armed Forces Bank, C-805-815-4845. CBC Federal Credit Union, C-805-988-2151. Navy Federal Credit Union-Port Hueneme Branch, C-1-866-454-3141.
Places to Eat: Flightline Cafe, C-805-989-7747. Base Galley, C-805-989-7747. Subway, C-805-989-7396.
Bowling: Mugu Lanes, C-805-989-7667.
Fitness Center: Point Mugu Gym, C-805-989-7728.
ITT/ITR: C-805-989-7628.
Military Museum: Seabee Museum Port Hueneme, C-805-982-5165.
Military Museum Website: http://www.history.navy.mil/museums/seabee_museum.htm
MWR: C-805-989-7628.
MWR Website: http://navylifesw.com/ventura/
MWR Facebook: https://www.facebook.com/pages/NBV C-MWR/215294089299
MWR Twitter: https://twitter.com/nbvcmwr
Swimming: Mugu Pool Aquatic Center, C-805-989-7788 offers lap swim and swim lessons. Mugu Beach Surf Lessons, C-805-982-4753.
Things To Do: Conveniently located near Channel Islands Harbor, which is

comprised of nine sparkling boating marinas, downtown Ventura is thriving with art galleries, book stores, a wide variety of restaurants and lively entertainment. Whether looking for a relaxing vacation, shopping adventures or a vibrant nightlife, Point Mugu offers it all within a short distance.
Walking Trails: Point Mugu has a nature walk and the Santa Monica Mountains State Park, a short driving distance from the facility, offers numerous hiking trails.

RV CAMPING & GETAWAYS
Point Mugu Beach Motel & RV Park

Reservation/Contact Number Info: C-805-989-8407, C-1-877-NAVY-BED. Fax C-805-989-5413.
RV Website: http://get.dodlodging.net/propertys/Na vy-Getaways-Point-Mugu-Beach-Hotel--RV-Park
Other Info Website: http://navylifesw.com/ventura/recreati on/recreationallodging/
GPS Coordinates: 34°6'01"N/119°6'11"W
Reservations: Reservations required and may be made 180 days in advance for AD, Ret, Res, Dep; 60 days in advance for DoD Civ. Military may reserve up to three rooms per ID; DoD may reserve up to two rooms. Cancellations must be made within 48 hours of arrival. Early departures must provide 24-hour notice. Check in at Bldg 774, Beach Motel: Check-in 1500 hours, check-out 1100 hours. RV/Camping: Check-in 1400 hours, check-out 1200 hours. Campground maximum stay 30 days, then seven days out before being able to return.
Season of Operation: Year-round.
Eligibility: AD, NG, Res, Ret, DoD-Civ, Dep and Base Contractors.
Camper/Trailer Spaces: RV Sites (71), Back-in and Pull-through, offering both 40' and 50' sites with E(30A/50A)/S/W hookup, picnic table, fire ring, beach access, Wi-Fi. Rates: $30 daily.

Tent Spaces: Primitive Beach Sites (16): picnic table, fire ring. Rates: $10 daily.
Yurt, A Frame, Cabin, Apt, Spaces: Motel Rooms: Standard Suites (2), sleeps 6, one queen bed, one queen sofa sleeper, dining table, microwave/fridge combo cabinet, two burner stove, full set of dining and cookware, CATV. Rates: $90 daily. Junior Suites (12), sleeps 6, slightly smaller than standard suite with one queen bed, one queen sofa sleeper, dining table, microwave/fridge combo cabinet, two burner stove, full set of dining and cookware, CATV. Rates: $80 daily. Queen Rooms (10): sleeps 4-6 with roll-away rental; two queen beds, dining table, microwave/fridge combo cabinet, two burner stove, full set of dining and cookware, CATV. Rates: $75 daily. Free laundry facility available 24 hours. Yurts are also available. Call to confirm current rates.
Support Facilities: Auto Craft Shop, Bath House, Beach, Bowling, Camping Equipment, Chapel, Exchange, Fire Rings, Gas, Grills, Ice, Laundry, Picnic Area, Playground, Pool, Rec Equipment, Restrooms*, Sewage Dump, Shoppette, Showers*, Skeet Range, Snack Bar, Sports Fields, Telephones, Tennis Courts, VCR Rental. * Handicap accessible.
RV Storage: None.
Activities: Bicycling, Duck Hunting*, Fishing*, Golfing, Jogging, Swimming. *Licenses required.
Credit Cards: MasterCard and Visa.
Restrictions: Pets not allowed in motel. Pets (two per site) allowed on leash in camping area. No firearms allowed unless approved by NAS Security. Fires allowed in fire rings only.
RV Driving Directions/Location: On Base. From CA-101/Ventura Freeway east or west: Take exit 55 south to Las Poses Rd S, which leads directly to the Las Poses Gate 3 (open 0530-1800 hours except Sat-Sun and holidays). Ask gate guard for map with instructions to RV camp. Continue southwest on Las Posas Road to end. Turn right on 13th Street. Turn left on Laguna Road and continue south across bridge to left turn on 18th Street to Mugu Beach Hotel and RV Park. If Gate 3 is closed make right turn just before gate and go north on Frontage Road (Naval Air Road on some maps) to Main Gate 2 which is open 24 hours daily on left side of road. Turn left on Mugu Road and ask gate guard for map with instructions to RV camp. Follow directions above.
Area Description: Located near beach along Pacific Ocean north of picturesque Point Mugu State Park and within easy driving distance of world-famous tourist attractions such as Six Flags Magic Mountain, Disneyland and Knott's Berry Farm. Full range of support facilities available on base.
RV Campground Physical Address: 774 Laguna Rd, Point Mugu, CA 93042.

Port Hueneme NCBC – Ventura County Naval Base

Address: 1000 23rd Avenue, Port Hueneme, CA 93043-4301.
Information Line: C-805-982-4571, DSN-312-551-4571.
Main Base Police: C-805-982-4591/2023, Emergencies dial 911.
Main Installation Website: http://www.cnic.navy.mil/regions/cnrsw/installations/navbase_ventura_county.html
Main Base Location: Naval Base Ventura County (NBVC) Port Hueneme/Point Mugu is located on the vast Oxnard plain, just 65 miles northwest of Downtown Los Angeles, California. The cities of Port Hueneme, Oxnard, and Camarillo are nearest to NBVC.
Directions to Main Gate: Traveling North on US-101/Ventura Freeway: Exit onto Oxnard Blvd and make a left towards the ocean. Drive to W Gonzalex Rd and make a right. Then drive to N Ventura Rd and turn left. Stay on N Ventura Rd for approximately 6.25 miles until reaching Sunkist St/23rd Ave and make a right directly to the Main Gate.
NMC: Los Angeles, 65 miles east.
NMI: Point Mugu, 8 miles southeast.

Base Social Media/Facebook:
https://www.facebook.com/NavalBase VenturaCounty
Base Social Media/Twitter:
https://twitter.com/NBVCCalifornia
Chapels: C-805-982-4487. DSN-312-551-4487.
Dental Clinic: C-805-982-5584.
Medical: C-805-982-6342. DSN-312-551-6342. Fax, C-805-982-1133, DSN-312-551-1133.
Veterinary Services: C-805-982-3271.
Beauty/Barber Shop: C-805-982-6820. DSN-312-551-6820.
Commissary: C-805-982-2400. DSN-312-551-2400.
Exchange Gas: C-805-982-6804.
Exchange: C-805-982-6801.
Financial Institutions: Armed Forces Bank, C-805-815-4845. CBC Federal Credit Union, C-805-988-2151. Navy Federal Credit Union-Port Hueneme Branch, C-1-866-454-3141.
Places to Eat: Officers' Club Bard's Mansion, Duke's Place, Nap's Southern Grill, C-805-982-2872, 19th Hole Snack Bar, C-805-982-4605, 9th Hole Snack Bar, C-805-982-4286, Flightline, C-805-989-7747 and Subway, C-805-989-7396. Navy Exchange Food Court, C-805-982-6800.
Bowling: NBVC Lanes Bowling Center, C-805-982-2619.
Fitness Center: Bee-Hive Gym and Boxing Facility, C-805-982-4749. Bee-Fit Wellness Center, C-805-982-4726. Warfield Gym, C-805-982-5173.
Golf: Seabee Golf Course, C-805-982-2620.
ITT/ITR: C-805-982-4284. C-1-877-323-1089.
Military Museum: Seabee Museum, C-805-982-5165.
Military Museum Website:
http://www.history.navy.mil/museums/seabee_museum.htm
MWR: C-805-982-5554.
MWR Website:
http://ventura.navylifesw.com/
MWR Facebook:
https://www.facebook.com/pages/NBVC-MWR/215294089299
MWR Twitter:
https://twitter.com/nbvcmwr

Outdoor Recreation: C-805-982-4282. Offers outdoor adventure gear rentals, outdoor programs, clinics, trips and more. The Gear Rental facilities carry sleeping bags, boogie boards, stoves, tents, fresh and saltwater fishing gear and much more.
Swimming: Seabreeze Aquatic Center, C-805-982-4752 or C-805-982-4753, offers swim lessons, recreational swim, lap swim, junior lifeguard program.
Things To Do: The area is noted for family fun whether it's pedaling a four-wheel surrey along a coastal bike path, hiking amidst colorful spring wildflowers, picnicking at Port Hueneme Beach Park, kart-racing at heart-pounding speeds, or enjoying Oxnard's white sandy beaches and Pacific blue waters offering a variety of sun and surf activities. The area is loaded with activities for the young and the young-at-heart. Within a 1.5 hour drive are Disneyland, Universal Studios, Santa Monica Pier, and Six Flags Magic Mountain. The Channel Islands National Park is a hub for boating, sport fishing, kayaking and whale-watching excursions. The harbor is also home to Ventura County Maritime Museum and fresh seafood restaurants.
Walking Trails: Contact Outdoor Recreation.

RV CAMPING & GETAWAYS
Fairways RV Resort

Reservation/Contact Number Info: C-1-877-NAVY-BED, C-805-982-6123, DSN-312-551-6123. Fax C-805-982-1564, DSN-312-551-1564.
Recreation Security: C-805-982-4591.
RV Website:
http://get.dodlodging.net/propertys/Fairways-RV-Resort-%E2%80%93-NB-Ventura-County-Port-Hueneme
Other Info Website:
http://navylifesw.com/ventura/recreation/recreationallodging/
GPS Coordinates:
34°10'23"N/119°12'24"W
Reservations: Reservations recommended and accepted one year in advance for AD; 6 months in advance

for Ret/DoD-Civ. Credit card required to hold reservation. Office hours 0900-1700 Mon-Fri. Maximum stay 30 days. Note: Victoria Gate is open to commercial traffic only for base entry at Port Hueneme.

Season of Operation: Year-round.
Eligibility: AD, NG, Res, Ret, 100% DAV, DoD-Civ.
Camper/Trailer Spaces: Camper Spaces: Hardstand: (85), Pull-thru, Maximum 40' in length, E(110V/15A)/S/W, picnic tables and grills. Rates: $30 daily. Additional charges may apply for non-military guests.
Support Facilities: Auto Craft Shop, Bath House, Bowling, Chapel, Commissary, Convenience Store, Diesel, Exchange, Fitness Center, Gas, Golf, Grills, Ice, Laundry/Free, Mechanic/Auto Repair, Pavilion, Picnic Area, Pool, Propane, Rec Center, Rec Equipment, Restrooms, RV Storage, Sewage Dump, Showers, Snack Bar, Sports Fields, Tennis Courts.
RV Storage: Available. Resort maintains full waiting list year-round, C-805-982-6123 for more information.
Activities: Golfing, Running, Shopping, Swimming.
Credit Cards: MasterCard and Visa.
Restrictions: Limit two pets per site. Pets must be leashed at all times. Owner must clean up after pet. No tent camping.
RV Driving Directions/Location: On Base. From Main Gate: Travel 23rd Avenue to Salsa Road. Take a right and follow to the RV Resort.
Area Description: Close to the Ventura Harbor and coastal shops, and only a mile from the beach. The area's cool temperate climate is great for year-round activities. Within short driving distance of the popular Los Angeles County beaches as well as the quieter Ventura County beaches. Port Hueneme also offers a great view of local 4th of July fireworks which are shot off over the Pacific Ocean.
RV Campground Physical Address: Fairways RV Resort, Salsa Street, Bldg 1534, Port Hueneme, CA 93042.

Presidio of Monterey

Address: 1759 Lewis Road, Suite 210, IMWE-POM Monterey, CA 93944.
Information Line: C-831-242-6601. DSN-312-768-6601.
Main Base Police: C-831-242-7860/7733. DSN-831-768-7860.
Main Installation Website: http://www.monterey.army.mil/Index.html
Main Base Location: The Presidio of Monterey (POM) is located in Monterey County in Monterey, California, about 117 miles south of San Francisco, on the Pacific coast.
Directions to Main Gate: From the north or south on CA-1 in Monterey: Take exit to Del Monte Blvd and travel west approximately two miles onto Lighthouse Avenue. Merge onto Foam Avenue then turn onto Reeside Avenue. Go left onto Lighthouse Avenue then right onto Private Bolio Road.
NMC: Monterey, within city limits.
NMI: Monterey Naval Postgraduate School, 2.7 miles southeast.
Base Social Media/Facebook: https://www.facebook.com/USAGPresidio
Base Social Media/Twitter: https://twitter.com/POMgarrison
Chapels: C-831-242-7620.
Dental Clinic: C-831-242-5613.
Medical: C-831-242-5741/5663.
Veterinary Services: C-831-242-7718/7721. DSN-312-768-7718.
Beauty/Barber Shop: C-831-647-9602.
Commissary: C-831-242-7668.
Exchange Gas: C-831-394-2443, C-831-372-0702.
Exchange: DLI, C-831-647-9602. Ord, C-831-899-2336.
Places to Eat: Hobson Java Cafe, C-831-242-7323; Combs Hall, C-831-242-5384; Belas Hall, C-831-242-5008 are on base. Monterey Joe's, Sardine Factory and The Whaling Station are within driving distance. Food Court offers Subway and Papa John's.
Fitness Center: C-831-242-5557.
Golf: C-831-242-5506. DSN-312-768-5506.
ITT/ITR: C-831-242-5506/6970.

Library: C-831-242-5572.
Military Museum: Presidio of Monterey Museum, C-831-646-3456.
Military Museum Website:
http://www.monterey.org/museums/Home.aspx
MWR: C-831-242-6995.
MWR Website:
https://presidio.armymwr.com/
MWR Facebook:
https://www.facebook.com/PresidioFMWR
MWR Twitter:
https://twitter.com/PresidioFMWR
Outdoor Recreation: C-831-242-5506. Offers rental of equipment for camping, golfing, biking, surfing, SCUBA diving, snorkeling, kayaking, fishing, skiing, snowboarding, and more.
Things To Do: Within minutes of many famous Monterey Peninsula tourist attractions: Monterey Bay Aquarium, Fisherman's Wharf, Cannery Row, Pebble Beach golf courses, Seventeen Mile Drive, Point Lobos, Carmel and Big Sur.

RV CAMPING & GETAWAYS

Eisenhower House

Reservation/Contact Number Info: C-831-242-5506. Fax C-831-242-6310.
Recreation Security: C-831-242-7851.
RV Website:
https://presidio.armymwr.com/programs/eisenhowerhouse
RV Email Address: info@pom-odr.com
Reservations: Reservations accepted one year in advance. A $100 booking fee required at time of reservation. Full rental payment is due no later than 30 days prior to first day of reservation, which includes the refundable $150 cleaning deposit. Cancellations must be made prior to 30 days before day of arrival for full refund. Sliding scale refund applicable thereafter. Check-in 1500 hours, check-out 1100 hours. Late fees apply. Minimum two-night stay required.
Season of Operation: Year-round.
Eligibility: AD, NG, Res, Ret, DoD/NAF-Civ and Ret; and dependents.

Yurt, A Frame, Cabin, Apt, Spaces: Cottage (1): Two bedrooms with one queen and one full size bed, one shared bath, complete kitchen, living room, fenced yard, BBQ grill, cable TV/DVD, internet. Fully furnished. Rates: Peak Season $225 nightly; Off Season $195 nightly.
Support Facilities: Commissary, Exchange, Fitness Center, ITT Office, Library, MWR, ODR. Full range of support facilities on base.
RV Storage: C-831-242-5506.
Activities: Beach, Fitness Center, Museum, ODR Rentals, Outdoor Activities, Playground, Shopping and more.
Credit Cards: Cash, Check, MasterCard, Visa.
Restrictions: A non-refundable $75 pet fee applies. An additional $7 per night after the 2nd night. Quiet hours apply.
RV Driving Directions/Location: From the Lighthouse Road Gate: Take Pvt Bolio Road to Kit Carson Road. Go left. Go left at Ewing Road to check in at ODR ahead.
Area Description: Monterey Bay area offers much to do! Enjoy whale watching tours, the beach, shopping at Cannery Row, or one of the many state and local parks along the shore.
RV Campground Physical Address: 567 Buffalo Soldier Trail, Bldg 364, POM, CA 93944.

Seal Beach Naval Weapons Station

Address: NWS Seal Beach, 800 Seal Beach Boulevard, Seal Beach, CA 90740.
Information Line: C-562-626-7011, DSN-312-873-7011.
Main Base Police: C-562-626-7229
Main Installation Website:
http://www.cnic.navy.mil/regions/cnrsw/installations/nws_seal_beach.html
Main Base Location: Seal Beach is located in Long Beach, California in the most western point of orange County adjacent to the San Pedro Bay.
Directions to Main Gate: From east or west on I-405: Exit onto Seal Beach Blvd heading south. Continue south for approximately one mile then turn left

onto Westminster Avenue. Main gate is located at the corner of Seal Beach Blvd and Forrestal Avenue.

NMC: Long Beach, adjacent.

NMI: Port Hueneme/Ventura County NB, 96 miles northwest.

Base Social Media/Facebook: https://www.facebook.com/pages/Naval-Weapons-Station-Seal-Beach/115671361809485

Exchange Gas: C-562-431-8983.

Exchange: C-562-431-8983.

Clubs: Eagle's Nest Clubhouse, C-714-889-1453.

Places to Eat: Visitors will find fast food, sushi, seafood, and breakfast a short drive away.

Golf: Navy Golf Course, C-714-889-1576.

ITT/ITR: C-562-626-6006.

MWR: C-562-626-7106.

MWR Website: http://navylifesw.com/sealbeach/

MWR Twitter: https://twitter.com/navylifesw

Outdoor Recreation: Outdoor Recreation Services, C-562-626-7026. Offers a variety of equipment for events to include party equipment, ice chests, chairs, tables, air mattresses, canopies, PA system and more.

RV CAMPING & GETAWAYS
Seabreeze RV Resort

Reservation/Contact Number Info: C-562-626-7106/6006, DSN-312-873-7106. Fax C-562-626-7893, DSN-312-873-7893.

Recreation Security: C-562-626-7229, DSN-312-873-7229.

RV Website: http://navylifesw.com/sealbeach/recreation/recreationallodging/

Other Info Website: http://get.dodlodging.net/propertys/Seal-Beach-RV-Park-(Seabreeze)-

RV Email Address: seabreezervresort@outlook.com

GPS Coordinates: 33°45'04.0"N 118°04'58.4"W

Reservations: Recommended. Reservations accepted up to 12 weeks in advance for AD; 10 weeks in advance for Res/Ret/100% DAV; 8 weeks in advance for DoD-Civ. Authorized patrons may sponsor up to one guest RV, however sponsors are required to make guest's reservation, register their guest to come onboard station and remain on premises in their own RV during the guest's stay. Cancellations made within 48 hours will be charged one night stay. Early departure requires 48-hour notice for refund. Check in at Registration Office, Bldg 35, Mon-Fri 0900-1600, closed for lunch 1230-1300. Camp host available after normal business hours. Check-in at 1300 hours, check-out 1100 hours.

Season of Operation: Year-round.

Eligibility: AD, NG, Res, Ret, DoD-Civ, Dep and 100% DAV.

Camper/Trailer Spaces: RV Sites: Hardstand (85): Full hookup, DirectTV, picnic table, free Wi-Fi and laundry. Rates: $35 daily; $39 daily for DoD-Civ three-person max. Guests may incur additional fees.

Support Facilities: State of the art Bathroom and Shower Complex, Beach, Cabana, Cafeteria, Exchange, Fishing Pier, Fitness Center, Golf, Grills, Horseshoe Pit, Ice, Laundry/free, Picnic Area, Playground, Rec Center, Rec Equipment, Restrooms, RV/Car Wash, RV Storage, Sewage Dump, Snack Bar, Sports Fields, Tennis Courts, Trails.

RV Storage: Can accommodate vehicles up to 50'. No time limit. C-562-626-7106, DSN-312-873-7106 for more information.

Activities: Basketball, Golf, Horseshoes, Softball, Running Trail, Volleyball.

Credit Cards: MasterCard and Visa.

Restrictions: Pets allowed on leash. No firearms. No feeding of animals from nearby wildlife refuge. Guests must be escorted by authorized patron if the guest travels outside the RV grounds on station.

RV Driving Directions/Location: On Base: From the Forrestal Ave Main Gate: Entrance to campground is straight through the Main Gate, approximately 500 yards to Chapel Drive, on the left. Please note: Large Class A RVs must call Security at 562-

626-7229 before entering base for specific instructions.

Area Description: Flat terrain with vegetation between RV stalls. Beautiful view of mountains in the distance, several sporting activities at the site. Numerous attractions are located nearby, including Disneyland, Knott's Berry Farm, Long Beach Aquarium, The Queen Mary and more.

RV Campground Physical Address: 800 Seal Beach Blvd, Bldg 35, Seal Beach, CA 90740-5000.

Travis Air Force Base

Address: 351 Travis Avenue, Bldg 660, Travis AFB, CA 94535.

Information Line: C-707-424-1110, DSN-312-837-1110.

Main Base Police: C-707-424-3294.

Main Installation Website: http://www.travis.af.mil/

Main Base Location: Travis Air Force Base is located in Solano County in Northern California near the cities of Fairfield, Suisun City, and Vacaville.

Directions to Main Gate: From SF Airport: Merge onto US-101 N toward San Francisco. Keep right to take I-80 E via Exit 433B toward Bay Bridge/Oakland/Seventh St/US-101 N (portions toll) for approximately 46 miles. Take the Air Base Pkwy Waterman Blvd exit toward Travis AFB. From Oakland IAP: Merge onto I-880 N toward Downtown Oakland. Keep right to take I-980 E toward CA-24/Walnut Creek. Merge onto I-580 W toward San Francisco for 5.8 miles then take I-80 E toward Vallejo/Sacramento (portions toll) for 34 miles. Take the Air Base Pkwy/Waterman Blvd exit toward Travis AFB.

NMC: San Francisco, 45 miles southwest.

NMI: Novato Coast Guard Facility, 45 miles southwest.

Base Social Media/Facebook: https://www.facebook.com/TravisAirForceBase/

Chapels: C-707-424-3217.

Dental Clinic: C-707-423-7300/7000.

Medical: C-707-423-3000, DSN-312-799-3000.

Veterinary Services: C-707-424-3010.

Beauty/Barber Shop: C-707-437-2848.

Commissary: C-707-437-4004.

Exchange Gas: C-707-437-2232/2678.

Exchange: C-707-437-4633.

Financial Institutions: Armed Forces Bank, N.A., C-707-437-3091. Travis Credit Union, C-707-449-4000.

Clubs: Delta Breeze Club, C-707-437-3711.

Places to Eat: Exchange Food Court, C-707-437-4633 offers Popeye's, Charley's Grilled Subs, Subway, Anthony's Pizza, Baskin-Robbins, Taco Bell Express, Cinnabon/Seattle's Best Coffee, Captain D's, and Manchu Wok.

Bowling: Travis Bowl, C-707-437-4737.

Fitness Center: C-707-424-2008.

Golf: Cypress Lakes Golf Course, C-707-424-5797.

ITT/ITR: C-707-424-0969.

Library: C-707-424-3279.

Marina: Travis Marina & Presidio Yacht Club, C-415-332-2319.

Military Museum: Travis Heritage Center, C-707-424-8180.

Military Museum Website: http://www.travis.af.mil/units/travisairmuseum.asp

MWR: C-707-424-0970/0969.

MWR Website: http://www.travisfss.com/

MWR Facebook: https://www.facebook.com/60FSS/?ref=hl

Outdoor Recreation: Travis Air Force Base Outdoor Recreation Services, C-707-424-0969. Offers a variety of recreational services: the Outdoor Adventure Program (OAP), equipment rentals, The Works bike & ski shop, Trail Mix resale shop, nearby park information, an indoor climbing wall, aquatic center, trap & skeet range, Xtreme paintball, FamCamp, RV storage, equestrian center, and ITT services.

Swimming: Travis Aquatic Center, C-707-424-5283 offers swimming lessons, water aerobics class or whitewater kayaking roll class. Pool parties available.

Things To Do: Visit San Francisco, The Napa Valley and Reno as well as various theme parks such as Six Flags Discovery Kingdom, and Aquarium of the Bay.

RV CAMPING & GETAWAYS

Travis AFB FamCamp

Reservation/Contact Number Info: C-707-424-3583, DSN-312-837-3583. Fax C-707-424-2568, DSN-312-837-2568.
Recreation Security: Emergencies dial 911.
RV Website: http://www.travisfss.com/
RV Email Address:
famcamp.tafb@gmail.com
GPS Coordinates:
38°16'17"N/121°57'12"W
Reservations: Accepted 30-90 days in advance. Deposit required. Less than 30 days first come, first serve. Office hours 0830-1530 Mon-Sat. Follow instructions for entering camp posted on office window. Check-out 1100 hours. Maximum stay 180 days per 12 months.
Season of Operation: Year-round.
Eligibility: AD, NG, Res, Ret, DoD-Civ and 100% DAV.
Camper/Trailer Spaces: Gravel (70): Back-in, E(110V/20/30/50A)/S/W, CATV, Wi-Fi, maximum length 40'. Rates: $20 daily.
Tent Spaces: Tent/Dry Sites (10): Primitive sites. Rates: $10 daily.
Support Facilities: Auto Craft Shop, Chapel*, Coin Laundry, Commissary, Convenience Store, Exchange, Fitness Center, Golf, Grills, Mess Halls*, Pavilion, Picnic Area, Playground, Pool*, Propane (Nearby), Rec Equipment, Restrooms, RV Storage*, Sewage Dump (for a fee), Showers, Sports Fields, Stables, Tennis Courts, Telephones. *On base.
RV Storage: Very busy year-round; generally reserved for AD. Call Outdoor Recreation, C-707-424-5659.
Activities: Biking, Bowling, Fishing*, Golfing, Sightseeing. *State license required.
Credit Cards: MasterCard and Visa.
Restrictions: Limit two dogs per site. Must be on leash and not allowed to annoy others. Owner must clean up after pet immediately. Designated pet friendly sites. No firearms allowed. No campfires. Quiet hours 2300-0800 hours.
RV Driving Directions/Location: On Base: From the Main Gate: Camp is immediately inside Main Gate on the right. Clearly marked.
Area Description: Located in state's famed valley region near Sacramento. Major water sports centers of San Pablo Bay and Lake Berryessa are nearby. Full range of support facilities available on base.
RV Campground Physical Address: FamCamp, 201 Fairfield St, Bldg 601, Travis AFB, CA 94535. Address: 60 SVS/SVRO, Attn: FAMCAMP Manager, 273 Ellis St, Travis AFB, CA 94535-5000.

Twenty-Nine Palms Marine Corps Air & Ground Combat Center

Address: 1551 Fifth Street, The Village Center, MCAGCC Twentynine Palms, CA 92278-8150.
Information Line: C-760-830-6000, DSN-312-230-6000.
Main Base Police: Emergencies dial 911.
Main Installation Website:
http://www.29palms.marines.mil/UnitHome.aspx
Main Base Location: Marine Corps Air Ground Combat Center (MCAGCC) is located in San Bernardino County in Southern California. MCAGCC covers more than 998 square miles of the high desert, which makes it larger than some small countries.
Directions to Main Gate: Arriving via Interstate 40 East: Take Highway 95 South at Needles, CA to Highway 62 West (29 Palms Highway) at the Vidal Junction. Take Highway 62 West to Adobe Road in 29 Palms then turn right. Adobe Road runs into the main gate.
NMC: Palm Springs, 60 miles southwest.
NMI: March Air Reserve Base, 100 miles southwest.
Base Social Media/Facebook:
https://www.facebook.com/thecombatcenter
Base Social Media/Twitter:
https://twitter.com/CombatCenterPAO
Chapels: C-760-830-6304.

Dental Clinic: C-760-830-7052.
Medical: C-760-830-2190, DSN-312-230-2190.
Veterinary Services: C-760-830-6896/7522, DSN-312-230-6896/7522.
Beauty/Barber Shop: Main Exchange, C-760-830-0342, C&E Complex, C-760-830-4101, Camp Wilson, C-760-830-4633.
Commissary: C-760-830-7572.
Exchange Gas: C-760-830-1573, 24-hour pumps.
Exchange: C-760-830-6163.
Clubs: Combat Center O Club, C-760-830-6610, Hashmarks SNCO, C-760-830-5035, Warrior Club, C-760-830-5613.
Places to Eat: Sandy Hill Lanes Snack Bar, C-760-830-1316, Quick Break, C-760-830-6163, Charlie's Coffee House, C-760-830-4103, Subway, C-760-830-1782, Carl's Jr., C-760-830-5607, Charlie's, Di Carlos Italian Café, Taco Bell, Jasmine's Espresso Cafe' and Warrior Club within short drive.
Bowling: Sandy Hill Lanes Bowling Center, C-760-830-6422.
Fitness Center: Camp Wilson Gym, C-760-830-4353. Community Center Gym, C-760-830-3350. East Gym, C-760-830-6440. West Gym, C-760-830-6451.
Golf: Desert Winds Golf Course, C-760-830-6132.
ITT/ITR: C-760-830-4067/4122.
Library: C-760-830-6875.
MWR: C-760-830-6163/6164.
MWR Website:
http://www.mccs29palms.com/
MWR Facebook:
https://www.facebook.com/MCCS29Palms
MWR Twitter:
https://twitter.com/mccs29palms
Outdoor Recreation: Outdoor Adventure Center, C-760-830-7235. Offers rental equipment for summer and winter sports, camping and other gear, paintball park and horse stables.
Swimming: Training Tank, C-760-830-6212, Officer/SNCO Pool, C-760-830-7250, Family Pool, C-760-830-6727, Crazy Horse Campgrounds' Lake Havasu, C-760-830-7235.
Things To Do: Five miles from Joshua Tree National Monument where the low Colorado and the high Mojave deserts come together. Many come from miles around to see the desert blooming with wildflowers.

RV CAMPING & GETAWAYS
Twilight Dunes

Reservation/Contact Number Info: C-760-830-6583, DSN-312-230-6583. Fax C-760-830-6557.
Recreation Security: C-760-830-3333.
RV Website:
http://www.mccs29palms.com/index.cfm/food-lodging/lodging/
GPS Coordinates:
34°12'20"N/116°3'8"W
Reservations: Reservations based on first come, first-serve basis. Maximum stay 30 days. Active Duty on orders may stay the duration of their assigned duty as stated in their orders. A $25 deposit required. Reservations accepted 24 hours daily. Check in at 1400 hours at Lodging Office, Bldg 690; check out 1200 hours. Mail services available.
Season of Operation: Year-round.
Eligibility: AD, NG, Res, Ret, DoD-Civ, Dep, 100% DAV and Guests.
Camper/Trailer Spaces: Hardstand (83): Back-in, Maximum 40' in length. E(110/220V/15/30/50A)/S/W, CATV, telephone hookups, picnic table, grill. Rates: $25 daily, $154 weekly, $300 monthly.
Support Facilities: Auto Craft Shop*, Bowling*, Chapel*, Coin Laundry, Commissary*, Convenience Store*, Diesel, Equipment Rental, Exchange, Family Pool, Fitness Center*, Gas, Golf*, Grills, Ice, Laundry/Pay, Mechanic/Auto Repair, Mess Hall, Pay Phone, Picnic Area, Playground, Propane (bottle & fill), Rec Equipment, Sewage Dump, Shoppette, Shuttle Bus, Snack Bar, Sports Fields, Swimming. *Handicap accessible.
RV Storage: C-760-830-6583.
Activities: Bicycling, Bowling, Golfing, Hiking, Rock Climbing.
Credit Cards: American Express, Discover, MasterCard and Visa.
Restrictions: Pets allowed, up to two per site, must be on a leash at all times.

Owners are responsible for cleaning up after their pets. Firearms not allowed.
RV Driving Directions/Location: On Base. From the Main Gate: Make a right at the first traffic light onto Del Valle Road. At the intersection of Del Valle Road and Saddleback Avenue, check in at the lodging office, Bldg 690. Continue on Del Valle Road, go past the commissary, make a right on Sunshine Road and proceed to RV park entrance, just past the housing area.
Area Description: Located ten miles from the Joshua Tree National Monument, where the low Colorado and the high Mojave deserts come together.
RV Campground Physical Address: 7941 Sunshine Peak, MCAGCC, Twentynine Palms, CA 92278-8150.

Vandenberg Air Force Base

Address: 706 Washington Avenue, Bldg 10122, Vandenberg AFB, CA 93437-6223.
Information Line: C-805-606-1110, DSN-312-276-1110.
Main Base Police: C-805-606-3911.
Main Installation Website:
http://www.vandenberg.af.mil/
Main Base Location: Vandenberg AFB (VAFB) is located on the central coast of California, near Lompoc and Santa Maria in northern Santa Barbara County.
Directions to Main Gate: From US-101 south: Exit westbound at Santa Maria onto Clark Avenue. Go 2.3 miles to left (south) on CA-135 which merges into CA-1. Continue southbound on CA-1 to Main Gate. From US-101 north to Buelton: Exit northwest onto CA-246. Just before Lompoc, bear right on Purisima Road which runs into CA-1. Follow CA-1 northwest to the Main Gate on left.
NMC: Santa Barbara, 55 miles southeast.
NMI: Camp San Luis Obispo, 60 miles north.
Base Social Media/Facebook:
https://www.facebook.com/30thSpace Wing

Base Social Media/Twitter:
https://twitter.com/30thSpaceWing
Chapels: C-805-606-5773.
Dental Clinic: C-805-606-1846.
Medical: C-805-606-2273, After Hours, C-1-888-252-3299, DSN-312-276-2273.
Veterinary Services: C-805-606-3019.
Beauty/Barber Shop: Barber, C-805-734-1259. Beauty, C-805-734-1264.
Commissary: C-805-734-3354 ext 254.
Exchange Gas: Bldg 14400 Express & Pumps, C-805-734-0967. Bldg 10317 Class 6, C-805-734-2250.
Exchange: C-805-734-5521, C-805-606-8153.
Financial Institutions: Coast Hills Federal Credit Union, C-805-733-7600, C-1-800-262-4488. Armed Forces Bank N.A., C-805-734-1777.
Clubs: Enlisted Club and Officers' Club, C-805-606-3330.
Places to Eat: Breakers Dining Hall, C-805-734-3997, Spare Time Grill, C-805-606-3209, The Turn, C-805-606-6262, Pacific Coast Club, C-805-606-3330. Additional restaurants within a short drive.
Bowling: Surf Lanes Bowling Center, C-805-606-3209.
Fitness Center: C-805-606-3832.
Golf: Marshallia Ranch Golf Course, C-805-606-6262.
ITT/ITR: C-805-606-7976.
Library: C-805-606-6414.
Military Museum: Space and Missile Heritage Museum, C-805-606-3595.
Military Museum Website:
http://www.vandenberg.af.mil/library/factsheets/factsheet.asp?id=4627
MWR: C-805-606-5031.
MWR Website:
https://www.vandenbergfss.com
MWR Facebook:
https://www.facebook.com/pages/30FSS-Vandenberg-AFB/126136854151715
Outdoor Recreation: Vandenberg Air Force Base Outdoor Recreation Services, C-805-606-5908. Offers full range of recreational equipment, lawn & garden supplies and even power equipment. Adventure programs include river rafting, sailing, scuba, hiking, biking and horseback riding trips.

Swimming: C-805-606-3581 offers a heated outdoor year-round swimming facility. The center has an eight lane 25-meter pool, a waterpark slide, a one meter diving board, a tot pool, and BBQ pit.

Things To Do: La Purisima Mission & State Historical Park, Sky-Dive Santa Barbara, Jalama Beach County Park, numerous wineries and vineyards, Santa Maria Speedway, Ostrich Land, Santa Maria Discovery Museum (for small children), Solvang Danish Village, Stearn's Fisherman's Wharf in Santa Barbara, Chumash Casino & Resort, Santa Barbara Zoo and Hearst Castle. Area Events: Lompoc Flower Festival, Lompoc Valley Dog Show, Spring Arts Festival, Santa Barbara County Vintners' Fest, Santa Maria Elks Rodeo, Strawberry Festival, Santa Barbara County Fair.

RV CAMPING & GETAWAYS

Vandenberg AFB FamCamp

Reservation/Contact Number Info: C-805-606-8579, DSN-312-276-8579. Fax C-805-606-1672.

Recreation Security: C-805-606-3911.

RV Website:
http://www.30fss.com/famcamp.html

GPS Coordinates:
34°43'21"N/120°33'1"W

Reservations: Reservations accepted 60 days in advance. Office hours 0730-1600 Mon-Fri. Check-in at FAMCAMP office Bldg 5010, check-out 1100 hours. After duty hours, use fee collection box located in front of FAMCAMP office and see office personnel the following day. It is advised that customers bring an alternate vehicle if they come in a motorhome so they will have access to all amenities the base/area offers; not required, but helpful.

Season of Operation: Year-round.

Eligibility: AD, NG, Res, Ret, 100% DAV and DoD-Civ.

Camper/Trailer Spaces: Hardstand (49) Pull-thru and Back-in, Any size, E(120V/50A)/S/W hookups. Rates: $24 daily, $158 weekly for pull-thru; $22 daily, $143 weekly for back-in. Dry Sites

(20): Back-in and Pull-through, any size, no hookups. Rates: $10 daily. Retirees and DoD Rates: $26 daily, $170 weekly. Max 180 cumulative day stay. Peak season may affect maximum stay.

Tent Spaces: Tent Spaces: Grass (20), fenced area, no hookups. Rates: $10 daily.

Support Facilities: Auto Craft Shop, Bathhouse, Beach, Boat Rental, Bowling, Cafeteria, Camping Equipment, Chapel, Commissary, Exchange, Fire Rings, Fishing Pier, Fitness Center, Game Room, Gas, Golf, Grills, Ice, Laundry/Pay, Lounge*, Mess Hall, Pavilion, Pay Phone, Picnic Area, Playground, Pool, Propane, Racquetball, Rec Center, Rec Equipment, Restrooms*, RV Storage, Sewage Dump, Showers*, Skeet Range, Snack Bar, Sports Fields, Stables, Tennis Courts, Trails, Vending Machines, Wi-Fi. * Handicap accessible.

RV Storage: Available through Outdoor Recreation, C-805-606-5908. FAMCAMP maintains waiting list year-round, C-805-606-8579 for more information.

Activities: Golfing, Hunting*, Lake Fishing*, Surf Fishing*. *State and base licenses required; some types of game require additional documentation.

Credit Cards: MasterCard and Visa.

Restrictions: Pets allowed, must comply with local license and leash laws. Must provide current vaccination information. Owner must clean up after pets. Firearms permitted during hunting season.

RV Driving Directions/Location: On Base. From the north on US-101: Exit at Orcutt and take the CA-1 to the Main Gate. Turn left on CA-1 to Santa Lucia Canyon Rd. Travel half mile to Lompoc Gate. From the south, on CA-1, half mile past Vandenberg Village take left exit on Santa Lucia Canyon Rd and travel half mile to Lompoc Gate. Note: RVs and trailers cannot enter the base via the Main Gate. For arrival after 1900, use Solvang Gate, located off Ocean Ave.

Area Description: Space and missile center. Installation covers over 98,000 acres. FAMCAMP is situated on main base and provides unlimited sightseeing and recreational opportunities. Full range of support facilities on base.

RV Campground Physical Address: FAMCAMP, 30 FSS/FSCO, 1036 California Blvd, Vandenberg AFB, CA 93437-5000.

COLORADO

Buckley Air Force Base

Address: 18500 East 6th Avenue, Aurora, CO 80011.
Information Line: C-720-847-9011, DSN-312-847-9011.
Main Base Police: C-720-847-9250. Emergencies dial 911.
Main Installation Website: http://www.buckley.af.mil
Main Base Location: Located on the doorstep of the Rocky Mountains, Buckley AFB is in Aurora, Colorado, a suburb just outside of Denver.
Directions to Main Gate: From Interstate 225: Take exit 9 for 6th Avenue/CO-30. Go east on 6th Avenue. Buckley AFB is 2.8 miles on the right. Online map sites or GPS use address: 18500 East Sixth Avenue, Aurora, CO 80011.
NMC: Denver, 21 miles west.
NMI: U.S. Air Force Academy, 62 miles south.
Base Social Media/Facebook: https://www.facebook.com/BuckleyAirForceBase
Base Social Media/Twitter: https://twitter.com/Buckley_AFB
Chapels: Chaplain, C-720-847-4631.
Dental Clinic: C-720-847-4118.
Medical: C-720-847-9355, DSN-312-847-6573.
Beauty/Barber Shop: Main Exchange, C-720-859-0933; Stylique, C-720-367-0011.
Commissary: C-720-847-7100.
Exchange Gas: C-720-859-0754.
Exchange: C-720-859-9626.
Financial Institutions: ENT Federal Credit Union, C-1-800-525-9623, C-719-574-1100.

Clubs: Panther Den Lounge, C-720-847-7197.
Places to Eat: Panthers Den, C-720-847-7197 and Rickenbacker's (Rocky Mountain Lodge), C-720-847-5899 are on base. Exchange Food Court offers Burger King, Domino's, Dunkin Donuts and Subway. Many restaurants within a short drive.
Fitness Center: Buckley FC, C-720-847-6679.
ITT/ITR: C-720-847-6100.
MWR: C-720-847-5278.
MWR Website: http://www.460fss.com
MWR Facebook: https://www.facebook.com/460FSS/
Outdoor Recreation: Outdoor Recreation Services, C-720-847-6100/6853. Offers camping gear, fishing rods, campers, trailers, skis, snowboards, ski apparel, ski racks, ski tune-up services, mountain rescue gear and more.
Things To Do: Visit Old West Attractions Overview, Colorado History Museum, Denver's Early History, Buffalo Bill Gravesite and Museum, Denver's Cowboy Culture, Mile High Thrill Rides, Elitch Gardens, Lakeside Amusement Park, Water World or take in a Colorado Rockies game.

RV CAMPING & GETAWAYS
Buckley AFB FamCamp

Reservation/Contact Number Info: C-720-847-6100.
RV Website: https://www.460fss.com/fam-camp/
RV Email Address: buckleyafb@gmail.com
Reservations: Reservations may be made 60 days in advance for AD, Res, NG; 30 days in advance for Ret, DoD Civ and Gov't Contractors. Office hours 0900-1730 Mon-Tue, Thur-Fri; 0900-1300 Wed; 0800-1400 Sat. Closed Sunday and holidays. Maximum stay 30 days with extensions granted on space available basis.
Season of Operation: Year-round.
Eligibility: AD, NG, Res, Ret, DoD-Civ and 100% DAV.

Camper/Trailer Spaces: RV Sites (38), Concrete pull-thru and back-in spaces with E/(30A/50A)S/W full hookups, picnic table, on-site restrooms and laundry, dumpster area. Rates: $22 daily, May-Oct; $20 daily Nov-April.

Tent Spaces: Campsites (5), no hook ups. Rates: $10 daily.

Support Facilities: Commissary, Community Center with eateries, Exchange, Gym.

RV Storage: C-720-847-6100. Limited availability.

Activities: Hiking, Trails, ITT Discount Tickets, Freshwater lakes nearby. ODR offers boat, canoe, kayaking rentals.

Credit Cards: Cash, Check.

Restrictions: Pets allowed. Dogs must be on leash. Owners must clean up after pets. Quite hours: 2200-0600. No firearms, no campfires. Charcoal grills only.

RV Driving Directions/Location: On Base. From the Mississippi Gate: Head north on Aspen Street. At third stop sign go right onto Steamboat. FamCamp is approximately 1.5 miles on left. Must use the commercial gate listed above.

Area Description: This area is known as the "Gateway to the Rockies" and offers many outdoor activities, scenic mountain views and tranquility. Denver is a short drive away.

RV Campground Physical Address: 538 S Aspen Street, Buckley AFB, CO 80011. Mailing Address: 18178 East A Basin Avenue, MS 90, Buckley AFB, CO 80011.

Farish Recreation Area

Address: 12005 Rampart Range Road, Woodland Park, CO, 80863.

Information Line: C-719-333-1110, DSN-312-333-1110.

Main Base Police: C-719-333-2000.

Main Installation Website: http://www.usafa.af.mil/

Main Base Location: A 650-acre paradise nestled in the mountains west of the Academy at an altitude of 9,000 feet.

NMC: Colorado Springs, 23 miles southeast via Woodland Park/Baldwin stoplight.

NMI: U.S. Air Force Academy, 30 miles southeast.

Commissary: Approximately 30 miles to the US Air Force Academy Commissary.

Exchange Gas: Approximately 30 miles to the Air Force Academy gas station, C-719-472-0395. Commercial gas station within 5 miles.

Exchange: Approximately 30 miles to the US Air Force Academy Base Exchange facility, C-719-472-0861.

Places to Eat: Fast food, breakfast, diners and fine dining are a short drive away.

MWR Website:
http://www.usafasupport.com/

MWR Facebook:
https://www.facebook.com/pages/10th-Force-Support-Squadron/243202264030?ref=ts

MWR Twitter:
https://twitter.com/10FSS

RV CAMPING & GETAWAYS

Farish Recreation Area

Reservation/Contact Number Info: C-719-687-9098. Fax C-719-687-1851.
Recreation Security: C-719-333-2000.
RV Website:
http://www.usafasupport.com/farish.html
GPS Coordinates: 39°0'7"N/105°0'35"W
Reservations: Highly recommended. Accepted up to 90 days in advance for AD; 60 days all others.
Cancellations/changes must be made no later than 14 days prior to reservation date to avoid charges. No reservations will be taken on weekends or holidays except for same/next day reservations. Credit card required to make reservations. Failure to make payment within 14 days will result in loss of reservation. Office hours 0830-1630 Mon-Fri. Check in at the Office/Store. Lodging Reservations: Check-in 1500 hours, check-out 1200 hours. RV/Camping: Check-in 1200 hours,

check-out 1100 hours. Resident caretaker on site for after hours check-in and emergencies. No check-in after 2200 hours.
Season of Operation: May-Oct. Closed Nov-Apr.
Eligibility: AD, NG, Res, Ret, DoD-Civ (AD/Ret), 100% DAV and Dep w/ID.
Camper/Trailer Spaces: RV/Camper Spaces: Pull Thru (5) Gravel, E/110V/15A. Picnic table, grill. Maximum Length 35'. Rates: $25 daily. Back in (8) Gravel, No Hookups. Picnic Table and Grill. Maximum Length 32'. Rates: $25 daily.
Tent Spaces: Tent Spaces: No hookups, picnic table, grill. Rates: $15 daily.
Yurt, A Frame, Cabin, Apt, Spaces: Duplexes: (6, 3 handicap accessible): Sleeps 5. Each has one bedroom and loft or second bedroom, private shower, private kitchenette w/ range top (no oven) and microwave, living room w/ satellite TV, linens, towels, cooking utensils. Rates: $100 daily. Cottage: (1) Rustic house, two-bedroom, sleeps eight, private shower, private kitchen, utensils, living room w/ gas-log fireplace, big screen TV/VCR, linens, towels, cooking utensils. Rates: $175 daily. Lodge: Rustic two-story building with four separately rented rooms. Kitchen and dining room for lodge guests is located in a separate building. Room 1: private bath, gas-log fireplace, TV, queen bed, bunk beds, and roll-away. Sleeps five. Rates: $75 daily. Room 2: shared bath downstairs, TV, queen bed, bunks, sleeps four. Rates: $50 daily. Room 3: shared bath (connected), gas-log fireplace, TV, queen bed, bunks, sleeps four. Rates: $60 daily. Room 4: shared bath down the hall, TV, queen bed, bunks, sleeps four. Rates: $50 daily. Camper Cabins: (8): Varying cabins with and without electricity. one-room log cabins, full bed frame and bunks w/ foam pads, (guests must provide sleeping bags or linens), port-o-johns, picnic table, porch swing, fire rings, sleeps fours. Rates: $35-$50 daily. Grace Lake Barn: Open bay sleeping sleeps 14 bunks w/ mattresses, (guests must provide sleeping bags or

linens), port-o-johns. Barn has electric, heat, but no running water. Rates: $100 daily.

Support Facilities: Bath House, Convenience Store, Diesel*, Equipment Rental, Fire Rings, Gasoline*, Grills, Ice, Laundry/Pay*, Long-Term RV Storage*, Mechanic/Auto Repair*, Pavilions (for a fee), Pay Phones**, Picnic Areas, Playground, Propane*, Restrooms, Sewage Dump Station*, Showers, Trails. *Off-Installation. **No phones in rooms. No cell phones service.

Activities: Fishing*, Hiking, Mountain Biking, Paddle Boats.

Credit Cards: MasterCard and Visa.

Restrictions: No weapons allowed. No smoking in any lodging facility. Guests staying in lodging may not bring pets. Pets are allowed on leash with day-use patrons and overnight in camper cabins, tents and RVs. Owner must pick up after pet. No sewage dump stations or water hookups. Potable water is available from water buffaloes located throughout the campground. All visitors are advised to call ahead for road and weather conditions prior to making the drive, especially in winter and spring. Entrance fee of $5/vehicle for day-use patrons. USAF Academy fishing permit is required for anglers 16 years and older; only daily or annual Academy permits are available for purchase at the office during business hours. Lakes are closed from 2300-0500 hours.

RV Driving Directions/Location: Off Base. From the Academy: Drive south on I-25 to Colorado Springs to exit 141. Travel west on Hwy 24 for 17 miles to Woodland Park. At third stoplight, turn right onto Baldwin (changes to Rampart Range Road). Follow road through four stop signs. Road forks just past water treatment facility, turn right and follow the Farish signs. Approximately two miles after the intersection, turn left onto Loy Creek Road and follow the signs to the new entrance into Farish. Facility is 6 miles past Woodland Park/Baldwin stoplight.

Area Description: Located on 655 acres of mountain woodlands with three fishing lakes, Farish is located within the Pike National Forest at an altitude of 9,000+ feet on Colorado's Front Range.

RV Campground Physical Address: 12005 Rampart Range Road, Woodland Park, CO 80863.

Fort Carson

Address: 6303 Wetzel Ave, Fort Carson, CO 80913.

Information Line: C-719-526-5811, DSN-312-691-5811.

Main Base Police: C-719-526-2333. Emergencies dial 911.

Main Installation Website: http://www.carson.army.mil/

Main Base Location: Fort Carson is located on the front range of the Rocky Mountains and is 60 miles South of Denver on Interstate 25 at Exit #135. The post is nestled in the extreme Southwest corner of Colorado Springs, beneath and in the shade of Cheyenne Mountain. You can also enter the post from State Highway 115 (Nevada Avenue).

Directions to Main Gate: From Denver: Take I-25 South to Colorado Springs. Take the South Academy Blvd exit at Exit 135. Keep right at the fork in the ramp. Merge onto south Academy Blvd heading West. The Front Range (mountains) is directly ahead. Pass the exit for Fort Carson Gate 4 at B-Street. Continue West towards the front range. Take the State Highway 115 exit South towards Canon City. Pass the Fort Carson Gate 2 exit. After approximately two miles, Fort Carson Gate 1 will be on left. Follow the brown signs to the In-processing/Welcome Center, open 24 hours or Colorado Inn billeting.

NMC: Colorado Springs, 7.5 miles north.

NMI: Schriever AFB, 25 miles east.

Base Social Media/Facebook: https://www.facebook.com/USArmyFortCarson

Base Social Media/Twitter: https://twitter.com/FtCarsonPAO

Chapels: Chaplain, C-719-526-5279.

Dental Clinic: Clinic 1, C-719-526-2200. Larson Clinic, C-719-526-3330. Smith Clinic, C-719-526-5400.

Medical: Appointment Line, C-719-526-2273. Information, C-719-526-7000.

Veterinary Services: C-719-526-3803.
Beauty/Barber Shop: Mini Mall, C-719-576-8013. Exchange Barber, C-719-540-9273; Stylique, C-719-576-6451. Ivy Express, C-719-524-0131. Wilderness Express, C-719-576-3693.
Commissary: C-719-503-8300.
Exchange Gas: Gate 3, C-719-527-4911. B Street, C-719-576-2108. Wilderness Express, C-719-226-0278.
Exchange: C-719-576-4000/4141.
Financial Institutions: Armed Forces Bank, N.A. C-719-576-6601, C-719-540-8418. Security Service Federal Credit Union, C-719-576-6401.
Clubs: Ivy Irish Pub, C-719-691-6646.
Places to Eat: Ivy Irish Pub, C-719-691-6646; Mulligan's Grill, C-719-526-2030 and Strike Zone Bar & Grill, C-719-526-5542 are on base. Eight dining facilities are located throughout the base. Exchange Food Court offers Anthony's Pizza, Burger King, Charley's, Starbucks, Subway and Taco Johns. Baskin Robbins, Dainty Kitchen, Domino's, Dunkin Donuts, Green Beans Coffee, Hunt Brothers Pizza, Jimmy John's, KFC, Korean Express, Pizza Hut, Qdoba and additional Starbucks, Subways and Burger Kings on base. Many restaurants within a short drive.
Bowling: Thunder Alley Bowling Center, C-719-526-5542.
Fitness Center: Garcia FC, C-719-526-3944. Iron Horse, C-719-526-2706. McKibben FC, C-719-526-2597. Waller, C-719-526-2742.
Golf Name and Phone Numbers: Cheyenne Shadows Golf Club, C-719-526-4102.
ITT/ITR: C-719-526-5366.
Library: Grant Library, C-719-526-2350.
Military Museum: The Mountain Post Historical Center, C-719-524-0915.
Military Museum Website: http://www.mountainposthistoricalcenter.org/
MWR: C-719-526-6452.
MWR Website: https://carson.armymwr.com
MWR Facebook: https://www.facebook.com/CarsonDFMWR

MWR
Twitter: https://twitter.com/carsonmwr
Outdoor Recreation: Outdoor Recreation Complex, C-719-526-1993. Offers camping gear, campers, fishing rods and boats, canoes, kayaks, paddle boards, outdoor sports equipment, party rentals, snow skiing gear, winter sport gear tune-ups, BBQ grills and more. Mountain Post Outfitters retail store on-site.
Swimming: Ellis Outdoor Pool, C-719-526-4456 offers recreational swim, water slides and snack bar. Iron Horse Pool, C-719-526-4093 offers open swim and swim lessons. Nelson Indoor Pool, C-719-526-3107 offers lap and open swim.
Things To Do: Visit Pikes Peak, Garden of the Gods, Glen Eyrie Castle, Cheyenne Mountain Zoo, Red Rock Canyon, Helen Hunt Falls or enjoy a more relaxing day of shopping and exploring unique boutique shops.
Walking Trails: Measured trails available, ask for Map at Check in.

RV CAMPING & GETAWAYS
Camp Falcon Recreation Area

Reservation/Contact Number Info: C-719-526-1993.
RV Website: https://carson.armymwr.com/programs/outdoor-recreation
Reservations: To reserve Camp Falcon, there is a onetime fee of $5, regardless of the number of consecutive nights reserved. The nightly fee is $3 per person per night. Special consideration can be given to groups who would like to perform a service project at Camp Falcon to help offset some of the fees. Office hours 0800-1800 Mon-Fri Closed weekends and all Federal Holidays.
Tent Spaces: Primitive camping area with no running water or electrical power. Sites provide one picnic table and a rocked fire pit. Charcoal grills at pavilion.
Support Facilities: Full range of support facilities on base.

RV Storage: C-719-526-1993. Storage facilities have electronic personal pin keypad entry control and are accessible 24/7.

Activities: Primitive location full of wildlife for excellent photography.

Restrictions: Bears and numerous other wild animals have been reported in and around Camp Falcon. Under no circumstances should any wildlife be fed by campers. No vehicle parking at campsites. Use designated parking area.

RV Driving Directions/Location: On Base. Access to Camp Falcon is available by entering base through Gate 6 between 0500-1800 hours or through Gate 1, 24 hours daily.

Area Description: Located near Colorado Springs at the base of the Rocky Mountains. The area is abundant in wildlife and natural beauty. Mountains and terrain make this an excellent location for skiing, hiking, sightseeing and exploration.

RV Campground Physical Address: Mailing Address: ITR, 7093 Specker Ave, Bldg 2429, Fort Carson, CO 80913.

United States Air Force Academy

Address: 2304 Cadet Drive, USAF Academy, CO 80840.

Information Line: C-719-333-1110, DSN-312-333-1110.

Main Base Police: C-719-333-2000.

Main Installation Website: http://www.usafa.af.mil/

Main Base Location: Located at the foothills of the beautiful Rocky Mountains, the US Air Force Academy is located northwest of Colorado Springs, Colorado in El Paso County. Spanning 18,000 spectacular acres, the Academy draws thousands of visitors from around the world each year. The Air Force Academy is the youngest of the U.S. service academies.

Directions to Main Gate: The Academy is located 60 miles south of Denver and is 10 miles northwest of downtown Colorado Springs. Approach Colorado Springs via I-25 from either north or south and take exit 156B (North Gate) or 150B (South Gate) to enter the Academy. The Academy is located between I-25 and the mountains.

NMC: Colorado Springs, eight miles south.

NMI: Peterson AFB, 22 miles southeast.

Base Social Media/Facebook: https://www.facebook.com/USAFA.Official

Base Social Media/Twitter: https://twitter.com/AF_Academy

Chapels: Chaplain, C-719-333-2856.

Dental Clinic: C-719-333-5190.

Medical: Appointment Line, C-719-524-2273. Information Line, C-719-333-5111.

Veterinary Services: C-719-333-4055.

Beauty/Barber Shop: Community Center Barber, C-719-472-1369; Stylique, C-719-472-1495. Fairchild Hall, C-719-472-1744.

Commissary: C-719-333-2227.

Exchange Gas: C-719-472-0395.

Exchange: C-719-472-0861.

Financial Institutions: Air Academy Federal Credit Union, C-719-593-8600, Armed Forces Bank, C-719-472-1090/0213.

Clubs: Falcon Club, C-719-333-8192. The Pub, C-719-333-8185.

Places to Eat: High Country Inn DFAC, C-719-333-4730; Ike's Grill, C-719-333-2606; Polaris Perk, C-719-472-7930; Ten Pin Grill, C-719-333-4252; Mitchell Hall Cadet DFAC and Falcon Club are on base. Burger King, Dunkin Donuts, Subway and Wing Zone are also on base. Many restaurants within a short drive.

Bowling: Academy Lanes Bowling Center, C-719-333-4709.

Fitness Center: C-719-333-4522. Satellite FC also on base.

Golf: Eisenhower Golf Course, C-719-333-2606.

ITT/ITR: C-719-333-7367.

Library: C-719-333-4665/3198.

MWR: C-719-333-4802.

MWR Website: http://www.usafasupport.com/

MWR Facebook: https://www.facebook.com/10th-Force-Support-Squadron-243202264030/

MWR Twitter: https://twitter.com/10FSS

Outdoor Recreation: Outdoor Recreation, C-719-333-4475. Offers information and access to a variety of outdoor adventures including skiing, fishing, hiking, boating and camping. Offers camping gear, campers, trailers, hiking and biking gear, lawn and garden equipment, party rental, picnic areas and more. Vandenberg ORC, C-719-333-4602 offers ski rentals and gear as well as retail sales and equipment tune-up. Transportation for Cadets provided for seasonal ski trips.

Swimming: Fitness Center Indoor Pool, C-719-333-4522 offers open swim and lap swim.

Things To Do: Located at the foot of the Rocky Mountains, near skiing and mountain resorts, there is much to do in the area. Also features a visitor's center, gift shop and exhibits.

Walking Trails: Running tracks are available on base.

RV CAMPING & GETAWAYS

Peregrine Pines FamCamp

Reservation/Contact Number Info: C-719-333-4980, DSN- 312-333-4356/4980. Fax C-719-333-6401. Off season, C-719-333-4602.

Recreation Security: C-719-333-2000.

RV Website: https://www.usafasupport.com/famcamp.html

GPS Coordinates: 39°0'23"N/104°50'24"W or 9022 Peregrine Pines Rd, Monument, CO 80840-5001.

Reservations: Recommended and accepted up to 90 days in advance for AD; 60 days in advance for all others during peak season. Off season availability first come, first serve basis. Credit card required for reservation. Payment due upon arrival. One night's stay charged for no shows. Maximum stay 30 days during peak season. Office hours 0900-2000 daily from 1 May-8 Oct. Check-in at FamCamp office during peak season, check FamCamp office door during off-season for self check-in packet and procedures. Check in 1200 hours, check out 1100 hours.

Season of Operation: Year-round. Office closed 8 Oct-20 May.

Eligibility: AD, NG, Res, Ret, Cadets, DoD-Civ and 100% DAV.

Camper/Trailer Spaces: Gravel (100), Back-in and Pull-through, Maximum 45' in length, E (110/220V/30/50A)/S/W hookups, picnic table, grill. Limited free Wi-Fi throughout park. Rates: $25-$27 daily for eligible, $30-$32 daily for sponsored guests during peak season. Contact staff for winter rates.

Tent Spaces: Gravel (10): No hookups, picnic table, grills. Rates: $12-$15 daily. Only available during peak season.

Support Facilities: Auto Craft Shop, Auto Repair, Bathhouse, Boat Rental/Storage, Bowling, Cafeteria, Camping Equipment, Chapel, Coin Laundry, Commissary, Convenience Store, Equipment Rental, Exchange, Falcon Trail, Fitness Center, Gas, Golf, Grills, Ice, Mess Hall, Pavilions, Pay Phones, Picnic Area, Playground, Pool, Propane, Rec Center, Restrooms, RV Storage, Sewage Dump, Shoppette, Shower, Snack Bar, Sports Fields, Stables, Tennis Courts, Trailer Rental, Trails.

RV Storage: Long term storage on installation; busy year-round. Some temporary storage available. Call Outdoor Recreation for availability: C-719-333-4356.

Activities: Bicycling, Bowling, Fishing*, Golfing, Horseback Riding, Hunting*, Jogging, Swimming, Skiing, Verizon Hot Spots available for rent, Hiking available on USAF Academy. Fishing/Rafting trips available through Outdoor Rec Center, C-719-333-4356. *State and base permits required for fishing. Limited hunting allowed with state and base licenses.

Credit Cards: Cash, MasterCard and Visa.

Restrictions: Pets allowed on leash, owner must clean up after pet. Pets must have current immunizations and must be under control at all times. Pets staying for more than two weeks must be registered with the Base Veterinary Services, 9037, C-719-333-4055. Quiet hours 2200-0800 hours. Do not feed

wild animals. Trees, flowers and nature's debris must remain undisturbed. No firearms allowed on base. No postal service at FAMCAMP. Mail may be shipped to Post Office for General Delivery at: Name @ FAMCAMP, USAF Academy, CO 80840.
RV Driving Directions/Location: On Base. From I-25 north of Colorado Springs: Take exit 150 and enter through the South Gate. FAMCAMP is just off Stadium Blvd approximately one block northeast of Falcon Stadium. From Denver: Take I-25 south and take exit 156 to enter through the North Gate. Turn left at the B-52 Bomber onto Stadium Blvd. Go approximately 1.25 miles. Look for FAMCAMP directional sign to turn left on Academy Drive. Take an immediate left on Peregrine Pines Drive and proceed to office.
Area Description: With an elevation of 7,000 feet, the camp is nestled in a peaceful, wooded area with views of the Front Range of the Rocky Mountains. Enjoy the seclusion, the varied attractions in the Colorado Springs area, and activities available through the Outdoor Recreation Center. The Academy has a Visitors Center (with Subway) on Academy Drive. Full range of support facilities available on base.
RV Campground Physical Address: 9022 Peregrine Pines Rd, USAF Academy, CO 80840-0249.

DELAWARE

Bethany Beach Training Site

Address: 163 Scannell Blvd, Bethany Beach, DE 19930-9770.
Information Line: HQ, C-302-323-3300.
Main Base Police: Emergencies dial 911.
Main Installation Website:
https://www.de.ng.mil/members/rti/
Main Base Location: The post is located three blocks from the Atlantic Ocean, approximately 14 miles from Ocean City, Maryland and 10 miles Rehoboth Beach, Delaware.
Directions to Main Gate: From US-13: Turn right onto US-113 N/Worcester Hwy. Take the ramp onto MD-90 E/Ocean City Expy. Turn left onto MD-528 N/Coastal Hwy. Continue to follow Coastal Hwy. Turn left onto Pennsylvania Ave. Take the first left. Turn right onto Scannell Blvd. Main Gate will be on the left.
NMC: Bethany Beach, within city limits.
NMI: Dover AFB, 45 miles northwest.
Places to Eat: Many restaurants within a short drive.
Fitness Center: Fitness Room on site.
Outdoor Recreation: Equipment Rental, C-302-854-7901. Offers volleyball court, cornhole boards, sports equipment, canoes, picnic areas and more.
Swimming: Beach swimming is available.
Things To Do: Enjoy leisurely beach days, stroll the boardwalk, visit Fenwick Island State Park, Fenwick Island Lighthouse or enjoy bird watching and plentiful shoreline for exploration.
Walking Trails: Padded track on base.

RV CAMPING & GETAWAYS
Bethany Beach RV Sites

Reservation/Contact Number Info: C-302-854-7901/7902. Fax C-302-854-7999, DSN-312-440-7999.
RV Website:
https://www.facebook.com/pg/BBTSBilletingOffice/services/
Other Info Website:
https://www.de.ng.mil/members/rti/
RV Email Address:
BBTSBilleting@gmail.com
GPS Coordinates:
32°54'32"N/75°3'47"W
Reservations: All requests must be submitted to the Bethany Beach Training Site, ATTN: Billeting Office, 163 Scannell Blvd, Bethany Beach, DE 19930-9770, faxed to C-302-854-7999 or emailed to BBTSBilleting@gmail.com. Telephone and/or Facebook requests not accepted. Lottery system in place. Please see Facebook page and click on

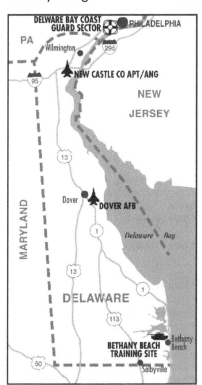

Support Facilities: Beach, Convenience Store, Fishing Pier, Fitness Center, Gas, Laundry, Marina, Pay Telephones, Picnic Area, Playground, Propane, Restrooms, Sewage Dump, Showers.

Activities: Amusement Rides, Basketball, Bicycling, Boardwalk, Canoe Rentals, Crabbing/Clamming, DVD Rentals, Fishing, Fitness Center, Golfing, Horseshoes, Jet Skiing, Jogging, Miniature Golf, Outlet Shopping, Rowboats, Rollerblading, Surfing, Swimming, Video Game Rentals, Volleyball.

Credit Cards: Discover, MasterCard and Visa.

Restrictions: No pets allowed. No firearms. Limit seven nights maximum stay, two-night minimum stay, three-night minimum on holidays and weekends. Posted speed limit 15 mph. One reservation per family at a time. Sponsor must be present during stay. No children under the age of 18 allowed alone in hotel.

RV Driving Directions/Location: On Base. Located on the west side of DE-1, approximately .5 miles north of DE-26 and DE-1 intersection Bethany Beach.

Area Description: Located on the Beach Highway, three blocks from the Atlantic Ocean, ten miles from Rehoboth Beach, DE, and 14 miles from Ocean City, MD. Many opportunities available for fun and enjoyment.

RV Campground Physical Address: Bethany Beach Training Site, Attn: Billeting Office Bldg 114, 163 Scannel Blvd, Bethany Beach, DE 19930-9770.

Dover Air Force Base

Address: 846 Sumner Drive, Bldg 846, Dover, DE 19901.

Information Line: C-302-677-3000, DSN-312-445-3000.

Main Base Police: Emergencies dial 911.

Main Installation Website: http://www.dover.af.mil/

Main Base Location: The base is located two miles south of the city of Dover, the capital of Delaware.

Directions to Main Gate: From BWI Airport: Start out going southeast toward I-195 W. Take I-195 W then take

"posts" for link to current year lottery information.

Season of Operation: Year-round.

Eligibility: The Delaware National Guard Bethany Beach Training Site is available for vacation use to the following personnel in priority sequence: (1) Current active/M-day personnel of the Delaware National Guard (1st Drawing) (2) Retired Delaware National Guard personnel (2nd Drawing) (3) Civilian employees of the Delaware National Guard (2nd Drawing) (4) All other non-Delaware National Guard Military Personnel and Retirees(3rd Drawing).

Camper/Trailer Spaces: Camper/RV Spaces: Hardstand (12), Back-in, maximum length 32', E(110/220V/15/30A)/S/W, CATV hookups. Gravel: (11), Pull-through, Any size, E(110V/15A)/S/W. Rates: $30 daily.

Yurt, A Frame, Cabin, Apt, Spaces: Mobile Home: Three-bedroom (22), 14'x70', furnished kitchen, A/C, heat, CATV/VCR. Rates: $90 daily. Official Use Rates: $45 daily.

MD-170 N/Exit 1 toward I-97/Annapolis/Bay Bridge. Merge onto Airport Loop/Aviation Blvd. Turn left onto MD-176 E/Dorsey Rd/Airport Loop. Continue to follow MD-176 E/Dorsey Rd. Merge onto I-97 S toward Annapolis/Bay Bridge. Take the MD-100/Exit 14B-A toward Gibson Island/Ellicott City. Merge onto MD-100 E via exit 14A on the left toward Gibson Island. Take MD-10 S/Arundel Expy toward Severna Park/MD-2. Take the 1st left onto Ritchie Hwy/MD-2 S. Continue to follow Ritchie Hwy. Merge onto US-301 N via the ramp on the left toward Bay Bridge tollway for approximately 37.5 miles. Turn right onto MD-302/Barclay Road, crossing into Delaware. MD-302/Barclay Rd becomes Arthursville Rd/SR-11. Turn right onto SR-44/Main Street continuing to follow SR-44. Turn left onto SR-8/Halltown Rd. Continue to follow SR-8 E. Turn right onto S Dupont Hwy S/US-13 S. Turn slight left onto S Bay Rd S. Merge onto SR-1 S toward Dover AFB/Beaches. Take exit 93 toward Dover AFB Main Gate Visitors.

NMC: Dover, five miles northwest.

NMI: New Castle County Airport/ANG, 45 miles north.

Base Social Media/Facebook: https://www.facebook.com/doverairforcebase/

Chapels: C-302-677-3932.

Dental Clinic: C-302-677-2846.

Medical: Appointment Line, C-302-730-4633.

Veterinary Services: C-302-677-5252.

Beauty/Barber Shop: Barber, C-302-734-1747.

Commissary: C-302-677-3919.

Exchange Gas: C-302-744-8049.

Exchange: C-302-678-2515.

Financial Institutions: Dover Air Force Base Federal Credit Union, C-302-678-8000, C-1-888-818-3328. Fort Sill National Bank, C-302-730-1466.

Clubs: The Landings Club, C-302-677-6024.

Places to Eat: King Pin Cafe, C-302-677-5323; Mulligans Sports Bar and Grill, C-302- 677- 6038 and Patterson DFAC, C-302-677-3926 are on base. Exchange

Food Court offers Burger King, Subway and Tim Horton's. Many restaurants within a short drive.

Bowling: Eagle Lanes Bowling Center, C-302-677-3950.

Fitness Center: Dover FC, C-302-677-3962.

Golf: Eagle Creek Golf Course, C-302-677-2988.

ITT/ITR: C-302-677-6772.

Military Museum: Air Mobility Command Museum, C-302-677-5938.

Military Museum Website: http://amcmuseum.org/

MWR: C-302-677-6372/6977.

MWR Website: https://www.doverafb436fss.com/

MWR Facebook: https://www.facebook.com/DoverAFBEvents

MWR Twitter: https://twitter.com/DoverAFBEvents

Outdoor Recreation: Outdoor Recreation Center, C-302-677-3959. Offers campers, camping gear, lawn and garden equipment, canoes, kayaks, paddle boards, fishing boats, trailers, outdoor sports equipment, party supplies and inflatables, mountain bikes, archery gear and more. Also offers an indoor climbing wall, park and pavilion rentals, bike shop and more.

Swimming: Oasis Seasonal Pool, C-302-677-3959 offers open and lap swim and a water slide.

Things To Do: Visit Dover Downs, the John Dickinson Plantation, Air Mobility Command Museum, Dover Downs Casino, the Old State House, First State Heritage Park or take a short 45-minute drive to Rehoboth and Dewey beaches.

Walking Trails: Indoor track at the Fitness Center.

RV CAMPING & GETAWAYS
Dover AFB FamCamp

Reservation/Contact Number Info: C-302-677-3959.

Recreation Security: C-302-677-6666.

RV Website: https://www.doverafb436fss.com/outdoor-rec

GPS Coordinates:
39°6'49"N/75°27'22"W
Reservations: Reservations are accepted for all 10 campsites up to 90 days in advance Office hours 0900-1700 Mon-Fri, and 0800-1300 on Sat (Apr-Sept). Closed Sundays and holidays. Payment must be made by credit card for the total number of days reserved. No refund for cancelled reservations within 3 days of arrival. Maximum occupancy and total reservation days: 1 Oct thru 30 Apr, 30 days; 1 May-30 Sep, 14 days.
Season of Operation: Year-round.
Eligibility: AD, NG, Res, Ret and DoD-Civ, base employees, dependents and guests.
Camper/Trailer Spaces: Camper/RV Sites: Gravel (10) back-in, maximum length 40", E (30A/50A)/S/W hookups, picnic table, grill. Rates: $20 daily. Overflow with utilities only, $15 daily. Newer bathhouse with coin-operated laundry facilities. Dump fees apply, $3.
Tent Spaces: Tent and Overflow Sites (5): Primitive sites. Rates: $8 daily.
Support Facilities: Auto Craft Shop, Auto Repair, Bath House, BBQ Grill, Beaches*, Bowling, Commissary, Dump Station, Exchange, Fitness Center, Gas Station, Golf, Grills, Horseshoes, Mess Hall, Pavilion, Picnic Area, Playground, Propane, Playground, Pool, Outdoor Recreation, Sewage Dump, Shoppette, Snack Bar, Sports Field, Tennis Courts. *Rehoboth and Dewey Beaches are located 45 minutes away.
Activities: Air Mobility Command Museum, Biking, Dover Downs*, Swimming, Tourist Attractions.
Credit Cards: American Express, MasterCard and Visa.
Restrictions: Pets allowed but must be attended to at all times and on a leash no longer than 6' when outdoors. Open fires not permitted on camp. Grills are provided along with a receptacle for hot coals. Quiet hours 2200-0700 hours. Guests are required to dispose of trash and debris at their site. Posted speed limit 5 mph.
RV Driving Directions/Location: On Base. East of DE-1/US-113 in Dover.

Clearly marked. Located on the south end of the base along Perimeter Road, near the Skeet Range.
Area Description: Several historic sites are located within the Dover area, including The John Dickinson Plantation. Rehoboth and Dewey beaches are just 45 minutes away.
RV Campground Physical Address: FamCamp, Bldg 67510, Dover AFB, DE 19902-7262.

FLORIDA

Avon Park Air Force Recreation Area

Address: Avon Park Air Force Range, 29 South Blvd, Avon Park, FL 33825.
Information Line: C-813-828-1110, DSN-312-968-1110.
Main Base Police: Emergencies dial 911.
Main Installation Website:
http://www.macdill.af.mil/
Main Base Location: Avon Park Air Force Range is a 106,000-acre military training facility located in Polk and Highlands County in south-central Florida.
NMC: Orlando, Fl 80 miles north.
NMI: MacDill AFB, 95 miles northwest.
Base Social Media/Facebook:
https://www.facebook.com/APAFROutdoorrec/
Exchange Gas: Commercial gas station available within 4 miles.
Places to Eat: Denny's, Wendy's, Subway, Arby's, Olive Garden, Outback Steakhouse, and much more are within a short drive.

RV CAMPING & GETAWAYS

Avon Park Air Force Range

Reservation/Contact Number Info: C-863-452-4254 option 0.
RV Website:
http://www.avonparkafr.net/
RV Email Address:
apafroutdoorrec@gmail.com

Reservations: Please check the forecast schedules on website or call office. Office hours and unit openings change weekly. Office closed Tue, Wed.

Season of Operation: Year-round.

Camper/Trailer Spaces: Primitive camping only. No electric hook-ups. Each campground has cold water showers and portables. Annual Military Park Permit $10.

Activities: Hunting*, fishing, hiking**. *Hunter's safety card is required for all hunt permit sales. **Hiking is not permitted during hunting season.

Credit Cards: Cash, MasterCard and Visa.

RV Driving Directions/Location: Off Base. Take County Road 64 East from Avon Park. From the Main Gate: Ask for directions to Outdoor Recreation, Bldg 600.

Area Description: Avon Park Air Force Range is a 106,000-acre military training facility located in Polk and Highlands Counties in south-central Florida.

RV Campground Physical Address: 29 S Blvd, Avon Park, FL 33825.

Blue Angel Naval Recreation Area

Address: BAP, 2100 Bronson Road, Pensacola, FL 32506.

Information Line: HQ Quarterdeck, C-850-452-4785/4786.

Main Base Police: C-850-452-2453/8888. Emergencies dial 911.

Main Installation Website: http://www.cnic.navy.mil/regions/cnrse/installations/nas_pensacola.html

Main Base Location: Pensacola is located in extreme Northwest Florida at the Florida/Alabama state line in Escambia County, 60 minutes east of Mobile, 45 minutes west of Ft. Walton Beach, and 500 miles Northwest of Orlando.

NMC: Pensacola, 15 miles east.

NMI: Pensacola Naval Air Station, 5 miles east.

Chapels: C-850-452-6376/6103.

Medical: C-850-452-6326, DSN-312-922-6326.

Commissary: Approximately 9 miles to NAS Pensacola Commissary, C-850-262-9200.

Exchange Gas: Approximately 9 miles to NAS Pensacola gas station, C-850-456-5502. Commercial gas station available within 7 miles.

Exchange: Approximately 9 miles to NAS Pensacola Exchange facility, C-850-453-5311.

Places to Eat: Lighthouse, C-850-452-2351 and O Club, C-850-452-3533. Barnhill's Country Buffet, C-850-456-2760 and Oyster Bar, C-850-455-3925 are within driving distance.

Fitness Center: Main, C-850-452-9845. Portside, C-850-452-7811/7810.

Golf: A.C. Read Golf Course, C-850-452-2454.

ITT/ITR: C-850-452-6354.

MWR: C-850-452-6701/6300.

MWR Website: http://www.navymwrpensacola.com/

Outdoor Recreation: At Blue Angel Recreation Area and Pensacola NAS and Corry Station there are beaches, disc golf, fitness center, a fishing pier, kayak, canoe and sunfish rentals, mountain bike rentals, paintball, equipment rentals, tennis courts, sports fields, picnic areas, playgrounds, mini-golf and much more.

Swimming: A swimming pool is available on Corry Station, C-850-452-6317. Barrancas Beach is walking distance while these beaches are a few miles away: Pensacola Beach, Perdido Key.

Things To Do: While here, see the miles of sugar-white sand beaches. Visitors can also participate in fishing, scuba diving or swimming. Don't miss the Saenger Theater of performing arts in Pensacola, watch the Blue Angels or tour the Navy Aviation Museum.

Walking Trails: Walking, jogging and nature trails are available.

RV CAMPING & GETAWAYS

Blue Angel Recreation Area

Reservation/Contact Number Info: C-850-390-6133.

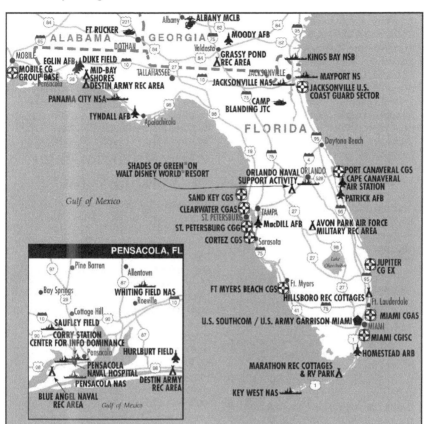

Recreation Security: C-850-452-2453. Emergency, C-850-452-8888.
RV Website:
http://www.navymwrpensacola.com/
Other Info Website:
http://get.dodlodging.net/propertys/Blue-Angel-Park
RV Email Address:
bapwelcomecenter@gmail.com
GPS Coordinates:
30°23'14"N/87°25'39"W
Reservations: RV sites and campgrounds are first come, first serve availability unless reserved. Reservations accepted 90 days in advance for AD, Ret; 60 days in advance for DoD-Civ. Office hours 0800-1700 Thur-Sun; 0800-1800 Fri-Sat. Check-in at Welcome Center 1400 hours, check-out 1100 hours. Maximum stay 90 days.
Season of Operation: Year-round.

Eligibility: AD, NG, Res, Ret, DoD-Civ (AD and Ret), 100% DAV, Dep and Guests.
Camper/Trailer Spaces: Anchor Cove: Grass area (80), back-in, maximum length 40', E(30A)/W, picnic table, grill. Rates: $16-$17.50 daily; $430-$470 monthly. Additional tents $8 daily. Battleship Row: Concrete Slabs (75), back-in, maximum length 40', E(50A)/S/W, picnic table. Rates: $23-$25 daily; $620-$675 monthly. Additional tents $8 daily. Bos 'N Court Trailers (12): Two bedroom, sleeps 6, one bath, full kitchen, with pull out sofa, fully furnished, picnic table, fire pit with grill. Rates: $70-$75 daily; $440-$475 monthly.
Tent Spaces: Primitive sites, no hookups, picnic table, grill. Rates: $7-$8 daily. Beachfront Platforms (4):

Primitive with running water nearby. Rates: $13-$14.50 daily.

Yurt, A Frame, Cabin, Apt, Spaces: Anchor Cove Cabins (7): Primitive. One room with full size bed, no cooking or bathroom facilities. Rates: $40-$45 daily.

Support Facilities: Bathhouse, Beaches, Boat Launch, Boat Rental/Dry Storage, Coin Laundry, Convenience Store, Diesel*, Equipment Rental, Exchange* (at Corry), Fire Rings, Fishing Pier, Fitness Center, Disc Golf, Gas*, Grills, Ice, Long-term RV Storage, Mechanic/Auto Repair*, Mini Golf, Pavilions, Picnic Areas, Playground, Propane, Restrooms, Sewage Dump, Shoppette, Showers, Sports Fields, RV Storage, Tennis Courts, Trails, Wi-Fi. *Off Base.

RV Storage: For AD/Ret only. Good availability. Rates: $35/month. For more information, C-850-390-6133.

Activities: Bicycling, Boating, Fishing*, Frisbee Golfing, Mini Golfing, Mountain Biking, Paintball, Swimming, Volleyball. *FL fishing license required for out of state visitors; license not required for FL residents.

Credit Cards: American Express, Discover, MasterCard and Visa.

Restrictions: Pets allowed on 6' leash in park. No pets or smoking allowed in cabins or mobile homes. Absolutely no firearms, bows and arrows, BB guns, or other items that could be considered weapons are allowed. No fireworks. Nominal admission charge for park, annual pass available.

RV Driving Directions/Location: Off Base. From I-10 east or west: Take exit 7 south on FL-297/Pine Forest Rd for 5.4 miles. Turn right (south) onto N Blue Angel Parkway. Travel 7.1 miles then turn right (west) onto US-98; follow for approximately four miles. Turn left onto Bronson Rd, follow for a short distance to the recreation area. Check-in at Welcome Center.

Area Description: Situated on Perdido Bay, with white sandy beaches, amidst oak trees and Spanish moss, the park offers spectacular camping, boating, swimming and picnic areas. As there are no currents or drop-offs in this part of the bay, its sandy bottom creates an ideal swimming area for children. Fifty acres of the complex have been reserved for youth activities. Full range of support facilities at Corry Station including Navy shopping mall and Navy hospital.

RV Campground Physical Address: 2100 Bronson Road, Pensacola, FL 32506.

Camp Blanding Joint Training Center

Address: Camp Blanding Joint Training Center, Florida National Guard, 5629 State Rd 16 West, Starke, FL 32091.

Information Line: C-904-682-3466, DSN-312-822-3466.

Main Base Police: C-904-682-3407.

Main Installation Website: http://www.floridaguard.army.mil/

Main Base Location: Clay County in North Central Florida.

Directions to Main Gate: From I-95 North or South: Exit 95A to FL 16 West for 31 Miles. Follow exit signs to support activities.

NMC: Jacksonville, 44 miles north.

NMI: NAS Jacksonville, 33 miles northeast.

Base Social Media/Facebook: https://www.facebook.com/FloridaNationalGuard

Base Social Media/Twitter: https://twitter.com/FLGuard

Chapels: C-904-682-3421/3366.

Medical: C-904-682-3911.

Beauty/Barber Shop: C-904-682-3195.

Exchange Gas: C-904-682-3513.

Exchange: C-904-682-3513.

Places to Eat: Conference Center, C-904-682-3197, Dining Hall, C-904-682-3166 are within driving distance of the facility.

Military Museum: Camp Blanding Museum and Memorial Park. C-904-682-3196.

Military Museum Website: http://www.campblanding-museum.org/

MWR: C-904-682-3104/3517.

Outdoor Recreation: Camp Blanding Recreation, C-904-682-3104. Offers camping, fishing pier, picnic area, playground, rec equipment, sports fields and tennis courts.

Swimming: Kingsley Lake is available.

Things To Do: Less than an hour drive to Gainesville, Jacksonville and St. Augustine. Three hours to Walt Disney World and the Orlando area.

RV CAMPING & GETAWAYS
Camp Blanding RV Park

Reservation/Contact Number Info: C-904-682-3104/3517, DSN-312-960-3104/3517. Fax C-904-682-3719.

Recreation Security: C-904-682-3462.

RV Website: https://www.facebook.com/CBJTCRecration/

GPS Coordinates: 29°57'13"N/81°59'20"W

Reservations: Reservations required for RV full hook-up sites. No reservations for primitive campsites. Reservations may be made 30 days in advance for association members; 90 days in advance for all other military. A deposit of half the stay plus one day is required within 72 hours after making a reservation and can be paid over the phone or by mail. Office hours 0800-1630 hours Mon-Fri. Check in at Recreation Dept. during business hours. After hours, check-in with Camp Host at primitive campground, located North of the RV Park in the Q-Hut Bldg. Check-out 1400 hours. Peak Season maximum stay 21 days. Main Gate open 24 hours.

Season of Operation: Year-round.

Eligibility: AD, NG, Res, Ret, 100% DAV and special "Associate Members" (Civilian) approved by commander.

Camper/Trailer Spaces: Primitive Park: Primitive sites with water hookup, burn pit and grill. Rates: $11 nightly; W/E hookup sites, burn pit and grill. Rates: $13.75 nightly; Full hookup E/W/S (5 sites), burn pit, grill. Rates: $24.75 nightly. Johnson RV Park (30): Full hookup E(30/50A)S/W with 50' slab, burn pit, picnic table, grill. Rates: $24.75 nightly. New RV Park (19): Full hookup E(30/50A)S/W with 60' slab, burn pit, picnic table, grill. Rates: $24.75 nightly.

Tent Spaces: Primitive sites with W hookup only. Two tents per site. Three bathhouses in area, two complete with hot showers. Rates: $11 nightly.

Support Facilities: Bathhouse, Beach, Boat Launch, Coin Laundry, Exchange, Fire Rings, Fishing Pier, Fitness Center, Ice, Mess Hall, Pavilion, Pay Phones, Picnic Area, Playground, Rec Equipment, Restrooms*, RV Storage, Sewage Dump, Showers, Sports Fields, Tennis Courts. *Handicap accessible.

RV Storage: Long-term RV storage is available for six months or one year. Availability limited; RV park maintains a waitlist year-round. Contact Recreation Office: C-904-682-3104 0800-1630 hours Mon-Fri, 0900-1300 hours Sat for more information.

Activities: Basketball, Boating, Fishing*, Hunting*, Jogging (only on Avenue A), Racquetball, Swimming, Volleyball. *State and base permits required.

Credit Cards: MasterCard and Visa.

Restrictions: Maximum of two pets allowed. Patrons must register all pets and provide a copy of shot records with the Recreation Department prior to arrival. Reservations are required to bring pets to post. Firearms must be registered with Range Control and at Main Gate. Boaters should stay clear of swimming areas, fishermen and private residences. Daily boat launch fee for Kingsley Lake is $5 for non-Florida NG; Florida NG and other DoD can buy annual stickers for $20.

RV Driving Directions/Location: On Base. From I-95 north or south, take exit 95 or 95A (located north of St. Augustine) onto FL-16 west for 31 miles to Camp Blanding. From US-301 north or south, at Starke, exit east onto FL-16 for 11 miles. Follow exit signs to Support Activities. After entering gate, go to first stop sign and turn left. Take the first right on Daytona Beach Road. Turn left on Avenue A/Lake Road. Facility ahead.

Area Description: Located on Kingsley Lake in Starke, Camp Blanding is a 70,380-acre wildlife management area leased to the army as a training center in 1939. An additional 140,000 surrounding acres were acquired for training purposes during World War II. There are two camping areas adjacent to each other. Basic campground (for trailers and tents) is wooded site on shores of Kingsley Lake, located on Avenue A south of NCO Lodge. Limited support facilities on post.

RV Campground Physical Address: Camp Blanding Recreation Department, 5629 State Rd, 16 West, Bldg 1530, Starke, FL 32091-9703.

Destin Army Recreation Area

Address: 557 Calhoun Ave, Destin, FL 32541.

Information Line: C-706-545-2011, DSN-312-835-2011.

Main Base Police: C-706-651-7400.

Main Installation Website: http://www.benning.army.mil/

Main Base Location: Just 220 miles south of Fort Benning, between Pensacola and Panama City, the resort is sprawled across 15 acres along the Choctawhatchee Bay, minutes from the Gulf of Mexico.

NMC: Fort Walton Beach, 10 miles west.

NMI: Eglin AFB, 17 miles north.

Commissary: Approximately 16 miles to Eglin AFB Commissary, C-850-609-3172 ext 2358.

Exchange Gas: Approximately 16 miles to Eglin AFB gas station. Commercial gas station within 2 miles.

Exchange: Approximately 16 miles to Eglin AFB Exchange facility, C-850-651-5621/5823.

Places to Eat: Cap't Dave's on the Gulf, C-850-837-2627, Destin Chops, C-850-654-4944 and Shoney's, C-850-837-9650 are within driving distance.

Marina: C-850-837-6423.

MWR: C-850-837-6423.

MWR Website: https://benning.armymwr.com/us/benning/programs/destin-army-recreation-area

MWR Facebook: https://www.facebook.com/destin.recreation/

Swimming: Swimming pool with splash park, ocean swimming at military beach nearby.

RV CAMPING & GETAWAYS

Destin Army Recreation Area

Reservation/Contact Number Info: C-850-837-6423.

Recreation Security: C-850-651-7400 for Okaloosa County Sheriff. Emergencies dial 911.

RV Website: https://benning.armymwr.com/programs/destin-army-recreation-area

GPS Coordinates: 30°24'38"N/86°29'54"W or 557 Calhoun Ave, Destin, FL 32541.

Reservations: Required for Villas, Hotel, Suites, Studios and RV Park. Reservations for Villas accepted up to six months in advance for AD; four months in advance for retirees and all others. Reservations accepted one year in advance for all other types of accommodations. Office hours 0700-2200 hours CST daily. Check-in at office 1600 hours, check-out 1100 hours. Rates vary based on season and rank. Additional fees apply for pets.

Season of Operation: Year-round.

Eligibility: AD, NG, Res, Ret, DoD-Civ and Foreign Military.

Camper/Trailer Spaces: Hardstand (46), Back-in, Maximum 40' in length, E(110V/30/50A)/S/W, CATV hookups. Rates: Summer: $21 to $24 daily. Winter: $21 to $23 daily. Summer Season maximum stay is 30 days. Winter Season maximum stay 120 days. Two pet maximum at each site.

Yurt, A Frame, Cabin, Apt, Spaces: Villas: Three-bedroom (4), alarm clock, private bath, kitchen, microwave, CATV, hair dryer, phone w/free local calls), pots/pans/utensils, linens, refrigerator. Rates: Summer: $139-$150 daily, E5 and below: $116-$126 daily. Winter: $123-$133 daily, E5 and below, $116-$126 daily. Additional fee for pets; $25 non-refundable deposit and $5 fee per day, per pet. Two-bedroom (13, 5 ADA accessible), private bath, kitchen, microwave, CATV, phone (free local calls), pots/pans, linens. Rates: Summer: $123-$128 daily, E5 and below, $100-$105 daily. Winter: $112-$118 daily, E5 and below, $100-$105 daily. Note: during Summer Season (1 Mar- 30 Sep): Villas require a 4-night minimum, with a maximum 7-day stay. Off-season (1 Oct to 28 Feb): Two-night minimum, with a 120-day maximum. Hotel: Rooms (14), two queen sized beds, sleeps four, microwave, refrigerator, coffee maker, CATV, phone. Rates: Summer: $80 daily, E5 and below, $55 daily. Winter: $80 daily, E5 and below, $55 daily weekly. Additional fee for pets; $25 non-refundable deposit and $5.00 fee per day, per pet. Maximum stay of seven days during peak season. 1-Bedroom Suites: Suites (14, 1 ADA Accessible), two queen size beds, kitchenette, utensils, CATV and phone. Rates: Summer: $112 daily, E5 and below, $90 daily. Winter: $102 daily, E5 and below, $90 daily. Note: during Summer Season (1 Mar- 30 Sep): Suites require a 3-night minimum, with a maximum 7-day stay. Off-season (1 Oct to 28 Feb): Two-night minimum, with a 120-day maximum. Studios: (20, 3 ADA Accessible), two queen size beds, cooktop, utensils, CATV and phone. Rates: Summer: $96-$102 daily, E5 and below, $74-$79 daily. Winter: $90-$96 daily, E5 and below, $74-$79 daily. Note: during Summer Season (1 Mar-30 Sep): Studios require a 2-night minimum, with a maximum 7-day stay. Off-season (1 Oct to 28 Feb): No minimum, with a 120-day maximum.

Support Facilities: RV Bathhouse, Boat Launch, Boat Rental, Boat Slip Rental (winter months only), Deep-Sea Charter, Fishing Pier, Grills, Laundry, Marina, Pavilion, Playground, Pool, Splash Park, Restrooms, Showers, Vending Machine and Wi-Fi Internet Access.

RV Storage: None.

Activities: Deep-Sea Fishing*, Fishing*, Jet Skis, Kayaks, Paddle boards, Pontoon Boats, Swimming. *State license required for fishing.

Credit Cards: American Express, MasterCard and Visa.

Restrictions: A maximum of two pets allowed in private RV's and pet friendly units. When making reservations a Pet friendly must be requested. Pets must be kept on leash in designated walking areas only. No firearms allowed. Quiet hours 2200-0700.

RV Driving Directions/Location: Off Base. From I-10 east: Take exit 56 to FL-85 south toward Fort Walton Beach, turn left (east) on US-98, then turn left on Benning Drive. At end of Benning Drive, turn left Calhoun Ave and immediately right into recreation area. From I-10 West: Take exit 85 onto US-331 South toward Freeport, proceeding for approx 25 miles, crossing the Clyde B Wells Bridge. Turn right on US-98 and proceed approx 19 miles. Turn right on Benning Drive. Follow directions as above.

Area Description: Located on 15-acre site on Choctawhatchee Bay in Destin, FL. Enjoy the sparkling sugar-white Gulf of Mexico beaches approximately two miles from recreation area. Area also offers golf at six public courses, two greyhound racetracks within 45 miles, deep sea fishing Cruiser, Destin Fishing Museum, Gulfariam, Zoo, and Indian Temple Mound Museum. Full range of support facilities available at Eglin AFB.

RV Campground Physical Address: 557 Calhoun Ave, Destin, FL 32541.

Eglin Air Force Base

Address: 502 W Van Matre Avenue, Bldg 205, Eglin AFB, FL 32542.

Information Line: C-850-882-1110, DSN-312-872-1110.

Main Base Police: C-850-882-2502.

Main Installation Website: http://www.eglin.af.mil/

Main Base Location: Eglin AFB is located in Okaloosa County, in northwest Florida, comprising over 640 square miles. This is a military friendly area and also a major tourist attraction due to the white sand beaches. Eglin is located 8 miles northwest of Fort Walton Beach, FL; 60 miles east of

Pensacola, FL and 65 miles west of Panama City, FL.

Directions to Main Gate: From I-10 east or west at Crestview: Take exit 12 south onto FL-85 south for 20 miles to Niceville. Go west (right) on John Sims Parkway/FL-20 to the East Gate of Eglin AFB and stay on Eglin Blvd to base.

NMC: Fort Walton Beach, seven miles south.

NMI: Hurlburt Field, 12 miles southwest.

Base Social Media/Facebook: https://www.facebook.com/TeamEglin

Base Social Media/Twitter: https://twitter.com/teameglin

Chapels: C-850-882-2111.

Dental Clinic: C-850-883-8324.

Medical: C-850-883-8242, DSN-312-872-8242.

Veterinary Services: C-850-882-2233.

Beauty/Barber Shop: Beauty, C-850-651-5224, Barber, C-850-651-8500.

Commissary: C-850-882-3172.

Exchange Gas: C-850-729-3720.

Exchange: C-850-651-2512/5823.

Financial Institutions: Coastal Bank and Trust, C-850-729-5510, C-1-800-840-8440. Federal Credit Union (Eglin Branch), C-850-862-0111, C-1-800-862-0111.

Clubs: Bayview Club, C-850-651-1010. Yacht Club, C-850-651-3122.

Places to Eat: Cafeteria, C-850-651-4821, Dining Facility, C-850-882-5053, Flight Kitchen, C-850-882-5014 and Legends Bar & Grill, C-850-678-5127 are within driving distance.

Bowling: Eglin Bowling Center, C-850-882-3352.

Fitness Center: C-850-882-2302, C-850-883-9127.

Golf: Eglin Golf Course, C-850-882-2949.

ITT/ITR: C-850-882-5930.

Library: C-850-882-5016.

Marina: C-850-882-7730.

Military Museum: Air Force Armament Museum, C-850-651-1808.

Military Museum Website: http://www.afarmamentmuseum.com/

MWR: C-850-882-5058.

MWR Website: http://www.eglinlife.com/

MWR Facebook: https://www.facebook.com/eglinlife

Outdoor Recreation: Outdoor Adventure Center, C-850-882-5058. Offers two FamCamp sites, Postl Point Marina, Ben's Lake Marina, Bear Creek Marina, a recreational vehicle storage lot, a pool, several picnic areas and beach operations. Boat storage is available with wet and dry slips at Ben's Lake Marina and wet slips at Bear Creek Marina.

Swimming: Eglin Pool, C-850-882-4959 and beaches nearby.

Things To Do: Close to the world's most beautiful white sand beaches, with crystal clear emerald waters. Some of the best deep-sea fishing and boating that you can experience anywhere.

Walking Trails: The Eglin Beach Park is located on Okaloosa Island just west of the Destin Bridge. Open during summer months to all DoD personnel, military dependents, retirees, civilian and federal personnel/contractors and guests with proper ID.

RV CAMPING & GETAWAYS
Eglin AFB FamCamp

Reservation/Contact Number Info: C-850-883-1243.

Recreation Security: C-850-882-2000.

RV Website: http://www.eglinlife.com/famcamp/index.html?ref=17134824

RV Email Address: EglinFamCamp@gmail.com

GPS Coordinates: 30°27'34"N/86°31'47"W

Reservations: No advance reservations. All sites first come, first serve. Camp Robbins Office hours 0800-1500 Mon-Fri; 0800-1200 Sat-Sun. Check-in at Bldg 1171, check-out 1000 hours. Max stay 60 days per visit.

Season of Operation: Year-round.

Eligibility: AD, NG, Res, Ret, DoD-Civ, Dep and 100% DAV.

Camper/Trailer Spaces: Camp Robbins: Concrete slab (60); pull-thru (45), back-in, any size, (15) E(110V/30/50A)/S/W, picnic table, bathhouse, laundry. Rates: Summer: $25 daily; $150 weekly; $450

monthly May-Sept; Winter monthly: $475 Oct-Apr; $30 daily guest fee with a 14-day guest max stay. Trailers (2), furnished but linens not provided. Rates: $60 daily, $120 weekly, $825 monthly. Reservations 90 days in advance with $50 deposit. Postl Point: Gravel (20), pull-thru, any size, E(110V/30A)/W, picnic table, CATV. Rates: $25 daily; $150 weekly; $450 monthly.

Tent Spaces: Camp Robbins: Grass (20); water, grill, picnic table. Rates: $7.50 daily.

Support Facilities: Auto Craft Shop, Bathhouse, Beach, Boat Launch, Boat Rental, Bowling, Chapel, Coin Laundry, Commissary, Convenience Store, Equipment Rental, Exchange, Fitness Center, Gas, Golf, Grills, Marina, Pavilion, Picnic Area, Playground, Pool, Propane Sales, Rec Center, Restrooms*, RV Storage, Sewage Dump, Shoppette, Showers*, Sports Fields, Stables, Tennis Courts, Trails. *Handicap accessible.

RV Storage: Waiting list with priority given to AD. Call Outdoor Recreation, C-850-882-5058.

Activities: Fishing*, Golfing, Hunting*, Jogging, Outdoor Adventure Program. *State license and Jackson Guard permit required.

Credit Cards: MasterCard and Visa.

Restrictions: Pets allowed; owner must clean up after pets. Sites limited to one RV and two vehicles. Quiet hours 2200-0700.

RV Driving Directions/Location: On Base. Camp Robbins located near Bear Creek Marina on Shambo Cove Road off Memorial Trail. Postl Point adjacent to the Outdoor Recreation Center off Flagler Road at Postl Point. Follow signs to to each camp.

Area Description: Located on a peninsula on the northern coast of the Gulf of Mexico in Fort Walton area off Choctawhatchee Bay. FamCamp is part of the base recreation area and is situated adjacent to the beach. Beautiful forested areas and fresh-water lakes also nearby. The boat rental marina is within walking distance of the beach. Full range of support facilities available on base.

RV Campground Physical Address: Eglin FamCamp, 404 N 7th St, Ste C, Eglin AFB, FL 82542-5498.

Hillsboro Recreational Cottages

Address: U.S. Coast Guard MWR Cottages, Hillsboro MWR Office, 907B Hillsboro Mile, Hillsboro Beach, FL 33062.

Information Line: PAO, C-305-415-6683.

Main Base Police: Emergencies dial 911.

Main Installation Website: http://www.atlanticarea.uscg.mil/Our-Organization/District-7/

Main Base Location: Located on the Coast Guard Light Station Hillsboro Inlet.

NMC: Pompano Beach, 5 miles southwest.

NMI: Miami CGAS, 35 miles south.

Exchange Gas: Commercial gas station available within 5 miles.

Places to Eat: There is a wide variety of restaurants nearby.

MWR: C-305-535-4565.

MWR Website: http://www.uscg.mil/BaseMiamiBeach/mwr/mwr_home.asp

Outdoor Recreation: MWR Equipment Rental, C-305-535-4565. Offers general beach activities including bicycling, hiking, swimming, snorkeling, scuba diving and fishing (license may be required). There is no boat ramp or docking available at the Recreational Cottages at Hillsboro.

Swimming: Ocean swimming is available.

Things To Do: Located near Miami, there is much to see and do within the city and in the great outdoors.

RV CAMPING & GETAWAYS
Hillsboro Recreational Cottages

Reservation/Contact Number Info: C-954-781-1817.

Recreation Security: C-954-427-6600.

RV Website:
https://www.dcms.uscg.mil/Our-Organization/Assistant-Commandant-for-Human-Resources-CG-1/Community-Services-Command-CSC/MWR/Coast-Guard-Lodging/

RV Email Address:
hillsboroinletreservations@gmail.com

Reservations: Reservations accepted via telephone and will be considered in the order received. When multiple cottages are reserved, the total nights reserved may not exceed 14 nights. Office hours 1000-1600 hours Mon-Fri. Cancellations must be made 10 days in advance of reservation date to receive full refund. There is a reservation and event restriction during the holiday period spanning the Monday before Thanksgiving to the Friday after New Year's. Maximum stay 14 days. All non-USCG patrons are limited to 60 days in advance reservation. Only one active reservation is permitted at a time. Check-in 1400 hours, check-out 1100 hours.

Season of Operation: Year-round.

Eligibility: AD, NG, Res, Ret, and their dependents; Widow/ers, DoD-Civ, 100% DAVs.

Yurt, A Frame, Cabin, Apt, Spaces: Beach House (1): Three-bedroom, two bath, ADA compliant main level; two queen size beds, three twin beds. Rates: $200 daily for O7-10; $175 daily for O5-6; $150 daily for E7+, O1-4, W2-4; $135 daily for E6 and below, honorably discharged. Inlet House (1): Three-bedroom, two bath, two queen size beds, three twin beds. Rates: $200 daily for O7-10; $175 daily for O5-6; $150 daily for E7+, O1-4, W2-4; $135 daily for E6 and below, honorably discharged. Inlet Bungalow (1): One-bedroom, two bath with one queen size bed, one pullout couch. Rates: $150 daily for O7-10; $135 daily for O5-6; $125 daily for E7+, O1-4, W2-4; $100 daily for E6 and below, honorably discharged, MOH Recipients.

Support Facilities: Lodging Amenities: Coffee Maker, Cooking Utensils, Dishes, Grills, Housekeeping upon check-out, Internet Access, Linens, Laundry Availability, Pots and Pans and Towels.

Activities: General beach activities including bicycling, hiking, swimming, snorkeling, scuba diving and fishing (license may be required). No boat ramp or docking available at the Recreational Cottages at Hillsboro. Contact MWR for more information.

Credit Cards: AMEX, DISC, MC, VISA.

Restrictions: No RVs, camping or pets allowed. Boat and trailers limited to 20'.

RV Driving Directions/Location: Off Base. From I-95: Take the Atlantic Blvd exit and head east. Make a left on A1A. Proceed north on A1A for approx 4 miles until you pass over the Hillsboro Inlet Bridge. Once over the bridge, make an immediate right and proceed to the security gate (of Hillsboro Club). The Lodge Host's office is located in the small building next to the flagpole. Note: Access to the Hillsboro Light Station and Cottages is via a private easement. For access to the facility, patrons must be a registered guest. Drop-in or day use of the facility is not permitted.

Area Description: The Recreational Cottages at Hillsboro are turn of the century cottages that were the occupied by the U.S. Coast Guard Light Keepers up until the full automation of the Hillsboro Lighthouse.

RV Campground Physical Address: 901 Hillsboro Mile, Hillsboro Beach, FL 33062.

Hurlburt Field

Address: Hurlburt Field AFR Center, 220 Lukasik Avenue, Bldg 90213, Hurlburt Field, FL 32544-5272.

Information Line: C-850-884-1110, DSN-312-579-1110.

Main Base Police: C-850-884-7114. Emergencies dial 911.

Main Installation Website:
http://www.hurlburt.af.mil/

Main Base Location: Hurlburt Field is located on the Gulf of Mexico in the Florida Panhandle, 35 miles east of Pensacola. Hurlburt Field is located in the city of Mary Esther, Florida and is very close to Eglin AFB.

Directions to Main Gate: From Interstate 10: Take exit 56/Old 12 in Crestview. Turn south on Highway 85 proceed about 14 miles to the intersection of Highway 123, veer to the right, continue on this road until it re-intersects with Highway 85. Go south for approximately 10 miles to Highway 98. Veer to the right towards Pensacola. Driving from the West via I-10: Take exit 31/Old 10 and turn right on Highway 87 and proceed about 20 miles to Highway 98. Turn left and proceed east for about 10 miles. Hurlburt Field sign is posted. The main gate is on the left.

NMC: Pensacola, 35 miles west.

NMI: Eglin AFB, 12 miles northeast.

Base Social Media/Facebook:
https://www.facebook.com/HurlburtFieldOfficial

Base Social Media/Twitter:
https://twitter.com/Hurlburt_Field

Chapels: C-850-884-7795.

Dental Clinic: C-850-884-7881.

Medical: C-850-883-8600, DSN-312-641-1020.

Beauty/Barber Shop: C-850-581-3524/8893.

Commissary: C-850-881-2138/2149/2150.

Exchange Gas: C-850-581-0488.

Exchange: C-850-581-0030/0031/8225/8226.

Financial Institutions: Eglin Federal Credit Union, C-850-862-0111. First National Bank and Trust, C-850-581-2222.

Clubs: The Reef, C-850-884-4970, The Soundside, C-850-884-7507 and The Riptide, C-851-881-5127/5128.

Places to Eat: Exchange Food Court, C-850-581-6008 offers Anthony's Pizza, Taco Bell and Einstein Bros. Bagels, Robin Hood, Church's Chicken, C-850-581-6656. Burger King, C-850-581-9111 and Velocity Subs, C-850-884-7365 are also available nearby. J.R. Rocker's Sports Cafe, C-850-884-6469 is within walking distance. Many fine restaurants are within driving distance.

Bowling: Hurlburt Lanes, C-850-884-6941.

Fitness Center: Commando Fitness Center, C-850-884-4412. Aderholt

Fitness, C-850-884-6884. Riptide Fitness, C-850-881–5121/5122.

Golf: Gator Lakes Golf Course, C-850-881-2251. Eglin AFB Golf Course, C-850-882-2949.

ITT/ITR: C-850-884-6795.

Library: C-850-884-6947.

Marina: Hurlburt Field Marina, C-850-884-6939.

MWR: C-850-884-6939.

MWR Website: http://myhurlburt.com/

MWR Facebook:
https://www.facebook.com/myhurlburt

Outdoor Recreation: Hurlburt Field Outdoor Recreation Center, C-850-884-6939. Offers boating, fishing, paintball, skeet and trap ranges, aquatic center, camping, FamCamp marina and much more.

Swimming: Hurlburt Aquatic Center, C-850-884-6866.

Things To Do: This area is also known as the Emerald Coast and is a major tourist attraction for its breathtaking white beaches and the emerald green waters. The fishing is great here! Destin is known as "The World's Luckiest Fishing Village." The area also has great beaches and many fine restaurants.

Walking Trails: Nature trails are available at the FamCamp.

Jacksonville Naval Air Station

Address: NAS Jacksonville, 6801 Roosevelt Ave, Jacksonville, FL 32212.

Information Line: Quarterdeck, C-904-542-2338, DSN-312-942-2338.

Main Base Police: C-904-542-2663.

Main Installation Website:
http://www.cnic.navy.mil/regions/cnrse/installations/nas_jacksonville.html

Main Base Location: Located in Duval County, along the west bank of the St. John's River in northeast Florida, it is a 20-minute ride to the heart of the City of Jacksonville.

Directions to Main Gate: From I-95 North from Daytona Beach: Take I-295 North over the Buchman Bridge. Exit at US-17 and go north for approximately 2.5 miles to NAS Jacksonville main gate. From I-95 South: Take I-10 West just after downtown Jacksonville. Stay in left lane and exit at US-17 South. Take US-17 South for about 6.5 miles to NAS Jacksonville main gate.

NMC: Jacksonville, 9 miles northeast.
NMI: Mayport Naval Station, 46 miles northeast.
Base Social Media/Facebook: https://www.facebook.com/NASJacksonville
Base Social Media/Twitter: https://twitter.com/NAS_Jax
Chapels: C-904-542-3051/3052.
Dental Clinic: C-904-542-3441.
Medical: Branch Medical Clinic, C-904-542-3500. Hospital, C-904-542-7300/3500, DSN-312-942-7300.
Veterinary Services: C-904-542-3786.
Beauty/Barber Shop: C-904-777-7228.
Commissary: C-904-317-3400, C-904-542-5311.
Exchange Gas: C-904-777-7142.
Exchange: C-904-777-7200/7286.
Financial Institutions: Vystar Credit Union, C-904-908-2715. ATM located in terminal.
Clubs: Fouled Anchor CPO Club, C-904-542-3900. Officers' Club T-Bar, C-904-542-3041.
Places to Eat: Galley, C-904-542-4245, Gutterball Grill, C-904-542-3295, Dewey's, C-904-542-3900, Bambinos, Mulligan's, C-904-542-2936, The Zone, C-904-542-3900 and McDonald's are within walking distance.
Bowling: Bowling Center, C-904-542-3493.
Fitness Center: C-904-542-2930.
Golf: NAS Jacksonville Golf Course, C-904-542-3249.
ITT/ITR: C-904-542-3318.
Marina: Mulberry Cove Marina, C-904-542-3260.
MWR: C-904-542-3111/3112.
MWR Website: http://www.navymwrjacksonville.com/
MWR Facebook: https://www.facebook.com/NASJAXMWR
Outdoor Recreation: Jacksonville Naval Air Station Outdoor Recreation Services, C-904-542-3111. Offers a golf course, bowling alley, picnic areas, and flying club. Marina, C-904-542-3260.

Swimming: Indoor Pool, C-904-542-3239. Seasonal outdoor pool. Beaches nearby.
Things To Do: Don't miss boating and water sports on over 74 square miles of inland waters. Visit the many golf courses and beautiful beaches that are boasted as Florida's finest.
Walking Trails: Nature walk behind the Navy Lodge.

RV CAMPING & GETAWAYS

Jacksonville NAS RV Park & Cottages

Reservation/Contact Number Info: RV Park, C-904-542-5898, DSN-312-942-5898. Fax C-904-542-5995, DSN-312-542-5995. Heritage Cottages, C-904-542-3138/3139.
Recreation Security: C-904-542-4539, DSN-312-942-4529.
RV Website: https://www.navymwrjacksonville.com
Other Info Website: http://get.dodlodging.net/propertys/Navy-Getaways-Jacksonville-RV-Park
GPS Coordinates: 30°13'10"N /81°40'27"W or Bldg 622, Birmingham Road, NAS Jacksonville, FL 32212.
Reservations: RV Park: Reservations accepted and up to 120 days in advance. Office hours 0800-2000 Mon, Thur, Fri, 0800-1600 Tue-Wed, 0900-1700 Sat-Sun. Check-in at Auto Skills Center, Bldg 622, on Birmingham Ave. Check-in 1400 hours, check-out 1100 hours. Reservations may be made for up to 30 days or in periods of 30 days not to exceed 180 days. After allotted time, must leave the park for 4 months. Cottages: Reservations accepted one year in advance for AD; 6 months in advance for all others. Check-in 1500 hours, check-out 1100 hours.
Season of Operation: Year-round.
Eligibility: AD, NG, Res, Ret and DoD-Civ (AD).
Camper/Trailer Spaces: Camper Spaces: (38): Full hookup sites. Rates: $14 daily. Partial hookup sites (6): Rates: $12 daily.
Yurt, A Frame, Cabin, Apt, Spaces: Cottage (16 - 2 ADA): Located on the

golf course. Two-bedroom, private full bath, fully furnished, can sleep up to six people. One queen bed, two twin beds, pull-out couch in living room, fully equipped kitchen, full-size refrigerator, microwave, stove, oven, TV/VCR/DVD, A/C and heat, laundry facility. Rates: $69 per day.

Support Facilities: Auto Craft Shop, Bathhouse, Boat Launch, Boat Rental/Storage, Bowling, Chapel, Commissary, Convenience Store, Diesel, Exchange, Fishing Pier, Fitness Center, Gas, Golf, Ice, Laundry, Marina, Mechanic/Auto Repair, Pavilion, Picnic Area, Playground, Pool, Propane, Restrooms, RV Storage, Sewage Dump, Showers, Shuttle Bus, Snack Bar, Sports Fields, Telephones, Tennis Courts, Trails.

RV Storage: Long term annual. Contact C-904-542-3227.

Credit Cards: American Express, Discover, MasterCard and Visa.

Restrictions: Pets allowed on leash and must be kept under control at all times. No pet can be left outside unattended at any time. Owners must clean up after pets. No firearms allowed.

RV Driving Directions/Location: On Base. From I-295 north or south: Take exit 10/Roosevelt Blvd/Hwy 17. Go north on Hwy 17 about one mile. Base is on right hand side. Enter either the Birmingham Gate or the Yorktown Gate. From Birmingham Gate go straight down Birmingham Avenue to the corner of Birmingham and Jason St. From the Yorktown Gate, go straight down Yorktown Ave. Take a right onto Jason St and go to the corner of Birmingham and Jason.

Area Description: The RV park is located on beautiful Manatee Point on the St. Johns River. While you are there, enjoy the nature walk area adjacent to the park. There are many opportunities for fishing, boating, and manatee watching. A full-service marina with boat rentals is convenient to the park. The NAS is a golfer's paradise with 27 holes of year-round golf within walking distance from the park. A full range of support facilities available on base, many within walking distance. Downtown Jacksonville is 20 minutes away. St. Augustine, the nation's oldest city, is just 30 minutes south.

RV Campground Physical Address: MWR RV Park, Bldg 1, Box 14, NAS Jacksonville, FL 32212-5000.

Key West Naval Air Station

Address: 600 Forrestal Ave, Bldg 324, Boca Chica Field, PO Box 9001, Key West, FL 33040.

Information Line: C-305-293-2268, DSN-312-483-2268.

Main Base Police: Emergencies dial 911.

Main Installation Website: http://www.cnic.navy.mil/regions/cnrse/installations/nas_key_west.html

Main Base Location: Naval Air Station (NAS) Key West is located on Boca Chica Key, the second to last major island in the Florida Keys. NAS has several annexes located on Key West itself.

Directions to Main Gate: From the Florida Turnpike or I-95 take US-1 South. Remain on US-1 for approximately 120 miles through the Florida Keys. Take ramp to right just before MM-8 and look for sign posted "Naval Air Station Next Right". All newly arriving personnel with orders to report to Naval Air Station Key West will first need to report to Boca Chica Field located on US-1 at mile marker 8.

NMC: Miami, 157 miles northeast.

NMI: Homestead ARB, 130 miles northeast.

Base Social Media/Facebook: https://www.facebook.com/naskeywest

Base Social Media/Twitter: https://twitter.com/naskeywest

Chapels: C-305-293-2318.

Dental Clinic: C-305-293-4600 ext 1362.

Medical: C-305-293-4600/4613.

Veterinary Services: Veterinary Clinic Resale, C-305-293-4191.

Beauty/Barber Shop: C-305-292-7200.

Commissary: Boca Chica Mini-Mart, C-305-292-7216. Commissary, C-305-293-4405. Trumbo Mini-Mart, C-305-292-7226.

Exchange Gas: C-305-292-2838.

Exchange: C-305-292-7200.

Clubs: Flying Conch Lounge, C-305-293-4208 at Truman Annex, Navigator's Bar & Grill, C-305-293-2468 at Boca Chica.

Places to Eat: Harbor Lights Seafood and Raw Bar, C-305-294-2727, Runaway Grill at Boca Chica, C-305-293-2116 and Beachside Grill at Truman Annex, C-305-293-5282 Cafe Sole, C-305-294-0230; Half Shell Raw Bar, C-305-294-7496 and PT's Late Night, C-305-296-4245 are within driving distance.

Bowling: Air Lanes Bowling Center, C-305-293-2976.

Fitness Center: C-305-293-2480/2683.

ITT/ITR: C-305-293-4173.

Marina: Sigsbee Marina, C-305-293-4434. Boca Chica Marina, C-305-293-2402/2468.

MWR: C-305-293-2112, C-888-539-7697.

MWR Website:
http://www.navymwrkeywest.com/

MWR Facebook:
https://www.facebook.com/NASKeyWestMWR/

MWR Twitter:
https://twitter.com/NASKeyWestMWR

Outdoor Recreation: Key West Naval Air Station Outdoor Recreation Services, C-305-293-2112. MWR Equipment Rentals, C-305-797-1275 offers tables, chairs bounce houses and other party needs. Truman Annex, C-305-293-5282 offers beach and bike rentals. Sigsbee Marina, C-305-293-4434 offers boat and gear rental.

Swimming: Trumbo Pool, C-305-293-4324 offers water slides, foam lily pads and lap lanes.

Things To Do: This is the place to kick back and relax by the ocean. Visit the Ernest Hemingway House Museum and Harry Truman Little White House. Visit www.keywest.com for attraction and event calendars. From Navy Gateway at Trumbo Point, the heart of Key West is a short, 20-minute walk away.

RV CAMPING & GETAWAYS

Sigsbee RV Park & Key West Vacation Rentals

Reservation/Contact Number Info: RV Park: C-305-293-4432, DSN-312-483-4432. Fax C-305-293-4413, DSN-312-483-4413. Townhomes/Trailers: C-305-293-5000/5001.

Recreation Security: C-305-293-2531.

RV Website:
http://get.dodlodging.net/propertys/Key-West-Campground

Other Info Website:
http://get.dodlodging.net/propertys/Key-West-Vacation-Rentals

RV Email Address:
rvsigsbee@yahoo.com

GPS Coordinates:
24°35'1"N/81°46'10"W or Sigsbee Rd, Key West, FL 33040. Key West Rentals: 24°34'46.4"N/81°46'21.9"W

Reservations: Reservations accepted one year in advance for AD. All others 6 months in advance. Office hours 0900-1500 Mon-Fri. Closed Thanksgiving, Christmas and New Years Day. Check-in at Bldg V-4113. Late or weekend arrivals check-in with Camp Host. Information posted on Office door. Townhomes and Trailers: Accepted one year in advance for AD; 6 months for all others. Same day arrivals must call office directly.

Season of Operation: Year-round.

Eligibility: AD, NG & Res (active only), Ret, DoD-Civ, Dep and 100% DAV, NATO Allied Service Members on orders to the U.S.

Camper/Trailer Spaces: RV Sites (93): Hardstand, pull-thru or back-in front row, full hookup. Rates $26 daily; $31 daily DoD-Civ. Dry Camp (500): No hookups, picnic area. Rates: $16 daily; $20 daily DoD-Civ.

Tent Spaces: Tent camping is available.

Yurt, A Frame, Cabin, Apt, Spaces: Mobile Home Trailers (12). Located near Old Town Key West. Two-bedroom, sleeps 4, double beds, full kitchens, dining room, private bath with tub and shower. Linens provided. Rates: $75 daily. Townhomes: Three-bedroom, sleeps 6, queen bed in each room, fully furnished, full kitchens, dining room, one full bath, one half bath, CATV. Linens provided. Rates: $130 daily.

Support Facilities: Auto Craft Shop, Bathhouse*, Beach, Boat Launch, Boat Rental/Storage, Bowling, Coin Laundry, Commissary, Convenience Store, Diesel,

Equipment Rental, Fenced Dog Park, Fitness Center, Gas, Golf, Ice, Internet Access**, Marina, Mechanic/Auto Repairs***, Pay Telephones, Playground, Pool, Propane/Bottle***, Restrooms*, RV storage, Sewage Dump, Showers, Sports Fields, Tennis Courts. * Handicap accessible. **Available at the Sigsbee Recreation Center. *** Available off base.

RV Storage: Available. Unlimited duration as long as appropriate registration, insurance and account balances are maintained. Call: C-305-293-4432 for more information.

Activities: Boating, Fishing, Snorkeling, Swimming, Water Sports.

Credit Cards: American Express, Discover, MasterCard and Visa.

Restrictions: RV Park: Pets allowed on leash, limit two. Must have complete and current immunizations. Owner must clean up after pets. No firearms allowed. No open campfires. Quiet hours 2300-0700 hours. Trailers: No smoking and no pets allowed.

RV Driving Directions/Location: Sigsbee RV Park: On Base. From the Main Gate: Ask for directions at gate or follow clearly marked signs to Sigsbee RV Park. Key West Vacation Rentals: For Trumbo Point Lodging: Enter Trumbo Point Annex Gate and building located off to right (six-story cream colored building). For Boca Chica and Truman Annex: Enter Boca Chica Gate and take first right to the second building on right.

Area Description: Key West has a long-standing reputation as being the premier tourist/vacation destination as the southernmost city in the Continental U.S. On waterfront. Excellent fishing, diving and snorkeling year-round (best in Apr-Sep). Historical sites include Fort Zachary Taylor and Ernest Hemingway House. Limited support facilities at Trumbo Point; full range of facilities available at Sigsbee Park.

RV Campground Physical Address: Bldg V-4113 Arthur Sawyer Road, Key West, FL 33040. Trailers: 1400H Flatley Ave NAS Trumbo Pt, Key West, FL 33040.

MacDill Air Force Base

Address: MacDill AFB, 6801 S. Dale Mabry Hwy, MacDill AFB, FL 33621-5313.

Information Line: C-813-828-1110, DSN-312-968-1110.

Main Base Police: C-813-828-3322. Emergencies dial 911.

Main Installation Website: http://www.macdill.af.mil/

Main Base Location: MacDill Air Force Base is located eight miles south of Tampa, Florida on the Southwestern tip of the Interbay Peninsula in Hillsborough County. The region is often referred to as "Tampa Bay" which is a seven-county region on Florida's west coast offering a diversity of communities.

Directions to Main Gate: From the North/Ocala: Take I-75 S to I-275 S to exit 41A to Southbound Dale Mabry. South Dale Mabry will end at the MacDill Main Gate. From the South/Miami: Take I-95 N to the Florida Turnpike. Take exit 54 to I-595. Then take exit for I-75 toward Naples. Take exit 256 for SR-618-TOLL//Crosstown Expressway. Take exit 1B right to S. Dale Mabry to MacDill Main Gate.

NMC: Tampa, five miles north.

NMI: Clearwater Coast Guard Air Station, 18 miles west.

Base Social Media/Facebook: https://www.facebook.com/MacDillAirForceBase

Base Social Media/Twitter: https://twitter.com/MacDill

Chapels: C-813-828-3621.

Dental Clinic: C-813-827-9400.

Medical: C-813-828-2273, DSN-312-651-2273.

Veterinary Services: C-813-828-3558.

Beauty/Barber Shop: C-813-840-0525/0087.

Commissary: C-813-828-3361.

Exchange Gas: C-813-840-2506/0640.

Exchange: C-813-840-0511.

Financial Institutions: Armed Forces Bank, N.A., C-813-840-8254. Grow Financial Federal Credit Union, C-800-839-6328.

Clubs: SeaScapes Beach Club, C-813-840-1451, Surf's Edge Club/Boomers BBQ, C-813-840-2220.

Places to Eat: Bowling Center, C-813-840-1516 is within walking distance. Fairways Grill, C-813-840-6906. Boomers, C-813-840-2020. Diners Reef, C-813-828-2412. Exchange Food Court, C-813-840-2200 offers Anthony's Pizza, Baskin-Robbins, Taco Bell, Subway, Charley's Grilled Subs, Dunkin Donuts and Manchu Wok.

Bowling: MacDill Lanes Bowling Center, C-813-828-4005.

Fitness Center: C-813-828-4496.

Golf: Bay Palms Golf Complex, C-813-840-6904.

ITT/ITR: C-813-828-2478.

Library: C-813-828-3607.

Marina: Coon's Creek Recreation Area, C-813-828-4983.

MWR: Marketing Office, C-813-828-3055.

MWR Website:
http://www.macdillfss.com/

MWR Facebook:
https://www.facebook.com/macdillfss/

MWR Twitter: https://twitter.com/6FSS

Outdoor Recreation: MacDill Air Force Base Outdoor Recreation Services, C-813-840-6919/6920. Offers equipment rentals including, boats, camping gear, fishing and other water sports equipment and much more. Trips to local attractions are also available through Outdoor Recreation.

Swimming: Beach swimming is available. There is also a base pool, C-813-828-6903, C-813-840-6919.

Things To Do: Local attractions include Busch Gardens, Tampa Aquarium, Adventure Island and more. This is an area with lots of interesting things to see.

RV CAMPING & GETAWAYS

MacDill AFB FamCamp

Reservation/Contact Number Info: C-813-840-6919/6920. Fax C-813-828-7507.

Recreation Security: Night Host for recreation area after 1800 hours, C-813-840-0875.

RV Website:
http://www.macdillfss.com/mainmenusub-rc.aspx?SectionID=436

RV Email Address:
macdillfamcamp@gmail.com

GPS Coordinates:
27°49'37"N/82°29'11"W

Reservations: Accepted up to one year in advance; AD have priority. Advance reservations require $100 deposit for stays 1-180 days and two-week stay reservations. All others, first come, first serve. Reservations for trailers may be made 90 days in advance with $100 deposit for 30' and $200 deposit for 40'. Cancellations require 24 hour notice. Office hours 1000-1800 hours daily Oct-Mar; closed Sunday Apr-Sept. Check-in at Outdoor Recreation, located on the right just prior to the entrance to the rec area. Campsite check-in 1200 hours, check-out 1100 hours. Trailers: Check-in 1400 hours, check-out 1100 hours.

Season of Operation: Year-round.

Eligibility: AD, NG, Res, Ret, 100% DAV and DoD-Civ if space available.

Camper/Trailer Spaces: RV Sites (380): Full hookup sites (359) E(20/30/50A)/S/W. CATV at all locations, picnic table. Rates: $16-$20 daily, $405-$520 monthly, depending on season. Partial Hookup Sites (21): Partial E(30/50A)/W hookups, picnic table. Rates: $13-$17 daily, $380-$460 monthly, depending on season.

Tent Spaces: Primitive Sites (40): Open space. Rates: $9-$10 nightly; $240-$270 monthly, depending on season.

Support Facilities: Auto Craft Shop, Auto Repair, Bathhouse, Beach, Boat Launch, Boat Rental/Storage, Bowling, Chapel, Coin Laundry, Commissary, Convenience Store, Equipment Rental, Exchange, Fishing Pier, Fitness Center, Gas, Golf, Grills, Ice, Marina, Mess Hall, Pavilion, Picnic Area, Playground, Pool (Seasonal), Propane, Rec Center, Restrooms, Sewage Dump, Shoppette, Showers, Skeet Range, Snack Bar, Sports Fields, Tennis Courts, Trails.

RV Storage: C-813-840-6919 for more information.

Activities: Aerobics, Arts and Crafts, Bowling, Fishing*, Golfing, Jogging,

Swimming, Walking. *State license required for all fishing, except for offshore fishing.

Credit Cards: MasterCard and Visa.

Restrictions: Limit two pets. Owners must have control of pet at all times. Owner must clean up after pets. Pets cannot be a nuisance to other campers and must be walked in designated area. All immunizations must be complete and current. Firearms must be registered at FAMCAMP office upon check-in. No open campfires. Quiet hours 2300-0700.

RV Driving Directions/Location: On Base. From the Main Gate: Stay on North Boundary Avenue and it turns then into South Boundary. At 4th light go left, then quick right to Bayshore Drive which becomes Golf Course Avenue. Follow Golf Course Avenue until a "Y" intersection at Marina Bay Drive. Go left onto Marina Bay Drive into the Recreation Area.

Area Description: Located on south end of installation in coastal peninsula. Recreation area consists of FamCamp, marina, beach, snack bar and pavilions. Fresh water lakes nearby, nature trail and an abundance of natural flora and fauna. Full range of support facilities on base.

RV Campground Physical Address: 9909 Marina Bay Dr, MacDill AFB, FL 33621-5000.

Mayport Naval Station

Address: Mayport Naval Station, Massey Avenue, Bldg 1, Mayport, FL 32228-0042.

Information Line: C-904-270-5401, DSN-312-270-5401.

Main Base Police: Emergencies dial 911.

Main Installation Website:
http://www.cnic.navy.mil/regions/cnrse/installations/ns_mayport.html

Main Base Location: Naval Station Mayport is located 15 miles east of Jacksonville, Florida, at the mouth of the St. Johns River in Duval County. NS Mayport is one of three major Navy installations in the Jacksonville area.

Directions to Main Gate: The Naval Station is located at the end of Mayport Road. From the north: Take I-95 South to the 9A exit. Get off on Atlantic Boulevard and drive east, crossing the Intracoastal Waterway. After crossing the waterway, take the first exit on the right to Mayport Road. Continue for approximately five miles to enter the Naval Station through the main gate.

NMC: Jacksonville, 10 miles west.

NMI: Jacksonville NAS, 46 miles northwest.

Base Social Media/Facebook:
https://www.facebook.com/pages/Naval-Station-Mayport/324867549652

Chapels: C-904-270-5212.

Dental Clinic: C-904-270-4460.

Medical: C-904-270-4444. Appointments, C-904-542-4677, DSN-312-270-4303.

Veterinary Services: C-904-270-7004.

Beauty/Barber Shop: C-904-242-3249.

Commissary: C-904-249-7524.

Exchange Gas: C-904-242-3278.

Exchange: C-904-249-8883.

Financial Institutions: Navy Federal Credit Union, C-1-888-842-6328.

Clubs: Foc'sle CPO Club, C-904-270-5431. Castaway's Lounge, C-904-270-7205.

Places to Eat: Bogey's, C-904-270-5143, Mayport Beach Club, C-904-270-7205 and Subway, C-904-242-0190 are within walking distance. Exchange offers McDonald's C-904-241-1486 and Taco Bell, C-904-242-2967. Arby's and Wendy's are within driving distance.

Bowling: Mayport Bowling Center, C-904-270-5377.

Fitness Center: C-904-270-5451.

Golf: Windy Harbor Golf Club, C-904-270-5328. NAS Jacksonville Golf Course, C-904-542-3249.

ITT/ITR: C-904-270-5145.

Library: C-904-270-5393.

Military Museum: Aircraft Heritage Park (outdoor static aircraft display).

Military Museum Website:
https://www.cnic.navy.mil/regions/cnrse/installations/nas_jacksonville/about/history/aircraft_heritage_park1.html

MWR: C-904-270-5228.,

MWR Website:
http://www.navymwrmayport.com/

MWR Facebook:
https://www.facebook.com/mwrmaypo
rt
MWR Twitter:
https://twitter.com/MWRMayport
Outdoor Recreation: Outdoor
Adventure Center C-904-270-5425.
Offers rental equipment for camping,
fishing, water sports, outdoor sports,
fishing and more.
Swimming: Seasonal Outdoor Pool
available at the Navy Lodge. Ocean
swimming. Aquatics, C-904-270-5425.
Things To Do: Located near Jacksonville
and historic St. Augustine. Adventure
Landing, Jacksonville Landing, the
Jacksonville Zoo and much more are
available. The area is well-known in
Florida for its beaches, where deep sea
fishing and collecting shark's teeth are
just some the many local activities.

RV CAMPING & GETAWAYS

Pelican Roost & Osprey Cove RV Parks

Reservation/Contact Number Info: C-
904-270-7808/7809, DSN-312-270-
7808. Fax C-904-270-7810, DSN-312-
270-7810.
Recreation Security: C-904-270-5583.
RV Website:
http://get.dodlodging.net/propertys/M
ayport-Recreational-Lodging
Other Info Website:
https://www.navymwrmayport.com
GPS
Coordinates: 30°23'39"N/81°24'1"W
Reservations: Reservations highly
recommended and accepted 180 days
in advance for AD, NG, Res; 120 days in
advance for Ret, 100% DAV; 60 days in
advance for DoD, MWR-Civ.
Reservations must be secured with
credit card. Reservations are accepted
by phone 0900-1700 Mon-Fri; 0900-
1600 weekends and holidays. Pelican
Roost max stay 14 days. Osprey Cove RV
Park minimum 30 days, maximum 6
months. Extensions permitted on a
space available basis. No refunds for
early departure. Check-in 1400 hours at
Pelican Roost Lodge during office hours.
Check-out 1200 hours. Late arrivals

check-in with Camp Host site 19/20.
Cabins: Two-night minimum stay.
Check-in 1400 hours, check-out 1000
hours.
Season of Operation: Year-round.
Eligibility: AD, NG, Res, Ret,
DoD/MWR/NAF-Civ, 100% DAV.
Camper/Trailer Spaces: Pelican Roost:
Hardstand: (47), Pull-thru (19)
maximum 40' in length; Back-in (30)
Maximum 40' in length, E(30/50A)/S/W,
CATV, picnic table. Rates: $19-$21 daily.
Osprey Cove (47): Hardstand, back-in,
maximum 45' in length, E(50A)/S/W,
CATV, picnic table. Rates: $18 daily.
Tent Spaces: Pelican Roost: No
hookups, two tents per site. Rates: $7
daily.
Yurt, A Frame, Cabin, Apt, Spaces:
Deluxe Camping Cabin at Osprey Cove
(3): Two queen beds, sleeps 6. Fully
furnished with kitchen amenities. Linens
provided. Rates: $50 daily.
Support Facilities: Auto Craft Shop,
Bathhouse, Beach, Boat Rental/Storage,
Bowling, Chapel, Commissary,
Convenience Store, Dive Shop,
Exchange, Fitness Center, Golf, Grills,
Ice, Laundromat, Mess Hall, Pavilion,
Pay Phones, Picnic Area, Playground,
Pool, Rec Center, Rec Equipment,
Restrooms, Showers, Shuttle Bus, Sports
Fields, Tennis Courts, Trails.
RV Storage: Contact MWR Vehicle
Storage, C-904-270-7022.
Activities: Bowling, Fishing, Fitness
Programs, Golfing, Racquetball, Surfing,
Swimming, Tennis.
Credit Cards: American Express,
Discover, MasterCard and Visa.
Restrictions: Pets allowed on leash;
owners must clean up after pets. One
car per assigned site, extra parking
available. No smoking. No pets allowed
in cabins. No group/rallies or sponsored
guest reservations accepted Oct-Apr.
RV Driving Directions/Location: On
Base. From Main Gate: Go to second
traffic light. Turn right onto Massey Ave.
Turn left on Bon Homme Richard Street
(beside Medical/Dental Clinic) and
continue past the ball fields. RV Park is
located on the right. From the north:
From I-95 take Route 9A exit toward the

beaches. From here directions are same as above. From the south: From I-95 take Route 9A toward the beaches. Continue north to Monument Road and make a right. Go approx. 3 miles to McCormick Rd. Make a right and follow directions above. RVs entering and exiting via the Main Gate must use the extreme right lane.

Area Description: Pelican Roost RV Park is located along the shore of the beautiful St. Johns River and within walking distance to Mayport Beaches on the Atlantic Ocean. Osprey Cove is nestled in a quiet, wooded area only minutes from Mayport Beaches and ocean.

RV Campground Physical Address: 1263 Bon Homme Richard Road, Bldg 2062, Mayport, FL 32228.

Mid-Bay Shores Maxwell-Gunter Recreation Area

Address: Mid-Bay Shores Recreation Area, 801 White Point Rd, Niceville, FL 32578.
Information Line: C-334-953-1110.
Main Base Police: Emergencies dial 911.
Main Installation Website:
http://www.maxwell.af.mil/
Main Base Location: Mid-Bay Shores boasts the beautiful white sandy shores of Choctawhatchee Bay. The gated entrance is just before the Mid-Bay Bridge, a toll bridge that connects Niceville and Destin. Located about three hours from Maxwell in Niceville, FL.
NMC: Fort Walton Beach, 18 miles west.
NMI: Eglin AFB, 16 miles west.
Commissary: Approximately 13 miles to the Eglin AFB Commissary, C-850-609-3172 ext 2358.
Exchange Gas: Approximately 13 miles to Eglin AFB gas station. Commercial gas station within 1 mile.
Exchange: Approximately 13 miles to the Eglin AFB Exchange facility, C-850-651-5621/5823.
Places to Eat: Waffle House, McDonald's, Pepito's Mexican Restaurant and First Choice Buffet are within walking distance.
MWR Website:
http://www.42fss.us/index.html
MWR Facebook:
https://www.facebook.com/42dfss

RV CAMPING & GETAWAYS

Mid-Bay Shores Recreation Area

Reservation/Contact Number Info: C-850-897-2411 information line only. Reservations, C-334-953-3509, DSN-312-493-3509.
Recreation Security: Police for recreation area (Eglin AFB): C-850-882-5360. Emergency, C-850-882-2000 ext 2502/2503.
RV Website:
https://www.lifeatthemax.us/mid-bay-shores/
RV Email Address:
mafbodritt@icloud.com
GPS Coordinates:
30°27'16"N/86°25'4"W
Reservations: May be made six months in advance for AD; four months for all others. Pre-pay at time of reservation. Two-night minimum stay; $15 charge for cancellation made within 7 days of reservation. Cancellations within 48 hours forfeit one night's stay. ID card required at check-in. Office hours 1000-1630 Mon-Fri. Rec Area Office Hours 0800-1700 daily. Check-in 1500-1700 hours check out 1100 hours. Wi-Fi at office and fitness center.
Season of Operation: Year-round.
Eligibility: AD, NG, Res, Ret, DoD-Civ, Dep (other than spouse must be over 21) and 100% DAV.
Camper/Trailer Spaces: RV Sites (26): Full hookup E(110/220V/15/30/50A)/S/W, picnic table, grill. Sites vary in length, with limited 40' spaces Rates: $25 daily; $125 weekly; $460 monthly. Overflow (6), partial hookup. Rates: $20 daily; $115 weekly. Some sites have maximum two week stay; all others confirm with reservations. New bathhouse with laundry facilities and fitness center.

Yurt, A Frame, Cabin, Apt,
Spaces: Cabins: Two-bedroom (26, 1 handicap accessible), one bathroom, alarm clock, central AC/heat, CATV, cookware/utensils, living room, kitchen, full size range, refrigerator, microwave, table/chairs, queen size sleeper sofa, main bedroom: queen size bed, second bedroom: queen size bed and twin bed, TV. Guests must provide own linens and towels. Rates: Start at $40 with 2-night minimum. Trailers (5): 3-bedroom, similar to cabins; pet friendly with $10 daily fee. Rates: $65-$90 daily, depending on rank. Weekly and monthly rates available for winter season. Check-in 1500-1700 hours, check-out 1100 hours. 1 Mar-30 Sept: 9-day max.
Support Facilities: Bathhouse, Beach, Boat Launch, Boat Rental/Storage, Convenience Store, Diesel*, Equipment rental, Fire Rings, Fishing Pier, Fitness Center, Gas*, Golf, Grills, Ice, Marina, Pavilion, Picnic Area, Playground, Propane*, Rec Center, Restrooms**, RV Storage, Sewage Dump, *Located Off Base, ** Handicap accessible.
RV Storage: Available, but generally very full. Rates: $35/month. C-334-953-3509 or C-850-897-2411.
Activities: Bicycling, Boating, Fishing*, Golfing, Hiking, Jogging, Sailing, Swimming. *FL or AL fishing license required.
Credit Cards: MasterCard and Visa.
Restrictions: No pets allowed in cabin area. Trailers pet friendly. Pets allowed at RV sites. No firearms or fireworks allowed. Bike helmets required. No open fires. Quiet hours 2200-0800 hours.
RV Driving Directions/Location: Off Base. From Pensacola: Merge onto I-10 E via the ramp on the left toward Tallahassee. Merge onto SR-85 S via exit 56 toward Niceville/Destin/Hurlburt Field/Eglin AFB/FTWalton Beach. Turn left onto SR-20 E/E John Sims Pky E. Continue to follow SR-20 E. Turn right onto White Point Road and follow to Rec Area.
Area Description: Located along Choctawhatchee Bay, facing beautiful sandy white beaches, located about three hours from Maxwell AFB in Niceville, FL.
RV Campground Physical Address: 801 White Point Road, Niceville, FL 32578-8913.

Panama City Naval Support Activity

Address: 101 Vernon Avenue, Panama City, FL 32407-7018.
Information Line: C-850-234-4011, DSN-312-436-4011.
Main Base Police: C-850-234-4332, DSN-312-436-4332. Emergencies dial 911.
Main Installation Website: http://www.cnic.navy.mil/regions/cnrse/installations/nsa_panama_city.html
Main Base Location: Naval Support Activity Panama City is located on beautiful St. Andrew Bay in Panama City Beach, Florida. It has direct, deep-water access to the Gulf of Mexico.
Directions to Main Gate: US Highways 231 and 98 are major highways to base. Highway 231 runs north and south, and crosses Highway 98. Highway 98 runs east and west and passes by the Naval Support Activity Panama City. Interstate 10 crosses North Florida and the Panhandle east and west and is approximately 50 miles north of Panama City. If traveling I-10: Look for Hwy 231 South. At the intersection of Hwy 231 and Hwy 98 (in Panama City), turn right and travel along Hwy 98 West. Cross over the Hathaway Bridge and prepare to turn left at the 2nd traffic light at Thomas Drive. Travel south on Thomas Drive and go approximately .25 miles and turn left to the Main Gate.
NMC: Panama City, within city limits.
NMI: Tyndall Air Force Base, 15 miles southeast.
Base Social Media/Facebook: https://www.facebook.com/NSAPC
Chapels: C-850-234-4084. After Duty Hours, C-850-625-1355.
Dental Clinic: C-850-234-4131.
Medical: C-850-234-4177. Appointments, C-1-877-879-1621.
Beauty/Barber Shop: C-850-234-4630.

Exchange: C-850-234-2407.
Financial Institutions: Navy Federal Credit Union, C-1-888-842-6328.
Places to Eat: C-Street Grill, C-850-234-4589 and The Main Deck, C 850-235-5502 are on base. Many restaurants are within a short drive.
Fitness Center: MWR Fitness Center, C-850-234-4370.
ITT/ITR: C-850-234-4374.
Marina: Hidden Cove Marina, C-850-234-4402.
MWR: C-850-234-4374.
MWR Website:
http://www.navymwrpanamacity.com/
MWR Facebook:
https://www.facebook.com/NSAPCMWR
Outdoor Recreation: Community Recreation, C-850-234-4402. Offers paddle boats, canoes, kayaks, home and garden equipment, sports gear, camping equipment and party rentals.
Swimming: Seasonal Outdoor Pool, C-850-234-4370 offers recreational swim and swim lessons. Beach swimming nearby.
Things To Do: While here, be sure to visit the Armament Museum, visit Florida's beautiful, sandy white beaches and enjoy sport fishing, swimming and snorkeling.

RV CAMPING & GETAWAYS
Panama City RV Park & Cabins

Reservation/Contact Number Info: C-850-234-4402. Fax C-850-230-7115, DSN-312-436-7115.
Recreation Security: C-850-234-4334.
RV Website:
http://get.dodlodging.net/propertys/Panama-City-RV-Parks--Cabins
Other Info Website:
http://www.navymwrpanamacity.com/programs/83dae9cf-377a-4920-9537-dad2de3cce96
GPS Coordinates:
30°10'55"N/85°45'14"W
Reservations: Reservations may be made 90 days in advance for AD, NG & AD Res, Ret, NSA DoD-Civ; 60 days for all others. Office hours 1000-1600 daily. Check-in 1500 hours at Marina Outdoor Recreation Office Bldg 327, check-out 1200 hours.
Season of Operation: Year-round.
Eligibility: AD NG, Res, Ret, 100% DAV, DoD-Civ/Ret
Camper/Trailer Spaces: Mainside RV Park (21), Full hookup (17) E(110V/30/50A)/S/W, CATV; Partial hookup (4) E(110V/30/50A)/W, CATV. Southside RV Park (24), Full hookup, E(110V/30/50A)/S/W, grill, picnic table, trash receptacle, CATV. Rates: $22 daily for AD/Ret, $24 daily for DoD. Monthly AD Rate: $540; DoD $600. Camplite Trailers (13): Can be used on or off site. Furnished campers with bathroom, kitchen and AC/Heat. Sleeps six. AD On-Site Rate: $40 daily; $45 daily DoD. AD Off-Site: $35 daily; $40 daily DoD
Yurt, A Frame, Cabin, Apt, Spaces: Log Cabins (8): One-bedroom, sleeps 6, sleeping loft, futon in living room, AC/Heat, alarm clock, CATV, coffee maker, cookware/utensils, iron/ironing board, kitchenette, bed linens, microwave, refrigerator, VCR, video rental. Guest must supply own towels. One ADA accessible cabin. Rates: $70 daily for AD/Ret; $80 for DoD.
Support Facilities: Auto Craft Shop*, Bath House*, Beach, Boat Rental/Storage, Bowling, Chapel, Convenience Store*, Equipment Rental, Exchange, Fishing Pier*, Fitness Center*, Golf, Grills, Ice, Laundry/Pay, Marina, Mess Hall*, Pavilion*, Picnic Area, Playground, Pool, Restrooms*, Showers, Snack Bar*, Sports Fields, Tennis Courts. *Handicap Accessible.
RV Storage: Limited with waiting list, C-850-230-4402.
Activities: The Marina offers bikes, canoes, kayaks, YOLO paddle boards, paddle boats, pontoon boats, fishing equipment, lawn and garden equipment, party equipment, pavilions, snorkeling gear and more. Sand volleyball and children's playground. Local dive shops and charter fishing available nearby. Florida fishing license required.
Credit Cards: American Express, MasterCard and Visa.

Restrictions: No pets or smoking in cabins. All pets must have current immunizations. Pets must be registered and identified at check-in. No firearms allowed. No campfires at sites.
RV Driving Directions/Location: On Base. From The Main Gate: Ask for directions at the gate. Open 24 hours daily.
Area Description: Located right on the St. Andrew's Bay with a beautiful view of the Hathaway Bridge and only minutes from the "World's Most Beautiful Beaches". Enjoy the sandy, white beaches and many outdoor activities.
RV Campground Physical Address: Panama City RV Parks & Cabins, 101 Vernon Ave, Panama City Beach, FL 32407.

Patrick Air Force Base

Address: 842 Falcon Avenue, Bldg 722, Patrick AFB, FL 32925-3439.
Information Line: C-321-494-1110, DSN-312-854-1110.
Main Base Police: C-321-494-2008. Emergencies dial 911. Cape, C-321-853-2121.
Main Installation Website: http://www.patrick.af.mil/
Main Base Location: Patrick AFB is located on the east coast of central Florida. Patrick AFB is three miles south of Cocoa Beach and approximately 12 miles north of Melbourne in Brevard County.
Directions to Main Gate: Directions to Main Gate: Take I-95 to exit 188. Travel on FL 404 East/Pineda Causeway for 10 miles. Make left onto SR A1A and travel 3 miles North. Main gate will be on left-hand side.
NMC: Orlando, 45 miles northwest.
NMI: Cape Canaveral Air Force Station, 17 miles north.
Base Social Media/Facebook: https://www.facebook.com/45thSpaceWing
Base Social Media/Twitter: https://twitter.com/45thSpaceWing
Chapels: C-321-494-4073.
Dental Clinic: C-321-494-6366.

Medical: Appointments, C-321-494-8241, DSN-312-854-8230.
Veterinary Services: C-321-494-6080.
Beauty/Barber Shop: Main Exchange, C-321-784-1061. C-321-784-1286. Cape Canaveral, C-321-853-3850. Beauty Shop, C-321-784-5432.
Commissary: C-321-494-5841.
Exchange Gas: C-321-494-6686.
Exchange: C-321-799-1300. Cape Canaveral, C-321-853-4262.
Financial Institutions: Space Coast Federal Credit Union, C-321-752-2222. Wire: Western Union available at exchange cashier cage.
Clubs: The Tides Collocated Club, C-321-494-4012.
Places to Eat: Bowling Center, C-321-494-2958; Golf Course Snack Bar, C-321-494-7856; The Beach House, C-321-494-4011 and Riverside Dining Facility, C-321-494-4248 are on base. Exchange Food Court offers Anthony's Pizza, Taco Bell, Dunkin Donuts and Charley's Grilled Subs. Cape Canaveral Exchange Food Court offers Subway. Burger King is on base. Many restaurants are within a short drive.
Bowling: The Alley Bowling Center, C-321-494-2958.
Fitness Center: Fitness & Sports Center, C-321-494-6697. CCAFS Fitness Center, C-321-853-3966.
Golf: Manatee Cove Golf Course, C-321-494-7856.
ITT/ITR: C-321-494-5158.
Library: C-321-494-6881.
Marina: Manatee Cove Marina, C-321-494-7455.
MWR: C-321-494-8081/5608.
MWR Website: http://www.gopatrickfl.com/
MWR Facebook: https://www.facebook.com/Patrick45FSS/
Outdoor Recreation: Patrick AFB Outdoor Recreation Services, C-321-494-2042. Offers party rentals, outdoor game rentals, outdoor water sport boat and sport rentals, scuba gear, lawn and garden equipment, picnic areas and more.
Swimming: Lap Pool, C-321-494-6697/4947.

Things To Do: Florida's "Space Coast" has much to see and do. Attractions include the U.S. Air Force Space Museum, the Kennedy Space Center, Disney World, Sea World, Epcot Center, Islands of Adventure, Universal Studios and Legoland.

RV CAMPING & GETAWAYS

Manatee Cove FamCamp & Beach Cottages

Reservation/Contact Number Info: C-321-494-4787.
RV Website:
http://www.gopatrickfl.com/outdoor-recreation.html
GPS Coordinates:
28°14'17"N/80°36'54"W
Reservations: Multi-million dollar RV Park renovation completed 2016. Reservations accepted for AD only. All other first come, first serve basis. Hosts are available for check-in while the office is closed until 2200 nightly. Guests checking in after 2200 hours must park in the Chevron Park parking area at the entrance to the campground and check in the following morning. Apr-Sep Office hours 0830-1230 Mon, Wed-Sat; Oct-Mar Office hours 0830-1600 Mon-Sat, 0900-1200 Sun. Beach Cottages: Reservations accepted up to one year in advance for all; 30-day cancellation policy. Credit card required. Peak Season (Mar-Sept) requires a minimum 2-night stay.
Season of Operation: Year-round.
Eligibility: AD, NG, Res, Ret and DoD/NAF-Civ.
Camper/Trailer Spaces: RV Sites (156); Riverfront sites 2-19, full hookup (46), Rates: $30 daily, $810 monthly. Standard Sites: Full hookup. Rates: $22-$24 daily, $595-$650 monthly. All sites gravel, back-in with picnic table. Access to 24-hour Community Center with full kitchen, TV and more. Limited 60' back-in spaces available. *Renovations slated for May 2016 include upgraded paved pads, all sites to full hookup and bathhouse renovations. Maximum stay 170 days and then vacate for 48 hours.

Tent Spaces: Tent Camping (10): Primitive, no hookups. Rates: $10 daily.
Yurt, A Frame, Cabin, Apt, Spaces: Beach Cottages (3): Sleeps (10), fully furnished, three bedroom, 3 bath, full kitchen, W/D. Linens provided. Peak Season Rates: $264 daily; 3-Day Thur-Sun: $772; 4-Day Sun-Thur: $946; Weekly: $1,493. Off Season Oct-Feb, minimum-night stay: Rates: $249 daily; 3-Day Thur-Sun: $647; 4-Day Sun-Thur: $796; Weekly: $1,318.
Support Facilities: Bath House, Bowling, Fishing Pier, Fitness Center, Golf, Ice, Laundry, Marina, Pavilions, Picnic Areas, Playground, Pool, Potable Water, Restrooms, Sewage Dump. Full Rental Store to include fishing & deck boats, ocean kayaks, canoes, surfboards, water skis, wakeboards, camping gear and fishing equipment. Beach House offers full-service menu.
RV Storage: C-321-494-2042 for more information.
Activities: Boating, Fishing*, Fitness Center, Golfing, Jogging, Scuba Diving, Sightseeing, Skeet/Trap Range, Surfing, Swimming, Wake Boarding, Water-Skiing, Outdoor AdventureTrips.
*License required.
Credit Cards: MasterCard and Visa.
Restrictions: No pets allowed in beach cottages. No weddings or other special functions allowed at beach house. Two pet limit at FAMCAMP. Must have proof of rabies vaccination upon entry to FAMCAMP.
RV Driving Directions/Location: On Base. From I-95 north or south: Take exit 191, located north of Melbourne. Go east onto Wickam Road/SR-509 for four miles then proceed east over Pineda Causeway/SR-404 for five miles. Turn left onto 1A and travel north for one mile. Turn left into the base's New Oversized Inspection Vehicle Area located on 1A. Exit the inspection area, taking Tech Road then turning right on S Patrick Drive, which becomes Atlas Ave. Turn right onto Atlas Ave and travel two miles west to Rescue Road. Turn left onto Rescue Road and travel one mile south to the FAMCAMP. Inspection area is open 0600-1700. After hours, RV's

must contact the Security Forces Desk at C-321-494-2008 to arrange entry through the truck inspection gate upon arrival. New Oversized Inspection Vehicle Area located on 1A. Call ahead for details.

Area Description: Tropical location on a barrier island in world famous Cocoa Beach Florida. The barrier island is separated by the Atlantic Ocean to the east and the Banana River to the west. Located just south of the Kennedy Space Center at Cape Canaveral Air Force Station and a little over one hour south of Orlando. Orlando is home to Disney World, Universal Studios, Sea World and other central Florida attractions. Full range of support facilities available on base.

RV Campground Physical Address: Manatee Cove FamCamp, P.O. Box 254740, Patrick AFB, FL 32925-4740.

Pensacola Naval Air Station

Address: NAS Pensacola, 150 Hase Rd, Pensacola, FL 32508-1051.
Information Line: Quarterdeck, C-850-452-4785. Information and Referral, C-850-452-2155.
Main Base Police: C-850-452-2453/8888. Emergencies dial 911.
Main Installation Website: http://www.cnic.navy.mil/regions/cnrse/installations/nas_pensacola.html
Main Base Location: Pensacola is located in extreme the Florida panhandle at the Florida/Alabama state line in Escambia County, 60 minutes east of Mobile, 45 minutes west of Ft. Walton Beach, and 500 miles Northwest of Orlando.
Directions to Main Gate: Four miles south of US-98, and 12 miles south of I-10. Take Navy Blvd from US-98 or US-29 directly to NAS.
NMC: Pensacola, 8 miles north.
NMI: Corry Station Center for Information Dominance, 5 miles north.
Area Cost of Living: Lower than the U.S. national average.
Main Base Population: 14,544 military personnel.

Main Base Area Population: 52,340 in Pensacola.
Base Social Media/Facebook: https://www.facebook.com/NASPPAO/
Base Social Media/Twitter: https://twitter.com/NASP_PAO
Chapels: C-850-452-2341.
Dental Clinic: Appointments, C-850-452-5660. C-850-375-1603 for after hour emergencies.
Medical: Clinic, C-850-452-5242. Naval Hospital, C-850-505-6601.
Veterinary Services: C-850-452-6882.
Beauty/Barber Shop: Exchange Mall: Barber, C-850- 458-8893. Beauty, C-850-458-8893. Aviation Plaza, C-850-458-8877.
Commissary: C-850-262-9200.
Exchange Gas: Exchange Mall, C-850-457-1228.
Exchange: Exchange Mall, C-850-453-5311. Aviation Plaza, C-850-458-8884.
Military Clothing: Aviation Plaza, C-850-458-8885/8835.
Financial Institutions: Pen Air Federal Credit Union, C-850-453-4341.
Clubs: Oaks Lounge, C-850-452-3859. Old Crow's Nest, C-850-452-6380. Portside Club, C-850-452-3364.
Places to Eat: Oaks Restaurant, C-850-452-3859; Cubi Bar Cafe, C-850-452-2643; Mustin Beach Club, C-850-452-2137 and Corry Grill, C-850-452-6380 are on base. Portside Food Court, C-850-457-6933 offers A&W, Taco Bell and Pizza Hut. Aviation Plaza Exchange Food Court offers Old Navy Yard Cafe, Panda Express, Starbucks and Subway. Exchange Mall Food Court offers Mama DeLuca's and Subway. Many restaurants are within a short drive.
Bowling: Corry Bowling Center, C-850-452-6380.
Fitness Center: Radford Fitness Center, C-850-452-9845. Family Fitness Center, C-850-452-6004. Portside Fitness Center, C-850-452-7810. Wenzel Fitness Center, C-850-452-6198. Navy Wellness Center, C-850-452-6802.
Golf: A.C. Read Golf Course, C-850-452-2454.
ITT/ITR: C-850-452-6354.
Library: C-850-452-4362.

Marina: Bayou Grande Sailing Marina, C-850-452-4152. Blue Angel Park Outpost Marina, C-850-281-5489. Sherman Cove Marina, C-850-452-2212.
Military Museum: National Naval Aviation Museum, C-850-452-3604.
Military Museum Website: http://www.navalaviationmuseum.org/
MWR: C-850-452-3806.
MWR Website: http://www.navymwrpensacola.com/
MWR Facebook: https://www.facebook.com/mwrpensacola
Outdoor Recreation: Community Recreation Outpost Rentals at Ski Beach, C-850-281-0134 offers picnic areas, fishing pier, water sport rentals, camping gear, bike rentals, party rentals and more. Outpost Rentals at Blue Angel Park, C-850-281-5489 offers pavilion rentals, camping equipment, sports equipment, water sport and sailboat rentals, disc golf, paintball and more.
Swimming: Mustin Beach Pool, C-850-452-8293 offers lap swim, open swim and water aerobics. Indoor Pool, C-850-452-9429 offers lap swim, open swim and swim lessons. Corry Pool, C-850-452-6317 offers lap swim and recreational swim. Barrancas Beach, C-850-452-5425 offers beach swimming and beach activities.
Things To Do: Enjoy the miles of sugar-white sand beaches. Visitors can also enjoy fishing, scuba diving or swimming. Don't miss the Saenger Theater of performing arts in Pensacola, watch the Blue Angels or tour the Navy Aviation Museum.

RV CAMPING & GETAWAYS

Oak Grove RV Park & Cottages

Reservation/Contact Number Info: C-850-452-2535. Fax C-850-452-2445.
Recreation Security: C-850-452-4153.
RV Website: http://get.dodlodging.net/propertys/Oak-Grove-Park-
Other Info Website: https://www.navymwrpensacola.com

GPS Coordinates: 30°20'33"N/87°18'50"W
Reservations: Reservations accepted 90 days in advance for AD, Ret; 60 days in advance for DoD-Civ and others. Reservations accepted with two-night deposit for reservations 10 days from arrival. Cancellations must be made 30 days prior to arrival to avoid fees. Cottages require a 2-night minimum stay with a maximum 14 day stay. Walk-in reservations are not accepted prior to 0900. Office hours 0800-1600 daily. Check in 1300-1600 hours at office adjacent to RV Park or host site, check-out 1000 hours. Visit http://www.navymwrpensacola.com/ for additional information.
Season of Operation: Year-round.
Eligibility: AD, NG, Res, Ret, DoD-Civ (AD and Ret, must show ID card), Dep and 100% DAV.
Camper/Trailer Spaces: Cement pads (51 total), Pull-thru (10), Back-in (41), maximum length 40', E(220V/30/50A)/S/W hookups, CATV, picnic table. Rates for sites 1-45: $23 daily/$600 monthly. Rates for sites 46-51 (waterfront): $27 daily two week maximum stay. No weekly rates available. Overflow RV sites start at $19/ day military or $21/ day DOD. Available only if RV sites are not available.
Tent Spaces: Grass/Dirt (8), no hookups, picnic table, grill. Rates: $7 daily/$42 weekly; Tent platforms (2), $10 daily/$60 weekly. No monthly rates.
Yurt, A Frame, Cabin, Apt, Spaces: Cottages (26): One-bedroom (12, 1 handicap accessible), Two-bedroom (14, 2 handicap accessible), alarm clock, CATV, cookware/utensils, TV DVD/VCR, full kitchen, iron/ironing board, linens (daily towel and linen exchange), kitchenette, microwave, refrigerator, private bath, furnished. Rates: $100-$120 daily.
Support Facilities: Auto Hobby Shop, Bath House, Beach, Boat Launch, Boat Rental/Storage, Bowling, Chapel, Coin Laundry, Commissary, Convenience Store, Diesel, Equipment Rental, Exchange, Fishing Pier, Fitness Center,

Gas, Golf, Grills, Ice, Marina, Mechanic/Auto Repair*, Picnic Areas, Playground, Pool, Propane, Restrooms, RV Storage, Sailing Facility, Sewage Dump, Showers, Sports Fields, Tennis Courts, Trails. *Off Base.

RV Storage: C-850-452-4152 for more information.

Activities: Bicycling, Boating, Fishing*, Golfing, Swimming. *License required for fishing on base.

Credit Cards: American Express, Discover, MasterCard, and Visa.

Restrictions: No smoking in cottages. No pets allowed in cottages. Pets are allowed on leash in RV Park and camping area but must under owner's control at all times. Owner must clean up after pet. Owners of loud or vicious dogs will be required to leave the park. No firearms or weapons of any type allowed. No fireworks. Speed limit in the park is 5 mph.

RV Driving Directions/Location: On Base. From I-10: Take exit 7 onto FL-297 south/Pine Forest Rd. Follow FL-297 to right (west) onto N. Blue Angel Pkwy/FL-173. Continue south approximately 12 miles to Back Gate of Pensacola NAS. After entering base on Radford Blvd, campground is approximately two miles further, on the right side of the road at the intersection of Radford and Shell Rd.

Area Description: Located in wooded area across from Naval Aviation Museum along a 1.5 mile Gulf of Mexico beachfront with historic lighthouse in center. Old Fort Pickens can be viewed from along beach. Full range of support facilities available on base.

RV Campground Physical Address: Oak Grove Park, Bldg 3696 Lighthouse Rd, Pensacola, FL 32508.

Tyndall Air Force Base

Address: 500 Minnesota Avenue, Tyndall AFB, FL 32403.

Information Line: C-850-283-1110, DSN-312-523-1110.

Main Base Police: C-850-283-2254.

Main Installation Website:
http://www.tyndall.af.mil/

Main Base Location: Tyndall Air Force Base is located in Bay County on the Gulf of Mexico in the Florida Panhandle, 12 miles east of Panama City. The Panama City area, best known for its sugar-white sand and emerald green waters, is a popular tourist destination.

Directions to Main Gate: From Tallahassee on I-10 W toward Pensacola: Take US-231 S/exit 130 toward Panama City. Turn left onto US-231 S/SR-75 S for approximately 39 miles. Turn left onto N Star Ave. Turn right onto E Highway 22/SR-22. Continue to follow SR-22. Turn left onto N Tyndall Pky/US-98 E/SR-30A E. Turn left onto US-98 E/US-98-BR E/S Tyndall Pky/SR-30 E/SR-30A E. Continue to follow US-98 E/S Tyndall Pky/SR-30 E and look for Tyndall AFB signs.

NMC: Panama City, 10 miles northwest.

NMI: Panama City Naval Support Activity, 15 miles northwest.

Base Social Media/Facebook:
https://www.facebook.com/325FWTyndall

Base Social Media/Twitter:
https://twitter.com/Tyndall_325FW

Chapels: C-850-283-2925.

Dental Clinic: C-850-283-7574.

Medical: C-850-283-2778, DSN-312-523-2778.

Veterinary Services: C-850-283-2434.

Beauty/Barber Shop: Barber Shop, C-850-286-4300. Flightline, C-850-286-1200.

Commissary: C-850-283-4826.

Exchange Gas: Bldg 3350, C-850-286-2400. Bldg 970, C-850-286-5826.

Exchange: C-850-286-5804.

Financial Institutions: Tyndall Federal Credit Union, C-850-769-9999.

Clubs: Oasis Sports Lounge, C-850-283-3222. Marina Club, C-850-283-3059.

Places to Eat: Berg-Liles Dining Facility, C-850-283-2239; Marina Club, C-85-283-3059; Horizons, C-85-283-4357; Strike Zone Snack Bar, C-850-283-2074 and Raptor Quick Turn, C-850-283-4345 are on base. Exchange Food Court offers Charlie's, Happy Cup Cake and Taco Bell, Subway and Burger King are also on base. Many restaurants are within a short drive.

Bowling: Raptor Lanes Bowling Center, C-850-283-2380.
Fitness Center: C-850-283-2631.
ITT/ITR: C-850-283-2495/3443.
Library: C-850-283-4287.
Marina: Beacon Beach Marina, C-850-283-3059. Bonita Bay ODR Complex, C-850-283-3199.
MWR: C-850-283-3199/44565.
MWR Website: http://325fss.com/
MWR Facebook:
https://www.facebook.com/iheartTY
MWR Twitter:
https://twitter.com/325fss
Outdoor Recreation: Bonita Bay Outdoor Recreation, C-850-283-3199. Offers canoe, kayak, sailboat and pontoon rentals, water sports gear rental, paintball field, skeet shooting range, archery range, sporting equipment, lawn and garden items, power tools, camping equipment and more.
Swimming: Seasonal Outdoor Pool, C-850-283-3199 offers open swim. Gulf Coast swimming is also nearby.
Things To Do: Enjoy beautiful white sand beaches, water sports, fishing and small friendly communities. This Gulf Coast area offers much in the way of beach and water activities.

RV CAMPING & GETAWAYS
Tyndall AFB FamCamp

Reservation/Contact Number Info: C-850-283-2798, DSN-312-523-2798.
Recreation Security: Emergencies dial 911.
RV Website:
http://www.325fss.com/famcamp
RV Email Address:
tyndallfamcamp@us.af.mil
GPS Coordinates:
30°5'41"N/85°36'46"W
Reservations: Reservations not accepted. Office hours 0800-1700 hours Mon-Sat, 0900-1600 hours Sun and holidays. Check-out 1100 hours. Late check-out fee $5. Evening host on duty for late check ins. Maximum stay 14 days. PCS and AD have priority. Cabins require 2-night minimum stay with $100 refundable deposit. Check-in 1400 hours, check-out 1100 hours.
Season of Operation: Year-round.
Eligibility: AD, NG, Res, Ret and DoD-Civ.
Camper/Trailer Spaces: RV Sites (100): E(220V/30A/50A)/S/W hookups, CATV hookups. Rates: $25 daily, $160 weekly, $500 monthly. Partial hookup sites (18). Call for rates. Note: Tents are permitted on trailer pads when available. Rates: $25 daily with max two tents per site.
Tent Spaces: Only on space available basis.
Yurt, A Frame, Cabin, Apt, Spaces: Cabins (3): Two-bedroom, sleeps six; two full-size beds, one queen sofa sleeper. CATV, fully furnished kitchen, full bath coin laundry, Must provide own linens and towels. Rates: $100 daily, $500 weekly.
Support Facilities: Arts & Crafts/Auto Hobby Shop, Beach, Public Boat Launch, Boat Rental, Equipment Rental, Bowling, Chapel, Coin Laundry, Base Exchange, Commissary, Convenience Store, Gazebo with Fire Pit, Fitness Center, Grills, Ice, Lawn Games, Marina, Paintball, Picnic Area, Pizza Pub, Playground, Pool, Pool Table, Propane, Rec Center*, Restrooms with Showers, RV Storage, Sewage Dump, Skeet Range, Sports Fields, Nature Trail, Veterinarian, Water Sports. *Rec Center has large screen tv, puzzles, and dart boards. Many activities are held in the Rec Center during the winter months.
RV Storage: Available. Bonita Bay Outdoor Recreation maintains sites, C-850-283-3199.
Activities: Boating, Fishing*, Hunting*, Swimming. *License required. Equipment/Boat Rental, C-850-283-3199.
Credit Cards: Cash, Check, Mastercard and Visa.
Restrictions: Open fires are prohibited. Domestic pets allowed. Must be on leash. Good behavior is required. Pets of any breed that are hostile or aggressive will not be tolerated. The camper may be asked to leave the campground. Pets may not be left unattended and tied up outside at

picnic tables, RV, trees or similar areas. No pets are permitted inside the recreation building, bathhouse, gazebo, or play areas. Pet owners will ensure their pets do not disturb other campers (constantly barking dogs). No pets allowed in rental cottages. No discharge of firearms or fireworks allowed. No smoking in any facilities. Swimming is not permitted in or around the water adjacent to the FAMCAMP area.

RV Driving Directions/Location: On Base. From US-98 southeast or northwest: Take exit to Tyndall AFB seven miles southeast of Panama City on the south side of US-98. The FAMCAMP is .25 miles on right after crossing Dupont Bridge.

Area Description: Located along the beautiful St. Andrew's Bay in the Gulf of Mexico. Offers pristine beaches along the Florida Panhandle and a variety of entertainment.

RV Campground Physical Address: 101 FamCamp Rd, Tyndall AFB, FL 32403-1045.

Whiting Field Naval Air Station

Address: 7550 USS Essex Street, Bldg 1401, Milton, FL 32570.
Information Line: C-850-623-7011, DSN-312-868-7011.
Main Base Police: C-850-623-7709, DSN-312- 868-7709.
Main Installation Website:
https://www.cnic.navy.mil/regions/cnrse/installations/nas_whiting_field.html
Main Base Location: NAS Whiting Field is located in the Northwest Florida Panhandle near the city of Milton. The Whiting Field/Milton area is noted for its pleasant overall quality of life and relaxed atmosphere. Located in Santa Rosa County, Milton along with neighboring city of Pace, has a large military retiree population and is definitely considered a Military Town.
Directions to Main Gate: From US-90 east: Exit FL-87 north for 8 miles to NAS on east side of FL-87.
NMC: Pensacola, 30 miles southwest.
NMI: Pensacola Naval Air Station, 38 miles southwest.

Base Social Media/Facebook:
https://www.facebook.com/naswhitingfield
Chapels: C-850-623-7211 ext 1.
Dental Clinic: C-850-623-7626/7627.
Medical: C-850-623-7508.
Veterinary Services: Pensacola NAS, C-850-452-3530.
Beauty/Barber Shop: C-850-626-9890.
Commissary: C-850-623-7131.
Exchange Gas: C-850-623-8088.
Exchange: C-850-623-8066. Whiting Pines Mini Mart, C-850-983-4758.
Financial Institutions: PenAir Federal Credit Union, C-850-623-6649.
Clubs: Aces Pub, C-850-623-7375.
Places to Eat: Bowling Alley, C-850-623-7545; Mulligan's Snack Bar, C-850-623-7521; North Field Snack Bar, C-850-623-2692; South Field Snack Bar, C-850-623-6574 and The Tower Cafe, C-850-623-7928 are on base. Exchange Food Court offers Subway. Many restaurants are within a short drive.
Bowling: Bowling Lanes, C-850-623-7313.
Fitness Center: C-850-623-7412.
ITT/ITR: C-850-665-6250.
Library: C-850-623-7274.
Marina: Whiting Park, C-850-623-2383.
MWR: C-850-623-7502.
MWR Website:
http://www.navymwrwhitingfield.com/
MWR Facebook:
https://www.facebook.com/WFMWR
MWR Twitter:
https://twitter.com/MWRNASWF
Outdoor Recreation: Whiting Field NAS Outdoor Recreation Services, C-850-623-7032. Navy water recreation facilities offers boat rentals, volleyball, basketball, horseshoes, a wading area and playground. Recreation on base includes disc golf, archery, and MWR trips including whitewater rafting, mountain biking, canoeing/kayaking, rock climbing, backpacking, geocaching, caving, surfing, paddle boarding, and more.
Swimming: Seasonal Outdoor Pool, C-850-623-7412. Please note that the pool is currently closed for the 2017 season due to renovations.

Things To Do: This facility is located in a small growing community, 25 miles northeast of Pensacola. The surrounding area includes a swimming pool, a bowling alley, a commissary and an Exchange. Visitors have a number of outdoor activities and sightseeing opportunities available to them when they stay here.

Walking Trails: Several trails are on base.

RV CAMPING & GETAWAYS
Clear Creek RV Park

Reservation/Contact Number Info: C-850-623-7670.

Recreation Security: C-850-623-7651.

RV Website: http://get.dodlodging.net/propertys/Clear-Creek-RV-Park

Other Info Website: http://www.navymwrwhitingfield.com/programs/c162a301-72f4-44a3-8118-c75b9f5f9581

Reservations: Recommended. Limited first come, first serve sites. Reservations accepted 90 days in advance for AD, Ret, and NAS Whiting DOD-Civ. All others, 60 days in advance. DOD contractors not permitted advance reservations. A 50% deposit required. Office hours 0800-1600 Mon-Fri, 0800-1200 Sat, Bldg 1475. Check-in 1400 hours, check-out 1200 hours. Late fees apply.

Season of Operation: Year-round.

Eligibility: AD and their dependents, Res, Ret, 100% DAV, and DOD-Civ.

Camper/Trailer Spaces: RV Sites (10), Full hookup, back-in with 40' max, picnic table. Handicapped accessible bathhouse and coin operated laundry facility. Wi-Fi and Cable/Satellite TV coming soon. Rates: AD/Ret: $22 daily, $140 weekly, $560.10 monthly; DoD-Civ: $25 daily, $162.47 weekly, $650.10 monthly.

Support Facilities: ATM, Bank, Bathhouse, Chapel, Coffee Shop, Commissary, Eateries, Exchange, Gymnasium, ITT, Outdoor Recreation.

RV Storage: C-850-623-7670 for more information.

Activities: Golfing, Hiking, Horseshoes, Picnic Area, Sand Volleyball, Sports Fields, Swimming Pool on base. Whiting Park offers fishing and waterski boat rentals, kayaks and canoes with a Convenience Store onsite.

Credit Cards: Mastercard, Visa, Debit Card.

Restrictions: Tent camping is not allowed, and ground fires are not permitted. One RV and one vehicle permitted per site (additional parking available nearby). Pets must be registered, and proof of current rabies shots required. Pets must be on leash at all times.

RV Driving Directions/Location: On Base. Located on the left side, just before Main Gate. Proper ID required.

RV Campground Physical Address: Clear Creek RV Park, 110 Magda Village, Milton, FL 32570.

GEORGIA

Albany Marine Corps Logistics Base

Address: Albany Marine Corps Logistics Base, 814 Radford Blvd, Suite 20311, Bldg 7200, Albany, GA 31704-1128.

Information Line: C-229-639-5000.

Main Base Police: C-229-639-5181. Emergencies, C-229-639-5911.

Main Installation Website: http://www.albany.marines.mil/

Main Base Location: Located in Southwest Georgia, just a few hours from some of Georgia's and Florida's most beautiful beaches.

Directions to Main Gate: From Atlanta, GA: Take Interstate 75 South to State-Highway 300 Cordele/Georgia/Florida Parkway. Follow Hwy 300 W for about 45 miles to Albany. Turn right onto Oglethorpe then take a left onto Mock Road. Follow Mock Road to Short Street, then turn left onto Short Street. At the end of Short Street turn left onto Fleming Road. Enter the installation through the Main Gate. From the South:

Take 75 N to 82 W/Tifton exit. Follow 82 W for about 45 miles to Albany. Take Business 82 W in Albany to Mock Road. Follow above directions to main gate.

NMC: Albany, three miles west.

NMI: Moody AFB, 82 miles southeast.

Base Social Media/Facebook: https://www.facebook.com/MCLBAlbany/

Base Social Media/Twitter: https://twitter.com/MCLBAlbany

Chapels: Chaplain. C-229-639-5284. Admin, C-229-639-5283/5282.

Dental Clinic: C-229-639-7871.

Medical: Appointment Line, C-229-639-7886.

Veterinary Services: C-229-639-5867.

Beauty/Barber Shop: C-229-435-9485.

Commissary: C-229-435-1721.

Exchange Gas: C-229-888-6801.

Exchange: C-229-888-6801.

Financial Institutions: Navy Federal Credit Union, C-229-435-0595, C-1-888-842-6328.

Clubs: Officers' Lounge, C-229-435-5227. SNCO Lounge, C-229-639-5223.

Places to Eat: Town and Country Restaurants, C-229-639-5223/5227 is on base. Exchange Food Court offers Subway. Bar & Grill, C-229-639-9490 for takeout before 1100 hours.

Bowling: Pin City Bowling Center, C-229-639-5233/5227.

Fitness Center: Daniels Family Fitness Center, C-229-639-6234. Thomason Gym, C-229-639-5246. HITT, C-229-639-6234.

Golf: Albany Driving Range, C-229-639-5246.

ITT/ITR: C-229-639-8177/8178.

Library: C-229-639-5242.

MWR: C-229-639-5268.

MWR Website: http://mccsalbany.com/

MWR Facebook: https://www.facebook.com/MCCS-Albany-795542963807997/

Outdoor Recreation: Outdoor Adventures, C-229-639-5221/5241. Offers campers, camping gear, canopies, grills, water slides, inflatables, trailers and more.

Swimming: MCLB Seasonal Outdoor Pool, C-229-639-5246/6234 offers lap swim, recreational swim and swim lessons.

Things To Do: Swim at beautiful Radium Springs, south of Albany, participate in outdoor sports, see a presentation of the local Concert Association, or visit the Little Theater. Albany is a trade and distribution center for Southwest Georgia, and there are many things to both see and do here.

RV CAMPING & GETAWAYS

Albany MCLB RV Park

Reservation/Contact Number Info: C-229-639-5234, DSN-312-567-5234. Fax C-229-639-6220, DSN-312-567-5234.

Recreation Security: C-229-639-5181.

RV Website: http://mccsalbany.com/index.cfm/retail/rv-park/

GPS Coordinates: 31°33'10"N/84°2'2"W

Reservations: Accepted. Office hours 0730-1630 hours Mon-Fri. Check-in at MCCS, Bldg 3600, between 0830-1630 Mon-Fri or with Campground Host. Oversize vehicles must use Truck Gate, 0530-1630 Mon-Fri. After hours and weekends use Main Gate. Maximum stay 30 days

Season of Operation: Year-round.

Eligibility: AD, NG, Res, Ret, DoD-Civ, Dep and 100% DAV.

Camper/Trailer Spaces: RV Sites (20): Hardstand, Gravel. Back-in (12), Pull-thru (8), E(110V/220V/15/30/50A)/S/W, CATV, Wi-Fi connection. No size restrictions and can accommodate a 5th wheel. Rates: $20 daily; $110 weekly; $350 monthly. Comfort Stations, Bldg 9251A. Coin operated laundry, bill changer.

Support Facilities: Bowling, Cafeteria, Chapel, Commissary, Diesel*, Equipment Rental, Exchange, Fitness Center, Gas, Grills, Laundry*, Mechanic/Auto Repair*, Pavilion, Picnic Area, Playground, Pool, Propane*, Restrooms, RV Storage*, Sewage Dump*, Snack Bar, Tennis Courts, Trails. *Off installation.

RV Storage: Available off base.

Activities: Bow Hunting*, Bowling, Fishing*, Movie Theater, Swimming. *State and Base License required.

Credit Cards: MasterCard and Visa.

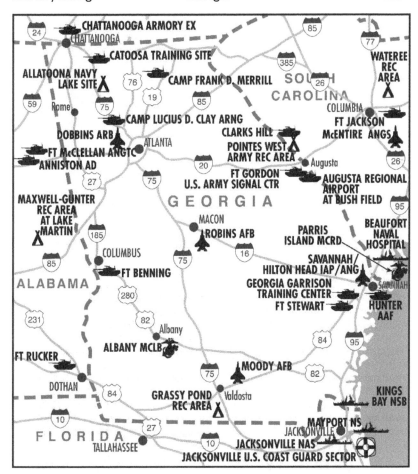

Restrictions: Pets allowed. Must be leashed at all times when outside the RV and must follow MCLB pet rules. State and base licenses required for fishing.

RV Driving Directions/Location: On Base: From the Main Gate: Check-in at MCCS main office.

Area Description: Located in southwest Georgia along the Flint River, Albany is known as the "Pecan Capital of the World." Enjoy the 3.1 mile Riverfront Trail that connects the Riverfront Park in downtown Albany. Many outdoor activities, including several parks, with hot summers and cool winters.

RV Campground Physical Address: Albany MCLB RV Park, MCCS, 814

Radford Blvd, Ste 20322, Bldg 3600, Albany, GA 31704.

Allatoona Navy Lake Site

Address: Allatoona Navy Lake Site, 166 Sandtown Rd, Cartersville, GA 30121.
Information Line: C-912-573-2000, DSN-312-573-2020.
Main Base Police: Emergencies dial 911.
Main Installation Website:
http://www.cnic.navy.mil/regions/cnrse/installations/navsubbase_kings_bay.html
Main Base Location: Lake Allatoona is situated on the Etowah River, a tributary of the Coosa River.
NMC: Atlanta, 40 miles southeast.
NMI: Dobbins ARB, 23 miles southeast.

Base Social Media/Facebook:
https://www.facebook.com/navylakesite/
Exchange Gas: Commercial gas station within 5 miles.
Exchange: Approximately 20 miles to Exchange at Dobbins ARB, C-770-428-1122.
Places to Eat: There are numerous restaurants within driving distance.
ITT/ITR: C-770-974-6309.
MWR: C-770-974-6309
MWR Website:
http://www.navymwrkingsbay.com/
MWR Facebook:
https://www.facebook.com/mwrkingsbay
Outdoor Recreation: Kings Bay NSB, Outdoor Adventure Center, C-912-573-8103.
Swimming: Lake swimming available.
Things To Do: Nearby Atlanta has plenty of activities and sightseeing opportunities to offer. Six Flags over Georgia and Underground Atlanta also offer theme park entertainment for visitors to the area. If seeking an outdoor adventure, climb Stone Mountain and watch the laser light show. Camping boating, fishing, hunting and hiking also available.
Walking Trails: Nature trails and hiking available on site.

RV CAMPING & GETAWAYS

Allatoona Navy Lake Site

Reservation/Contact Number Info: C-770-974-6309. Fax C-1-770-974-1927.
Recreation Security: C-770-919-6394.
RV Website:
http://get.dodlodging.net/propertys/Navy-Lake-Site-Allatoona
RV Email Address:
navylakesite@yahoo.com
GPS Coordinates: 34°6'1"N/84°42'42"W or 166 Sandtown Rd. Cartersville, GA 30121.
Reservations: Reservations accepted via phone daily. First night's stay charged at the time of reservation as a non-refundable deposit. Office hours 0900-1700 daily. Check-in between 1500-1700 hours, check-out 1100 hours.
Season of Operation: Year-round.

Eligibility: AD, NG, Res, Ret and DoD-Civ (Active & Ret), Dep and 100% DAV with VA card showing access to MWR facilities.
Camper/Trailer Spaces: RV Sites: Paved, Back-in (11), Pull-through (1), Maximum 40' in length, E(110V/30A)/W hookups. Rates: $16 daily. Notes: Only one site is Big Rig Friendly. Campgrounds are heavily wooded.
Tent Spaces: Primitive (12). Rates: $10 per tent daily.
Yurt, A Frame, Cabin, Apt, Spaces: Cabins: (10, 6 handicap accessible): Four-bedroom (1), furnished, microwave, pots/pans, dishes, A/C, TV, linens. Rates: $75-$120 seasonal. Three-bedroom (1), furnished, microwave, pots/pans, dishes, A/C, TV, linens. Rates: $65-$110 seasonal. Two-bedroom (6), handicap accessible, furnished, microwave, pots/pans, dishes, A/C, TV, linens. Rates: $55-$100 seasonal. One-bedroom (2), furnished, microwave, pots/pans, dishes, A/C, TV, linens. Rates: $45-$90 seasonal. Camper cabins and trailer also available. Check-in 1500-1700 hours, check-out 1100 hours. All units are non-smoking. Camper Cabins: (3). Primitive. 12' by 12', one twin and one full bed, mini-fridge, table, three chairs A/C, grill and picnic table, electric. No water, kitchen, bathroom or shower. Bathhouse is nearby. Rates: $30 daily.
Support Facilities: Bath House, Beach, Boat Launch, Boat Rental/Storage, Convenience Store, Fuel Dock, Equipment Rental, Fire Rings, Fishing Pier, Gas Grills, Ice, Marina, Pavilions (For a Fee), Picnic Areas, Playground, Restrooms*, Sewage Dump, Showers. * Handicap accessible. Marina has 96 wet slips, Pontoon & Deck Boat rentals, Canoes, Kayaks, Paddleboards, Paddletoons and Stand Up Paddleboard Rentals.
RV Storage: Available.
Activities: Boating, Fishing, Swimming, Water Skiing.
Credit Cards: American Express, Discover, MasterCard and Visa.
Restrictions: Pets are permitted in RV and tent camping areas only but must

be on leash at all times. Owners must clean up after their pets. No firearms allowed. Cabin rentals have two-day minimum on weekends.

RV Driving Directions/Location: Off Base: From I-75 north of Atlanta: Take exit 283 then turn right (east) on Old Allatoona Road. Proceed 3.8 miles to marked entrance on the left to Allatoona Landing Rd.

Area Description: Located in a 52-acre park on Lake Allatoona reservoir. Ideal spot for many outdoor recreational activities.

RV Campground Physical Address: 166 Sandtown Road, Cartersville, GA 30121.

Dobbins Air Reserve Base

Address: 1430 First Street, Dobbins ARB, GA 30069-5009.

Information Line: C-678-655-5000, DSN-312-325-5000.

Main Base Police: C-678-655-4909. Emergencies dial 911.

Main Installation Website: http://www.dobbins.afrc.af.mil/

Main Base Location: Dobbins ARB is located in Marietta, Georgia, a suburb about 20 miles northwest of Atlanta, in Cobb County, Georgia.

Directions to Main Gate: Driving From North Georgia: Take I-575 to I-75 southbound. Merge onto I-75 S. Take exit 261 towards GA-280/Lockheed/Dobbins AFB. Keep right at the fork in the ramp. Stay straight to go onto Delk Rd SE/GA-280 S. Dobbins located immediately on the right.

NMC: Atlanta, 16 miles southeast.

NMI: Camp Frank D. Merrill, 75 miles northeast.

Base Social Media/Facebook: https://www.facebook.com/DobbinsAir ReserveBase/

Base Social Media/Twitter: https://twitter.com/dobbinsarb

Chapels: Chaplain, C-678-655-2427.

Dental Clinic: C-678-655-3009.

Medical: C-678-655-4995.

Beauty/Barber Shop: C-770-425-3092.

Exchange: C-770-428-1122.

Clubs: Lakeside Lounge Consolidated Club, C-678-655-4594.

Places to Eat: The Dobbins Club, C-678-655-4594. Subway is on base. Many restaurants are within a short drive.

Fitness Center: Dobbins Fitness & Sports Center, C-678-655-4872. Human Performance Center, C-678-655-9517,

ITT/ITR: C-678-655-4797.

MWR: C-678-655-4975.

MWR Facebook: https://www.facebook.com/MWRHapp enings

Outdoor Recreation: Outdoor Recreation & Rental Services, C-678-655-4594. Offers boat and camper rentals, indoor/outdoor sports equipment, gardening tools and more.

Things To Do: Enjoy excellent fishing and boating opportunities around the Metro Atlanta area at Lake Allatoona and Lake Lanier. Visit underground Atlanta, the Cyclorama, Stone Mountain Park which has a nightly laser show, Fort Gillem, Six Flags, White Water Amusement Park and the Jimmy Carter Presidential Library, the Atlanta Zoo and the Atlanta Aquarium.

RV CAMPING & GETAWAYS

Dobbins Lakeside FamCamp

Reservation/Contact Number Info: C-678-655-4870, DSN-312-625-4870. Fax C-678-655-5992, DSN-312-625-5992.

Recreation Security: C-678-655-4908/4909.

GPS Coordinates: 33°55'14"N/84°31'16"W

Reservations: Availability based on first come, first serve basis with the exception of 4 sites. Patrons should park RV on available site and report to Bldg 558 to register. Office hours 0800-1700 hours. Check-out at 1200 hours. Late arrivals should call base security for entry to Gate 2. Maximum stay 90 days.

Season of Operation: Year-round.

Eligibility: AD, NG, Res, Ret and DoD-Civ.

Camper/Trailer Spaces: RV Sites: Hardstand (18), Back-in, E(110V/30A)/W hookups, picnic table, grill. Rates: $16.12 daily.

Tent Spaces: Allowed at RV spaces. Rates: $16.12 daily.

Support Facilities: Bath House, Chapel (Nearby), Dump Site, Exchange, Fitness Center, Gas*, Grills, ITT Office*, Laundry/Pay, Picnic Area, Playground, Rec Center/Lounge, Rental Center, Restrooms, RV Storage, Sewage Dump, Shoppette*, Showers, Sports Fields, Tennis Courts. * Located at Camp Lucius Clay (formerly Atlanta NAS).

RV Storage: Available. FAMCAMP usually maintains a short waiting list. Rates: $25 monthly. Yearly rate accepted.

Activities: Horseshoes, Jogging, Volleyball.

Credit Cards: Cash, MasterCard and Visa.

Restrictions: Pets allowed on leash. No swimming or fishing allowed.

RV Driving Directions/Location: On Base: From Gate 2: Gate open 0600-1700 hours Mon-Fri. Front gate does not allow entry with campers. Ask security guards for directions to FAMCAMP. Limited gate hours on weekends of UTA training.

Area Description: Offers many recreational and leisure activities. Conveniently located for sightseeing in Atlanta and surrounding area. Geese, ducks, beavers and other wildlife frequent the picnic/playground area adjacent to the FAMCAMP. Support facilities available on base and at Camp Lucius Clay (formerly Atlanta NAS), adjacent to Dobbins ARB.

RV Campground Physical Address: Recreational Services, 1335 Dozer Circle, Bldg 558, Dobbins ARB, GA 30069-4510.

Fort Benning

Address: 7117 Baltzell Avenue, Fort Benning, GA 31905.

Information Line: C-706-545-2011, DSN-312-835-2011.

Main Base Police: C-706-545-5222. Emergencies dial 911.

Main Installation Website: http://www.benning.army.mil/

Main Base Location: Fort Benning is located in an area commonly known as the "Tri-Community", comprised of Columbus and Fort Benning, Georgia,

and Phenix City, Alabama. Columbus is Georgia's third-largest city.

Directions to Main Gate: From Hartsfield International Airport: Take ramp left onto I-285/Atlanta Airport/Montgomery. At exit 61, turn right onto ramp towards I-85/Atlanta/Montgomery. Take ramp left onto I-85 towards I-85/Columbus/Montgomery. At exit 21 take ramp right onto I-185 towards I-185 Columbus. Fort Benning is directly at the end of I-185 South.

NMC: Columbus, five miles northwest.

NMI: Robins AFB, 100 miles northeast. Or Maxwell AFB, AL, 100 miles west.

Base Social Media/Facebook: https://www.facebook.com/FortBenningMCoE/

Base Social Media/Twitter: https://twitter.com/FortBenning

Chapels: Chaplain, C-706-545-2289, C-706-545-2218.

Dental Clinic: Bernheim Dental Clinic, C-706-545-3030. Harmony Church, C-706-706-544-5696. MACH Clinic, C-706-544-3034. Salomon, C-706-544-8338.

Medical: Appointment Line, C-706-544-2273, DSN-312-784-2273. Information Desk, C-762-408-2605.

Veterinary Services: Appointment Line, C-706-545-4444.

Beauty/Barber Shop: Main Exchange, C-706-687-2436; Stylique, C-706-687-2743, C-706-617-1747. Chaffee, C-706-685-0027. Harmony Church, C-706-685-4837. MCOE, C-706-689-0044. Mini Mall, C-706-682-0011. Sand Hill, C-706-687-8618.

Commissary: C-706-544-3965.

Exchange Gas: Harmony Church, C-706-682-5343.

Exchange: C-706-685-3242.

Financial Institutions: Columbus Bank & Trust Co., C-706-649-2622. TIC Federal Credit Union, C-706-320-8500. Wells Fargo, C-706-685-7101.

Clubs: Bennings Brew Pub, C-706-545-8426. Fiddler's Green, C-706-682-0640. Infantry Bar, C-706-687-1861.

Places to Eat: Breezeway Snackbar and; Lounge, C-706-844-5766; Destiny Dogs, C-706-685-4466; El Zapata, C-706-689-9009; Jack's 19th Hole, C-706-545-0397;

Java Cafe Main, C-706-626-0232; Java Cafe Harmon Church, C-706-626-2971, Java Cafe Bldg 35, C-706-545-3938; Lexington Room, C-706-687-1861; Little Caesars, C-706-682-2799; Subway Mai, C-706-687-8274; Subway Sand Hill, C-706-687-4919 and Zaxby's, C-706-683-0066 are on base. Exchange Food Court offers Arby's, Boston Market, Burger King, Charley's, Manchu Wok, Pizza Hut, Starbucks and Taco Bell. Dunkin Donuts, Domino's, Popeye's Chicken and Wing Zone are also on base. Many restaurants are within a short drive.

Bowling: Family Entertainment Center, C-706-545-4272. Mall Bowling Center, C-706-682-7781.

Fitness Center: Audie Murphy's HPC, C-706-545-1940. Breezeway FC, C-706-545-1687. Smith FC, C-706-545-4388. Whittington HPC Harmony Hill, C-706-544-7528. Santiago FC Sand Hill, C-706-544-9486.

Golf: Fort Benning Golf Course, C-706-545-0397.

ITT/ITR: C-706-626-7644.

Library: MWR Library, C-706-545-4911.

Marina: Uchee Creek Campground Marina, C-706-545-4053/7238.

Military Museum: National Infantry Museum, C-706-685-5800.

Military Museum Website: https://www.nationalinfantrymuseum.org/

MWR: C-706-545-4468.

MWR Website: https://benning.armymwr.com/

MWR Facebook: https://www.facebook.com/BenningFMWRfans/

MWR Twitter: https://twitter.com/BenningMWR

Outdoor Recreation: Outdoor Recreation, C-706-545-7978. Offers boat rentals, campers, moving trucks, generators, mowers, inflatable bounce houses and slides, super cookers and catering supplies, camping equipment, sound systems, tables and chairs, fans, games as well as outdoor activities to include paintball and more.

Swimming: Smith Fitness Center, C-706-545-5709 offers open and recreation swim. Briant Wells Indoor Pool, C-706-545-4726 offers lap and open swim. Carey Outdoor Seasonal Pool, C-706-545-1687 offers open swim, kiddie pool, dive boards and splash park. Breezeway Seasonal Pool and Splash Pad, C-706-545-1687 offers lap swim, splash pad, and open swim.

Things To Do: Visit the Infantry Museum, the Columbus Museum, The National Civil War Naval Museum, the Lunchbox Museum, Columbus Riverwalk, historical homes in the area, Flat Rock Park, Coca-Cola Space Science Center or sign up for one of the many rafting and tubing adventures in the area.

Walking Trails: Follow Me Fitness Trail is on base.

RV CAMPING & GETAWAYS
King's Pond

Reservation/Contact Number Info: C-706-545-7978.

RV Website: https://benning.armymwr.com/programs/parks-ponds-trails

GPS Coordinates: 32°21'52.3"N/84°48'10.1"W

Reservations: Reservations not required except when MWR events are scheduled.

Season of Operation: Year-round.

Eligibility: AD, NG, Res, Ret and Dep.

Tent Spaces: Primitive Sites: Charcoal grill, fire pit, restrooms. Rates: No charge.

Support Facilities: Boat Launch, Fishing Pier, Pavilion, Playground, Restrooms. Full range of support facilities on base.

Activities: Enjoy fishing, boating, picnicking or the great outdoors.

Credit Cards: American Express, MasterCard and Visa.

RV Driving Directions/Location: On Base. From the Outdoor Recreation Center, take a right out of the parking lot onto Gillespie Street. Turn left onto Burr Avenue. Then turn right onto Ingersoll Street. Go left onto Dixie Road, then bear right on 1st Division Road and follow for approximately five miles. Bear right onto 8th Division Road. Follow 8th Division approximately four miles to the end and go left on Hourglass Road. Follow Hourglass for approximately one mile and bear right onto the tank trail that leads to Kings Pond.

Area Description: Located on base. King's Pond is a favorite hangout for relaxation, Family Campout activities, boating (no combustion-type), fishing and other great outdoor activities.

RV Campground Physical Address: Ft Benning ODR, Bldg 1707 Gillespie St, Ft Benning, GA 31905.

Uchee Creek Army Campground & Marina

Reservation/Contact Number Info: C-709-545-4053/7238.

Recreation Security: C-706-545-5222.

RV Website: https://benning.armymwr.com/progra ms/uchee-creek-campground-and-marina

GPS Coordinates: 32°21'25"N/84°53'54"W

Reservations: Accepted for cabins and RV sites. May be made up to 6 months in advance for AD; 4 months for all others. Call for availability on camper spaces. Sites selected at time of arrival on first come, first serve basis. Cabins and chalets require 2-night minimum. No reservations for tent spaces. Reservations taken 0800-2000 hours. Check in 1600 hours, check-out 1100 hours at the Country Store. Camp Host on duty nightly until 2200 hours.

Season of Operation: Year-round. Closed Thanksgiving, Christmas Day and New Year's Day.

Eligibility: AD, NG, Res, Ret and DoD-Civ stationed at Fort Benning.

Camper/Trailer Spaces: RV Sites: Full hookup sites (30/50A). Rates: $23 daily with $10 dump fee. Mobile park homes: Sleeps 4 with 1 full-sized bed, sofa and loft with 2 floor mattresses. Rates: $50 daily based upon rank.

Tent Spaces: Campsites: Rates: $8 daily; $48 weekly.

Yurt, A Frame, Cabin, Apt, Spaces: Chalets: Executive Chalet: (5), two bedrooms with two queen beds and one bunk bed. Private bath, kitchen,

refrigerator, microwave, stove, utensils, linens/towels, central A/C and heat, washer/dryer, phone, CATV, DVD/VCR. Rates: $140-$120 daily, $720-$840 weekly depending on rank. Classic Chalets: (10), two bedrooms with full size bed, loft with 2 full size beds, sleeps eight, private bath, kitchen, refrigerator, microwave, stove, utensils, linens/towels, central A/C and heat, phone, CATV, DVD/VCR. Rates: $95-$110 daily, $570-$660 weekly depending on rank. Cabins: Large (10), one-bedroom, loft, sleeps six, private bath, kitchen, refrigerator, microwave, stove, utensils, linens/towels, A/C, heat, phone, CATV, DVD/VCR. Rates: $70-$85 daily, $420-$510 weekly depending on rank. Medium (10), one-bed room, sleeps four, private bath, kitchen, refrigerator, microwave, stove, utensils, linens/towels, A/C, heat, CATV, DVD/VCR. Rates: $65-$75 daily, $390-$450 weekly depending on rank. Small (10), sleeps four, private bath, kitchen, refrigerator, microwave, stove, utensils, linens/towels, A/C, heat, CATV, DVD/VCR. Rates: $60-$70 daily, $360-$420 weekly depending on rank.

Support Facilities: Bathhouse, Boat Dock, Boat Launch, Boat Rentals, Boat Slips, Country Store, Deer Stands, Fire Pit, Fishing Pier, Gas, Golf, Grills, Ice, Laundry, Lodge, Marina, Pavilion, Picnic Area, Playground, Pool (Seasonal), Rec Equipment Rentals, Restrooms, RV Rally Site and Activity Center (Seats 500), Sewage Dump, Showers, Snack Bar, Sports Fields and country store.

RV Storage: None.

Activities: Basketball, Fishing*, Golfing, Hunting*, Softball, Swimming, Volleyball, Walking Trails. *License required.

Credit Cards: American Express, MasterCard and Visa.

Restrictions: Pets allowed in private RVs and designated cabins. Pets must be on a leash when outdoors. Quiet hours 2200-0900 hours.

RV Driving Directions/Location: On Base: From Atlanta/Columbus: Take I-85 S. Exit onto I-185 S to Columbus/exit 21. Take I-185 to Hwy 80 W/exit 10. Take

Hwy 80 to Hwy 280/431/80 S (Hwy 80 last exit). *Take Hwy 280/431/80 to Hwy 431 S. Take Hwy 431 to Hwy 165 South (left turn). Take Hwy 165 to 101st Airborne Rd (left turn). Stay on 101st Airborne Rd and follow signs to Uchee Creek Rd and Uchee Creek Campground. From Montgomery, Alabama: Take 1-85 N to Hwy 280 E/exit 62 in Opelika. Take Hwy 280 (which turns into 280/431/80) to Hwy 431 S. Continue as above from *. From Eufaula, Alabama: Take 165 N (off of Hwy 431) to 101st Airborne Rd (right turn). Stay on 101st Airborne Rd and follow signs to Uchee Creek Rd and Uchee Creek Campground.

Area Description: The geography and climate are ideal for most outdoor activities. National Infantry Museum, Golf Course, Restaurants, and full range of support facilities available on post.

RV Campground Physical Address: Mailing Address: Business Operations Division, ATTN: ATZB-PAB Uchee Creek Campground/Marina P.O. Box 52358, Fort Benning, Georgia, 31905. Campground Address: 7 Uchee Creek Rd, Fort Mitchell, Al 36856.

Victory Pond

Reservation/Contact Number Info: C-706-545-7978.

RV Website: https://benning.armymwr.com/progra ms/parks-ponds-trails

GPS Coordinates: 32°22'00.0"N/84°49'56.4"W

Reservations: Contact ODR Office for details.

Season of Operation: Year-round.

Eligibility: AD, NG, Res, Ret and Dep.

Tent Spaces: Primitive sites only.

Support Facilities: Full range of support facilities on base.

Activities: Enjoy fishing on this well stocked pond.

Credit Cards: American Express, MasterCard and Visa.

RV Driving Directions/Location: On Base. From 8th Division ACP, take Left at lights onto 8th Division Road. Follow 8th Division past the Armor School area, and the pond will be on the right.

Area Description: Located on base, just a short drive to the recreation area.

RV Campground Physical Address: Ft Benning ODR, Bldg 1707 Gillespie St, Ft Benning, GA 31905.

Weems Pond

Reservation/Contact Number Info: C-706-545-7978.

RV Website: https://benning.armymwr.com/progra ms/parks-ponds-trails

GPS Coordinates: 32°18'26.8"N/84°50'31.1"W

Reservations: Contact ODR for reservation details.

Season of Operation: Year-round.

Tent Spaces: Primitive sites only.

Support Facilities: Full range of support facilities available on base.

Activities: Enjoy fishing on this well stocked pond.

Credit Cards: American Express, MasterCard and Visa.

RV Driving Directions/Location: On Base. From 8th Division ACP, take Right at lights onto 8th Division Road. Turn Left on Jamestown Road and follow it for approximately 4.5 miles. Weems Pond ahead on the left.

Area Description: Located on base, just a short drive to the recreation area.

RV Campground Physical Address: Ft Benning ODR, Bldg 1707 Gillespie St, Ft Benning, GA 31905.

Fort Gordon – U.S. Army Signal Center

Address: 307 Chamberlain Avenue, Fort Gordon, GA 30905.

Information Line: C-706-791-0110, DSN-312-780-0110.

Main Base Police: C-706-791-4537/4380.

Main Installation Website: http://www.gordon.army.mil/

Main Base Location: Fort Gordon is located just a few miles southwest of the city of Augusta, Georgia in Richmond County, GA.

Directions to Main Gate: From Interstate 20: Take exit 194 to Belair Road and Dyess Parkway. Follow the Dyess Parkway signs, and also the Fort

Gordon signs. Dyess Parkway will lead directly into the post through Gate 1.
NMC: Augusta, 12 miles northeast.
NMI: Robins AFB, 130 miles southwest.
Base Social Media/Facebook:
https://www.facebook.com/ftgordonga
Base Social Media/Twitter:
https://twitter.com/FGPAO
Chapels: Chaplain, C-706-791-5653.
Dental Clinic: Snyder Clinic, C-706-787-7050. Tingay Clinic, C-706-787-5102. Hospital, C-706-787-2601.
Medical: Appointment Line, C-706-787-7300. Information Desk, C-706-787-5811, DSN-312-773-5811.
Veterinary Services: C-706-787-3815.
Beauty/Barber Shop: Main Exchange, C-706-793-0230. Hospital, C-706-787-7282. Troop Store, C-706-796-8646.
Commissary: C-762-333-7160.
Exchange Gas: Gate 5 Express, C-706-793-1160.
Exchange: C-706-793-7171.
Financial Institutions: Fort Gordon Community Credit Union, C-706-793-0012. Wells Fargo, C-706-771-5960.
Clubs: Heroe's Sports Bar, C-706-791-3446.
Places to Eat: Alternate Escapes Cafe, C-706-791-0785; Bogey's Grill, C-706-791-2433; Huddle House, C-706-798-3722; Jackpot Cafe at Bingo Palace, C-706-791-5106; Kegler's Cafe, C-706-771-6907; Lift-A-Latte, C-706-791-2647; MWR Cafe - Darling Hall, C-706-791-1330; and Tower's Cafe, C-706-791-5849 are on base. Burger King, Domino's Pizza and Me Me's and Bo Bo's Express Chinese are also on base. Exchange Food Court offers Arby's, Boston Market, Charley's, Popeye's Chicken, Starbucks, Subway and Taco Bell. Many restaurants within a short drive.
Bowling: Gordon Lanes, C-706-791-3446.
Fitness Center: Cyber FC, C-706-791-7370. Gordon FC, C-706-791-2369. Nelson FC, C-706-791-6872. Victory FC, C-706-791-2864.
Golf: Gordon Lakes Golf Course, C-706-791-2433.
ITT/ITR: Aladdin Travel, C-706-771-0089.

Library: Woodworth Library, C-706-791-7323.
Marina: Pointes West Army Resort, C-706-541-1057.
Military Museum: Signal Corps Museum, C-706-791-2818.
Military Museum Website:
http://www.signal.army.mil/OLD/ocos/Museum/
MWR: C-706-791-6779.
MWR Website:
http://www.fortgordon.com/
MWR Facebook:
https://www.facebook.com/FortGordonMWR
MWR Twitter:
https://twitter.com/FortGordonMWR
Outdoor Recreation: Outdoor Recreation, C-706-791-5078. Offers multiple locations for outdoor fun including Freedom Park, Freedom Park Trail, Hilltop Riding Stables, Sportsman's Complex and Pointes West Army Resort. Offers bicycle rentals, outdoor equipment, fishing boats, archery equipment and more.
Swimming: Indoor Pool, C-706-791-3034 offer lap and fitness swim. Courtyard Seasonal Outdoor Pool and Spray Park, C-706-791-8053 offers recreational swim, water slides, dive boards and kiddie slide.
Things To Do: Fort Gordon is a great location for many different water and outdoor activities. Enjoy the Augusta Riverwalk, Augusta Museum of History, Augusta Canal Discovery Center, Brick Bond Park, Woodrow Wilson's Childhood Home, Greeneway Trail or enjoy unique shopping and eateries.
Walking Trails: Fort Gordon nature trails on base.

RV CAMPING & GETAWAYS
Leitner Lake Recreation Complex

Reservation/Contact Number Info: C-706-791-5078.
RV Website:
http://fortgordon.com/programs/leisure/outdoor/leitner-lake-recreation-complex/

GPS Coordinates: 33°22'2.6"N/-82°15'17.2"W

Reservations: Campsites first-come, first served basis. Camper rental accepted 60 days in advance. Cancellations must be received no less than 3 days prior to check-in to avoid fee. Office hours 1000-1800 Tue-Fri, 0900-1700 Sat, 1300-1700 Sun. All guests must check in at ODR, Bldg 445.

Season of Operation: Year-round.

Eligibility: AD, NG, Res, Ret DoD-Civ, 100% DAV.

Camper/Trailer Spaces: RV/Camper Sites (22), full hook-up sites with E(30/50A)/S/W, picnic table, grill. Rates: $20 daily; $15 daily 62+, 100% DAV. Trailer (1), sleeps 4-5, 2 bedrooms, shower, heat/air, complete kitchen with microwave, pots/pans, dishes for 6, TV. Two-night minimum. Rates: $50 daily, $135 3-day rental, $300 weekly.

Tent Spaces: Primitive camping area and picnic area, lake front view. Rates: $3 daily.

Support Facilities: Leitner Lake includes a new comfort station with bathroom, showers and washer and dryers. Easy access to full range of support and commercial facilities available at Fort Gordon.

RV Storage: None.

Activities: Easy access to fishing*, hunting**, outdoor equipment rental, bicycles, fishing boats, archery equipment and firearms for target practice. Skeet and Trap fields and sporting clays course are also nearby. *license required. ** License and Georgia Hunter Education Course required. Required licenses and hunting course are available on Fort Gordon.

Credit Cards: American Express, MasterCard and Visa.

Restrictions: No pets are allowed inside rental units. Campers under the age of 18 must be accompanied by an adult. Before departing trailer units, customers must remove all trash and debris to the dumpster; wash, dry and put away dishes used; remove sheets and pillowcases from bed and place used linens in a pile; sweep floor.

RV Driving Directions/Location: On Base. From Outdoor Recreation: Take a left on Carter Road. Turn left on Range Road, then right on Gibson. Take immediate left at fork onto Gibson Road and continue to MWR Lake Park Drive. Turn right to enter Leitner Lake Recreation Complex.

Area Description: Located on the serene Leitner Lake and minutes from the heart of Fort Gordon, location is ideal for camping, hiking and freshwater activities.

RV Campground Physical Address: MWR Lake Park Drive, Fort Gordon, GA 30905.

Fort Stewart

Address: General Stewart Way & Memorial Dr, Hinesville, GA 31313.

Information Line: C-912-767-1411, DSN-312-870-1411.

Main Base Police: C-912-767-4264.

Main Installation Website: http://www.stewart.army.mil/

Main Base Location: Fort Stewart is located in Hinesville, a small coastal Georgia town in Liberty County. Approximately 41 miles southwest of the city of Savannah.

Directions to Main Gate: On I-95 North: Take exit 76/Midway and Sunbury Rd. Turn left on US Hwy 84 West. Travel approximately 15 miles to General Stewart Way and turn right. Follow directions to the Fort Stewart main gate. On I-95 South: take exit 87/Coastal Highway/GA Hwy 17 and turn left on GA Hwy 17 South. Travel 4.5 miles to GA Hwy 196 West. Veer to the right on GA Hwy 196 West. Travel 8.9 miles to US Hwy 84 West, turn right at the T-junction. Travel 4.3 miles to General Stewart Way and turn right.

NMC: Savannah, 35 miles northeast.

NMI: Hunter Army Airfield, 40 miles northeast.

Base Social Media/Facebook: https://www.facebook.com/3rd.Infantry.Division

Base Social Media/Twitter: https://twitter.com/3rd_infantry

Chapels: Chaplain, C-912-767-4418. Winn Army Hospital, C-912-435-6661.

Dental Clinic: Central Appointment Line, C-912-435-6777.
Medical: Appointment Line, C-912-435-6633.
Veterinary Services: C-912-767-4194.
Beauty/Barber Shop: Brigade, C-912-876-0325. 2nd Brigade Mini Mall, C-912-877-2103. 6th St Mini Mall, C-912-368-1716. Main Exchange, C-912-876-0934; Stylique, C-912-877-0774.
Commissary: C-912-767-2076.
Exchange Gas: Marne Express 24-Hour Pumps, C-912-876-8434.
Exchange: C-912-876-2850.
Financial Institutions: Fort Stewart Georgia Credit Union, C-912-368-2477. The Heritage Bank, C-912-408-6440.
Clubs: Club Stewart, C-912-767-4717.
Places to Eat: Thunder Run, C-912-767-4372; Marne Strike Zone Snack Bar, C-912-767-3293; Stewart Lanes Corner Cafe, C-912-767-4273 and Marne Bistro, C-912-767-4197 are on base. Exchange Food Court offers Arby's, Boston Market, Charley's, Starbucks and Subway. Burger King, Coldstone Creamery and Popeye's Chicken are also on base. Many restaurants are within a short drive.
Bowling: Marne Bowling, C-912-767-4866. Stewart Lanes, C-912-767-4273.
Fitness Center: Caro FC, C-912-767-4763. Johnson FC, C-912-435-9306. Jordan FC, C-912-767-5742. Newman FC, C-912-767-3031.
Golf: Taylor's Creek Golf Course, C-912-767-2370.
ITT/ITR: C-912-767-2841/8609.
Library: Hays Library, C-912-767-2828.
Military Museum: Fort Stewart Museum, C-912-767-7885.
Military Museum Website:
https://www.facebook.com/pages/Fort-Stewart-Museum/124845484197425
MWR: C-912-767-5117.
MWR Website:
https://stewart.armymwr.com
MWR Facebook:
https://www.facebook.com/FortStewartHunterFMWR
MWR Twitter:
https://twitter.com/fortstewartfmwr
Outdoor Recreation: Lowcountry Outdoor Center, C-912-435-8205. Offers paintball, park/pavilion rentals, party rentals, camping gear, trailers, kayaks, canoes, fishing boats, water skis, paddle boards, outdoor games, costumers, archery range, skeet and trap range and more.
Swimming: Johnson Pool, C-912-435-9306 offers open and lap swim. Newman Pool, C-912-767-3034 offers open swim, lap swim and classes. Corkan Recreational Facility, C-912-767-8575 offers seasonal open swim, recreational swim and Splashpark; adventure golf, fun center and more. Bryan Village Outdoor Seasonal Pool, C-912-767-2701 offers open and recreational swim.
Things To Do: Local recreational activities include hunting, fishing, tennis and golf. Ocean beaches are within driving distance and historic Savannah is 40 miles northeast with many attractions. Visit Old Liberty County Jail, the Hinesville Farmers Market and other historical sites.
Walking Trails: Hiking and walking trails are on base.

RV CAMPING & GETAWAYS

Holbrook Pond Recreation Area & Campground

Reservation/Contact Number Info: C-912-435-8213. Fax C-912-435-8212.
Recreation Security: C-912-767-4264.
RV Website:
https://stewarthunter.armymwr.com/programs/campground
GPS Coordinates:
31°52'9"N/81°34'18"W
Reservations: Accepted up to 30 days in advance with one day deposit. Payment in full required upon arrival. Office hours 1100-1730 daily summer; Tue-Sat winter. Closed Thanksgiving, Christmas and New Year's Day. Check-in during office hours, Bldg 8340. After hour check in with Camp Host Site 1. Check-out 1200 hours. Discounts available to holders of Golden Age and Golden Access Passports. Wi-Fi available. Maximum stay 90 days.
Season of Operation: Year-round.

Eligibility: AD, NG, Res, Ret, 100% DAV and DoD-Civ AD/Ret, Dep.

Camper/Trailer Spaces: Camper Spaces: Concrete (30): sites 1-19 partial hookup, picnic table, fire pit, grill. Sites 20-30 full hookup, picnic table, fire pit, grill. Rates: $22 daily; Golden Age Pass $17 daily. Sites 1-19 $550 monthly; Sites 20-30 $675 monthly.

Tent Spaces: Primitive (8): No hookups, picnic table, grill. Rates: $8 daily.

Support Facilities: Auto Craft Shop, Bathhouse, Beach, Boat Launch, Boat Rental/Storage, Bowling, Cafeteria, Chapel, Commissary, Convenience Store, Equipment Rental, Exchange, Fire Rings, Fishing Pier, Fishing Pond, Fitness Center, Golf, Grills, Ice, Internet Access, Laundry, Pavilion, Picnic Area, Playground, Pool, Recreation Center, Restrooms, RV Storage, Screen Pavilion, Sewage Dump, Shoppette, Showers, Shuttle Bus, Skeet Range, Snack Bar, Sports Fields, Stables, Tennis Courts, Trails, Volleyball Court.

RV Storage: Available. All storage requires proper paperwork, C-912-425-8205/8209 for more information.

Activities: Boating, Fishing*, Golfing, Hiking, Hunting*. *Licenses and Area Access Passes required. Visit Fort Stewart Pass and Permit, C-912-435-8061 (Bldg 8091 on Highway 144).

Credit Cards: MasterCard and Visa.

Restrictions: Pets allowed (breed restrictions apply, call for information) on leash and must be under owner control at all times. No firearms in the open. Loaded firearms prohibited. No generators.

RV Driving Directions/Location: On Base. From I-95 north or south: Take exit 90 and proceed west on Hwy 144 approximately 17 miles. Watch for the Holbrook Pond Recreation Campground entrance on the left, Fort Stewart Road 48B. Continue down Fort Stewart Rd 48B about .25 miles to the Equipment Checkout Center. For late check-in continue straight ahead down Fort Stewart Road 48B around the pond to the campground (approximately one mile) stop at Campsite #1 and see the Camp Host.

Area Description: Campground view is of Holbrook Pond located on Ft. Stewart, nestled among the towering Georgia pines. Very quiet and secluded. Full range of support facilities available at Fort Stewart, approximately 2.5 miles away.

RV Campground Physical Address: Hwy 144E, Bldg 8340, Holbrook Pond, Fort Stewart, GA 31314. Mailing Address: Outdoor Recreation, 688 Fort Stewart Rd #48, Bldg 8325, Fort Stewart, GA 31314-7500.

Grassy Pond Recreation Area

Address: 5360 Grassy Pond Drive, Lake Park, GA 31636.

Information Line: C-229-257-1110, DSN 312-460-1110.

Main Base Police: C-229-257-3108. Emergencies dial 911.

Main Installation Website: http://www.moody.af.mil/

Main Base Location: Grassy Pond is a 500+ acre recreation area in Southern Georgia in Lake Park.

NMC: Valdosta, 12 miles north.

NMI: Moody AFB, 28 miles north.

Base Social Media/Facebook: http://www.facebook.com/moodygrassypond

Chapels: C-229-257-3211, C-229-257-3501 (after duty hours).

Medical: C-229-257-2778, DSN-312-460-2778.

Commissary: Approximately 27 miles north at Moody AFB Commissary, C-229-257-3384. Shoppette, C-229-257-3451.

Exchange Gas: Approximately 27 miles to Moody AFB gas station, C-229-257-3431. Commercial gas station within 3 miles.

Exchange: Approximately 27 miles north at Moody AFB Base Exchange, C-229-257-3431/3432.

Places to Eat: There are limited restaurants within driving distance of Recreation Area. Moody AFB offers Quiet Pines Dining Facility, C-229-257-3651, Turn N' Burn Flight Kitchen, C-229-257-3048, Bowling Center Snack Bar, C-229-257-3872, Moody Field Club,

C-229-257-3792, Quiet Pines Snack Bar, C-229-257-5850 and Wright Bros Cafe, C-229-257-4530. Exchange Food Court offers Taco Bell, Anthony's Pizza, Burger King and Church's Chicken, C-229-257-3431 and Family Pizza House, C-229-244-1845 is near.

Fitness Center: C-229-257-1621.
Golf: Quiet Pines Golf Course, C-229-257-3297.
ITT/ITR: C-229-257-3280.
MWR: C-229-257-4428.
MWR Website:
http://www.moodyfss.com/
MWR Facebook:
https://www.facebook.com/moodyfss
Outdoor Recreation: Grassy Pond, C-229-559-5840. Grassy Pond has a playground, water play area, fishing, boating, hunting and equipment rentals including boats, outdoor sports and more. Outdoor Adventure Center, C-229-257-1375, at Moody AFB offers trips to Florida and surrounding areas of Georgia to enjoy deep sea fishing, scalloping, snorkeling, kayaking, canoeing, archery, horseback riding, water sports, a yearly wilderness challenge and much more. Splatter Swamp Paintball, C-229-257-1375, is also available.

Swimming: Lake swimming is available at recreation area. Moody AFB has an Indoor Pool, C-229-257-5655 and Outdoor Pool with large water slide and children's area, diving board and lap lanes, C-229-257-3244.

Things To Do: Grassy Pond Recreation Area is located in a wooded area near the GA/FL state line. There are many opportunities for outdoor activities. Tour the Crescent mansion in Valdosta and visit the freshwater lakes for fishing and water sports. Visit the Wild Adventures Theme Park. Dove, quail, turkey and other wild game hunting season is also popular seasonally.

Walking Trails: 3.1 and 1 mile nature trails are available at recreation area.

RV CAMPING & GETAWAYS
Grassy Pond Recreation Area

Reservation/Contact Number Info: C-229-559-5840.
Recreation Security: Sheriff's Office, C-229-333-5133.
RV Website:
http://moodyfss.com/grassy-pond/
RV Email Address:
GPS Coordinates:
0°39'27"N/83°14'19"W
Reservations: Reservations accepted one year in advance for AD; 6 months in advance for all others. Payment required at time of reservation. Office hours 0900-1700 hours daily. Cancellations require 15 day notice prior to arrival to avoid fee for all reservations. Cabins: Reservations required for cabins. Telephone reservations preferred. One night's stay deposit required. Payment in full prior to arrival. Cabins: Check-in 1500 hours; check-out 1100 hours. Check in at Bldg 2019.
Season of Operation: Year-round.
Eligibility: Open to public. Park entry is free for Military/DoD ID cardholders, and $5 per vehicle up to six passengers and $2 per each additional person for the public.
Camper/Trailer Spaces: Camper Spaces: Gravel (39), Maximum 60' in length; 30 sites have E(110V/30/50A)/S/W hookups, 9 sites have E(110V/30A)/S/W hookups. RV Rates: $25 daily; $150 Weekly; $475 Monthly. Military discounts available for all military and DOD cardholders.
Tent Spaces: Rates: $12 daily; $50 weekly. Electric and water provided. Military discounts available for all military and DOD cardholders.
Yurt, A Frame, Cabin, Apt, Spaces: Cabins (19) Two and three-bedroom cabins, private bath, kitchen, dishes, pots/pans, CATV. Patrons must provide bath/kitchen towels, washcloths, paper towels, detergent for dishes. Rates: $80-$100 nightly; $500-$575 weekly. Two-bedroom Cottage:

Private bath, kitchen, pots/pans, dishes, CATV. For all cabins: Linens are not provided but can be rented for a fee. Rates: $85 daily, $525 weekly. Military discounts available for all military and DOD cardholders.

Support Facilities: Playground, Basketball Court, Volleyball Court, Picnic Area, Fishing, Boating, Boat Rentals, Boat Ramp, Hiking & Nature Trails, Shoppette, Splash Pool, Dump, Sewer, Water, Electric, Cabins, Mobile Units, RV Site, Laundry, Showers, Game Room, Pet Friendly and more!

RV Storage: None.

Activities: Basketball, Boating, Fishing*, Horseshoes, Nature Trail, Volleyball. *Base and state permits required. *Only Moody AFB fishing licenses sold on-site.

Credit Cards: MasterCard and Visa.

Restrictions: Pets allowed in some cabins. Pet fee applies. Up to two pets allowed at campsite. Pet must be on leash; owner must clean up after pet. No firearms allowed. Quiet hours 2200-0800 hours.

RV Driving Directions/Location: Off Base. From I-75 S/GA-401 S toward Lake City: Take the GA-376/Lakes Blvd exit 5 toward Lake Park. Turn right onto Lakes Blvd/GA-376. Turn left onto Loch Laurel Road. Turn left onto Grassy Pond Road and look for signs for facility.

Area Description: The 500-acre recreational area is similar to a state park with cabins, RV sites, tent sites, group shelters, a recreational boat area, nature trails, grills and other amenities. The major fishing area offers a variety of accommodations and activities for guests such as a boat launch for personal boats, equipment rentals and fishing contests.

RV Campground Physical Address: Grassy Pond, 5360 Grassy Pond Dr, Lake Park, GA 31636-5000.

Hunter Army Airfield

Address: 171 Haley Avenue, Hunter Army Airfield, GA 31409.

Information Line: C-912-767-1411, DSN-312-870-1411.

Main Base Police: C-912-315-6133.

Main Installation Website: http://www.stewart.army.mil/units/home.asp?id=186

Main Base Location: Hunter Army Airfield is located in Savannah, GA.

Directions to Main Gate: From I-95: Take exit I-16 east and then take exit 164A to I-516. Go approximately 4 miles to the end of I-516. Before 2100 hours, exit right onto Montgomery Street. ID, safety belt and proof of insurance are required at the gate. Enter Post on Duncan Drive.

NMC: Savannah, in southwest part of city.

NMI: Ft. Stewart, 45 miles.

Base Social Media/Facebook: https://www.facebook.com/HunterArmyAirfield/

Chapels: C-912-315-5111.

Dental Clinic: Appointment Line, C-912-439-6777 option 3. Clinic, C-912-315-5417.

Medical: Tuttle Clinic, C-912-315-6500, DSN-312-729-6500. Winn Army Community Hospital, C-912-435-6633.

Veterinary Services: Appointments, C-912-912 767-4194.

Beauty/Barber Shop: C-912-692-0101.

Commissary: C-912-315-5219.

Exchange Gas: C-912-459-1223.

Exchange: C-912-315-8380/5336/2558.

Financial Institutions: Federal Credit Union, C-912-354-6420.

Places to Eat: Popeye's and Burger King are within walking distance. Many restaurants within a short drive.

Fitness Center: Tominac FC, C-912-315-5078.

Golf: Hunter Golf Course, C-912-315-9115.

ITT/ITR: C-912-315-3674.

Marina: Lotts Island Recreation Area, C-912-315-9354/9554.

MWR: Fort Stewart, C-912-767-5133.

MWR Website: https://stewarthunter.armymwr.com/

MWR Facebook: https://www.facebook.com/FortStewartHunterFMWR

MWR Twitter: https://twitter.com/fortstewartfmwr

Outdoor Recreation: Outdoor Recreation, C-912-315-9354/9554.

Offers hunting, fishing, a shooting range, camping, equipment rentals, marina, parks, picnic areas and much more.

Swimming: Hunter Outdoor Seasonal Pool, C-912-315-5786 offers lap and open swim. Tominac Indoor Pool, C-912-315-2819 offers lap swim, open swim and classes.

Things To Do: Enjoy historic Savannah with its cobblestone streets and antebellum architecture. Visit Forsyth Park, Owens-Thomas House, Mercer-Williams House Museum, unique shopping and eateries, or enjoy the beautiful coastline.

Walking Trails: Hallstrom Lake Recreation Area offers walking trails.

RV CAMPING & GETAWAYS
Lotts Island RV Park

Reservation/Contact Number Info: C-912-315-9554. Fax C-912-315-9574.
Recreation Security: C-912-315-9308.
RV Website:
https://stewarthunter.armymwr.com/programs/lotts-island
GPS Coordinates:
31°59'16"N/81°11'4"W
Reservations: Reservations accepted. Office hours 1000-1630 Mon, Thur, Fri; 0730-1430 Sat-Sun. Check-in 1100 hours. Maximum stay 90 days.
Season of Operation: Year-round.
Eligibility: AD, NG, Res, Ret, 100% DAV, Dep and DoD-Civ. (AD and Ret), Civilians with ID.
Camper/Trailer Spaces: Camper Spaces: Gravel: (16), Pull-through (11), Back-in (5), Maximum 40' in length, E(110/220V/30/50A)/S/W, Ask about CATV. Rates: $25 daily, $550 monthly. Discount for holders of Access/Golden Age Passports, Rates: $20 daily.
Tent Spaces: Grass/Dirt: (6) W Hookups only. Rates: $6 daily.
Support Facilities: Auto Craft Shop, Boat Launch, Boat Docks, Boat Rental/Storage, Cafeteria, Camping Equipment, Camper Rental, Convenience Store, Equipment Rental, Exchange, Fire Rings, Fishing Pier, Fitness Center, Gasoline, Golf, Grills, Ice, Laundry, Long-term RV Storage, Marina, Mechanic/Auto Repair, Mess Hall, Pavilions (for a fee), Picnic Areas, Playground, Pool, Recreation Center, Restrooms, Sewage Dump Station, Skeet Range, Sports Fields, Tennis Courts, Trails.
RV Storage: Available. Rates: $10-$20 monthly. Call C-912-315-9554 for more information.
Activities: Boating, Fishing*, Golfing, Seasonal Hunting*. *Post permit and state license required.
Credit Cards: MasterCard, Visa.
Restrictions: Pets allowed, must be on leash at all times. No firearms. No tents allowed in RV park.
RV Driving Directions/Location: On Base: From I-95 take GA-204 exit 94. Take GA-204 north (east). Cross the Forest River Bridge and turn left at the next traffic light onto Rio Road. Gate is on the left. Park is located immediately inside the gate to the left.
Area Description: Located at Lotts Island, the RV Park is conveniently close to the many water-related activities of the inland harbor. Located only five miles from the Savannah Historic District. Mall and library are located across from the campground.
RV Campground Physical Address: Outdoor Recreation, 313 Stratofortress Road, Hunter Army Airfield, Savannah, GA 31409-5000.

Kings Bay Naval Submarine Base

Address: Kings Bay Naval Submarine Base, 1063 USS Tennessee Avenue, Kings Bay, GA 31547.
Information Line: C-912-573-2000/2001.
Main Base Police: Emergencies dial 911.
Main Installation Website:
http://www.cnic.navy.mil/regions/cnrse/installations/navsubbase_kings_bay.html
Main Base Location: Kings Bay borders the cozy, historic town of St. Marys, Georgia in the southeastern corner of Coastal Georgia, just north of the Florida border.

Directions to Main Gate: From Interstate 95: Take either exit 1, 3, or 6. Exit 1 leads to St. Marys Road and ends at the Franklin Gate. From Exit 3: Take Georgia State Route 40 east to St. Mary's and turn east onto Kings Bay Road, which ends at Stimson Gate. Exit 6 leads to Kings Bay Road and to the Stimson Gate.

NMC: Jacksonville, FL 40 miles south.

NMI: Jacksonville Naval Air Station, 50 miles south.

Base Social Media/Facebook: https://www.facebook.com/nsbkingsbay

Chapels: C-912-573-4501.

Dental Clinic: C-912-573-4212.

Medical: Appointment Line, C-912-573-6450.

Veterinary Services: C-912-573-0755.

Beauty/Barber Shop: Barber, C-912-882-6228. Beauty, C-912-882-6152.

Commissary: C-912-573-3310.

Exchange Gas: C-912-573-3104.

Exchange: C-912-882-6098.

Financial Institutions: Navy Federal Credit Union, C-912-573-2180, C-1-800-842-6328.

Clubs: K.B. Finnegan's Irish Pub, C-912-573-9429.

Places to Eat: O'Brien's Bunker, C-912-573-0008; Pirate's Cove Galley, C-912-573-9639 and Starbucks are on base. Domino's and McDonald's are also on base. Exchange Food Court offers Subway. Many restaurants within a short drive.

Bowling: Rack-N-Roll Lanes, C-912-573-9492.

Fitness Center: Kings Bay FC, C-912-573-3990.

Golf: Trident Lakes Golf Course, C-912-573-8475.

ITT/ITR: C-912-573-1157.

Military Museum: St Mary's Submarine Museum, C-912-882-2782.

MWR: C-912-573-2538.

MWR Website: http://www.navymwrkingsbay.com/

MWR Facebook: https://www.facebook.com/mwrkingsbay

Outdoor Recreation: Outdoor Rentals, C-912-573-8103. Offers fishing boat rentals, kayaks, canoes, paddle boards, party rentals, trailers, camping gear, park and pavilion rentals and more.

Swimming: Fitness Complex Pool, C-912-573-3001 offers lap swim and recreational swim year-round. Heated outdoor pool.

Things To Do: From the beauty and history of old Savannah to the beaches of the Golden Isles near Brunswick and the Cumberland Island National Seashore, coastal Georgia offers everything from sightseeing to fishing and hunting.

Walking Trails: Several parks on base with nature trails.

RV CAMPING & GETAWAYS
Eagle Hammock RV Park

Reservation/Contact Number Info: C-1-877-NAVY-BED, C-912-573-5262. Fax C-912-573-3308.

Recreation Security: C-912-573-2271/2145/2146. Emergenices dial 911.

RV Website: http://get.dodlodging.net/propertys/Eagle-Hammock-RV-Park

Other Info Website: http://www.navymwrkingsbay.com/programs/c4353e59-afa4-4bb7-be62-0fcb74186d06

RV Email Address: eaglehammock@tds.net

GPS Coordinates: 30°46'36"N/81°33'14"W Note: Please do not use the physical address.

Reservations: Reservations accepted one year in advance for AD, NG, Res; 6 months in advance for Ret, DoD-Civ. Credit card holds reservation. Reservations may be made in 90-day increments as space is available. Office hours 0900-1600 Mon-Fri, Nov-Mar; 0900-1300 Mon-Fri, Apr-Oct. Check-in 1400 hours at RV Park office, check-out 1200 hours. Camp Host available for after-hours arrival.

Season of Operation: Year-round.

Eligibility: AD, NG, Res, Ret, DoD-Civ, 100% DAV, Dep and Sponsored Guests.

Camper/Trailer Spaces: Hardstand (60): Pull-thru (16), Back-in (44), E(110/220V/15/30/50S)/S/W hookups, maximum 40' in length, CATV, Wi-Fi, picnic tables, fire ring, grills. Rates: $19-$21 daily.

Tent Spaces: Tents are not allowed at RV park; only at On Base Etowah Park, approximately 5 miles away. Grass (6), Primitive tent sites; no electricity, no potable water in area. Grills, fire rings, and bathroom facilities at campground. Contact Outdoor Adventures for directions, C-912-573-8103.

Yurt, A Frame, Cabin, Apt, Spaces: Cabins (2): sleeps 6, one bedroom, one bath, fully furnished with full kitchen. Linens provided. Rates: Call for rates and information.

Support Facilities: Auto Hobby Shop, Bathhouse, Boat Rental/Storage, Bowling, Cafeteria, Chapel, Commissary, Convenience Store, Diesel, Equipment Rental, Exchange, Fire Rings, Fishing Pier, Fitness Center, Gas, Golf, Grills, Ice, Laundry, Long Term RV Storage, Marina, Mechanic/Auto Repair, Mess Hall, Pavilion, Picnic Area, Playground, Pool, Propane, Recreation Center, Restrooms, RV Storage, Sewage Dump, Shoppette, Showers, Snack Bar, Sports Fields, Tennis Courts, Trails.

RV Storage: C-912-573-8103.

Activities: Boating, Fishing, Hunting, Kayaking. All need appropriate Georgia State Licenses. Fishing and Hunting also need Base Permits.

Credit Cards: American Express, Discover, MasterCard, Visa and Cash.

Restrictions: Pets allowed, must be under owner control at all times. Limit two pets per site. Owner must clean up after pet immediately. No fencing or external structures may be erected. Written verification of pet's current vaccinations must be provided. Firearms must be declared and checked in at the front gate before entering base property.

RV Driving Directions/Location: On Base: Note: Please do not use physical address for GPS directions. Base access Mon-Fri 0500-1800, USS Benjamin Franklin Drive, Kings Bay, GA or after-hours Fri-mon 1830-0500, USS Henry L Stimson Drive, Kings Bay, GA. From the Main Gate: Use right lane when entering through gate. Go to second stoplight and turn right onto USS Daniel Webster Rd. Park is .5 miles on left. If Franklin Gate is closed: Make left at stoplight and drive one mile to Stimpson Gate.

Area Description: Situated in a peaceful and quiet part of the base, with open terrain. Woods surround the perimeter, and a 270-acre lake is accessible from the park. Canoes, kayaks, and boats are available for rent from Outdoor Adventures. Close to historical town of St. Mary's. Submarine Museum, restaurants, shops and access to Cumberland Island National Seashore via ferry. Short drive to St. Simons, Jekyll Island, Okefenoke Swamp and Fernandina Beach, FL.

RV Campground Physical Address: 937 USS Daniel Webster Road, Kings Bay, GA 31547.

Pointes West Army Recreation Area

Address: Lake Thurmond, 6703 Washington Road, Appling, GA 30802.
Information Line: C-706-791-0110, DSN-312-780-0110.
Main Base Police: Emergencies dial 911.
Main Installation Website: http://www.gordon.army.mil/
Main Base Location: Fort Gordon is located just a few miles southwest of the city of Augusta, Georgia in Richmond County, GA.
NMC: Augusta, 25 miles southeast.
NMI: Fort Gordon, 26 miles south.
Chapels: C-706-791-4684.
Dental Clinic: C-706-787-7050.
Medical: C-706-787-5811, DSN-312-773-5811.
Beauty/Barber Shop: C-706-793-7171.
Commissary: Approximate 26 miles to Fort Gordon Commissary, C-706-791-3718.
Exchange Gas: Approximately 26 miles to Fort Gordon gas station, C-706-793-7171. Commercial gas station within 1 mile.
Exchange: Approximately 26 miles to Fort Gordon Post Exchange, C-706-793-7171.

Places to Eat: There are a limited restaurants within driving distance of the facility.

Fitness Center Phone Numbers: C-706-791-6872.

Golf: Gordon Lakes Golf Course, C-706-791-2433.

ITT/ITR: Aladdin Travel, C-706-771-0089.

Marina: Pointes West Army Recreation Area Marina, C-706-541-1057.

MWR: 706-791-6491.

MWR Website:
http://www.fortgordon.com/

MWR Facebook:
https://www.facebook.com/FortGordonMWR

MWR Twitter:
https://twitter.com/FortGordonMWR

Outdoor Recreation: Fort Gordon Outdoor Recreation Program, C-706-791-5078. Offers swimming at Lake Thurmond, picnic areas, children's playgrounds, boating and fishing available at Pointes West Recreation area. Water sports and camping equipment rentals are also available.

Swimming: Swimming at Lake Thurmond from 21 May 2011 through Labor Day weekend. Fort Gordon Indoor Pool, C-706-791-3034. Courtyard Outdoor Pool, C-706-791-3550.

Things To Do: Located on a 904-acre site with a 1200-mile shoreline along Thurmond Lake on the Georgia/South Carolina line. It is a great location for many different water and outdoor activities.

Walking Trails: Bartram Trails are available on-site.

RV CAMPING & GETAWAYS
Pointes West Army Recreation Area

Reservation/Contact Number Info: C-706-541-1057. Fax C-706-541-1963

Recreation Security: C-706-541-1057.

RV Website:
https://gordon.armymwr.com/pwar

GPS Coordinates:
33°41'21"N/82°18'54"W

Reservations: Reservations required for motel, cabins, cottages and campers.

Accepted 150 days in advance for AD; 80 days in advance for all others. RV/Tent Camping first come, first serve. Office hours 1000-1800 daily. Campground: Check-in 1430 hours, check-out 1400 hours. Max stay 30 days within 60-day period. Extensions need prior approval. Motel, Cabins, Cottages: Credit card holds reservation. Check-in 1500 hours, check-out 1230 hours. Minimum 2-night stay for all reservations. One-night stays will be handled on walk-in, space available basis.

Season of Operation: Year-round.

Eligibility: AD, NG, Res, Ret, DoD-Civ, 100% DAV.

Camper/Trailer Spaces: RV Sites: Gravel (58): Back-in, maximum 40' in length, E(110/220V/30/50A)/S/W hookups, picnic table, grill, fire ring. Rates: $20 daily; Ret & DAV $14 daily. Partial: Gravel (20), Back-in, maximum 40' in length, E(20A), picnic table, fire ring, grill. Rates: $10 daily.

Tent Spaces: Primitive sites in 4 tent areas, no hookups. Rates: $7 daily.

Yurt, A Frame, Cabin, Apt, Spaces: Motel Suites (12): sleeps 2-4, two queen beds, fully furnished kitchenette, bathroom with separate vanity area, patio, central heat/air, satellite TV, phone. Linens provided. Rates: $99 daily. Rustic Cabins (8): Three-bedroom cottage (6), sleeps 3-5 with two queen beds, one twin; Two-bedroom cottage (2), sleeps 3-4 with one queen bed, two twins. Each cabin fully furnished with one bathroom, private bedrooms, kitchen, dining area, living space, and a deck with patio furniture. All overlooking Lake Thurmond. Linens provided. Rates: $105 daily. Cottages (5): two-bedroom cottages with loft, sleeps 4-6. Each two-story cottage fully furnished and features two bedrooms, two baths, two fold out couches, kitchen, dining area, living space and deck with patio furniture. Linens provided. Rates: $120 daily.

Support Facilities: Bathhouse, Beach (Summer), Bicycles, Boat Launch, Boat Sheds/Slips, Camping Equipment, Canoes, Country Store (Apr-Sept 1000-

1800 daily), Marina, Pavilions, Pedal Boats, Picnic Area, Playground, Restrooms, Sewage Dump, Showers, Trails, TV Room.

RV Storage: None.

Activities: Boating, Fishing*, Hiking, Picnicking, Swimming, Biking. *License required.

Credit Cards: American Express, MasterCard and Visa.

Restrictions: No pets in cabins or swimming area. Pets allowed on leash in other areas; owners must clean up after pets. Firearms, bows and arrows, explosives, fireworks and all sporting devices capable of causing death or injury are prohibited. No ATVs, dirt/mini motor bikes, or go-carts allowed.

RV Driving Directions/Location: Off Base. From I-20 east or west: Take exit 183/Appling to GA-47 north to Washington Road. Turn left (northwest) onto Washington Road and follow to Recreation Area.

Area Description: Located on 904-acre site with a 1200-mile shoreline along Thurmond Lake, formerly Clarks Hill Lake, on Georgia/South Carolina line. Ideal for wide range of outdoor activities in fresh-water lakes and rivers of the area. Savannah about 120 miles southeast. Easy access to full range of support facilities available at Fort Gordon.

RV Campground Physical Address: Lake Thurmond, 6703 Washington Road, Appling, GA 30802. Mailing Address: Pointes West Recreation Area, PO Box 67, Appling, GA 30802-5000.

Robins Air Force Base

Address: Highway 247, Robins AFB, GA 31098-2235.

Information Line: C-478-926-1110/1113, DSN-312-468-1110.

Main Base Police: C-478-926-2187. Emergencies dial 911.

Main Installation Website: http://www.robins.af.mil

Main Base Location: Robins AFB is located in middle Georgia, 100 miles south of Atlanta and 16 miles south of Macon.

Directions to Main Gate: Driving from Atlanta: Take I-75 south until Macon. Merge onto I-475 south to bypass Macon. Merge back onto I-75 south. Take exit 146 on the right for Centerville. Turn left onto Watson Blvd/247 Connector. Drive down Watson Blvd all the way to base, which leads to the main gate.

NMC: Macon, 15 miles northwest.

NMI: Fort Benning, 100 miles southwest.

Base Social Media/Facebook: https://www.facebook.com/RobinsPublicAffairs/

Base Social Media/Twitter: https://twitter.com/RobinsAFB_GA

Chapels: C-478-926-2821.

Dental Clinic: C-478-327-8056.

Medical: C-478-327-7850, DSN-312-497-7850.

Veterinary Services: C-478-327-8448.

Beauty/Barber Shop: Barber, C-C-478-923-5421. Stylique, C-478-923-7027. Heritage Club, C-478-923-9593 by appointment only.

Commissary: C-478-222-7618.

Exchange Gas: C-478-923-7292.

Exchange: C-478-923-5536.

Financial Institutions: Robins Federal Credit Union, C-478-923-3773, C-800-241-2405. SunTrust Bank, C-478-329-5710.

Clubs: Heritage Club, C-478-327-7979.

Places to Eat: Afterburner, C-478-222-7827; Base Restaurant, C-478-926-6972; Fairways Grille, C-478-923-1717; On Spot Cafe, C-478-926-5240; Pizza Depot, C-478-926-0188 and Wynn DFAC and Flight Kitchen, C-478-926-6596 are on base. Exchange Food Court offers Charley's, Dunkin Donuts, Popeye's Chicken, Qdoba and Subway. Burger King is also on base. Many restaurants within a short drive.

Bowling: Bowling Center, C-478-926-2112.

Fitness Center: Main FC, C-478-926-2128. FC Annex, C-478-926-2840.

Golf: Pine Oaks Golf Course, C-478-926-4103.

ITT/ITR: C-478-926-2945.

Library: C-478-327-8761/8762.

Military Museum: Museum of Aviation, C-478-926-6870.
Military Museum Website: http://www.museumofaviation.org/
MWR: C-478-926-5491
MWR Website: http://robinsfss.com
MWR Facebook: https://www.facebook.com/78FSS/
Outdoor Recreation: Outdoor Recreation, C-478-926-4001. Offers canoes, fishing boats, kayaks, paddle boards, trailers, camping equipment, lawn and garden tools, party rentals, outdoor sporting equipment, park and pavilion rentals and more.
Swimming: Heritage Seasonal Pool, C-478-926-4001 offers lap swim, open swim and Splash Pad.
Things To Do: Visit Macon, the Cherry Blossom Capital of the World (if seasonal), the Museum of Aviation, Johnston-Felton-Hay House, Cannonball House, the Allman Brothers Band Museum, Ocmulgee National Monument, the Tubman Museum or enjoy Sandy Beach Water Park of the Amerson River Park.
Walking Trails: Robins Fitness Center offers a 5K paved jogging trail with exercise stations.

RV CAMPING & GETAWAYS
Robins AFB FamCamp

Reservation/Contact Number Info: C-478-926-4500, DSN-312-468-4500.
Recreation Security: C-478-926-2187.
RV Website: https://robinsfss.com/outdoor-recreation/
RV Email Address: robinsfamcamp@gmail.com
GPS Coordinates: 32°35'33"N/83°33'59"W. GPS Address: 1201 12th Street, Warner Robins, GA 31098.
Reservations: Reservations may be made up to three months in advance. Non-refundable deposit of $25 required for all reservations. Reservations may be made via email or telephone. Check-in 12:00 hours at FamCamp office, Bldg 1305; check-out 11:00 hours.
Season of Operation: Year-round.

Eligibility: AD, NG, Res, Ret, DoD-Civ, Dep and 100% DAV.
Camper/Trailer Spaces: Camper/Pull-Thru Spaces (27): Hardstand, paved sites; Pull-thru (5), maximum length 40', E(110/220V/30/50A)/S/W hookups, picnic table. Rates: $25 daily; $120 weekly; $360 monthly. Overflow area available with no hookups $10 nightly.
Tent Spaces: Tent Sites (3): No hookups, picnic table. Rates: $6 daily.
Support Facilities: Bathhouse with coin operated washer ($1.75) and dryer ($1.50). Clubhouse with TV, Wi-Fi, refrigerator, microwave, and covered deck. Luna Lake, Waters Edge Pavilion, fire pits, grills, nature trail, and playgrounds.
RV Storage: C-478-926-4001.
Activities: Bicycling, Fishing*, Golfing, Hiking, Hunting*. *Georgia license required for fishing for all guests ages 16 and up. Georgia license, base permit, and completion of Robins AFB hunting safety class required for hunting. For more information about fishing/hunting call: C-478-926-4001.
Credit Cards: Cash, Check, MasterCard and Visa.
Restrictions: Pets allowed on leash. Firearms are prohibited. For fishing and hunting information, C-478-926-4001.
RV Driving Directions/Location: On Base: From Commercial Truck Gate 4: All recreational vehicles must enter this gate. Turn left into gate. Continue straight on Peacekeeper Way to second stop sign and turn right onto Robins Pkwy. Follow to 4th traffic light and turn left onto 10th St. At first light, turn right onto Macon St. At next stop sign, turn left onto 12th St. Follow 12th St past Turner Housing (on right) around Scout Lake. At the end of the lake take the left hand fork through the woods to Luna Lake. At far end of Luna Lake go to the right to the FAMCAMP office (Bldg 984) on left.
Area Description: Nestled among the tall Georgia pines, the FAMCAMP is located in the southeast corner of Robins AFB, adjacent to Lake Luna. Centrally located, only 92 miles from Atlanta.

RV Campground Physical Address: Outdoor Recreation (FSCO), Bldg 984, Robins AFB, GA 31098.

GUAM

Andersen Air Force Base

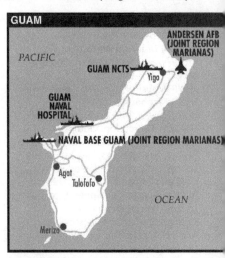

Address: Andersen AFB (Joint Region Marianas), Bonins Boulevard, Bldg 21000, Yigo, Guam 96543.
Information Line: C-671-366-1110, DSN 315-366-1110.
Main Base Police: Emergencies dial 911.
Main Installation Website: http://www.andersen.af.mil
Main Base Location: Andersen Air Force Base (AFB), Guam is located on the north end of Guam, approximately 15 miles from the capital, Agana (or Hagan-ya). Andersen AFB is in the village of Yigo (pronounced "Jeego"). Guam is the most southern island in the Marianas Island chain.
Directions to Main Gate: Andersen AFB is located at the northernmost tip of Guam. The main road on Guam is Marine Corps Drive (Route 1). Upon arrival into the Guam International Airport Authority, exit the parking area and take a left at the traffic light. Proceed on this road until you reach Route 1, then take a right. Stay on this road until reaching the front gate of Andersen AFB.
NMC: Agana, 15 miles southwest.
Base Social Media/Facebook: https://www.facebook.com/36WGPA
Base Social Media/Twitter: https://twitter.com/36WingPA
Chapels: C-671-366-6139, C-671-366-2913 (Non-Duty Hrs).
Dental Clinic: C-671-366-9355.
Medical: C-671-366-9355/2456, DSN-315-366-9355.
Veterinary Services: C-671-366-3205.
Beauty/Barber Shop: C-671-653-8598/8599.
Commissary: C-671-366-5134.
Shoppette, C-671-653-8143/8144.

Exchange Gas: C-671-653-4677.
Exchange: C-671-653-1141/1136 ext.110.
Financial Institutions: Pentagon Federal Credit Union, C-671-653-6555/6490. Bank/Currency Exchange: Hours: 0900-1700, C-671-653-8371, 1.5 miles away.
Clubs: Top of the Rock Collocated Club, C-671-366-6166. Consolidated Club, C-671-366-1201.
Places to Eat: Meridian Cafe, C-671-366-4654. Burger King, C-671-653-0782, Bowling Alley, C-671-366-5117, Subway, C-671-653-2925 and Robin Hood, C-671-653-7149 are within walking distance. AMC Terminal, C-671-366-8283, Magellan Inn, C-671-366-3623 and Palm Tree Golf Course, C-671-362-4654, Cafe Latte', C-671-366-2233, Bamboo Willies, C-671-653-9814 are within driving distance.
Bowling: Gecko Lanes Bowling Center, C-671-366-5085/5117.
Fitness Center: C-671-366-6100/8282.
Golf: Palm Tree Golf Course, C-671-366-4653.
ITT/ITR: C-671-366-2586/1476.
Library: C-671-366-4291/4294.
MWR: C-671-366-4550.
MWR Website: http://www.militarymwrguam.com/
MWR Facebook: https://www.facebook.com/36FSS
MWR Twitter: https://twitter.com/36FSS

Outdoor Recreation: Outdoor Recreation, C-671-366-5197. Offers a skate park, paintball, surfing, dive shop, fishing, snorkeling, hiking trips, various classes and much more.

Swimming: Swimming Pool, C-671-366-6100 offers a diving board, baby pool, slide and aquatic toys. Ocean swimming nearby.

Things To Do: Lots of sunshine, beaches, coral reefs and exciting WWII shipwrecks to explore for scuba enthusiasts. Hikers can enjoy tropical mountains and jungles. The weather is beautiful here year-round. Visit Underwater World Guam, Lost Pond/Shark's Hole, Two Lovers Point, Guam's Coral Reefs, Chamorro Village's Wednesday Night Market and War in the Pacific National Historical Park.

Walking Trails: Hiking is available. Contact Outdoor Recreation for more information.

RV CAMPING & GETAWAYS

Tarague Beach Campsites

Reservation/Contact Number Info: C-671-366-5197/5204. Fax C-671-653-5152.

Recreation Security: C-671-366-2913, DSN-315- 366-2913.

RV Website: http://aafb.militarymwrguam.com/recreation

GPS Coordinates: 13°34'21"N/144°56'33"E.

Reservations: Accepted. Office hours 0900-1800 Mon-Fri, 0900-1200 Sat-Sun.

Season of Operation: Year-round.

Eligibility: AD, NG, Res, Ret and DoD-Civ.

Tent Spaces: Beach camp sites (33), no hookups. Rates: $10 daily.

Support Facilities: Full range of support facilities on base.

Activities: Bicycling, Fishing, Golfing, Hiking, Swimming.

Credit Cards: MasterCard and Visa.

Restrictions: No pets. No firearms allowed. No glass bottles. No entry to water without a lifeguard on duty. Limit ten people per site.

RV Driving Directions/Location: On Base: On the north end of the island, accessible from Marine Drive (GU-1). Sites are located on Tarague Beach.

Area Description: Lots of sunshine, beaches, coral reefs, exciting WWII shipwrecks to explore for scuba enthusiasts. Hikers enjoy tropical mountains and jungles.

RV Campground Physical Address: 36 FSS/FSCO, Unit 14002, APO AP 96543-4003.

Naval Base Guam

Address: Naval Base Guam (Joint Region Marianas), PSC 455, Box 157, FPO AP 96540-1157.

Information Line: C-671-355-1110, DSN-315-355-1110.

Main Base Police: C-671-339-3414.

Main Installation Website: http://www.cnic.navy.mil/regions/jrm/installations/navbase_guam.html

Main Base Location: Guam is a tropical island and is the largest and southernmost island in the Marianas Archipelago, which consists of Guam, Rota, Tinian, Saipan and ten other smaller islands. Guam is about three-quarters of the way from Hawaii to the Philippines and is across the International Dateline from mainland United States.

Directions to Main Gate: From the airport: Exit the airport by taking a left onto Route 10A West. Pass Home Depot located on the right. At the next traffic light take a left onto Route 1/Marine Corps Drive. Follow Route 1 South for approximately fourteen miles from the airport to the Main Gate of Naval Base Guam. Route 1 South runs directly into Naval Base Guam. To obtain a temporary pass the Naval Base Guam Visitor Control Center (VCC) is located about a quarter mile south of the Naval Base Guam's main gate on Marine Corps Drive, just behind the Navy Housing Office Building.

NMC: Agana, 10 miles northeast.

Base Social Media/Facebook: https://www.facebook.com/USNavalBaseGuam

Base Social Media/Twitter:
https://twitter.com/nbguam
Chapels: C-671-339-2126/2334.
Dental Clinic: C-671-339-3175/5146,
Dental Clinic at Naval Hospital: C-671-339-7118.
Medical: Hospital, C-671-344-9340.
Clinic, C-671-339-7118/4224.
Veterinary Services: Veterinary Clinic,
Andersen AFB, C-671-366-3205, Boller
Veterinary Clinic, C-671-333-3225.
Beauty/Barber Shop: C-671-564-3131/3110.
Commissary: C-671-339-5177.
Exchange Gas: C-671-564-1446.
Exchange: C-671-564-4639; Mini-Mart,
C-671-565-3231, C-671-564-3285, C-671-343-5250.
Financial Institutions: Navy Federal
Credit Union, C-1-800-842-6328.
Places to Eat: Exchange Food Court
offers McDonald's, C-671-564-2480,
Pizza Hut, Taco Bell, Del Taco, C-671-564-4124, Domino's Pizza, C-671-564-3030, Popeye's Chicken, C-671-564-4125 and Subway, C-671-564-5500 all
within walking distance. Nap's Alabama
Barbeque, C-671-564-1833, Winchells,
C-671-564-3030, Hot Stuff Pizza/Mean
Gene's Hamburgers, C-671-564-1000
and Molly McGee's Irish Pub, C-671-564-1834 are also available on base.
Hard Rock Cafe, Lonestar Steakhouse,
Outback Steakhouse and TGI Friday's
are within driving distance of the
facility.
Bowling: Orote Point Lanes, C-671-564-1828.
Fitness Center: C-671-333-2049.
Golf: Driving Range, C-671-333-2049.
Palm Tree Golf Course at Andersen AFB,
C-671-366-4653.
ITT/ITR: C-671-989-2301.
Library: C-671-564-1836.
Marina: Sumay Cove Marina, C-671-564-1846.
Military Museum: The Marianas
Military Museum, C-617-339-3319.
Military Museum Website:
http://www.guam.net/pub/milmuseum/visitinfo.htm
MWR: C-671-333-2147, C-671-687-2589.

MWR Website:
http://www.militarymwrguam.com/
MWR Facebook:
https://www.facebook.com/GuamMWR
MWR Twitter:
https://twitter.com/MWRGUAM
Outdoor Recreation: Rec 'N Crew at
Sumay Marina, C-671-564-1826. Rec 'N
Crew at Sumay Marina offers a variety
of rental gear for outdoor sports, water
sports, camping gear, games, party
supplies and much more. They also
offer information regarding trips to local
outdoor attractions. Sumay Cove
Marina, C-671-564-1846 offers boat
rentals, fishing, diving, dolphin watching
tours and more.
Swimming: NBG Swimming Pool, C-671-564-1822, NCTS Swimming Pool, C-671-355-5091, C-671-564-1822, Naval
Hospital Pool, C-671-344-9009, C-671-564-1822 are available on base. Ocean
swimming is also available.
Things To Do: These quarters are within
walking distance of all base support
facilities. Scuba diving and other beach-related activities are popular. Visit
World War II Historical Sites, Latte
Stone Park, Puntan Dos Amantes (Two
Lovers' Point) and the War in the Pacific
National Historic Park & Talofofo Bay.
Walking Trails: Hiking trips are available
through Outdoor Recreation.

RV CAMPING & GETAWAYS
Guam Naval Station Cabanas

Reservation/Contact Number Info: C-671-564-1826.
Recreation Security: C-671-366-2913,
DSN-315-366-2913.
RV Website:
http://nbg.militarymwrguam.com/recreation
GPS Coordinates:
13°26'35"N/144°39'14"E
Reservations: Accepted. Office hours
1100-1800 Mon, Thur, Fri; 0800-1800
Sat, Sun and holidays. Closed Tue, Wed,
Bldg 1986.
Season of Operation: Year-round.
Eligibility: AD, NG, Res, Ret and DoD-Civ.

Yurt, A Frame, Cabin, Apt, Spaces: Cabanas: Gab Gab Beach: $20 per cabana per day; Fantasy Island, $5 per campsite per day; Clipper Landing, $10 per cabana per day; San Luis Beach, No Fee; Polaris Point, No Fee. Camping fees are for a 24-hour period, 0800-2000 hours. Picnic fees are from 0800-2200. Cabana camping allowed with a 2-day Cabana rental only. Patrons are only allowed to use utilities from the site reserved. Strict adherance to rules.

Support Facilities: Beaches, Marina, Outdoor Recreation Rentals.

Activities: Boating, Kayaking, Paddleboards, Picnic Areas, Scuba Diving, Swimming.

Credit Cards: None.

Restrictions: No pets. No firearms. No fishing. No lifeguard on duty at San Luis and Polaris Point Beaches. Bring plastic bags to dispose of trash. No camping near Pool area and west side of Gab Gab beach.

RV Driving Directions/Location: On Base: South on Marine Drive (GU-1) from Agana, through Main Gate, on west side of island. Clearly marked. Cabanas are located near the marina on San Luis Beach, along shoreline at Gab Gab Beach and along shoreline of Polaris Point Beach.

Area Description: Lots of sunshine, beaches, coral reefs, exciting WWII shipwrecks to explore for scuba enthusiasts. Hikers enjoy tropical mountains and jungles.

RV Campground Physical Address: Guam NS MWR, PSC 455, Box 169, FPO AP 96540-1099.

HAWAII

Barbers Point Recreation Area

Address: Barbers Point Beach Cottages, White Plains Beach, Bldg 1797, Barbers Point, HI 96707.

Information Line: C-808-449-7110, DSN-315-449-7110.

Main Base Police: Emergencies dial 911.

Main Installation Website: http://cnic.navy.mil/regions/cnrh/install ations/jb_pearl_harbor_hickam.html

Main Base Location: The Beach Cottage Rental Program includes 24 cottages located at White Plains Beach, Nimitz Beach and Nimitz Cove, on the island of Oahu.

NMC: Pearl Harbor, 15 miles northwest.

NMI: Pearl Harbor-Hickam Joint Base, 21 miles east.

Base Social Media/Facebook: https://www.facebook.com/greatlifeha waii

Base Social Media/Twitter: https://twitter.com/greatlifehawaii

Medical: C-808-433-6661. Emergencies dial 911.

Commissary: Approximately 20 miles east to Pearl Harbor Commissary, C-808-471-8402 ext 155.

Exchange Gas: Approximately 20 miles to Pearl Harbor gas station, C-808-423-3229. Commercial gas station within 4 miles.

Exchange: Approximately 20 miles east at the Pearl Harbor Exchange, C-808-423-3344/3274.

Places to Eat: Galley-Silver Dolphin Bistro, C-808-473-0983, Bowling Alley Food Frame, 19th Puka Snack Bars, Kapolei Shopping Center, Kentucky Fried Chicken and Taco Bell are within driving distance.

Fitness Center: Naval Station Gym, C-808-473-2494/2437.

Golf: Barbers Point Golf Course, C-808-682-2098, Mamala Bay Golf Course, C-808-449-2304, Ke'alohi Golf Course, C-808-448-2318, Navy-Marine Golf Course, C-808-471-0142.

ITT/ITR: C-808-682-2019.

MWR Website: http://www.greatlifehawaii.com/

MWR Facebook: https://www.facebook.com/greatlifeha waii

MWR Twitter: https://twitter.com/greatlifehawaii

Outdoor Recreation: Outdoor Adventure Center, C-808-473-1198. Offers surfboard rentals and lessons, golf, and fishing.

Swimming: Private ocean beaches and seven sparkling pools throughout Joint Base Pearl Harbor-Hickam.

Things To Do: Located on the west coast of Oahu, 13 miles from Pearl Harbor and 29 miles from Honolulu. Have fun surfing or sunning on the beautiful beaches. Nearby attractions include: Pearl Ridge Phase I and II, Ala Moana Park, Wainae Beach parks, Pearl Harbor Park and Ice Palace. Full range of support facilities available on base.

RV CAMPING & GETAWAYS

Barbers Point Recreation Area

Reservation/Contact Number Info: C-808-682-3085, C-1-877-NAVY-BED.
Recreation Security: C-808-684-6222/6223.
RV Website:
http://get.dodlodging.net/propertys/Barbers-Point-Beach-Cottages
Other Info Website:
https://jbphh.greatlifehawaii.com/housing-lodging-/navy-getaways-barbers-pt-beach-cottages
GPS Coordinates:
21°20'31"N/158°4'23"W
Reservations: Reservations accepted one year in advance for AD, Res and Dep; 6 months in advance for Ret, Dod-Civ. Credit card required for deposit. Payment due at check in. Reservations accepted via phone, or online. Two-night minimum stay required. Cancellations require 30-day notice to avoid fee. Office hours 0900-1800 daily; 0900-1500 holidays. Check in 1500 hours at BPT Beach Cottage Reservations; ITT Office, Bldg 1797; check out 1100 hours. Late check out fee applies. Maximum stay 14 days.
Season of Operation: Year-round.
Eligibility: AD, NG, Res, Ret, DoD-Civ.
Yurt, A Frame, Cabin, Apt, Spaces: Cottages (25): Two-bedroom, duplex units (18). Rates: $115-$120 daily. One-bedroom ADA duplex units (2). Rates: $95-$100 daily. Deluxe Cedar Cottages (2). Rates: $140-$155 daily. Three-bedroom, deluxe cottages (2). Rates: $155-$170 daily. DVQ three-bedroom home (1). Rates: $170 daily. All cottages are fully furnished with refrigerator, stove, microwave, coffee maker, TV, cable, dishes, flatware, cooking utensils, cookware and grill. Linens and towels are provided.

Support Facilities: Bathhouse, Beach, Fishing Area, Fishing Pier, Golf Course with Cafe', Mini Mart/Gas Station, Party Patios, Surf Shack.
RV Storage: None.
Activities: Golfing, Surfing, Swimming. Enjoy beautiful beaches, relaxation and tranquility.
Credit Cards: MasterCard and Visa.
Restrictions: No pets allowed. No firearms, smoking or fire pits. Guests must depart by 2200 hours Mon-Fri; 2400 weekends. Quiet hours after 2200.
RV Driving Directions/Location: Off Base. From airport travel westbound on H-1 and take Exit 2, continue in left lane. Turn left on Makakilo Dr and travel straight on Fort Barrett Rd. Turn left on Roosevelt Rd. Turn right on Essex Rd. Check-in at Barbers Point Golf Course Clubhouse.
Area Description: Enjoy a relaxing stay and nourish your mind, body and spirit. Located on the west coast of Oahu, 13 miles from Pearl Harbor and 29 miles from Honolulu. Have fun surfing or sunning on the beautiful beaches. Nearby attractions include: Pearl Ridge Phase I and II, Ala Moana Park, Pililiaau Beach parks, Pearl Harbor Park and Ice Palace (skating). Full range of support facilities available on base.
RV Campground Physical Address: Address: MWR Dept, Attn: ITT@NEX Mall Pearl Harbor, 915 North Rd, Bldg 161, Pearl Harbor, HI 96860-4456

Barking Sands Pacific Missile Range Facility

Address: P.O. Box 128, Kekaha, HI 96752-0128.
Information Line: C-808-335-4234/4235, DSN-315-471-6234/6235.
Main Base Police: Emergencies dial 911.
Main Installation Website:
http://www.cnic.navy.mil/regions/cnrh/installations/pacific_missile_range_facility_barking_sands.html

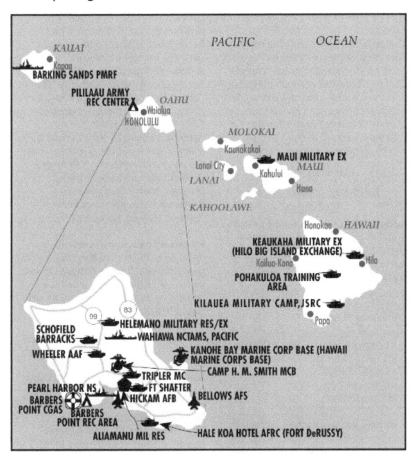

Main Base Location: Pacific Missile Range Facility, Barking Sands, Kauai, is located on the west side of the island of Kauai on the Mana Plain. Barking Sands is a long, narrow site bordered on the west by the Pacific Ocean.

Directions to Main Gate: Located at mile 30 of Hwy 50 (four miles west of Kekaha).

NMC: Lihue, 30 miles east.

NMI: Pearl Harbor-Hickam Joint Base, 103 air miles southeast.

Base Social Media/Facebook: https://www.facebook.com/PacificMissileRangeFacility

Medical: AD Branch Clinic, C-808-335-4203.

Beauty/Barber Shop: C-808-335-4450.

Exchange Gas: C-808-335-4347.

Exchange: C-808-335-4300.

Places to Eat: Shenanigans, C-808-335-4706 is on base. Many restaurants are within a short drive.

Fitness Center: C-808-335-4983.

ITT/ITR: C-808-335-4195.

MWR: C-808-335-7936.

MWR Website: http://pmrf.greatlifehawaii.com/

MWR Facebook: https://www.facebook.com/greatlifehawaii

MWR Twitter: https://twitter.com/greatlifehawaii

Outdoor Recreation: Community Recreation Center, C-808-335-4195. Offers beach chairs, boogie boards, surfboards, snorkel gear, kayaks, camping gear and more.

Swimming: Mana Splash Pool, C-808-335-4391/4379 offers seasonal swim, lap swim, swim lessons and recreational swim.

Things To Do: This is truly the Navy's "Best Kept Secret In Paradise!" Captain Cook's historic landing place, Waimea Canyon, "the Grand Canyon of Hawaii," and a seven-mile strip of white sandy beach are all nearby. MWR on post can provide tickets to island attractions at military prices.

RV CAMPING & GETAWAYS

Barking Sands Beach Cottages

Reservation/Contact Number Info: C-808-335-4752. Fax C-808-335-4769, DSN-315-471-6769.

Recreation Security: C-808-335-4523.

RV Website:
http://get.dodlodging.net/propertys/Navy-Getaways-Barking-Sands

Other Info Website:
https://pmrf.greatlifehawaii.com/lodging-navy-getaways/beach-cottages-at-pmrf

RV Email Address:
pmrfcottages.fct@navy.mil

GPS Coordinates:
21°58'39"N/159°44'57"W

Reservations: Reservations accepted one year in advance for AD; 6 months for all others. Reservations accepted via phone, email, or online. Office hours 0830-1700 Mon-Fri; 1000-1400 Sat, Sun and holidays. After hours arrivals must take Cottage Packet to Housing Gate. Contact office for more information. Check-in 1400 hours at OAC, Bldg 1293. Minimum 2-night stay; maximum 14-day stay.

Season of Operation: Year-round.

Eligibility: AD, Ret, DoD-Civ, MWR, NEX or NAF employees and contractors working on board the installation with approval from CO.

Yurt, A Frame, Cabin, Apt, Spaces: Beach Cottages (24): Beachfront (12), Oceanview (12), Standard and deluxe cottages; (1) VIP. Fully furnished with refrigerator, stove, washer, dryer, microwave, coffee maker, TV, DVD/VCR, basic cable, telephone, internet access, dishes, flatware, cooking utensils, cookware and BBQ grill. Linen and towels provided. Bedrooms with A/C. Rates: From $80 daily depending on rank. Call for current rates.

Support Facilities: All Hands Club, Beach, Driving Range, Exchange, Fitness Center, Gas, Grills, Outdoor Adventure Center, Rec Equipment, Shoppette, Skate Park, Sports Fields, Theater.

Activities: Fishing, Golfing, Kayaking, Swimming, Tennis. Enjoy leisure beach activities and the scenic, lush foliage.

Credit Cards: American Express, Discover, MasterCard and Visa.

Restrictions: No pets allowed. No firearms allowed. No housekeeping service.

RV Driving Directions/Location: On Base. From the Main Gate: Take the first right onto Nohili Road. Cottages ahead on the left. If after hours, continue straight on Tartar to Housing Gate once through Main Gate.

Area Description: Located on the picturesque Garden Island of Kauai near Captain Cook's Landing Place. Although the island is small, there are many scenic areas to explore. Waimea Canyon (the Grand Canyon of Hawaii) is 12 miles from the base. Limited support facilities available on base.

RV Campground Physical Address: Beach Cottages Reservations, Bldg 1293, Nohili Road, Barking Sands, HI 96752.

Bellows Air Force Station

Address: Bellows Air Force Station, 220 Tinker Road, Waimanalo, HI 96795.

Information Line: C-808-259-8080.

Main Base Police: C-808-448-4916/4200.

Main Installation Website:
https://www.bellowsafs.com/

Main Base Location: Bellows AFS is located on the northern portion of Waimanalo Bay and includes a stretch of white sandy beach that curves around the bay.

Directions to Main Gate: From the airport: Take H-1 West Waianae Lane. Take exit 13B/H-3 Kaneohe/Honolulu to get onto H-3. Take exit

11/Kamehameha Hwy/Kaneohe and turn right to get onto Kamehameha Hwy. Turn left onto Kalaniana'ole Hwy to go toward Kailua/Waimanalo. At the third light, next to Castle Medical Center, turn right. Remain on Kalaniana'ole Hwy Drive through the town of Waimanalo. Bellows AFS main gate will be on the left.
NMC: Kaneohe, nine miles northwest.
NMI: Pearl Harbor-Hickam Joint Base, 15.5 miles west.
Base Social Media/Facebook:
https://www.facebook.com/bellowsafs/
Base Social Media/Twitter:
https://twitter.com/bellowsafs
Exchange Gas: C-808-853-4699.
Exchange: C-808-853-4699.
Clubs: Braddah's Brewhouse, C-808-259-4136/4137.
Places to Eat: Braddah's Brewhouse, C-808-259-4136/4137, Turtle Cove Retail Store, and Subway, C-808-853-4672 are on base. Exchange Services offers snacks, C-808-853-4699.
Golf: Driving Range and Miniature Golf, C-808-259-4136/4137.
ITT/ITR: C-808-259-4136/4137.
MWR Website:
http://www.bellowsafs.com
MWR Facebook:
https://www.facebook.com/bellowsafs/
MWR Twitter:
https://twitter.com/bellowsafs
Outdoor Recreation: Outdoor Recreation Services, C-808-259-4136/4137. Offers equipment rentals, paintball, biking, body boarding, kayaking, snorkeling and more.
Swimming: Ocean swimming is available.
Things To Do: Located on Oahu's north west coast, about 16 miles from downtown Waikiki, these cottages offer a beautiful and relaxing way to "get away from it all." Turquoise waters and gorgeous beaches await your arrival to this beachfront recreation center.
Walking Trails: A 2.8 mile nature trail walk and loop trail on base.

RV CAMPING & GETAWAYS
Bellows Recreation Area
Reservation/Contact Number Info: C-808-259-8080.
Recreation Security: C-808-259-4200.
RV Website:
http://www.bellowsafs.com/
GPS Coordinates:
21°21'8"N/157°42'28"W
Reservations: Reservations accepted and encouraged. Online reservations accepted 13 months in advance; phone reservations accepted one year in advance. Applicable to all lodging and campsites. Office hours 0630-1830 Mon-Fri. Peak Summer Season: Cabins and Condos require 2-night minimum; 14-day maximum not to exceed 21 days within 60-day period. Off Season allows for 21-day stay. Camping Facilities: No minimum stay; maximum stay 21-day stay. All reservations require a minimum one-night deposit. Reservations for extended stays of 15-21 nights require a 25% non-refundable deposit. Failure to provide proper payment within ten days of initial booking will result in cancellation. Cancellations made 14 days prior to the arrival date will receive a refund of deposit (excluding extended stays). Check-in 1500 hours, check-out 1100 hours.
Season of Operation: Year-round.
Eligibility: AD, NG, Res, Ret and DoD-Civ.
Camper/Trailer Spaces: RV Sites (2): No hookups, picnic table, charcoal grill. Rates: $22 daily.
Tent Spaces: Family Campsites (55), No hookups, bathhouses with hot showers, picnic table, charcoal grills. Three site locations: Menhune, Ocean are Oceanside; Lettered is Mountainside. No campfires, generators. Two tent max, 10 person max. Rates: $22 daily. Group campsites available (5): Sink, fire pit, picnic tables. Max 75 people; 15 tents per site. Rates: $110 daily.
Yurt, A Frame, Cabin, Apt, Spaces: Beach Side Cabins (109): Sleeps 4 adults, fully equipped kitchen,

dining/living area, charcoal grill, picnic table, Wi-Fi, TV. DVD player. Cribs available; extra linens and guests incur fee. ADA cabins available. Guests are allowed to pitch one canopy per cabin (15'x15' maximum). Rates: $105 daily. Nā Mokulua Condos (8): Two-bedroom beach side ocean views, sleeps 4 adults. Offers breakfast nook, fully equipped kitchen, dining/living area, A/C, Wi-Fi, TV/DVD, outside patio area. Cribs available; extra linens and guests incur fee. ADA units are available. Rates: $132 daily. Cedar Camper Cabins (10): No electricity, kitchen or bathrooms; bathhouse offers hot showers. Cabins offer one double size bed and one twin size bunk bed, charcoal grill, picnic tables. Linens for fee. Rates: $33 daily.

Support Facilities: Basketball Courts, Bathhouses, Beach, Camping Equipment, Gas, Golf Driving Range, Laundry, Mini Golf, Picnic Area, Pub, Shoppette, Snack Bar, Tennis Courts, Volleyball Courts.

Activities: Biking, Body Boarding, Fishing*, History Tours, Kayaking, Lei Making Classes, Loop Trail, Massage, Paintball, Snorkeling, Swimming. *State fishing permits required.

Credit Cards: MasterCard and Visa.

Restrictions: No pets allowed. No firearms or metal detectors allowed. Hiking and Hunting are prohibited on Bellows AFS. Quiet hours 2200-0800. Guest pass required for all visitors.

RV Driving Directions/Location: On Base. From the Main Gate: Follow directions to Reservations, Bldg 220, on the right-hand side.

Area Description: An oceanfront recreation facility on the southeast coast of the Island of Oahu, 16.5 miles from the Honolulu business district. One of the oldest places of habitation in the Hawaiian Islands. Three miles of beautiful beachfront. Some support facilities available on base; full range at Hawaii MCB (formerly Kaneohe Bay), 10 miles northwest.

RV Campground Physical Address: Bellows Reservation Office, 220 Tinker Rd, Waimanalo, HI 96795-1010.

Kaneohe Bay Marine Corps Base

Address: D Street & Mokapu Road, Building 216, Box 63073, MCBH Kaneohe Bay, HI 96863.

Information Line: C-808-449-7110.

Main Base Police: C-808-257-9111.

Main Installation Website: http://www.mcbhawaii.marines.mil/

Main Base Location: Marine Corps Base Hawaii (MCBH) Kaneohe Bay is fondly referred to as K-Bay. It's located on the island of Oahu's Windward side on Mokapu Peninsula and is 20 miles northeast of the Honolulu International Airport.

Directions to Main Gate: From I-H1: Exit to I-H3 north to Main Gate of Kaneohe Bay MCB. From Honolulu IAP: Take HI-1 west to H-3 interchange. Take HI-3 east to Kaneohe and continue to main gate, located off Mokapu Blvd and Kaneohe Bay.

NMC: Honolulu, 14 miles southwest.

NMI: Bellows AFS, 18 miles southeast.

Base Social Media/Facebook: https://www.facebook.com/MarineCorpsBaseHawaii

Base Social Media/Twitter: https://twitter.com/MCBHawaii

Chapels: C-808-257-3552/5138.

Dental Clinic: C-808-457-3100.

Medical: Appointment Line, C-808-473-0247. Naval Clinic at K-Bay, C-808-257-3365. Tripler Army Medical Center, C-808-433-6661

Veterinary Services: C-808-257-3643.

Beauty/Barber Shop: Mokapu Mall, C-808-254-6585/6588.

Commissary: C-808-257-1465.

Exchange Gas: C-808-254-2775.

Exchange: C-808-254-3890. Annex, C-808-254-7616.

Financial Institutions: Navy Federal Credit Union, C-866-605-1271. Bank of Hawaii, C-808-254-1551. Windward Community Federal Credit Union, C-808-254-3566. Bank/Currency Exchange: Hours: 0900-1500 Mon-Thu, 0900-1600 Fri, C-808-254-1551, 0.5 mile away.

Clubs: The Officers' Club, C-808-254-7650. SNCO Club, C-808-254-5592.

Kahuna's Sports Bar & Grill, C-808-254-7660/7661.

Places to Eat: Sam Adams Sports Grill, C-808-254-5592; Flying Leatherneck Inn, C-808-254-5828; Strikers Grill, C-808-254-7663; Daily Grind, C-808-254-9500 and the Lava Java Coffee Cart are on base. Mokapu Mall offers Chowmein Express, Ninja Sushi, Authentic Parma Italian, Subway, Starbucks, Taco Bell and Pizz Hut Express. McDonald's, Papa John's and K-Bay Garden are on base. Many restaurants within a short drive.

Bowling: K-Bay Lanes, C-808-254-7693.

Fitness Center: K-Bay, C-808-254-7597. HITT Center, C-808-254-7594. Kulia, C-808-257-3822.

Golf: Kaneohe Klipper Golf Course, C-808-254-1745.

ITT/ITR: Mokapu Mall, C-808-254-7563/7562.

Library: C-808-254-7624.

Marina: Kaneohe Bay Marina, C-808-254-7666/7667.

MWR: C-808-254-7679.

MWR Website: http://mccshawaii.com/

MWR Facebook: https://www.facebook.com/mccshawaii

MWR Twitter: https://twitter.com/mccshawaii

Outdoor Recreation: Outdoor Recreation Services, C-808-254-7666. Offers sailing classes, water sports equipment, party rentals, marina and much more.

Swimming: K-Bay Pool, C-808-254-7655 offers lap and recreational swim. Hilltop Officers' Pool, C-808-254-7655 offers lap and open swim. Manana Pool, C-808-474-6207, C-808-254-7655 offers lap and open swim.

Things To Do: MCB's full support facilities are available to guests of this resort. Relaxing on the beaches or boating off the coast are some of the activities to enjoy. Visit The Byodo-In Temple, Mokoli'i Island (Chinaman's Hat), Ho'omaluhia Botanical Garden, Kualoa Regional Park or the Stairway To Heaven known as Haiku Stairs. Tiki Island on base offers miniature golf, batting cages, and bumper boats. Skate Park on base.

RV CAMPING & GETAWAYS

Kaneohe Bay Beach Cottages & Cabanas – Hale Koa Campground

Reservation/Contact Number

Info: Cottages and Cabanas, C-808-254-2806. Campground, C-808-254-7666.

Recreation Security: C-808-257-2123.

RV Website: http://mccshawaii.com/cottages/

Other Info Website: http://mccshawaii.com/cabanas/

RV Email Address: http://mccshawaii.com/marina/

GPS Coordinates: 21°27'39"N/157°45'53"W

Reservations: Accepted. Cabanas and Cottages: AD Marines stationed at K-Bay and Camp Smith up to four months in advance; All other Marines three months in advance; All other AD, Res, Ret two months in advance; DoD-Civ AD/Ret one month in advance. Minimum 3-night stay over weekends; 4-night stay over holiday weekends. One night stay deposit required at time of reservation. Cancellations require 48 hours or forfeit deposit. Check in for all lodging facilities in the Inns of the Corps lobby located by the front gate entrance open 24 hours daily. Check-in 1500, check-out 1100. Maximum stay for Cabanas 14 days; 7-days for cottages. Hale Koa Campground: Reservations accepted 60 days in advance. Office Summer hours 0800-1700 Mon-Fri; 0800-1900 Sat-Sun and holidays. Winter hours 0800-1700 daily. Check-in 1300, check-out 1300 at OREC Bldg 6800. Maximum stay 14 days.

Season of Operation: Year-round.

Eligibility: AD, NG, Res, Ret and DoD-Civ.

Tent Spaces: Campsites (17): Beachfront (11), Roadside (6). No more than ten people or two tents per site. Rates: $15 daily.

Yurt, A Frame, Cabin, Apt, Spaces: Cottages (13), Two-bedrooms with full kitchen, living and dining areas, cable TV, complimentary Wi-Fi, ceiling fans, lanai, BBQ grill and daily housekeeping services offered. Rates: $155 daily; Seabee Beach Cottages $160 daily. Cabanas (29): Bedroom studios with one king or two queen size beds, a sitting area with a small table and chairs, cable TV, Wi-Fi, washing sink, mini refrigerator, charcoal grills, A/C. The on-site community men's and women's restrooms have bathrooms, shower stalls, changing areas with benches, and are secured through guest room key card. Housekeeping services daily. Rates: $78 daily.

Support Facilities: Auto Craft Shop, Beach, Boat Launch, Boat Rental/Storage, Chapel, Commissary, Convenience Store, Exchange, Fire Rings, Fishing Pier, Fitness Center, Gas, Golf, Grills, Ice, Laundry, Marina, Pavilion (For a Fee), Picnic Area, Playground, Pool, Rec Equipment, Shoppette, Showers, Snack Bar, Sports Fields, Stables, Telephones, Tennis Courts.

RV Storage: None.

Activities: Boating, Fishing, Golfing, Scuba Diving, Swimming, Tennis. OREC Equipment Rentals for boating, water activity rentals, pavilion and park rental. Beautiful beaches for leisure activities.

Credit Cards: American Express, Discover, MasterCard and Visa.

Restrictions: No pets allowed. No ground fires. No tents on beach. Quiet hours 2300-0800.

RV Driving Directions/Location: On Base. From H-1 east or west: Exit to H-3 north to the Main Gate of Kaneohe MCAS. The temporary lodging facility (TLF) office is on the right at first traffic light. Clearly marked off Mokapu Blvd and Kaneohe Bay Drive. Campground located off Mokapu Blvd. Drive across runway and make first left, crossing the old abandoned Runway called "West Field". Make a hard right onto Perimeter Road. Drive .25 miles and take the left-hand turn at the signs for Hale Koa Recreation Area.

Area Description: Located in a secluded area overlooking beautiful Kaneohe Bay. Cottages are across the airstrip along the coastline, near Pyramid Rock. Campsites and Cabanas are near the northern area of the base in a sheltered cove with an excellent view. Full range of support facilities on base.

RV Campground Physical Address: Cottages and Cabanas: Inns of the Corp, Kaneohe Bay, Bldg 6534 MCB Hawaii, Kaneohe Bay, HI 96863. Campground: MCCS Marina, Bldg 6800, Kaneohe Bay MCBH, HI 96863-3037.

Kilauea Military Camp – Joint Services Recreation

Address: KMC at Kilauea Volcano, Attn: Reservations, P.O. Box 48, 99-252 Crater Rim Drive, Hawaii Volcanoes National Park, 96718-0048.

Information Line: C-808-967-8333/7315.

Main Base Police: Fire and paramedic services are available on site.

Main Installation Website: http://kilaueamilitarycamp.com/

Main Base Location: On the island of Hawaii, 216 air miles southeast of Honolulu, 32 miles southwest off HI-11 from Hilo International Airport.

Directions to Main Gate: From Hilo Airport: Turn left onto Hwy 11 and travel south for about 28 miles until reaching the main entrance of Hawaii Volcanoes National Park, mile marker 28. It will take about 1 hour. From Kona International Airport: Take Hwy 19 south which will become Hwy 11 south until reaching the main entrance of Hawaii Volcanoes National Park. It is about 105 miles away and it will take about 3 hours. Enter the park to get to KMC. Drive 1 mile past the Kilauea Visitor Center and steam vents. On the right-hand side, there will be a grassy front lawn and row of cottages. In the center of the row is the Headquarters/Front Desk building for check-ins.

NMC: Hilo, 32 miles northeast.

NMI: Pearl Harbor-Hickam Joint Base, 214 air miles northwest.

Base Social Media/Facebook: https://www.facebook.com/pages/Kilauea-Military-Camp/100485131338

Base Social Media/Twitter:
https://twitter.com/kmcvolcano
Chapels: Chapel is available.
Medical: Paramedic services are available, C-808-967-8333/7315, Direct Dial from Oahu, C-438-6707 for more information.
Commissary: Mini mart on site.
Exchange Gas: C-808-967-7315.
Exchange: C-808-967-8364/8362.
Places to Eat: KMC Crater Rim Cafe, Java Cafe, and 10-Pin Grill Snack Bar are within walking distance. Volcano House, C-808-967-7321 and Volcano Golf & Country Club Restaurant, C-808-967-8228 are also within walking distance. Kilauea Lodge, C-808-967-7366, Lava Rock Cafe, C-808-967-8526, Kiawe Kitchen, C-808-967-7711 and Thai, C-808-967-7969 are within driving distance.
Bowling: Bowling Center is on site.
Fitness Center: Exercise room available at location.
Golf: Discounted golf packages are available at the Recreation Lodge.
ITT/ITR: C-808-967-8333.
MWR Website:
http://kilaueamilitarycamp.com/accommodations/
MWR Facebook:
https://www.facebook.com/pages/Kilauea-Military-Camp/100485131338
MWR Twitter:
https://twitter.com/kmcvolcano
Outdoor Recreation: Playground, tennis, basketball, bowling, island tours, helicopter tours and more, including a discounted 18-hole golf at a nearby course. Scenic waterfalls, tropical botanical gardens, black sand beaches and hot springs can be enjoyed. Local activities include hiking, mountain biking and visiting the beach.
Swimming: Beach swimming is available.
Things To Do: Located on the rim of the active Kilauea Crater at 4,000 feet in Hawaii Volcanoes National Park, the state's number one visitor attraction. These quiet guest cottages create a perfect place to relax, unwind and have fun. Endless lava fields and lush rainforests create a tranquil setting with numerous hiking trails and rare wildlife. Up close views of active lava flows when conditions permit, and great stargazing.
Walking Trails: Hiking is available.

RV CAMPING & GETAWAYS
Kilauea Military Camp

Reservation/Contact Number Info: C-808-967-8333. Fax C-808-967-8343.
Recreation Security: Park Dispatch, C-808-985-6170. Emergencies dial 911.
RV Website:
http://kilaueamilitarycamp.com/accommodations/
RV Email Address: reservations@kmc-volcano.com
GPS Coordinates:
19°26′5″N/155°16′29″W
Reservations: Reservations required and accepted up to a year in advance. Reservations can be made by phone or the on-line system 24 hours daily. One night's stay deposit required within 15 days of booking. Cancellations must be made 30 days prior to reservation date. Please contact reservations for stays longer than 14 days. Peak periods reserved for AD, Ret. Check-in 1500 hours, check-out 1100 hours.
Season of Operation: Year-round.
Eligibility: AD/Ret Armed Forces, NG, Res, CG-Civ, DoD Civ, (AD & Ret), Dep, US Public Health Service, NOAA, and sponsored guest. Other personnel on official business with DoD may also be eligible.
Yurt, A Frame, Cabin, Apt, Spaces: Cottages and Apartments: One, two and three bedrooms (90). All with private bath and fireplaces. Handicap accessible units are available. Coffee maker, CATV, flashlights, hair dryer, iron & ironing board, microwave, mini-refrigerator, umbrella. Linens provided for all cottages and apartment. Rates: One-bedroom apt: $72-$160, w/jetted tub: $86-$180. One-bedroom cottage: $80-$170, w/jetted tub: $95-$190. Two-bedroom cottage: $107-$210, w/kitchen: $125-$235, w/kitchen & jetted tub: $138-$250. Three-bedroom apt: $130-$250. Three bedroom cottage w/kitchen & jetted tub: $168-$295. Six

bedroom cottage (1): 3 baths, kitchen and full side Jacuzzi hot tub in adjacent bldg. Fully furnished. Rates: $468-$720 daily. House (1): Seven bedrooms, fully furnished. Rates: $428-$695 daily. Eisenhower House (1): Rank restricted. Rates: $259-$350 daily. All rates based on rank. Dormitory: Common baths and showers. Rates: $16-$24 per person per night. Wi-Fi available.

Support Facilities: Bowling Lanes, Café, Chapel, Coffee Bar Kiosk, Conference and Catering Services, Fitness Center, Gas Station, Grill/Picnic Areas, General Store, Hilo Airport Shuttle, Lounge, Playground, Recreation Lodge, Snack Bar, Theater, Tour/Charter Service.

RV Storage: None.

Activities: Baseball, Basketball, Bicycling, Bowling, Golf, Helicopter Tours, Island Tours, Hiking, Hula Show, Live Bands and Tennis.

Credit Cards: American Express, MasterCard and Visa.

Restrictions: Pets, firearms, and fireworks are prohibited.

RV Driving Directions/Location: On Base. Off HI-11 approximately one mile inside Hawaii Volcanoes National Park, southwest of Hilo on island of Hawaii. Honolulu is 216 air miles northwest. Scheduled shuttle from Hilo airport to Kilauea Military Camp (KMC), 48-hour advance reservations required.

Area Description: Kilauea Military Camp (KMC) proudly serving America's Military since 1916, is located in Hawaii's number one visitor attraction, Hawaii Volcanoes National Park. The surrounding landscape ranges from lush tropical rainforests to stark lava fields. At 4,000 feet above sea level, the temperatures are cooler than typical Hawaiian weather and layered dressing recommended.

RV Campground Physical Address: Kilauea Military Camp, Attn: Reservations, P.O. Box 48, 99-252 Crater Rim Drive, Hawaii National Park, HI 96718-0048.

Pililaau Army Recreation Center

Address: Pililaau Army Recreation Center, Bldg 4065, 85-010 Army Street, Wai'anae, HI 96792.

Information Line: C-808-449-7110, DSN-315-449-7110.

Main Base Police: Emergencies dial 911.

Main Installation Website: http://www.garrison.hawaii.army.mil/

Main Base Location: Pililaau Army Recreation Center (PARC) located on the Pokai Bay and is one of the best beach facilities on the island. It captures the essence of "old Hawaii" with beachfront property surrounded by rustic farms and homes.

NMC: Honolulu, 35 miles southeast.

NMI: Schofield Barracks, 20 miles northeast.

Chapels: C-808-655-9307.

Commissary: Approximately 25 miles away at Schofield Barracks, C-808-655-6252.

Exchange Gas: Approximately 25 miles to Schofield Barracks gas station, C-808-624-3316. Commercial gas station within 1 mile.

Exchange: Approximately 25 miles away at Schofield Barracks, C-808-622-1773.

Clubs: All Ranks Club.

Places to Eat: The Beach House by 604 is within walking distance. Many restaurants within a short drive.

Fitness Center: Martinez Physical Fitness, C-808-655-0900.

Golf: Leilehua Golf Course, C-808-655-4653.

ITT/ITR: Ticket Office, C-808-655-9971. Travel Office, C-808-655-6055.

MWR: C-808-655-0037.

MWR Website: http://www.himwr.com/

MWR Facebook: https://www.facebook.com/fmwr.hawaii

MWR Twitter: https://twitter.com/FMWRArmyHawaii

Outdoor Recreation Unique: Outdoor Recreation, C-808-655-0143.

Outdoor Recreation Text: Offers surfing, hiking, mountain biking, stand-up paddleboard instruction, kayaking, Hawaiian canoeing, paintball, snorkeling, SCUBA instruction and tours, fishing and more.

Swimming Pools Name, Phone, and Text: Beach swimming is available. Swimming pools are available at Schofield Barracks.

Things To Do: Located on the western side of Oahu, this facility has some of the best beaches in Hawaii. Visitors can enjoy snorkeling, surfing and swimming.

Walking Trails: Beach walking is available.

RV CAMPING & GETAWAYS

Pililaau Recreation Center

Reservation/Contact Number Info: C-808-696-4158 from Oahu, C-800-333-4158 from mainland. Fax C-808-696-7841.

Recreation Security: C-808-696-2811/6633.

RV Website: https://hawaii.armymwr.com/programs/pillar-army-recreation-center-parc

RV Email Address: parcreservations@kmc-volcano.com

GPS Coordinates: 21°20'17"N/158°10'51"W

Reservations: Reservations required and accepted up to one year in advance for all eligible military categories and DoD-Civ. Office hours 0700-2000 daily. Reservations accepted by phone or mail 0800-1700 daily. One night's stay deposit required. Check-in 1630-1930 hours, check-out 1200 hours. Notify front desk of late check in for instruction. Late check out fee applicable. Maximum 21-day stay.

Season of Operation: Year-round.

Eligibility: AD, NG, Res, Ret, DoD-Civ and Fed Emp.

Yurt, A Frame, Cabin, Apt, Spaces: Cabins: Beachfront (31, 2 DV), A/C, ceiling fans, CATV, full kitchen, cooking utensils, dishware, linens, grill, housekeeping, sundeck. Rates: Studios $77-$87; Makai Hale One Bedroom $72-$82; Two-bedroom $102-$112; Makai Hale Two Bedroom $89-$99; Three-bedroom $117-$127; Sergeants Majors Hale E9+ $134; Waianae Hale O6+ $159. All rates rank dependent. Additional amenity fees may apply. Wi-Fi service at Sunset Cafe.

Support Facilities: Beach, Beach Equipment Rental, Club (All Ranks), First Aid Station, Golf, Grills, Laundry, Package Store, Pavilions (For a Fee), Picnic Areas, Rec Equipment, Restrooms, Showers, Snack Bar.

RV Storage: None.

Activities: Kayaking, Snorkeling, Surfing, Swimming. Outdoor sports facilities are a five-minute walk from camp.

Credit Cards: American Express, Discover, MasterCard and Visa.

Restrictions: No pets allowed. No firearms or fireworks. One room reservation per ID holder.

RV Driving Directions/Location: Off Base. On west coast of Oahu. Take H-1 west to HI-93/Farrington Highway and travel northwest for approximately 10.5 miles. Turn left on Army Street (the third left after the Waianae Police Station) and proceed all the way to the security gate; front office is to the right of the gate. From Honolulu International Airport: Start out going north on Rodgers Blvd toward N Nimitz Hwy. Turn left onto N Nimitz Hwy/HI-92 W. Take the HI-92 W/HI-99 W/I-H1 W ramp. Merge onto I-H1 W. I-H1 W becomes HI-93 W. Turn left onto Army Street, which is just past Guard Street. The facility is ahead.

Area Description: Located along beach of Pokai Bay in once quiet fishing and plantation village. One of the favorite swimming, surfing and fishing spots on Oahu. The facility is one of the finest on the island. Full range of support facilities at Schofield Barracks.

RV Campground Physical Address: Address: Pililaau Army Recreation Center, Bldg 4070, 85-010 Army Street, Waianae, HI 96792.

IDAHO

Boise Air Terminal – Gowen Field ANG

Address: 4040 W Guard Street, Boise ID 83705.
Main Base Police: Emergencies dial 911.
Main Installation Website:
http://www.124thfighterwing.ang.af.mil/
Main Base Location: The Gowen Field complex is adjacent to the Boise International Airport and is located on 576 acres, with the Gowen Field Training.
Directions to Main Gate: From I-84 east or west: Take Orchard Street exit (exit 52 south). Turn left and remain on Gowen Road as it goes behind the airport. Watch for Gowen Field sign near tanks. Turn left into Main Gate.
NMC: Boise, five miles north.
NMI: Mountain Home AFB, 35 miles southeast.
Base Social Media/Facebook:
https://www.facebook.com/124FW/
Base Social Media/Twitter:
https://twitter.com/124FighterWing
Chapels: C-208-422-5394.
Medical: Clinic, C-208-422-5369.
Places to Eat: Dining Facility on base. Many restaurants within a short drive.
Fitness Center: Fitness Center on base.
Military Museum: Idaho Military History Museum, C-208-272-4841.
Military Museum Website:
https://twitter.com/124FighterWing
Things To Do: Visit the Old Idaho Penitentiary Museum and State Historical Museum or enjoy one of the ski areas nearby.

RV CAMPING & GETAWAYS

Gowen Field RV Park

Reservation/Contact Number Info: C-208-272-4451. DSN-312-422-4451.
Recreation Security: C-208-272-3683, DSN-312-422-3683.
RV Website:
https://www.facebook.com/Gowen-Field-Billeting-1818594495021724/

GPS Coordinates:
43°33'33"N/116°14'0"W or 4484 W Ellsworth St. Bldg. 720 Boise, ID 83705.
Reservations: Accepted 30 days in advance. Office hours 0800-1630 Mon-Fri. Check in at the Gowen Field Billeting Office, Bldg 720. Check-out 1200 hours.
Season of Operation: Year-round.
Eligibility: AD, NG, Res and Ret.
Camper/Trailer Spaces: Camper Spaces: Concrete (7), Back-in, Maximum 45' in length, 35' back-in pad, plenty of room for overhang, E(110/220V/20/50A)/S/W hookups. Rates: $15 daily; Winter: $12 daily.
Support Facilities: Exchange, Fitness Center, MWR Activities Center Bldg 710, Coffee Shop, Grill and Club.
RV Storage: C-208-272-4451.
Activities: Fishing*, Hunting*, Skiing, Water Sports, hiking, bicycling and golfing. *License required.
Credit Cards: American Express, MasterCard and Visa.
Restrictions: Pets allowed.
RV Driving Directions/Location: On Base: From the West: Take Exit 52 off of I 84 then turn right on South Orchard (which will turn into Gowen Rd.) Continue down Gowen Rd. Turn left to enter the main gate on Farman Street. Contractor's gate available too. Continue down Gowen Rd and turn left on Zeppelin Street. From the East: Take exit 57 and turn left onto Gowen Rd. Continue down Gowen Road approximately three miles. Turn right onto Zeppelin Street to access contractor's gate or continue down Gowen Road and turn right onto General Manning Ave to access the main gate.
Area Description: Located at the edge of the high desert, near Treasure Valley, within an hour of the Snake River.
RV Campground Physical Address: Gowen Field RV Park, 4484 West Ellsworth, Bldg 720, Boise, ID 83705-8033.

Mountain Home Air Force Base

Address: 575 Gunfighter Avenue, Mountain Home AFB, ID 83648-5237.

Information Line: C-208-828-2111.
Main Base Police: C-208-828-2256.
Emergencies dial 911.
Main Installation Website:
http://www.mountainhome.af.mil/
Main Base Location: Located on a high-desert plateau between two large mountain ranges in southwestern Idaho.
Directions to Main Gate: From Boise: Take I-84 east toward Mountain Home. Take exit 90 for I-84 toward State Hwy 51/State Hwy 67/Mountain Home/Bruneau. Merge onto I-84 BUS E/Old US 30/Sunset Strip. Continue to follow I-84 BUS E/Old US 30 E. Continue onto W 6th St, which turns into Airbase Rd after the overpass. This leads directly to the base gate. From the Twin Falls and East: Take I-84 west toward Mountain Home. Take exit 95 and go left at the end of the exit. You will be on American Legion Blvd. Follow American Legion Blvd until it ends. Go left onto I-84 BUS E/Old US 30. Continue onto W 6th St, which turns into Airbase Rd after the overpass. This leads directly to the base gate.
NMC: Boise, 50 miles northwest.
NMI: Boise ANG/Gowen Field, 35 miles northwest.
Base Social Media/Facebook:
https://www.facebook.com/366FW/
Base Social Media/Twitter:
https://twitter.com/GunfighterSnow
Chapels: Chaplain, C-208-828-6417.
Dental Clinic: C-208-828-7300.
Medical: C-208-828-7900, DSN-312-728-7900.
Veterinary Services: C-208-828-2221.
Beauty/Barber Shop: Barber Shop, C-208-832-7191; Stylique, C-208-832-4090.
Commissary: C-208-828-2163.
Exchange Gas: C-208-832-4660.
Exchange: C-208-832-4353/4613.
Financial Institutions: Pioneer Federal Credit Union, C-208-832-4675.
Clubs: Gunfighters Club, C-208-828-2105.
Places to Eat: Hackers Bistro, C-208-828-6151; Jet Stream Java, C-208-828-5674; Strikers Grill, C-208-828-2567; Tin Star Cafe, C-208-828-2105 and Wagon Wheel DFAC, C-208-828-6420 are on base. Exchange Food Court offers Popeye's Chicken and Taco Bell. Burger King, Pizza Hut and Subway are also on base. Several restaurants within a short drive.
Fitness Center: Mountain Home FC and Annex, C-208-828-2381.
Golf: Silver Sage Golf Course, C-208-828-6151.
ITT/ITR: C-208-828-6229 located at the Community Skills Center.
Library: C-208-828-2326.
Marina: Strike Marina, C-208-834-2723.
MWR: C-208-828-4296.
MWR Website:
http://www.mhafbfun.com/
MWR Facebook:
https://www.facebook.com/366FSS
MWR Twitter:
https://twitter.com/366fss
Outdoor Recreation: Outdoor Recreation Services, C-208-828-6333. Offers trips, trap and skeet, archery, mini golf, camping equipment, utility trailers, canoes, kayaks, stand up paddle boards, fishing boats, ski boat rentals, jet skis, inflatables, party supplies, winter sports gear and more.
Swimming: Indoor Pool, C-208-828-6620 offers open swim, lap swim, swim lessons and family fun nights.
Things To Do: Idaho is abundant with outdoor activity. There are numerous geothermal hot springs in Idaho. White water rafting, hiking, golf and skiing are a few activities available. The Snake River and its gorges, the Oregon Trail and the Bruneau Dunes are a short drive. Boise is 45 miles away with all the excitement a city has to offer.
Walking Trails: Indoor and outdoor running tracks on base.

RV CAMPING & GETAWAYS

Mountain Home AFB FamCamp

Reservation/Contact Number Info: C-208-828-6333, DSN-312-728-6333. Fax C-208-828-1748.
Recreation Security: C-208-828-2256.

RV Website:
https://mhafbfun.com/directory_listing/fam-camp/
GPS Coordinates:
43°3'38"N/115°51'50"W
Reservations: No advance reservations. Office hours 0830-1700 Mon-Fri; closed Wed. Check-in at FamCamp at self check-in station located across from campsite #1 and register. Place envelope with fee in the safe. Credit Card payments accepted at the Outdoor Adventure Program, Bldg 2800 during operating hours. Check-out 1100 hours. Host on site in summer.
Season of Operation: Year-round.
Eligibility: AD, NG, Res, Ret and Dep.
Camper/Trailer Spaces: Camper Spaces: Concrete (19), pull-thru, maximum length 60', handicap accessible, E(220V/50A)/S/W hookups. Rates: $15 daily. Grass/Dirt: (3) back-in, maximum length 60', E(220/50A). Rates: $15 daily.
Tent Spaces: Campsites: Unlimited, no hookups. Rates: $8 daily.
Support Facilities: Auto Hobby Shop, Bathhouse, Bowling, Chapel, Commissary, Community Center, Convenience Store, Equipment Rentals, Exchange, Fitness Center, Golf, Grills, Laundry, Marina*, Mess Hall, Pavilion, Pay Phones, Picnic Area, Pool, Restrooms, Sewage Dump, Showers, Skeet/Trap Range, Tennis Courts.
RV Storage: None.
Activities: Boating, Fishing (seasonal), Golfing, Hunting, Snow Skiing (nearby). Outdoor Recreation operates a marina 20 miles south of the base with boat

rentals and good fishing. Jet ski and ski boat rentals, whitewater rafting trips.
Credit Cards: MasterCard and Visa.
Restrictions: Limit two pets allowed; leashes are required. Quiet hours 2300-0800.
RV Driving Directions/Location: On Base. From I-84 north or south at Mountain Home City: Exit 95 west, follow road through Mountain Home to Air Base Road/ID-67, 10 miles to Main Gate on south side of ID-67. Enter AFB on Gunfighter Street. Travel .5 miles then turn right onto Aardvark Street. Continue for .5 miles to right turn onto Falcon Street for .5 miles to FAMCAMP on right.
Area Description: FAMCAMP offers shade on many sites and a covered

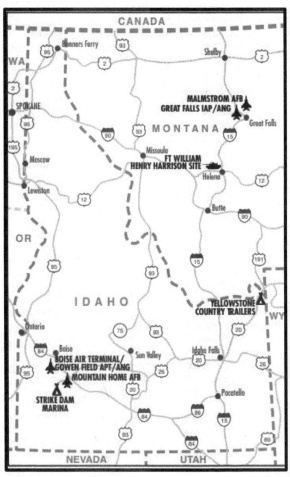

camping area. Near many beautiful natural areas, national forests, state parks, ghost towns, ski resorts, gem collecting. Located in open country surrounded by mountains, close to Snake and Boise Rivers. Sun Valley is approximately 100 miles northeast. Excellent access to vast public lands and recreation. A full range of support facilities is available on base.
RV Campground Physical Address: 366 FSS/Outdoor Recreation, 665 Pine St, Bldg 2800, Mountain Home AFB, ID 83648-5125.

Strike Dam Marina

Address: C. J. Strike Marina, North Park Boat Launch C.J. Strike Dam, Mountain Home, ID 83648.
Information Line: C-208-828-1110, DSN-312-728-1110.
Main Base Police: Emergencies dial 911.
Main Installation Website: http://www.mountainhome.af.mil/
Main Base Location: Located at the C.J. Strike Reservoir near Grand View on the Snake and Bruneau Rivers.
NMC: Boise, 60 miles northwest.
NMI: Mountain Home AFB, 15 miles northeast.
Places to Eat: Dining is limited, but cafe's, restaurants and fast food are within driving distance.
Marina: Strike Dam Marina, C-208-834-2723.
MWR Website: http://www.mhafbfun.com/marina/index.html
MWR Facebook: https://www.facebook.com/366FSS
Outdoor Recreation: Marina Equipment Rental, C-208-828-6333. Offers trips, camping, trap and skeet, a marina, rental equipment, and much more.
Things To Do: Fish for bass, trout, perch, catfish, crappie, or bluegill. Wakeboard, water ski, or tube behind a ProCraft 115. Take your family out on a pontoon boat or cruise on a Jet Ski. Spend a day, a weekend, or an entire week!

RV CAMPING & GETAWAYS
Strike Dam Marina

Reservation/Contact Number Info: C-208-834-2723, C-208-828-6333. Fax C-208-828-1748.
Recreation Security: C-208-828-2256, DSN-312-728-2256.
RV Website: https://mhafbfun.com/directory_listing/cj-strike-marina/
GPS Coordinates: 42°57'14"N/115°58'12"W
Reservations: Accepted two weeks in advance. Must contact Outdoor Recreation during operating hours, 0830-1700 Mon-Fri; closed Wed. Marina hours: 0900-1700 Mon-Fri, 0800-1800 Sat-Sun during summer; 0900-1700 hours Tue-Fri; 0800-1800 Sat-Sun during winter. Open federal holidays.
Season of Operation: Memorial Day-Labor Day.
Eligibility: AD, NG, Res, Ret and DoD-Civ.
Yurt, A Frame, Cabin, Apt, Spaces: Cabins (3): Sleeps 6, provides small fridge/microwave unit, one queen bed, one bunk bed, one pull-out futon couch/bed. Primitive bathroom facilities. Rates $40 daily. No linens or running water.
Support Facilities: Boat Docks, Boat Launch, Boat Rental, Golf (nearby), Grills, Marina, Picnic Area, Restrooms, Snack Bar, Water Sports Equipment Rental.
RV Storage: None.
Activities: Boating, Fishing*, Golfing, Jet Skiing, Pontoon Boat, Sailing, Water Skiing, Wind Surfing. *State license required.
Credit Cards: MasterCard and Visa.
Restrictions: No pets.
RV Driving Directions/Location: Off Base. From I-84 north or south at Mountain Home: Take exit 95 west and follow road through Mountain Home to Air Base Road/ID-67. Continue past AFB for approximately 20 miles to the C. J. Strike Reservoir on the Snake River south of ID-67. From MHAFB: Take

Airbase Road to Grandview turnoff. Travel 13.9 miles to Simplot Cattle Lot and turn left. Travel 2.1 miles and then go left for 7.0 miles until reaching a stop sign. Go left again for approximately 0.7 miles passing the Idaho Power Park until reaching Strike Marina.

Area Description: Situated along Snake River and surrounded by mountains. Full support for water sports and picnic activities. Full range of support facilities at Mountain Home AFB.

RV Campground Physical Address: C. J. Strike Dam Marina, Mountain Home AFB Camping/Cabins, Mountain Home AFB, ID 83648. Mailing Address: Address: 366 SVS/SVRM, Attn: Strike Dam Marina, Bldg 2800, Mountain Home AFB, ID 83648-5125.

Yellowstone Country Trailers

Address: 4133 Quakie Lane, Island Park, ID 83429.

Main Installation Website:
http://www.mountainhome.af.mil/

Main Base Location: Yellowstone Country Trailers are located on the east side of Island Park, Idaho approximately 21 miles west of West Yellowstone, Montana on Hwy 20.

Directions to Main Gate: Turn West off Highway 20 onto Sawtelle Peak Rd. Take the first right onto and Quakie Lane. Facility ahead.

NMC: West Yellowstone, MT, 20 miles northeast.

NMI: Mountain Home AFB, 335 miles southwest.

Places to Eat: West Yellowstone, MT offers a variety of dining options.

Things To Do: Visit Henry's Fork of the Snake River, Henry's Lake State Park, Harriman State Park or enjoy the views of the Sawtelle and Jefferson Mountains. And of course, Yellowstone National Parks is a short drive. West Yellowstone offers the Grizzly and Wolf Discovery Center, Yellowstone Aerial Adventures, gift shops and more.

RV CAMPING & GETAWAYS
Yellowstone Country Trailers

Reservation/Contact Number

Info: Mountain Home AFB, C-208-828-6333.

Recreation Security: Emergencies dial 911.

RV Website:
https://mhafbfun.com/directory_listing/outdoor-adventure-program/

Other Info Website:
http://www.sawtellemountainresort.com/

GPS Coordinates:
44°31'23"N/111°19'45"W

Reservations: Reservation instructions are specific: Rentals from Memorial Day weekend through June, call on the first business day of April. Rentals for July call on the first business day of May. Rentals for August and September, call on the first business day of June. The telephones will be very busy on these dates but keep trying. Flexibility in trip dates increases chances even several days after the initial bookings have started. Personnel stationed at Mountain Home AFB may make walk-in reservations three working days prior to the nationwide reservation date. Office hours 0900-177 hours Mon, Tues, Thurs and Fri. Closed Wed, Sat, Sun and holidays. Cancellations must be received 30 days prior to arrival less $25 cancellation fee. Camp host on site.

Season of Operation: Memorial Day through mid-September.

Eligibility: AD, Res, Ret and Dep and DoD Civ.

Camper/Trailer Spaces: Trailers On Site (8): 26' modern trailers fully equipped with cooking and eating utensils and small shower. Sleeps 6 (queen bed, bunk beds and converting couch). Guests must provide own linens, pillows, towels, cleaning supplies and other necessities. Rates: $120 nightly with 2-night minimum.

Support Facilities: General store nearby, laundry and shower facilities on site.

Activities: On-site pool, hot tub/sauna, horseshoe pits, pavilion, swing set, and volleyball net. ATV/UTV rentals on location. Yellowstone National Park offers many fun and exciting activities for the whole family. Horseback rides are available at Mammoth Hot Springs, Roosevelt Lodge, and Canyon Lodge. Stagecoach rides offer visitors a memorable jaunt through rolling sagebrush covered hills. Stagecoach rides depart from Roosevelt Lodge throughout the day. Bridge Bay Marina offers sight-seeing cruises of Yellowstone Lake or rent an outboard motorboat. Guided fishing boats are available for charter on Yellowstone Lake.

Credit Cards: American Express, MasterCard and Visa.

Restrictions: Pets are not permitted.

RV Driving Directions/Location: Turn West off Highway 20 onto Sawtelle Peak Rd. Take the first right onto and Quakie Lane. Facility ahead.

Area Description: Enjoy the majestic scenery, lots of trees, and plenty of fresh air. Pristine lakes, mountains, wildlife and an abundance of outdoor activities make this area the perfect retreat.

RV Campground Physical Address: 4133 Quakie Lane, Island Park, ID 83429.

ILLINOIS

Great Lakes Naval Training Center

Address: 2601 E. Paul Jones Street, Great Lakes, IL 60088-2845.

Information Line: C-847-688-3500, DSN-312-792-3500.

Main Base Police: C-847-688-3333. Emergencies dial 911.

Main Installation Website: https://www.cnic.navy.mil/regions/cnrma/installations/ns_great_lakes.html

Main Base Location: Naval Station Great Lakes is a military town, located on the shores of Lake Michigan, approximately one hour north of Chicago, Illinois and one hour south of Milwaukee, Wisconsin.

Directions to Main Gate: If arriving by auto, NAVSTA is located approximately 3 miles east of Hwy 41 and approximately 15 miles east of Interstate 94/294 at US Rt 137/Buckley Rd. Coming north from the Chicago area using the bypass Interstate 294 north, to Rt 137. Make a right turn on Rt 137/Buckley Road and go east approximately 6 miles.

NMC: Chicago, 30 miles south.

NMI: General Mitchell IA/ARS, 52 miles north.

Base Social Media/Facebook: https://www.facebook.com/NavalStationGreatLakes

Base Social Media/Twitter: https://twitter.com/navstaglakes

Chapels: C-847-688-4461. Training Support Center, C-847-688-5610/

Dental Clinic: Fischer Clinic, C-847-688-3331.

Medical: Appointment Line, C-800-941-4501. Information Line, C-847-688-7500. Fischer Clinic, C-847-88-2092.

Veterinary Services: C-847-688-5740.

Beauty/Barber Shop: Burky Mall, C-847-257-0530. Main Exchange, C-847-578-6348.

Commissary: C-847-688-2644.

Exchange Gas: C-847-578-6358.

Exchange: C-847-578-6329.

Financial Institutions: Armed Forces Bank, C-847-473-5833/2824. Navy Federal Credit Union, C-1-888-842-6328.

Clubs: Legends Sports Club, C-847-688-4641. Sam Adam's Brewhouse, C-847-688-6946.

Places to Eat: Buckley's, C-847-688-4593; Galley, C-847-688-2894 ext 342; Legends Sports Club, C-847-688-4641; Sam Adam's Restaurant, C-847-688-6946; Spinz, C-847-688-7898 and Zapper's Snack Bar, C-847-688-5858 are on base. Main Exchange Food Court offers Dunkin Donuts, McDonald's, Panda Express, Subway, Taco Bell and Pizza Hut. Burky MAll offers Subway. Many restaurants within a short drive.

Bowling: Bowling Center, C-847-688-4641.
Fitness Center: Field House, C-847-688-3419. Great Lakes FC, C-847-688-5649. Gym 4, C-847-688-7769.

Golf: Willow Glen Golf Course, C-847-688-4593.
ITT/ITR: C-847-688-3537.
Library: C-847-688-4617.

Marina: Great Lakes Marina, C-847-688-5417/6978.
Military Museum: Great Lakes Naval Museum, C-847-688-3154.
Military Museum Website: http://www.greatlakesnavalmuseum.org/
MWR: C-847-688-2110/2020.
MWR Website:
http://www.navymwrgreatlakes.com/
MWR Facebook:
https://www.facebook.com/MWRGreatLakes
MWR Twitter:
https://twitter.com/NavyGreatLakes
Outdoor Recreation: Great Lakes Rental Center, C-847-688-5417/6978. Offers camping gear, campers, a wide variety of boats from fishing to water skiing, canoes, kayaks, party inflatables, sports equipment and gear rental for both winter and summer sports. Pavilion rental available as well as an archery range is on base.
Swimming: Field House Indoor Pool, C-847-688-3419 offers lap and recreational swim as well as lessons and lifeguard training. Nunn Beach is available seasonally.
Things To Do: Visit Chicago via the train, enjoy sailing or golfing right on base, visit the Illinois Beach State Park, Six Flags Great America, Gurnee Mills Mall, Market Square in Lake Forest or visit Libertyville and enjoy quaint shopping and eateries.
Walking Trails: Indoor and outdoor tracks available on base.

RV CAMPING & GETAWAYS
Great Lakes RV Park

Reservation/Contact Number Info: C-847-688-6675, DSN-312-792-6675. Fax C-847-688-5421, DSN-312-792-5421.
Recreation Security: C-847-688-2035.
RV Website:
http://get.dodlodging.net/propertys/Great-Lakes-RV-Campground
Other Info Website:
http://www.navymwrgreatlakes.com/programs/8bed3a80-f9d6-4211-a93d-cadb1a3e8dab
RV Email Address: marina@mwrgl.com

GPS Coordinates:
42°19'14"N/87°49'53"W
Reservations: Accepted. Seasonal daily office hours: 0830-1700 hours 1 Mar-30 Apr; 0830-1800 hours 1 May-30 Sept; 0830-1800, 1 Oct-1 Dec. Office and facilities closed 1 Dec-31 Jan. Check-in 1300 hours and check-out 1300 hours. One day charge for cancellations. Maximum stay 30 days.
Season of Operation: February-November.
Eligibility: AD, NG, Res, Ret, DoD-Civ, DoD Civ Ret, Dep, 100% DAV and other U.S. Gov Civ Employees.
Camper/Trailer Spaces: Camper Spaces: Paved: (20) Back-in, Maximum 50' in length, E(220V/30A), restrooms, showers nearby; (12) E(220V/50A) sites. Rates: $17-19 daily, $450-$465 monthly. Water and sewage services available at Bldg 13.
Tent Spaces: Seabee Park Sites: (10), no hookups, grill, picnic table. Rates: $12-14 daily. Group camp available. Rates: $100 daily.
Support Facilities: Bath House, Beach, Boat Launch, Boat Rental/Storage, Bowling, Cafeteria, Chapel, Commissary*, Equipment Rental, Diesel, Exchange, Fire Rings, Fishing Pier, Fitness Center, Gas (on installation for authorized users only), Golf, Grills, Ice, Laundry/Pay, Marina, Mechanic/auto repair*, Microwave, Pavilion, Picnic Area, Playground, Propane (bottle or fill), Restrooms, RV Storage*, Sewage Dump, Shoppette, Showers, Shuttle Bus, Soda/Snack Vending, Sports Fields, Tennis Courts, Trails. *off base.
RV Storage: Available, C-847-688-2110. Maintains year-round waiting list.
Activities: Beaches, Bicycling, Bowling, Camping*, Charter Fishing Trips, Fishing**, Golfing, Hiking, Hunting***, Pools, Sailboats*, Sea Kayaks*, Skiing*, Swimming, Theater. * Instructional courses are available. **The required state fishing permits are sold on site. *** Must be in compliance with Illinois rules and regulations.
Credit Cards: American Express, Discover, MasterCard and Visa.

Restrictions: Pets allowed on leash. No firearms. Camp passes mandatory.

RV Driving Directions/Location: On Base. RV's need to enter through Gate 5 located north of Main Gate. From Main Gate: Follow main road to the end and turn right. Stay in the left lane and turn left onto Decatur. Beyond the theater, turn right onto Mahan and follow to bottom of hill where Mahan becomes Ziegemeier Street. Marina and campground are at bottom of hill.

Area Description: The RV sites are located on the waterfront of beautiful Lake Michigan. Biking/running trail just outside Front Gate goes all the way south to Chicago. Easy train ride into Chicago with a great deal of tourist points of interest, jazz clubs and endless shopping. Full range of support facilities available on base.

RV Campground Physical Address: MWR, 2601 Paul Jones, Great Lakes, IL 60088-5000.

Scott Air Force Base

Address: 10 Seibert Drive, Scott AFB, IL 62225-5359.

Information Line: C-618-256-1110, DSN-312-576-1110.

Main Base Police: C-618-256-6000. Emergencies dial 911.

Main Installation Website: http://www.scott.af.mil/

Main Base Location: Scott is located in southern Illinois and is part of the "Metro-East" portion of the greater St. Louis area. The base is located near historic Belleville, Illinois in St. Clair County, approximately 20 miles east of St. Louis, which is the largest city near the base.

Directions to Main Gate: From I-64/Northern Illinois: Take exit 19-A/Scott AFB. Turn left at second stop light and travel to Main Gate. From Westbound I-70: Turn right (west) onto I-64. Follow directions as above. From Southern Missouri: Take I-270 south toward Memphis. I-270 becomes I-255 east. Follow I-255 east to I-64. Turn east onto I-64. Follow directions as above. From Kansas City: Take I-70 east to I-270 north toward Chicago. Follow I-270

across the Mississippi River into Illinois. Take I-255 toward Memphis. Turn onto I-64 east. Take exit 19A (Scott AFB). Follow directions as above.

NMC: St. Louis, 25 miles west.

NMI: St. Louis Army Human Resources Command, 30 miles northwest.

Base Social Media/Facebook: https://www.facebook.com/ScottAirForceBase

Base Social Media/Twitter: https://twitter.com/ScottAFB

Chapels: C-618-256-4060.

Dental Clinic: C-618-256-6667.

Medical: Appointment Line, C-618-256-9355, DSN-312-576-9355. Scott Family Health Clinic, C-618-256-7804.

Veterinary Services: C-618-256-3989/5452.

Beauty/Barber Shop: C-618-746-2097.

Commissary: C-618-212-3898.

Exchange Gas: C-618-744-9253.

Exchange: C-618-744-9830.

Financial Institutions: Scott Credit Union, C-618-345-1000.

Clubs: Scott Event Center, C-618-256-5501.

Places to Eat: Cardinal Creek Cafe, C-618-256-2385; Common Grounds, C-618-256-1540; Nightingale Inn DFAC, C-618-256-2909; Rickenbacker's, C-618-256-5501 and Zeppelin's, C-618-256-5501 and Stars and Strikes Snackbar, C-618-256-4054 are on base. Exchange Food Courts offers American Eatery, Anthony's, Charley's, Domino's, Panda Express, Robin Hood Sandwiches, Starbucks and Taco Bell. Burger King, Joe's Asian Cuisine and McAlister's Deli are also on base. Many restaurants within a short drive.

Bowling: Stars & Strikes Bowling Center, C-618-256-4054.

Fitness Center: Scott FC, C-618-256-1218. James Sports Center, C-618-256-4524.

Golf: Cardinal Creek Golf Course, C-618-744-1400 or C-618-256-2385.

ITT/ITR: C-618-256-5919.

Library: C-618-256-5100.

Military Museum: Scott Field Heritage Air Park, C-618-233-2015.

Military Museum Website: http://www.scottfieldairpark.org/

MWR: C-618-256-3766.
MWR Website:
http://www.375fss.com/
MWR Facebook:
https://www.facebook.com/375thForce
SupportSquadron/
MWR Twitter:
https://twitter.com/375fss
Outdoor Recreation: Outdoor
Recreation Services, C-618-256-2067.
Offers camping gear, trailers, canoes,
kayaks, fishing boats, pontoon boats,
sailboats, lawn and garden equipment,
party supplies, inflatables and more.
Fishing available at Scott Lake and
pavilion rentals available.
Swimming: Seasonal Pool, C-618-256-
2067 offers open swim.
Things To Do: Near the "Gateway to the
West," visitors can enjoy the cultural,
sporting and outdoor activities that St.
Louis has to offer. Visit Union Station,
Busch Stadium, St. Louis Zoo, Eckert's
Belleville Farm, the Labor and Industry
Museum, Skyview Drive-In, Rock Springs
Park and many orchards.

INDIANA

Camp Atterbury

Address: 3008 Hospital Rd, Edinburgh,
IN 46164-5000.
Information Line: C-812-526-1499,
DSN-312-569-2499.
Main Base Police: C-812-526-
1234/1109. Emergencies dial 911.
Main Installation Website:
http://www.atterburymuscatatuck.in.ng
.mil/
Main Base Location: Located between
the two communities of Franklin, 13
miles north, and Columbus, 15 miles
south. Adjacent to Nineveh, Edinburgh,
and Taylorsville.
Directions to Main Gate: From I-65,
take exit 76B/US-31 north. Turn left at
Hospital Road. Enter post on Eggleston
Street at Main Gate. Use 3008 Hospital
Road for GPS.
NMC: Indianapolis, 45 miles north.

NMI: Grissom Air Reserve Base, 109
miles north.
Base Social Media/Facebook:
https://www.facebook.com/CampAtter
buryIndiana/
Base Social Media/Twitter:
https://twitter.com/Camp_Atterbury
Chapels: C-812-526-1499 ext 62020.
Medical: C-812-526-1120.
Beauty/Barber Shop: C-812-526-1163.
Exchange: C-812-526-1140.
Clubs: The House - All Ranks Club, C-
812-526-1143.
Places to Eat: A dining facility and
Subway are on base. Several restaurants
within a short drive.
Fitness Center: C-812-526-1499 ext
2309.
Golf: Golf Driving Range, C-812-526-
1499 ext 62952.
Military Museum: Camp Atterbury
Museum. Contact Public Affairs, C-812-
526-1386
Military Museum Website:
http://www.atterburymuscatatuck.in.ng
.mil/NewsMedia/PublicAffairsInformati
on/Museums.aspx
MWR: C-812-526-1499 ext 62962.
MWR Website:
http://www.atterburymuscatatuck.in.ng
.mil/Home/MWR.aspx
Outdoor Recreation: Outdoor
Recreation, C-812-526-1499 ext 62952.
Offers camping gear, boats, outdoor
sports equipment, bikes, sports fields,
golf clubs, driving range, picnic areas
and more.
Swimming: Seasonal Outdoor Pool, C-
812-526-1149 ext 61952 offers open
swim, lap swim and slide.
Things To Do: Visit the indoor and
outdoor museum and World War II
Prisoner of War Chapel on base or enjoy
one of the many on-base activities
provided. Take a day trip to Indianapolis
or explore the outdoor opportunities in
the area.

RV CAMPING & GETAWAYS
Farrell Recreation Area Cabins

Reservation/Contact Number Info: C-
812-526-1128. Fax C-812-526-1764.

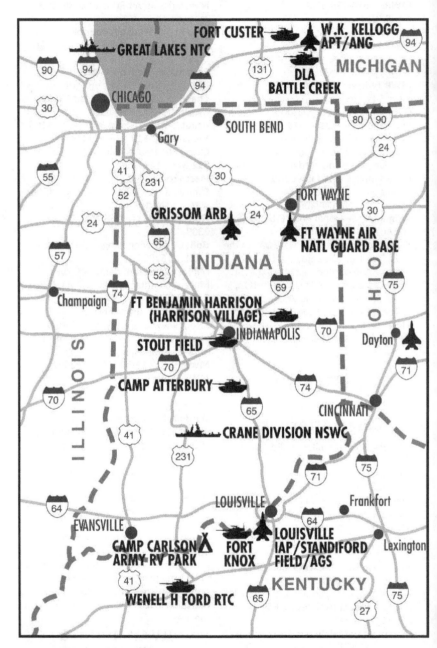

RV Website:
https://www.atterburymuscatatuck.in.n
g.mil/Staying-with-Us/Cabin-Rentals/
Reservations: Accepted no earlier than
the first working day of the month prior
to the month desired reservation
month. Contact reservations office,
0730-1600 Mon-Fri. Confirmations
made 14 days out of arrival. Maximum
stay 5 days. Check-in to be confirmed at

time of reservation, check-out 1200 hours.

Season of Operation: Year-round.

Eligibility: AD, NG, Res, Ret, their dependents; Widow/ers; DoD-Civ, DoD-Civ Ret, DAVs.

Yurt, A Frame, Cabin, Apt, Spaces: Cabins at Farrell Recreation Area (3): Two-bedroom (2), full size kitchen, dining room, living room, washer/dryer, TV/DVD, gas fireplace, patio. Secluded with lake access. Rates: $50 daily. Three-bedroom Cabin (1): Recently renovated, full kitchen, dining room, living room, washer/dryer, TV/DVD, gas fireplace, patio. Secluded with lake access. Rates: $90 daily. DV/VIP Cabin (1): Four-bedroom, four bath, living room, dining room, full-size kitchen, patio, gas fireplace, TV/VCR, washer and dryer. Rates: Reservations through Protocol Office.

Credit Cards: MasterCard and Visa.

Restrictions: Pets are not permitted in cabins.

RV Driving Directions/Location: From the Main Gate: Take an immediate left onto Headquarters' Road. Turn right onto Clark Street to Bldg 402, the second building on the right and enter the parking lot.

Whitaker Place Campgrounds

Reservation/Contact Number Info: C-812-526-1128. Fax C-812-526-1764.

Recreation Security: C-812-526-1499 DSN-312-569-2499. Police for campground: C-812-526-1109.

RV Website: https://www.atterburymuscatatuck.in.n g.mil/Staying-with-Us/Lodging-Chargeable-Transient-Quarters/

GPS Coordinates: 39°21'17"N/86°01'39"W

Reservations: RV Sites: Reservations accepted 30 days in advance in person at Bldg 402 or via telephone. Office hours 0730-1600 Mon-Fri.

Season of Operation: Year-round.

Eligibility: AD, NG, Res, Ret, DoD-Civ (Active and Retired), Dependents and Camp Atterbury Emp.

Camper/Trailer Spaces: RV Sites (33): Gravel (7), pull-thru, (26) back-in, maximum 45' in length, E(110V/30A/50A)/S/W hookups, CATV, picnic table, grill. Rates: $20 daily, $350 monthly. Primitive (4), no hookups. Rates: $10 daily.

Support Facilities: Archery Range, Barber Shop, Bathhouse*, Boat Launch, Chapel, Coin Laundry*, Enlisted Club, Exchange, Fire Rings, Fitness Center, Golf, Grills, Ice, Library, Mail service, Nature Trail, Officers' Club, Pavilion, Picnic Area, Playground, Pool, Rec Equipment, Restrooms*, RV Storage, Shelters, Showers*, Snack Bar, Sports Fields, Telephones, Tennis Courts. * Handicap accessible.

RV Storage: Long-term RV storage and sewage dump station available on post. Call for more information.

Activities: Bicycling, Boating, Canoeing, Fishing*, Hiking, Hunting*, Swimming. *State permits required.

Credit Cards: MasterCard and Visa.

Restrictions: Pets allowed must be on leash while outside. Owners must clean up after pets. No firearms. No ATVs or off-road vehicles allowed. Quiet hours 2200-0600 hours.

RV Driving Directions/Location: On Base. From the Main Gate: Turn left on Headquarters Rd. go right onto Durbin Street. Camp is located .25 miles ahead.

Area Description: Limited support facilities on post. Located in a heavily wooded, quiet and pristine area with a pond and abundant wildlife.

RV Campground Physical Address: Camp Atterbury Campground, Bldg 433, Mailing Address: P.O. Box 5000, Edinburgh, IN 46124-5000.

Crane Naval Support Activity

Address: 300 Hwy 361 Code N1, Bldg 3219, Crane, IN 47522.

Main Base Police: Emergencies dial 911.

Main Installation Website: https://www.cnic.navy.mil/regions/cnr ma/installations/nsa_crane.html

Other Info Website: http://www.navsea.navy.mil/Home/Wa rfare-Centers/NSWC-Crane/

Main Base Location: The Crane Division (NSWC Crane), located in Crane, Indiana is a shore command of the U.S. Navy. NSWC Crane is under the Naval Sea Systems Command headquartered in Washington DC.

Directions to Main Gate: From the airport follow the signs to I-465 South. Take I-465 South approximately 7 miles to Indiana-37 South. Take Ind-37 South approximately 43 miles to Indiana 45 South. Take Ind-45 South approximately 20 miles to the Ind-45 and Ind-58 junction (blinking red light). Turn right and proceed for approximately 10 miles. Turn left onto Ind-558 (sign for Crane visible). The Visitor Center is located on the left about 1 mile before the gate. Visitors are processed and provided a badge. Once badge is received visitor may proceed to gate for entry.

NMC: Bloomington, 30 miles northeast.

NMI: Grissom Air Reserve Base, 109 miles north.

Base Social Media/Facebook: https://www.facebook.com/NSACrane/

Base Social Media/Twitter: https://twitter.com/NAVSEACrane

Commissary: C-812-854-1297.

Exchange Gas: C-812-854-0234.

Exchange: C-812-854-0230.

Financial Institutions: Crane Federal Credit Union, C-812-863-7000.

Places to Eat: Crane Cafeteria, C-812-854-3290 is on base. Many restaurants within a short drive.

Fitness Center: Crane FC, C-812-854-6057.

ITT/ITR: C-812-854-6255.

Marina: Lake Greenwood Marina, C-812-854-3947.

MWR: C-812-854-3773.

MWR Website: http://www.navymwrcrane.com/

MWR Facebook: https://www.facebook.com/MWRCrane/

Outdoor Recreation: Lake Greenwood Marina Rentals, C-812-854-3947. Offers water sport rentals to include jon boats, canoes, kayaks, sailboats and powerboats. Also offers pavilion rentals, fishing, cornhole rental and more.

Swimming: Seasonal Outdoor Pool, C-812-854-1923 offers open and lap swim.

Things To Do: Visit Holiday World Amusement and Water Park, Amish community, WonderLab, Lake Monroe, Fairfax State Recreation Area, Hoosier National Forest, Indiana University Art Museum, Grunwald Gallery of Art, Indiana Heritage Quilt Show, Indiana Limestone Sculpture Symposium, Lotus World Music and Arts Festival, Theta Antique and Decorative Arts Sale, Week of Chocolate, Wine and Food Festival.

RV CAMPING & GETAWAYS

Crane MWR Campgrounds & Lake Greenwood Cabins

Reservation/Contact Number Info: C-1-877-NAVY-BED, C-812-854-1176, DSN-312-482-1176. Fax C-812-854-1032, DSN-312-482-1032.

Recreation Security: C-812-854-3300.

RV Website: http://get.dodlodging.net/propertys/Lake-Greenwood

Other Info Website: http://www.navymwrcrane.com/programs/0b93104b-99e7-41d2-861f-3b7caaede86c

GPS Coordinates: RV Entrance Gate: 38°53'28"N, 86°49'52"W Campgrounds: 38°52'37"N/86°49'17"W

Reservations: Required. A minimum of four campsites will be kept open for daily/weekly rentals. Half of total stay due at time of reservation. Reservations for the coming season are accepted after January 1 of that year. Maximum cabin stay 14 days; maximum RV stay 30 days. Check-in 1500 hours at Bldg 3329, check-out 1100 hours.

Season of Operation: 1 Apr-31 Oct.

Eligibility: AD, NG, Res, Ret, DoD-Civ, Dep and NSWC-Civ. Gov't Contractors.

Camper/Trailer Spaces: RV Sites (48): All sites with electric hookups, bathhouse, picnic table, fire ring. Rates: $20 daily. Call for weekly and monthly rates.

Tent Spaces: Primitive Screen Houses (4), Wooden Platform, no hookups. Picnic table, fire ring. Rates: $10 daily.

Grass (8), no hookups. Picnic table, fire ring. Rates: $10 daily.

Yurt, A Frame, Cabin, Apt, Spaces: Cabins: Loft Cabin (1), Sleeps seven. One full size bed in loft, two sets of bunk beds in private BR, one person futon in main room, one full bathroom, kitchenette w/small refrigerator, two burner counter top stove (no oven) microwave, single sink, coffee pot and toaster, A/C, heat. Rates: Call for current rates. Cabins: Small Cabins (4), sleeps 4, One private BR with full size bed, one full bathroom. Main room with 1 set of bunk beds, small refrigerator, microwave, toaster, coffee pot. A/C, heat. Rates: $35 daily. Cabins: Bunkhouse (1), sleeps 10, Main room has 5 sets of bunk beds, two full bathrooms, full kitchen w/ cookware, utensils, coffee pot, toaster, toaster oven, Main room has big screen TV, VCR (no cable), A/C, heat. Rates: $70 daily

Support Facilities: Bathhouse, Beach, Boat Launch, Boat Rental/Storage, Bowling, Cafeteria, Commissary, Exchange, Fire Rings, Fishing Pier, Fitness Center, Gas, Golf, Grills, Ice, Laundry/Pay, Marina, Mini-Mart w/Video Rental, Pavilion, Picnic Area, Playground, Pool, Propane, Rec Center, Restrooms, RV Storage, Sewage Dump, Showers, Snack Bar, Sports Fields, Swimming Pool, Tennis Courts, Trails, Vending.

RV Storage: C-812-854-3947.

Activities: Boating, Fishing*, Golfing, Hiking, Hunting*, Swimming, Volleyball. *License required.

Credit Cards: MasterCard and Visa.

Restrictions: No pets allowed in cabins nor tied up outside of cabins. Pets allowed on leash in campsites but must be leashed at all times. Owner must clean up after pet. No firearms. No jet skis. No open fires. Possession of fireworks is prohibited. Unlicensed motor bikes or mini bikes are not permitted in campground.

RV Driving Directions/Location: On Base. From Crane Gate: Turn left at 1st stop light. Proceed to 4-way stop and turn left. Check in at Navy Gateway Inns and Suites, Bldg 3329. To Campground: Proceed through two stoplights, then turn left at Bldg 2045 onto Constitution Grove Road.

Area Description: Located on an 800-acre lake in an area offering fishing, hunting, boating and hiking. Campgrounds located adjacent to the marina. Full range of support facilities available on base.

RV Campground Physical Address: MWR Campgrounds, Bldg 3319, 300 Highway 361, Crane, IN 47522-5001.

KANSAS

Fort Riley

Address: 7264 Normandy Drive, Fort Riley, KS 66442.

Information Line: C-785-239-3911, DSN-312-856-1110-3911.

Main Base Police: C-785-239-6767. Emergencies dial 911.

Main Installation Website: http://www.riley.army.mil/

Main Base Location: Located in both Geary and Riley counties, Fort Riley is located in northeastern Kansas, one hour west of Topeka, the state capital.

Directions to Main Gate: Directions from Kansas City International Airport (KCI): Take 435 south from airport then travel on 435 South to the exit for I-70 west to the Turnpike incurring small fee. Stay on the Turnpike until reaching the Topeka exit where there are only two and it does not matter which one. Look for signs showing I-70 west toward Manhattan, Salina and Denver. Remain on I-70 west and take exit 301. Look for signs.

NMC: Topeka, 50 miles east.

NMI: Salina Kansas ANGRTI, 60 miles southwest.

Base Social Media/Facebook: https://www.facebook.com/FortRiley

Base Social Media/Twitter: https://twitter.com/FortRiley

Chapels: Chaplain, C-785-239-3359.

Dental Clinic: Clinic 1, C-785-239-7955/7510. Clinic 2, C-785-240-7411/7410. Clinic 3, C-785-239-

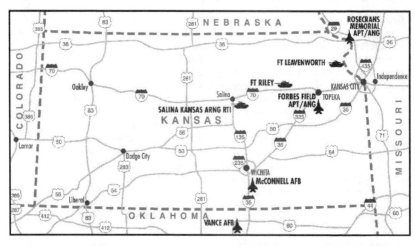

4261/4262. Clinic 4, C-785-239-4174/1765.

Medical: Appointment Line, C-785-239-3627. Information Desk, C-785-239-7000.

Veterinary Services: C-785-239-3886.

Beauty/Barber Shop: Custer Hill: C-785-307-0093, C-785-492-2214, C-785-492-2222. Forsyth, C-785-492-2340.

Commissary: C-785-239-3737.

Exchange Gas: Forsyth, C-785-784-2993/4900. Riley Big Red 1, C-785-717-2893.

Exchange: C-785-784-2026.

Financial Institutions: Armed Forces Bank, C-785-784-4400, C-800-826-8137. Credit Union 1, C-785-784-3100.

Places to Eat: Custer Hill Bowling Center, C-785-239-4366; Demon Diner DFAC, C-785-239-4998; Devils Den DFAC, C-785-239-1697; Outdoor Rec Snackbar, C-785-239-2363 and Riley Center, C-785-784-1000 are on base. Custer Hill Exchange Food Court offers Charley's, Subway, Taco Bell and Wing Zone. Forsyth Food Court offers Burger King, Charley's, Manchu Walk, Popeye's Chicken, Starbucks and Subway. Austin Blues BBQ, Domino's, Hunt Brother's Pizza and J Walken Chicken are also on base. Many restaurants within a short drive.

Bowling: Custer Hill Bowling Center, C-785-239-4366.

Fitness Center: Craig FC, C-785-239-5562. King Field House, C-785-239-3868. Leonard FC, C-785-239-5771.

Long FC, C-785-239-4683. Robinson FC, C-785-239-4480. Whiteside FC, C-785-239-2573.

ITT/ITR: C-785-239-5614.

Library: C-785-239-5305.

Marina: Fort Riley Marina, C-785-463-5253.

Military Museum: Ft Riley Museums, C-785-239-2737.

Military Museum Website: https://www.facebook.com/FtRileyMuseums

MWR: C-785-239-3467.

MWR Website: https://riley.armymwr.com/

MWR Facebook: https://www.facebook.com/rileymwr

MWR Twitter: https://twitter.com/RileyMWR

Outdoor Recreation: Outdoor Recreation Services, C-785-239-2363. Offers camping gear, campers and trailers, canoes, kayaks, fishing boats, party supplies, inflatables, trailers, outdoor sports equipment, archery, driving range, ATV track, paintball, parks, pavilion rentals and more.

Swimming: Eyster Indoor Pool, C-785-239-4854 offer open swim, lap swim and recreational swim. Long Training Pool, C-785-239-4684 offer lap swim. Custer Aquatic Park, C-785-239-4854 offers recreational swim, lazy river, and splash pad.

Things To Do: Visit the Custer House or the U.S. Cavalry Museum to explore the history of Fort Riley. In Topeka visit

Great Overland Station, Evil Knievel Museum, Combat Air Museum, Kansas Museum of History, Lake Shawnee or one of the many outdoor recreation parks.

Walking Trails: Outdoor running track at Long FC. Indoor track at Whiteside FC.

RV CAMPING & GETAWAYS

Fort Riley Marina Campsites

Reservation/Contact Number Info: C-785-463-5253, C-785-307-3798.

RV Website: https://riley.armymwr.com/programs/marina

Reservations: No reservations. Call Marina for availability. Marina Office hours 1100-1900 Fri, Mon; 0700-2000 Sat-Sun. Contact Outdoor Recreation, C-785-239-2363/6368 for additional information if Marina closed.

Season of Operation: Late April-mid October.

Eligibility: AD, Ret, Dep, Dod-Civ.

Tent Spaces: Primitive Sites (20), no hookups, no bathhouse. Picnic table, fire ring provided. Rates: $7 daily.

Support Facilities: Full range of support facilities available on base.

RV Storage: Contact Outdoor Recreation, C-785-239-2363/6368.

Activities: Boating, Climbing Wall, Hiking, Kayaking, Paintball, Seasonal ODR Trips. See full range of activities on base.

Credit Cards: Cash, Check, Mastercard and Visa.

Restrictions: No RV's at campsites. No 4-wheelers allowed.

RV Driving Directions/Location: On Base. From I-70 take exit 295 and turn north on Hwy 77. Travel 25 miles and turn left on Hwy 82 (Wakefield). Go 1 mile west and turn left at Fort Riley Marina sign. Located on the north side of Milford Lake.

Area Description: Milford Lake is the largest man-made lake in Kansas, with over 15,000 acres of water. Some of the attractions you will find at Milford Lake include a nature center, camping, boating, swimming, hiking, wildlife watching, off-road vehicle trails and much more.

RV Campground Physical Address: Physical Address: Fort Riley Marina, 7112 Highway 82, Fort Riley, KS 66442. Mailing Address: Outdoor Recreation, 1806 Buffalo Soldier Rd, Fort Riley, KS 66442.

McConnell Air Force Base

Address: 52802 Kansas Street, McConnell AFB, KS 67221-3606.

Information Line: C-316-759-6100, DSN-312-743-6100.

Main Base Police: C-316-759-3976. Emergencies dial 911.

Main Installation Website: http://www.mcconnell.af.mil/

Main Base Location: McConnell AFB is located in Wichita, KS approximately three hours north of Oklahoma City and three hours southwest of Kansas City, MO.

Directions to Main Gate: From the North on the Kansas Turnpike/I-35: Take the east Wichita exit and travel .5 miles on US 54/Kellogg Avenue. Turn left on Rock Road. Four stop lights down and base is on the right. From the South on the Kansas Turnpike: Take the K-15 exit. Turn right and go north to 31st Street. Turn right and then left at the George Washington Boulevard stop sign. The west gate is approximately .5 miles ahead.

NMC: Wichita, six miles northwest.

NMI: Salina Kansas ANGRTI, 95 miles north.

Base Social Media/Facebook: https://www.facebook.com/22ARW

Base Social Media/Twitter: https://twitter.com/22ARW

Chapels: C-316-759-3562.

Dental Clinic: C-316-759-5181.

Medical: Appointment Line, C-316-691-6300.

Veterinary Services: C-316-759-5190.

Beauty/Barber Shop: C-316-686-2128; Stylique, C-316-689-8716.

Commissary: C-316-759-5621.

Exchange Gas: C-316-685-0291.

Exchange: C-316-685-0231.

Financial Institutions: Bank of America-Military Bank, C-316-759-5450. Freedom First Credit Union, C-316-759-5457.

Clubs: Tanker Tavern Consolidated Club, C-316-759-2076.

Places to Eat: Chisholm Trail DFAC, C-316-759-6114; McJava Cafe, C-316-759-6187; Tanker Tavern, C-316-759-2076 and Twisters Cafe, C-316-759-6187 are on base. Exchange Food Court offers Charley's. Burger King and Hunt Brothers Pizza are also on base. Many restaurants within a short drive.

Bowling: Tornado Alley Bowling Center, C-316-759-6187.

Fitness Center: McConnell FC, C-316-759-4009.

ITT/ITR: C-316-759-6007.

Library: McConnell Library, C-316-759-4207.

Military Museum: Kansas Aviation Museum, C-316-683-9242.

Military Museum Website: http://www.kansasaviationmuseum.org/

MWR: Admin, C-316-759-4980.

MWR Website: http://www.refuelmcconnell.com

MWR Facebook: https://www.facebook.com/BoomerBMcConnell/

MWR Twitter: https://twitter.com/McConnell22FSS

Outdoor Recreation: Outdoor Recreation Services, C-316-759-4435/4432/4645. Offers camping equipment, campers and trailers, fishing boats, canoes, kayaks, ski boats, wave runners, lawn and garden equipment, inflatables, outdoor sports equipment, ATVs, party rentals, Krueger Recreation Area rentals and activities and more.

Swimming: McConnell FC Indoor Pool, C-316-759-4009 offers lap swim and open swim. Outdoor Seasonal Pool, C-316-759-4435 offers open swim, recreational swim and water slides.

Things To Do: Visit Old Cowtown Museum, Museum of World Treasures, Exploration Place, Sedgwick County Zoo, Great Plains Nature Center, The Wichita Gardens (Botanica), Arkansas River Trail and The Keeper of the Plains, Old Town, Lawrence-Dumont Stadium and more.

Walking Trails: Indoor running track at McConnell FC. Krueger Recreation Area offers over 160 acres of park and nature activities.

RV CAMPING & GETAWAYS

Krueger Recreation Area

Reservation/Contact Number Info: C-316-759-6999, DSN-312-743-6999. Fax C-316-759-4190. ODR Primitive Camp, C-316-759-4435/4639. Fax C-316-759-4729.

Recreation Security: C-316-759-3976.

RV Website: http://www.refuelmcconnell.com/recreation/outdoor-recreation/krueger-recreation-area/

RV Email Address: Outdoor.Recreation@us.af.mil

GPS Coordinates: 37°37'26"N/97°14'43"W

Reservations: Not accepted. First come, first serve. Register at Lodging Office, Bldg 196. Check-in 1400 hours, check-out 1100 hours. A credit card is required at check-in and payment due in advance for up to 15 days. Primitive Camp must register with ODR.

Season of Operation: Year-round.

Eligibility: AD, NG, Res, Ret, DoD-Civ, 100% DAV.

Camper/Trailer Spaces: RV Sites (10): Concrete/Paved, back-in, E(110V/20A/30A)/W hookups, dump station. Rates: $18 daily.

Tent Spaces: Primitive Sites: Rates: $5 daily.

Support Facilities: Auto Craft Shop, Boat Rental/Storage, Bowling, Central Sewage Dump, Chapel, Commissary, Convenience Store, Exchange, Fitness Center, Gas, Grills, Ice, Laundry, Pavilion, Picnic Area, Playground, Pool, Rec Center, Rec Equipment, Shoppette, Snack Bar, Sports Fields, Tennis Courts.

RV Storage: Contact Outdoor Recreation, C-316-759-4432.

Activities: Bowling, Fishing*, Fitness Center, Golfing, Swimming, Tennis. *State permit required.

Credit Cards: MasterCard, Visa and Services Club Card.

Restrictions: Pets allowed on leash; owner must clean up after pet. No firearms or open fires.

RV Driving Directions/Location: On Base. From the Main Gate: Air Capital Inn is the first building on the left, 24 hours daily. Guests must check in with Lodging before going to the FAMCAMP. Ask for directions to Primitive Campsites.

Area Description: Wichita is located along the Arkansas River and lies four miles from the Air Force Base. The area offers modern city conveniences, entertainment and is home to Wichita State University.

RV Campground Physical Address: Mailing Address: McConnell FamCamp, 22FSS/FSVL, Bldg 196, Suite 1, 53050 Glen Elder, McConnell AFB, KS 67221-5000.

KENTUCKY

Camp Carlson Recreational Area

Address: Camp Carlson, Army Recreational Area, Attn: Manager, 9210 US Route 60, Muldraugh, KY 40155-2015.

Information Line: C-502-624-1000/1181, DSN-312-464-0111/1181.

Main Base Police: Emergencies dial 911.

Main Installation Website: http://www.knox.army.mil/

Main Base Location: Near Fort Knox.

NMC: Fort Knox, 7 miles southeast.

NMI: Louisville, 30 miles north.

MWR: C-502-624-4836.

MWR Website: https://knox.armymwr.com/us/knox

RV CAMPING & GETAWAYS

Camp Carlson Recreational Area

Reservation/Contact Number Info: C-502-624-4836, DSN-312-464-4836. Fax C-502-624-8144, DSN-312-464-8144.

Recreation Security: C-502-624-2111. Emergency, C-502-624-0911.

RV Website: https://knox.armymwr.com/programs/carlson-campgrounds

GPS Coordinates: 37°54'13"N/86°1'32"W

Reservations: Required for family and group cabins. May be made up to one year in advance. Advance payment equal to one day rental fee for the family cabins and 50% for the group cabins required at time of reservation. Cancellations require 30 days for full refund. Rescheduling is allowed for notices less than 30 days and within 48 hours of scheduled arrival date. For RV park and tents, reservations can be made up to 3 months in advance for water/electric sites only. Full hookups are first come, first serve. Summer (1 May-24 Dec): 0830-1700 hours Mon-Sat; 0830-1230 Sunday; winter: 0830-1700 hours Mon-Sat. Closed on Sundays and all federal holidays. Check-in 1300 hours, check-out 1100 hours. Note: Check with office regarding limits of stay for cabins and RV Park.

Season of Operation: Year-round.

Eligibility: AD, NG, Res, Ret, DoD-Civ, Dep, 100% DAV and DoD contractors or technical representatives.

Camper/Trailer Spaces: RV Sites (53): Full hookup sites (35); partial hookup (18). Access to bathhouse, 24-hour laundry. Rates: Peak season $25-$35 daily; Low season $20-$30 daily.

Tent Spaces: Primitive Sites (14): Rates: $8 daily for up to 6 people; $1 for each additional person. Showers, bathrooms and laundry facilities nearby. Reservations not accepted. Three water spigots are located in the tent camping area. Each site has a burn-ring, picnic table and grill.

Yurt, A Frame, Cabin, Apt, Spaces: Family Cabins: Total (10). Single Sleeper Cabins, sleeps 2, one room w/bath, sat TV, microwave, phone. Rates: $55 daily Sun-Th; $60 daily Fri-Sat. Ranch Cabins (6): One-bedroom, sleeps 4, living room, kitchen and bath. Rates: $65 daily Sun-Fri; $70 daily Fri-Sat. Double Ranch Cabins: Two bedrooms, sleeps 8, living

room, kitchen and bath. Rates: $75 daily Sun-Thu; $80 daily Fri-Sat. Group Cabins: Two bedrooms (3), 16 bunks, with a minimum of 10 persons, maximum of 16. Rates: $10 per person daily. Guests must provide linens.
Support Facilities: A-Liner Rental*, Auto Craft Shop*, Bathhouse, Boat Rental*, Bowling*, Chapel*, Coin Laundry, Commissary*, Community Center, Convenience Store*, Equipment Rental*, Exchange*, Fitness Center*, Free Wi-Fi, Fire Rings, Gas*, Golf*, Grills, Ice, Pavilion, Picnic Area, Playground, Pool*, Restrooms, RV Storage*, Sewage Dump, Showers, Snack Bar*, Sports Fields, Telephones, Trails, Vending Machine. *Available on post.
RV Storage: 285 slots; good availability. For more information, C-502-624-2314.
Activities: Bicycling, Bowling, Fishing*, Golfing, Hunting*, Swimming. *State permits required for fishing in Carlson Lake.
Credit Cards: MasterCard and Visa.
Restrictions: Pets are not allowed in the cabins or any building. Pets must be kept on leash and cleaned up after. Pets must not be left unattended. Park speed limit is 10 MPH and strictly enforced. No firearms or fireworks. Fires in grills or fire rings only. Quiet hours: 2300-0900.
RV Driving Directions/Location: Off Base. From I-65 north or south: Take exit 102 West onto Hwy 313. Stay on 313 until you reach Hwy 60. Turn right (east) onto Hwy 60. Go 4 miles. Entrance to campground will be on the left side of the road at the bottom of the hill. The park office is at the entrance. Park in the parking lot next to the office to register.
Area Description: Camp Carlson Army Recreational Area is located amidst 65 acres of natural beauty, with a 25-acre lake stocked with Catfish, Bluegill & Crappie.
RV Campground Physical Address: Camp Carlson Army Recreational Area, Attn: Manager, 9210 US Hwy 60, Muldraugh, KY 40155-2015.

Fort Campbell

Address: 5661 Screaming Eagle Blvd, Fort Campbell, KY 42223.
Information Line: C-270-798-2151, DSN-312-635-2151.
Main Base Police: C-270-798-7111/7112, DSN-312-635-7111.
Main Installation Website: http://www.campbell.army.mil
Main Base Location: Fort Campbell Kentucky lies on the Kentucky/Tennessee border between the towns of Hopkinsville, KY and Clarksville, TN about 60 miles northwest of Nashville.
Directions to Main Gate: Directions from the Airport or from the East: Start out going South on Terminal Drive. Merge onto I-40 W toward Nashville I-65/I-24. Keep right to take I-24 W via exit 211B toward Clarksville/ I-65 North/ Louisville. Keep left to take I-24 W via exit 88B toward Clarksville. Take exit 86 US-41Alt toward Hopkinsville/Fort Campbell. Turn Left onto US-41A South/Fort Campbell Blvd at the light. In approximately 4.2 miles from here, Turn Right to Gate 4 (main gate).
NMC: Nashville, TN, 50 miles southeast.
NMI: Nashville IA/ANG, 65 miles southeast.
Base Social Media/Facebook: https://www.facebook.com/FortCampbell
Base Social Media/Twitter: https://twitter.com/FortCampbell
Chapels: Chaplain, C-270-798-6124.
Dental Clinic: Byrd/Atkins Clinic, C- 412-6027/6028. Epperly Clinic, C-270-798-3544/3675. LaPointe/Kuhn Clinic, C-270-412-2787. Taylor Clinic, C-270-798-6362/5429. Oral Surgery Clinic, C-270-956-0382.
Medical: Appointment Line, C-270-798-4677, C-931-431-4677. Information, C-270-798-8400.
Veterinary Services: C-270-798-3614.
Beauty/Barber Shop: Main Exchange, C-270-439-0198; Stylique, C-270- 439-1023. Airfield Mini Mall, C-270-640-3539. Troop Store, C-931-431-4231. Gardner Hill, C-270-640-4843.
Commissary: C-270-640-4008.

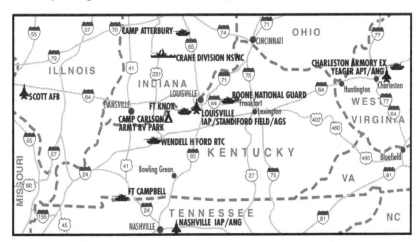

Exchange Gas: Kentucky Express, C-270-439-1914. Tennessee Express, C-270-431-4944. Mini-Mall, C-931-431-2410/2026.

Exchange: C-270-439-1841.

Financial Institutions: Bank of America Military Bank, C-931-431-4280. Federal Credit Union, C-931-431-6800, C-1-800-821-5891.

Clubs: Warrior Zone, C-270-461-0603.

Places to Eat: 19th Hole Snack Bar, C-270-798-4906; Artillery Grille, C-270-798-0766; Cole Park Eatery, C-270-798-4610; Hooper Grille, C-270-798-5887 and Smokehaus, C-270-798-4993 are on base. Flo's Dining Facility, C-270-798-8079 is located at the hospital. Exchange Food Court offers Boston Market, Burger King, Charley's, Einstein Bros Bagels, Qdoba, Popeye's Chicken and Sarku Japanese Cuisine. Domino's, Green Beans Coffee, Hunt Brothers Pizza, Kentucky Fried Chicken, Pizza Hut, Smoothie King, Starbucks, Subway and Taco Bell are also on base. Many restaurants within a short drive.

Bowling: Hooper Bowling Center, C-270-798-5887.

Fitness Center: Clarksville Base FC, C-270-412-5285. Fratellenico FC, C-270-798-9418. Gertsch FC, C-270-798-2753. Lozada FC, C-270-798-5830. Olive FC, C-270-798-4101. Sabo FC, C-270-798-7355. Shaw FC, C-270-461-2294. Estep Wellness Center, C-270-798-4023.

Golf: Cole Park Golf Course, C-270-798-4906.

ITT/ITR: C-270-798-7436/0509.

Library: Robert F Sink Memorial Library, C-270-798-5729.

Military Museum: Don F. Pratt Museum, C-270-798-3215/4986.

Military Museum Website: http://fortcampbell.com/museums/don-f-pratt-museum/

MWR: C-270-798-7535.

MWR Website: https://campbell.armymwr.com/

MWR Facebook: https://www.facebook.com/FortCampbellMWR/

MWR Twitter: https://twitter.com/FortCampbellMWR

Outdoor Recreation: Outdoor Recreation Services, C-312-352-7854. Gear to Go Equipment Rental, C-270-798-3919/6806. Offers an archery range, camping, challenge course, golfing, fishing, hunting, multiple parks and recreation areas, paintball, riding stables and much more. Gear to Go Rentals offers campers and camping equipment, inflatables, lawn and garden tools, sports equipment, trailers, vehicle rental, water sports equipment and boats, canoes, kayaks and more.

Swimming Pools Name, Phone, and Text: Seasonal Outdoor Pools Dolan, C-270-798-5350; Baldanado, C-270-798-5207; and Singles, C-270-798-4247 offer open swim. Gardner Indoor Pool, C-270-798-6310 offers lap and open swim.

Things To Do: Stroll Clarksville's Public Square and architectural district for turn-of-the-century buildings. Visit local watershed lakes for fishing and picnicking. Nashville is approximately 50 miles to the east.

Walking Trails: Five parks are on base.

RV CAMPING & GETAWAYS

Eagle's Rest RV Park and Fletcher's Fork RV Park & Cabins

Reservation/Contact Number Info: C-270-798-2175, DSN 635-2175. Fax C-270-798-4666.

Recreation Security: C-270-798-7112.

RV Website:
https://campbell.armymwr.com/programs/camping

GPS Coordinates:
36°35'6"N/87°28'25"W

Reservations: Eagles' Rest and Fletcher's Fork RV: No advance reservations. Upon arrival, occupy a site then pay Outdoor Recreation, Bldg 6645, during normal business hours, 0730-1630 daily. After hours arrivals must pay first thing in morning. Check-out 1200 hours. Cabins: Reservations required. Non-refundable deposit equal to first night's stay required. Check-in 1500-1630 hours, check-out 1000 hours.

Season of Operation: Year-round.

Eligibility: AD, NG, Res, Ret, DoD-Civ and Public.

Camper/Trailer Spaces: Eagles Rest RV Park (24): Concrete slabs, Back-in, (22) with maximum length 30'; Pull-thru (2) with maximum length 40'. All have E(110V/220V/20A/50A)S/W hookups, picnic table. Rates: $25 daily, $600 monthly. Fletcher's Fork (22): Paved, Pull-thru, (20) with maximum length 40'; Back-in, (2) with maximum length 30'. All have E(110V/220V/20A/50A)S/W hookups, picnic table. Rates: $25 daily, $600 monthly. Golden Age Access Passports and America the Beautiful, Rates: $23 daily.

Yurt, A Frame, Cabin, Apt, Spaces: Fletchers Fork: Rustic Cabins and Cottages (8): Each provides a double bed, bunk beds, table and two chairs, small refrigerator, microwave, HVAC, front porch swing (cabins only), ceiling fans (cottages only). No indoor plumbing. Bathhouse provided. Linens not provided. Rates: $40 daily. Deluxe Cabins (3): Each provides a double bed, bathroom, bunk beds, table and two chairs, small refrigerator, microwave, HVAC, and handicap accessible unit. Linens not provided. Rates: $60 daily.

Support Facilities: Auto Craft Shop, Bath House, Boat Launch, Boat Rental/Storage, Bowling, Chapel, Commissary, Convenience Store, Equipment Rental, Exchange, Fishing Pier, Fitness Center, Golf, Grills, Ice, Laundry, Pavilion, Picnic Area, Playground, Pool, Recreation Center, Restrooms*, Sewage Dump, Showers*, Sports Fields, Stables, Tennis Courts. * Handicap accessible.

RV Storage: C-270-956-1611.

Activities: Fishing*, Golfing, Hiking*, Hunting*. *License and Post Permit required.

Credit Cards: Cash, Check, Discover, MasterCard and Visa.

Restrictions: Pets allowed on leash at all time and may not be left unattended. No Handguns. Firearms are permitted for hunting but must be registered with the installation. No smoking, no pets in cottages or cabins.

RV Driving Directions/Location: On Base. The ODR Main Office is located in the red building on the right side at the traffic light, adjacent to Destiny Parks. The campgrounds are straight through the light. Eagle's Rest is the first right and Fletcher's Fork is down the hill and across the bridge on the right, next to the MWR Skeet Range.

Area Description: Located near the Land Between the Lakes (LBL) Area, between Clarksville, TN and Hopkinsville, KY. Tennessee Valley Authority manages LBL, an extensive reservoir complex on the Tennessee River along KY/TN line. Unlimited water recreational opportunities.

RV Campground Physical Address: Mailing Address: Outdoor Recreation, 6645 101st Airborne Division Rd, Fort Campbell, KY 42223-5000.

LOUISIANA

Alligator Lake RV Park

Address: Bldg 8590 Alligator Loop, Fort Polk, LA 71459.
Information Line: C-337-531-2911, DSN-312-863-2911.
Main Base Police: C-337-531-2677.
Main Installation Website:
http://www.jrtc-polk.army.mil/
Main Base Location: Alligator Lake RV Park is located approximately one mile away from Fort Polk JRTC.
NMC: Alexandria, 60 miles northeast.
NMI: Fort Polk JRTC, one mile

RV CAMPING & GETAWAYS

Alligator Lake RV Park

Reservation/Contact Number Info: C-337-531-5350.
Recreation Security: C-337-531-2677.
RV Website:
https://polk.armymwr.com/programs/alligator-lake
GPS Coordinates:
31°08'31.9"N/93°09'08.5"W
Reservations: Reservations required and accepted 60 days in advance via telephone or in person at Bldg 8590. Office hours 0800-1600 Mon, Thur, Fri; 0900-1700 Sat-Sun. Maximum stay 30 days. Check-in upon arrival.
Season of Operation: Year-round.
Eligibility: AD, NG, Res, Ret, DoD-Civ, Dep, 100% DAV, Gov't Contractors.
Camper/Trailer Spaces: RV Sites (15): Full hookup, picnic table, grill. Rates: $20 daily, $105 weekly, $370 monthly.
Tent Spaces: Primitive, no hookups. Rates: $5 daily.
Support Facilities: Bathhouse, Batting Cages*, Beach, Canoe Boat Rental, Equipment Rental, Fire Rings, Fishing Equipment, Fishing Pier, Grills, Laundry, Pavilions, Picnic Areas, Playgrounds, Restrooms, Sewage Dump, Shoppette*, Showers, Splash Park*, Sports Fields, Trails. Fort Polk located one mile away.
Activities: Canoeing, Fishing, Softball, Volleyball.

Credit Cards: Cash, Check, Mastercard and Visa.
Restrictions: Pets allowed on leash. Firearms must be registered with Fort Polk security. Quiet hours apply.
RV Driving Directions/Location: Off Base. Located one mile from base. Take Hwy-28 to where it intersects with Hwy-469. Travel 1-2 miles and watch for signs for Alligator Lake Recreation Site.
Area Description: Located amidst tree-lined water, the Recreation Area is approximately one mile from Fort Polk. This park-like setting provides plenty of outdoor fun and relaxation.
RV Campground Physical Address: Bldg 8590 Alligator Loop, Fort Polk, LA 71459.

Barksdale Air Force Base

Address: 413 Curtiss Road, Barksdale AFB, LA 71110-2426.
Information Line: C-318-456-1110, DSN-312-781-1110.
Main Base Police: C-318-456-2551.
Main Installation Website:
http://www.barksdale.af.mil/
Main Base Location: Barksdale Air Force Base (BAFB) is located in the northwest corner of Louisiana, in Bossier Parish near Shreveport which is located just across the Red River from Bossier City in Caddo Parish.
Directions to Main Gate: Barksdale is located on the Southwest side of Bossier City and can be easily accessed from interstates 20 and 49. Traveling from the east on I-20: Take exit 22/Airline Drive and turn left at the traffic light. Take another left at the next light onto Old Minden Road/LA-72. Stay in the right lane as it merges onto Northgate Drive, ending at the Bossier gate of Barksdale, open until 2100 hours. The Main Gate or West Gate can be accessed by taking exit 20C/Barksdale Blvd. Continue straight, then turn left on West Gate Drive/the 6th light, which ends at the main gate open 24 hours.
NMC: Shreveport, one mile west. Co-located with Bossier City, four miles northwest.

NMI: Red River Army Depot, TX, 100 miles northwest.

Base Social Media/Facebook: https://www.facebook.com/TeamBarksdale/

Base Social Media/Twitter: https://twitter.com/teambarksdale

Chapels: Chaplain, C-318-456-2111/2151.

Dental Clinic: C-318-456-6718/6719.

Medical: Appointment Line, C-318-456-6555.

Veterinary Services: C-318-456-3923.

Beauty/Barber Shop: Main, C-318-741-3114. Stylique, C-318-746-5930. Flightline, C-318-456-3769.

Commissary: C-318-456-8263.

Exchange: C-318-318-752-9227.

Financial Institutions: Barksdale Federal Credit Union, C-318-549-8240, C-1-800-647-2328. Chase Bank, C-318-226-2722.

Clubs: Barksdale Club and Hangar II Lounge, C-318-456-4926.

Places to Eat: Bowling Center Snack Bar, C-318-456-4162; Caddie Corner Grille, C-318-456-4195; Flight Kitchen, C-318-456-4769; Pelicans Snack Bar, C-318-456-0119; Red River DFAC, C-318-456-8068 and The Source, C-318-456-5985 are on base. Exchange Food Court offers Charley's, Johnny's Pizza House, Smoothies-n-Things, Starbucks, Subway and Taco Bell. Many restaurants within a short drive.

Bowling: Bomber Alley, C-318-456-4133.

Fitness Center: Bell FC, C-318-456-4135. The Pump House, C-318-456-4135.

Golf: Fox Run Golf Course, C-318-456-2263.

ITT/ITR: C-318-456-1866.

Library: Barksdale AFB Library, C-318-456-4101.

Military Museum: Barksdale Global Power Museum, C-318-752-0055.

Military Museum Website: http://barksdaleglobalpowermuseum.com/

MWR: C-318-456-6955.

MWR Website: http://barksdalelife.com/

MWR Facebook: https://www.facebook.com/2FSSBarksdale

Outdoor Recreation: Outdoor Adventures and Equipment, C-318-456-3426. Offers boat rentals, bounce houses, campers, lawn and garden equipment, park and pavilion rentals, sporting equipment, trailers and more. Outdoor Adventures offers archery, paintball, and trips.

Swimming: Outdoor Seasonal Pool, C-318-456-3482 offers lap and open swim, swim lessons, water slides and a children's pool.

Things To Do: Visit the Shreveport Water Works Museum, the Gardens of the American Rose Center located in a 118-acre wooded park, the Red River District or enjoy one of the many seasonal festivals and events.

Walking Trails: East Reservation offers 3 and 7-mile trails.

RV CAMPING & GETAWAYS

Barksdale AFB FamCamp & Trailers

Reservation/Contact Number Info: C-318-456-2679, C-318-453-7176. DSN-312-456-2679. Fax C-318-742-5236.

Recreation Security: C-318-456-2551.

RV Website: http://barksdalelife.com/index.php?src=gendocs&ref=FamCamp

Other Info Website: http://barksdalelife.com/index.php?src=gendocs&ref=Lodging%20Recreational&category=Recreation2

RV Email Address: Outdoorrecreation@barksdale.af.mil.

GPS Coordinates: 32°30'37"N/93°37'4"W.

Reservations: No advance reservations for sites 1-42 but required for sites 43-62. Office hours 0800-2100 daily. Camping unit must be present at time of check-in. Check-out 1200. After hours check-in with Camp Host at sites 1 and 2. Recreational Lodging Units: Reservations accepted 90 days in advance. One night's stay due at time of reservation. Check-in during normal operating hours, check-out 1200. Maximum 30-day stay for all recreational facilities. Park area and

pavilion may be reserved up to 90 days in advance with $25 deposit.
Season of Operation: Year-round.
Eligibility: AD, NG, Res, Ret and DoD-Civ.
Camper/Trailer Spaces: RV Sites (63): Paved, maximum 45', E(110/220V/20/30/50A)/S/W, Wi-Fi. Rates: $20 daily, $120 weekly, $500 monthly. Clubhouse with living room, fireplace, flat screen TV, computers and Wi-Fi. Laundry, bathhouse and showers adjacent.
Tent Spaces: Primitive, no hookups. Rates: $4 daily.
Yurt, A Frame, Cabin, Apt, Spaces: Trailers (12): Three-bedroom, one and two bath, fully furnished, laundry in sites 7-12. Rates: $55-$65 daily. Pets allowed with applicable daily fee. Clubhouse accessible.
Support Facilities: Auto Craft Shop, Auto Repair, Bathhouse, Boat Launch, Boat Rental, Bowling, Chapel, Coin Laundry, Commissary, Convenience Store, Equipment Rental, Exchange, Fire Rings, Fishing Pier, Fitness Center, Gas, Golf, Grills, Ice, Mess Hall, Pavilions, Picnic Area, Playground, Pool, Propane, Rec Center, Restrooms, RV Storage, Sewage Dump, Shoppette, Showers*, Sports Fields, Tennis Courts, Trails, Currently Upgrading the Wi-Fi system. * Handicap accessible.
RV Storage: Call C-318-456-3426 for more information.
Activities: Bicycling, Boating, Canoeing, Fishing*, Golfing, Hiking, Hunting*, Jogging, Trap/Skeet.
Credit Cards: MasterCard and Visa.
Restrictions: Pets allowed on leash. No swimming in lakes or ponds.
RV Driving Directions/Location: On Base: From Industrial Drive travel approximately 200 yards and turn left to the Commercial Traffic Gate. From the Gate: Go left on Lindberg Rd and proceed approximately 1.5 miles. Take the first left onto Range Rd. Follow Range Rd for approximately 2.5 miles. FamCamp is on the right-hand side. Check-in at clubhouse.
Area Description: Camp is situated in alternating open and wooded areas shaded by many oaks and hickories. Three lakes and eleven ponds on base offer opportunities for fishing and boating. Also, Toledo Bend, Caddo, Cross and Bistineau Reservoir lakes are conveniently located for a variety of water-oriented recreation. Full range of support facilities available on base.
RV Campground Physical Address: FamCamp, 6341 Range Road, Barksdale AFB, LA 71110-2164. Mailing Address: Barksdale FAMCAMP, P.O. Box 59, Barksdale AFB, LA 71110-2164.

Camp Minden

Address: Camp Minden Training Site, 100 Louisiana Blvd, Minden, LA 71055.
Information Line: C-318-382-4153.
Main Base Police: Emergencies dial 911.
Main Installation Website: http://geauxguard.la.gov/installations/camp-minden-training-site/
Main Base Location: Approximately 18 miles east of Shreveport, LA.
Directions to Main Gate: From I-20: Take exit 38 to Hwy 80 then left for .5 miles.
NMC: Shreveport, 18 miles east.
NMI: Barksdale AFB, approximately 30 miles west.
Exchange: C-318-382-4170.
Clubs: Enlisted Club, C-318-382-4170.
Places to Eat: Enlisted Club, C-318-382-4170. Post Exchange offers food items. Many restaurants within a short drive.
MWR: C-318- 382-4170.
MWR Website: http://geauxguard.la.gov/installations/camp-minden-training-site/camp-minden-mwr/
Things To Do: Shreveport is a large city with many interesting attractions. Visit Sci-Port: Science Center, Jubilee Zoo, The Boardwalk and multiple museums.

RV CAMPING & GETAWAYS

Camp Minden Trailers & Bunkhouse

Reservation/Contact Number Info: C-318-382-4170/4141.
RV Website: http://geauxguard.la.gov/installations/c

amp-minden-training-site/camp-minden-mwr/

Reservations: Reservations not accepted.

Season of Operation: Year-round.

Camper/Trailer Spaces: Pull-thru (14): 30A sites. Reservations not accepted. Rates: $10 daily. Available during hunting season and weekends.

Yurt, A Frame, Cabin, Apt, Spaces: Barracks: Open bay with showers and bathrooms, HVAC. Reservations not accepted. Rates: $10 daily.

Support Facilities: All Ranks Club on base.

RV Driving Directions/Location: On Base. From the Main Gate: Ask for directions at gate.

Area Description: Located in northwestern Louisiana, the area is full of history and many outdoor recreational activities. Visit the Minden Cemetery, which includes Civil War gravesites or the Germantown Colony and Museum.

RV Campground Physical Address: 5090 Dutch Harbor Ave, Minden, LA 71055.

New Orleans Naval Air Station – JRB

Address: 400 Russell Avenue, Belle Chasse, LA 70037-5000.

Information Line: Automated Information Line, C-504-678-3284.

Main Base Police: C-504-678-3518/3530/3235.

Main Installation Website:
http://www.cnic.navy.mil/regions/cnrse/installations/nas_jrb_new_orleans.html

Main Base Location: Naval Air Station Joint Reserve Base (NAS JRB) New

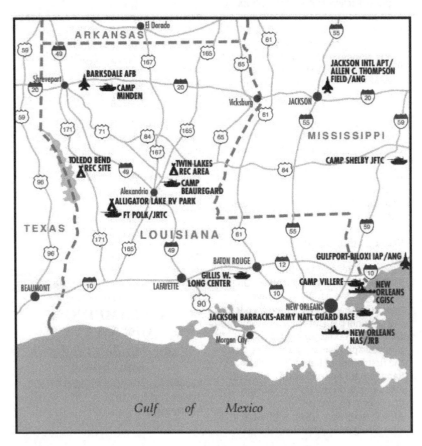

Orleans is located in Belle Chasse, Louisiana, a quiet suburb 11 miles from New Orleans.

Directions to Main Gate: Take I-10 to US-90 Business West. Cross the Crescent City Connection Bridge to the Westbank Expressway. Exit at Lafayette Street. Make a left turn at the traffic light. Keep straight on LA-23/Belle Chasse Highway and go through a tunnel. After the tunnel, stay on LA-23 for approximately 4 miles and go to Main Gate.

NMC: New Orleans, 10 miles north.

NMI: New Orleans Coast Guard ISC, less than one mile north.

Chapels: Chaplain, C-504-678-3525

Dental Clinic: C-504-678-7965.

Medical: Appointment Line, C-504 678-7914. Information, C-504-678-3660.

Veterinary Services: C-504-678-4600.

Beauty/Barber Shop: Exchange, C-504-678-2724.

Commissary: C-504-678-2587.

Exchange: C-504-678-2057.

Military Clothing: C-504-678-2780.

Financial Institutions: Navy Federal Credit Union, C-1-888-842-6328. NAS JRB Credit Union, C-504-678-3563. Wire: Bldg 300, Hours: 1000-1730 Tue-Sun, C-504-678-3580.

Clubs: Boondoggles, C-540-678-3034.

Places to Eat: Bayou Bowl, C-504-678-3514; Bayou Grill, C-504-678-4529 and the Galley, C-504-678-3421 are on base. Exchange Food Court offers Subway. Many restaurants within a short drive.

Bowling: Bayou Fun Time Bowl, C-504-678-3514.

Fitness Center: NASJRB FC, C-504-678-3230.

ITT/ITR: C-504-678-3508.

Library: C-504-678-3078.

MWR: C-504-678-3231.

MWR Website: http://www.navymwrneworleans.com/

MWR Facebook: https://www.facebook.com/MWRNOLA

MWR Twitter: https://twitter.com/mwrnasjrbnola

Outdoor Recreation: Outdoor Gear Rental, C-504-678-3142. Offers outdoor equipment, camping gear, canoes, kayaks, trailers, and boating gear.

Archery and paintball are also available on base.

Swimming: Seasonal Outdoor Pool, C-504-678-3524 offers lap swim, recreational swim, swim lessons, water slides and a children's wading pool.

Things To Do: The New Orleans area is a great location for travel and sporting activities as well as hosting a wealth of popular tourist centers. The exciting French Quarter, first class museums, the Audubon Zoo and Audubon Aquarium, historic plantations, professional sporting facilities, and unparalleled special events and festivals make New Orleans one of the country's favorite vacation destinations and a great place to live.

Walking Trails: Running track is on base.

RV CAMPING & GETAWAYS
Aviation Arbor RV Park

Reservation/Contact Number Info: C-504-678-3500, C-1-877-NAVY-BED.

Recreation Security: Emergencies dial 911.

RV Website: http://get.dodlodging.net/propertys/Aviation-Arbor-RV-Park

Other Info Website: http://www.navymwrneworleans.com/programs/446857b9-0c4b-43f0-a20f-6d46b7529d0c

RV Email Address: NORL.N92_AVATION_ARBOR@navy.mil

GPS Coordinates: 29-49'-12"N/90-1'-14"W

Reservations: Reservations may be made up to 1 year in advance for AD, 6 months in advance for Ret/DoD-Civ. Same day reservation arriving after 1600 hours. All reservations first come, first served. Office hours 0830-1630. Must reserve RV pull-thru.

Season of Operation: Year-round.

Eligibility: AD, NG, Res, Ret, DoD-Civ, Dep, 100% DAV and Medal of Honor Winners.

Camper/Trailer Spaces: RV Sites (45): Back-in, pull-thru concrete pads, 40" max with limited 50' at some sites, picnic table, Rates: $21.50 daily; $125

Weekly; $405 monthly. Maximum stay 30 days. Additional site available for RV living for AD military and geo-bachelors. Rates: $360 monthly.

Support Facilities: Archery Range, ATM, Basketball Court, Bathhouse, Bike Rentals, Boat Rental, Canoe Rental, Concrete Pads, Covered Picnic Area, Dump Station, Equipment Rental, Fishing, Free Wi-Fi, Full Hook-up Sites, General Store, Grill Area, Internet Access, Laundry Facilities, Near Golf Course.

RV Storage: C-504-678-3448.

Activities: Audubon Aquarium, Insectarium, and IMAX, Audubon Zoo, Gray Line Bus and Walking Tours, Jean Lafitte Swamp Tours and World War II Museum.

Credit Cards: Cash, Visa, MasterCard, Discover or American Express.

Restrictions: Call for pet policy.

RV Driving Directions/Location: On Base. From Main Gate: Turn left at 4-way stop sign. Drive 1 block and follow signs to the RV Park.

Area Description: Located approximately 20 minutes from Downtown New Orleans, the area offers something for everyone. Enjoy the New Orleans nightlife, the Gulf beaches or the tranquility of Belle Chasse.

RV Campground Physical Address: Mailing Address: Aviation Arbor, 400 Russell Ave, Bldg 579A, NASJRB Belle Chasse, LA 70037.

Toledo Bend Recreational Site

Address: 1310 Army Recreation Road, Florien, LA 71429.

Information Line: C-888-718-9088.

Main Base Police: C-337-531-2677.

Main Installation Website:
http://www.jrtc-polk.army.mil/

Main Base Location: Located on the largest man-made reservoir in the south, 45 miles northwest of Fort Polk.

NMC: Leesville, 35 miles east.

NMI: Fort Polk, 42 miles southeast.

Exchange Gas: Commercial gas station within 20 miles.

Marina: Toledo Bend Marina, C-888-718-9088.

MWR: C-337-531-8312.

MWR Website:
https://polk.armymwr.com/us/polk

MWR Facebook:
https://www.facebook.com/fortpolkmwr

MWR Twitter:
https://twitter.com/FortPolk_MWR

Swimming: Beach available.

Things To Do: Toledo Bend is the largest man-made lake in the south and fifth largest in the country. Excellent fishing and swimming area. Campsite located on 26 acres of wooded land. Hodges Gardens and Fort Jesup offer sightseeing opportunities. Full range of support facilities available at Fort Polk.

RV CAMPING & GETAWAYS

Toledo Bend Recreational Site

Reservation/Contact Number Info: C-1-888-718-9088, C-318-565-4484. Fax C-318-565-3084.

Recreation Security: C-337-531-2911, DSN-312-863-2911. Police for recreation site: C-318-531-6825.

RV Website:
https://polk.armymwr.com/programs/toledo-bend-army-recreation-site

GPS Coordinates: 31°15'57"N/93°34'32"W.

Reservations: Accepted for AD between the 1st and 8th days of the month for the following month, 9th day on for all others. Tent sites first come, first serve. Summer Office hours 0800-1700 Mon-Fri, 0700-1900 Sat-Sun. Winter hours 0800-1700 daily. Cancellations require 48-hour notice to avoid fee. Reservations require one night's stay deposit with credit card. Check-in 1500 hours, check-out 1200.

Season of Operation: Year-round.

Eligibility: AD, NG, Res, Ret, DoD-Civ, Dep, 100% DAV, Gov't Contractors.

Camper/Trailer Spaces: RV Sites (28): Gravel (13), E(220V/50A)/W hookups, back-in, up to 35', picnic table, grill. Rates: $15 daily. Concrete (15), E(50A/30A)/W/S hookups, sites 1-6 30A only, back-in, maximum 30', picnic table, grill. Built in 2012. Rates: $20 daily. Weekly and monthly discounts available for all sites.

Tent Spaces: Primitive (15), no hookups, picnic table, grill. Rates: $5 daily.

Yurt, A Frame, Cabin, Apt, Spaces: Standard Cabins (13): One and two-bedroom, full bath, full kitchen, cooking utensils, microwave, central heat/air, TV, rollaways. Patrons must provide linens and towels. Rates: $80 daily. Texas Two-Step (2): Two-bedroom, full bath, full kitchen, cooking utensils, microwave, central heat/air, TV. Patrons must provide linens and towels. Rates: $100 daily. Yurts (5): Single room with microwave, refrigerator, window A/C unit. Patrons must provide linens and towels. Rates: $35 daily.

Support Facilities: Bathhouse, Beach, Boat Launch, Boat Rental, Equipment Rental, Fire Rings, Fishing Equipment, Fishing Pier, Grills, Ice, Laundry, Marina, Pontoon Party Barges, Pavilions, Picnic Areas, Playgrounds, Equipment, Restrooms, Sewage Dump, Shoppette, Showers, Trails.

RV Storage: None.

Activities: Boating*, Fishing**, Hiking, Kayaking, River Running Trips, Swimming, Volleyball. *Safety course required. **License required.

Credit Cards: American Express, Cash, Check, MasterCard and Visa.

Restrictions: Pets friendly cabins. No firearms. Fishing licenses available on-site.

RV Driving Directions/Location: Off Base: North of Leesville, from US-171 north or south, turn left onto Hornbeck. Turn left on LA-392. Proceed .5 miles, then turn right onto LA-473. Continue for seven miles, turn left onto LA-191 and continue for 2.1 miles to Recreation Site on right side at large Army RV Park sign.

Area Description: Toledo Bend is the largest man-made lake in the south and fifth largest in the country. Excellent fishing and swimming area. Campsite located on 26 acres of wooded land. Hodges Gardens and Fort Jesup offer sightseeing opportunities. Full range of support facilities available at Fort Polk, including Alligator Lake Recreation Site, which covers approximately 20 acres along a man-made lake.

RV Campground Physical Address: 1310 Army Recreation Rd, Florien, LA 71429.

Twin Lakes Recreation Area

Address: Camp Beauregard, 301 F Street Pineville, LA 71360-3737.

Information Line: C-318-641-5600.

Main Base Police: Park Police, C-318-641-5666.

Main Installation Website: http://geauxguard.la.gov/installations/camp-beauregard/

Main Base Location: Located on Buckhorn Road at the Camp Beauregard Range Complex.

NMC: Alexandria, 13 miles southwest.

NMI: Camp Beauregard, 7 miles west.

Exchange Gas: Commercial gas station within 1 mile.

Exchange: Approximately 7 miles away at Camp Beauregard, C-318-641-9661.

Places to Eat: Esler Field Diner, C-318-290-6281, McDonald's, Pizza Hut and Popeye's Chicken, Lee J's of the Levee, C-318-487-4628 Paradise Catfish House, C-318-640-5032 and Tunk's Cypress Inn, C-318-487-4014 are within driving distance.

Outdoor Recreation: Recreation Services at All Ranks Club, C-218-641-5619. Offers ATV trails, bicycling, boating, fishing* and hunting*(*state license required). Equipment for all courts and fields is available Recreation Services through the All Ranks Club on base.

Swimming: Pool available on base.

Things To Do: Explore the great outdoors at this recreation area located in a state wildlife management area.

Walking Trails: Trails are available at recreation area.

RV CAMPING & GETAWAYS

Twin Lakes Recreation Area

Reservation/Contact Number Info: C-318-641-5669.

Recreation Security: C-318-641-5666.

RV Website:
http://geauxguard.la.gov/installations/camp-beauregard/camp-beauregard-mwr/
Reservations: Contact Lodging, Bldg 302, for reservation information and details.
Season of Operation: Year-round.
Eligibility: AD, NG, Ret, 100% DAV.
Camper/Trailer Spaces: Sites (11): Trailers (6): Provide refrigerator, freezer, air/hear, radio, hot water, microwave, coffee pot, shower, and toilet. RV Sites offer full hookups. Rates: $20 daily trailer, $10 daily RV.
Tent Spaces: Sites (10). Primitive sites with access to male/female showers and latrines. Rates: $5 daily.
Support Facilities: Limited facilities. Exchange located on post.
RV Driving Directions/Location: Off Base: From US-165, about 1.5 miles north of Alexandria: Exit to LA-116 right (east) and follow for about four miles to Recreation area.
Area Description: Remote and primitive location.
RV Campground Physical Address: Twin Lakes Recreation Area, 301 F Street, Camp Beauregard, LA 71360-3737.

MAINE

Great Pond Outdoor Adventure Center

Address: Great Pond Outdoor Adventure Center, 9 Dow Pines Road, Great Pond, ME 04408.
Information Line: C-207-438-1000.
Main Base Police: Emergencies dial 911.
Main Installation Website:
http://cnic.navy.mil/regions/cnrma/installations/portsmouth_ns.html
Main Base Location: Located in Great Pond, Maine on a 375-acre reservation.
NMC: Bangor, 30 miles southwest.
NMI: Bangor ANG, approximately 38 miles southwest.
Exchange Gas: Commercial gas station within 22 miles.

Places to Eat: Local take out approx 7.5 miles seasonal from End of May to September. Small general store approx 9 miles that has eat-in or take out availability.
MWR Website:
http://www.navymwrportsmouthshipyard.com/
Outdoor Recreation: Great Pond Outdoor Adventure Center, C-207-584-2000. Offers a boat launch with boat rental, a camp store, CATV, dump station, equipment rental, fire rings, picnic area, playground, recreation center and restrooms. Also offers canoeing, fishing*, hiking, kayaking, mountain biking, swimming, cross country skiing, ice fishing, snowshoeing and snowmobiling. *State license required for patrons ages 16 and up. Children younger than sixteen must be accompanied by adult with a state license.
Swimming: Lake swimming is available.
Things To Do: Beautiful remote lakeside setting with two more lakes nearby; water access available. Cabins and some campsites in wooded area by the water. Acadia National Park is only a 90-minute drive away.
Walking Trails: Trails available, ask for information.

RV CAMPING & GETAWAYS

Great Pond Outdoor Adventure Center

Reservation/Contact Number Info: C-207-584-2000.
Recreation Security: C-207-438-1000, DSN-312-684-1000.
RV Website:
http://get.dodlodging.net/propertys/Great-Pond-Outdoor-Adventure-Center
Other Info Website:
http://www.navymwrportsmouthshipyard.com/programs/4d2ef246-5528-4fa9-8b2a-6126415c24bc
RV Email Address:
greatpondoac@rivah.net.
GPS Coordinates:
44°57'12"N/68°16'55"W.
Reservations: Reservations accepted and may be made up to one year in

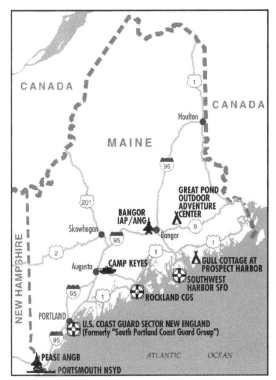

All others provide basic furnishings, one futon, table, four chairs, gas grill, heat, microwave, picnic table, fire ring and outhouse, TV/VCR/DVD. Four accessible by car. Rates: $30-$35 daily. Cabins (12): Sleep six, fully furnished. Rates: $135 daily. Bigelow (1): sleeps eight. fully furnished, with a galley kitchen, cooking utensils, dishes, bathroom with shower, large fieldstone fireplace, gas grill, lake views with access, canoe. Linens provided. Rates: $160 daily. Maine Lodge (1): Sleeps ten. fully furnished with two bathrooms, large kitchen with cooking utensils, dishes, linens, towels, three fieldstone fireplaces, washer and dryer, glass sunroom, deck and satellite TV.

advance for AD; 6 months for all others. Credit card required. Cancellations must be made 30 days in advance. If cancelled within 30 days patrons will be charged one night's stay. Office hours 0800-2000 daily. Two-night minimum stay required. Check-in 1500 hours, checkout 1100 hours. Maximum stay 7 days.
Season of Operation: Cabins: Year-round. Campsites: May-October.
Eligibility: AD, NG, Res, Ret, DoD-Civ and 100% DAV.
Camper/Trailer Spaces: Back-in (11): Partial hookups, fire ring and picnic tables. Rates: $25 daily. Dump station available.
Tent Spaces: Camp Sites (13): E/W hookups, picnic tables and fire rings. Rates: $20 daily. Wilderness Sites: No hookups. Rates: $10 daily.
Yurt, A Frame, Cabin, Apt, Spaces: Yurt (6,1 remote): Sleeps five. E/W hookups. Remote location accessible by boat only; sleeps two, no hook ups, outhouse, fire ring, picnic table, chairs.

Rates: $200 daily. Tumbledown Cabin (1), sleeps 5, two bedrooms and sleeper sofas. Fully furnished, washer and dryer. Available May-Nov. Rates: $135 May 1-Oct 3, $90 Nov 1-Apr 30. Tiny House (1): Sleeps 2 adults and 2 children, refrigerator, microwave, utensils. Bathhouse a short walk. Guests must provide linens. Rates: $50 daily.
Support Facilities: Bathhouse, Boat Launch, Boat Rental, Camp Store, CATV, Dump Station, Equipment Rental, Fire Rings, Charcoal grills, Ice, Laundry facility, Picnic Area, Playground, Recreation Center, Restrooms, and Trails.
RV Storage: None.
Activities: Canoeing, fishing*, hiking, kayaking, mountain biking, swimming, cross country skiing, ice fishing, snowshoeing and snowmobiling. *State license required for patrons ages 16 and up. Children younger than sixteen must be accompanied by adult with a state license.

Credit Cards: American Express, Discover, MasterCard, Visa, Cash.

Restrictions: Pets allowed $10 daily/pet fee for cabins and yurts. Pets must be on leash. Max two tents per site. Quiet hours 2200-0700 hours. No ATVs. No smoking in cabins or yurts.

RV Driving Directions/Location: Off Base. From New Hampshire border: Take the Maine Turnpike north (I-95N) to Exit 44 (signs for South Portland/I-295 North). Continue on I-295N until it merges with I-95N. Continue on I-95N to Exit 182A, which is I-395. Travel I-395 to Exit 6A, Route 1A South. Turn left on Route 46. Turn right on Route 49 for approximately 14 miles. Turn left at the Great Pond business district sign (first left after Route 179) Continue for 1.4 miles. Turn left onto Great Pond Road. Continue seven miles then take slight left onto Dow Pines Road.

Area Description: Beautiful remote lakeside setting with two more lakes nearby; water access available. Cabins and some campsites in wooded area by the water. Acadia National Park is only a 90-minute drive away.

RV Campground Physical Address: Great Pond Outdoor Adventure Center, 9 Dow Pines Rd, Great Pond, ME 04408.

Gull Cottage at Prospect Harbor

Address: 115 Lighthouse Point Road, Prospect Harbor, ME 04669-0229.

Information Line: C-207-438-2700.

Main Base Police: Emergencies dial 911.

Main Installation Website:
http://cnic.navy.mil/regions/cnrma/inst allations/portsmouth_ns.html

Main Base Location: Located in the picturesque fishing village of Prospect Harbor, ME.

NMC: Bangor, 50 miles northwest.

NMI: Southwest Harbor CGG, 20 miles southwest.

Exchange Gas: Commercial gas station within 10 miles.

Exchange: Approximately 20 miles away, at USCG Southwest Harbor, ME, C-207-244-5670.

Places to Eat: There are local seasonal restaurants available within driving distance of the facility. There are restaurants located in Ellsworth, that are open year-round.

MWR Website:
http://www.navymwrportsmouthshipya rd.com/

Things To Do: Visit Acadia National Park, enjoy shopping in downtown Bar Harbor or sea kayaking, biking, and whale watching from Bar Harbor.

RV CAMPING & GETAWAYS
Gull Cottage

Reservation/Contact Number Info: C-207-584-5099.

Recreation Security: C-207-667-7575.

RV Website:
http://get.dodlodging.net/propertys/Gu ll-Cottage

Other Info Website:
http://www.navymwrportsmouthshipya rd.com/programs/3fe94bd4-72ac-40fc-a356-2ffed51be931

RV Email Address:
greatpondoac@rivah.net.

GPS Coordinates:
44°24'20"N/68°1'5"W.

Reservations: Accepted. One year in advance AD, 6 months in advance all others. Credit Card required. Reservations are accepted between 0800 and 2200 hours. Check-in after 1500 hours at Administration Bldg 112. Check-out no later than 1200 hours to avoid extra charges. Two-night minimum stay, 7 night maximum.

Season of Operation: Year-round.

Eligibility: AD, NG, Res, Ret, Dep, 100% DAV and DoD-Civ.

Yurt, A Frame, Cabin, Apt, Spaces: Cottage: Two-bedroom (1), alarm clock, CATV, cookware/utensils, Cribs, cots/rollaways, fireplace, hair dryer, linens, microwave, refrigerator, telephone, toiletries, TV/VCR, living room, study, kitchen and bath. Larger groups (6 or more) require OIC's approval. Rates: $125 daily.

Support Facilities: Extremely limited. Laundry in basement of cottage. Local restaurants and shops.

RV Storage: None.

Activities: Fishing. No license required unless fishing off of boat.

Credit Cards: American Express, Discover, Mastercard, Visa.

Restrictions: No pets. Groups of six or more people require approval by OIC.

RV Driving Directions/Location: Off Base. From I-95 north or south at Bangor: Take exit 282A to I-395. From I-395 north or south: Take exit 6A to US-A1 southeast through Ellsworth. Take a left at the fourth light and stay on US-1. Follow US-1 to Gouldsboro. Take ME-195/Pond Road to Prospect Harbor. Turn left onto ME-186 and take first right onto ME-195/Corea Rd. Bear right onto Lighthouse Point Rd.

Area Description: Cottage and lighthouse, landmarks of unparalleled quality, are located on Maine's rugged Atlantic Coast. Acadia National Park nearby. Limited support facilities.

RV Campground Physical Address: Gull Cottage at Prospect Harbor, 115 Lighthouse Road, Prospect Harbor, ME 04669.

MARYLAND

Aberdeen Proving Ground

Address: 2201 Aberdeen Boulevard, Aberdeen Proving Ground, MD 21005-5000,

Information Line: C-410-278-5201, C-410-306-1403.

Main Base Police: C-410-306-2222. C-410-436-2222.

Main Installation Website:
https://www.apg.army.mil/

Main Base Location: Located 23 miles northeast of Baltimore, in Harford County, just off Maryland's beautiful Chesapeake Bay.

Directions to Main Gate: Leave the highway at Aberdeen Interchange 85: Turn right onto State Route 22 East/Aberdeen Thruway and proceed to the Aberdeen Proving Ground on Hartford Road to the Military Police Gate approximately three miles down. This gate is closed at 8 p.m. If traveling after 8 p.m. travel from Route 22. Turn off ramp at US Route 40 west and stay on the left, merging onto US Route 40 west. Proceed on Route 40 west until exit 715 on the right. Proceed onto the ramp until arriving at the Aberdeen Proving Ground Military Police Gate.

NMC: Baltimore, 30 miles southwest.

NMI: Martin State AP/Warfield ANG, 27 miles southwest.

Base Social Media/Facebook:
https://www.facebook.com/APGMd

Base Social Media/Twitter:
https://twitter.com/USAGAPG

Chapels: C-410-278-4333. After Hours Duty Cell, C-410-306-4736.

Dental Clinic: APG North, C-410-278-1795/1796. APG South, C-410-436-3481.

Medical: Kirk Medical Clinic, C-410-278-5475/1724.

Veterinary Services: C-410-278-4604.

Beauty/Barber Shop: C-410-272-7886.

Commissary: C-410-278-3101.

Exchange Gas: C-410-671-6097.

Exchange: C-410-272-6828.

Financial Institutions: Bank of America Military Bank-Main Banking Center, C-410-278-8100. Bank of America Military Bank- Beards Hill Plaza (APG) Banking Center, C-410-272-7290. Bank of America Military Bank-Proving Ground Banking Center, C-410-272-6907. APG Federal Credit Union, C-410-278-5347, C-410-272-4000.

Places to Eat: Exton Cafe, C-410-436-2213; Strike Force Cafe, C-410-278-4041 and Sutherland Grille, C-410-278-0534 are on base. Exchange Food Court offers Subway and Express Food services. Burger King is on base. Many restaurants are within a short drive.

Bowling: APG Bowling Center, C-410-278-4041.

Fitness Center: APG Athletic Center, C-410-278-7934/7933. AA Fitness Center, C-410-278-9725. Hoyle Fitness Center, C-410-436-7134.

Golf: Exton Golf Course APG South, C-410-436-2213. Ruggles Golf Course APG North, C-410-278-9452.

ITT/ITR: C-410-278-4011/4907.

Library: C-410-278-3417.
Marina: C-410-278-4124.
MWR: C-410-278-4698/7952.
MWR Website:
http://www.apgmwr.com/
MWR Facebook:
https://www.facebook.com/APGMWR
MWR Twitter:
https://twitter.com/APGMWR
Outdoor Recreation: Outdoor
Recreation, C-410-278-4124. Offers
equipment rental, skeet shooting,
stables, boating, fishing, golfing, hunting
and bounce house rentals.
Swimming: APG North Olympic Pool, C-
410-278-4124 and APG South Bayside
Pool, C-410-278-4124 offer lap swim
and open swim.
Things To Do: Historic waterfront city of
Havre de Grace approximately five miles
away has many summer activities, such
as boating, fishing, kayaking, a seafood
festival, and arts festival. This
installation is on the beautiful
Chesapeake Bay and offers hiking trails
and historical sites including the
Concord Point Lighthouse, the Maritime
Museum and the Decoy Museum. The
Cal Ripken Museum and Ripken Stadium
in the city of Aberdeen is approximately
3-5 miles away. Baltimore is 30 miles
south, Washington, D.C. is 75 miles
south and Philadelphia is 92 miles
north.

Walking Trails: Hiking and nature trails
are available.

RV CAMPING & GETAWAYS
Marylander RV Park

Reservation/Contact Number Info: C-
410-278-4124. Fax C-410-278-4160.
After hours, C-443-910-6259.
Recreation Security: C-410-306-2222,
DSN-312-458-2222.
RV Website:
https://aberdeen.armymwr.com/progra
ms/campgrounds
RV Email Address: APGR-USAG-MWR-
OutdoorRec@conus.army.mil.
GPS Coordinates: Located off Maryland
Avenue, on Atlantic Court.
Reservations: Reservations required.
APG Campground rules must be read
(see website), signed and returned to
office via scan, email or Fax C-410-278-
4160. Online registration available on
website. ODR Office hours 0900-1700
Mon-Fri, Bldg 2184. Reservations must
be paid in full at time of reservation and
eligibility confirmed. Refunds are only
given in emergency situations. Check-in
1500-1700 Mon-Fri, check-out 1200
Mon-Sun. Maximum 14-day stay.
Season of Operation: 1 April-1
November. Weather permitting,
exceptions may be made.

Eligibility: AD, NG, Res, Ret, DoD-Civ and 100% DAV.

Camper/Trailer Spaces: Marylander RV Park (11): Concrete pad, full utility service, picnic table, fire pit. Rates: AD $20 daily; Ret $30 daily; DoD $35 daily; Sponsored Guest $50 daily. Weekly and monthly discounts. Pin code for water for utilities provided at check-in.

RV Storage: Yes. C-410-278-4124/5789.

Activities: Boating, Fishing*, Golfing, Hiking, Hunting**. *State license required. **State license and base permit required. Contact ODR for full rules and regulations.

Credit Cards: American Express, Discover, MasterCard and Visa.

Restrictions: Pets allowed on leash. Campfires allowed (weather permitting). All firearms must be stored with installation police until departure.

RV Driving Directions/Location: On Base: Ask for directions at Gate. Located off Maryland Avenue, on Atlantic Court.

Area Description: Located near the mouth of the Susquehanna River, where the river enters the Chesapeake Bay, offering a wide array of water and outdoor activities and events. The southside is bordered by the Gunpowder River. The installation lies on two peninsulas separated by the Bush River.

RV Campground Physical Address: Mailing Address: ODR, Bldg 2184, Swan Creek Dr, USAG, Aberdeen Proving Ground, MD 21005-5001.

Shore Park Travel Camp & Cabins

Reservation/Contact Number Info: C-410-278-4124.

RV Website: https://aberdeen.armymwr.com/progra ms/campgrounds

GPS Coordinates: 39°28'49.6"N/76°07'18.2"W

Reservations: Reservations accepted by phone 120 days in advance for AD; 90 days in advance for all others. Office hours (Oct- March) 1000-1600 Mon-Fri. Summer: (Apr-Sept) 0800-1600 Mon, 1000-1600 Tues-Thurs, 0800-1700 Friday Minimum 2-night stay required

for weekends. Maximum stay 30 days. Cabins require deposit equal to one night's stay. Proof of eligibility must be provided. IAW AR 215-1: Patrons are allowed to stay in one RV site 60 days in peak season (Apr 1- Oct 31), 90 days in non-peak season (Nov 1- Mar 30). Check-in 1400 hours Mon-Fri, check-out 1200 hours Sat-Sun. Arrival after 1700 hours considered late arrival and must be arranged through ODR office.

Season of Operation: Year-round.

Eligibility: AD, NG, Res, Ret, and their dependents; Widow/ers; DoD-Civ, DoD-Civ Ret and their dependents w/ID; DAVs.

Camper/Trailer Spaces: Back-in (24): Full hookup sites, 60' maximum. Laundry facilities, bathhouse and recreation room available. Rates: $35 daily for AD/Ret; $40 daily for DoD Civ/Ret; $45 daily for APG Contractors; $60 daily for sponsored guests. Handicap accessible site available.

Yurt, A Frame, Cabin, Apt, Spaces: Cabins (5): Two bedrooms with loft, sleeps 10, private bath, microwave, refrigerator, dining area, living area with flat screen TV, coffee maker, utensils, porch swing. Linens not provided. Rates: AD/Ret $$75-85 daily; DoD $$85-95 daily; APG Contractor $95-$110 daily; Sponsored Guest $120 daily.

Support Facilities: Full range of support facilities on base. Laundry facility, bathhouse, recreation room on site.

Activities: Enjoy boating on Swan Creek, or just the tranquility of this new Travel Camp and Cabin recreation area.

Credit Cards: American Express, Discover, MasterCard and Visa.

Restrictions: Pets are not permitted at these facilities.

RV Driving Directions/Location: On Base. Take Route 40 to 715, using the right lane (#5) when entering the 715 gate. Travel through approximately 6 red lights to Aberdeen Blvd. Go to the 3rd red light at Bel Air Street and turn left. At the Bel Air Street dead end, turn right on to Swan Creek Drive. Pass ODR Bldg 2184 and turn left onto Park Drive. Turn left at the stop sign onto School

Street. School Street turns into Sydney Park. Facility ahead.

Area Description: Located off of Sidney Park Drive near Shore Park Picnic Area and Swan Creek.

RV Campground Physical Address: Outdoor Recreation, Bldg 2184 Swan Creek Drive, APG, MD 21005.

Andrews Air Force Base

Address: 1832 Robert M Bond Drive, Andrews AFB, MD 20762.

Information Line: C-301-981-1110, DSN-312-858-1110.

Main Base Police: C-301-981-2001, DSN-312-858-2001.

Main Installation Website: http://www.jba.af.mil/

Main Base Location: Joint Base Andrews is located in Prince George's County, Maryland, approximately 10 miles outside the Washington, D.C. city limits. The base is physically located in the town of Camp Springs, MD, and is bordered by three other towns (Clinton, Morningside, and Forestville).

Directions to Main Gate: From I-95 north/east portion of Capital Beltway, I-495: Take exit 9 and at the first traffic light after leaving the exit ramp, make a left turn. At the next traffic light, turn right into the Main Gate of AFB. From I-395 north: Exit South Capitol Street and cross the Anacostia River and bear left to Suitland Parkway east. Exit at Morningside on Suitland Road east to Main Gate of AFB.

NMC: Washington D.C., 10 miles northwest.

NMI: Indian Head Division, NSWC, 30 miles southwest.

Base Social Media/Facebook: https://www.facebook.com/jointbaseandrews

Base Social Media/Twitter: https://twitter.com/JBA_NAFW

Chapels: C-301-981-2111/0501.

Dental Clinic: C-240-857-5029.

Medical: C-301-981-5029/2806, DSN-312-587-5029/2806. Appointments, C-1-888-999-1212.

Veterinary Services: C-240-857-2651.

Beauty/Barber Shop: Barber, C-301-420-9874. Beauty, C-301-735-1988.

Commissary: C-301-541-1370.

Exchange Gas: C-301-735-2764.

Exchange: C-301-568-1500.

Financial Institutions: Andrews Federal Credit Union, C-1-800-487-5500, C-301-702-5500.

Clubs: Hangar One Officers' Club and Tatum's Enlisted Lounge are both located within The Club at Andrews, C-301-568-3799

Places to Eat: Freedom Hall Dining Facility, C-301-981-6516; In-Flight Kitchen, C-301-981-3543; The Landing Zone, C-301-981-4084 and Smokehouse 54, C-301-736-4887 are all on base. Exchange Food Court offers Charley's, Anthony's Pizza and Taco Bell. Burger King, Starbucks, Domino's Pizza and Subway are within walking distance. Many restaurants within a short drive.

Fitness Center: West Fitness Center, C-301-981-7101. East Fitness Center, C-301-981-1610. 24-Hour Tactical Fitness Center.

Golf: The Courses at Andrews, C-301-736-4595.

ITT/ITR: C-301-981-4041.

Library: C-301-981-6454.

MWR: C-301-981-5211/4109.

MWR Website: http://andrewsfss.com/

MWR Facebook: https://www.facebook.com/AndrewsFSS

MWR Twitter: https://twitter.com/AndrewsFSS

Outdoor Recreation: Outdoor Recreation, C-301-981-4109/5663. Offers FamCamp, an archery range, paintball field, swimming pool & splash park, and a ticket office are available on base. Yuma and Freedom Park are nearby. Rental facility offers a wide variety of camping and recreational equipment and a large fleet of rental boats.

Swimming: Pool and Splash Park, C-301-981-4109/5663 offers lap swim, lap swim, swim lessons, wading pool and scuba classes.

Things To Do: Andrews is the military aerial gateway to Washington, D.C. for most overseas VIPs and the home of Air Force One. Visit one of the many nearby museums, historical sites, or take in a seasonal football game at FedEx Field.

RV CAMPING & GETAWAYS

JB Andrews FamCamp

Reservation/Contact Number Info: C-301-981-3279.

Recreation Security: C-301-981-2001.

RV Website:
https://www.andrewsfss.com/fam-camp

RV Email Address:
andrewscampground@hotmail.com

GPS Coordinates:
38°47'4"N/76°52'53"W

Reservations: Reservations required for all secured sites. Overflow parking/sites first come, first serve. AD can make reservations 6 months in advance, Ret 4 months in advance, and Res 2 months in advance. Summer Reservation Policy (1 Apr- 30 Sept): Reservations can be made 15 days at a time with the option to request another 15 days when space is available. Winter Reservations Policy (1 Oct- 31 March): Reservations can be made 30 days at a time with the option to request another 30 days when space is available. Make checks payable to JBA Andrews FAMCAMP. Hours vary. Guest should call ahead. Check-in after 1200 hours, check-out 1100 hours. Maximum stay 60 days during summer; maximum stay 179 days during winter max if space available.

Season of Operation: Year-round.

Eligibility: AD, NG, Res, Ret and DoD-Civ.

Camper/Trailer Spaces: Concrete (30), Back-in, Maximum 40' in length, E(110/120V/30A)/S/W hookups. Rates: $20 daily. Concrete (6), Back-in, Maximum 30' in length, E(110/120V/30A) hookup. Rates: $16 daily. Pull-thru Electric only site (1). Rates: $12 daily.

Tent Spaces: Primitive Sites available. Rates: $12 daily.

Support Facilities: Bathhouse, Grills, Golf, Lake, Laundry, Picnic Area, Playground, Restrooms, Sewage Dump, Showers, Telephone, TV Lounge.

RV Storage: Yes, C-301-981-5663/4109.

Activities: Fishing*, Golfing, Horseshoes. *No license necessary for fishing on base. Catch and release only.

Credit Cards: Check, Mastercard and Visa.

Restrictions: Pets allowed on leash. Fenced dog walk area available. All firearms must be registered with security police. No ground fires. Clotheslines not permitted. Water lines must be disconnected when outside temperatures are below freezing. No feeding of wildlife.

RV Driving Directions/Location: On Base: From any direction on I-495: Take exit 11-A (MD Rt 4 South). At the third light turn right onto Dower House Rd. After approximately 8/10 mile take the first right into the base through the Pearl Harbor/Commercial Delivery gate. After inspection, go through the first stop sign. At the second stop sign turn left onto East Perimeter Road and follow it 2.2 miles to the south end of the base. Travel past the runways on the right and past the base lake on the left. Turn left on Wheeling Road and FamCamp ahead.

Area Description: Aerial gateway to Washington, D.C., and home of Air Force One, the President's aircraft. There is much to do in the way of entertainment, monuments, parks, museums, restaurants, theaters, zoo, aquariums, etc. Three excellent 18-hole golf courses within walking distance of FAMCAMP. Full range of support facilities available on base.

RV Campground Physical Address: JB Andrews FAMCAMP, 4520 Wheeling Rd, JB Andrews, MD 20762

Edgewood Area – APG

Address: Edgewood Chemical Biological Center, 5183 Black Hawk Road, Edgewood, MD 21010.

Information Line: C-410-436-1159, Fax C-410-436-6529.

Main Base Police: C-410-436-2222, DSN-312-584-2222.

Main Installation Website:
https://www.ecbc.army.mil/

Main Base Location: Located 23 miles northeast of Baltimore, in Harford

County, Aberdeen Proving Ground (APG) is home to nearly 70 tenant organizations. Located just off Maryland's beautiful Chesapeake Bay.

Directions to Main Gate: From Baltimore take I-95 North to exit 77A, MD Route 24 South. Proceed approximately 4 miles to the Edgewood Area gate.

NMC: Baltimore, 25 miles southwest.

NMI: Aberdeen Proving Ground, 12 miles northeast.

Base Social Media/Facebook: https://www.facebook.com/Edgewood ChemBioCenter/

Base Social Media/Twitter: https://twitter.com/EdgewoodChemBio

Beauty/Barber Shop: C-410-676-8160.

Commissary: Aberdeen PG, C-410-278-3101.

Exchange: C-410-671-6097.

Places to Eat: Exton Cafe, C-410-436-2213. Subway, C-410-671-9446.

Fitness Center: C-410-436-7134, DSN-312-584-7134.

Golf: Exton Golf Course, C-410-436-2213.

MWR: C-410-278-4402.

MWR Website: http://www.apgmwr.com/

MWR Facebook: https://www.facebook.com/APGMWR/

Outdoor Recreation: MWR Outdoor Recreation, C-410-278-4124/5789/2134/2135. Offers boating, fishing*, golfing and hunting* (*state license required).

Swimming: C-410-436-2713, DSN-312-584-2713.

Things To Do: There are many attractions in nearby Havre de Grace, including Concord Lighthouse, Decoy Museum, Stafford Furnace and the Susquehanna Museum. The Carter Mansion, Jersey Toll House, and Rock Mill Run are all in Susquehanna State Park.

Walking Trails: Nature trails are available.

RV CAMPING & GETAWAYS
Skipper's Point Campground

Reservation/Contact Number Info: C-410-278-4124/5789/2134/2135. After hours, C-443-356-1856. Fax C-410-278-4160.

Recreation Security: C-410-436-2222, DSN-312-584-2222.

RV Website: https://aberdeen.armymwr.com/progra ms/campgrounds

RV Email Address: APGR-USAG-MWR-OutdoorRec@conus.army.mil.

GPS Coordinates: 39°24'27"N/76°16'49"W

Reservations: Reservations required. APG Campground rules must be read (see website), signed and returned to office via scan, email or fax. Online registration available on website. ODR Office hours 0900-1700 Mon-Fri, Bldg 2184. Reservations must be paid in full at time of reservation and eligibility confirmed. Refunds are only given in emergency situations. Call to confirm additional check-in procedures.

Season of Operation: 1 March-30 October.

Eligibility: AD, NG, Res, Ret, DoD-Civ and 100% DAV.

Tent Spaces: Wooded Area (15), no hookups. Picnic table and grill. Rates: $5 daily.

Support Facilities: Boat Launch, 20', Boat Rental**, Chapel*, Gas*, Golf*, Grills, Gym*, Nature Trail, Pavilion, Picnic Area, Playground, Port-a-Potties. Located in Edgewood Area ** Located in the Aberdeen Area, 17 miles away.

RV Storage: Yes.

Activities: Boating, Fishing*, Golfing, Hiking, Hunting**. *State license required. **State license and base permit required. Contact ODR for full rules and regulations.

Credit Cards: American Express, Discover, MasterCard and Visa.

Restrictions: Pets allowed on leash. Campfires allowed (weather permitting). All firearms must be stored with installation police until departure.

RV Driving Directions/Location: On Base. To check-in location: From I-95, take exit 85. Go east on MD-22 for three miles to Main Gate. From US-40 north, go east on MD-22 to entrance to Main Gate. To recreation facility: From I-95, take exit 77A. Go southeast on MD-24, then left on MD-755 east and follow two miles to Main Gate. From US-40, take MD-755 east to Main Gate.

Area Description: This is a primitive camping facility located on a gravel road beside the Bush River, approximately ten miles from Aberdeen Proving Ground. There are many attractions in nearby Havre de Grace, including Concord Point Lighthouse, Decoy Museum, Stafford Furnace, and the Susquehanna Museum. The Carter Mansion, Jersey Toll House, and Rock Mill Run are all in Susquehanna State Park. Limited support facilities in the Edgewood Area, full range available at Aberdeen Proving Ground.

RV Campground Physical Address: Mailing Address: ODR, Bldg 2184, Swan Creek Dr, USAG, Aberdeen Proving Ground, MD 21005-5001.

Fort George C. Meade

Address: 830 Chisholm Ave, Fort Meade, MD 20755.
Information Line: C-301-677-6261.
Main Base Police: C-301-677-6622.
Main Installation Website:
http://www.ftmeade.army.mil/
Main Base Location: Located in Maryland, midway between the cities of Baltimore, Annapolis and Washington, DC.
Directions to Main Gate: BWI Airport is a convenient 20 minutes away from Fort Meade. At BWI Airport follow signs for I-195 W: Take exit 2B for MD 295 S/Balt/Wash Pkwy toward Washington DC; Merge onto MD295 S: Exit onto Annapolis Rd/Jessup Rd/ MD 175 E/Odenton Rd toward Odenton. Continue to follow Annapolis Rd/MD-175 E for 2.5 miles and turn right at Reece Rd into the Ft Meade Main Gate and Visitor Center.
NMC: Baltimore, 18 miles northeast.

NMI: Fort Detrick Army Garrison, 55 miles northwest.
Base Social Media/Facebook:
https://www.facebook.com/FtMeade
Base Social Media/Twitter:
https://twitter.com/ftmeademd
Chapels: Chaplain, C-301-677-4337.
Dental Clinic: Kimbrough, C-301-677-8955. EPES, C-301-677-6078.
Medical: Appointment Line, C-301-677-8606. C-301-677-8392, DSN-312-622-8392.
Veterinary Services: C-301-677-1300.
Beauty/Barber Shop: C-410-551-2053. NSA Annex, C-410-672-0583. Town Center, C-410-674-7170. Beauty Shop, C-410-674-2262.
Commissary: C-301-677-4316.
Exchange Gas: C-410-672-1183, C-301-677-7425. 32 Gate Express, C-410-305-4682.
Exchange Main: C-410-305-8625.
Financial Institutions: Ft Meade Credit Union, C-410-551-5300. PNC Bank, C-410-551-5300.
Clubs: Brass Lounge, C-301-677-6969. The Lounge at The Lanes, C-301-677-5541.
Places to Eat: The Pin Deck Cafe, C-301-677-5541 is on base. Exchange Food Court offers Boston Market, Charley's, Domino's, Starbucks and Subway. Burger King, Arby's and Dunkin Donuts are within walking distance. Many restaurants are within a short drive.
Bowling: The Lanes at Ft Meade, C-301-677-5541.
Fitness Center: Gaffney Fitness Center, C-301-677-3716/3724. Murphy Field House, C-301-677-2402.
ITT/ITR: C-301-677-7354.
Library: C-301-677-5522/4509.
Military Museum: Fort Meade Museum, C-301-677-6966.
Military Museum Website:
http://www.ftmeade.army.mil/museum/
MWR: C-301-677-6635.
MWR Website:
https://meade.armymwr.com/
MWR Facebook:
https://www.facebook.com/FtMeadeMWR
MWR Twitter:
https://twitter.com/fortmeadefmwr

Outdoor Recreation: Outdoor Recreation, C-301-677-3810/3825. Offers fishing, outdoor sports, and camping equipment rentals. Also offers campers, bounce houses, dunk tank, canopies, chairs, winter recreation gear rental and trailers.

Swimming: Gaffney Fitness Center Indoor Pool, C-301-677-7916 offers lap swim, open swim and swim lessons.

Things To Do: Visit Baltimore's Fort McHenry National Monument, the Inner Harbor or see Annapolis' quaint shopping areas. Washington, D.C. is also a short drive from Fort Meade.

Walking Trails: Burba Park offers paved path around the lake.

RV CAMPING & GETAWAYS

Camp Meade RV Park

Reservation/Contact Number Info: C-301-677-6196, C-1-888-722-4237, DSN-312-622-6196.

Recreation Security: C-301-677-3662.

RV Website: https://meade.armymwr.com/programs/camp-meade-rv-park

RV Email Address: outdoor@ftmeademwr.com.

GPS Coordinates: 39°5'40"N/76°43'46"W

Reservations: Required by phone, in person at the Outdoor Recreation Branch, or online. Active duty on orders to Fort Meade may stay up to sixty days, maximum fourteen-day stay all others. Extensions may be granted on last day of reservation if space available.

Season of Operation: Year-round.

Eligibility: AD, NG, Res, Ret, DoD-Civ and EPA Emp.

Camper/Trailer Spaces: Concrete Pads (50): Back-in (29); Pull-thru (21) with max 55' length, E(110V/20/30/50A)/S/W hookups. Rates: $40-60 daily.

Tent Spaces: Primitive tent camping area, access to bath house. Rates: $17 daily per tent. Group Rates: $38 for 3-8; $133 daily for large groups.

Yurt, A Frame, Cabin, Apt, Spaces: Camper Cabins (4): Primitive, One handicap accessible. Two bedroom, sleeps 2 adults and up to 4 children, table, fridge, heat and A/C, picnic table, fire ring. No plumbing; nearby bathhouse with showers, restrooms and laundry facilities. Rates: $60 daily. Cabin with Back-In RV Site package. Rates: $86 daily.

Support Facilities: Auto Craft Shop, Ballfields, Burba Lake Park, Bowling Center, Camp Store/Propane, Chapel, Commissary, Conference Room Rental, Convenience Stores/Gas, Equipment Rental, Exchange, Fitness Centers with Indoor Pool, Library, Pet Boarding & Grooming, Playgrounds, Post Theater, Ticket Sales.

RV Storage: C-301-677-6159/3825.

Activities: Boating Rentals, Fishing*, Sightseeing, Shopping, Volleyball. *Fishing license from any state required for patrons ages 16 and up. Children younger than sixteen must be accompanied by an adult with a state license.

Credit Cards: American Express, MasterCard and Visa.

Restrictions: Pets are not allowed in cabins or lounge. Pets must be on leash and under positive control.

RV Driving Directions/Location: On Base. From I-95 north or south: Exit onto Rt 32 east. Go approximately two miles and take exit 198 for Laurel and Fort Meade. Bypass the Main Gate and enter base through the NSA/Truck delivery gate. Make a left on Mapes Rd and take a right onto Ernie Pyle St. Continue straight through Llewellyn Ave and turn right onto 85th Medical Battalion St. Road dead-ends at Wilson St. Go left and the Camp Meade RV Park is located immediately to the left. Park office is on the left. For alternate routes please call the Reservation Line.

Area Description: Centrally located between Baltimore, Annapolis and Washington, D.C., the area is rich in cultural and tourist activities. Approximately three miles south of Arundel Mills Mall and Bass Pro Shops Outlet. Public train station to Baltimore and Washington, D.C. is one mile from the park. Bus transportation is provided to Walter Reed Army Medical Center three times a day on weekends. Kimbrough Ambulatory Care Center, located on Fort Meade, is a primary care clinic with limited non-prime appointment availability and no emergency care services.

RV Campground Physical Address: Attn: Camp Meade RV Park, 2300 Wilson St, Fort Meade, MD 20755-5071.

Patuxent River Naval Air Station

Address: 21993 Bundy Road, Bldg 2090, Patuxent River, MD 20670-1132.

Information Line: C-301-342-3000, DSN-312-342-3000.

Main Base Police: C-301-757-4667/4669, DSN-312-757-4667/4669. Emergencies dial 911.

Main Installation Website: https://www.cnic.navy.mil/regions/ndw/installations/nas_patuxent_river.html

Main Base Location: Naval Air Station Patuxent River stretches across approximately 12 miles of shoreline at the mouth of the Patuxent River in St. Mary's county, overlooking the picturesque Chesapeake Bay.

Directions to Main Gate: From Baltimore/Washington International Airport: Take I-97 south to Route 3 south. Route 3 will become Route 301 south. From 301 south exit to Route 4 south. Continue through Prince Frederick and over the Governor Thomas Johnson Bridge. Go to the traffic light at the intersection of Routes 4 and 235 and turn left onto Route 235. Gate 1 is on the left at the intersection of Route 235 and Pegg Road. Gate 2 is on the left at the intersection of Route 235 and Great Mills Road (Route 246). Both intersections have a stop light.

NMC: Washington, D.C., 65 miles northwest.

NMI: Indian Head Division, NSWC, 55 miles northeast.

Base Social Media/Facebook: https://www.facebook.com/NASPaxRiver

Base Social Media/Twitter: https://twitter.com/naspaxriverpao

Chapels: C-301-342-3811.

Dental Clinic: C-301-342-1407/1408. CDO After Hours, C-301-342-1506

Medical: C-301-342-1506/1418, DSN-312-342-1506.

Beauty/Barber Shop: C-301-342-0611.

Commissary: C-301-342-3789.

Exchange Gas: C-301-863-1258.

Exchange: C-301-342-0614.

Financial Institutions: Cedar Point Federal Credit Union, C-301-863-7027.

Clubs: Bald Eagle Club, C-301-342-3656.

Places to Eat: Eddie's, Cafe 300 Snack Bar, C-301-342-3994 and River's Edge, C-301-342-3656 are on base. Exchange Food Court offers McDonald's, NAVAIR Cafeteria and Subway. Many restaurants are within a short drive.

Bowling: Pax Bowling Center, C-301-342-3994.

Fitness Center: Drill Hall Fitness Center, C-301-757-3943.

Golf: Cedar Point Golf Course, C-301-342-3597.

ITT/ITR: C-301-342-3648.

Marina: West Basin Marina, C-301-342-3573.

Military Museum: Patuxent River Naval Air Museum, C-301-863-1900.

Military Museum Website: http://paxmuseum.com/

MWR: C-301-342-3510.

MWR Website: http://www.navymwrpaxriver.com/

MWR Facebook: https://www.facebook.com/mwrpaxriver

MWR Twitter: https://twitter.com/mwrpaxriver

Outdoor Recreation: Community Recreation, C-301-342-3573. Offers canoes, kayaks and stand up paddle board rentals; picnic and pavilion reservations.

Swimming: Aquatics Center, C-301-342-5960 offers lap swim, open swim and swim lessons. Seasonal Outdoor Pool, C-301-342-4225 offers lap swim, open swim and swim lessons. Cedar Point Beach is on base.

Things To Do: Visit Calvert Cliffs, Drum Point Lighthouse, Solomon's Recreation Area, historic St Mary's City or enjoy crabbing and fishing along the Maryland shore. Follow the Patuxent Wine Trail, Check Out Sotterley Plantation or Explore Civil War History at Scenic Point Lookout State Park.

Walking Trails: Walking and nature trails are available on base.

RV CAMPING & GETAWAYS

Goose Creek – Hog Point – Paradise Grove Campgrounds

Reservation/Contact Number Info: C-301-342-3573, C-1-877-628-9233.
Recreation Security: C-301-342-3208/3218.
RV Website:
http://get.dodlodging.net/propertys/Goose-Creek-Campgrounds
Other Info Website:
http://www.navymwrpaxriver.com/programs/055f315f-3b68-45bf-9ffa-71a6a2072aa0
GPS Coordinates:
38°17'20"N/76°23'2"W
Reservations: Reservations accepted one year in advance for AD, 6 months for all others. Office hours 0730-1600 Mon-Fri. Check-in 1500 hours at Marina, 46970 Bauhof Rd; check-out 1200 hours. Max 30 day stay. Hog Point primitive trailer sites require reservations.
Season of Operation: Year-round. Goose Creek, Feb-Nov.
Eligibility: AD, NG, Res, Ret, DoD-Civ.
Camper/Trailer Spaces: Goose Creek (39): Gravel (25), back-in, maximum 48' in length, E(110V/30A)/W hookups. AD Rates: $15.75 daily, $94.50 weekly, $283.50 monthly; All others: $21 daily, $126 weekly, $378 monthly. Primitive Sites (14), no hookups. AD Rates: $12 daily, $72 weekly, $216 monthly; All others: $15.75 daily, $94.50 weekly, $283.50 monthly. Comfort station with bath and showers.
Tent Spaces: Hog Point (2 camping areas): Primitive sites, no hookups. Rates: $12 daily for AD; $14 daily all others. Paradise Grove (11): Primitive, no hookups. Rates: $12-$15.75 daily for AD; $15.75-$21 daily all others. Weekly and monthly rates available.
Support Facilities: Auto Craft Shop, Bathhouse, Beach, Boat Launch, Boat Rental, Camping Equipment, Chapel, Commissary, Convenience Store, Exchange, Fire Rings, Fishing Pier, Fitness Center, Gas, Golf, Grills, Ice, Laundry, Marina, Pavilion, Picnic Area, Playground, Pool, Rec Center, Rec Equipment, Restrooms, Sewage Dump, Shoppette, Snack Bar, Sports Fields, Tennis Courts.
Activities: Crabbing, Fishing*, Golfing, Hunting*, Jogging, Swimming Pool. *State and base licenses required for ages 16 and up. Children younger than sixteen must be accompanied by adult with a state license.
Credit Cards: American Express, Discover, MasterCard and Visa.
Restrictions: Pets allowed on leash. No firearms.
RV Driving Directions/Location: On Base: From Main Gate: Pass through the gate and continue on Cedar Point Rd. Turn left on Tate Road and follow signs to West Basin Marina for check-in.
Area Description: The campground at Goose Creek is located along the Chesapeake Bay on Cedar Point Road. The Naval Air Station offers a wide range of recreational facilities and a full range of support facilities.
RV Campground Physical Address: Goose Creek, 47476 Keane Road, Patuxent River, MD 20670. West Basin Marina, Bldg 2655, Old Bank Bldg, Patuxent River NAS, MD 20670-5423.

Solomons Navy Recreation Center

Address: Solomons Navy Rec Center, 13855 Solomons Island Road S., Solomons, MD, 20688
Information Line: C-301-342-3000, DSN-312-342-3000.
Main Base Police: C-301-757-4669, C-301-995-1941. Emergencies dial 911.
Main Installation Website:
http://www.cnic.navy.mil/regions/ndw/installations/nas_patuxent_river.html
Main Base Location: Nestled on a peninsula bound by the picturesque Patuxent River and the Chesapeake Bay.
NMC: Washington, D.C., 65 miles northwest.
NMI: Patuxent River NAS, 10 miles south.
Chapels: C-301-342-3811.

Medical: Naval Health Clinic, C-301-342-1506/1418, DSN-312-342-1506.
Commissary: Approximately 10 miles away at Patuxent River NAS, C-301-342-3789 ext 3001.
Exchange Gas: Approximately 10 miles away at Patuxent River NAS. Commercial gas station within 2 miles.
Exchange: Approximately 10 miles away at Patuxent River NAS, C-301-342-0614.
Places to Eat: Bald Eagle Pub, C-301-342-3656. River's Edge Catering & Conference Center, C-301-342-3656, Menu Line: C-301-342-1683. There are also numerous restaurants within driving distance.
Golf: Cedar Point Golf Course, C-301-342-3597.
ITT/ITR: C-301-342-3648.
Marina: Point Patience Marina, C-410-326-2859.
MWR Phone Number: C-301-342-3510.
MWR Website:
http://www.navymwrsolomons.com/
Outdoor Recreation: MWR, C-301-342-3648. Solomons Recreation offers a multitude of activities and recreation opportunities to include a 124-slip marina, fishing pier, swimming pools, beach, miniature golf, driving range, basketball courts and tennis courts and much more. Park and picnic reservations, C-410- 286-7302; Point Patience Marina, C-410-286-8022/8023, Sunset Pier/Marina, C-410-286-8023, West Basin Marina, C-301-342-3573 and Adventure Zone, C-410-286-8046/8047.
Swimming: Riverside Aquatics Complex, C-410-394-2845. Base pool, C-301-342-5449, C-301-757-1293.
Things To Do: This is a complete recreational area. Full support facilities are at Patuxent River NAS. St. Mary's City, Calvert Cliffs, Calvert Marine Museum, Farmers' Market, charter fishing and Point Lookout State Park are all available sources of entertainment.
Walking Trails: Nature trails available at nearby parks.

RV CAMPING & GETAWAYS

Solomons Navy Recreation Center

Reservation/Contact Number Info: C-1-877-NAVY-BED, C-410-392-6872/3719. Fax C-410-394-3758.
Recreation Security: C-410-326-2980. Emergencies dial 911.
RV Website:
http://www.navymwrsolomons.com/
RV Email Address: info.mwr-solomons.fcm@navy.mil
GPS Coordinates:
38°20'32"N/76°28'3"W.
Reservations: Required. Reservations accepted one year in advance for all AD; six months in advance for Ret/Dod-Civ. Online reservations preferred. Summer Office hours 0800-2100 Mon-Thur; 0700-2300 Fri; 0800-2200 Sat-Sun. Cancellations must be made within 30 days of arrival to avoid fees. 90-day maximum stay for RV Sites. Complimentary Leisure Passes provided, depending on reservation. Additional passes may be purchased for fee. Comfort Stations throughout the Recreation Area are under renovation. Expected completion Summer 2016.
Season of Operation: Year-round.
Eligibility: AD, NG, Res, Ret and DoD-Civ.
Camper/Trailer Spaces: RV Sites (146), Concrete pads, E(110V/30A50A)/S/W full hookups, back-in, maximum 60' picnic table and grill. Rates: $30-$41 daily depending on length of stay and on/off seasonal rates; Concrete pads, (152), E(120V/30A/50A)/W partial hookups, back-in, maximum 60', picnic table and grill. Rates: $25-$36 daily depending on length of stay and on/off seasonal rates.
Tent Spaces: Camper/Tent Spaces: (56), no hookups, charcoal grill, picnic table. Rates: $5-$20 daily depending on length of stay and on/off seasonal rates. Group Sites (15), no hookups. Rates: $45-$70 daily, depending on season.
Yurt, A Frame, Cabin, Apt, Spaces: Waterfront Cottages (6): Two, four and five-bedroom cottages fully furnished

with CATV. Linens provided. Rates: $115-$205 daily. Cottages (7): Two, three, four and five-bedroom cottages fully furnished with CATV. Linens provided. Rates: $110-$200 daily. Apartments (2): One, two, three and four-bedrooms, fully furnished with CATV. Rates: $90-$165 daily. Deluxe Cottages (21): Three bedroom, recently renovated, fully furnished with CATV. Linens provided. Rates: $110-$145. All rates depending on reservation status and on/off seasonal rates. Deluxe Cabins/Upgraded Cabins (5): Furnished cabins with CATV. Single Rates: $95-$125 daily; Full Rates: $150-$220 daily. Yurts (2): Furnished but primitive in nature; 24' diameter structure. Linens not provided. Rates: $15-$35 depending on reservation status and on/off seasonal rates. Basic Cabins (3): Primitive in nature. Linens not provided. Rates: $25-$50 daily.

Support Facilities: Bait/Tackle, Ball Fields, Beach, Boat Launch, Boat Rental, Boat Slip Rental, Camper Rental, Camping Equipment, Driving Range, Fish/Crab Pier, Gazebo, Grills, Ice, Laundry, Marina, Miniature Golf, Party Pavilions, Picnic Area, Playground, Pools, Racquetball Court, Restrooms, RV Storage, Sewage Dump, Showers, Softball Field, Sports Equipment, Tennis Courts, Video Arcade.

RV Storage: C-410-326-2924 for long term storage information.

Activities: Basketball, Bicycling, Boating, Crabbing*, Duck Hunting*, Fishing*, Horseshoes, Special Events, Swimming, Volleyball, Windsurfing. *License required.

Credit Cards: American Express, Discover, MasterCard and Visa.

Restrictions: Pets are not allowed inside lodging units. Pet owners must have proof of shots and register pet at the Reservation and Information Center; pet must be in a kennel. Open fires prohibited except in group site areas where fire rings are provided.

RV Driving Directions/Location: Off Base. On the Patuxent River. From US-301 North or South: Take MD-4 southeast to Solomons on right. From MD-5 southeast: Take MD-235, then MD-4 northeast to Solomons on left.

Area Description: Located in southern Maryland on approximately 260 acres with extensive frontage on the Patuxent River and the Chesapeake Bay. The area is known as "The land of pleasant living."

RV Campground Physical Address: 13855 Solomons Island Road, Solomons, MD 20688. Mailing Address: Solomons Navy Recreation Center, PO Box 147, Solomons, MD 20688.

United States Naval Academy – Annapolis NSA

Address: 121 Blake Road, U.S. Naval Academy Administration, Annapolis, MD 21402-5073.

Information Line: C-410-293-1000, DSN-312-281-1000.

Main Base Police: C-410-293-5763.

Main Installation Website: https://www.cnic.navy.mil/regions/ndw /installations/nsa_annapolis.html

Other Info Website: https://www.usna.edu/homepage.php

Main Base Location: The U.S. Naval Academy (USNA) is located in Annapolis, Maryland on the banks of the Severn River and on the shores of the Chesapeake Bay. Annapolis is located in Anne Arundel County.

Directions to Main Gate: From Washington, DC: Take US 50 East. Cross over the Severn River Bridge and take exit 27 to the Naval Academy. Go 1 mile and at first light turn left onto MD Rt 648. Follow the road to next light. Turn right at light onto Kinkaid Rd. Follow the road to the first guard shack. Continue on Kinkaid Road through housing then bear left onto Bennion Road. The first building on the left at 168 Bennion Road. Parking and entrance is located at the rear of the building.

NMC: Annapolis, within city limits.

NMI: Fort George Meade, 20 miles north west.

Base Social Media/Facebook: https://www.facebook.com/NSAAnnap olis/

Base Social Media/Twitter:
https://twitter.com/NavalAcademy
Chapels: C-410-293-1100.
Dental Clinic: C-410-293-3756/3788.
Medical: C-410-293-2273, C-1-800-475-9365, DSN-312-281-2273.
Beauty/Barber Shop: C-410-757-5870 ext 3701/3700. Naval Academy, C-410-293-3200.
Commissary: C-410-972-0049.
Exchange Gas: C-410-757-5870.
Exchange: C-410-757-5870. Midshipmen Store, C-410-293-2392.
Financial Institutions: Navy Federal Credit Union, C-1-888-842-6328.
Clubs: The Club at Greenbury Point, C-410-293-4679. Naval Academy Club, C-410-293-2633.
Places to Eat: Drydock Restaurant, C-410-293-2434, Steerage, C-410-293-2950 and The Alley are located at the Naval Academy. Exchange Food Court offers Subway and Panda Express. Many restaurants are within a short drive.
Fitness Center: C-410-293-9204. Naval Academy Brigade Sports Complex, C-410-293-9700.
Golf: United States Naval Academy Golf Club, C-410-293-9747.
ITT/ITR: C-410-293-9200.
Library: Nimitz Library, C-410-293-6945.
Marina: Carr Creek Marina and Mill Creek Pier, C-410-293-2058/3731.
Military Museum: United States Naval Academy Museum, C-410-293-2108.
Military Museum Website:
http://www.usna.edu/Museum/
MWR: C-410-293-9210/9200.
MWR Website:
http://www.navymwrannapolis.com/
MWR Facebook:
https://www.facebook.com/FFRAnnapolis
Outdoor Recreation: Outdoor Recreation Services, C-410-293-9200. Offers of camping supplies, sports equipment and party supplies including inflatables. Marina offers sailing lessons and boat rentals.
Swimming: North Severn Pool Outdoor Pool, C-410-293-2082 offers lap swim, open swim, swim lessons and aquatic classes. South Severn Outdoor Pool, C-410-293-3033 offers lap swim, open swim and swim lessons.

Things To Do: Don't miss a trip to the waterfront shopping and restaurant area. Visit the Naval Academy Chapel and historic buildings and walk around this historic capital city.
Walking Trails: Appointed walking trails are on base.

RV CAMPING & GETAWAY
Annapolis Campground

Reservation/Contact Number Info: C-410-293-9200, C-1-877-NAVY-BED.
Recreation Security: C-410-293-5760.
RV Website:
http://get.dodlodging.net/propertys/Annapolis
Other Info Website:
http://www.navymwrannapolis.com/programs/ddaaad0e-8b94-4e6b-8aab-796b571b801b
RV Email Address: market.mwr-nsaa.fcm@navy.mil
GPS Coordinates:
38°59'09.55"N/76°27'53.97"W
Reservations: Reservations required. Accepted by phone or online www.dodlodging.net. Check-in at Blue Jacket Community Recreation Center, Bldg 46. Office hours 0530-2000 Mon-Fri, 0900-1700 Sat-Sun, 0900-1700 Federal holidays. Closed Thanksgiving. Christmas, and New Year's Day.
Season of Operation: Year-round, tent camping Apr-Oct.
Eligibility: AD, NG, AD Res, Ret, DoD-Civ AD/Ret.
Camper/Trailer Spaces: Hardstand (14), Concrete pad, back-in, limited sites can accommodate 38'-40', depending on style, E(110V/30A)/W hookups. Rates: $22 daily.
Tent Spaces: Primitive (12), no hookups. Rates: $3 daily/person.
Support Facilities: Auto Skills Shop, Boat Rental, Equipment Rental, Fitness Center, Gas, Golf, Grills, Marina, Mini Mart, Picnic Area, Playground, Pools (seasonal), Racquetball Courts, Rec Center, Restrooms, Sewage Dump, Showers, Sports Fields.
RV Storage: None.
Activities: Crabbing*, Fishing*, Golfing, Racquetball, Swimming, Tennis. * State

license required for patrons ages 16 and up. Children younger than sixteen must be accompanied by adult with a state license.

Credit Cards: American Express, Discover, MasterCard and Visa.

Restrictions: Pets allowed on leash. No firearms. No open fires. No swimming in area waterways.

RV Driving Directions/Location: On Base. From Washington DC: Take Route 50 East. Cross the Rte 50 Bridge over the Severn River. Take the first exit to Naval Academy/Rte 450. Bear right on Rte 450. Proceed about 1-1.5 miles to the stoplight at Rte 450 and 648. Turn left onto Rte 648 (DON'T go over the bridge to the Naval Academy). Follow the signs to the Navy Exchange/Commissary. At the "Y" in the road, stay to the right which becomes Greenbury Point Road. Continue another block and turn right at the stoplight onto Kinkaid Road. Follow Kinkaid through to the Guard Gate. Stop at the gate. Bear left at the guard gate and down the big hill at which point the road becomes "Bennion" Road. Continue down the big hill to the Blue Jacket Community Recreation Center, Bldg 46, on the left. Register at Customer Service Desk.

Area Description: Located in one of America's most historic cities. The area boasts great seafood, boating, and a vibrant waterside scene. The new Visitor's Center is conveniently located in the heart of city. Be sure to visit many of its historical sites, including the burial site of Revolutionary War hero John Paul Jones. The Annapolis Yacht Club draws many spectators to its yacht races.

RV Campground Physical Address: Annapolis Campground, 328 Kinkaid Road, Annapolis, MD 21402.

MASSACHUSETTS

Cuttyhunk Island Recreational Facility

Address: Boston Coast Guard Integrated Support Command, 427 Commercial St, Boston, MA 02109.

Information Line: C-617-223-3312.

Main Base Police: Emergencies dial 911.

Main Installation Website: http://www.uscg.mil/baseboston/

Main Base Location: Cuttyhunk Island is 15 miles over water from New Bedford. Ferry reservations at least three weeks in advance highly recommended.

NMC: Boston, approximately 72 miles north (via ferry).

NMI: Newport Naval Station, RI 48 miles west (via ferry).

Commissary: Approximately 30 miles away at Hanscom AFB, C-781-377-4210.

Exchange: Gas available at close-by Cuttyhunk Town Marina.

Exchange: Approximately 30 miles away at Hanscom AFB, C-781-862-0580.

Places to Eat: There are two small restaurants and a small convenience store on the island.

Outdoor Recreation: MWR Recreation, C-617-223-3458. Offers beach swimming, hiking, bicycles rentals and a basketball court.

Swimming: Swimming at the beach.

Things To Do: The dwelling site, a former Coast Guard lifeboat station, is approximately 300 yards from the ferry landing and is within easy walking distance of the local community. As the community is very small and depends on ferry service for delivery of supplies, prices will be understandably higher than on the mainland. A small grocery store is available on the island, but visitors are advised to bring adequate food and laundry supplies to meet most of their needs during their stay. Full range of support facilities at Newport Naval Station, RI. On the island there are great beaches and many activities, including fishing, bicycling, boating, hiking and swimming. Martha's

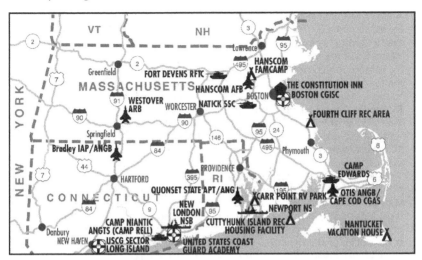

Vineyard, with its nature preserves and historical sights, is to the east. Each rental unit also has use of a gas-powered golf cart. Filling the cart up at the end of the week is the responsibility of the occupants.

RV CAMPING & GETAWAYS

Cuttyhunk Island Housing Facility

Reservation/Contact Number Info: 617-223-3458.

Recreation Security: C-617-223-3333.

RV Website:
https://www.dcms.uscg.mil/Our-Organization/Assistant-Commandant-for-Human-Resources-CG-1/Community-Services-Command-CSC/MWR/Coast-Guard-Lodging/

RV Email Address:
USCG.Boston.MWR@uscg.mil.

GPS Coordinates:
41°18'5"N/71°5'58"W.

Reservations: Recommended. Priority One: AD and their dependents. Priority Two: All other MWR patrons, Ret, Res, DHS/NAF-Civ employed by the Coast Guard, members of the Coast Guard Auxiliary and 100% DAV. C-617-223-3181, 0600-1400 hours Mon-Fri. Check-in 1000 hours Sun at Cuttyhunk Island Landing Dock, check-out 1000 hours Sat.

Season of Operation: 1 May-30 Nov.

Eligibility: AD, NG, Res, Ret, DHS/CG-Civ Emp and 100% DAV.

Yurt, A Frame, Cabin, Apt, Spaces: Apartment: Three-bedroom apartment upstairs (1) and two-bedroom apartment downstairs (1). Each apartment has private kitchen and bathroom facilities. Both apartments are fully furnished, including bed linen, towels, blankets, radio, pots, pans, dishes, glasses, silverware, etc. Cribs and folding beds are available on the premises. There is a common room for all guests with a television, VCR and basic satellite television service. Movie rentals are available on the island. A laundry room with washer and dryer is located on the first floor. Guests are responsible for washing their own bed linen and towels and leaving them clean for incoming occupants. Rates: $500-$900 weekly (depending on rank and size of apartment). Units are non-smoking. Note: There are no TVs or telephones in individual units. No housekeeping service. Facility also provides two golf carts and bicycles for getting around the island.

Support Facilities: Beach and Convenience Store. Marina has NO handicap or medical facilities.

RV Storage: None.

Activities: Bicycling, Boating, Fishing*, Hiking, Swimming, Nature Trails, Picnic

Area, Playground. *Saltwater fishing, no license required.

Credit Cards: Check or Money Order.

Restrictions: Pets allowed. No vehicles. No firearms. Units are non-smoking. Renters are encouraged to bring a lock to secure valuables.

RV Driving Directions/Location: Off Base: On Cuttyhunk Island. From I-195 east or west, take exit 15 south on MA-18 in New Bedford. Take Downtown exit. Continue straight on Water Street. Take left onto Union Street to bottom of road. Look for signs to the boat and state pier. Transportation to the island is via ferry M/V ALERT, C-508-992-1432, or Cuttyhunk Ferry Co, Inc, C-508-992-0200 (call for arrival/departure times. WEB: www.cuttyhunkferryco.com). Cuttyhunk Island is 15 miles over water from New Bedford. Directions from ferry to house will be given at time reservations are made. Ferry reservations at least three weeks in advance highly recommended.

Area Description: The dwelling site, a former Coast Guard lifeboat station, is located 14 miles south off the coast of New Bedford and just west of Martha's Vineyard. It is approximately 300 yards from the ferry landing and is within easy walking distance of the local community. As the community is very small and depends on ferry service for delivery of supplies, prices will be understandably higher than on the mainland. A small grocery store is available on the island, but visitors are advised to bring adequate food and laundry supplies to meet most of their needs during their stay. NOTE: The Island Market and Raw Bar only take cash or checks. No credit or debit cards. Full range of support facilities at Newport Naval Station, RI.

RV Campground Physical Address: USCG Boston MWR, 427 Commercial Street, Boston, MA 02109-1027.

Fourth Cliff Recreation Area

Address: Fourth Cliff Recreation, 348 Central Ave, Humarock, MA 02047.
Information Line: C-781-225-1110.

Main Base Police: C-781-225-5000. Emergencies dial 911.

Main Installation Website: http://www.hanscom.af.mil/

Main Base Location: Fourth Cliff Family Recreation Area is a 56-acre seaside resort located in Humarock (Scituate) on Massachusetts' South Shore.

NMC: Boston, 30 miles north.

NMI: Hanscom AFB, 46 miles northwest.

Chapels: C-781-225-5501.

Medical: C-781-225-6789 for appointments, DSN-312-845-6789.

Exchange Gas: Commercial gas station within 7 miles.

Places to Eat: The Recreation Hall offers a seasonal snack bar and beer and wine bar. There are many restaurants within driving distance. On Hanscom AFB there is the E Club, C-781-377-2123, Minuteman Commons, C-781-225-6501, Duke's Bar and Grill, C-781-274-0300, Burger King, C-781-274-7970, Dunkin Donuts, C-781-274-9910, Bowling Center, C-781-377-2237 and Pizza Sub Shop, C-781-274-0133 are within walking distance. Cafe Luigi, C-781-271-0666, Chili's, C-781-273-9309 and Great Wall, C-781-275-7007 are within driving distance.

Fitness Center: C-781-225-6630.

Golf: Hanscom Patriot Golf Course, C-781-687-2396, approximately 3 miles from base.

ITT/ITR: C-781-225-6505.

Library: C-781-225-2766.

MWR: C-781-225-1359.

MWR Website: http://www.hanscomservices.com/

Outdoor Recreation: Outdoor Recreation office at Hanscom AFB, C-781-225-6621. Swimming, fishing, and beachcombing are available on site. Martha's Vineyard is also nearby. Outdoor Recreation office at Hanscom AFB offers a wide variety of summer rental equipment such as gear for boating, camping, outdoor sports, bicycling and much more. Outdoor Recreation also offers winter sports rentals including snowboarding, skiing, and other winter sports equipment.

Swimming: Beach swimming is available. Indoor Olympic swimming pool, C-781-225-6638 is available on Hanscom AFB.

Things To Do: Easy access to Boston, Cape Cod, Martha's Vineyard and Nantucket Islands. Located on a cliff overlooking the Atlantic and scenic North River, this is an excellent place for a vacation. Near Hanscom AFB, delve into U.S. history by visiting Minute Man National Historical Park, Boston Children's Museum, Battle Road near Fiske Hill in Lexington, the Wayside Unit, the homes of Louisa May Alcott and Nathaniel Hawthorne, and the Lexington Green.

Walking Trails: The gym has an indoor running track.

RV CAMPING & GETAWAYS

Fourth Cliff Recreation Area

Reservation/Contact Number Info: C-1-800-468-9547, C-781-837-9269. Fax C-781-837-4921.

Recreation Security: Local Police, C-781-545-1212.

RV Website: https://www.hanscomfss.com/fourth-cliff

RV Email Address: Fourth-cliff@comcast.net (For information only)

GPS Coordinates: 42°9'37"N/70°42'22.75"W

Reservations: Accepted. Hanscom AFB AD 120 days in advance; AD all branches including NG/Res 80 days in advance; Retirees 75 days in advance; DAV 70 days in advance. Office hours 0800-1630 Mon-Fri. Check-in 1400 at Fourth Cliff Recreation Hall, Bldg 7; check-out 1100 hours. Cancellation policy adhered to; early departures and cancellations generally result in forfeiture of payment. Peak season reservations limited to 7-day max. For late/early check-ins and for off-season hours, C-781-837-6785. Ask about special discounts. RV sites generally require reservations; check-out 1200.

Season of Operation: Year-round. May-October for RV and camping.

Eligibility: AD, NG, Res, Ret, DoD-Civ and 100% DAV.

Camper/Trailer Spaces: Concrete (11), back-in, Maximum 42' in length. E(110V/30/50A)/S/W, CATV hookups. Rates: $40 daily; primitive $15 daily.

Tent Spaces: Primitive, no hookups, Rates: $16 daily per tent.

Yurt, A Frame, Cabin, Apt, Spaces: Cottages: Three-bedroom, sleeps 8 (4, 2 handicap); Fully furnished 2-floor cottage, winterized; gas log fireplace. Two queen beds, two twins and crib. Linens and towels provided for up to four occupants. Rates: $150 daily. Chalets: Two-bedroom, sleeps 6 (11); Fully furnished and winterized, gas log fireplace. One queen bed, two twins and crib. Linens and towels provided for up to four occupants. Rates: $135 daily. Efficiencies (4, 1 handicap); One-room with pull-out sofa and queen bed, furnished, modified kitchen with microwave, full fridge but no stove; winterized, gas log fireplace. Linens and towels provided for up to four occupants. Rates: $100 daily. Coin-operated laundry available in Bldg 6. Charcoal grills, all rentals with water views.

Support Facilities: Bathhouse, Beach, Boat Launch, Chapel, Convenience Store, Equipment Rental, Gas, Golf, Grills, Ice, Laundry/pay, Pavilion, Picnic Area*, Playground, Propane, Rec Center, Rec Equipment, Restrooms, Showers, Snack Bar, Telephone/Pay, Trails.* May be rented for group picnics, reservation required. Arrangements can be made for sewage dump.

RV Storage: None.

Activities: Fishing, Horseshoes. Visitor information display is available for local sights and attractions. Discount passes and season tickets are available and may be reserved.

Credit Cards: MasterCard and Visa.

Restrictions: All units are non-smoking. Pets are not allowed inside any cabins or on the porches. In other areas, pets must be leashed or tied at all times and must not annoy other guests. Firearms and/or hunting equipment not allowed. No open fires.

RV Driving Directions/Location: Off Base: From the north and Hanscom AFB:

Take I-95 South, continue to I-93 North, watching for signs to I-93N/Boston/Braintree/US-1 N, until intersecting with Route 3 South. From Boston: Take I-93 South until it intersects with Route 3 South. Take Route 3 south to exit 12 to Marshfield/Pembroke). **Turn right (East) on to Route 139 toward Marshfield. Drive 1.5 miles to the fourth traffic light (first light at exit) and make a left turn at the fourth traffic light onto Furnace St. Continue to the "T" intersection then take a left turn onto Ferry St, continuing until it intersects with Sea St at the Bridgeway Inn restaurant. Make a right turn on to Sea St and cross over the bridge. Make a left turn onto Central Ave and drive north to the fork in the road, then bear left to the Fourth Cliff gate. Open the gate and proceed to check-in at Bldg 7. From the South Route 3 northbound: Follow the directions above, starting at the exit, count three traffic lights. From Logan Airport or Boston: Take I-93 South to MA Rt. 3 South and follow directions above, starting at the right turn east onto Route 139. Do not take exit 12 off I-93 South when coming from Boston. Note: All vehicles, including recreational vehicles, must enter and exit through the Main Gate. Gate is not locked; please close when entering or exiting.

Area Description: Fourth Cliff is a 56-acre military family recreation area situated atop a cliff on the tip of a small peninsula overlooking the Atlantic Ocean to the east and the scenic North River to the west. Easy access to Boston, Cape Cod, Martha's Vineyard, Nantucket Islands and a host of recreational activities. Full support facilities available at Hanscom AFB.

RV Campground Physical Address: Fourth Cliff Recreation Area, 348 Central Ave, P.O. Box 479, Humarock, MA 02047-5000.

Hanscom Air Force Base FamCamp

Address: 1003 South Road, Bedford, MA 01730.

Information Line: C-781-225-1110, DSN-312-845-1110.

Main Base Police: Emergencies dial 911.

Main Installation Website: http://www.hanscom.af.mil/

Main Base Location: Left off of South Street 2 miles from base.

NMC: Boston, 20 miles southeast.

NMI: Hanscom AFB, two miles southwest.

Commissary: Approximately 4 miles away at Hanscom AFB, C-781-377-4210.

Exchange Gas: Approximately 4 miles away at Hanscom AFB. Commercial gas station within 3 miles.

Exchange: Approximately 4 miles away at Hanscom AFB, C-781-862-0580.

MWR Website: http://www.hanscomservices.com/

RV CAMPING & GETAWAYS
Hanscom AFB FamCamp

Reservation/Contact Number Info: C-781-225-3953. Off season, C-781-225-6621. Fax C-781-225-3954.

Recreation Security: C-781-225-5000. Bedford, C-781-275-1212.

RV Website: https://www.hanscomfss.com/outdoor-recreation

GPS Coordinates: 42°28'23"N/71°16'48"W GPS address: 499 South Road, Bedford, MA 01730.

Reservations: No reservations needed; first come, first serve basis. Office hours 0800-1600 Mon-Fri, 0900-1400 Sat-Sun. Check-in at Campground Office, Bldg 1003 after 1300 hours, check-out 1300 hours.

Season of Operation: Year-round. Summer: 1 May-31 Oct; Winter: 1 Nov-30 Apr.

Eligibility: AD, NG, Res, Ret and DoD-Civ at Hanscom AFB.

Camper/Trailer Spaces: RV Sites (73): Hardstand (56), E(30/110V/50A)/S/W hookups. Rates: $26 daily. Gravel (17), E(20A/30A/50A)/W partial hookups. Rates: $24 daily. New larger full hookup sites $29 daily.

Tent Spaces: Sites (10), no hookups. Rates: $10 daily.

Support Facilities: Auto Repair, Basketball Courts, Bikes, Bathhouse, Bike Path, Bowling, Chapel, Commissary, Convenience Store, Fitness Center, Gas, Golf, Grills, Ice, Laundry**, Long-Term RV Storage** Pavilion, Picnic Area, Playground, Pool, Propane (Fill)**, Rec Equipment, Restrooms*, Sewage Dump**, Showers*, Trails, * Handicap accessible. Off-Season all washrooms, bathrooms, and laundry are shut off. Several spots with heating elements to keep water from freezing. Must be self-contained.

RV Storage: C-781-225-3953. Off season, C-781-225-6621, Fax C-781-225-3954 for RV storage details.

Activities: Bicycling, Golfing, Horseshoes, Sightseeing.

Credit Cards: Cash, Checks, MasterCard and Visa.

Restrictions: Pets must be on leash and under physical control; owner must clean up after pet. Firearms allowed only after Firearms Identification Document has been obtained from local Chief of Police. Quiet hours 2200-0700 hours.

RV Driving Directions/Location: Off Base: Northwest of Boston, from I-95 north or south: Take exit 31B west onto MA-4/225/Bedford Street for .6 miles to right exit onto circle to Hartwell Avenue going southwest. Continue on Hartwell Avenue for .5 miles to right onto Maguire Road and continue for .3 miles. Turn left onto Summer Street for .4 miles. Turn left onto South Street for .4 miles to FAMCAMP.

Area Description: Located in wooded section adjacent to base, six miles from Concord Bridge (site of "the shot heard round the world") and other Revolutionary War historical sites. Easy drive to Boston and the cultural and social world of the city known as the Hub of the Universe. Full range of support facilities on base.

RV Campground Physical Address: 499 South Road, Bedford, MA 01730. Mailing Address: Outdoor Recreation, Bldg 1530, 98 Barksdale Street, Hanscom AFB, MA 01731-1807.

Nantucket Vacation House

Address: 4 Low Beach Rd, Siasconset, MA 02564.

Information Line: C-508-968-4386/4387.

Main Base Police: C-508-968-4303. Emergencies dial 911.

Main Installation Website: http://www.102iw.ang.af.mil/

Main Base Location: Located on Nantucket.

NMC: Boston, 60 miles northwest.

NMI: Otis ANGB/Cape Cod CGAS, 21 miles south of Martha's Vineyard and 48 miles southeast of Nantucket Vacation Houses.

Chapels: Cape Cod AS, C-508-968-6341. Otis ANGB, C-508-968-4508.

Medical: Keahler Clinic, C-508-968-6582.

Exchange Gas: Commercial gas station within 7 miles.

Places to Eat: Activity Center Snack Bar, C-508-968-6478, Crosswind Bar and Pub, C-508-968-6517, and Pizza Hut, C-508-563-3373, Golf Course Snack Bar, C-508-968-6454 and Galley at CGAS, C-508-968-6426 are on base.

Fitness Center: MWR Pool available.

Golf: Falcon Golf Course at Otis ANGB, C-508-968-6453.

ITT/ITR: C-508-968-6447.

MWR: C-508-968-6479.

MWR Website http://www.mwrcapecod.com/

MWR Facebook: https://www.facebook.com/MoraleWellBeingRecCapeCod

MWR Twitter: https://twitter.com/MWRCapeCod

Outdoor Recreation: MWR Cape Cod, C-508-968-6479. Offers a golf course, softball, volleyball, basketball, racquetball, driving range, tennis courts, swimming pool, fitness center and much more on base. Beach access within walking distance of facility.

Swimming: MWR Pool, C-508-968-6476. Beach swimming also available.

Things To Do: Otis has a nine-hole golf course and driving range. The Newport mansions, beaches, Martha's Vineyard and Nantucket Islands are wonderful island communities. They offer great beaches, nature preserves, historical sights, museums, swimming, fishing and boating.

Walking Trails: Hiking and walking trails available on base.

RV CAMPING & GETAWAYS

Nantucket House

Reservation/Contact Number Info: C-508-968-6461. Fax C-508-968-6637.

RV Website: http://www.mwrcapecod.com/facilities/mwr-lodging/nantucket-house/

RV Email Address: mwrlodgingbcc@gmail.com

GPS Coordinates: 41°17'23"N/70°5'33"W

Reservations: Reservations required and online only. Season Requests: 6 June-4 Sept accepted April 1-7; Off Season Requests: 15 May-4 June accepted March 1-7; 5 Sept-Oct 15 accepted August 1-7. Patrons may only rent once per calendar year. Weighted lottery system used for same day reservation requests. Office hours 0800-1600 hours Mon- Fri, 0900-1400 Sat. Follow check in procedures found in Confirmation Letter. Caretakers phone number will be in letter. Early arrivals are not permitted without prior approval Cancellations must be done 14 days prior to receive full refund. Check-in 1800, check-out 1100. Late check-out fees apply.

Season of Operation: 15 May-15 October.

Eligibility: AD, Res, Ret, auxiliary personnel of Armed Forces, DHS-Civ Emp of CG and uniformed personnel of PHS and NOAA when assigned to CG.

Yurt, A Frame, Cabin, Apt, Spaces: Ranch Style Guesthouse (1): Sleeps 8. Three-bedroom, two bath, garage, queen bed, full bed, and 2 sets of bunk beds, sleeper sofa. Fully furnished with towels and linens. Within walking distance to beach. Summer Season: $1794 weekly Sat-Fri; Off Season Rates: $250 daily with 3 night minimum and 7 day max.

Activities: Boating, Fishing*, Swimming. *State license required for patrons ages 15 and up. Children younger than fifteen must be accompanied by adult with a state license.

Credit Cards: American Express, Discover, MasterCard and Visa.

Restrictions: No pets. No smoking.

RV Driving Directions/Location: Off Base: House is located in Siasconset on Nantucket Island, which is accessible via ferry from West Yarmouth, Cape Cod. In order to take vehicles to the islands, reservations are required with the island ferry. Note: Reservations are very difficult to obtain and costly. It is advised to contact The Steamship Authority, C-508-477-8600 to make reservations once reservation confirmed.

Area Description: Nantucket offers a wonderful island community with great beaches, nature preserves, historical sights and museums, fishing and boating.

RV Campground Physical Address: 4 Low Beach Rd, Siasconset, MA 02564. Mailing Address: Reservation Office, 5204 Ent Street, Buzzards Bay, MA 02542.

Otis ANG Base – Cape Cod Coast Guard Air Station

Address: Otis ANG, 156 Reilly Street, Otis ANGB, MA 02542. Cape Cod Coast Guard Air Station, 5205 Ent Street, Buzzards Bay, MA 02542.

Information Line: C-508-968-4386.

Main Base Police: C-508-968-4303. Emergencies dial 911.

Main Installation Website: http://www.102iw.ang.af.mil/

Main Base Location: Cape Cod curls into the Atlantic for 70 miles. South of it lies Nantucket, Martha's Vineyard and the Elizabethan Islands, which guard the entrance to Buzzards Bay. The Cape Cod Canal joins Buzzards Bay and Cape Cod Bay.

Directions to Main Gate: To Otis ANGB, South of Plymouth: Travel south on MA-28 (MacArthur Blvd) to Otis Rotary.

Take third right off rotary onto Connery Avenue approximately 1.5 miles to Bourne/Buzzards Bay Gate. From US-6: Take exit 2 south onto MA-130. Go south approximately 4.3 miles to Snake Pond Road. Take right onto Snake Pond Road and follow to Sandwich Gate. From MA-151: Turn north on Old Sandwich Road and travel about 1.7 miles to Falmouth Gate. Note: Otis Air National Guard Base and Cape Cod Coast Guard Air Station share several support facilities.

NMC: Boston, 60 miles northwest.
NMI: Camp Edwards, 7 miles north.
Base Social Media/Facebook: https://www.facebook.com/102IW/
Base Social Media/Twitter: https://twitter.com/102IW
Chapels: C-508-968-4508/6343.
Dental Clinic: CG, C-508-968-6582.
Medical: Keahler Clinic, C-508-968-6582. ANG, C-508-968-4091.
Exchange Gas: C-508-968-6683.
Exchange: CGX, C-508-563-2495.
Places to Eat: C Side Snack Shack, C-508-968-6517; Falcon Deli, C-508-968-6454 and USCG Galley, C-508-968-6426 are on base. Many restaurants within a short drive.
Bowling: C Side Lanes, C-508-968-6477.
Fitness Center: C Side FC, C-508-968-6689.
Golf: Falcon Golf Club, C-508-968-6453.
ITT/ITR: C-508-968-6447.
MWR: C-508-968-6479.
MWR Website: http://www.mwrcapecod.com/
MWR Facebook: https://www.facebook.com/MoraleWelIBeingRecCapeCod
Outdoor Recreation: Gear Issue, C-508-968-6447. Offers lawn and garden equipment, table and chair rental, outdoor sporting equipment and games, trailers and more.
Swimming: Outdoor Seasonal Pool, C-508-968-6476 offers recreational swim.
Things To Do: Bourne Scenic Park on the banks of the Cape Cod Canal is located nearby. The canal is well known for its superb sport fishing, scenic bike rides and for carrying ships flying the flags of all nations. The annual Bourne Scallop Festival, which is held in early September each year, brings visitors from across the nation.

RV CAMPING & GETAWAYS

MWR RV Park – CGAS

Reservation/Contact Number Info: C-508-968-6461. After hours check-in contact JOOD, C-508-968-6331.
RV Website: http://www.mwrcapecod.com/rv_park.php
RV Email Address: MWRLodgingBCC@gmail.com
GPS Coordinates: 41°39'33"N/70°34'3"W.
Reservations: RV Park: Reservations accepted 90 days in advance via email, US postal service or online reservations. Office hours 0900-1500 Mon-Fri. Payment due at time of reservation. No refunds except in cases of emergency as defined on website. Check-in 1300 hours, check-out 1100. Maximum stay 14-days with space available extensions not to exceed 28 days.
Season of Operation: Year-round.
Eligibility: AD, NG, Res, Ret, DoD-Civ AD/Ret, Dep.
Camper/Trailer Spaces: Gravel Sites (5); Cement pad, E(30A/50A)/W/S hookups, picnic table, fire ring. Hardshell campers only; no pop-ups. Laundry available at Wings Inn. No shower/restroom facilities available at the RV Park. Rates: $30 daily.
Support Facilities: Bowling, Chapel, Exchange, Fitness Center, Gas, Golf (9 holes), Laundry, Recreation Center, Rec Equipment, Sports Fields, Swimming Pool, Theater, Vending Machine.
RV Storage: None.
Activities: Fitness Center, Fishing, Golfing, Swimming.
Credit Cards: American Express, Discover, MasterCard and Visa.
Restrictions: RVs are allowed to park 1 additional vehicle on their site. RVs are required to place drip pans under engines while parked.
RV Driving Directions/Location: On Base: From the Main Gate: Take first right at Hospital Road to split. At split,

stay to the left. Continue through stop sign to first right at Ent Street to Bldg 5204, 2nd building on left. After hours check in with JOOD at CGAS. From Main Gate: Continue straight to rotary and take 3rd exit to CG Air Operations. Go right at stop sign onto Herbert Road to the gate. JOOD, Bldg 3159, on left. JOOD C-508-968-6331.

Area Description: Located in Flatrock Hill in the northwest corner of the base and a short drive to the Cape Cod Bay. The area offers great hiking and climbing for the outdoor enthusiast, beautiful scenery and tranquil surroundings.

RV Campground Physical Address: CGAS, Temporary Quarters, Bldg 5204 Ent St, Otis ANGB/Cape Cod CGAS, MA 02542-5024.

Base Cape Cod Recreation House

Phone: C-508-968-6461.
Email: mwrlodgingbcc@gmail.com
Reservation Website: http://mwrcapecod.com/facilities/mwr-lodging/base-cape-cod-recreation-house/
Information: Contact facility for reservations.
Address: 5204 Ent Street Buzzards Bay, MA 02542.
Directions from Main Gate: From Bourne Gate: Take first right at Hospital Road. At the split, bear left. At stop sign, go straight to first right onto ENT Street. Facility ahead .8 miles from the Wings Inn.
Check In/Check Out: Call to confirm.
Office Hours: 0800-1600 hours Mon-Fri; 0900-1500 hours Sat-Sun, closed federal holidays
Payment Methods: AMEX, DISC, MC, VISA.
Eligibility: AD, NG, Res, Ret, and their dependents; Widow/ers; DoD-Civ, DoD-Civ Ret, and their dependents; 100% DAVs.
Seasonal Availability: Year-round.
Types of Rooms and Rates: Three Bedroom House (1): Fully furnished with well-equipped kitchen, one bathroom, sleeps 8, large living room and breakfast area; cable TV and Wi-Fi. Large backyard. Rates: $150-$199 daily depending on season.

Westover Air Reserve Base

Address: 975 Patriot Ave, Chicopee, MA 01022.
Information Line: C-413-557-1110.
Main Base Police: C-413-557-3557. Emergencies dial 911.
Main Installation Website: http://www.westover.afrc.af.mil/
Main Base Location: Located in Chicopee, Massachusetts, in the northeast region of the U.S.
Directions to Main Gate: From 91 North or South: Take exit 12 to Route 391 and get off at exit 3, Chicopee exit. Follow the Westover signs to the base. From Connecticut: Take Route 91 North to Route 291 in Springfield to Fuller Road and take exit marked Westover ARB. From Boston: Take the Mass Pike/Route 90 West to exit 5 in Chicopee. Follow signs.
NMC: Springfield, eight miles south.
NMI: Bradley IA/ANG, 30 miles south.
Base Social Media/Facebook: https://www.facebook.com/Westover.Patriot
Base Social Media/Twitter: https://twitter.com/439westover
Chapels: C-413-557-3360.
Beauty/Barber Shop: C-413-557-2080.
Exchange Gas: C-413-593-3288.
Exchange: C-413-593-5583/2901.
Clubs: Westover Club, C-413-557-2039.
Places to Eat: The Grind, C-413-557-3418; Bowling Center Snackbar, C-413-557-2039 and Westover Club, C-413-557-2039 are on base. Exchange Food Court offers Subway. Many restaurants within a short drive.
Bowling: Bowling Center, C-413-557-3990.
Fitness Center: Westover FC, C-413-557-3958.
ITT/ITR: C-413-557-2192.
MWR: Four Seasons, C-413-557-2192.
MWR Website: http://www.westoverservices.com/
Outdoor Recreation: Outdoor Recreation/Four Seasons, C-413-557-

2192. Offers camping gear, canoes, kayaks, boats, outdoor sporting games, lawn and garden equipment, winter sports rentals to include skis and snowboards as well as winter sports equipment maintenance.

Things To Do: Visit the Basketball Hall of Fame, Springfield Symphony Hall, the Titanic Historical Society, Forest Park Zoo, Six Flags New England or enjoy a variety of outdoor activities at one of the many outdoor parks and recreation areas.

RV CAMPING & GETAWAYS
Westover ARB FamCamp

Reservation/Contact Number Info: C-413-557-2192, DSN-312-589-2192. Fax C-413-557-2528.
Recreation Security: C-413-557-3557/3558.
RV Website: http://www.westoverservices.com/outdoor/campguide.html
RV Email Address: services@westover.af.mil
GPS Coordinates: 42°10'26"N/72°34'39"W.
Reservations: No advance reservations. Sites available on first come, first serve basis. Office hours 0830-1630 Mon-Fri; 0800-1300 Sat. Check-in 1400 hours, check out at 1100 hours. All campers must register at the camp office during normal operating hours. Late arrivals check-in at Flyer's Inn, Bldg 2201. Late arrivals must register by 0900 hours the next day at camp office. Maximum 14-day stay; extensions may be granted.
Season of Operation: Year-round.
Eligibility: AD, NG, Res, Ret, Dep, DoD-Civ and 100% DAV.
Camper/Trailer Spaces: Concrete sites (20). Pull-thru (2), Back-in (18), Maximum 40' in length, E(110/220V/20/30/50A)/W hookups, picnic table, grill. Rates: $20 daily, $120 weekly.
Tent Spaces: Tent Sites (15); No hookups, picnic table, grill. Rates: $10 daily, $60 weekly.
Support Facilities: Bathhouse, Bowling, Chapel, Coin Laundry, Convenience Store, Equipment Rental, Exchange, Fire Rings, Fitness Center, Gas, Golf, Grills, Mess Hall, Pavilion, Picnic Area, Propane, Rec Center, Restrooms, RV Storage, Sewage Dump, Shoppette, Showers, Snack Bar, Sports Fields, Tennis Courts, Trails.
RV Storage: Available on first come, first serve basis. Rates: $25 monthly. Call Outdoor Recreation: C-413-557-2192 for more information.
Activities: Basketball, Bowling, Golf (nearby), Horseshoes, Swimming, Sports Field, Tennis.
Credit Cards: MasterCard and Visa.
Restrictions: Pets allowed on leash; owner must have control of the pet at all times and must clean up after it. Quiet hours 2200-0700 hours. Firearms and/or hunting equipment not allowed. No fireworks.
RV Driving Directions/Location: On Base. From Boston: From the Main Gate: Ask for directions to FamCamp at gate.
Area Description: Located at the foothills of the Berkshire mountains and knows as the "Gateway to the Northeast". The campground is surrounded by woods with adjoining fields and is within walking distance of all major service facilities.
RV Campground Physical Address: Outdoor Recreation, Bldg 5346, Westover ARB, MA 01022-1636.

MICHIGAN

Alpena ANG Combat Readiness Training Center

Address: 5884 A Street, Alpena, MI 49707-8125.
Information Line: C-989-354-6203.
Main Base Police: C-989-354-6268. Emergencies dial 911.
Main Installation Website: http://www.alpenacrtc.ang.af.mil/

Main Base Location: Located in the northeastern part of Michigan's lower peninsula along Lake Huron.
Directions to Main Gate: Five miles west of Alpena on MI-32, (north side of MI-32). From I-75, take exit 232 to MI-32. Continue on MI-32 until reaching the airport.
NMC: Alpena, 5 miles east.
NMI: Traverse City Coast Guard Air Station, 95 miles southwest.
Base Social Media/Facebook:
https://www.facebook.com/alpenacrtc
Exchange Main Phone Number: C-989-354-6272.
Clubs: River Club, C-989-354-6279.
Places to Eat: River Club offers dining menu. Base Exchange offers food items. Many restaurants within a short drive.
Fitness Center: Fitness Center on base.
MWR Website:
http://www.alpenacrtc.ang.af.mil/
Outdoor Recreation: MWR Recreation Services, C-989-354-6536. Offers a variety of sports equipment, canoes, kayaks, paddle boats, fishing poles, life jackets, golf clubs, board games, movies, fitness equipment and more.
Things To Do: Alpena is located along the shores of Lake Huron. Many seasonal activities from summer festivals, top-rated golf courses, beautiful fall color tours and many winter activities to include skiing, snowmobiling, sledding and cross-country skiing.

RV CAMPING & GETAWAYS

Alpena CRTC RV Campground

Reservation/Contact Number Info: C-989-354-6536/6316.
Recreation Security: C-989-354-6268. Emergencies dial 911.
RV Website:
http://www.alpenacrtc.ang.af.mil/
GPS Coordinates:
45°04'59"N/83°34'29."W
Reservations: Reservations accepted via telephone 30 days in advance on a space available basis. UTA, active duty and Military operation exercises take

priority. Office hours 0745-1630 Mon-Fri. Maximum stay 14 days.
Season of Operation: Memorial Day - Labor Day.
Eligibility: AD, NG, Res, and Ret.
Camper/Trailer Spaces: Sites (24): 18 Sites with W/E hookup only and (6) primitive sites. Bath house with showers and restrooms, picnic table and fire pit. Rates: $15.28 daily.
Support Facilities: Boat Launch, Laundry Facilities, MWR Services and Rentals, Pavilion and Shoppette.
Activities: MWR Services offers canoes, kayaks, bikes and rowboats.
Credit Cards: Check, MasterCard and Visa.
Restrictions: Pets allowed on a leash. Quiet hours 2200-0600 daily.
RV Driving Directions/Location: Five miles west of Alpena on MI-32, (north side of MI-32). From I-75, take exit 232 to MI-32. Continue on MI-32 until reaching the airport.
Area Description: Alpena is located along the shores of Lake Huron. Many seasonal activities from summer festivals, top-rated golf courses, beautiful fall color tours and many winter activities to include skiing, snowmobiling, sledding and cross-country skiing.

Camp Grayling Joint Maneuver Training Center

Address: 2450 West North Down River Rd, Grayling, MI 49738-5000.
Information Line: C-989-344-6100.
Main Base Police: C-989-344-6120. Emergencies dial 911.
Main Installation Website:
http://grayling.minationalguard.com/
Main Base Location: In Crawford County, central northern Michigan in the center of the Lower Peninsula.
Directions to Main Gate: Located 3 miles west of city of Grayling, just off I-75. Main Gate is at the end of MI-93. I-75 north to exit 251. Turn left. Go to end of Four Mile Road and turn right. Go to the end of Military Road and turn

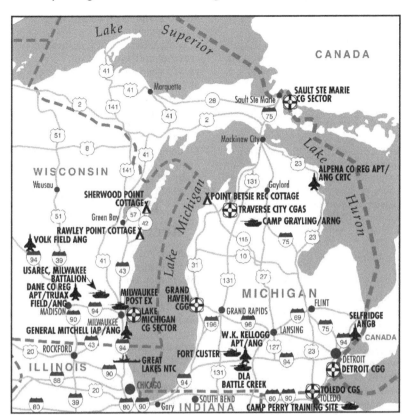

left into the Main Gate. I-75S to exit 259. Follow signs.

NMC: Grayling, 3 miles east.

NMI: Traverse City Coast Guard Air Station, 55 miles northwest.

Base Social Media/Facebook: https://www.facebook.com/michguard

Base Social Media/Twitter: https://twitter.com/minationalguard

Chapels: C-989-344-6752.

Exchange: C-989-348-4781.

Clubs: Officers' Club, C-989-348-9033. NCO Club, C-989-344-6244.

Places to Eat: Dining Hall, C-989-344-6733 is on base. Several restaurants within a short drive.

Fitness Center: C-989-344-6742.

MWR: C-989-344-6114/6670.

MWR Website: http://grayling.minationalguard.com/mwr/

Outdoor Recreation: MWR Beach House, C-989-344-6670. MWR Beach House offers sporting equipment.

Things To Do: Visit one of the many lakes, golf resorts, mountain resorts and seasonal festivals in beautiful northern Michigan. Many outdoor recreation areas are nearby.

RV CAMPING & GETAWAYS

Camp Grayling RV Park & Cottages

Reservation/Contact Number Info: RV, C-989-344-6246, C-989-348-9033. Cottages, C-989-344-6213.

Recreation Security: C-989-344-6120.

RV Website: http://grayling.minationalguard.com/mwr/

Other Info Website: http://grayling.minationalguard.com/quarters/

RV Email Address: Oclub@frontier.com
GPS Coordinates:
44°38'1"N/84°46'34"W
Reservations: Cottages: Reservations accepted 6 months in advance official duty and 90 days for leisure. Cancellations made within 24 hours of arrival will be charged $100 cancellation fee. Office hours 0800-1700 Mon-Fri Oct-Mar and 0800-2000 Mon-Fri Apr-Sept. Cottage Check-in: 1500 hours, check-out 1000 hours. RV Sites: Contact facility for reservations. Check-in 1400 hours, check-out 1400 hours.
Season of Operation: Campground: 2nd Saturday in May through the 3rd Sunday of September. Cottages: 1 May-31 Oct.
Eligibility: AD, NG, Res, Ret and DoD-Civ.
Camper/Trailer Spaces: Sites (70): Full hookup sites (50); partial hookup (20); Back-in and Pull-thru, Maximum of 43' in length, Rates: $17 daily; $450 monthly; $925 seasonally. Five (5) sites are reserved for larger rigs with 50A.
Yurt, A Frame, Cabin, Apt,
Spaces: Cottages: (4) Sleeps 8, three bedroom, two-story, king room, queen room, twin room with two twin beds and queen sofa sleeper, CATV. Fully furnished homes on Lake Margarethe. Furnished deck with grill. Rates: $130 daily for official; $161 for leisure.
Support Facilities: Barn (for group events), Bath House, Beach, Boat Launch, Boats, Grills, Laundry*, Picnic Area, Playground, Restrooms, Showers. *On post.
Activities: Boating, Fishing*, Hiking, Swimming. *Michigan state rules apply.
Credit Cards: Cash, check or money order.
Restrictions: Pets at campsites must be caged or chained, $2 security deposit required. Firearms not allowed. Quiet hours after 2300 hours. Motorized two and three wheeled vehicles are prohibited in trailer park. Parents will be held responsible for the actions of their children at all times.
RV Driving Directions/Location: On Base: From Main Gate: RV park is located to the right of security.

Area Description: The largest National Guard training site in the country, Camp Grayling is conveniently located in the center of northern Michigan's vacationland, close to major highways and recreational areas. Local activities include excellent in-season hunting and fishing opportunities, as well as camping, boating, golf, trail riding, skiing and snowmobiling.
RV Campground Physical Address: Camp Grayling Trailer Park, c/o Officers' Club, 311 Howe Road, Camp Grayling, MI 49738.

Pointe Betsie Recreation Cottage

Address: Point Betsie Cottage, 3720 Pt. Betsie Road, Frankfort, MI 49635.
Information Line: C-616-850-2511/2500.
Main Base Police: Emergencies dial 911.
Main Installation Website:
http://www.uscg.mil/d9/sfograndhaven/
Main Base Location: Point Betsie Cottage is located in northwest lower MI on the eastern shore of Lake Michigan, located to the west and with Crystal Lake to the east in Benzie county.
NMC: Traverse City, 45 miles east.
NMI: Traverse City Coast Guard Air Station, 45 miles east.
Exchange Gas: Commercial gas station within 5 miles.
Places to Eat: Many restaurants within a short drive.
Outdoor Recreation: Hiking, skiing, golf, fishing, and beachcombing are all within 10 miles, or closer, of the cottage.
Things To Do: Crystal Lake and Betsie Bay resorts are nearby. Shopping, restaurants, and a city market are located in Frankfort, 5 miles south.
Walking Trails: Beach strolling is available.

RV CAMPING & GETAWAYS
Pointe Betsie Recreation Cottage

Reservation/Contact Number Info: C-616-850-1601.

Recreation Security: Emergencies dial 911.

RV Website: http://reservations.vacationrentaldesk.com/pika9qdlqr1.html

GPS Coordinates: 44°41'25"N/86°15'15"W

Reservations: Reservations required via telephone or online link. Reservations accepted 120 days in advance for AD; 60 days in advance for all others. Payment for full reservation must be paid 30 days in advance. Minimum stay 3 days; maximum stay 7 days. Check-in and check-out at: Coast Guard Station Frankfort, 100 Coast Guard Drive, Frankfort, MI 49635. Check-in 1400 hours; check out 1000 hours.

Season of Operation: Year-round.

Eligibility: AD, NG, Res, Ret DoD-Civ.

Yurt, A Frame, Cabin, Apt, Spaces: Cottage: Two-bedroom (1), sleeps seven, furnished, cookware, kitchen, refrigerator, microwave, utensils, gas grill, telephone (local calls only), television (satellite). Bed linens and towels are not provided. Rates: $60 daily.

Support Facilities: There are no support facilities at the cottage. Facilities are nearby or within a short driving distance.

RV Storage: None.

Activities: Boating, Fishing*, Golfing, Hunting*, Snow Skiing, Swimming, Water Skiing. *State rules apply.

Credit Cards: Check or online credit card payment.

Restrictions: No pets allowed. No smoking. On-site local telephone, C-231- 352-5088 provided. Sparse cell phone service.

RV Driving Directions/Location: Off Base. From Route 115 to Frankfort: Take the last exit off of MI-115 and proceed west to Frankfort, MI. In Frankfort, follow the road signs to the US Coast Guard Station, located at the end of the main road in town. After checking in at the Coast Guard Station, proceed north on Route 22 approximately 5 miles. Turn left on Pt. Betsie Road. The cottage is .25 miles east of the lighthouse.

Area Description: Located in northwest Michigan on eastern shores of Lake Michigan south of Sleeping Bear Dunes National Lakeshore. Crystal Lake and Betsie Bay resorts nearby.

RV Campground Physical Address: 3720 Pt. Betsie Road, Benzie County, MI 49635. Mailing Address: Commanding Officer, USCG SFO, 650 South Harbor Drive, Grand Haven, MI 49417-5000.

MINNESOTA

Camp Ripley Training Center

Address: 15000 Highway 115, Little Falls, MN 56345-4173.

Information Line: Command Post, C-320-616-2699.

Main Base Police: C-320-632-7375. Emergencies dial 911.

Main Installation Website: http://www.minnesotanationalguard.org/camp_ripley/

Main Base Location: Central Minnesota, approximately 40 miles north of St Cloud.

Directions to Main Gate: From I-94 W/US-52 N: At exit 167B, take ramp right for MN-15 toward St. Cloud. Take ramp and follow signs for US-10. Take ramp right for MN-371 toward Brainerd. Take ramp right for CR-47/MN-115 toward Randall. Turn left onto MN-115/CR-47. Watch for Camp Ripley Training Center signs.

NMC: Little Falls, 7 miles south.

NMI: Grand Forks Air Force Base, ND, 140 miles northwest.

Base Social Media/Facebook: https://www.facebook.com/CampRipley/

Chapels: C-320-616-2708.

Medical: C-320-616-3152.

Exchange: C-320-632-7446.

Clubs: Viking Club, C-320-632-7046.

Places to Eat: Dining Facility, C-320-616-3173 and Snack Bar, C-320-632-7412 are on base. Several restaurants within a short drive.

Fitness Center: Recreation & Training Center offers wellness facilities.

Military Museum: Minnesota Military Museum, C-320-616-6050.

Military Museum Website: https://www.mnmilitarymuseum.org/

MWR: MWR Services, C-320-616-2705.

MWR Website: https://minnesotanationalguard.ng.mil/camp-ripley-mwr/

Outdoor Recreation: MWR Services, C-320-616-2705. Offers cross country skiing, softball, baseball, tennis, basketball, biking, horseshoes, volleyball, running track, fishing, boating, canoes, badminton, archery, picnic areas and swimming.

Things To Do: The Mississippi River runs through Camp Ripley, bringing easy access to fishing and water recreation. Miles of wooded areas are perfect for camping, hiking or just getting away to relax.

Walking Trails: Running track and courses on base.

RV CAMPING & GETAWAYS
DeParcq Woods

Reservation/Contact Number Info: C-320-616-3140, DSN-312-871-3140. Fax C-320-632-7787, DSN-312-871-7787.

Recreation Security: C-320-632-7339/75.

RV Website: https://minnesotanationalguard.ng.mil/camp-ripley-fac02/#deparcq

RV Email Address: heather.berens@mn.ngb.army.mil.

GPS Coordinates: 46°5'35"N/94°22'2"W.

Reservations: Accepted. Payment due upon check-in, Bldg 6-76. Office hours 0600-2300 Mon-Thu, 0600-2400 Fri, 0700-2300 Sat, 0600-2200 Sun. Check-in 100 hours, check-out 1100 hours.

Season of Operation: 1 May-30 Oct.

Eligibility: AD, NG, Res, Ret, DoD-Civ, Dep, 100% DAV, MN State Employees.

Camper/Trailer Spaces: Hardstand, (15), back-in, maximum length 40', E(110/220V/15/30A)/W, picnic table, grill, Wi-Fi. Rates: $17 daily.

Tent Spaces: Grass/Dirt: No hookups, picnic table. Rates: $7 nightly. Some tent spaces can be used for camper/trailers.

Support Facilities: Bath House/Shower Facility, Boat Launch, Boat Rental/Storage, Bowling, Chapel, Convenience Store, Equipment Rental, Fire Rings, Fitness Center, Gas, Grills, Ice, Laundry, Mess Hall, Pavilion, Picnic Area, Playground, Rec Center, Restrooms, Sewage Dump, Snack Bar, Sports Fields, Tennis Courts.

RV Storage: None.

Activities: Biking, Fishing*. *State license required for patrons ages sixteen and up. Children younger than sixteen must be accompanied by adult with a state license.

Credit Cards: MasterCard and Visa.

Restrictions: Pets allowed on leash. Pets not allowed within 50' of pavilion.

RV Driving Directions/Location: On Base: From the Main Gate: Check-in at Bldg 6-76.

Area Description: Located adjacent to the Mississippi River.

RV Campground Physical Address: DeParcq Woods, 15000 Hwy 115, Camp Ripley, Little Falls, MN 56345.

MISSISSIPPI

Camp Shelby Training Site

Address: Camp Shelby JTC, Bldg T900, 1001 Lee Avenue, Camp Shelby, MS 39407-5500.

Information Line: C-601-558-2000, DSN-312-286-2000.

Main Base Police: C-601-558-2232/2251. Emergencies dial 911.

Main Installation Website: http://ms.ng.mil/installations/shelby/Pages/default.aspx

Main Base Location: Camp Shelby is in southern Mississippi just outside Hattiesburg, encompassing more than 134,000 acres.

Directions to Main Gate: From Hattiesburg: Take US-49 south or take US-98 east from Hattiesburg to MS-29 south, which bisects the training site. Follow signs.

NMC: Hattiesburg, 10 miles north.

NMI: Keesler Air Force Base, 58 miles south.

Chapels: C-601-558-2378/4078.

Medical: C-601-558-2221.

Beauty/Barber Shop: Available on base.

Exchange: C-601-558-0801.

Financial Institutions: First Southern Bank, C-601-450-2181; Citizens National Bank, C-601-264-2528.

Clubs: Camp Shelby Clubs, C-601-558-2749, NCO, C-601-558-2427.

Places to Eat: Dining in Bldg 3514, C-601-558-2131. Louisiana Sisters Cafe, C-601-543-0779 is just outside the gate and many other restaurants within driving distance.

Fitness Center: Bldg 1300, C-601-558-2397.

Military Museum: Armed Forces Museum, C-601-558-2757.

MWR: C-601-558-2397.
MWR Website:
http://ms.ng.mil/installations/shelby/ss
/mwr/Pages/default.aspx

Outdoor Recreation: MWR Services, C-601-558-2397. Offers camper rentals, outdoor activities, seasonal outdoor pool and more.

Swimming: Seasonal Outdoor Pool, C-601-558-2397.

Things To Do: Museums, walking tour of Hattiesburg and the Hattiesburg Zoo are easy to visit attractions close by or enjoy a daytrip to the Gulf Coast.

Walking Trails: Outdoor running track available.

RV CAMPING & GETAWAYS

Lake Walker Family Campgrounds & Cabins

Reservation/Contact Number Info: C-601-558-2397, DSN-312-286-2397. Fax C-601-558-2067.

Recreation Security: C-601-558-2232.

RV Website:
http://ms.ng.mil/installations/shelby/housing/Pages/Cabins.aspx

GPS Coordinates:
31°12'27"N/89°12'33" W

Reservations: RV Sites: All sites available on a first come, first serve basis. Recommend calling for availability. AD personnel have priority during annual training while training at Camp Shelby. Office hours 0600-1630 Mon-Fri. Payment due upon arrival. Check-in at Bldg 1300 on Forrest Avenue. Cabins: Maximum 3-night stay. Cancellations must be made within 48 hours of arrival to avoid fee. Check-in 1300-1600 hours; Check-out 0830. Late checkout requires approval to avoid fee.

Season of Operation: Year-round.

Eligibility: AD, NG, Res, Ret, DoD-Civ, Dep and 100% DAV.

Camper/Trailer Spaces: Hardstand (31): Pull-thru (3), back-in (29), maximum 42' in length, E(110/220V/15/30/50A)/S/W hookups, picnic table. Rates: $15 daily, $90 weekly, $300 monthly.

Tent Spaces: Primitive (3): No hookups, picnic table. Rates: $10 daily.

Yurt, A Frame, Cabin, Apt, Spaces: Large Cabins: Full size beds w/private bath, Kitchen, Cable, Sleeps six, fully equipped. Rates: $45 daily. Small Cabins: Full size beds w/private bath, Kitchen, Cable, Sleeps four, fully equipped; Rate: $40 daily. Cabin rentals are for MWR purposes only. Cabins are not authorized for Official Use. Extended stays require approval.

Support Facilities: Bath House, Boat Launch, Boat Rental, Cafeteria, Chapel, Convenience Store, Exchange, Fire Rings, Fishing Pier, Gas, Grills, Laundry (Free), Pavilion, Picnic Area, Restrooms, Sewage Dump Station, Showers, Sports Fields, Tennis Courts. An additional picnic area located at Dogwood Lake, about three miles away.

RV Storage: None.

Activities: Boating, Fishing*. Ages 16+ require military ID for fishing on post. A state license is required for fishing off post. Children under the age of sixteen must be accompanied by an adult with the appropriate ID/license.

Credit Cards: Cash or Check.

Restrictions: RV: Pets allowed on leash. Owner must clean up after pet. No firearms allowed. Open fires in designated areas only. Cottages: No pets allowed.

RV Driving Directions/Location: On Base. From the South Gate: Check in at Bldg 1300. Continue on Forrest Road to Lee Road. Turn onto 16th Street and signs for campground visible.

Area Description: Located on the edge of the DeSoto National Forest, Camp Shelby is one hour away from the Gulf Coast and enjoys a mild climate year-round. The campground is beside Lake Walker. Limited support facilities available on post, full range available at Gulfport Naval Construction Battalion Center, 60 miles south.

RV Campground Physical Address: 1001 Lee Avenue, Bldg 1300, Camp Shelby JFTC, MS 39407-5500.

Gulfport Naval Construction Battalion Center

Address: Gulfport Naval Construction Battalion Center, 3502 East 8th Street at Pass Road, Gulfport, MS 39501.

Information Line: C-228-871-2555, DSN-312-868-2555.

Main Base Police: C-228-871-2361. Emergency Line, C-228-871-2222/2333. Emergencies dial 911.

Main Installation Website:
http://www.cnic.navy.mil/regions/cnrse/installations/ncbc_gulfport.html
Main Base Location: Located in Harrison County in the city of Gulfport, Mississippi on the Gulf of Mexico. Gulfport, along with Biloxi, Pascagoula, Ocean Springs and Bay St. Louis, is one of the cities that line the beachfront of Mississippi.
Directions to Main Gate: Pass Road Gate: Take the I-10 Exit 34 to south on Hwy 49 towards Hwy 90/Beaches. At the Burger King on the NW corner, turn right on Pass Road and head west directly to the gate, approximately .5 miles.
NMC: Gulfport, within city limits.
NMI: Keesler AFB, 14 miles east.
Base Social Media/Facebook:
https://www.facebook.com/NCBCGulfport
Base Social Media/Twitter:
https://twitter.com/SeabeeCenter
Chapels: C-228-871-2454.
Dental Clinic: C-228-871-2605/2606.
Medical: Appointment Line, C-228-871-4033. Branch Clinic, C-228-871-2810.
Beauty/Barber Shop: Barber, C-228-871-2350. Beauty, C-228-863-4820.
Commissary: C-228-871-2039.
Exchange Gas: C-228-864-8565.
Exchange: C-228-864-6877.
Financial Institutions: Navy Federal Credit Union, C-228-871-4000.
Clubs: Anchors & Eagles Club, C-228-871-4607. The Hive, C-228-871-4009.
Places to Eat: Colmer Dining Facility, C-228-871-3463; Subway, C-228-871-5799 and The Grill, C-228-871-2494 are on base. Many restaurants are within a short drive.
Fitness Center: NCBC Fitness Center, C-228-871-2668.
ITT/ITR: C-228-871-2231.
Library: MWR Digital Library, C-228-871-2231.
Military Museum: Seabee Museum, C-228-871-4779.
Military Museum Website:
http://www.seabeehf.org/the-museum/
MWR: C-228-871-2538.

MWR Website:
http://www.navymwrgulfport.com/
MWR Facebook:
https://www.facebook.com/gulfportmwr
MWR Twitter:
https://twitter.com/mwrgulfport
Outdoor Recreation: Outdoor Recreation Services, C-228-871-2127. Offers camping equipment, mountain bikes, sail boats, jon boats, outdoor games, party supplies and more. Seabee Park and Recreation Area has a dog park, soccer/football field, paintball course, batting cages and driving range. Camping and fishing are available at Shields RV Park on base.
Swimming: CBC Outdoor Pool, C-228-871-2668 offers lap, open and recreational swimming. Swim lessons are offered. Heated year-round pool.
Things To Do: Swimming, fishing, sailing, windsurfing, sunning and beach combing in the summer are popular. Casinos are nearby. Visit Beauvoir (Confederate President Jefferson Davis' home), Gulf Islands National Seashore, Gulf Island Water Park, Biloxi Lighthouse, Lynn Meadows Discovery Center, Seabee Memorial Museum and the Shearwater Pottery showroom.
Walking Trails: Walking/Fitness trail at Seabee Lake.

RV CAMPING & GETAWAYS
Shields RV Park

Reservation/Contact Number Info: C-1-877-NAVY-BED, C-228-871-5435, DSN-312-868-5435.
Recreation Security: C-228-871-2361.
RV Website:
http://get.dodlodging.net/propertys/Shields-RV-Park
Other Info Website:
http://www.navymwrgulfport.com/programs/57527bde-b606-40cd-b96b-cdaba37ef0a8
GPS Coordinates:
30°22'39"N/89°6'36"W
Reservations: No advance reservations accepted. All spots are first come, first served. Office hours 0800-1600 Mon-Sat; 0800-1400 Sun. Check-in at campground office, Bldg 456, between

0800-1600 hours, check-out 1200 hours.
Season of Operation: Year-round.
Eligibility: AD, NG, Res, Ret, DoD-Civ and Dep.
Camper/Trailer Spaces: Shields RV Park 9th Street (68): Pull-thru (53) maximum length 44', Back-in (15), maximum length 40', E(20-30-50A)/S/W, CATV hookups, Wi-Fi picnic table, grill. Rates: $20 daily, $120 weekly, $381 monthly. Shields RV Park West Perimeter (35): Full hookup back-in sites, bathrooms and showers, dump station. Call for current rates.
Support Facilities: Auto Craft Shop, Auto Repair, Basketball Court, Bathhouse and Restrooms*, Boat Rental/Storage, Chapel, Coin Laundry, Commissary, Convenience Store, Dog Park (fenced), Equipment Rental, Exchange, Fitness Center, Gas, Grills, Mess Hall, Pavilions, Pier, Playground, Pool, Propane, Restrooms, RV Storage, Sewage Dump, Showers, Volleyball Court (Grass). RV Park features Rec. Park featuring 4 practice golf holes, chipping green, driving range, paint ball, football, soccer fields, and 1/2 mile walking trail. *Handicap Accessible.
RV Storage: Yes. C-228-871-5435.
Activities: Bicycling, Fishing*, Swimming. *License not required on base but is required off base.
Credit Cards: American Express, Discover, MasterCard and Visa.
Restrictions: Firearms prohibited. Two pets per campsite allowed. Must be on leash at all times when outside. One extra vehicle per RV is authorized to be parked in designated lots.
RV Driving Directions/Location: On Base. Shields RV 9th Street: From the Pass Road Gate: Continue through to RV Park, visible on the right. From the NCBC Broad Gate: Take the first right at Marvin Shields Blvd, which turns into Decatur Ave at the first bend to the left. At 7th Street, go right. Go left onto Olson Avenue to RV park entrance. Shields RV Park W Perimeter: Located near the Navy Community Rec Center. Ask for specific directions.

Area Description: Gulfport NCBC is located on the beautiful Mississippi Gulf coast near twenty-six miles of white sandy beaches and twelve coastal casinos. The facility boasts a seven-acre lake and many on-base activities.
RV Campground Physical Address: 453 Katrina Court, Gulfport, MS 39501-5000.

Keesler Air Force Base FamCamp

Address: Keesler Fam Camp, 201 Atkinson Road, Biloxi, MS 39531.
Information Line: C-228-377-1110, DSN-312-597-1110.
Main Base Police: C-228-377-3040. Emergencies dial 911.
Main Installation Website: http://www.keesler.af.mil/
Main Base Location: Located between the Back Bay of Biloxi and the Mississippi Sound.
NMC: Biloxi, within city limits.
NMI: Keesler AFB, 3 miles east.
Commissary: Approximately 4 miles to commissary at Keesler AFB, C-228-377-3933/4972/2830/4288.
Exchange Gas: Gas station at Keesler AFB approximately 4 miles away. Commercial gas station within 2 miles.
Exchange: Approximately 4 miles to Base Exchange at Keesler AFB, C-228-435-2524.
Golf: Bay Breeze Golf Course, C-228-377-3832
ITT/ITR: C-228-377-3818.
Marina: Keesler Outdoor Recreation Area/Marina, C-228-377-3160.
MWR: C-228-377-0002.
MWR Website: http://www.keesler81fss.us/
MWR Facebook: https://www.facebook.com/Keesler81FSS
MWR Twitter: https://twitter.com/81FSS
Outdoor Recreation: Outdoor Recreation Services at Keesler, C-228-377-3160. Offers a variety of rental equipment, adventure programs and a marina. Call for details.
Swimming: Beach swimming.

Things To Do: Enjoy swimming, boating, historical tours of the area, casinos and more.

Walking Trails: Beach strolling.

RV CAMPING & GETAWAYS

Keesler AFB FamCamp

Reservation/Contact Number Info: C-228-377-9050.

Recreation Security: C-228-377-3040.

RV Website:
https://www.discoverkeesler.com/fun/f amcamp

RV Email Address:
81.svs.cc@keesler.af.mil

GPS Coordinates:
30°24'28"N/88°57'20"W. GPS Address: 2003 Atkinson Rd, Biloxi, MS 39534.

Reservations: Reservations required. Office hours 0800-1600 Mon-Fri; 1000-1400 Sat-Sun. Hosts on duty during office hours. Check-in at office. After hours arrival information posted on office door.

Season of Operation: Year-round.

Eligibility: AD, NG, Res, Ret and DoD-Civ.

Camper/Trailer Spaces: RV Sites (52), E(115V/30/50A)/S/W, CATV hookups, Wi-Fi. Rates: $22 daily, $140 weekly, $420 monthly. Overflow sites available, no hookups. Rates: $10 daily. Waste Removal fee: $5.

Support Facilities: Beach, Boat Rental, Chapel, Equipment Rental, Gas, Golf, Grills, Laundry/pay, Marina, Picnic Area, Playground, Pool, Quick Shop, Showers, Snack Bar, Sports Fields, Tennis Courts.

RV Storage: 25' or less, $25/monthly. Over 40', $40. C-228-377-3160.

Activities: Bicycling, Boating, Casinos, Fishing*, Golfing, Hiking, Jogging, Sailing, Swimming. *State license required for patrons ages sixteen and up. Children younger than sixteen must be accompanied by adult with a state license. Hunting/Fishing licenses can be obtained at Marina Store, C-228-377-3160.

Credit Cards: Cash, Checks, MasterCard and Visa.

Restrictions: No open fires on beach without city approval.

RV Driving Directions/Location: Off Base. From I-10 take exit 41 south/Cedar Lake to Popps Ferry Road and turn right. Travel south, crossing over drawbridge to the next light at Atkinson Road. Go left (east) directly to FamCamp.

Area Description: Mississippi Gulf Coast holds a wealth of history. In Biloxi, tours are available daily at Beauvoir, the home of Jefferson Davis. The marina is located off Ploesti Drive on Back Bay and offers a park, boating and fishing. Numerous large casinos line the beach in Biloxi and Gulfport. Free certificates are available at the FAMCAMP Information Center. Full range of support facilities available on base.

RV Campground Physical Address: Keesler FamCamp, 200 Annex Road, Biloxi, MS 39531.

Meridian Naval Air Station

Address: NAS Meridian, 255 Rosenbaum Avenue, Meridian, MS 39309.

Information Line: C-601-679-2211, DSN-312-637-2211.

Main Base Police: C-601-679-2508. Emergencies dial 911.

Main Installation Website:
http://www.cnic.navy.mil/regions/cnrse /installations/nas_meridian.html

Main Base Location: Naval Air Station, Meridian Mississippi is approximately 15 miles northeast of the city of Meridian, in Lauderdale County, between State Highways 39 and 45.

Directions to Main Gate: From I-20/59: Take exit 154B to State Highway 39 North out of Meridian. Posted signs will provide directions off of Highway 39 and down the Stennis Drive access road to the NAS Meridian main gate.

NMC: Meridian, 15 miles southwest.

NMI: Meridian Regional Airport/ANGB, 18 miles south.

Base Social Media/Facebook:
https://www.facebook.com/NASMeridian

Chapels: C-601-679-3635/2139. Duty Chaplain, C-601-604-2015/2115.

Dental Clinic: C-601-679-2383.

Medical: Appointment Line, C-601-679-2210. Aviation, C-601-679-2208.
Beauty/Barber Shop: C-601-679-2641.
Commissary: C-601-679-2554.
Exchange Gas: C-601-679-2662.
Exchange: C-601-679-2665.
Financial Institutions: Navy Federal Credit Union, C-1-888-842-6328.
Clubs: Rudders Pub, C-601-679-2636.
Places to Eat: Sandtrap Grille, C-601-679-2780; Subway at McCain Bowling Center, C-601-679-9947; Tutto Bene Pizza, C-601-679-2345 and Wheat Galley for AD and RCTA, C-601-679-2712 are on base. Many restaurants within a short drive.
Bowling: McCain Recreation Center, C-601-679-2651.
Fitness Center: Sonny Montgomery FC, C-601-679-2379.
Golf: Ponta Creek Golf Course, C-601-679-2526.
ITT/ITR: Ponta Creek Clubhouse, C-601-679-2526/2609.
Library: Andrew Triplett Library, C-601-679-2326.
MWR: C-601-679-2551.
MWR Website:
http://www.navymwrmeridian.com/
MWR Facebook:
https://www.facebook.com/MWRMeridian
Outdoor Recreation: Outdoor Recreation Services, C-601-679-2526/2609. Offers Lake Tant and Lake Martha for recreational use with accessible pavilions. Horseback riding, fishing, boat rental, driving range, disc and foot golf, paint ball, trailers, camping gear and more.
Swimming: Seasonal Outdoor Pool, C-601-679-2379 offers lap and open swim.
Things To Do: Take a driving tour of the historic Natchez Trace or visit a local flea market. Visit Flora's Petrified Forest and the Choctaw Fair for American Indian life and lore.
Walking Trails: Jogging, walking and biking trails are available on base.

RV CAMPING & GETAWAYS
Lake Martha Primitive Sites
Reservation/Contact Number Info: C-601-679-2526/2609.
RV Website:
https://www.navymwrmeridian.com/programs/a2c23a09-2b33-4bf8-9f6c-88af6a3e2254
Reservations: Reservations not accepted. Best to contact facility for availability.
Season of Operation: Year-round.
Eligibility: AD, NG, Res, Ret, Dep and DoD-Civ.
Tent Spaces: Primitive camp spaces available with picnic table, fire ring, showers and bathrooms.
Support Facilities: Full range of facilities on base.
Activities: Enjoy boating, pavilions, outdoor recreation areas, Ponta Creek Golf Course, seasonal outdoor pool facility, McCain Recreation Center, fitness centers.
RV Driving Directions/Location: Located adjacent to the pavilion area on base.
Area Description: Lakeside primitive campsites on base, along the shoreline of Lake Martha.

MISSOURI

Lake of the Ozarks Recreation Area

Address: FLW Lake Recreation Area (LORA), 789 Olney Circle, Linn Creek, MO 65052.
Information Line: C-573-596-0131.
Main Base Police: C-573-596-6141. Emergencies dial 911.
Main Installation Website:
https://leonardwood.armymwr.com/
Main Base Location: LORA is located 57 miles Northeast of Fort Leonard Wood on the Grand Glaize arm of the Lake of the Ozarks.
NMC: Jefferson City, 66 miles northeast.

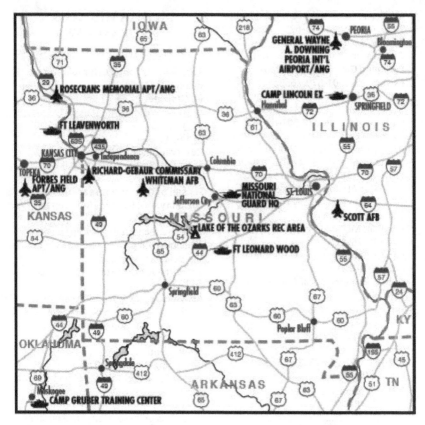

NMI: Fort Leonard Wood, approximately 49 miles southeast.
Exchange Gas: Commercial gas station within 15 miles.
Places to Eat: Many restaurants within a 30-minute drive.
Fitness Center: C-573-596-4359.
Golf: Piney Valley Golf Course, C-573-329-4770.
ITT/ITR: C-573-329-TKTS (8587).
Marina: C-573-346-5640.
MWR: C-573-596-0117.
MWR Website:
https://leonardwood.armymwr.com/us/leonardwood
MWR Facebook:
https://www.facebook.com/mwr.ftwood
MWR Twitter:
https://twitter.com/FLWMWR
Outdoor Recreation: Outdoor Adventure Program, C-573-596-4223. Outdoor Adventure and LORA offer hunting, fishing, archery, trap and skeet ranges, paintball and rental equipment for camping, water sports and more.
Swimming: Lake swimming is available.
Things To Do: This is a large and fully equipped recreational area including a marina, fishing pier, and much more.
Walking Trails: Nature trails are available on site.

RV CAMPING & GETAWAYS
Lake of the Ozarks Recreation Area

Reservation/Contact Number Info: C-573-346-5640. Fax C-573- 346-3578.
Recreation Security: Sheriff, C-573-346-2243.
RV Website:
https://leonardwood.armymwr.com/programs/lake-ozarks-recreation-area-lora

GPS Coordinates:
38°5'58"N/92°36'22"W.

Reservations: Required by phone or in person at the LORA Office, Bldg 528, between 0900-1700 hours Mon-Fri. Summer hours 0800-1900 Mon-Fri; 0800-2000 Sat-Sun Memorial Day-Labor Day. Credit card deposit required. Accepted one year in advance for AD, 180 days in advance for all others. Summer season requires a 2-night minimum Fri-Sat. Cancellations must be received within 48-hours of arrival date to avoid cancellation fee. Check-in at office, Bldg 528. Check-in 1500 hours, check-out 1100 hours. Call for after-hours arrival instructions.

Season of Operation: Year-round.

Eligibility: AD, NG, Res, Ret, 100% DAV, DoD/NAF-Civ (AD/Ret), Dep, Sponsored Guests and FLW Contractors.

Camper/Trailer Spaces: RV Sites (27): Cement, pull-thru and back-in, Maximum 54' in length, E(220V/50A)/S/W hookups, picnic table, grill. Rates: $30 daily. Partial hookups, picnic table, grill. Rates: $25 daily.

Tent Spaces: Rustic Sites (21): No hookups, picnic table, grill. Rates: $15 daily.

Yurt, A Frame, Cabin, Apt, Spaces: Cabins (29): Three-bedroom (3), furnished, two queen beds, one full bed, two baths, kitchen, microwave, refrigerator, cookware/utensils, linens, A/C, TV, DVD/VCR, satellite TV. Rates: High Season: $100 daily. Two-bedroom (6), furnished, two queen beds, two bath, kitchen, microwave, refrigerator, cookware/utensils, linens, A/C, TV, DVD/VCR, satellite TV. Rates: High Season: $95 daily. One-bedroom (10), furnished, full bed, carpeted sleeper loft, kitchen, TV/VCR, satellite TV. Rates: High Season: $85 daily. Log Cabins: Three-bedroom (5), furnished, three queen beds, loft, one baths, kitchen, microwave, refrigerator, cookware/utensils, linens, A/C, TV, DVD/VCR, satellite TV. Rates: High Season: $125 daily. Two-bedroom (5), furnished, three queen beds, one bath, kitchen, microwave, refrigerator, cookware/utensils, linens, A/C, TV,

DVD/VCR, satellite TV. Rates: High Season: $110. ADA accessible units available. Housekeeping not provided.

Support Facilities: Bath House, Beach, Boat Launch, Boat Rental, Boat/RV Storage, Convenience Store, Equipment Rental, Fire Rings, Fishing Pier, Golf (nearby), Grills, Ice, Laundry, Marina, Party Barges, Pavilion (fee), Picnic Area, Restrooms, Sewage Dump, Showers, Ski Boats, Telephones, Trails.

RV Storage: C-573-346-5640 for rates and information.

Activities: Camping, Boating, Swimming, Water skiing, Fishing and other outdoor activities at Missouri's scenic playground.

Credit Cards: American Express, MasterCard, Visa.

Restrictions: No firearms, fireworks, hunting or open fires. No ATV's. Pets must be on leash and have all shots (tags displayed). Owner must pick up after pets. No swimming except in beach area. Pets are allowed in cabins with an additional charge of $30 daily.

RV Driving Directions/Location: Off Base. From east or west on I-70: Take exit 128-A at Columbia south to US-63 towards Jefferson City. Go right (south) on US-54. Turn left (east) onto SR-A. Follow SR-A approximately six miles. Turn left (north) on McCubbins Drive (formerly A-33). Continue straight for 4.7 miles to LORA. Turn left on Olney Circle to bottom of hill. Directions from Fort Leonard Wood: Take I-44 west 11 miles to Lake of the Ozarks exit. Turn right off exit onto Route 7. Travel 9.3 miles on Route 7 to Route A. Turn right on Route A and travel 19.8 miles to McCubbins Drive (formerly A-33). Turn right on McCubbins Drive and travel North 4.7 miles to LORA. Turn left on Olney Circle to bottom of hill. Facility ahead.

Area Description: Located on the Lake of the Ozarks in the center of a State Wildlife Refuge. Very peaceful setting situated on 360-acre reserve with excellent fishing and beautiful scenery.

RV Campground Physical Address: LORA, 789 Olney Circle, Linn Creek, Missouri 65052.

MONTANA

Fort William Henry Harrison Site

Address: JFHQ, 1956 Mt. Majo Street, P.O. Box 4789, Fort Harrison, MT 59636-4789.
Information Line: C-406-324-3000.
Main Base Police: C406-324-3970. Emergencies dial 911.
Main Installation Website:
http://www.montanaguard.com/trainingsite/html/fort_harrison.cfm
Main Base Location: Located in Lewis and Clark County. Fort Harrison is located outside the city of Helena.
Directions to Main Gate: Traveling East: Head east on US-12. Turn left onto Williams Street, turning right to stay on Williams Street. Take the 3rd left onto Mt. Defensa Avenue/South Avenue. Traveling West: Head west on US-12W/Euclid Avenue. Turn right onto Williams Street, turning right to stay on Williams Street. Take the 3rd left onto Mt. Defensa Avenue/South Avenue.
NMC: Helena, 2 miles east.
NMI: Malmstrom AFB, 72 miles northeast.
Base Social Media/Facebook:
https://www.facebook.com/MTGUARDOFFICIAL/
Chapels: C-406-324-3375.
Beauty/Barber Shop: Barber shop located in post exchange.
Exchange: C-406-443-0837.
Places to Eat: Three dining facilities on base. Many restaurants within a short drive.
Fitness Center: Fitness Center on base.
Military Museum: Montana Military Museum, C-406-324-3550.
Military Museum Website:
https://www.montanamilitarymuseum.org/
Things To Do: Visit St. Helena Cathedral, The Montana Historical Society, Montana State Capitol, Great Northern Carousel, Original Governor's Mansion, Holter Museum of Art or enjoy one of the many outdoor recreation areas.

RV CAMPING & GETAWAYS

Fort William Henry Harrison RV Park

Reservation/Contact Number Info: C-406-324-3355.
Recreation Security: Emergencies dial 911.
Reservations: Reservations recommended and accepted on a first come, first serve basis. Credit card required. Payment due in full upon arrival. Office hours 0700-1700 Mon-Fri. Check-in 1400 hours, check-out 1000 hours. Maximum stay 14 days. All extension require approval.
Season of Operation: May-October.
Eligibility: AD, NG, Res, Ret.
Camper/Trailer Spaces: RV Sites (12): (30A/50A)/W/S hookups, gazebo area, showers. Rates: $21 daily.
Support Facilities: Chapel, Dining Facilities, Exchange, Fitness Center, Showers, Thrift Shop.
Activities: Running Track, Fitness Center, Softball Field.
Credit Cards: Cash, Check. MasterCard and Visa.
Restrictions: No pets allowed. Firearms must be registered with Security.
RV Driving Directions/Location: On Base. On US 12 in West Helena. From I-15 Exit on the Cedar St: Follow signs for Fort Harrison, the VA Hospital, or west bound US 12. Continue to Joslyn St and turn right. Travel approximately 1.5 blocks and veer left onto Country Club Ave. Continue to the end of Country Club Ave. The Main Gate a tight fit for small rigs. Follow road to the right to North Gate and once through, travel to the Training Site Support Facility, Bldg 1011, which is kitty corner to the first stop sign. Check in at desk during business hours; otherwise, after hours check-in is for those with reservations. Key is in a lockbox. Limited RV parking in front of Bldg 1011. Continue right out of lot to get to the RV park.
Area Description: Located just outside of Helena, the state capital. The area is full of outdoor exploration, with surrounding features like the

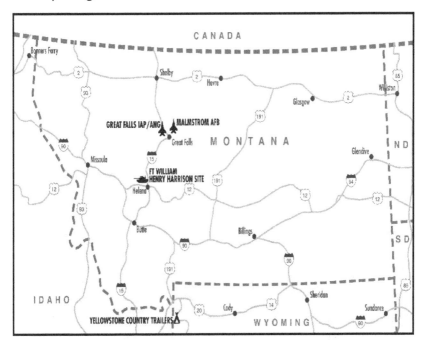

Continental Divide, a plethora of state parks and the Helena National Forest. Freshwater lakes, mountains and open country provide swimming, hiking, biking and year-round outdoor activities.

RV Campground Physical Address: 1956 Mt. Majo Street, Ft Harrison, MT 59636.

Malmstrom Air Force Base

Address: 312 73rd St N, Malmstrom AFB, MT 59402-7511.

Information Line: C-406-731-1110, DSN-312-632-1110

Main Base Police: C-406-731-4958. Emergencies dial 911.

Main Installation Website: http://www.malmstrom.af.mil/

Main Base Location: Malmstrom is located in Great Falls, Montana amidst scenic beauty and natural wonders.

Directions to Main Gate: From I-90 south of Butte: Merge onto I-90 E/I-15 N via the ramp on the left. Merge onto I-15 N via exit 129 toward Helena. Travel 148 miles and merge onto US-89 S/MT-200 E/MT-3 S via exit 278 toward 10th Ave South. Turn left onto US-87-

BYP N/57th St S. Turn right onto 2nd Ave N. 2nd Ave N becomes Goddard Ave. Turn right onto Tamarack Circle. Take the 1st left onto Ponderosa Lane and turn right onto Goddard Avenue which will become Goddard Drive. Turn left onto 73rd St N and facility on left.

NMC: Great Falls, 1 mile west.

NMI: Great Falls IA/ANG, 10 miles west.

Base Social Media/Facebook: https://www.facebook.com/MalmstromAirForceBase/

Base Social Media/Twitter: https://twitter.com/341MissileWing

Chapels: Chaplain, C-406-731-3721.

Dental Clinic: C-406-731-4633.

Medical: C-406-731-4633.

Beauty/Barber Shop: Family Hair Care, C-406-453-5715.

Commissary: C-406-731-3432.

Exchange Gas: C-406-454-1301.

Exchange: C-406-454-1301.

Financial Institutions: 1st Liberty Federal Credit Union, C-1-800-824-0585, C-406-761-8300. US Bank, C-406-454-8857.

Clubs: Grizzly Bend, C-406-731-3359.

Places to Eat: Elkhorn Diner, C-406-731-2008; Grizzly Bend Club and Coffee

Shop, C-406-731-3359 and Aces High Snack Bar, C-406-731-2494/2495 are on base. Exchange Food Court offers Popeye's Chicken and Subway. Burger King and Five Loaves Coffeehouse and Bakery are also on base. Many restaurants within a short drive.

Bowling: Aces High Bowling Center, C-406-731-2695.

Fitness Center: Malmstrom FC, C-406-731-3621.

ITT/ITR: C-406-731-3263.

Library: Arden G Hill Library, C-406-731-4638.

Military Museum: Malmstrom Museum, C-406-731-2705.

Military Museum Website: http://www.malmstrom.af.mil/About-Us/Malmstrom-Museum/

MWR: C-406-731-4141.

MWR Website: http://341fss.com/

MWR Facebook: https://www.facebook.com/341fss

Outdoor Recreation: Outdoor Recreation Center, C-406-731-3263. Offers camping equipment, watercraft sport and accessories, fishing equipment, hunting gear, mountain bikes, outdoor sports gear, seasonal sport rentals, lawn and garden equipment, party supplies, inflatables and more.

Swimming: Seasonal Outdoor Pool, C-406-731-3263 offers open and recreational swim.

Things To Do: Visit the Lewis and Clark Interpretive Center, C.M. Russell Museum, Giant Springs State Park, River's Edge Trail, Ryan Dam or enjoy shopping in Great Falls as well as many seasonal events and activities.

Walking Trails: Indoor and outdoor running tracks available on base.

RV CAMPING & GETAWAYS

Gateway FamCamp & Gateway Annex

Reservation/Contact Number Info: C-406-731-3263/5140.

Recreation Security: Annex, C-406-731-5140. FamCamp, C-406-731-3263.

RV Website: http://341fss.com/famcamp

GPS Coordinates: 47°30'2"N/111°12'18"W.

Reservations: No advance reservations, first come, first serve for both Gateway and Annex. Reservation must be paid in full upon arrival. Office hours 0800-1700 daily, closed Tue-Wed; 0800-1400 Sat-Sun; closed holidays. No refunds except in emergencies. Self check-in and registration via cash or check. Credit card payments made in person at ODR office, Bldg 1222. Payment receipt required from Fee Station prior to occupancy of site. Check-in with FamCamp host or ODR office, check-out 1200 hours. Three week max stay for FamCamp.

Season of Operation: Mid-April to mid-October.

Eligibility: AD, NG, Res, Ret, 100% DAV, DoD-Civ, NAF Civ Emp and sponsored guests.

Camper/Trailer Spaces: Gateway FamCamp: Hardstand (25), pull-thru, max 45' in length, E(220V/50A)/S/W hookups, local/sat TV, Wi-Fi, picnic table, grill. Rates: $25 daily, $130 weekly. Overflow: Paved (25), no hookups. Rates: $10 daily. Must be coordinated with Camp Host or Outdoor Rec Staff. Gateway Annex (30): Hardstand (25), E(220V/30A)/S/W, local/sat TV, picnic table, grill. Rates: $20 daily, $100 weekly. Partial hookups (5): Picnic table, grill. Rates: $15 daily. Overflow: No hookups; must be coordinated with Camp Host or Outdoor Rec staff. Rates: $8 daily. Dump Fee: $2 daily.

Tent Spaces: Gateway Annex Tent Sites: No hookups, Rates: $8 daily.

Support Facilities: Auto Craft Shop, Auto Repair, Boat Rental/Launch, Bowling, Chapel, Coin Laundry, Commissary, Convenience Store, Exchange, Fitness Center, Fitness Trail, Golf, Gas/Propane, Grills, Ice, Mess Hall, Pavilion, Pay Phones, Picnic Area, Pool, Rivers Edge Trail, Rec Equipment, Restrooms, RV Storage, Sewage Dump, Showers, Snack Bar, Sports Fields, Stables, Taxi, Tennis Courts, Wi-Fi.

RV Storage: C-406-731-3263.

Activities: Bicycling, Canoeing, Fishing*, Golfing, Hiking, Hunting*, Rafting, Swimming, Tennis. *State licenses required for patrons ages twelve and up. Children younger than twelve must be accompanied by an adult with appropriate state licenses. Montana Hunters' Safety Education Course required in order to obtain a state hunting license.

Credit Cards: MasterCard and Visa.

Restrictions: Pets allowed on leash but must be under the physical control of owner; owner must clean up after pet. Discharging of firearms prohibited on base, patrons possessing firearms must comply with state laws and base regulations. No open fires except in grills. Quiet hours 2200-0700 hours.

RV Driving Directions/Location: Gateway FamCamp: Off Base. Located approximately .5 miles south of the base main gate. Gateway Annex: On Base. From the Main Gate: Continue to Goddard Drive and turn right. At 76th Street, turn left and continue two blocks. Facility ahead on the right.

Area Description: Situated in open terrain surrounded by Highwoods and Little Belt range of the Rockies. Close to the Missouri River. Rich in Lewis and Clark history. Full range of support facilities available on base.

RV Campground Physical Address: Mailing Address: Outdoor Recreation, 500 76th Street N, Malmstrom AFB, MT 59402-7515.

NEBRASKA

Camp Ashland

Address: 220 County Road A, Ashland, NE 68003-6000.

Information Line: C 402-309-7170. Nebraska HQ, C-402-309-8210.

Main Base Police: Emergencies dial 911.

Main Installation Website: https://ne.ng.mil/RTI

Main Base Location: A small town located in southeastern Nebraska just a 30-minute drive from either Omaha or Lincoln.

Directions to Main Gate: Take I-80: Take exit 432 to NE-31 N in Melia-Forest City. Turn left on US-6 W. Drive approximately 1 mile, then make a right on County Road A. Keep right at split in road and follow to Nebraska Ave. Make a right to the gate.

NMC: Omaha, 20 miles northeast.

NMI: Offutt Air Force Base, 18 miles east.

Base Social Media/Facebook: https://www.facebook.com/NebraskaNationalGuard/

Chapels: C-402-309-8491/8492.

Exchange: C-402-944-2750.

Places to Eat: Several restaurants within a short drive.

Fitness Center: Fitness Center on base.

Military Museum: SAC Aerospace Museum, C-402-944-3100.

Military Museum Website: https://sacmuseum.org/

Things To Do: Visit the SAC Museum, Mahoney State Park, Wildlife Safari Park, Ashland Country Club, Henry Doorly Zoo or the State Capital. Enjoy fishing, swimming and boating in the Platte River.

RV CAMPING & GETAWAYS

Camp Ashland Recreation Area

Reservation/Contact Number Info: C-402-309-7267.

GPS Coordinates: 41°03'54.0"N/96°20'00.3"W

Reservations: Approval for usage prior to arrival. Maximum stay 14 days. Office hours 1700-100 hours Mon-Fri. Check in at Bldg 23, Lodging Office. Late arrivals after 1500 hours check-in and check-out with Camp Ashland Guards at gate.

Season of Operation: Year-round.

Eligibility: Valid ID cardholders, State employees affiliated with State of Nebraska military department.

Camper/Trailer Spaces: RV/Camper pads (12): Limited hookups with E/W, picnic tables, fire rings. No charge.

Support Facilities: Picnic Shelter with grill, Port-a-Potties.

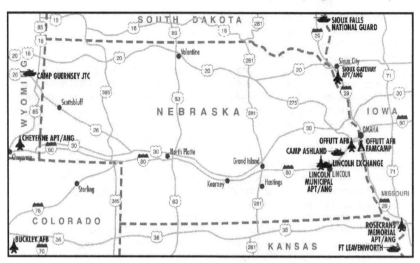

Activities: Canoeing, Fishing*, Swimming. *Nebraska Game and Fishing laws apply.

Restrictions: No motorized boats. Swimming at own risk. No personal firearms allowed. Open fires in designated pits only. Pets must be on leash.

RV Driving Directions/Location: On Base. From the Main Gate: Check in at Lodging Office, Bldg 23 during normal business hours.

Area Description: Three of Nebraska's main tourism attractions, The SAC Museum, Mahoney State Park and the wildlife Safari, are located within four miles of Ashland. Outdoor activities and rural atmosphere with a hometown feel make this a great spot for relaxation.

RV Campground Physical Address: Main Gate: 220 County Road A, Bldg 23 Ashland, NE 68003-6000.

Offutt Air Force Base FamCamp

Address: Offutt FamCamp, Lake Drive East, Bellevue, NE 68005.

Information Line: C-402-294-1110, DSN-312-271-1110.

Main Base Police: Emergencies dial 911.

Main Installation Website:
http://www.offutt.af.mil/

Main Base Location: Offutt Base Lake Recreation Area is located on 183 acres east of Offutt AFB.

NMC: Omaha, 12 miles north.

NMI: Offutt AFB, 1 mile east.

Commissary: Approximately 5 miles to commissary at Offutt AFB, C-402-294-6783.

Exchange Gas: Gas station at Offutt AFB approximately 5 miles away. Commercial gas station within 7 miles.

Exchange: Approximately 5 miles to Exchange facility at Offutt AFB, C-402-291-9100.

MWR: MWR/FSS, C-402-294-4049.

MWR Website:
http://www.offutt55fss.com/

MWR Facebook:
https://www.facebook.com/offutt55fss

MWR Twitter:
https://twitter.com/Offutt55FSS

Outdoor Recreation: Outdoor Recreation Services, C-402-294-4049. Offers household items, lawn and garden equipment, party supplies including a large inventory of inflatable's, trailers, boats, canoes, campers and outdoor adventure gear.

RV CAMPING & GETAWAYS
Offutt AFB FamCamp

Reservation/Contact Number Info: C-402-294-2108.

Recreation Security: Emergencies dial 911.

RV Website:
http://offutt55fss.com/base-lake/

GPS Coordinates:
41°6'44"N/95°52'47"W

Reservations: Advance reservations accepted during summer season, 20 April-13 October. Reservations accepted 3-days in advance. Holiday weekend reservations 45 days in advance for AD. Summer office hours 1030-1800 daily. Non-refundable first night's payment due at time of reservation. Must request late arrival to hold reservation. Off-season is first come, first serve with on-site self-registration. Maximum stay 30-days. Extensions approved on case-by-case basis. Reservations for sponsored guest 14 days in advance; 7 day limit. Sponsored campers are not authorized between Memorial Day and the 4th of July Weekend or during Labor Day weekend. Check-in 1200 hours, check-out 1100 hours. Tent Reservations: Tent campers must check in and register at Cast-A-Ways Boathouse or after hours with the FamCamp host, Site 20.

Season of Operation: Year-round with water service limited to a central fill-up point during the winter.

Eligibility: AD, NG, Reservists, Retired, 100% DAV, DOD Civilians.

Camper/Trailer Spaces: RV Sites (40): Concrete pads, E(50A)/W/S, picnic table. Rates: $20 daily, $550 monthly; Sponsored Guests: $25 daily. Overflow (6): Gravel pads, no hookups, picnic table. Rates: $12 daily. Laundry and showers available near Cast-A-Ways Boathouse, 24 hours daily with access code. Wi-Fi throughout FamCamp; computer available in the Cast-A-Ways Boathouse during season. Propane refills, Bldg 362.

Tent Spaces: Tent Sites: $9 daily, $50 weekly. Sponsored Guest: $12 nightly, $75 weekly. Group Camp: Max 10 tents: $40 nightly. Additional tent $4 nightly.

Support Facilities: Auto Craft Shop, Bait, Bathhouse, Boat Launch, Boat Rental, Bowling, Chapel, Coin Laundry, Commissary, Convenience Store, Equipment Rental, Exchange, Fire Rings, Fishing Pier, Fitness Center, Gas, Golf (On Base), Grills, Ice, Marina, Mess Hall, Pavilion, Picnic Area, Playground, Pool, Propane, Racquetball, Rec Center, Restrooms, RV Storage, Shoppette, Showers, Skeet/Trap Range, Snack Bar, Sports Fields, Stables, Tennis Courts, Trails.

RV Storage: Available with Equipment Rental on base. Rates vary depending on size of RV, C-402-294-4049.

Activities: Boating, Fishing*, Golfing, Hunting*. *State and base fishing licenses and state hunting license required for patrons ages sixteen and up. Children younger than sixteen must be accompanied by an adult with appropriate licenses.

Credit Cards: MasterCard and Visa.

Restrictions: Pets allowed on leash. Owners must clean up after pets. No firearms allowed. Campfires allowed in designated fire pits only. Quiet hours 2200-0600 hours. No swimming or wading in base lake.

RV Driving Directions/Location: Off Base. From I-80 Eastbound: Exit I-80 at Exit 439 turning right onto Nebraska Hwy 370 East towards Bellevue. Continue on Hwy 370 for 12 miles. Exit right onto Hwy 75 South towards Plattsmouth and continue for 3.4 miles. Turn left onto Hwy 34 and continue east for 2.0 miles. Turn left onto Harlan Lewis Road and continue north for 2.5 miles. Turn right into the Offutt Base Lake Entrance and stop at unguarded railroad crossing. Cross over RR Tracks, turn right and continue around lake to check in at the Cast-a-Ways Boathouse. I-80 Westbound: Exit I-80 by taking left exit, 1-29S towards Kansas City. Continue south on I-29 then take exit 35B, Hwy 34 west towards South Bellevue. Turn right onto Hwy 34 and continue west for 4.5 miles. Follow directions from this point as listed above.

Area Description: The Offutt Base Lake Recreation Area is located on 183 acres east of Offutt. Facilities include a large indoor pavilion available for parties and special events, covered picnic shelters, disc golf course, archery range, sand volleyball courts, basketball court, horseshoe pits, and two playgrounds. The lake is stocked with a variety of fish. Nebraska fishing laws apply.

RV Campground Physical Address: Outdoor Recreation: 55FSS/FSCO, 105 Union Lane Bldg 362, Offutt AFB, NE 68113-2084. FamCamp: 55FSS/FSCO, Lake Drive, Bellevue, NE 68005.

NEVADA

Desert Eagle RV Park

Address: 4907 FamCamp Drive, Las Vegas, NV 89115-1917.
Information Line: C-702-652-1110.
Main Base Police: Emergencies dial 911.
Main Installation Website: http://www.nellis.af.mil/
Main Base Location: Located in the desert with mountains on one side and Lake Mead National Recreation area on the other with an easy drive to the Grand Canyon.
NMC: Las Vegas, eight miles southwest.
NMI: Nellis Air Force Base, adjacent.
Commissary: Approximately 2 miles to the Nellis AFB commissary, C-702-632-5500.
Exchange Gas: Nellis AFB gas station approximately 2 miles away. Commercial gas station within 2 miles.
Exchange: Approximately 2 miles to the Nellis AFB Exchange, C-702-643-3526.
MWR Website: https://nellislife.com/
MWR Facebook: https://www.facebook.com/nellisforcesupport/

RV CAMPING & GETAWAYS
Desert Eagle RV Park

Reservation/Contact Number Info: C-702-643-3060. Fax C-702-643-3702.
Recreation Security: Emergencies dial 911.
RV Website: https://nellislife.com/desert-eagle-rv-park/

RV Email Address: reservations@nellislife.com
GPS Coordinates: 36°14'57"N/115°3'2"W
Reservations: Accepted up to six months in advance. Office hours 0800-1900 Mon-Fri, 0900-1900 Sat-Sun. Check-in at office RV Park, Bldg 2889, check-out 1100 hours.
Season of Operation: Year-round.
Eligibility: AD, NG, Res, Ret and DoD-Civ. Foreign military must have written permission from base commander.
Camper/Trailer Spaces: Hardstand (226), Back-in and Pull-through, Maximum 60' in length, E(110V/30/50A)/S/W hookups. Rates: $22-$26 daily depending on site. Partial hookups (4): Hardstand, back-in and pull-thru, maximum 60' in length, E(110V/30/50A)/W hookups. Rates: $20 daily. Maximum six-month stay.
Tent Spaces: Tent Sites: No hookups. Rates: $8 daily.
Support Facilities: Boat Rental/Storage, Chapel, Coin Laundry*, Commissary, Convenience Store, Covered Patio*, Dog Run*, Exchange, Fitness Center, Gas, Golf, Grills*, Pavilion*, Picnic Area*, Playground*, Racquetball, Rec Equipment, Rec Lounge, Restrooms*, RV Storage, Sewage Dump*, Shoppette, Showers*, Sports Fields, Tennis Courts, Wi-Fi hot spot*. *Located at Desert Eagle RV Park, all others on base.
RV Storage: Yes. C-702-652-2514.
Activities: Boating, Fishing*, Golfing, Snow Skiing, Swimming. *State license required.
Credit Cards: MasterCard and Visa.
Restrictions: Pets allowed on leash; owner must clean up immediately after pets. No open fires.
RV Driving Directions/Location: Off Base. From I-15 north of Las Vegas: Take Apex exit 58 to south on Las Vegas Blvd/NV-604. Turn right on Range Road and follow RV Park Signs. From US-93/95 south of Las Vegas: Take I-15 north (Salt Lake City exit) to east onto Craig Road to north on Las Vegas Blvd/NV-604. Go left on Range Road and follow RV park signs.

Main Base
Location: Located amidst the natural beauty of the Northern Nevada high desert in Churchill County, Nevada.
Directions to Main Gate: From Reno/Sparks: Take I-80 East to the Fernley/Fallon exit 48 and veer right. Continue through one light and over bridge and at the round-about make three quarter circle onto Alternate US-50. Alternate US-50 leads directly into Fallon. In Fallon, US-50 turns into Williams Avenue. Continue down Williams to Taylor Street/US-95 south. Turn right onto Taylor Street. Approximately 5 miles out of town turn left on Union Lane. Proceed east to Pasture Road. Turn left onto Pasture Road. The main gate will be approximately .25 miles on the right.
NMC: Reno, 72 miles west.
NMI: Reno-Tahoe IA/ANG, 70 miles west.
Base Social Media/Facebook: https://www.facebook.com/pages/Naval-Air-Station-Fallon/126636387376605
Base Social Media/Twitter: https://twitter.com/fallon_nas
Chapels: Chaplain, C-775-426-2959/2768.
Dental Clinic: C-775-426-2811.
Medical: Appointment Line, C-775-426-3125.
Beauty/Barber Shop: C-775-426-2547.
Commissary: C-775-426-3420.
Exchange Gas: C-775-426-2583.
Exchange: C-775-426-2818.
Financial Institutions: Navy Federal Credit Union, C-888-842-6328.

Area Description: Located in the desert with mountains on one side and Lake Mead National Recreation Area on the other. Easy drive to Grand Canyon. Fifteen minute drive to main Las Vegas attractions. Full range of support facilities.
RV Campground Physical Address: Desert Eagle RV Park, 4907 FamCamp Dr, Las Vegas, NV 89115-5000.

Fallon Naval Air Station

Address: 4755 Pasture Road, Fallon, NV 89496-5000.
Information Line: C-775-426-3000, DSN-312-890-3000.
Main Base Police: C-775-426-2803. Emergencies dial 911.
Main Installation Website: http://www.cnic.navy.mil/regions/cnrsw/installations/nas_fallon.html

Clubs: Sage & Sand CPO Club, C-775-426-2482. Silver State Officer's Club, C-775-426-2625.

Places to Eat: Kingpin Pizzeria, C-775-426-2454 and Take 5ive Grille, C-775-426-2445 are on base. Exchange Food Court offers Subway. Many restaurants within a short drive.

Bowling: Sagebrush Bowl, C-775-426-2451.

Fitness Centers: Warrior Fitness Complex, C-775-426-2251.

Golf: Driving Range, C-775-426-2598.

ITT/ITR: C-775-426-2275.

MWR: C-775-426-2550.

MWR Website:
http://navylifesw.com/fallon/

Outdoor Recreation: Outdoor Gear Rentals, C-775-426-2598. Offers camping gear, fishing poles, mountain bikes, golf clubs, snowboards, skis, camping trailers, boats, canoes, outdoor sport games, paintball park, lawn care equipment and more.

Swimming: Desert Springs Indoor Pool, C-775-426-2791 offers open and lap swim.

Things To Do: At the Carson River and Lake Lahontan, fishing, boating, swimming, water skiing and rock collecting are areas of interest. Call MWR for special rates to Reno, Tahoe, Carson City, Virginia City and other points of interest.

RV CAMPING & GETAWAYS

Fallon RV Park & Recreation Area

Reservation/Contact Number Info: C-775-426-2598, DSN-312-890-2598, C-1-800-NAVY-BED. Fax C-775-426-2492.

Recreation Security: Emergencies dial 911.

RV Website:
http://get.dodlodging.net/propertys/Fallon-RV-Park

Other Info Website:
https://fallon.navylifesw.com/programs/86b79b18-e464-4d34-b6e9-197fe3435b87

GPS Coordinates:
39°25'36"N/118°43'16"W

Reservations: Accepted 30 days in advance by phone or online: www.navygetaways.com. Check-in at Equipment Rental, Bldg 393, 1000-1800 hours Mon-Fri, Closed Holidays. Check-out 1200. Maximum stay 30 days.

Season of Operation: Year-round.

Eligibility: AD, NG, Res, Ret, DoD-Civ, Dep and 100% DAV.

Camper/Trailer Spaces: Pull-Thru Spaces: Hardstand (25), Pull-thru, Any size, E(220V/50A)/S/W hookups. Free Cable and WI-FI. Rates: $30 daily, $160 weekly, $400 monthly. DoD-Civ: $40 daily, $240 weekly, $475 monthly.

Support Facilities: Auto Skills by appointment only, Bath House, Bowling, Chapel, Commissary, Convenience Store, Equipment Rental, Exchange, Fitness Center, Gas, Laundry, Movie Theater, Pay Phones, Picnic Area, Playground, Pool, Restrooms, RV Storage, Sewage Dump, Showers, Sports Fields, Go Karts, Golf Driving Range, Tennis Courts, Wi-Fi.

RV Storage: Rates: $35 monthly, C-775-426-2598.

Activities: Boating, Sightseeing.

Credit Cards: Cash, MasterCard and Visa.

Restrictions: Pets allowed on leash; owner must clean up after pet. Must use designated pet area. No firearms.

RV Driving Directions/Location: On Base. From I-80 north or south: Take exit 46/Fernley east on ALT US-50 for 30 miles to Fallon. Continue through four traffic lights. Travel 1.5 miles past hospital to Crook Rd. and turn right. Continue to dead end and make a left at the stop sign onto Wildes Rd. Take the first right onto Pasture Road (one mile) to the Main Gate on the left at Cottonwood Drive. Main Gate only accessible to cars. RVs must use South Gate. To reach South Gate follow directions to Main Gate, then continue past the Main Gate on right. Turn left on Berney Rd to the gate. South Gate hours: 0600-1200 Mon-Fri. Weekends: C-755-426-2803 for Security to unlock gate for entrance. Call the same number when leaving the campground after hours or on the weekend. After entering

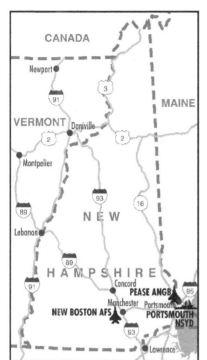

NEW HAMPSHIRE

New Boston Air Force Station

Address: 23rd Space Operations Squadron, 317 Chestnut Hill Road, New Boston, NH 03070-5125.
Information Line: C-603-471-2451/2000/2234.
Main Base Police: Emergencies dial 911.
Main Installation Website: http://www.schriever.af.mil/About-Us/Fact-Sheets/Display/Article/275805/23rd-space-operations-squadron/
Main Base Location: Located in Hillsborough County in south central New Hampshire, occupying more than 2,800 acres in three towns.
Directions to Main Gate: From I-93 north: Take I-293 west to NH-144 north. Take a left on New Boston Road, and drive approximately eight miles. New Boston Air Station is on the right.
NMC: Manchester, 8 miles northeast.
NMI: Hanscom AFB, 50 miles south.
MWR: C-603-471-2234.
MWR Website: https://50fss.com/new-boston-outdoor-rec/
Outdoor Recreation: C-603-471-2451/2452. Offers skis, snowboards, poles, boots, snowmobiles, popup trailers, kayaks, canoes and boats and more.

RV CAMPING & GETAWAYS

New Boston Recreation Area

Reservation/Contact Number Info: C-603-471-2451.
RV Website: https://50fss.com/new-boston-outdoor-rec/new-boston-camping-campgrounds/
RV Email Address: rodney.hooper@us.af.mil
GPS Coordinates: 42°56'09.1"N/71°38'26.8"W
Reservations: Contact facility for reservations. Office hours 0700-1530 Mon-Fri. Primitive sites do not require reservations.

park, check-in at Bldg 393 is left at the stop sign and on right side of street. It is the second building on right and not visible from RV Park.
Area Description: Nearby Carson River and several lakes offer fishing, boating, swimming, and water skiing. Call MWR for special rates to Reno, ghost towns, Virginia City, and other points of interest. Full range of support facilities available on base.
RV Campground Physical Address: Fallon RV Park & Recreation Area MWR, Department, Pony Express Outfitters, 4755 Pasture Road, Bldg 393, Fallon NAS, NV 89406-5000.

Eligibility: AD, NG, Res, Ret, DoD-Civ and Dep.

Camper/Trailer Spaces: RV (25): Full hookup site, firepit, picnic table. Rates:

Tent Spaces: Primitive (25): No hookups, firepit, picnic table. Rates: $20 daily. Located at Johnson Point and Upper and Lower Ice Pond.

Yurt, A Frame, Cabin, Apt, Spaces: Cabins (2): Two-bedrooms, sleeper sofa, full kitchen and one bath. Space heaters, deck and firepit. Linens and towels not provided. Sleeps 5. Rates: $70 daily.

RV Storage: Yes. C-603-471-2451.

Credit Cards: MasterCard, Visa, Cash and Check.

RV Driving Directions/Location: From the main gate: Travel to first T intersection and turn left to facility ahead on the left.

Area Description: Enjoy tranquil grounds, boating or just enjoying undisturbed nature in the heart of New England. Many outdoor activities.

RV Campground Physical Address: New Boston Air Force Station: New Boston Recreation Area, 317 Chestnut Hill RD, New Boston, NH 03070-5125.

NEW JERSEY

Cape May Coast Guard Training Center

Address: 1800 Pennsylvania Ave, Cape May, NJ 08204-4017.

Information Line: C-609-898-6995.

Main Base Police: C-609-898-6244.

Main Installation Website: http://www.forcecom.uscg.mil/Our-Organization/FORCECOM-UNITS/TraCen-Cape-May/

Main Base Location: Sewell Point, a peninsula at the southern tip of the New Jersey Shore.

Directions to Main Gate: Enter Cape May on Route 109 S. Cross two bridges to Lafayette Street. Turn left one block after crossing the second bridge, Sydney Street. Take another left onto Washington Street and an immediate right on Texas Avenue at the C-View Inn. Follow this road to Pittsburgh Avenue. Travel about .5 miles to the blinking yellow light and make a left on Pennsylvania Ave. Proceed to Training Center Cape May's main gate.

NMC: Atlantic City, 45 miles northeast.

NMI: Atlantic City IA/ANG, 45 miles northeast.

Base Social Media/Facebook: https://www.facebook.com/USCoastGuardBootCamp/

Chapels: C-609-898-6974.

Dental Clinic: C-609-898-6960.

Medical: Appointment Line, C-609-898-6610.

Beauty/Barber Shop: C-609-898-6939.

Exchange: C-609-898-6940.

Clubs: Harborview, C-609-898-6359/6397. Oceanside, C-609-898-6935/6396.

Places to Eat: Harborview, C-609-898-6937/6396 and Etheridge Hall, C-609-898-2138 are on base. Many restaurants within a short drive.

Fitness Center: C-609-898-6973.

Golf: Driving range on base.

MWR: C-609-898-6922.

MWR Website: http://www.forcecom.uscg.mil/Our-Organization/FORCECOM-UNITS/TraCen-Cape-May/Recreation-Morale/

MWR Facebook: https://www.facebook.com/TRACENCAPEMAYMWR/

Outdoor Recreation: MWR Equipment Rental, C-609-374-0767. Offers campers, camping gear, canoes, kayaks, sports equipment, lawn and garden equipment and more.

Swimming: Fitness Center Indoor Pool, C-609-898-6973 offer open and lap swim. Closed Sunday.

Things To Do: Fishing, boating, beaches, boardwalk amusement parks, museums and parks all provide entertainment for visitors to the "Garden State."

Walking Trails: Running trails on base.

RV CAMPING & GETAWAYS

Tracen Cape May Camping

Reservation/Contact Number Info: C-609-898-6922. Fax C-609-898-6884.
RV Website: https://www.forcecom.uscg.mil/Our-Organization/FORCECOM-UNITS/TraCen-Cape-May/Recreation-Morale/Camping/
RV Email Address: D05-SMB-TRACENCM-MWR@USCG.MIL
Reservations: Reservations required and require patron to submit completed application with full payment. Accepted 90 days in advance. Applications accepted at MWR office in gymnasium, via mail, fax or email. Upon approval, site is assigned. Cancellations must be made within 72 hours of arrival to avoid fee. Check-in 1200-1600 hours, check-out 1100 hours. Maximum 14 day stay not to exceed 28 days within one year.
Season of Operation: Memorial Day-Columbus Day.
Eligibility: AD, Military ID holders, Sponsored Guests.
Tent Spaces: Primitive Sites (8): No hookups, picnic table, fire ring and trash/recycling receptacle. Showers available at MWR gym. Max 2 tents and 10 people. Rates: No charge. Tent camping only.
Support Facilities: Covered Picnic Pavilion, Equipment Rental, Playground, Sand Volleyball Court, Softball Field, Golf Range, Tennis Courts.
Activities: Beaches nearby.
Restrictions: Fire permits required. Beach tags required and available at MWR. Pets must be on a leash. Quiet hours 2200-0600.
RV Driving Directions/Location: On Base. From the Main Gate: Located at the south end of Training Center Cape May off Frasier Avenue.
Area Description: Campsites located on 2 acres near base activities. Beach swimming within walking distance in designated areas.
RV Campground Physical Address: Mailing Address: USCG Training Center, ATTN: MWR Office, 1 Munro Avenue, Cape May, NJ 08204.

Earle Naval Weapons Station

Address: 201 Route 34 S, Colts Neck, NJ 07722-5001.
Information Line: C-732-866-2500.
Main Base Police: C-732-866-2291. Emergencies dial 911.
Main Installation Website: http://www.cnic.navy.mil/regions/cnrma/installations/nws_earle.html
Main Base Location: Located in Monmouth County and nestled within an upscale community of horse farms, fruit orchards and country estates in Colts Neck, New Jersey.
Directions to Main Gate: From the North Garden State Parkway South: Take exit 123/Route 9/Sayreville/Old Bridge. Travel several miles then merge onto Route 18 South via ramp on left toward Asbury Park/Shore Points. Continue on Route 18 South for several miles to exit 19B/Route 34 South/Pt. Pleasant. The base will be approximately one mile on the left on Route 34 South. From the south: Take the NJ Turnpike north to exit 7A (Shore Points) to 195 east to exit 35B to Rte 34 north. Proceed to circle and stay in right lane. Take Rte 34 north to first traffic light after the circle. Base is on the right. From the north: Take Garden State Pkwy south, exit 100A, Route 33 west toward Freehold. At traffic circle follow Rte 34 for approximately 2 miles. Proceed to first traffic light. The Main Gate is on the right.
NMC: Newark, 50 miles north.
NMI: JB McGuire-Dix-Lakehurst, 30 miles south.
Base Social Media/Facebook: https://www.facebook.com/NWSEarleNJ/
Dental Clinic: C-732-866-2255/2257.
Medical: C-732-866-2300., DSN-312-449-2300/7493.
Beauty/Barber Shop: C-732-866-2285.
Exchange: C-732-866-2893.
Financial Institutions: Navy Federal Credit Union, C-1-888-842-6328.

Places to Eat: Johnny J's Cafe, C-732-866-2106. Many restaurants within a short drive.

Fitness Center: Mainside FC, C-732-866-2119. Baybreeze FC, C-732-866-7059.

ITT/ITR: C-732-866-2103.

MWR Phone Number: C-732-866-2608.

MWR Website:
http://www.navymwrearle.com/

MWR Facebook:
https://www.facebook.com/earlemwr/

Swimming: Pavilion Outdoor Pool, C-732-866-2351 offers lap and open swim.

Things To Do: Absecon Lighthouse, Aviation Museum Naval Air Station Wildwood, Battleship New Jersey, Cape May Historic District/Mid-Atlantic Center for the Arts, Cape May

Lighthouse, East Jersey Olde Towne Village, Ellis Island, Statue Cruises at Liberty State Park.

RV CAMPING & GETAWAYS
Earle NWS RV Park

Reservation/Contact Number Info: C-732-866-2448.

RV Website:
http://get.dodlodging.net/propertys/Navy-Getaways-Deer-Run-RV-Park

Other Info Website:
https://www.navymwrearle.com/lodging/navy-getaways

RV Email Address:
dianna.lauterwasser@navy.mil

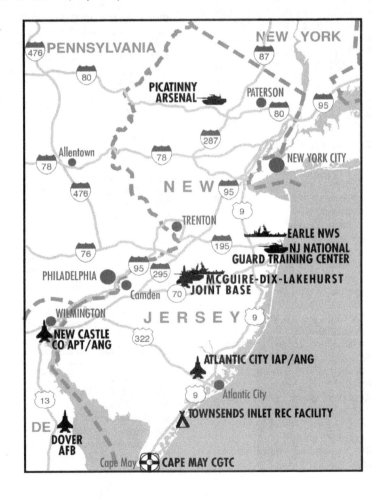

GPS Coordinates:
40°15'50"N/74°9'26"W.

Reservations: Reservations accepted online at www.dodlodging.net and by telephone, 24 hours daily. RV guest's check-in after 1200. Check in with base security to pick up check-in package.

Season of Operation: Seasonally, April-November 15, weather permitting.

Eligibility: All AD, Res, Retirees, DOD Civilian, 100% DAV.

Camper/Trailer Spaces: Concrete (15), Back-in, Any size, E(110/220/50A)/S/W, picnic table, grill, Wi-Fi access. Sites are large and roomy (10X62'), with 11X25 patio, concrete pads, plenty of side room for slide-outs, set on knoll surrounded by pinewoods in quiet, pastoral area. Rates: $25 daily.

Support Facilities: Auto Skills Shop, Fitness Center and Gymnasium, Min-Mart. Mainside Sports Complex including the (2) regulation softball fields, tennis courts, picnic pavilion, seasonal pool and basketball/volleyball courts.

RV Storage: C-732-866-2448 with limited availability.

Activities: Within a ten mile radius: Atlantic Ocean Beaches, Birding*, Charter/Party Fishing Boats, Dessert and Dinner Theaters, Discount Outlet Mall, Fishing**, Horse race tracks (2), Hunting*, Lighthouses, Live Theater (Professional and Amateur), Multi-Screen Movie Theaters (At Mall), NASCAR Race Track, National Recreation Area, Restaurants (75), Surf Fishing***. * Base and state licenses required for patrons ages ten and up. Children younger than ten must be accompanied by an adult with the appropriate licenses. ** Base license required for patrons ages sixteen and up. Children younger than sixteen must be accompanied by an adult with a base license. ***No license necessary.

Credit Cards: American Express, Discover, MasterCard and Visa.

Restrictions: Pets allowed in RV spaces, must be well behaved, leashed, up to date immunizations. No firearms permitted.

RV Driving Directions/Location: On Base. From the Main Gate: Check in with security and map will be provided to RV Park.

Area Description: Located on beautifully wooded acres, the RV facilities are an easy drive from New York City, Atlantic City, and Philadelphia. For history buffs, there are many Revolutionary War sites, memorials, state and county parks, museums and homes in the area, as well as pastoral lands. Historic Twin Lights, once the brightest beacon on the East Coast, and Sandy Hook Lighthouse, the oldest continuously operating lighthouse in the United States, are popular nearby attractions. Also popular are Barnegat Lighthouse and Cape May Lighthouse, both within a 90 minute drive. Birding along the Eastern Flyway is excellent at Sandy Hook (ten miles) and Cape May (ninety miles). Shopping malls and Jackson Outlet Mall are nearby, as well as major chain supermarkets, country food markets, green grocers, and specialty shops.

RV Campground Physical Address: Earle NWS RV Park, 201 Highway 34, Colts Neck, NJ 07722.

Fort Dix Army Support Activity (JB-MDL)

Address: 2270 Fort Dix Road, Fort Dix, NJ 08640.

Information Line: C-609-754-1110.

Main Base Police: C-609-562-6001.

Main Installation Website:
http://www.jointbasemdl.af.mil/

Main Base Location: Dix and McGuire are located in beautiful southern central New Jersey, approximately 15 miles from Trenton, 50 minutes from Philadelphia and Atlantic City.

Directions to Main Gate: From NJ Turnpike: Exit at Bordentown, NJ Turnpike exit 7. Bear left after the toll to Dix. Take Route 206 South for approximately .25 miles then turn left onto Route 68. Proceed for about 8 miles to the Dix entrance and checkpoint.

NMC: Trenton, 17 miles northwest.

NMI: Earle Naval Weapons Station, 36 miles northeast.

Base Social Media/Facebook: https://www.facebook.com/JBMDL

Base Social Media/Twitter: https://twitter.com/jointbasemdl

Chapels: Religious Services & Programs, C-609-754-4673.

Dental Clinic: Main Dental Clinic, C-609-754-3786. Lakehurst Dental, C-732-323-2158.

Medical: Main Clinic Appointment Line, C-866-377-2778. Lakehurst Appointment Line, C-732-323-5323.

Veterinary Services: C-609-562-6636.

Beauty/Barber Shop: Main Exchange Barber, C-609-723-5190; Stylique, C-609-723-7377. MCSS, C-609-723-9400. Pomona Retail Store Barber, C-609-761-6336. The Hairport at Pudgey's, C-609-754-4348. NEX Barber, C-732-323-1081.

Commissary: Lakehurst, C- 732-323-1220. McGuire, C-609-754-2153.

Exchange Gas: Bldg 5359 Express, C-609-723-0469/0044. Bldg 2841 Express, C-609-723-4705.

Exchange: JB Exchange, C-609-723-6100. Lakehurst NEX, C-732-323-7680.

Financial Institutions: Wells Fargo Bank, C-609-724-7570.

Clubs: Pudgy's Pub, C-609-724-0443.

Places to Eat: Doughboy Loop Snack Bar, C-609-562-6895 and Fountain Green Golf Course Grill, C-609-562-5443 (weekends only) are on base as well as eligible patron only Dining Facilities. JB McGuire-Dix-Lakehurst Exchange Food Court offers Arby's, Boston Market, Charley's, Popeye's Chicken and Smoothie King. Burger King, Dunkin Donuts and Pizza Hut are also available. Many restaurants within a short drive.

Bowling: Doughboy Loop Bowling Center, C-609-562-6895.

Fitness Center: Doughboy Gym, C-609-562-5780. Griffith Field House, C-609-562-4888.

Golf: Fountain Green Golf Club, C-609-562-5443.

ITT/ITR: Fort Dix, C-609-562-6667/4208. Lakehurst, C-732-323-1362/4565.

Library: See McGuire AFB.

Military Museum: Army Reserve Mobilization Museum, C-609-562-2334.

Military Museum Website: http://www.dix.army.mil/Services/TMD/Museum.aspx

MWR: C-609-754-5327.

MWR Website: http://www.gomdl.com/

MWR Facebook: https://www.facebook.com/87FSS

MWR Twitter: https://twitter.com/gomdl

Outdoor Recreation: Fort Dix ODR, C-609-562-6667/4208. Lakehurst ODR, C-732-323-2583. Offers a variety of adventure programs as well as canoes, trailers, fishing boats, fishing gear, kayaks, camping gear, outdoor sports equipment, party and picnic supplies, ski and snowboard rentals, winter ski equipment service and more. John F Mann Recreational Park, C-609-562-6667 offers go-karts, mini-golf, batting cages, basketball courts and more. Lakehurst offers a variety of adventure programs as well as canoes, camping gear, sports equipment and more.

Swimming: Indoor Pool Bldg 5901, C-609-562-2808 offers lap and open swim, swim lessons and aerobic classes. Outdoor Seasonal Pool Bldg 6046, C-609-562-2808 offers lap and open swim. SCUBA diving classes and Lifeguard training also offered. Pine Ridge Pool Seasonal Outdoor Pool, C-732-323-2473 offers lap and open swim.

Things To Do: Six Flags Great Adventure Amusement Park is located in Jackson, NJ, approximately 15 miles away. Visit Trenton 17 miles northwest, historic Smithville Park, Smithville Mansion, Underground Railroad of Burlington County, Union Transportation Trail, Sea Girt Beach and Boardwalk and many local vineyards and wineries.

Walking Trails: Indoor running track at Griffith Field House.

RV CAMPING & GETAWAYS
Willow Pond RV Camping

Reservation/Contact Number Info: C-609-562-6667/4210. Fax C-609-562-4212, DSN-312-562-4212.

Recreation Security: C-609-562-6001.

RV Website:
http://gomdl.com/activities/outdoor-recreation/fam-camps/
GPS Coordinates:
40°0'44"N/74°36'32"W
Reservations: Reservations and deposits accepted at Dix ODR. Office hours 1000-1700 Mon-Fri, 0900-1600 Sat-Sun. No restrictions on length of stay. Check-in during operational hours, check-out 1200 hours.
Season of Operation: Year-round.
Eligibility: AD, NG, Res, Ret, DoD-Civ (AD and Ret), Dep, 100% DAV, Emp- Civ with ID access to base.
Camper/Trailer Spaces: Gravel (8), Back-in, Maximum 50' in length, E(220V/30A)/S/W. Rates: $20 daily; $100 weekly; $400 monthly.
Tent Spaces: Camp Dix Sites (6): Primitive, no hookups, fire rings, picnic table. Rates*: $10 nightly. *Also available for Boy/Girl Scout troop camping. Rates: $3 daily/scout.
Support Facilities: Auto Repair, Beach, Boat Launch, Boat Storage, Bowling, Cafeteria, Chapel, Commissary, Convenience Store, Equipment Rental, Exchange, Fishing Pier, Fitness Center, Gas, Golf, Grills, Ice, Laundry* Marina, Mess Hall, Pavilion, Pay Phones, Picnic Area, Playground, Pool, Propane, Rec Center, Restrooms, RV Storage, Sewage Dump, Shoppette, Showers, Shuttle Bus, Sports Fields, Stables, Tennis Courts, Trails. *Located Outside the RV Camp.
RV Storage: C-609-562-6667.
Activities: Bicycle & Hiking Trails, Canoeing, Fishing*, Hunting*, Kayaking, Museums, Seaside Heights, Six Flags/Hurricane Harbor, Six Flags Outlet Shopping, Swimming. * State and base licenses required for patrons ages sixteen and up. Children younger than sixteen must be accompanied by an adult with appropriate licenses.
Credit Cards: MasterCard and Visa.
Restrictions: Pets allowed. Owner must clean up after pet.
RV Driving Directions/Location: On Base. From north of Fort Dix: Take NJ Turnpike to exit 7 (Fort Dix) onto Rte 206 south, which is second traffic light about .5 miles, to Rte 68 (left fork from Rt 206). Rte 68 leads to Fort Dix to the SSG Terry Hemingway Reception Center. Once inside the gate, drive through traffic circle and take first exit out of circle. Follow the road to a stop sign/flashing light and make a left onto Lemontown Rd. Take left onto 8th Street. Continue on 8th St until reaching an intersection and take a right onto Doughboy Loop Road. Check-in at Outdoor Recreation, Bldg 6045, on Doughboy Loop. RV Park is located on Willow Pond at the corner of Texas Ave and Eighth Street.
Area Description: Located on Fort Dix next to Willow Pond. Enjoy the biking and hiking trails, as well as fresh-water fishing. Local attractions include Six Flags Amusement Park and Hurricane Harbor.
RV Campground Physical Address: Willow Pond RV Camping, Fort Dix Outdoor Recreation, Bldg 6045, Doughboy Loop, Fort Dix, NJ 08640.

New Jersey National Guard Training Center

Address: 100 Camp Drive, Sea Girt, NJ 08750.
Information Line: C-732-974-5900.
Main Base Police: C-732-974-5977.
Main Base Location: Located in Monmouth County in Sea Girt along the Atlantic Ocean.
Directions to Main Gate: From the West: Take I-195 East. I-195 turns into 138E. Take Rt 35 South SEA GIRT exit. Stay on Rt 35 South for approximately 2.5 miles. Make left onto Sea Girt Avenue. Continue on Sea Girt Ave for approx 1.5 miles to intersection of Rt 71. Cross over Rt 71 - proceed approx 50 yards and bear right after crossing railroad tracks. Make right turn into National Guard Training Center.
Places to Eat: Many restaurants within a short drive.
Fitness Center: Fitness Center on base.
Military Museum: New Jersey Militia Museum, C-732-974-5966.
Military Museum Website:
https://www.nj.gov/military/museum/
Swimming: Ocean swimming on base beach.

Things To Do: Enjoy the Sea Girt boardwalk and beaches or visit the Sea Girt Lighthouse. Unique shopping and dining in nearby downtown area.

RV CAMPING & GETAWAYS

Sea Girt NGTC RV Park

Reservation/Contact Number Info: C-732-974-5951.

GPS Coordinates: 40°07'10.1"N/74°01'57.3"W

Reservations: Must contact facility for reservations accepted every Wednesday from 0900-1200. Two-night minimum required. Maximum stay 14 days.

Season of Operation: Year-round.

Eligibility: AD, NG, Res, Ret and Dep.

Camper/Trailer Spaces: RV Sites (9): Full hookup site, bathhouse accessible with key. Rates: 20' $30 daily; larger RV $35 daily.

Restrictions: Pets are not permitted.

RV Driving Directions/Location: From Gate: Follow Camp Drive to RV area.

Area Description: Enjoy beautiful beaches, the Sea Girt Boardwalk or explore the area.

Picatinny Arsenal

Address: Picatinny Arsenal. Farley Avenue & Buffington Road, Picatinny Arsenal, NJ 07806.

Information Line: C-800-831-2759.

Main Base Police: C-973-724-7273. Emergencies dial 911.

Main Installation Website: http://www.pica.army.mil/Picatinny/

Main Base Location: Picatinny Arsenal is located in Morris County in Northwest New Jersey.

Directions to Main Gate: From the Newark airport: Bear left at main exit to I-78 westbound, following the signs toward. Exit I-78 westbound to Route 24 westbound to I-287 northbound. Take I-80 westbound and take exit 34 to Route 15 northbound/Sparta & Picatinny Arsenal. Go through traffic light and bear right to Picatinny entrance up a small hill before underpass.

NMC: Newark, 30 miles southeast.

NMI: U.S. Military Academy, West Point, 66 miles northeast.

Base Social Media/Facebook: https://www.facebook.com/PicatinnyAr senal

Base Social Media/Twitter: https://twitter.com/Picatinny_NJ

Chapels: C-973-724-4139.

Dental Clinic: West Point, C-732-532-7063.

Medical: Keller Army Community Hospital, C-845-938-5169, DSN-312-688-5169. AD Health Clinic, C-973-724-2113.

Veterinary Services: West Point, C-845-938-3817.

Commissary: C-973-724-5510.

Exchange: C-973-989-2411.

Financial Institutions: Picatinny Credit Union, C-973-989-2612.

Places to Eat: Bucky's, C-973-724-9621; Choices Marketplace, C-973-724-5788; Gunpowder Grill, C-973-724-2405 and Sam Adams Pub, C-973-724-4630 are on base. Many restaurants within a short drive.

Fitness Center: Forge Fitness, C-973-724-4629.

Golf: Picatinny Golf Course, C-973-724-4653.

ITT/ITR: C-973-724-4186.

MWR: C-973-724-4157.

MWR Website: https://picatinny.armymwr.com/

MWR Facebook: https://www.facebook.com/PicatinnyAr senalFMWR

Outdoor Recreation: Outdoor Recreation Services, C-973-724-4484. Offers camping gear, outdoor sports equipment including winter sports gear, inflatables, canoes, kayaks, trailers, dunk tank, SCUBA gear, paintball, clubs and more. Lake Denmark Pavilion rental available as well.

Swimming: Frog Fall Aquatic Park, C-973-724-7275 offers seasonal recreational swim, splash pads, water slides, snack bar and more.

Things To Do: Enjoy many outdoor recreation areas and parks. Visit the Ford Mansion and Museum, historic Speedwell, Morristown National

Historic Park or visit New York City, which is only about 35 miles east.

Walking Trails: Hiking is available at recreational facilities.

RV CAMPING & GETAWAYS

Picatinny Arsenal MWR Recreational Cabins

Reservation/Contact Number Info: C-973-724-8855, DSN-312-880-8855. Fax C-973-724-6721.

Recreation Security: Emergencies dial 911.

RV Website: https://picatinny.armymwr.com/programs/recreational-lodging

GPS Coordinates: 40.957581/74.526082. GPS Address: Snake Hill Rd, Picatinny Arsenal, NJ 07806.

Reservations: Reservations accepted online on a first come, first serve basis. Confirmation email provided when accepted or approved. Office hours 0800-1500 Mon-Fri. Closed weekends and federal holidays. Military in PCS Status may request lodging 120 days in advance. 30 day maximum stay unless otherwise approved. Cancellations must be made within 7 days of arrival to avoid $100 cancellation fee. Failure to cancel fee equal to 2-night's stay. Check-in 1500 hours, check-out 1000 hours.

Season of Operation: Year-round.

Eligibility: AD, NG, Res, Ret, DoD-Civ.

Camper/Trailer Spaces: RV sites coming soon. Please check with MWR or website for updates.

Yurt, A Frame, Cabin, Apt, Spaces: Two Bedroom Cabins (3): Queen size bed and three twin size beds; private bath, living area, dining area, full kitchen, washer/dryer, TV/Cable. Rates: $100-$125 nightly; $2,300-$2,950 monthly. An additional pet fee of $6 per night applies.

Support Facilities: Full range of support facilities available on base.

Activities: Frog Falls Aquatic Park, Hiking, Fishing, Scenic Trails.

Credit Cards: MC, VISA.

Restrictions: Pets must be on a leash. Limited pet-friendly units. No smoking.

RV Driving Directions/Location: On Base. From Main Gate: Follow Parker Road to Cannon Gate. Go left on 1st Street, take first right on Ramsey Avenue. Follow around sharp corner to Bldg 34N on the right. Cabins located of Snake Hill Road on Hart Road.

Area Description: Many hiking trails and scenic areas in this pristine location in Northern New Jersey.

RV Campground Physical Address: Mailing Address: FMWR Recreational Lodging Office, Bldg 34N, Picatinny Arsenal, NJ 07806-5000.

Townsend Inlet Recreation Facility

Address: Townsends Inlet Recreational Facility, 8101 Landis Avenue, Sea Isle City, NJ 08243.

Information Line: C-609-677-2227, Fax C-609-813-3850.

Main Base Police: Duty Officer, C-609-677-2226. Emergencies dial 911.

Main Installation Website: https://www.atlanticarea.uscg.mil/Our-Organization/District-5/District-Units/Air-Station-Atlantic-City/

Main Base Location: Recreation Facility is located off base at the Old Coast Guard lifesaving station in Sea Isle City, NJ, two blocks from the beach.

NMC: Atlantic City, 25 miles northeast.

NMI: Cape May Coast Guard Training Center, 20 miles southwest.

Chapels: C-609-898-6974.

Exchange Gas: Commercial gas station within 6 miles.

Exchange: Approximately 23 miles away at USCG Training Center Cape May, C-609-898-6940.

Places to Eat: Resort area with many restaurants nearby.

Fitness Center: C-609-898-6973.

ITT/ITR: C-609-263-3722.

MWR Phone Number: C-609-263-3722.

MWR Website: http://www.uscg.mil/d5/airstaAtlanticCity/mwr.asp

Outdoor Recreation: MWR Facility Services, C-609-263-3722/6922. Call for details. All Hands Clubs, the Harbor

View Community Club and the Oceanside Community Club, C-609-898-6396. Tennis courts, driving range, ball fields and racquetball courts available.

Swimming: Pool available, C-609-898-6973. Ocean swimming also available.

Things To Do: This peaceful location is a short walk from the beach, an area for outdoor games, premier fishing, ocean kayaking, sailing, windsurfing and excellent bird watching.

Walking Trails: Oceanside walking is available near lodging facility.

RV CAMPING & GETAWAYS

Townsend Inlet Recreation Facility

Reservation/Contact Number Info: C-609-263-3722.

Recreation Security: Duty Officer, C-609-677-2226. Emergencies dial 911.

RV Website: https://www.atlanticarea.uscg.mil/Our-Organization/District-5/District-Units/Air-Station-Atlantic-City/MWR/Townsend-Inlet-Recreational-Facility/

GPS Coordinates: 39°7'44"N/74°42'34"W.

Reservations: Reservations required; online only. See website for reservation procedures. Reservations accepted 90 days in advance beginning Monday for Sunday reservation for AD, Res, NG, Service Academy Cadet, PHS, NOAA. Reservations accepted 60 days in advance beginning Wednesday for Sunday reservations for Ret, DHS, DoD Civ and CG Aux. Office hours 0800-1600 hours Mon-Fri. Check-in 1400-1630 hours on premises, check-out 1000 hours. Maximum stay 7 days.

Season of Operation: Year-round.

Eligibility: AD, NG, Res, Ret, Dep, Foreign Service, DHS-Civ and U.S. Public Health Service Emp.

Yurt, A Frame, Cabin, Apt, Spaces: Apartments (4 units): Communal kitchen, refrigerator, microwave, cookware/utensils and dining room, cribs, cots/rollaways, highchairs, linens, toiletries, washer/dryer, telephone, A/C, CATV/DVD, Wi-Fi. Two units with private bath. All four apartments may be rented by same group. Summer Rates: $70-$90 daily; Winter: $40-$45 daily. Fees according to rank.

Support Facilities: Basketball Court, Bath House, Beach, Bicycling, Grills, Picnic Area, Volleyball Court.

RV Storage: None.

Activities: Basketball, Bicycling, Fishing, Horseshoes, Shuffleboard, Swimming, Volleyball.

Credit Cards: Checks, MasterCard and Visa.

Restrictions: No pets allowed. Firearms prohibited. No smoking.

RV Driving Directions/Location: Off Base. From the north: Take the Garden State Pkwy exit 17. Travel east on Rt 625 (Sea Isle Blvd) into Sea Isle City and follow to Landis Ave. Turn right on Landis and continue to 82nd St. From the South: Take the Garden State Pkwy exit 13. Travel east on Rt 601 (Avalon Blvd) and follow to Ocean Drive. Drive north along Ocean Dr, which changes to Landis Ave. The building is located on a full city block at the intersection of Landis Ave and 82nd St.

Area Description: Old Coast Guard lifesaving station in Sea Isle City, NJ. Two blocks from beach. Located in southern New Jersey, midway between Cape May and Atlantic City, this Victorian house is one block from the ocean and two blocks from the bay. Facility provides all amenities to enjoy a stay here, including beach badges.

RV Campground Physical Address: 8101 Landis Ave, Sea Isle City, NJ 08243.

NEW MEXICO

Holloman Air Force Base

Address: 490 First Street, Holloman AFB, NM 88330.

Information Line: C-575-572-1110, DSN-312-572-1110.

Main Base Police: C-575-572-7171. Emergencies dial 911.

Main Installation Website:
http://www.holloman.af.mil/
Main Base Location: Located six miles southwest of the central business district of Alamogordo in Otero County.
Directions to Main Gate: From the Alamogordo Airport: Take Airport Road to Highway 70 and turn left following the signs to Holloman AFB. Recommended to arrive via El Paso IAP.
NMC: Las Cruces, 50 miles southwest.
NMI: White Sands Missile Range, 40 miles northwest.
Base Social Media/Facebook:
https://www.facebook.com/HollomanAirForceBase
Base Social Media/Twitter:
https://twitter.com/HollomanAFB
Chapels: Chaplain, C-575-572-7211.
Dental Clinic: C-575-572-3742.
Medical: Appointment Line, C-575-572-2778.
Veterinary Services: C-575-572-3303.
Beauty/Barber Shop: Barber, C-575-479-4449; Beauty Salon, C-575-479-2748.
Commissary: C-575-572-7572.
Exchange Gas: C-575-479-2201/6004.
Exchange: C-575-479-1509.
Financial Institutions: Otero Federal Credit Union, C-575-439-2400. Wells Fargo Bank, C-575-479-6153.
Places to Eat: 49er Lounge, C-575-572-8198; Brewed Awakenings; Oasis Bar and Grill, C-575-572-4444; Shenanigan's, C-575-572-4444, Shifting Sands DFAC, C-575-572-5859 and Ten Pin Cantina, C-575-572-7010 are on base. Exchange Food Court offers Charley's, Subway and Taco Bell. Domino's, McDonald's and Popeye's Chicken are on base as well. Many restaurants within a short drive.
Bowling: Desert Lanes, C-575-572-7378.
Fitness Center: Domenici FC & Sports Center, C-575-572-2529.
Golf: Apache Mesa Golf Course, C-575-572-3574.
Library: Ahrens Memorial Library, C-575-572-3939.
MWR: C-575-572-5597.
MWR Website:
http://www.hollomanfss.com/

MWR Facebook:
https://www.facebook.com/HollomanFSS/
Outdoor Recreation: Outdoor Recreation Services, C-575-572-5369. Offers camping gear, campers, trailers, lawn and garden tools, sports equipment, winter ski rentals, bikes, party supplies, inflatables and more. Enjoy archery and paintball courses.
Swimming: Indoor Pool, C-575-572-2529 offers lap swim and swim lessons.
Things To Do: Visit Carlsbad Caverns and see one of the world's largest underground chambers, as well as countless rock formations. Tours are offered year-round. See the local pistachio farms and wineries or take a short drive to White Sands National Park.

RV CAMPING & GETAWAYS
Holloman AFB FamCamp

Reservation/Contact Number Info: C-575-572-5369, DSN-312-572-5369. Fax C-575-572-3695.
Recreation Security: C-575-572-7171.
RV Website:
https://www.hollomanfss.com/famcamp
RV Email Address:
hollomanodr@gmail.com
GPS Coordinates:
32°49'54"N/106°4'14"W.
Reservations: No advance reservations. First come, first serve. Full payment due at check-in. Park in open site and check in with camp host at site 19 to make payment. Office hours 0900-1700 Mon-Fri, 0900-1300 Sat-Sun. Check-out 1100 hours. Maximum 30-day stay with extension on space available basis.
Season of Operation: Year-round.
Eligibility: AD, NG, Res, Ret and DoD/NAF-Civ.
Camper/Trailer Spaces: Hardstand (36), Pull-thru, Maximum 40' in length, E(110V/20/30/50A)/S/W hookups, picnic table, CATV, Wi-Fi. Rates: $20 daily, $120 weekly, $500 monthly. Dry camping available for $7 daily if sites are full.
Support Facilities: Auto Craft Shop, Auto Repair, Bathhouse, Bowling, Chapel, Commissary, Convenience

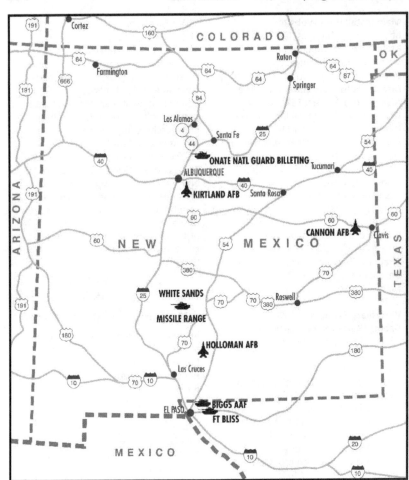

Store, Equipment rental, Exchange, Fitness Center, Gas, Golf, Grills, Ice, ITT, Laundry, Mess Hall, Pavilion, Pay Phones, Picnic Area, Playground, Pool, Propane, Rec Center, Restrooms, Sewage Dump Station, Shoppette, Showers, Shuttle bus, Snack Bar, Sports Fields, Stables, Tennis Courts.

RV Storage: C-575-572-5369.

Activities: Bicycling, Fishing*, Hiking, Hunting*, Swimming, River Rafting, Skiing, Snowboarding, Tennis, Softball, Skeet/Trap, Paintball. *State license required. Licenses can be purchased at Apache Sports Range.

Credit Cards: MasterCard and Visa.

Restrictions: Pets must be on leash and have current immunizations; owner must clean up after pet. Firearms must be approved by security forces. No open campfires. Quiet hours 2100-0800 hours.

RV Driving Directions/Location: On Base. From the Main Gate: Turn left on Alamogordo Blvd, then left onto Andrews Dr. Make a right onto Mesquite. FamCamp ahead on the left.

Area Description: Situated on open, semi-arid terrain, the FAMCAMP has limited trees, but is surrounded by shrubs. Nearby attractions include Space Center Hall of Fame, planetarium, zoo, White Sands National Park, horse racing and winter sports. Full range of support facilities available on base.

RV Campground Physical Address:
Holloman FAMCAMP, 661 Delaware
Avenue, Building 234, Holloman AFB,
NM 88330-5000. Mailing address:
Holloman FamCamp, Outdoor
Recreation, P.O. Box 734, Holloman
AFB, NM 88330-5000.

Kirtland Air Force Base

Address: 1451 4th Street SE, Kirtland
AFB, NM 87117.
Information Line: C-505-846-0011.
Directory Assistance, C-505-853-4636.
Main Base Police: C-505-846-
7926/7913. Emergencies dial 911.
Main Installation Website:
http://www.kirtland.af.mil/
Main Base Location: Kirtland AFB is
located in Bernalillo County, in the
southeast section of Albuquerque
occupying over 52,000 acres.
Directions to Main Gate: Travel either I-
40 east/west to exit 164
South/Wyoming Boulevard and look for
signs. Travel 1-25 north/south to exit
222/Gibson Boulevard and look for
signs.
NMC: Albuquerque, 1 mile northwest.
NMI: Cannon AFB, 215 miles southeast.
Base Social Media/Facebook:
https://www.facebook.com/KirtlandAir
ForceBase
Base Social Media/Twitter:
https://twitter.com/KIRTLAND377ABW
Chapels: C-505-846-5691.
Dental Clinic: C-505-846-3027.
Medical: Appointment Line, C-505-846-
3200. Information, C-505-846-3395.
Veterinary Services: C-505-846-4276.
Beauty/Barber Shop: Barber C-505-266-
5181; Stylique, C-505-266-6430.
Commissary: C-505-846-4902.
Exchange Gas: Eastside Express, C-505-
265-9093.
Exchange: C-505-232-8771.
Financial Institutions: Wells Fargo Bank,
C-505-254-0135.
Clubs: Mountain View Club/Relativity
Bar & Grill, C-505-846-5165.
Places to Eat: Relativity Bar and Grill, C-
505-846-5165; Bogey Bar and Grill, C-
505-846-1169; Jitters Coffee Shop, C-
505-853-3223; Sparetime Grill, C-505-

846-6851 and Thunderbird DFAC, C-
505-846-8048 are on base. Exchange
Food Court offers Charley's, Domino's,
Dunkin Donuts, Popeye's Chicken and
Subway. McDonald's is also on base.
Many restaurants within a short drive.
Bowling: Kirtland Lanes, C-505-846-
6851.
Fitness Center: East Gym, C-505-846-
1102. West Gym, C-505-846-1068.
Golf: Tijeras Arroyo Golf Course, C-505-
846-1169.
ITT/ITR: C-505-846-2924.
MWR: C-505-846-1644.
MWR Website:
http://www.kirtlandforcesupport.com/
MWR Facebook:
https://www.facebook.com/KirtlandFor
ceSupport
MWR Twitter:
https://twitter.com/377ForceSupport
Outdoor Recreation: Outdoor
Recreation Services, C-505-846-1499.
Offers outdoor gear equipment,
outdoor sports equipment, camping
gear, trailers, campers, lawn and garden
tools, party supplies, boats, paddle
boards, canoes, kayaks, winter sports
gear, winter equipment tune-ups and
more.
Swimming: Indoor Pool, C-505-846-
5485 offers lap and open swim. Outdoor
Seasonal Pool, C-505-846-5821 offers
open swim, lap swim and kiddie pool.
Things To Do: While in the Albuquerque
area, take the tram to the Sandia
Mountains or investigate the National
Atomic Museum and Old Town
Albuquerque, founded in 1706. Also,
enjoy local skiing, the State Fair in
September and the International Hot Air
Balloon Fiesta each October.
Walking Trails: Outdoor running tracks
on base.

RV CAMPING & GETAWAYS

Kirtland AFB FamCamp

Reservation/Contact Number Info: C-
505-846-0337.
Recreation Security: C-505-846-7926.
RV Website:
https://kirtlandforcesupport.com/famca
mp/

RV Email Address:
Kirtland.ODR@us.af.mil.
GPS Coordinates:
35°3'19"N/106°32'25"W
Reservations: No advance reservations. Prepayment required. Office hours 0800-1600 hours Mon-Fri, 24 hour registration box. Checkout 1100 hours.
Season of Operation: Year-round.
Eligibility: AD, NG, Res, Ret and DoD and Other U.S. Gov Civ, if installation access is allowed.
Camper/Trailer Spaces: West Campground (32): Full hookup sites with E(110/220V/30/50A)/S/W hookups. Rates: $18 daily. East Campground (38): Full hookup sites with E(110/220V/30/50A)/S/W hookups. Rates: $18 daily. Bathhouses available at both East and West campgrounds.
Tent Spaces: Grass sites; no hookups. Rates: $6 daily.
Support Facilities: Auto Craft Shop, Bathhouse, Boat Rental/Storage, Bowling, Chapel, Commissary, Diesel, Exchange, Fitness Center, Gas, Golf, Grills, Ice, Laundry/Pay, Mechanic/Auto Repair*, Mess Hall, Pavilions, Picnic Area, Playgrounds, Pool, Propane, Restrooms, Sewage Dump, Shoppette, Showers, Snack Bar, Sports Fields, Tennis Courts. *Off Base.
RV Storage: C-505-846-1499/1275.
Activities: Bicycle, Fishing*, Golfing, Hiking, Hunting*, Outdoor Sports, Swimming. *Licenses Required.
Credit Cards: MasterCard and Visa.
Restrictions: Pets must be on leash, no exceptions; owner must clean up after pets immediately. No firearms allowed. Quiet hours 2200-0600 hours. No generators 2200-0600 hours. 14-day limit. No vehicle washing. Must sign in before using any facilities.
RV Driving Directions/Location: On Base. From Eubank Gate: Continue on Eubank Blvd SE for approximately .9 miles. Turn right on "G" Ave SE and continue for approx .25 miles. Turn right onto Frost "F" Ave SE and proceed approximately .15 miles. FAMCAMP will be on right. From the Main Gate: Turn left onto Frost Avenue. Turn left onto

12th Street then take first right and continue for two blocks. FAMCAMP will be to the left. Check-in instructions are on the wall of the office. Note: Eubank Gate is closed after 1800 and on weekends.
Area Description: Located adjacent to base housing. Sandia and Manzano Mountains are east of the base. Sandia Crest Recreation Area and aerial tram nearby. Full range of support facilities available on base.
RV Campground Physical Address: For Fedex/Ups Delivery only: Kirtland FAMCAMP at Outdoor Recreation, 8351 Griffin Ave, Bldg 20410, Kirtland AFB, NM 87117. For USPS: 1551 First Street, Bldg 20350, Kirtland AFB, NM 87117.

White Sands Missile Range

Address: Headquarters Ave, White Sands Missile Range, NM 88001
Information Line: C-575-678-2121.
Main Base Police: C-575-678-1234. Emergencies dial 911.
Main Installation Website:
http://www.wsmr.army.mil
Main Base Location: White Sands Missile Range (WSMR) is located in the Tularosa Basin of south-central New Mexico.
Directions to Main Gate: From Las Cruces, NM: Take Hwy 25 north to Hwy 70 East, also referred to as Main Street. Turn right onto Hwy 70 East towards WSMR or Alamogordo. Continue on Highway 70 East for about 25 miles over the San Augustine Pass and exit just after mile marker 169. Turn right onto Owen Rd. The Las Cruces/Alamogordo Main Post Gate is approximately 3 miles after the exit.
NMC: Las Cruces, 20 miles east.
NMI: Holloman AFB, 40 miles southeast.
Base Social Media/Facebook:
https://www.facebook.com/WSMissileRange
Base Social Media/Twitter:
https://twitter.com/wsmissilerange
Chapels: Chaplain, C-575-678-2615.
Dental Clinic: C-575-674-3597/3500.
Medical: Appointment Line, C-575-674-3500.

Beauty/Barber Shop: C-575-674-2040.
Commissary C-575-678-2313.
Exchange Gas: C-575-678-4877.
Exchange: C-575-678-2498.
Financial Institutions: WSFCU, C-575-674-1217/1734.
Clubs: Frontier Club, C-575-678-2055. Sparetime Lounge, C-575-678-3465.
Places to Eat: Coyote Snack Bar, C-575-678-3465 and Frontier Club are on base. Exchange Food Court offers Subway. Several restaurants within a short drive.
Bowling: Roadrunner Lanes, C-575-678-3465.
Fitness Center: Bell Gym, C-575-678-3374.
ITT/ITR: C-575-678-4134.
Library: C-575-678-5820.
Military Museum: White Sands Missile Range Museum, C-505-678-3358.
Military Museum Website: http://www.wsmr-history.org/
MWR: C-575-678-6103.
MWR Website: http://www.wsmrmwr.com/
MWR Facebook: https://www.facebook.com/WSMR-FMWR-359595167318/
Outdoor Recreation: Outdoor Recreation, C-575-678-1713. Offers camping gear, campers, carnival games, sports equipment, park and pavilion rentals and more.
Swimming: Aquatic Center, C-575-678-1068 offers lap swim, open swim, recreational swim area and kiddie pool area.
Things To Do: Las Cruces' blending of three cultures and New Mexico State University supply great local entertainment. Visit the International Space Hall of Fame in Alamogordo, White Sands National Monument and El Paso, the gateway to the Southwest and Mexico.

RV CAMPING & GETAWAYS
RV Travel Camp
Reservation/Contact Number Info: C-575-678-1713, DSN-312-258-1713.
RV Website: https://whitesands.armymwr.com/programs/outdoor-recreation

GPS Coordinates: 32°22'37"N/106°29'33"W
Reservations: Recommended. Office hours 0900-1700 Mon-Fri; 0800-1220 Sat (summer only). Checkout 1100 hours. Maximum stay 21 days within 60-day consecutive period.
Season of Operation: Year-round.
Eligibility: AD, NG/Res (Active), Ret, DoD-Civ (AD/Ret), Dep and Contractors w/ WSMR.
Camper/Trailer Spaces: Gravel (8), Pull-through, maximum 40'-60' in length, E(110/220V/15/30/50A)/S/W hookups, canopy, picnic table, and grill. Rates: $10 daily.
Support Facilities: ACOE Lodge/Pavilion (fee), Auto Craft Shop, Bowling, Cafeteria, Chapel, Commissary, Equipment Rental, Exchange, Fitness Center, Gas, Golf, Grills, Ice, Laundry/Pay, Pay Phones, Picnic Area, Playground, Pool, Propane (bottle), Rec Center, Restrooms, RV Storage, Shoppette, Showers, Snack Bar, Sports Fields, Tennis Courts.
RV Storage: C-575-678-1713.
Activities: Fishing*, Golfing, Hiking, Hunting**, Skeet/Trap Range, Snow Skiing, Tours***. * State license required for patrons ages twelve and up. Children younger than twelve must be accompanied by an adult with a state license. All state licenses can be purchased online at http://www.wildlife.state.nm.us/hunting/. Rate: $6 ages 12-15, $25 ages 16 and up. ** State license required. Outdoor Recreation Center sells licenses for Deer, Bear, Barbary sheep, Turkey and Cougar. Hunting of all other types of animals, including oryx, are approved by draw or special hunt. For more information, call C-505-678-1713 or visit http://wildlife.state.nm.us/recreation/index.htm. ***Tours to Trinity Site, location of world's first nuclear explosion, are conducted on first Saturday in April and first Saturday in October. Arrangements may be made through Public Affairs Office. C-575-678-1134/1135/1700.
Credit Cards: Cash, Checks, MasterCard and Visa.

Restrictions: Pets must be on leash. Owner must clean up after pets. Must have current vaccination records. No firearms. No tents allowed.

RV Driving Directions/Location: On Base. From the Headquarters Avenue Gate: Follow Headquarters Avenue past the HQ Building, Bldg 100, and immediately turn right on to Aberdeen. Follow Aberdeen until it forks. Follow the left fork and turn left at Aerobee Ave. Follow this road until camping spots visible. Entry to installation controlled by Military Police. Visitor pass required.

Area Description: Many outdoor sports to be found within 100-mile radius. To the east is Cloudcroft Ski Area, horse racing at Ruidoso Downs, Apache Indian Reservation with Ski Apache, a first-class ski area, and Inn of the Mountain Gods, a resort of international repute. El Paso, where you can cross border into Mexico, is to the south. To the north are Caballo and Elephant Butte Lakes featuring state-operated recreational areas with RV facilities, boating, water skiing, fishing and swimming. Full range of support facilities on post.

RV Campground Physical Address: Bldg 445 Flagler St, White Sands Missile Range, NM 88002-5035. Mailing address: Outdoor Recreation, P.O. Box 400, White Sands Missile Range, NM 88002.

NEW YORK

Fort Drum

Address: 4330 Conway Road, Bldg P-4330, Fort Drum, NY 13602.
Information Line: C-315-772-6011, DSN-312-772-6011.
Main Base Police: C-315-772-7771. Emergencies dial 911.
Main Installation Website:
http://www.drum.army.mil/
Main Base Location: Located near Watertown, NY, in Jefferson County, Fort Drum is situated in one of the most unique and beautiful areas of the

United States. Fort Drum is approximately 30 miles from Canada, with the Great Lakes to the west and the Adirondack Mountains to the east.

Directions to Main Gate: From Syracuse: Follow I-81 North and take exit 48A I-781 East. Travel approximately 4.1 miles to the gate at Fort Drum.
NMC: Watertown, 6 miles south.
NMI: Syracuse-Hancock IA/ANG, 82 miles southwest.
Base Social Media/Facebook:
https://www.facebook.com/drum.10th mountain
Base Social Media/Twitter:
https://twitter.com/drum10thmtn
Chapels: Chaplain, C-315-772-5591.
Dental Clinic: Clark Hall Clinic, C-315-772-8891. John Sayre Marshall Clinic, C-315-772-9415. Stone Clinic, C-315-5576.
Medical: Appointment Line, C-315-772-2778, DSN-312-772-2778. General Inquiries, C-315-772-4312,
Veterinary Services: C-315-772-4262.
Beauty/Barber Shop: Main Exchange, C-315-772-3498; Stylique, C-315-773-1990. Mini-Mall, C-315-772-5106. Sweet Complex, C-315-772-3497. Wheeler Express, C-315-772-1254.
Commissary: C-315-774-9130.
Exchange Gas: Mini-Mall, C-315-773-4149/7594. Nash Express, C-315-773-8015. North Gate, C-315-773-1005. Wheeler Express, C-315-773-8327.
Exchange: C-315-773-0061.
Financial Institutions: AmeriCU Federal Credit Union, C-315-772-5244. Key Bank, C-315-773-0155.
Clubs: The Commons All Ranks Club, C-315-772-6222.
Places to Eat: Buster's Brew Pub C-315-772-1900; Pine Plains Snack Bar, C-315-772-6601; The Commons at Dillenbeck's Corner, C-315-772-6222 and Winner's Circle Sports Bar, C-315-772-7673 are on base. Exchange Food Court offers Boston Market, Charley's, Manchu Wok, Qdoba, Starbucks and Subway. The Mini-Mall offers Popeye's and Subway. Wheeler Express offers Burger King. Jack T Sweet Complex offers Domino's and Subway. Many restaurants within a short drive.

Bowling: Pine Plains Bowling Center, C-315-772-6601.
Fitness Center: Atkins Fitness Facility, C-315-772-3377. Magrath Sports Complex, C-315-772-9670. Monti Center, C-315-772-4936.
ITT/ITR: C-315-772-8222.
Library: McEwen Library, C-315-772-9099/6005.
Military Museum: 10th Mountain Division & Fort Drum Museum, C-315-772-0355/0391.
Military Museum Website: https://www.facebook.com/FortDrum Museum/
MWR Phone Number: C-315-772-5685.
MWR. Website: http://drum.armymwr.com
MWR Facebook: https://www.facebook.com/DrumFMWR
Outdoor Recreation: Outdoor Recreation, C-315-772-8222. Offers a wide variety of recreational and event equipment. Summer items include canoes, tents, bicycles, campers, sleeping bags and more. Winter Items include ice-fishing, skiing, and snowboarding packages.
Swimming: Magrath Indoor Pool, C-315-772-9673 offers lap swim. Monti Indoor Pool, C-315-772-4936 offers open and lap swim.
Things To Do: Visit the Sackets Harbor Battleground, site of the War of 1812 battle. or see the fascinating 1,000 Islands, which are rich in water recreation. Canada is also 45 minutes away. Many parks and recreational areas nearby.
Walking Trails: Hiking available at Remington Park. Outdoor and indoor running tracks on base.

RV CAMPING & GETAWAYS
Pine Lane Cabins

Reservation/Contact Number Info: C-315-774-7331, DSN 315-774-7331.
RV Website: https://drum.armymwr.com/programs/recreational-lodging
GPS Coordinates: 44°01'52.1"N/75°44'54.6"W
Reservations: Reservations accepted via telephone. Contact reservations for details. Office hours 0800-1700 hours Mon-Fri. Closed weekends and holidays.
Season of Operation: Year-round.
Eligibility: AD, NG, Res, Ret, and their dependents; Widow/ers; DoD-Civ, DoD-Civ Ret and their dependents w/ID; DAVs.
Yurt, A Frame, Cabin, Apt, Spaces: Cabins: Two-story, two bedroom with loft; queen bed and twin beds (4), private bath, two-burner stove top, full-sized refrigerator, microwave, gas grill, utensils, CATV. Rates: $85 daily, $400 weekly; $1,450 monthly. Linens not provided but available to rent.
Support Facilities: Full range of support facilities on base.
Credit Cards: MasterCard and Visa.
Restrictions: Pets are permitted at this facility. An additional $5 per day fee applies. No deposit required.
RV Driving Directions/Location: On Base. From the Iraqi Freedom Drive Gate: Continue ahead and turn right onto Mt Belvedere Blvd. Go left onto Enduring Freedom Drive. Turn right onto Euphrates River Valley Road. Check in at The Commons at Dillenbeck Corners ahead on the right.
Area Description: Located in a quiet, serene area on base. Enjoy nature and a tranquil setting.

Pine Lane Cottages

Reservation/Contact Number Info: C-315-774-7331, DSN 315-774-7331.
RV Website: https://drum.armymwr.com/programs/recreational-lodging
GPS Coordinates: 44°01'52.1"N/75°44'56.4"W
Reservations: Reservations accepted via telephone. Contact reservations for details. Office hours 0800-1700 hours Mon-Fri. Closed weekends and holidays.
Season of Operation: Year-round.
Eligibility: AD, NG, Res, Ret, and their dependents; Widow/ers; DoD-Civ, DoD-Civ Ret and their dependents w/ID; DAVs.
Yurt, A Frame, Cabin, Apt, Spaces: Cottages (7): One bedroom with queen bed, pull out sofa (most units) private

bath, microwave, compact refrigerator, coffee maker, utensils, washer/dryer. Small House Cottages (2): Two bedroom with queen beds, pull out sofa, full kitchen with dishwasher, dining area, living area, washer/dryer, CATV. Rates: Single Bedroom Cottage: $80 daily; $375 weekly; $1,400 monthly. Two Bedroom Cottage with full kitchen $90 daily; $425 weekly, $1,500 monthly. Linens not provided but available to rent.

Support Facilities: Full range of support facilities on base.

Credit Cards: MasterCard and Visa.

Restrictions: Pets are permitted at this facility. An additional $5 per day fee applies. No deposit required.

RV Driving Directions/Location: On Base. From the Iraqi Freedom Drive Gate: Continue ahead and turn right onto Mt Belvedere Blvd. Go left onto Enduring Freedom Drive. Turn right onto Euphrates River Valley Road. Check in at The Commons at Dillenbeck Corners ahead on the right.

Area Description: Located in a quiet, serene are of old post. Enjoy nature and tranquility at these cottages.

RV Campground Physical Address: Pine Lane, Fort Drum, NY 13603.

Remington Park Cabins & RV Park

Reservation/Contact Number Info: C-315-774-7331, DSN 315-774-7331.

RV Website: https://drum.armymwr.com/programs/recreational-lodging

Other Info Website: https://drum.armymwr.com/programs/remington-park-rv-campground

Reservations: Reservations can be made by calling Fort Drum Outdoor Recreation Mon-Sat 0900-1600. Check-in 1400-1700; Check-out 0900-1100.

Season of Operation: The Cabins at Remington Park are open year round. The Remington RV Campground is open 1 May-1 Oct. Remington Pond Beach area is open 1 Jun-Labor Day weekend.

Eligibility: AD, Ret, Dep, DoD ID card holders and guests.

Camper/Trailer Spaces: Pull-through spaces on concrete pads (10): E(20,30,50A)/W/S hookups. Hardstand hookups (4) located in Officer's Loop area of Fort Drum seasonally. Rates: $35 daily; $175 weekly; $500 monthly.
Tent Spaces: Tent sites (5) with water, electricity, picnic tables with campfire ring. Five (5) Adirondack style lean-tos. Rates: $10 daily; $50-$60 weekly; $200-$240 monthly.
Yurt, A Frame, Cabin, Apt, Spaces: Cabins: Each cabin offers sleeping accommodations for 6 adults, a kitchenette, a comfortable seating or lounge area in a quiet wooded area. Linens are not provided but available to rent. Rates: $75 daily; $350 weekly; $1,250 monthly.
Support Facilities: Dog Park, Hiking and Biking Trails, Playgrounds, Picnic Areas, Pavilions, Fishing, Beach and Swimming Area, with paddle boat and kayak rentals. Handicap accessible.
RV Storage: RV storage in open outdoor lot. $20/month, minimum 6 months. Call C-315-722-8222.
Activities: Cabins: Located within walking distance of wilderness trails, playgrounds, a sandy beach and swimming area. Handicap accessible.
Credit Cards: American Express, Discover, MasterCard and Visa.
Restrictions: Pets allowed at RV Campground and walking trails. Dog Park is also available. No pets permitted at Remington Pond Beach or Pavilions.
RV Driving Directions/Location: On Base. From the Main Gate: Ask for directions at gate.
Area Description: The park is located on the shores of Fort Drum's Remington Pond.
RV Campground Physical Address: Pech Road, Fort Drum, NY 13602

Lake Frederick Recreation Area

Address: Lake Frederick Recreation Area, 206 Smith Clove Road, Central Valley, New York 10917.
Information Line: C-845-938-4011.
Main Base Police: C-845-938-3333/3312/4172.

Main Installation Website:
http://www.westpoint.army.mil/
Main Base Location: A short drive from the U.S. Military Academy at West Point, within mountains and nature.
NMC: New York City, 50 miles southeast.
NMI: U.S. Military Academy, West Point, 3 miles east.
Commissary: Approximately 15 miles away at West Point Academy, C-845-938-3663.
Exchange Gas: West Point Academy gas station approximately 15 miles away. Commercial gas within 2 miles.
Exchange: Approximately 15 miles awat at West Point Academy, C-845-446-5404/5405/5406.
Golf: West Point Golf Course, C-845-938-2435.
ITT/ITR: ITR Office, C-845-938-3601.
Marina: C-845-938-3011.
MWR: C-845-938-2103.
MWR Website:
https://westpoint.armymwr.com/us/westpoint
MWR Facebook:
https://www.facebook.com/westpointfmwr

RV CAMPING & GETAWAYS
Lake Frederick Recreation Area

Reservation/Contact Number Info: C-845-938-2503/3860, DSN-312-688-2503. Fax 845-938-3788. Off-season information, C-845-938-8811.
Recreation Security: Emergencies dial 911.
RV Website:
https://westpoint.armymwr.com/programs/lake-frederick-recreation-area
GPS Coordinates:
41°20'21.1"N/74°05'48.8"W
Reservations: Required and accepted starting the first Tuesday after Martin Luther King holiday for AD; the first Tuesday after President's Day holiday for Ret, DoD-Civ. Reservations limited to two sites per sponsor. Payment due at time of reservation. Cancellations require 72 hours prior to reservation. Office hours 1 April-Labor Day 0800-

1700 daily. Off-season office hours, 1000-1400 Mon-Fri. Maximum stay 14 days.

Season of Operation: April-October.

Eligibility: All patrons must be authorized IAW AR 215-1. Eligibility restrictions are waived for all Scouts/Scout groups. Eligible personnel must be present at all times with their guests.

Tent Spaces: Tent Sites/Scouts: Primitive (50), no hookups. Rates: $38 daily. Maximum 25 people per site.

Yurt, A Frame, Cabin, Apt, Spaces: A-Frame Cabins (8): Bunk beds, mini-refrigerator, kitchen table/chairs, outdoor grill, picnic table and boat access. A-Frames: $75 per night Apr-Nov. Minimum 2-night minimum. Special event/season rates apply. 14 bunk beds limited 110-volt receptacles inside and 30 amp RV plug outside, outdoor grill and two picnic tables. Nov-April four (4) bunkhouses with heat available. No space heaters.

Support Facilities: Bathhouse, Recreation Building, Beach, Boats, Picnic Sites and Volleyball/Horseshoes areas. Campfire pits and BBQ.

Activities: Fishing, Swimming, Lake Rentals.

Credit Cards: Cash, Check, Master Card and Visa.

Restrictions: Pets are to be leashed at all times and are prohibited inside A-frames, beach and swim area. Owners are to ensure they clean up after their pets. Dogs that bark and disturb others will be asked to leave. RVs, ATVs, motorboats, motorized scooters, firearms and bows & arrows are prohibited. Quiet hours: 2200-0700.

RV Driving Directions/Location: Off Base. From the South: Take Palisades Interstate Parkway North to the Rte 6 exit. At the traffic circle, stay on Route 6. Follow Rte 6 to the exit ramp for Newburgh/Suffer/Rte 32 and Central Valley. Turn right at the traffic light onto Rte 32 and drive approximately 1.2 miles into Central Valley. Turn right onto Smith Clove Road. Drive for approximately 2 miles, and then take the first right after the Falkirk Estate and Country Club (golf course) onto the Lake Frederick access road. From the North: Take I-87 (NYS Thruway) south to exit 16 (Harriman/Rte 17). Merge onto Rte 17W then take the exit ramp toward US 6 East/NY 17 South/NY 32 and Harriman. Turn right at the traffic light onto Rte 32 and drive for approximately 1.2 miles into Central Valley. Follow directions as above.

Area Description: Beautiful lake area with hiking trails and all that nature has to offer. Scenic and peaceful surroundings.

RV Campground Physical Address: 206 Smith Clove Road, Central Valley, NY 10917. One mile to the left.

New York Coast Guard Sector

Address: 212 Coast Guard Dr, Staten Island, NY 10305.

Information Line: C-718-354-4037.

Main Base Police: C-718-354-4353. Gateway National Park Police, C-718-338-3988. Emergencies dial 911.

Main Installation Website: http://www.atlanticarea.uscg.mil/Our-Organization/District-1/District-Units/Sector-New-York/

Main Base Location: Located on historical Fort Wadsworth and part of the Gateway National Recreation Area, a 26,000-acre recreation area located in the heart of the New York metropolitan area.

Directions to Main Gate: To Fort Wadsworth: Take exit 13 off the NJ Turnpike/I-95 to Gothels Bridge. Take Staten Island Expressway/I-278 to exit 15/Lilly Pond Ave/Bay Street, which is the last exit before bridge. Go left at end of ramp and follow Lilly Pond Ave to next light which is Bay Street. Turn right and the entrance to the Fort is .25 miles. Fort Hamilton U.S. Army Garrison is located in Brooklyn, New York at the base of the Verrazano Bridge.

NMC: New York City, 10 miles north.

NMI: Fort Hamilton, 4 miles northeast.

Chapels: C-718-354-4421. Fort Hamilton, C-718-630-4969.

Medical: C-718-354-4414. Ainsworth Army Health Clinic at Fort Hamilton, C-

718-630-4417/4860/4129, Pharmacy, C-718-630-4268.

Commissary: Approximately 4 miles away at Fort Hamilton, C-718-630-4960.

Exchange Gas: Gas station at Fort Hamilton approximately 4 miles away, C-718-748-3440. Commercial gas station within 1 mile.

Exchange: Fort Wadsworth CG Exchange, C-718-815-6519/6823. Fort Hamilton, approximately 4 miles away, C-718-630-3415/3440.

Places to Eat: Galley, C-718-354-4360 and many other restaurants are within driving distance.

Fitness Center: C-718- 354-4417.

ITT/ITR: C-718-354-4407.

MWR: C-718-354-4407.

MWR Website: http://secnymwr.com/

MWR Facebook: https://www.facebook.com/pages/Coast-Guard-New-York-MWR/134010083358795

Outdoor Recreation: MWR Recreation, C-718-354-4407. Contact MWR for information and details regarding available rental facilities and equipment.

Things To Do: Downtown Manhattan is a short trip away; just take the Staten Island Ferry, which is a ten-minute drive away. There is parking available for patrons to make the visit even more convenient. You can also escape the city and visit the vineyards on Long Island. Free wine tasting tours are held every weekend in the summer.

Walking Trails: Nature trails available at Gateway National Recreation Area.

RV CAMPING & GETAWAYS

Fort Wadsworth Guest Quarters

Reservation/Contact Number Info: C-718-354-4407.

Recreation Security: Emergencies dial 911.

RV Website: http://secnymwr.com/guest-quarters-1/

Other Info Website: https://www.dcms.uscg.mil/Our-Organization/Assistant-Commandant-for-Human-Resources-CG-1/Community-Services-Command-CSC/MWR/Coast-Guard-Lodging/

RV Email Address: d01-mwrsecny@uscg.mil

Reservations: Reservations required and accepted one year in advance. Payment due at time of reservation. Office hours 0800-1630 Mon-Fri. Cancellations incur $35 fee. Any cancellation within 48-hours of arrival incurs 50% of full stay penalty. Check-in 1500 hours, check-out 1100 hour. Arrivals after 1630 should check in at UPH, 215 Drum Road.

Season of Operation: Year-round.

Eligibility: AD, NG, Res, Ret.

Yurt, A Frame, Cabin, Apt, Spaces: Guest Quarter Apartments (2): Two-bedroom (1), Three-bedroom (1), fully furnished, full bath, living room, dining room, kitchen with cooking utensils, A/C, deck w/grill. Linens provided. Rates: $109-$114 daily.

Support Facilities: Equipment Rental, Exchange, Fitness Center, Visitor's Center.

Activities: Staten Island Ferry is short 10-minute drive. Visit the Gateway National Park Visitors Center for tours and information.

Credit Cards: American Express, MasterCard and Visa.

Restrictions: No pets allowed in guest quarters.

RV Driving Directions/Location: On Base. From the Main Gate: Make a right onto Coast Guard Drive. Go left onto Molony Drive. MWR office is located in the gymnasium.

Area Description: Located at the historical Fort Wadsworth, a short scenic ferry ride from Manhattan, the heart of New York City.

RV Campground Physical Address: 204 Molony Drive, Fort Wadsworth, Staten Island, New York 10305.

Round Pond Recreation Area

Address: Round Pond Recreation Area, 1348 Round Pond Road, West Point, New York 10996.

Information Line: C-845-938-4011, DSN-312-688-1110.

Main Base Police: Emergencies dial 911.
Main Installation Website:
http://www.westpoint.army.mil/
Main Base Location: The Round Pond Recreation area is located in a rocky, woody area, just three miles from the United States Military Academy. Round Pond is a clear mountaintop lake surrounded by a beach, playground, picnic areas and campsites.
NMC: New York City, 50 miles southeast.
NMI: U.S. Military Academy, West Point, 3 miles east.
Medical: C-845-938-5169, DSN-312-688-5169.
Commissary: Approximately 4 miles away at West Point Academy, C-845-938-3663.
Exchange Gas: West Point Academy gas station approximately 4 miles away. Commercial gas station within 5 miles.
Exchange: Approximately 4 miles away at West Point Academy, C-845-446-5404/5405/5406.
Golf: Located one mile from campground.
ITT/ITR: LTS Office, C-845-938-3601.
MWR
Website: https://westpoint.armymwr.com/us/westpoint
Outdoor Recreation: West Point Outdoor Recreation, C-845-938-0123. Offers camping, swimming, fishing, boating, basketball and volleyball courts and much more.
Swimming: Round Pond Swimming Area and Crandall Pool, C-845-938-3066 are available.
Walking Trails: Nature trails are available.

RV CAMPING & GETAWAYS
Round Pond Recreation Area

Reservation/Contact Number Info: C-845-938-2503/3860. Fax C-845-938-3788. Off-season information, C-845-938-8811.
Recreation Security: C-845-938-3333.
RV Website:
https://westpoint.armymwr.com/programs/round-pond-recreation-area

GPS Coordinates:
41°22'39"N/74°1'36"W
Reservations: Required. Accepted starting the first Tuesday after Martin Luther King holiday for Active Duty and the first Tuesday after President's Day holiday for Retired Military and DoD-Civilians. Reservations are limited to two sites per sponsor. Maximum stay two weeks. Pre-payment of full amount required. Cancellation policy requires notice be given 72 hours before the start of the reservation. 1 April-Memorial Day: 0800-1700 hours daily; Memorial Day-Columbus Day: 0800-1800 hours daily, Columbus Day-31 Oct: 0800-1700 hours daily. Check-in at campground main office: Check-in 1300 hours, check-out 1100 hours. Cottages: Check-in 1400 hours, check-out 1100 hours.
Season of Operation: 1 Apr-31 Oct.
Eligibility: AD, NG, Res, Ret, DoD-Civ, Dep, 100% DAV and Guests.
Camper/Trailer Spaces: Camper: (28), Back-in, Maximum 45' in length, E(110/220V/15/30/50A)/W hookups. Rates: $2 daily $3 Holiday/ Football weekends. Popup sites (2). E(110/220V/15/30/50A)/W hookups. Rates: $20 daily; $15 without hookups.
Tent Spaces: Dirt/Grass (20), no hookups. Rates: $15 daily Fri-Sun; $10 all other days.
Yurt, A Frame, Cabin, Apt, Spaces: Cottage (1) Queen Bed, (2) Futons, sleeps Six. A/C, kitchen, refrigerator, stove, sink, appliances, cookware/utensils, bathroom and shower. Cottage has both electricity and water. Guests must supply own linens. Rates: $125 per night (5 consecutive nights) $150 per night (2 night min) $172 per night (Holidays/ Football Weekends, 3 night min). Check-in 1400 hours, check-out 1100 hours. Mini Log Cabin: (10, 1 handicap accessible), sleeps four, electric only, no water hookup. Guests must supply own linens. Rates: $60 per night; $75 per night holiday/ football weekends, 2-day minimum.
Support Facilities: Bait Shop, Bathhouse*, Beach**, Bicycle Rental,

Boat Launch, Boat Rental/Storage, Coin Laundry, Equipment Rental*, Fire Rings, Grills, Ice, Pavilions, Picnic Area, Playground*, Propane, Sewage Dump, Trails. *Handicap accessible.
**Memorial Day-Labor Day.
RV Storage: Yes. C-845-938-3926.
Activities: Located on Academy property in rocky, wooded area near old Ramapo mines. Mountain-top setting with natural spring-fed pond. Full range of support facilities available at U.S. Military Academy.
Credit Cards: Cash, Check, Master Card and Visa.
RV Driving Directions/Location: Off Base: Located three miles west of West Point on NY-293. From I-87: Take exit 16 to US-6 east. Follow US-6 east for about three miles, bear left and get onto NY-293. Proceed on NY-293 for approximately six miles to the recreation area. Turn left at the Round Pond Recreation Area sign. From I-84 east: Take exit 4E to NY-17 east. Drive on NY-17 east for 17 miles, then take exit 130A onto US-6 east and follow directions above. From I-84 west, take exit 10S into 9W south and proceed for 12 miles. Take NY-293 and drive for one mile to the recreation area. Make a right turn at the sign for Round Pond Recreation Area.
Area Description: Located in the beautiful Hudson Valley.
RV Campground Physical Address: Physical Address: Round Pond Recreation Area, 1348 Round Pond Road, West Point, New York 10996. Mailing Address: USMA MWR, Attn: Round Pond Recreation Area, Building 681 Hardee Place, 2nd Floor, West Point, New York 10996.

United States Military Academy – West Point

Address: 681 Hardee Place, West Point, NY 10996-1985.
Information Line: C-845-938-2022.
Main Base Police: C-845-938-3333.
Main Installation Website:
https://www.westpoint.army.mil/
Other Info Website:
http://www.usma.edu/

Main Base Location: Located in the scenic Hudson River valley of Orange County, only 50 miles from New York City, the U.S. Military Academy at West Point is a four-year academic institution and a nationally-renowned historic site.
Directions to Main Gate: Palisades Interstate Parkway Directions: Take the Parkway north until it ends at the Bear Mountain Bridge circle. Proceed 3/4 of the way around the circle, following signs for West Point onto Route 9W North. Stay on Route 9W for approximately three miles then exit onto Route 218 North. As entering the Village of Highland Falls on Rt. 218, continue to bear right to the Thayer Gate of West Point. Autos without a DoD decal for West Point should access the installation through the Stoney Lonesome gate from 0500-2300 hours or the 24-hour Thayer Gate from Highland Falls.
NMC: West Point, within city limits.
NMI: Camp Smith, 11 miles southeast.
Base Social Media/Facebook:
https://www.facebook.com/USAGWest Point
Base Social Media/Twitter:
https://twitter.com/USAGWestPoint
Dental Clinic: Saunders Dental Clinic, C-845-938-3121/2505/2106.
Medical: Appointment Line, C-845-938-7992. Front Desk, C-845-938-5169. Referral Assistance, C-845-938-5373.
Veterinary Services: C-845-938-3817/3838.
Beauty/Barber Shop: Main Exchange, C-845-839-0019. Club Barber, C-845-938-2749.
Commissary Phone Numbers: C-845-938-3663.
Exchange Gas Phone Number: C-845-446-3666.
Exchange Main Phone Number: C-845-446-5404.
Military Clothing: C-845-446-1019/5446.
Financial Institutions: Federal Credit Union, Pentagon, C-845-446-4946, C-1-800-431-1404.
Postal Services: USCC Post Office, C-845- 446-8750. West Point, C-845-446-8749.

Clubs: West Point Club and Benny Havens Lounge, C-845-938-5120.

Places to Eat: Benny Havens Lounge, C-845-936-5120; WP Bowling Center, C-845-938-2140; WP Golf Course Snack Bar, C-845-938-2435 and USMAPS Dining Facility, C-845-938-1957/1958 are on base. Exchange Food Court offers Burger King and Taco Bell. Starbucks and Subway are also on base. Many restaurants are within a short drive.

Bowling: West Point Bowling Center, C-845-938-2140.

Fitness Center: West Point FC, C-845-938-6490.

Golf: West Point Golf Course, C-845-938-2435.

ITT/ITR: C-845-938-3601.

Library: Reference Desk. C-845-938-8325.

Marina: West Point Yacht Club, C-845-938-3011.

Military Museum: West Point Museum, C-845-938-2203/3590.

Military Museum Website: https://www.westpoint.army.mil/museum.html

MWR: C-845-938-8250.

MWR Website: http://www.westpointmwr.com/

MWR Facebook: https://www.facebook.com/westpointfmwr/

Ski Area: Victor Constant Ski Slope Hotline, C-845-938-2475.

Outdoor Recreation: Outdoor Recreation and Equipment Rental, C-845-938-0123. Offers camping gear, canopies, rock climbing equipment, canoes, kayaks, stand up paddle boards, water sport gear, archery gear, paintball gear, mountain bikes, outdoor sports games, grills and more.

Swimming: Crandall Pool, C-845-938-2985 offers open and lap swim. Round Pond Swimming Area, C-845-938-2503 offers seasonal swimming.

Things To Do: Part of the U.S. Armed Forces Recreation System, sporting events and special vacation packages are available at the castle-like Thayer Hotel overlooking the Hudson River. Enjoy many outdoor activities in both the winter and summer.

Walking Trails: Nature trails available at recreation areas.

RV CAMPING & GETAWAYS

Bull Pond Recreation Area

Reservation/Contact Number

Info: Reservations Office at Round Pond, C-845-938-2503. Fax C-845-938-3788.

Recreation Security: C-845-938-3333.

RV Website: https://westpoint.armymwr.com/programs/bull-pond-recreation-area

Reservations: Reservations are accepted on a lottery basis conducted at the Victor Constant Ski Slope Lodge beginning at 0900 the first Saturday in April for Active Duty Military ONLY. One chip per active duty military member, no exceptions will be granted. Proxies are limited to one per person. Pre-registration required starting March 23rd, C-845-938-2503. Reservations will continue for all other eligible personnel on the following Monday at 0800 am at the Round Pond office on a first-come first-served basis for any remaining dates. Full payment due at time of approved reservation. Office hours 1 April-Memorial Day, 0800-1700 hours daily. Memorial Day-Columbus Day, 0800-1800 hours daily. Columbus Day-31 October, 0800-1700 hours daily. Off Season, 1000-1400 hours Mon-Fri. Cancellations: Campers unable to use their Bull Pond reservation are committed to securing an eligible replacement to assume their reservation. Round Pond will assist campers in securing replacements through waiting lists and post media. No refunds will be granted. Check-in 1400 hours, check-out 1000 hours.

Season of Operation: Year-round.

Eligibility: All renters must be authorized IAW Army Regulation AR 215-1 and be 21 years of age or older.

Yurt, A Frame, Cabin, Apt, Spaces: Cottages (2): Stone House Cottage: One king size bed and a double pull-out couch. Full bath with tub/shower, and bath/hand towels. Living room with one couch, loveseat, and chair, a full service kitchen with table with benches. Linens provided. Rates: $340-$360 Mon-Fri; $300-$320 Fri-Mon. July 4th weekend, $690, Graduation Weekend, $650. Guest House: The Guest House accommodates five persons, three single and one double bed, full bath with shower with bath/hand towels, living room with two couches, full kitchen. Linens provided. Rates: $340-$360 Mon-Fri; $300-$320 Fri-Mon. July 4th weekend, $690; Graduation Weekend $650.

Support Facilities: Sand beach swim area with aluminum raft, paddle boat, canoe and V-bottom rowboat moored at a boat house with pool table and boating amenities provided for use.

Activities: Boating, Fishing*, Swimming. *Anglers age 16 and older must have a current NYS fishing license and West Point permit available at Round Pond.

Credit Cards: MasterCard and Visa.

Restrictions: No pets or firearms permitted.

RV Driving Directions/Location: On Base. Located on the West Point Reservation. Ask for directions at time of reservation.

Area Description: Located on the federal military reservation known as West Point in Orange County, NY. Near the Hudson River and many lakes and natural beauty.

RV Campground Physical Address: Bull Pond Rd, Rt 293, West Point, NY 10996.

NORTH CAROLINA

Camp LeJeune Marine Corps Base

Address: 818 Holcomb Blvd, Camp Lejeune, NC 28542.

Information Line: C-910-451-1113, DSN-312-751-1113.

Main Base Police: C-910-451-3004/3005

Main Installation Website: http://www.lejeune.marines.mil/

Main Base Location: Onslow county in southeastern North Carolina. Camp Lejeune and the City of Jacksonville are adjacent to the New River flowing to the Onslow Beach area.

Directions to Main Gate: From the north on I-95: Fifteen miles south of Smithfield take I-40 East. At Magnolia take US-903 East for approximately 8 miles to Kenansville. Turn right onto State Hwy 24 East to Jacksonville. Follow Camp Lejeune signs to the Main Gate. From the south on I-95: Exit on State Hwy 24 East to Jacksonville. Follow Camp Lejeune signs to the Main Gate.

NMC: Jacksonville, 3 miles northwest.

NMI: New River MCAS, 20 miles west.

Base Social Media/Facebook: https://www.facebook.com/camp.lejeune/

Base Social Media/Twitter: https://twitter.com/camp_lejeune

Chapels: Chaplain, C-910-451-3210/5647.

Dental Clinic: Courthouse Bay, C-910-.440-7147. Naval Hospital, C-910-450-4740.

Medical: Naval Hospital, C-910-450-4300, DSN-312-750-4300. Courthouse Bay, C-910-440-7338.

Veterinary Services: C-910-450-1607.

Beauty/Barber Shop: Main Mall, C-910-451-2400. Bldg 1, C-910-451-1820. Courthouse Bay, C-910-440-7193. French Creek, C-910-451-5237. Hadnot Point, C-910-451-2395. Naval Hospital, C-910-450-4592. II MEF, C-910-451-8181.

Commissary: C-910-451-5071.

Exchange Gas: Courthouse Bay, C-910-440-7345. Central, C-910-451-2443.

Exchange: C-910-451-5030.

Financial Institutions: First Citizens Bank and Trust, C-910-353-3113, C-910-451-5877. Marine Federal Credit Union, C-910-451-2492, C-800-225-3967.

Clubs: Paradise Point Officers' Club, C-910-451-2465. The SNCO Club, C-910-450-9556. Heroz, C- 910-450-6428.

Places to Eat: Berkeley Express, C-910-451-9073; Domino's, C-910-451-3888;

Duffer's Retreat, C-910-451-0148; Dunkin-Donuts/Baskin Robbins, C-910-451-2599; Heroz Sports Grill, C-910-450-6428; Industrial Grill, C-910-451-8680; Jimmy John's, C-910-449-8850; Papa John's, C-910-450-7272; Smedley's O Club, C-910-451-2465; Spare Time Sports Grill, C-910-451-5731; University Cafe, C-910-450-9567; Warrior's Command Post, C-910-451-8822; Starbucks, Subway, Taco Bell and Wendy's are on base. The Sandbar at Courthouse Creek, C-910-440-7024; French Creek Snack Bar, C-910-451-2382; Chops at Hadnot Point, C-910-451-3896 and La Casita Loca at Hadnot Point, C-910-450-9606 are on base. Domino's at Tarawa Terrace, C-910-353-3111. MCX Food Court offers American Treats, Honey Baked Ham Cafe, Panda Express, Papa John's, Subway, Taco Bell and Wendy's. Many restaurants are within a short drive.

Bowling: Bonnyman Bowling Center, C-910-451-5121.

Fitness Center: Area 2, C-910-451-8209. Courthouse Bay, C-910-440-7447. French Creek, C-910-451-5430. HITT, C-910-451-0122. Morgan Bay, C-910-451-1676. Tarawa, C-910-450-1681. Wallace Creek, C-910-450-7649.

Golf: Paradise Point Golf Course, C-910-451-5445.

ITT/ITR: All Points Travel, C-910-451-3535.

Library: Harriet B Smith, C-910-451-3026. John A LeJeune Education Center, C-910-450-9845.

Marina: Courthouse Bay Marina, C-910-440-7386. Gottschalk Marina, C-910-451-8307.

MWR: C-910-451-5173.

MWR Website:
http://www.mccslejeune-newriver.com/

MWR Facebook:
https://www.facebook.com/mccslejeunenewriver

Outdoor Recreation: Outdoor Adventures, C-910-451-1440. Camp LeJeune Equipment Rentals, C-910-451-1368/2360. Offers outdoor games, lawn care equipment rental, cookers, camping gear, sports equipment and party supplies as well as many adventure trips.

Swimming: Area 2 Indoor Pool, C-910-451-2024 offers open and lap swim. Paradise Point Seasonal Officers' Pool, C-910-451-1316 offers recreational swim. Tarawa Community Seasonal Pool, C-910-450-1610 offers recreational swim. Wallace Pool, C-910-450-7659 offers lap swim only.

Things To Do: Visit Fort Macon, Jones Lake, Hammocks Beach, Hanging Rock, Cape Hatteras National Seashore, national forests and local festivals. Onslow Beach offers swimming, surfing and picnicking.

Walking Trails: Walking and running and mountain bike trails throughout the base

RV CAMPING & GETAWAYS
Brewster Recreation Area

Reservation/Contact Number Info: C-910-451-1440.

Recreation Security: Emergencies dial 911.

RV Website: http://www.mccslejeune-newriver.com/outdoor/#camp

GPS Coordinates:
34°43'24.5"N/77°22'20.0"W

Reservations: Reservations must be made 48 hours prior to arrival and will be confirmed upon payment. Payment accepted at Outdoor Adventures Office, Bldg 728 0900-1600 hours Mon-Fri. Check-in 1200 hours, check-out 1100 hours. Contact ODR for late arrivals or check-out procedures.

Season of Operation: Year-round.

Eligibility: AD, NG, Res, Ret and Dep.

Tent Spaces: Primitive Sites (8): Picnic Shelter, picnic table, fire ring; Potable water, port-a-johns. Rates: $15 nightly with max 12; Group Campsite (1): $30 nightly with max 40.

Support Facilities: Full range of support facilities on base.

Activities: Canoe and kayak launch on site.

Restrictions: Pet are permitted and must be supervised. Quiet hours 2200-0600. Hot Rocks permit required for fires. Children under the age of 10 must be supervised at all times.

RV Driving Directions/Location: On Base. From Brewster Blvd turn right onto Wilson Blvd. Facility ahead on the right.

Area Description: Wooded recreation area on base along the river. Canoe and kayak launch on site.

Onslow Beach Recreation Area

Reservation/Contact Number Info: C-910-440-7502, DSN-312-484-7502. Fax C-910-440-7258.

Recreation Security: C-910-451-3004/3005

RV Website: http://www.mccslejeune-newriver.com/beach/

GPS Coordinates: 34°34'18"N/77°16'6"W

Reservations: Accepted by telephone or in person. Reservations for RV/Camping and lodging may be made 20 weeks in advance for AD stationed at Camp Lejeune, Cherry Point and MCAS New River; 18 weeks in advance for Retirees and 16 weeks in advance for DOD civilians. Full payment required at the time of booking. Cancellations require 7-day notice to avoid fee. Office hours 0800-1800 daily Mon-Fri and 0900-1700 Sat, Sun and Holidays. Lodging packages available for 3, 4 or 7 nights only. Lodging check-in 1600 hours, check-out 1000 hours. RV/Campground check-in 1200 hours, check-out 1100 hours. Maximum stay for lodging is 7 days and 30 days for RV full hookup sites.

Season of Operation: Year-round.

Eligibility: AD, NG, Res, Ret, DoD-Civ and Dep.

Camper/Trailer Spaces: Gravel (39), Back-in, maximum 40' length, E(220V/30A/50A)/S/W hookups, CATV, picnic table with awning. Rates: $32 daily.

Tent Spaces: Tent Sites (5): Located within RV area. Rates: $12 daily. Dry sites: Located near lodges. Rates: $8 daily.

Yurt, A Frame, Cabin, Apt, Spaces: Lodges (44): One-bedroom, one bath, sleeps 2-4, furnished, A/C, alarm clock, heat, TV/DVD, refrigerator, utensils, linens. Rates: $210 for 3 nights, $280 for 4 nights, $490 weekly.

Support Facilities: Auto Craft Shop, Auto Repair, Bait/Tackle, Bathhouse*, Beach*, Boat launch, Boat Rental/Storage, Bowling, Cafeteria, Chapel, Coin Laundry, Commissary, Conference Facilities, Convenience Store, Equipment Rental, Exchange*, Fishing Pier, Fitness Center, Gas, Gazebo, Golf, Grills, Ice, Marinas (2)/on base, Mess Hall, Pavilions*, Picnic Area, Playgrounds (Fenced), Pool, Propane, Rec Center, Restrooms*, RV Storage**, Shoppette, Sewage Dump, Showers, Shuttle, Snack Bar, Sports Fields, Tennis Courts, Trails, Wi-Fi. *Located in recreation area. All other support facilities are elsewhere on base. **Available off base.

RV Storage: Yes. C-910-451-8307.

Activities: Fishing*, Golfing, Hunting*, Surfing, Swimming**. *State and base licenses required for patrons ages sixteen and up. Children younger than sixteen must be accompanied by an adult with appropriate licenses. **Lifeguard swimming area Memorial Day-Labor Day.

Credit Cards: American Express, Discover, MasterCard and Visa.

Restrictions: Pets allowed in a few select units. Must not be on restricted breed list. Pets must be on leash at all times and may not be walked outside of the RV Park unless transported by vehicle to the pet walking area on the beach. No firearms allowed. No fires are allowed on the beach, in the campgrounds or at any of the cabins and cottages.

RV Driving Directions/Location: On Base. From Wilmington: Take Hwy 17 north. Turn right on Hwy 172, heading to Sneads Ferry. Go to back gate. Once inside Camp Lejeune take right at third traffic light (Beach Rd). Proceed over drawbridge (ICW) to Onslow Beach. Reservations office is behind Exchange on left. From Swansboro: Take Hwy 24 west. Turn left on Hwy 172, stay left when Hwy 172 and Sneads Ferry merge. Take left at traffic light onto Beach Rd.

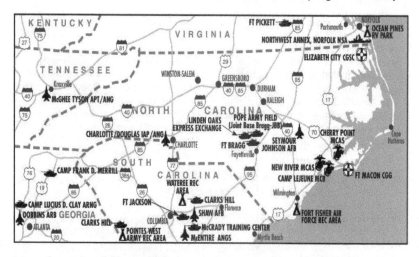

Proceed over drawbridge and follow directions as above. From Jacksonville: Enter Camp Lejeune Main Gate on Hwy 24. Proceed from Main Gate on Holcomb Blvd to left on Sneads Ferry Rd. Merge with Hwy 172 and take left at traffic light onto Beach Road. Follow directions as above.

Area Description: Located on island between Inner Coastal Waterway and Onslow Bay. Campsites are on beach or in wooded area. Many commercial fishing and beach areas also available. ITT Office on base has information on recreational activities and discount tickets. Full range of support facilities available on base.

RV Campground Physical Address: 275 Beach Road, Camp Lejeune, NC 28547-2539.

Cherry Point Marine Corps Air Station

Address: Cherry Point Marine Corps Air Station, Bldg 4335, C Street, Havelock, NC 28532.

Information Line: C-252-466-2811.

Main Base Police: C-252-466-5123/4366. Emergencies dial 911.

Main Installation Website: http://www.cherrypoint.marines.mil/

Main Base Location: Cherry Point is located approximately 20 miles west of Morehead City/Atlantic Beach off Rt. 70 on Highway 101 and 16 miles east of New Bern. Located in Craven County, it is surrounded by Carteret, Pamlico, and Jones counties.

Directions to Main Gate: From New Bern: Take US-70 Branch/Broad St toward Middle Street. At roundabout, take first exit where road name changes to US-70 E Branch. Take ramp left for US-70 East toward Havelock. Bear right onto US-70/W Main Street then bear left onto NC-101/Fontana Blvd. Turn left onto Cunningham Blvd and arrive at Marine Corps Air Station Cherry Point ahead on the right.

NMC: New Bern, 17 miles northwest.

NMI: Fort Macon CGG, 20 miles south.

Base Social Media/Facebook: https://www.facebook.com/MCASCherryPoint

Base Social Media/Twitter: https://twitter.com/MCASCPPA

Chapels: C-252-466-4000. Chaplain Duty Line, C-252-229-7248.

Dental Clinic: Appointments, C-252-466-0921.

Medical: Appointments, C-252-466-0921. Marine Centered Same Day, C-252-466-3956 Option 1 or 2.

Veterinary Services: C-252-466-2166/2409.

Beauty/Barber Shop: MCX, C-252-444-1835. Troop Store, C-252-444-4002.

Commissary: C-252-466-0800.

Exchange Gas: Marine Mart, C-252-463-1639. Convenience Store, C-252-720-1626.

Exchange: C-252-464-1628.
Financial Institutions: First Citizens Bank & Trust, C-252-447-2077. First Flight Federal Credit Union, C-252-444-3190 on base, C-252-447-0691 off base. Navy Federal Credit Union, C-888-842-6328 off base.
Clubs: Rockers SNCO Lounge, C-252-466-9927. The Roadhouse & Bar, C-252-466-5555. Alfred A Cunningham Officers' Lounge, C-252-466-9169.
Places to Eat: Wings Restaurant, C-252-466-9132; Crows Nest, C-252-466-9147; Five Guys, Hungry Harrier, Library Cafe, Mayberry Cafe, McDonald's, New City Deli, Rice King, Snack-a-Tach and Subway are on base. 7 Day Troop Store also offers a food bar. Many restaurants are within a short drive.
Fitness Center: Hancock Fitness Center, C-252-466-4018. Devil Dog Gym, C-252-466-2713. HITT, C-252-466-7201. Marine Dome, C-252-466-2566.
Golf: Sound of Freedom Golf Course, C-252-466-3044.
ITT/ITR: Crystal Coast, C-252-466-2197/2172.
Library: Marine Warrior, C-252-466-3552.
Marina: Hancock Marina, C-252-466-2762.
MWR: C-252-466-3001/2301.
MWR Website:
http://www.mccscherrypoint.com/
MWR Facebook:
https://www.facebook.com/mccschpt
MWR Twitter:
https://twitter.com/cherrypointmccs
Outdoor Recreation: Outdoor Connection Rentals, C-252-466-4058. Offers inflatables, camping gear, kayaks, canoes, paintball and sports equipment, lawn mowers, garden tools, and more.
Swimming: Marine Dome Indoor Pool, C-252-466-2510 offers lap swim and open swim. Cedar Creek Pool Seasonal Outdoor Pool, C-252-466-2277 offers open, recreational swim and seasonal swim lessons. Hancock Seasonal Outdoor Pool, C-252-466-2168 offers open and recreational swim.
Things To Do: Historical downtown New Bern has the Tryon Palace, museums, shops and restaurants. There are several other historical attractions in the area: Fort Macon (Atlantic Beach), Maritime museum and Blackbeard's museum in Beaufort, sailing center at Oriental, fishing and boating on the nearby Outer Banks, Cape Lookout National Seashore are popular local activities.
Walking Trails: Many walking trails throughout the base.

RV CAMPING & GETAWAYS

Pelican Point RV Park – Oak Grove Campground - ODR Camping

Reservation/Contact Number Info: C-252-466-2762. Fax C-252-466-6751.
Recreation Security: C-252-466-2811.
RV Website:
http://mccscherrypoint.com/recreation-entertainment/marinas-picnic-camping/
GPS Coordinates:
34°54'33"N/76°53'42"W
Reservations: Recommended for RV park. Required for Bartlett, Duck and LoneTree Point campsites. RV Park office hours 0800-1630 Mon-Fri. Sites assigned according to length of stay and availability. Check-in 1200, check-out 1100. Late arrivals check in with camp host, site 23. Maximum stay 30 days. Oak Grove Campground: Reservations required at least 3 days in advance. Weekend camping only. Check-in and check-out at Pelican Point RV Park 0800-1600 Fri-Mon. Small boat dock and launch on site.
Season of Operation: Year-round. Oak Grove: Mid May-August.
Eligibility: AD, NG, Res, Ret, DoD-Civ, Dep and MCCS Emp.
Camper/Trailer Spaces: RV Sites (30): Concrete pads, E(110/220V/30/50A)/S/W hookups, CATV, Wi-Fi. Summer Rates: $25 daily, $150 weekly, $550 monthly. Bathhouse, marina and convenience store nearby.
Tent Spaces: Bartlett and Duck Pond, LoneTree Point: Primitive sites with bathrooms/outhouses. No running water at Duck Pond. Rates: No cost but reservations required. Oak Grove

Campground (2) sites: Group camping allowed, picnic tables, grills. Call for rates.

Support Facilities: Auto Skills Center, Boat Rental, Bowling, Camping Equipment Rental*, Chapel, Commissary, Convenience Store, Exchange, Fishing Areas, Fitness Center, Golf, Marina, Picnic Area, Pool, Recreation Center, Tennis Courts, Walking/Bike Trails. *Pig cooker, propane refill, fishing rods, etc.

RV Storage: None.

Activities: Fishing*, Golfing, Hunting*, Movie theater. * For fishing, state and base licenses required for patrons ages sixteen and up. For hunting, state license and hunter's safety course required for patrons ages twelve and up (no charge for ages twelve to fifteen). Children younger than sixteen must be accompanied by an adult with a state license.

Credit Cards: American Express, Discover, MasterCard and Visa.

Restrictions: Pets allowed on leash. RV Quiet hours 2200-0730. No tents allowed at RV sites.

RV Driving Directions/Location: On Base: From the Main Gate: Follow Roosevelt Blvd to Franklin Rd. Turn left on Franklin Rd. RV Park is located at the end of Franklin Rd on the right side. Ask for directions to Bartlett, Duck and LoneTree Point campgrounds. Oak Grove Park located off-base in Pollocksville. Ask for directions at time of reservation or at check-in with Pelican Point.

Area Description: Located near Neuse Waterway and Outer Banks area, it is also about eight miles from Croatan National Forest. The RV Park is within walking distance of most support facilities on base.

RV Campground Physical Address: Pelican Point RV Park, 4908 Monroe Drive, Cherry Point MCAS, NC 28533. Mailing Address: MCCS, Attn: ITT Director, PSC 8009, Cherry Point MCAS, NC 28533-0009.

Elizabeth City Coast Guard Support Center

Address: Commanding Officer, U.S. Coast Guard Base Support Unit, 1664 Weeksville Rd, Bldg 35, Elizabeth City, NC 27909-5006.

Information Line: C-252-335-6000.

Main Base Police: C-252-335-6588. Emergencies dial 911.

Main Installation Website: http://www.dcms.uscg.mil/Our-Organization/Director-of-Operational-Logistics-DOL/Bases/Base-Elizabeth-City/

Main Base Location: Located off the Albemarle Sound in Pasquotank County and an hour's drive to the Outer Banks and Kitty Hawk area.

Directions to Main Gate: From US-17 in Elizabeth City, NC: Take NC-34/Halstead Blvd/Weeksville Rd south to the Main Gate of the CG Base Elizabeth City.

NMC: Elizabeth City, within city limits.

NMI: Norfolk Naval Station, VA, 50 miles north.

Base Social Media/Facebook: https://www.facebook.com/BaseElizabethCity/

Chapels: C-252-335-6202.

Dental Clinic: C-252 335-6460.

Medical: C-252-335-6460.

Beauty/Barber Shop: C-252-335-1011.

Exchange: C-252-335-1011.

Clubs: Hangar 7 Club, C-252-335-6389.

Places to Eat: Many restaurants are within a short drive.

Fitness Center: C-252-335-6397.

ITT/ITR: C-252-335-6482.

MWR: C-252-335-6482.

MWR Website: http://www.dcms.uscg.mil/Our-Organization/Director-of-Operational-Logistics-DOL/Bases/Base-Elizabeth-City/Base-Elizabeth-City-MWR-Branch/

Outdoor Recreation: MWR Hobby Shop Rentals, C-252-335-6412. Offers boats, canoes, kayaks, sports equipment, camping gear, lawn and garden rentals.

Things To Do: Visit Kitty Hawk and the Outer Banks. This is a beautiful part of the east coast. Enjoy boating on the Albemarle Sound and the Intracoastal

Waterway, as well as many other seasonal events in Elizabeth City.

Walking Trails: Trails are available on base.

RV CAMPING & GETAWAYS
Elizabeth City RV & Recreation

Reservation/Contact Number Info: C-252-335-6482. Fax C-252-335-6296.

Recreation Security: C-252-335-6588/6855.

RV Website: https://www.dcms.uscg.mil/Our-Organization/Assistant-Commandant-for-Human-Resources-CG-1/Community-Services-Command-CSC/MWR/Coast-Guard-Lodging/

RV Email Address: ecity-mwr@uscg.mil.

GPS Coordinates: 36°16'10"N/76°10'46"W.

Reservations: Accepted up to 90 days in advance. Payment required upon arrival Office hours 0730-1600 Mon-Fri. Closed weekends and holidays. Check-in 1500 hours at Watchstander office, located in Bldg 5 (Gym). Must check in before gym closes. Check-out 1000 hours.

Season of Operation: Year-round.

Eligibility: AD, NG, Res, CG Aux, Ret, 100% DAV, Dep, DHS (Ret), DoD-Civ and NASA-Civ.

Camper/Trailer Spaces: Concrete (10), Back-in, Maximum 40' in length, E(110/220V/30/50A)/S/W. Rates: $20 daily. Gravel (4), Back-in, Maximum 40' in length, E(110/220V/50A)/S/W. Rates: $18 daily.

Yurt, A Frame, Cabin, Apt, Spaces: Mobile Homes: Two and three-bedroom (6), sleeps six, private bath, kitchen, satellite TV, limited utensils, A/C, W/D available in Bldg 16G. Rates: $50 daily. Cabins: One-bedroom (3), sleeps six, one loft, screened porch. Rates: $60 daily.

Support Facilities: Beach, Boat Launch, Camping Equipment, Chapel, Convenience Store, Driving Range, Exchange, Fishing Pier, Fitness Center, Gas Station, Grills, Hobby Shop. Laundry, Pavilion, Picnic Area, Playground, Rec Center, Restrooms, Sewage Dump, Snack Bar, Sports Fields, Trails.

RV Storage: Yes. C-252-335-6397.

Activities: Boating, Fishing, Swimming*. *Swim at own risk on Sandy Beach on Pasquotank River.

Credit Cards: Cash, Check, MasterCard and Visa.

Restrictions: No pets in cabins or mobile homes. Pets allowed in RV park. Must be on a leash at all times. Service Dogs are allowed in cabins and trailers with valid certificate prior to check-in date. No firearms allowed. No Smoking. No open flames.

RV Driving Directions/Location: On Base. From the Main Gate of CG Support Center: Check in at MWR offices located in the gym, Bldg 5.

Area Description: Located off the Albemarle Sound. Small beach on base on the Pasquotank River. Attractions include the Outer Banks and Kitty Hawk, only one hour drive away. Wide range of support facilities available on base.

RV Campground Physical Address: Elizabeth City CGSC MWR, 1644 Weeksville Road, Bldg 5, Elizabeth City, NC 27909.

Fort Bragg

Address: Soldier Support Center, Building 4-2843 Normandy Street, Fort Bragg, NC 28310.

Information Line: C-910-396-0011, DSN-312-236-0011.

Main Base Police: C-910-396-0391. Emergencies dial 911.

Main Installation Website: http://www.bragg.army.mil/

Main Base Location: Fort Bragg is located just west of Fayetteville, North Carolina.

Directions to Main Gate: From I-95 South: Take exit 56 toward Fayetteville/Fort Bragg/Pope AFB and US 301 South. Make a right at the first light on to Grove Street/NC-24/NC-210 and at the end turn right onto Bragg Blvd/NC-24/NC-210. Continue to follow Bragg Blvd to Santa Fe Drive. Turn left on Santa Fe Drive. At the next light merge onto the All American Fwy which leads to Fort Bragg.

NMC: Fayetteville, 10 miles southeast.
NMI: Pope AFB, adjacent.
Base Social Media/Facebook:
https://www.facebook.com/fortbraggnc
Base Social Media/Twitter:
https://twitter.com/ftbraggnc
Chapels: C-910-396-1121/7168.
Dental Clinic: WAMC Dental Clinic, C-910-907-6974. Davis Clinic, C-910-432-4227/6190. Joel Clinic, C-910-907-1076/1080. LaFlamme Clinic, C-910-432-3515/4821. Rhode Clinic, C-910-432-2526. Smoke Bomb Clinic, C-910-396-1571/1572.
Medical: Appointment Line, C-910-907-2778. Womack, C-910-907-8500. Clark Clinic, C-910-907-2525. Joel Clinic, C-910-907-5635. Robinson Clinic, C-910-907-8282. Byars Troop and Family Clinic, C-910-907-7673. Woodland, C-910-908-9663. Hope Mills, C-910-908-4673. Linden Oaks, C-910-908-6257. Troop Medical, C-910-396-8115. Robinson Health Clinic, C-910-907-8282, DSN-312-337-8282. Womack Medical Center, C-910-907-6000/9262, DSN-312-337-6000. Womack Family Practice Clinic, C-910-907-6451.
Veterinary Services: C-910-396-9120.
Beauty/Barber Shop: North Post, C-910-497-0789; Stylique, C-910-436-9090. South Post, C-910-436-0202; Stylique, C-910-436-2228. Smoke Bomb, C-910-493-0489. Airborne Troop Store, C-910-436-0101. Honeycutt Express, C-910-497-3800. Mini Mall, C-910-436-4011. Womack AMC, C-910-907-7093.
Commissary: North Commissary, C-910-396-2316. South Commissary, C-910-853-7333.
Exchange Gas: Butner Road, C-910-436-1600. Old Glory Express, C-910-436-4278. Pine Express, C-910-436-0602.
Exchange: North Post, C-910-436-4888. South Post, C-910-436-2166.
Military Clothing: C-910-436–2200.
Financial Institutions: Bragg Mutual Federal Credit Union, C-910-488-3515. Fort Bragg Federal Credit Union, C-910-864-2232, C-1-800-793-2328. First Citizens Bank & Trust, C-910-436-7300.
Clubs: Sports USA, C-910-907-0739/2373.

Places to Eat: Books and Beans, C-910-396-0178; Mugs Coffee Hardy Hall, C-910-908-1514; Mugs Coffee Soldier Support Center, C-910-432-9481; McKellar's Lodge, C-910-907-5253; Smoke Bomb Grille, C-910-907-4976; Strike Zone Airborne Lanes, C-910-432-6900; Strike Zone Dragon Lanes, C-910-907-2695 and The Divot at Ryder Golf Course, C-910-432-8122 are on base. South Post Exchange Food Court offers Charley's, Domino's, Manchu Wok, Popeye's, Starbucks and Subway. North Post offers Anthony's Pizza, Burger King, Captain D's, Charley's and Subway. Pine Express offers Burger King. Smoke Bomb Hill offers Arby's, Boston Market, Hunt Brothers Pizza, Qdoba and Subway. Old Glory Express offers Burger King and KFC. Airborne Troop Store offers Burger King, Charley's, Dunkin Donuts, Pizza Hut, Popeye's, Subway and Taco Bell. Mini Mall offers Charley's, Burger King, Manchu Wok, Starbucks, Subway and Wing Zone. Mallonee Plaza offers Coldstone Creamery, Popeye's and Starbucks. Butner Express offers Papa John's and Quiznos. Womack AMC offers dining facility and Grab and Go services. Many restaurants within a short drive.
Bowling: Airborne Lanes, C-910-432-6900. Dragon Lanes, C-910-907-2695.
Fitness Center: Blackjack FC, C-910-432-7922*. Callahan Athletic Center, C-910-396-3037. Dahl FC, C-910-236-6226. Frederick PEC, C-910-432-7949*. Funk FC, C-910-432-8772. Hosking FC, C-910-432-6489*. Iron Mike FC, C-910-432-5679. Patriot Point FC, C-910-908-2766. Ritz-Epps FC, C-910-432-1031. Towle Courts FC, C-910-432-6493. Tucker PEC, C-910-432-3573. Warfighter FC, C-910-396-9660. *Denotes locations that are temporarily closed.
Golf: Ryder Golf Course, C-910-907-4653. Stryker Golf Course, C-910-396-3980.
ITT/ITR: C-910-396-8747.
Library: Throckmorton Library, C-910-396-3526.
Military Museum: 82nd Airborne Division War Memorial, C-910-436-

1735. U.S. Army John F. Kennedy Special Warfare Museum, C-910-432-4272.
Military Museum Website:
http://www.82ndairbornedivisionmuseum.com/
MWR: C-910-396-7632.
MWR Website:
https://bragg.armymwr.com
MWR Facebook:
https://www.facebook.com/fortbraggmwr/
Outdoor Recreation: Recreation Equipment Center, C-910-396-7060. Outdoor Recreation Excursion, C-910-643-4569. Offers campers, canoes and kayaks, moon bouncers, climbing wall, picnic and party equipment, canopy tents, tables and chairs, grills and super cookers, propane fill-up station, dunk tanks, lawn and garden equipment and more. Outdoor Excursions offers adventure trips.
Swimming: Tolson Indoor Pool, C-910-643-8533 offers rec swim weekends only. Tucker Indoor Pool, C-910-908-3198 offers lap swim. Outdoor Seasonal Pools: Atchley, C-910-498-6187 offers lap swim. Normandy, C-910-432-5465 offers lap swim rec swim and diving board. Twin Lions, C-910-432-7266 offers lap swim, rec swim and Splash Pad.
Things To Do: The 82nd Airborne Division War Memorial Museum has more than 3,000 objects for viewing. The Historic Fayetteville Foundation gives walking tours of historical sites. Check out the Cleland Ice and Indoor Skating Rink, offering organized sports, a skate park and more, C-910-396-5127. Cape Fear River Trail is nearby.
Walking Trails: Many parks and recreation areas available on base.

RV CAMPING & GETAWAYS

Smith Lake Recreation Area – Army Travel Camp

Reservation/Contact Number Info: C-910-396-5979, DSN-312-326-5979. Fax C-910-907-2397.
Recreation Security: C-910-396-0391

RV Website:
https://bragg.armymwr.com/programs/smith-lake-recreation-area
GPS Coordinates:
35°8'10"N/78°55'19"W
Reservations: Reservations required; accepted 90 days in advance. One night stay deposit required. Cancellations within 7 days of arrival for refund. Unreserved cabins are on first come, first serve basis. Smith Lake office hours 0800-1700 Thur-Mon. RV pull-thru sites 14 day maximum stay. Extended stays based on availability. Discounts available to holders of Golden Age and Golden Access Passports. Check-in 1500 hours, check-out 1200 hours.
Season of Operation: Year-round.
Eligibility: AD, NG, Res, Ret, DoD APF/NAF Civ, DoD contract personnel, eligible family Members.
Camper/Trailer Spaces: RV Sites: Hardstand, Back-in and pull-thru sites, maximum 50' in length, E(110V/30/50A)/S/W hookups, picnic tables at most sites. Rates: $23 daily back-in; $25 daily pull-thru. Partial hookup $18 daily.
Tent Spaces: Primitive Sites: No hookups. Rates: $12 daily per tent.
Yurt, A Frame, Cabin, Apt, Spaces: Primitive Log Cabins (12): 1 double bed, 1 set of bunk beds, table and four chairs. Electricity, refrigerator, microwave, heat, outdoor grill, picnic table, near the bathhouse, no kitchen, bath or running water. Must provide own linens. Rates: $55 daily. Large Two-bedroom Cabin (2), Sleeps eight; 1 double bed, 1 set of bunk beds and loft with futon sleeper, living area full size bathroom, kitchenette with table and four chairs, AC/Heat. Must provide own linens. Minimum 2-night stay. Rates: $135 daily.
Support Facilities: Auto Craft Shop, Bathhouse, Camping Equipment, Chapel*, Coin Laundry, Commissary, Convenience Store, Exchange, Fitness Center, Gas, Golf, Grills, Ice, Pavilion, Picnic Area, Playground, Rec Center, Rec Equipment, Restrooms, Sewage Dump, Shoppette, Showers, Stables, Tennis

Courts. *On base approximately 5 miles away.

RV Storage: None.

Activities: Canoeing, Fishing, Golfing, Kayaking, Mountain Bike Trails, Paintball, Swimming, Wake Zone Water Skiing.

Credit Cards: MasterCard and Visa.

Restrictions: No pets allowed in cabins. Pets allowed on leash in campground.

RV Driving Directions/Location: On Base. From the North: Take exit 58 off I-95 south onto I-295. Road ends at Ramsey St/Rte 401 and go right. Go left at Andrews Road and then another left at McArthur Road. Go right at Honeycutt Road then a left at Smith Lake Road and follow to camp office. From the South: Take I-95 to Business Loop I-95/US-301 to Owen Drive (changes to All-American Freeway). Follow freeway to Santa Fe Drive. At the exit, turn right. Follow Santa Fe to Bragg Blvd. Keep straight across to Shaw Road and follow to NC-210. Turn left onto NC-210 north and follow to Honeycutt Road. Take a right on Honeycutt Road. Turn right at Smith Lake Road. Note: Smith Lake access road CLOSED. Facility is approximately five miles from the base.

Area Description: JFK Special Warfare Museum and 82d Airborne Division Museum on post; Pinehurst Resort is nearby. Full range of support facilities available on post.

RV Campground Physical Address: Smith Lake Recreation Area, Bldg Q-2816, Smith Lake Rd, Fort Bragg, NC 28310.

Fort Fisher Air Force Recreation Area

Address: Fort Fisher Rec Area, 118 Riverfront Road, Kure Beach, NC 28449.

Information Line: C-919-722-1110, DSN-312-722-1110

Main Base Police: C-919-722-0911. Emergencies dial 911.

Main Installation Website: http://www.seymourjohnson.af.mil/

Main Base Location: Fort Fisher lies between the Cape Fear River and the Atlantic Ocean in southeastern North Carolina.

NMC: Wilmington NC, 20 miles northwest.

NMI: Camp Lejeune, 65 miles northeast.

Exchange Gas: Commercial gas station within 2 miles.

Places to Eat: Beach House Bar and Grill, Kure Beach and Carolina Beach offer several local restaurants.

Fitness Center: Weight Room in Recreation Hall – June – August only.

MWR Phone Number: C-919-722-1106.

MWR Website: http://www.sjfss.com

MWR Facebook: https://www.facebook.com/sjfss

Outdoor Recreation: Fort Fisher Recreation, C-910-458-6549. Offers beach umbrellas/chairs, boogie boards, fishing poles, canoes, kayaks, boat launching ramp, as well as nearby public beach access, swimming pool and more. Contact Seymour Johnson AFB Outdoor Recreation for additional rentals.

Swimming: Swimming pool located near Recreation Hall – June – August only, Ocean.

Things To Do: The North Carolina Aquarium at Fort Fisher, the Fort Fisher State Historic Site Civil War Museum, the USS North Carolina Battleship Memorial, Poplar Grove Plantations, and Downtown Wilmington.

RV CAMPING & GETAWAYS
Fort Fisher

Reservation/Contact Number Info: C-910-279-6888.

RV Website: http://ftfishermilrec.com/

RV Email Address: reservations@fort-fisher.com

GPS Coordinates: 33°58'52"N/77°54'51"W

Reservations: Accepted. All SJAFB 180 days in advance. All other active duty 150 days in advance. Retirees, 100% Military Disabled, DoD Civilians 120 days in advance. Lodges 30 days in advance. Office hours 0900-1700 daily. Cottages and Lodges: Check-in 1600, check-out 1100. RV and Tent Camping: Check-in 1400, check-out 1400.

Season of Operation: Year-round.
Eligibility: AD, Ret, 100% DAV and DoD Civilian.
Camper/Trailer Spaces: Hardstand (18), Back-in (primarily) and Pull-through, Maximum 45' in length, E(110/220V/30A)/S/W/CATV hookups. Rates: $25 daily. Overflow: Grass (7), Maximum 45' in length, no hookups. Rates: $15 daily. PLEASE NOTE: RV sites will be undergoing renovations March 2018 and an additional 8 sites are to be added. RV Park will remain open during all renovations and additions.
Tent Spaces: Primitive: One 8-man two 4-man tents per site. Rates: $10 daily per site.
Yurt, A Frame, Cabin, Apt, Spaces: Cottages: One, three and four-bedroom cottages. Private baths, full kitchen with refrigerator, stove and microwave; coffee pot, TV and linens. Larger cottages offer two bathrooms, queen beds and twin beds. Rates vary depending on season and rank. Please contact facility for current rates. Lodges: Hercules and Old Hickory Halls offer full size bed, shared bathroom, mini-fridge, coffee pot and cable TV. Rates: $40 daily.
Support Facilities: Beach, Boat Launch, Camping Equipment, Exercise/Weight Room, General Store, Gift/Beach Shop, Grills, Laundry, Picnic Area, Picnic Tables, Pool, Rec Center, Rec Equipment, Restaurant, Restrooms, Sauna, Sewage Dump, Showers, Tennis Courts.
RV Storage: Limited amount of spaces.
Activities: Beach, Boating, Canoeing, Clamming, Fishing*, Sailing, Sightseeing, Swimming. *State license required.
Credit Cards: Mastercard, Visa, Check, Money Order or Cash.
Restrictions: No pets allowed in accommodations; kennel available. Pets allowed on leash in designated areas only, owner must clean up after pet. No smoking in any of the lodging facilities or on any of the porches.
RV Driving Directions/Location: Off Base: Fort Fisher is located on Pleasure Island between Cape Fear River and the Atlantic Ocean. From Wilmington:

Follow Carolina Beach Rd/US-421 south. At Myrtle Grove Junction, keep right to stay on US-421 and follow 8.5 miles to bridge. Continue straight over bridge onto Pleasure Island. Stay on US-421/Carolina Beach Rd and travel south through Carolina and Kure Beaches, approximately 9 miles. Recreation Area on the west side of US-421. Ample signs for Rec Area all along US-421.
Area Description: Fort Fisher is located on Pleasure Island between Cape Fear River and Atlantic Ocean, within walking distance of beaches.
RV Campground Physical Address: Fort Fisher Air Force Recreation Area, 118 Riverfront Road, Kure Beach, NC 28449-3321.

New River Marine Corps Air Station

Address: New River Marine Corps Air Station, 90 Curtis Road, Jacksonville, NC 28540.
Information Line: C-910-451-1113.
Main Base Police: C-910-449-4248/4249. Emergencies dial 911.
Main Installation Website: http://www.newriver.marines.mil/
Main Base Location: MCAS New River is located four miles south of downtown Jacksonville on Hwy 17 S, in Onslow County, North Carolina.
Directions to Main Gate: Driving from the North: Take exit 81 off I-95 South onto 40 East. Approximately 25 minutes later take exit 373. Make a left turn at the stop sign and go straight for six miles until reaching a light and a sign with directions to Jacksonville. Make a right turn onto Hwy 24 East traveling 49 miles to Jacksonville. 24 East flows into Hwy 17, which runs North and South. Make a right onto 17 South. The Air Station is approximately 3 miles down the road on the left side. Look for a small green sign on the right indicating "Air Station" to the left.
NMC: Jacksonville, 2 miles northeast.
NMI: Camp Lejeune, 20 miles east.
Base Social Media/Facebook: https://www.facebook.com/mcasnewriver

Base Social Media/Twitter:
https://twitter.com/MCASNewRiver
Chapels: Chaplain, C-910-449-6801.
Dental Clinic: MCAS, C-910-449-6515/6516. Camp Geiger, C-910-449-0545. Camp Johnson, C-910-450-0971.
Medical: Naval Hospital Camp Lejeune, C-910-450-4300, DSN-312-750-4300. Camp Geiger, C-910-449-0545. MCAS Medical, C-910-449-6500.
Veterinary Services: C-910-450-1607.
Beauty/Barber Shop: C-910-449-0593.
Commissary: C-910-449-6395.
Exchange Gas: C-910-449-6092.
Exchange: C-910-449-0539.
Financial Institutions: Fort Sill National Bank, C-1-800-749-4583. Marine Federal Credit Union, C-910-577-7333.
Clubs: New River Officers' Club, C-910-449-6409/6531. New River Enlisted Club, C-910-449-0589.
Places to Eat: Corner Cafe, C-910-449-7669; Flightline Grill, C-910-449-6731; Heavenly Brew Cafe, C-910-449-4529; New River Bowling Center, C-910-449-4918; Noble Roman's, C-910-449-0513; Rally Point, C-910-449-0152; Subway and Wendy's are on base. Papa John's Camp Johnson, C-910-450-7272 and Heavenly Brew Camp Johnson, C-910-787-9180 are on base. Stone Bay Shooter's Grill, C-910-440-2572 and MARSOC Grill are on base. Many restaurants are within a short drive.
Bowling: New River Bowling Center, C-910-449-4921/4922.
Fitness Center: AS 400, C-910-449-0294. Camp Geiger, C-910-449-0609. Camp Johnson, C-910-450-1250. HITT, C-910-449-7698/5854. New River, C-910-449-4961. Stone Bay, C-910-440-2055.
Golf: Paradise Point Golf Course Camp Lejeune, C-910-451-5445.
ITT/ITR: All Points Travel, C-910-449-6530.
Library: Station Library, C-910-449-6715. Camp Johnson, C-910-450-0844.
Marina: New River Marina, C-910-449-6578.
MWR Phone Number: C-910-451-5173.
MWR Website:
http://www.mccslejeune-newriver.com/

MWR Facebook:
https://www.facebook.com/mccslejeunenewriver
Outdoor Recreation: Outdoor Adventures, C-910-451-1440. Camp LeJeune Equipment Rentals, C-910-451-1368/2360. Offers outdoor games, lawn care equipment rental, cookers, camping gear, sports equipment and party supplies as well as many adventure trips.
Swimming: New River Indoor Pool, C-910-449-4309/4307 offers swim lessons and open swim. New River Outdoor Pool, C-910-449-6231 offers recreational swim. Camp Johnson, C-910-451-0768.
Things To Do: Visit Fort Macon, Jones Lake, Hammocks Beach, Hanging Rock, Cape Hatteras National Seashore, national forests and local festivals.
Walking Trails: Perimeter Road jogging trail nearby Recreation Area 8.

RV CAMPING & GETAWAYS
New River MCAS Marina

Reservation/Contact Number Info: C-910-449-6578, DSN-312-752-6578. Fax C-910-449-6907, DSN-312-752-6578.
Recreation Security: C-910-449-6111.
RV Website: http://www.mccslejeune-newriver.com
GPS Coordinates:
34°38'59"N/77°25'42"W
Reservations: None accepted. Deposit of $3 required. Office hours 0800- 1830. Check in at Marina Building located at 2800 Perimeter Road. Checkout 1200 hours.
Season of Operation: Year-round.
Eligibility: AD, NG, Res, Ret, DoD-Civ (AD and Ret), 100% DAV and Dep ID card holders.
Tent Spaces: Primitive (9), no hookups. Picnic Table and grill. Rates: $5 daily.
Support Facilities: Auto Craft Shop, Bathhouse, Beach, Boat Launch, Boat Rental/Storage, Boat Slip Rental, Bowling, Chapel, Commissary, Convenience Store, Exchange, Fire Rings, Fishing Pier, Fitness Center, Gas, Golf, Grills, Ice, Laundry, Marina*, Mess Hall, Pavilion, Picnic Area, Playground,

Pool, Rec Center, Rec Equipment, Restrooms, Shoppette, Showers, Snack Bar, Sports Fields, Tennis Courts, Trails. * Patio Room at Marina for parties, by reservation.
RV Storage: Yes. C-910-449-6578.
Activities: Basketball, Boating, Bowling, Canoes, Fishing, Horseshoes, Jet Skiing, Kayaking, Softball, Swimming, Tennis, Volleyball, Water Skiing.
Credit Cards: MasterCard and Visa.
Restrictions: Pets are permitted on leash in camping area, but not on beach. No firearms.
RV Driving Directions/Location: On Base. From the main Gate: Follow Curtis Rd until it ends. Turn left onto East Perimeter Road. Marina is .25 mile on the right.
Area Description: Situated along the New River in Morgan Bay. Area offers water sports and picnic areas. Improvements to facilities at camping area are currently under construction.
RV Campground Physical Address: New River MCAS, 2800 Perimeter Rd, Jacksonville, NC 28540-0128. Mailing Address: MCCS, New River MCAS, ATTN: Marina, PO Box 4128, Jacksonville, NC 28540-0128.

Seymour Johnson Air Force Base

Address: 1510 Wright Brothers Avenue, Suite 100, Seymour Johnson AFB, NC 27531.
Information Line: C-919-722-1110, DSN-312-722-1110.
Main Base Police: C-919-722-1211/1212.
Main Installation Website: http://www.seymourjohnson.af.mil/
Main Base Location: Located in the southeast section of Goldsboro, North Carolina in the middle of Wayne County midway between Raleigh and the coast.
Directions to Main Gate: From the Raleigh/Durham airport: Take I-40 east for approximately 10 miles. Stay in the left lane and exit onto Interstate 440 East to Goldsboro. Exit onto Highway 70 East to Goldsboro. Once into Goldsboro, take the exit to Seymour Johnson AFB, remaining on Hwy 70 East. Exit at the Seymour Johnson/Snow Hill exit to Berkeley Boulevard which leads directly into the Main Gate of the base.
NMC: Raleigh, 50 miles west.
NMI: Fort Bragg, 70 miles west.
Base Social Media/Facebook: https://www.facebook.com/SeymourJohnsonAirForceBase
Chapels: C-919-722-0315.
Dental Clinic: C-919-722-1933.
Medical: Appointment Line, C-919-722-1802.
Veterinary Services: C-919-722-1465.
Beauty/Barber Shop: Exchange, C-919-735-9442. ODR, C-919-722-7760.
Commissary: C-919-722-0321.
Exchange Gas: Bldg 3703, C-919-734-7235.
Exchange: C-919-735-8511/8512.
Financial Institutions: North Carolina Community Federal, C-919-722-1174.
Clubs: Kitty Hawk Lounge, C-919-722-1192 currently undergoing renovations. Spitfire Club, C-919-722-1340.
Places to Eat: 10-Pin Cafe, C-919-722-0349; Afterburner Flight Kitchen, C-919-722-4085/8383; Southern Eagle DFAC, C-919-722-5295/5298 and Three Eagles Cafe, C-919-722-0394 are on base. Exchange Food Court offers Subway. Many restaurants are within a short drive.
Fitness Center: Fitness and Sports Complex, C-919-722-0408. BellaMorphosis Women's Center, C-919-722-0413.
Golf: Three Eagles Golf Course, C-919-722-0395.
ITT/ITR: C-919-722-1104.
Library: Watkins-Das Learning Center. C-919-722-5825.
MWR: C-919-722-1106/8532.
MWR Website: http://www.sjfss.com
MWR Facebook: https://www.facebook.com/sjfss
Outdoor Recreation: Outdoor Recreation Services, C-919-722-1104.
Outdoor Recreation Text: Offers canoes, kayaks, bounce houses, costume rental, tools and equipment, outdoor games, sports equipment, camping equipment, adventure programs and more.

Swimming: Outdoor Seasonal Pool, C-919-722-1104/7437 offers lap swim, recreational swim, kiddie pool, water slide, and a Splash Pad.

Things To Do: Located near Goldsboro. Visit the Cliffs of the Neuse River or enjoy picnicking, fishing, swimming, rental rowboats and museums. Also visit historic Fort Macon, the Cape Hatteras National Seashore and Kure Beach.

RV CAMPING & GETAWAYS

Seymour Johnson AFB FamCamp

Reservation/Contact Number Info: C-919-722-1104/7437.

Recreation Security: C-919-722-6911.

RV Website: https://www.sjfss.com/outdoor-recreation/

GPS Coordinates: 35°21'37"N/77°58'1"W.

Reservations: No advance reservations. Availability first come, first serve basis. Office hours 0900-1700 Mon-Fri. Check-in and check-out at ODR office.

Season of Operation: Year-round.

Eligibility: AD, NG, Res, Ret, DoD-Civ (AD and Ret), Dep and 100% DAV.

Camper/Trailer Spaces: Hardstand (16), Back-in, Maximum 40' in length, handicap accessible, E(220V/30A)/S/W hookups, picnic table, grill. Rates: $20 daily, $120 weekly, $450 monthly. Low season rates may be lower. Overflow area: Gravel, back-in and pull-through, maximum 40' in length, E(220V/30A)/W. Rates: $10 daily.

Support Facilities: Auto Craft Shop, Bath House, Boat Rental, Bowling, Cafeteria, Chapel, Coin Laundry, Commissary, Exchange, Fitness Center, Gas, Golf, Grills, Ice, Laundry, Mess Hall, Pavilion, Picnic Area, Playground, Pool, Racquetball Court, Rec Center, Rec Equipment, Restrooms, RV Storage, Sewage Dump, Shoppette, Showers, Skeet/Trap Range, Snack Bar, Sports Fields, Telephones, Tennis Courts.

RV Storage: C-919-722-1104.

Activities: Bowling, Golfing, Jogging, Nature Trail, Swimming.

Credit Cards: MasterCard and Visa.

Restrictions: Pets allowed on leash only. Firearms must be registered with security forces.

RV Driving Directions/Location: On Base. From Back Gate off Slocum Street: Continue straight to Jabara Ave and turn left. Turn left on Fickel St. FamCamp located on the right. Note: The back gate must be used for security purposes.

Area Description: Surrounded by heavily forested areas and is within walking distance of many of support facilities available on base.

RV Campground Physical Address: Outdoor Recreation, 1515 Goodson Street, Goldsboro, NC 27531-5000.

NORTH DAKOTA

Grand Forks Air Force Base

Address: Steen Blvd, Grand Forks AFB, ND 58205.

Information Line: C-701-747-3000, DSN-312-362-3000.

Main Base Police: C-701-747-5351. Emergencies dial 911.

Main Installation Website: http://www.grandforks.af.mil/

Main Base Location: Located in the Heart of the Red River Valley at the junction of the Red Lake River and the Red River of the North.

Directions to Main Gate: From the north or south on I-29: Approach the city of Grand Forks. Take exit 141 and head West on US-2W for 12.4 miles. Exit toward Emerado/Grand Forks Air Base/Mekinock for 1.1 miles. Turn left onto the Avenue of Flags to the Main Gate. Driving from the West on US-2W: Take the Emerado/Grand Forks Air Base/Mekinock exit onto County Road 5. Turn left and go over the bridge. Stay on this road for 1.1 miles to the Avenue of Flags. Turn left to the Main Gate.

NMC: Grand Forks, 15 miles east.

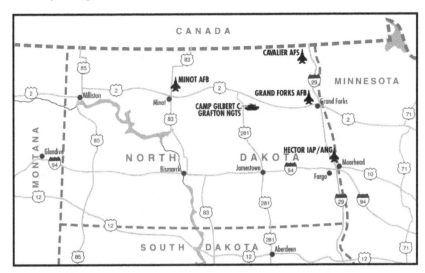

NMI: Camp Gilbert C. Grafton NGTC, 78 miles west.
Base Social Media/Facebook: https://www.facebook.com/grandforks airforcebase/
Base Social Media/Twitter: https://twitter.com/319ABW
Chapels: C-701-747-5673.
Dental Clinic: C-701-747-5393.
Medical: Appointment Line, C-701-747-5601.
Veterinary Services: C-701-747-3375.
Beauty/Barber Shop: C-701-594-2122.
Commissary: C-701-747-3083.
Exchange Gas: C-701-594-5684.
Exchange: C-701-594-5542.
Financial Institutions: Alerus Financial Credit Union, C-701-594-3347.
Clubs: J.R. Rockers. C-701-747-3392.
Places to Eat: Strike Zone Snack Bar, C-701-747-3050 and J.R. Rockers. C-701-747-3392 are on base. Airey Dining Facility is currently undergoing renovations for 2018. Exchange Food Court offers Burger King, Erbert and Gerbert's and Little Bangkok. Many restaurants within a short drive.
Bowling: Dakota Lanes, C-701-747-3050.
Fitness Center: Grand Forks FC, C-701-747-4738.
Golf: Plainsview Golf Course, C-701-747-4279.
ITT/ITR: C-701-747-3688.

Library: C-701-747-3046.
Military Museum: Air Park on base.
MWR: C-701-747-3283
MWR Website: http://www.forksupport.com/
MWR Facebook: https://www.facebook.com/319.FSS/
MWR Twitter: https://twitter.com/@319FSS
Outdoor Recreation: Outdoor Recreation Services, C-701-747-3688. Offers campers, camping gear, trailers, boats, canoes, kayaks, hunting and fishing gear, inflatables, outdoor sports rentals, ski equipment and much more.
Swimming: Indoor Pool, C-701-747-3305 offers open swim, lap swim and swim lessons.
Things To Do: Check out the Waterworld Water Slide Park in Grand Forks. Also visit the North Dakota Museum of Art, Center for Aerospace Sciences and Flood Memorial Monument. Canada is approximately 60 miles north of the base.
Walking Trails: Indoor running track at fitness center.

RV CAMPING & GETAWAYS

Grand Forks AFB FamCamp

Reservation/Contact Number Info: C-701-747-3688, DSN-312-362-3688.

Recreation Security: C-701-747-5351/5352. Emergencies dial 911.
RV Website: https://319fss.com/
GPS Coordinates:
47°58'6"N/97°22'40"W
Reservations: No advance reservations accepted. Office hours 0800-1700 Mon, 1000-1700 Tue-Thur, 0800-1800 Fri, 0700-1200 Sat. Closed Sundays and holidays. Check-in at Bldg 621. Alternate check-in: Fill out registration envelope available at Bathhouse and deposit with money in locked box. Check-out 1100 hours.
Season of Operation: 1 May-1 Oct, weather permitting.
Eligibility: AD, NG, Res, Ret, DoD-Civ, Dep, 100% DAV.
Camper/Trailer Spaces: Gravel (21), Back-in, Maximum 40' in length, E(30A/50A)/S/W, CATV hookups, picnic table, grill. Rates: $20 daily.
Tent Spaces: Grass (40): No hookups. Rates: $7 daily. Access to showers, laundry and Wi-Fi.
Support Facilities: Auto Craft Shop, Boat Rental, Bowling, Chapel, Commissary, Equipment Rental, Exchange, Fitness Center, Gas, Golf, Grills, Ice, Laundry, Pavilion, Picnic Area, Playground, Pool, Rec Center, Restrooms, RV Storage, Shoppette, Showers, Snack Bar, Sports Fields, Stables, Tennis Courts, Trails.
RV Storage: Yes. C-701-747-3688. Rates: $15 monthly, minimum two months.
Activities: Birdwatching, Boating (Nearby), Fishing (Nearby)*, Golfing, Hiking, Hunting (Waterfowl)*, Tennis. * State license required for patrons ages sixteen and up. Children younger than sixteen must be accompanied by an adult with a state license.
Credit Cards: MasterCard and Visa.
Restrictions: Pets allowed on leash. Firearms are prohibited in the FAMCAMP. For information on hunting and fishing contact the North Dakota Fish and Game Department in Bismarck at C-701-221-6300.
RV Driving Directions/Location: On Base. From I-29 at Grand Forks exit 141: Take US-2 14 miles west to County Road B-3 (Emerado/Air Base). Exit north on B-3 for one mile to Grand Forks AFB, located on the west side of B-3. The best entrance for motorhomes/coaches towing an auto, or for vehicles with fifth wheel or trailer, is through the South Gate (Cargo Gate). After entering through gate, stay straight on Eielson St to north end of base (approximately four miles) and bear right at end of road. FAMCAMP is straight ahead after one quarter mile or ask directions to FAMCAMP at gate.
Area Description: Located in an open area. Wide variety of recreational activities available. Two-hour drive to Canada. Full range of support facilities available on base.
RV Campground Physical Address: Outdoor Recreation, 784 Eielson Street, Bldg 621, Grand Forks Air Force Base, ND 58205-5000.

Minot Air Force Base

Address: 196 Missile Avenue, Minot AFB, ND 58705-5003.
Information Line: C-701-723-7979.
Main Base Police: C-701-723-3096. Emergencies dial 911.
Main Installation Website: http://www.minot.af.mil/
Main Base Location: Minot AFB is located in Ward County, 13 miles north of Minot, North Dakota and only 50 miles from the Canadian border.
Directions to Main Gate: From Minot on US-83 N travel approximately 13 miles then turn left onto Missile Ave to main gate.
NMC: Minot, 13 miles south.
NMI: Camp Grafton, 140 miles southeast.
Base Social Media/Facebook: https://www.facebook.com/minotaf
Base Social Media/Twitter: https://twitter.com/TeamMinot
Chapels: C-701-723-2456.
Dental Clinic: C-701-723-5565.
Medical: Appointment Line, C-701-723-5633, DSN-312-453-5633.
Veterinary Services: C-701-723-6449.
Beauty/Barber Shop: Barber, C-701-727-4868. Stylique, C-701-727-5545.
Commissary: C-701-723-4559.
Exchange: C-701-727-4973.

Exchange: C-701-727-4717.
Financial Institutions: Northern Tier Credit Union, C-701-727-6111. Wells Fargo Bank, C-701-857-1780.
Clubs: Rockers Bar and Grill, C-701-727-7625.
Places to Eat: B-50 Brew, C-701-727-4377; Dakota Inn; Fly By Inn; Kelley's Place, C-701- 727-4714; Rockers Bar and Grill, C-701-727-7625 and Rough Riders, C-701-727-4377 are on base. Exchange Food Court offers Charleys, Popeye's Chicken, Subway and Taco Bell. Burger King and Papa John's are also on base. Many restaurants within a short drive.
Bowling: Rough Rider Lanes, C-701-727-4715.
Fitness Center: McAdoo FC, C-701-723-2145.
Golf: Roughrider Golf Course, C-701-723-3164.
ITT/ITR: C-701-727-6669.
Library: C-701-723-3344.
Military Museum: Dakota Territory Air Museum, C-701-852-8500.
Military Museum Website: http://www.dakotaterritoryairmuseum.com/
MWR: C-701-723-6707.
MWR Website: http://5thforcesupport.com/
MWR Facebook: https://www.facebook.com/5thforcesupport
Outdoor Recreation: Outdoor Recreation, C-701-723-3648. Offers camping equipment rentals, archery ranges, paintball fields, playgrounds, boat rentals and more.
Swimming: Indoor Pool, C-701-723-3648 offers open swim and lap swim. Seasonal outdoor pool features a water slide and children's wading pool.
Things To Do: Visit General Custer's command post at Fort Lincoln State Park and the International Peace Garden on the Manitoba/North Dakota border or visit Roosevelt Park and enjoy the zoo, tennis courts and public pools.
Walking Trails: Indoor running track at fitness center.

RV CAMPING & GETAWAYS
Minot AFB FamCamp

Reservation/Contact Number Info: C-701-723-3648, DSN-312-453-3648. Fax C-701-723-4334.
Recreation Security: C-701-723-3096.
RV Website: http://5thforcesupport.com/activities/outdoor/
GPS Coordinates: 48°25'31"N/101°20'32"W
Reservations: No advance reservations. Availability first come, first serve basis. Prepayment required. Office hours 0800-1700 Mon; 1000-1700 Tue, Thur; 0800-1800 Fri; 1000-1400 Sat. Closed Wed, Sun.
Season of Operation: May-Oct.
Eligibility: AD, NG, Res, Ret, 100% DAV, DoD/NAF-Civ and family.
Camper/Trailer Spaces: RV Sites (6): E(30A)/W hookups, sewage dump on site. Rates: $15 daily, $90 weekly.
Support Facilities: Gas, Golf, Grills, Laundry, Mechanic/Auto Repair, Pavilions, Picnic Area, Playground, Pools (Indoor/Outdoor), Restrooms, Sewage Dump, Sports Fields, Stables, Track.
RV Storage: C-701-723-3648.
Activities: Archery, Boating, Fishing*, Golfing, Hiking, Horseback riding, Hunting*, Rock Climbing, Snow skiing, Swimming. *State license required. Contact Outdoor Recreation fro more information, C-701-723-3648.
Credit Cards: MasterCard and Visa.
Restrictions: Pets allowed on leash. Firearms are prohibited. For information on hunting and fishing contact North Dakota Fish and Game Department at C-701-328-6300.
RV Driving Directions/Location: On Base. From the Main Gate: Continue on Missile Ave to the end and take a left into FAMCAMP.
Area Description: Located in the north central area of North Dakota. Theodore Roosevelt National Park, North Dakota Badlands, and Fort Lincoln State Park nearby. Thirty-five miles to Canada. Full range of support facilities on base.

RV Campground Physical Address:
FamCamp/ODR, 146 Missile Avenue,
Minot AFB, ND 58705-5000.

OHIO

Camp Perry Training Site

Address: 1000 Lawrence Road, Port Clinton, OH 43452-9578.
Information Line: C-614-336-6245.
Main Base Police: Emergencies dial 911.
Main Installation Website:
http://www.ong.ohio.gov/campperry/
Main Base Location: On the southern shore of Lake Erie, at Port Clinton, Ohio.
Directions to Main Gate: From Cincinnati/Dayton: Take I-75 North toward Dayton for approximately 179 miles. Take exit 179/Napoleon/Fremont onto US-6 East toward Fremont. Continue to follow US-6 East for approximately 28 miles then take exit onto OH-53 North toward Port Clinton. Travel 13.1 miles and turn left to take ramp onto OH-2 West toward Toledo traveling 4.2 miles. Look for facility signs.
NMC: Toledo, 35 miles west.
NMI: Selfridge ANGB, MI, 65 miles northeast.
Chapels: C-614-336-6218.
Exchange: C-419-635-0101.
Places to Eat: Several restaurants within a short drive.
MWR: C-614-336-6213.
Outdoor Recreation: Troop Recreation Area, C-614-336-6213. Offers a park and pavilion. Call for more information.
Swimming: Beach swimming is available.
Things To Do: Camp Perry is situated along Lake Erie approximately 30 miles from the Canadian border. Limited support facilities available on post. Fishing/ license, swimming, fishing pier, grills, picnic area.

RV CAMPING & GETAWAYS

Camp Perry RV Park & Cottages

Reservation/Contact Number Info: C-1-888-889-7010, C-614-336-6214.
RV Website:
http://www.cplcc.com/rates.html
RV Email Address:
cplccinfo@gmail.com
Reservations: Reservations accepted. Cancellations must be made by 1500 hours day of arrival to avoid fee.
Season of Operation: Year-round. RV Park open May-Oct.
Eligibility: AD, Res, Ret with ID.
Camper/Trailer Spaces: RV Sites: Back-in sites only; full hookup sites with access to showers and bathrooms. Rates: $45 daily.
Tent Spaces: Primitive sites (10): No hookups. Access to bathhouse. Rates: $23.50 daily.
Yurt, A Frame, Cabin, Apt, Spaces: Cottages (27): Range from sleeping 4-9 persons. Fully furnished lakeside cottages with private baths, kitchens, linen exchange. No housekeeping services. Rates: $289 daily in season; $145 daily off season.
Support Facilities: Conference Center on site.
Credit Cards: American Express, Discover, MasterCard, and Visa.
Restrictions: Pets are prohibited.
RV Driving Directions/Location: On Base. From the Main Gate: Ask for directions at gate.
Area Description: Located on the Camp Perry Military Reservation, on the shores of Lake Erie, near Port Clinton, Ohio.
RV Campground Physical Address: 1000 Lawrence Rd, Bldg 600, Port Clinton, OH 43452.

Wright-Patterson Air Force Base

Address: 2000 Allbrook Drive, Wright-Patterson AFB, OH 45433-5315.
Information Line: C-937-257-1110.

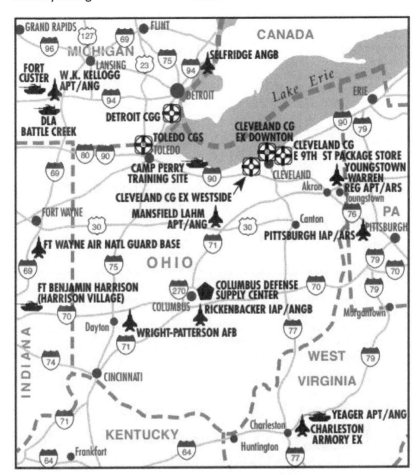

Main Base Police: C-937-904-2923. Emergencies dial 911.

Main Installation Website: http://www.wpafb.af.mil/

Main Base Location: Wright-Patterson AFB is located less than one mile from the city of Fairborn, Ohio, in Greene and Montgomery Counties and located six miles northeast of Dayton.

Directions to Main Gate: From Columbus: Take I-70W to exit 44/I-675 to Rt 444 exit. Turn right and proceed through town via Broad Street to Gate 1C. From Indianapolis, IN: Take I-70E to exit 44/I-675 to Rt 444 exit. Turn right and proceed through town via Broad Street to Gate 1C. From Cincinnati, OH: Take I-75 to I-675N to I-844 to WPAFB area A. Proceed straight to gate 26A.

NMC: Dayton, 10 miles southwest.

NMI: Columbus Defense Supply Center, 70 miles northeast.

Base Social Media/Facebook: https://www.facebook.com/WPAFB

Base Social Media/Twitter: https://twitter.com/WrightPattAFB

Dental Clinic: C-937-257-8761.

Medical: Appointment Line, C-937-522-2778. Information Line, C-937-257-0837.

Veterinary Services: C-937-257-6853.

Beauty/Barber Shop: Barber, C-937-879-5171; Stylique, C-937-879-5281. Barber, C-937-656-1746. Annex Barber, C-937-255-6038. Area B, C-937-255-5261. Hospital, C-937-257-7304. Bldg 262, C-937-257-7860.

Commissary: C-937-257-2060.

Exchange Gas: C-937-878-7985.
Exchange: C-937-879-5730.
Military Clothing: C-937-257-2800/6808.
Financial Institutions: Wright-Patt Credit Union: Area A, C-937-256-5470, Area B, C-937-256-2157, Kittyhawk, C-937-878-3077.
Clubs: Wings Grille & Lounge, C-937-522-2172.
Places to Eat: Canteen 10, C-937-255-3511; Java Street Cafe 1, C-937-257-6082; Java Cafe 2, C-937-522-2960; Mandarin Chef, C-937-257-2679; Sphinx Cafe, C-937-257-4417; Valkyrie Cafe, C-937-255-2735; Young's Cafe, C-937-257-4728 and Wings Grill, C-937-522-2172 are on base. Exchange Food Court offers Burger King and Charley's. Einstein Bros Bagels, Starbucks and Subway are also on base. Many restaurants within a short drive.
Bowling: Kittyhawk Lanes, C-937-257-7796.
Fitness Center: Dodge FC, C-937-257-4225. Jarvis FC, C-937-257-4469. Wright Field FC, C-937-255-1961. Health Club, C-937-257-4402.
Golf: Prairie Trace Golf Course, C-937-257-7961. Twin Base Golf Course, C-937-257-4130.
ITT/ITR: C-937-257-7670.
Library: C-937-257-4815.
Military Museum: National Museum of the USAF, C-937-255-3286.
Military Museum Website: http://www.nationalmuseum.af.mil/
MWR: C-937-257-8220.
MWR Website: http://www.88thfss.com/
MWR Facebook: https://www.facebook.com/88FSS
Outdoor Recreation: Outdoor Recreation Services, C-937-257-9889. Offers camping gear and campers, fishing boats, trailers, canoes, kayaks, aquatic recreation equipment, lawn and garden tools, sports equipment, carnival games, picnic and pavilion rentals and more.
Swimming: Dodge Indoor Pool, C-937-257-3044 offers lap swim, open swim and classes. Patterson Seasonal Pool, C-937-257-3764 offers open and lap swim.

The Prairies Seasonal Pool, C-937-255-8566 offers open and lap swim.
Things To Do: Visit the Air Force Museum on base, Carillon Historical Park, The Wright Cycle Company Complex, Sunwatch Indian Village, Paul Lawrence Dunbar House or one of the many parks and outdoor exploratory areas.
Walking Trails: Indoor and outdoor running tracks on base.

RV CAMPING & GETAWAYS
FamCamp at Bass Lake

Reservation/Contact Number Info: C-937-271-2535.
Recreation Security: C-937-257-6516.
RV Website: https://www.wrightpattfss.com/fun/famcamp
RV Email Address: campground@wpafb.af.mil
GPS Coordinates: 39°50'9"N/84°3'9"W
Reservations: Accepted up to six months in advance. Deposit of $25 due at reservation. Payment due in full upon arrival. Cancellations require notice to avoid fee. Office hours 1200-1700 daily. Check-in 1500 hours, check-out 1200 hours.
Season of Operation: Year-round.
Eligibility: AD, NG, Res, Ret, Dep and DoD-Civ.
Camper/Trailer Spaces: Hardstand (40), Back-in, limited pull-thru, E(110V/30/50A)/S/W hookups, picnic table. Rates: $25 daily. Partial (14): Hardstand, E(110V/30/50A)/W, dump station available, picnic table. Rates: $22 daily. Primitive overflow area available. Wi-Fi, laundry facilities and bathhouse available.
Tent Spaces: Primitive Sites: No hookups. Rates: $10 daily.
Support Facilities: Auto Craft Shop, Bathhouse, Boat Launch, Boat Rental/Storage, Bowling, Cafeteria, Chapel, Coin Laundry, Commissary, Community Center, Convenience Store, Equipment Rental, Exchange, Fire Rings, Fitness Center, Gas, Golf, Grills, Library, Mess Hall, Pavilion, Picnic Area, Playground, Pool, Rec Center, Post

Office, Rec Equipment, Restrooms, Sewage Dump, Showers, Tennis Courts, Wi-Fi.

RV Storage: C-937-257-9889.

Activities: Bicycling, Boating, Fishing*, Golfing, Jogging, Roller blading. *Base license required for patrons ages twelve and up. Children younger than sixteen must be accompanied by an adult with a state license.

Credit Cards: MasterCard and Visa.

Restrictions: Pets allowed on leash. Owner must clean up after pet and be in control of pet at all times. Firearms must be checked with Security.

RV Driving Directions/Location: On Base. From Gate 12A: Make the first left through gate. At the stop sign, go right onto Skeel Road. Remain on Skeel Road to Mitchell Rd, which becomes Loop Rd. Bass Lake signs visible. Go past the sign and FamCamp is just ahead.

Area Description: Home of world's largest and most complete military aviation museum and Wright Brothers Memorial. Full range of support facilities available on base.

RV Campground Physical Address: Bass Lake Campground, Area C, Wright-Patterson AFB, OH 45433-1234.

Youngstown Air Reserve Station

Address: 3976 King Graves Rd, Vienna, OH 44473.

Information Line: C-330-609-1000, DSN-312-346-1000.

Main Base Police: C-330-609-1299. Emergencies dial 911.

Main Installation Website: http://www.youngstown.afrc.af.mil/

Main Base Location: Located in northeast Ohio, in the Mahoning Valley area between Cleveland, Ohio and Pittsburgh, Pennsylvania. The Mahoning Valley area includes the area of Trumbull and Mahoning Counties, Ohio.

Directions to Main Gate: From OH-11: Take the exit for King Graves Road. Go east on King Graves Road, the ARS is on the right. Base is clearly marked.

NMC: Youngstown, 10 miles south.

NMI: Pittsburgh IA/ARS, 74 miles southeast.

Base Social Media/Facebook: https://www.facebook.com/YoungstownARS/

Base Social Media/Twitter: https://twitter.com/910AW

Chapels: C-330-609-1393.

Medical: C-330-609-1233.

Exchange: C-330-609-1395.

Clubs: Eagle's Nest Club, C-330-609-1139.

Places to Eat: Several restaurants within a short drive.

Fitness Center Phone Numbers: Sports and Fitness Center, C-330-609-1281.

Things To Do: Be sure to visit Six Flags Amusement Park. Downtown Youngstown is home to the Arms Family Museum, the Butler Institute of Art, the War Vet Museum and the Youngstown Symphony Orchestra. There are also several golf courses available in the area.

RV CAMPING & GETAWAYS

Youngstown ARS FamCamp

Reservation/Contact Number Info: C-330-609-1501.

Recreation Security: C-330-609-1117.

GPS Coordinates: 41°15'59N/80°40'12"W

Reservations: Reservations accepted via telephone 90 days in advance. Credit card required to hold reservation. Cancellations must be made 24-hours in advance of arrival to avoid fee or patrons will be charged one night's stay. Maximum length of stay is 180 days. Check in at at Fitness Center, Bldg 104. Check-in: 1300-1600 hours; Check-out: 1100 hours.

Season of Operation: Year-round.

Eligibility: AD, NG, Res, Ret and Dep.

Camper/Trailer Spaces: RV Sites (16): Full hookup (sites 1-5 50A) and partial with water and electric (sites 6-16 30A). Dump station on site. Rates: $10/$15 daily; $60/$95 weekly; $235/$375 monthly.

Support Facilities: Exchange, Fitness Center, Laundry Facilities, Pavilion, Restrooms, Running Track.

Activities: Enjoy on base amenities to include outdoor recreation rentals and events, pavilion, running track, and fitness center.

Credit Cards: Cash, Check, MasterCard and Visa.

Restrictions: Pets are limited to two. Quiet hours 2200-0800.

RV Driving Directions/Location: From Main Gate: Once through gate, take first left and follow road around to back side of base and take another left to FamCamp ahead on the left.

Area Description: Located on base adjacent to the Field House and running track. Youngstown is among the foothills of the Appalachian Mountains, along the Mahoning River. The Pennsylvania border is a short 10 miles to the east.

OKLAHOMA

Altus Air Force Base

Address: Falcon Road and N. Veterans Drive, Building 2000, Altus AFB, OK 73523-5000.

Information Line: C-580-482-8100, DSN-312-866-1110.

Main Base Police: C-580-481-7444. Emergencies dial 911.

Main Installation Website: http://www.altus.af.mil

Main Base Location: Altus OK is located in the southwest corner of Oklahoma at the intersection of US Highway 62 and State Highway 283.

Directions to Main Gate: From US-62 traveling west from Lawton: Make a right turn heading north on Veteran Drive in Altus. Stay in the right lane and follow the road to the Main Gate on Falcon Road.

NMC: Lawton, 56 miles east.

NMI: Fort Sill, 52 miles east.

Base Social Media/Facebook: https://www.facebook.com/97AMW

Base Social Media/Twitter: https://twitter.com/97AMW

Chapels: C-580-481-7485.

Dental Clinic: C-580-481-5235.

Medical: Appointment Line, C-580-481-5235, DSN-312-866-5235.

Beauty/Barber Shop: C-580-482-8221.

Commissary: C-580-481-6529.

Exchange Gas: C-580-482-8733.

Exchange: C-580-482-8733.

Financial Institutions: Federal Credit Unions, C-580-481-7148. NBC, Altus AFB Branch, C-580-477-1100, C-580-481-7722.

Clubs: Club Altus and May's Lounge, C-580-481-7034.

Places to Eat: Charlie's, C-580-481-6224; Club Altus, C-580-481-7034; Flight Kitchen, C-580-481-7220; Galaxy Grill, C-580-481-6420; Hangar 97, C-580-481-7881; May's Lounge, C-580-481-7034 and Wild Brew Yonder, C-580-481-7411 are on base. Many restaurants within a short drive.

Bowling: Galaxy Lanes, C-580-481-6704.

Fitness Center: Altus FC, C-580-481-7440.

Golf: Windy Trails Golf Course, C-580-481-7207.

ITT/ITR: C-580-481-6600.

Library: C-580-481-6302.

MWR: C-580-481-1310.

MWR Website: http://altusfss.com/

MWR Facebook: https://www.facebook.com/altusfss2

MWR Twitter: https://twitter.com/Altus_FSS

Outdoor Recreation: Outdoor Recreation Services, C-580-481-7696. Offers camping and off-road gear, boating equipment, party activities, bicycles, lawn and garden equipment, miniature golf and more.

Swimming: Seasonal Outdoor Pool, C-580-481-7696 offers open and recreational swim.

Things To Do: Visit the Museum of the Western Prairie for the saga of the area's wild west roots. Quartz Mountain State Park hosts the county fairs, rodeos and roundups that are part of everyday life here. Wichita Wildlife Refuge is a 40 minute drive.

RV CAMPING & GETAWAYS

Altus AFB FamCamp

Reservation/Contact Number Info: C-580-481-7696.

Recreation Security: C-580-481-7444.

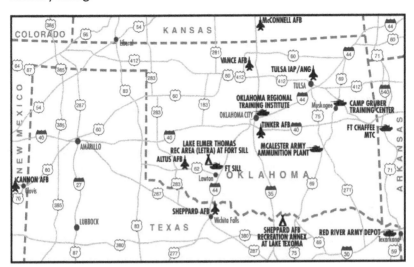

RV Website:
http://www.altusfss.com/odr/
GPS Coordinates:
34°38′45″N/99°17′2″W
Reservations: Accepted up to 30 days in advance. Office hours 1000-1700 Mon, Tue, Thur, Fri; 0800-1200 Sat. Closed Sun, Wed. Check-in at ODR Bldg 343 during hours of operation. Check-out 1200 hours.
Season of Operation: Year-round.
Eligibility: AD, NG, Res, Ret and DoD-Civ.
Camper/Trailer Spaces: Gravel (7), E(110V/30A)/S/W hookups. Rates: $17 daily.
Support Facilities: ATV Track, Auto Craft Shop, Boat Rentals, Bowling Alley, Cafeteria, Chapel, Family Bowling, Equipment Rentals, Fitness Center, Gas, Golf, Grills, Mess Hall, Paintball, Pavilion, Pay Phones, Picnic Area, Playground, Pool, Port-a-Potties, Recreation Center, Rec Equipment, Restrooms, RV Storage, Sewage Dump, Showers (At Gym), Snack Bar, Sports Fields, Swimming Pool (In Summer), Tennis Courts, Wood Hobby Shop.
RV Storage: C-580-481-7696.
Activities: Biking, Fishing*, Golfing, Hunting*, Jogging, Swimming, Tennis, Water Skiing. * State license required for patrons ages fourteen and up. Children younger than fourteen must be accompanied by an adult with a state license.
Credit Cards: American Express, MasterCard and Visa.
Restrictions: Pets allowed on leash. Signature required for action to be taken in event of severe weather.
RV Driving Directions/Location: On Base. From the Main Gate: Take the first right to the campground.
Area Description: Located in the southwest corner of Oklahoma along the Red River and near the Texas border.
RV Campground Physical Address: Altus FamCamp, Outdoor Recreation, Bldg 343, Altus AFB, OK 73523-5000.

Camp Gruber Training Center

Address: Camp Gruber Training Center, P.O. Box 29, Braggs, OK 74423.
Information Line: C-918-549-6001, DSN-312-628-6001.
Main Base Police: C-918-549-6021.
Main Installation Website:
http://ok.ng.mil/Pages/camp-gruber/default.aspx
Main Base Location: Eastern Oklahoma lying east of the Arkansas River and State Highway 10 in Muskogee and Cherokee counties.
Directions to Main Gate: From I-40 exit at Webber Falls/exit 287. Take Hwy 100

which merges into I-64 north to Gore, OK. Pass through town and take first left after First St. Take Hwy 10 northwest approximately 12 miles to Braggs. Pass through Braggs and the take second entrance into camp.

NMC: Muskogee, OK. 7 miles NW.
NMI: McAlester Army Ammunition Plant, 95 miles south west.
Base Social Media/Facebook: https://www.facebook.com/campgruber/
Chapels: Thunderbird Chapel on base.
Exchange: C-918-549-6284.
Places to Eat: Dining facility available on base, C-918-549-6126. Many restaurants within a short drive.
Fitness Center: Fitness Center on base.
Things To Do: The Muskogee area offers abundant outdoor recreation as well as diverse Native American cultural events, bull riding championships, a real WWII submarine and a Medieval castle, historical shopping districts and unique eateries.
Walking Trails: Two-mile running track on base.

RV CAMPING & GETAWAYS
Blackhawk RV Park

Reservation/Contact Number Info: C-918-549-6065/6060. Fax C-405-606-7656.
Recreation Security: C-918-549-6021.
RV Website: http://ok.ng.mil/Pages/camp-gruber/facilities/billeting.aspx
GPS Coordinates: 35°40'10"N/95°11'41"W
Reservations: Accepted by phone 0700-1600 hours Tues-Fri. Must have military ID. Open for check-in only when operating for training. Closed on some holidays.
Season of Operation: Dates vary.
Eligibility: AD, NG, Res, Ret, DoD-Civ, Dep and 100% DAV.
Camper/Trailer Spaces: Gravel (12): Back-in. Rates: $9 daily, $54 weekly, $189 monthly.
Support Facilities: Fitness Center, Shoppette, Sewage Dump.
Activities: Fishing*, Hunting*. *License required.

Credit Cards: MasterCard and Visa.
Restrictions: Pets must be on a leash.
RV Driving Directions/Location: On Base. From the second entrance into camp: Follow signs to billeting at check in at Bldg 117 on Rhineland Rd.
Area Description: Located in Braggs, near the Arkansas River.
RV Campground Physical Address: Mailing Address: Camp Gruber Billeting, P.O. Box 29, Braggs, OK 74423.

Fort Sill

Address: Fort Sill, B4700 Mow-Way Road, Fort Sill, OK 73503-5100.
Information Line: C-580-442-8111, DSN-312-639-7090.
Main Base Police: C-580-442-2101/2102. Emergencies dial 911.
Main Installation Website: http://sill-www.army.mil/
Main Base Location: Located in southwest Oklahoma, Comanche County, and adjacent to the city of Lawton.
Directions to Main Gate: From Oklahoma City Will Rogers World Airport: Exit the terminal building onto Meridian Road northbound. In approximately 1.5 miles, head east on Airport Road. At the intersection of I-44 and exit south on I-44 at MM 116. Portions are toll. Remain on I-44 for approximately 80 miles looking for the Key Gate sign and take that exit at MM41. Look for facility signs.
NMC: Lawton on the south boundary of Fort Sill. Oklahoma City, 75 miles northeast.
NMI: Altus AFB, 52 miles west.
Base Social Media/Facebook: https://www.facebook.com/FiresCenterofExcellence
Base Social Media/Twitter: https://twitter.com/FCoE_TeamSill
Chapels: Chaplain, C-580-442-3302.
Dental Clinic: Allen Dental Clinic, C-580-442-6106. Cowan Clinic, C-580-442-3143.
Medical: Appointment Line, C-580-558-2000. Information Desk, C-580-558-2800.
Veterinary Services: C-580-442-3416/4951.

Beauty/Barber Shop: Main Exchange Barber, C-580-353-5697; Stylique, C-580-353-6104. Quarry Hill Barber, C-580-353-8918. Family Hair Care C-580-353-5788.

Commissary: C-580-442-4515.

Exchange Gas: Fort Sill Express, C-580-357-0786. Sheridan Road Express, C-580-355-8106.

Exchange: C-580-351-0504.

Financial Institutions: Fort Sill Federal Credit Union, C-580-353-2124, C-800-654-9885. Fort Sill National Bank, C-800-749-4583, C-580-357-9880.

Clubs: Jack Daniel's Lounge, C-580-442-6595. Patriot Club, C-580-442-5300.

Places to Eat: Mulligans, C-580-442-5391 and Strike Zone, C-580-442-2882 are on base. Exchange Food Court offers Burger King, Charley's, Starbucks, Subway and Taco Bell. Sheridan Road Express offers Pizza Hut. Quarry Hill offers Subway. Popeye's is also on base. Many restaurants within a short drive.

Bowling: Twin Oaks Bowling Center, C-580-442-2882.

Fitness Center: FIRES FC, C-580-442-2445. Goldner FC, C-580-442-2740. Honeycutt FC, C-580-442-4670. Rinehart FC, C-580-442-6712/6652.

Golf: Fort Sill Golf Course, C-580-442-5493.

ITT/ITR: Adventure Travel, C-580-250-4040.

Library: Nye Library, C-580-442-2048/3806.

Military Museum: Fort Sill Museum, C-580-442-5123.

Military Museum Website: http://sill-www.army.mil/museum/FSNHLM/index.html

MWR: C-580-442-3113/6472.

MWR Website: https://sill.armymwr.com

MWR Facebook: https://www.facebook.com/FortSillMWR

MWR Twitter: https://twitter.com/Ft_Sill_MWR

Outdoor Recreation: Outdoor Adventure and Equipment Center, C-580-355-8270. Offers camping gear, fishing boats, inflatables, party supplies, sports equipment, park and pavilion rentals, and more.

Swimming: Rinehart Indoor Pool, C-580-442-6200/6175 offers lap swim, open swim and swim lessons. Quinette Seasonal Pool, C-580-442-6435 offers open and recreational swim. Seasonal Spray Park, C-580-442-4697 offers padded splash area. Swimming activities also available at LETRA.

Things To Do: Fort Sill offers plenty to keep you entertained. Check out the Fort Sill Golf Course, a parkland wooded course that is rare in southwest Oklahoma. Fort Sill Museum has 26 buildings filled with artifacts, insignia, flags and more. Enjoy the nearby restaurants, the movie theater and a bowling alley. Off-Post, Lawton is home to the historic Mattie Beal Home, Comanche National Museum and Museum of the Great Plains. Lake Elmer Thomas and the scenic Wichita Mountains Wildlife Refuge are nearby.

Walking Trails: Parks and recreation areas on or near the base are available.

RV CAMPING & GETAWAYS
Medicine Creek RV Park

Reservation/Contact Number Info: C-580-355-8270.

Recreation Security: C-580-442-2101/2102. Emergencies dial 911.

RV Website: https://sill.armymwr.com/programs/equipment-checkout-center

Other Info Website: http://www.adv-travel.com

GPS Coordinates: 34°40'59.7"N/98°24'09.9"W

Reservations: Reservations accepted any time and must be pre-paid. On-line reservations available at www.adv-travel.com. Office hours Mon/Tues/Fri 0900-1600 and Saturday 0800-1200. Closed Wed/Thurs/Sun and Holidays. Cancellations must be received three days prior to day or arrival to avoid one night's fee charge. Check-in 1200 hours; Check-out 1200 hours.

Season of Operation: Year-round.

Eligibility: AD, NG, Res, Ret and dependents.

Camper/Trailer Spaces: RV Sites (8): Shaded, full hookup sites (six sites 50

amp and two sites 30 amp), picnic table, BBQ. Rates: $17 daily. Primitive Sites (3): No hookups. Rates: $5 daily. Tent camping is not permitted.

Support Facilities: Full range of support facilities on base.

RV Storage: C-580-355-8270.

Activities: Creek fishing (seasonal) at RV Park.

Credit Cards: Cash, Check, MasterCard and Visa,

Restrictions: Pets are permitted but must be on leash. Quiet hours 2200-0600.

RV Driving Directions/Location: On Base. From Sheridan Road Gate: Continue on Sheridan Road and turn left onto NW Currie Rd. Continue approximately 1.5 miles. Facility ahead on the right.

Area Description: Quiet, shaded area on base with seasonally stocked fishing creek. Lake Elmer Thomas and the scenic Wichita Mountains Wildlife Refuge are nearby.

RV Campground Physical Address: Check-in: OAC, 2503 Ringgold Road, Fort Sill, OK 73503.

Lake Elmer Thomas Recreation Area (LETRA)

Address: 7463 Deer Creek Canyon Road, Fort Sill, OK 73503-0307.

Information Line: C-580-442-8111, DSN-312-639-7090.

Main Base Police: C-580-442-2426. Emergencies dial 911.

Main Installation Website: http://sill-www.army.mil/

Main Base Location: Located 12 miles NW of the main post, LETRA can be reached by registered vehicles using Apache Gate on Hwy 49 and all other by Sheridan Road Gate.

NMC: Lawton on the south boundary of Fort Sill. Oklahoma City, 75 miles northeast.

NMI: Fort Sill, 12 miles southwest.

Chapels: C-580-442-3319/3302.

Dental Clinic: C-580-442-6106.

Medical: C-580-558-2000, DSN-312-495-2800.

Veterinary Services: C-580-442-3340/3416/4951.

Commissary Phone Numbers: Approximately 9 miles to the commissary at Fort Sills, C-580-442-2305/3601.

Exchange Gas Phone Number: C-580-355-8106.

Exchange Main Phone Number: Approximately 9 miles to the Ft. Sill Post Exchange, C-580-351-0504.

Military Clothing: C-580-248-3802, C-580-442-5007.

Financial Institutions: Fort Sill Federal Credit Union, C-580-353-2124, C-1-800-654-9885. Fort Sill National Bank, C-1-800-749-4583, C-580-357-9880.

Clubs: Historic Patriot Club, C-580-442-5300 and Impact Zone Club, C-815-442-0023 are on Fort Sill.

Places to Eat: Mulligan's, C-580-442-5441, Java Cafe, C-580-442-6630 are on Fort Sill Base. Many restaurants within short drive.

Bowling: Twin Oaks Bowling Center, C-580-442-2882.

Fitness Center: Fort Sill, C-580-442-2740/0952.

Golf: Fort Sill Golf Course, C-580-442-5493.

ITT/ITR: C-580-250-4040.

Library: Fort Sill, C-580-442-3806.

Military Museum: Fort Sill FCOE Directorate of Museums and Military History. Fort Sill Museum. U.S. Army Air Defense Artillery Museum, C-580-442-0201/0267/5123/0374.

MWR: C-580-442-3001.

MWR Website: https://sill.armymwr.com/

MWR Facebook: https://www.facebook.com/FortSillMWR

MWR Twitter: https://twitter.com/Ft_Sill_MWR

Outdoor Recreation: RecPlex Fort Sill, C-580-355-8270. Offers tents, canoes, campers and camping supplies, moon bounces, carnival games, boats and more.

Swimming: Seasonal pool and waterslide, C-580-442-6200.

Things To Do: Fort Sill offers plenty to keep you entertained. Check out the Fort Sill Golf Course, a parkland wooded course that is rare in southwest Oklahoma. Fort Sill Museum has 26 buildings filled with artifacts, insignia, flags and more. Enjoy the nearby restaurants, the movie theater and a bowling alley. Off-Post, Lawton is home to the historic Mattie Beal Home, Comanche National Museum and Museum of the Great Plains. Lake Elmer Thomas and the scenic Wichita Mountains Wildlife Refuge are nearby.

RV CAMPING & GETAWAYS

LETRA

Reservation/Contact Number Info: C-580-442-5858/5854, DSN-639-5854/5858. Fax C-580-442-8184, DSN-312-639-8184.

Recreation Security: Emergencies dial 911.

RV Website: http://www.adv-travel.com/letra-cabins-reservations.html

Other Info Website: https://sill.armymwr.com/programs/letra

GPS Coordinates: 34°43'11"N/98°30'54"W

Reservations: Accepted two months in advance and must be prepaid. Online and telephone reservations accepted. Cancellations require three day notice without penalty. Office hours 0900-1800 hours Mon-Fri. Check-in 1500, check-out 1100 hours.

Season of Operation: Year-round.

Eligibility: AD, NG, Res, Ret, DoD-Civ (active & retired), Dep, 100% DAV, U.S. Govt Civ and General Public.

Camper/Trailer Spaces: Gravel (45): Pull-through, Maximum 45' in length, E(220V/30/50A)/S/W, cable and Internet hookups, picnic table and grill. Peak Season Rates: $25 daily; $115 weekly; $400 monthly.

Tent Spaces: Grass (15), no hookups. Picnic table and grill. $10 daily.

Yurt, A Frame, Cabin, Apt, Spaces: Cabins (10): One-bedroom (4), A/C, heat, alarm clock, CATV/DVD, cookware/utensils, hair dryer, kitchenette, microwave, refrigerator, Wi-Fi. Rates: $70 daily. Two-bedroom (3), A/C, heat, alarm clock, CATV/DVD,

cookware/utensils, hair dryer, kitchenette, microwave, refrigerator, Wi-Fi. Rates: $80 daily. Three-bedroom (3), A/C, heat, alarm clock, CATV/DVD, cookware/utensils, hair dryer, kitchenette, microwave, refrigerator, Wi-Fi. Rates: $90 daily.

Support Facilities: Auto Craft Shop, Bathhouse, Beach, Boat Launch, Boat Rentals, Bowling, Chapel, Coin Laundry, Commissary, Convenience Store, Diesel*, Equipment Rental, Exchange, Fishing Pier, Fitness Center, Gasoline, Golf, Grills, Ice, Marina, Mechanic/Auto Repair, Mess Hall, Picnic Area, Pavilions, Playgrounds, Pool, Propane*, Recreation Center, Restaurant, Restrooms, RV Storage, Sewage Dump, Shoppette, Showers, Snack Bar, Sports Fields, Tennis Courts, Trails. *Located off-installation.

RV Storage: Yes.

Activities: Archery, Fishing*, Hiking, Horse Shoes, Miniature Golf, Frisbee Golf, Paintball, Picnicking, Playgrounds, Swimming, Water Activities**, Water Slide**. * State license required for patrons ages sixteen and up. Children younger than sixteen must be accompanied by an adult with a state license. **May-Sep only.

Credit Cards: Cash, Check, MasterCard, Visa and Amex.

Restrictions: No pets in cabins. Pets allowed in RV area but must be on leash and owner must clean up after pets.

RV Driving Directions/Location: Off Base: Take I-44 north or south to exit 45. Turn left at Fort Sill Truck Entrance. Turn right on North Boundary Road. Drive approximately 8 miles and LETRA is on right. Check in at Country Store. OR From I-44: Take the Hwy 62/Rogers Lane exit and head West. Exit to the right on Sheridan Road northbound. Enter Fort Sill and turn left at Mow-Way Road (1st light). Turn right on Tower Two Road, being cautious of the water crossing. Go approximately four miles and turn left on North Boundary Road. Go another four miles and LETRA will be on the right.

Area Description: Located in the Wichita Mountains of southwestern

Oklahoma, the recreation area offers a 360-acre lake and a wildlife refuge in the Wichita Mountains.

RV Campground Physical Address: LETRA at Fort Sill, 7463 Deer Creek Canyon Road, Fort Sill, OK 73503-0307. Mailing Address: MWR, P.O. Box 33307, Fort Sill, OK 73503-0307.

McAlester Army Ammunition Plant

Address: McAlester Army Ammunition Plant, 1 C Tree Road, McAlester, OK 74501-9002.

Information Line: C-918-420-7200, DSN-312-956-7200.

Main Base Police: C-918-420-6642. Emergencies dial 911.

Main Installation Website: http://www.mcaap.army.mil/

Main Base Location: Located in Pittsburg County, Oklahoma a few miles outside of McAlester.

Directions to Main Gate: McAlester Army Ammunition Plant is located in Southeastern Oklahoma with Hwy 69 running north and south and US Highway 270 east and west. The Indian Nation Turnpike also serves the area and Interstate 40 is only 40 miles to the north.

NMC: Tulsa, 90 miles north.

NMI: Camp Gruber, 90 miles northeast.

Base Social Media/Facebook: https://www.facebook.com/MCAAP/

Medical: Health Clinic, C-.918-420-7496.

Exchange: C-918-320-6388.

Financial Institutions: McAlester Federal Credit Union, C-918-420-6377.

Places to Eat: Bullet Express Food Truck, C-918-420-6669; Landview Restaurant, C-918-420-6669 and Ruth's Snack Shack, C-918-420-7587 are on base. Many restaurants within a short drive.

Bowling: MCAAP Bowling Center, C-918-420-6673.

Fitness Center: Sports/Fitness Complex, C-918-420-7335.

ITT/ITR: C-918-420-6288/6780.

MWR: C-918-420-6780.

MWR Website: https://mcalester.armymwr.com/

MWR Facebook: https://www.facebook.com/MCAAPFMWR/

Outdoor Recreation: Equipment Issue Center, C-918-420-7484. Offers boat rental to include pontoons, motorboats, fishing boats, wave runners; water sport rental equipment, camping gear, outdoor sporting equipment and games, lawn and garden rentals, trailers and more.

Swimming: Summer Pool Passes available through the Fitness Center, C-918-420-7335.

Things To Do: Lake Eufaula, third largest artificial lake in the U.S., is a 30-minute drive away. Many other lakes are nearby for fishing and boating. Visit historic McAlester Scottish Rite Masonic Temple and the Oklahoma State Penitentiary Museum, which chronicles famous inmates, early chain gangs and prison escapes. The nearby town of Krebs is known as Oklahoma's Little Italy and is famous for its great cuisine.

Walking Trails: Walking track available at the Fitness Center.

RV CAMPING & GETAWAYS

Lakefront Cottages on Brown Lake

Reservation/Contact Number Info: C-918-420-7484.

Recreation Security: C-918-420-6642.

RV Website: https://mcalester.armymwr.com/programs/lake-front-cottages

GPS Coordinates: 34°50'02.1"N/95°52'38.0"W

Reservations: Accepted up to one year in advance. Reservations may be made by phone or in person 0630-1700 Mon-Wed, 0630-1730 Thurs, Thur, 0830-170 Fri, closed Sat-Sun. Deposit required for confirmed reservation. Cancellation must be made three weeks in advance to avoid cancellation fee. Check-in between 1400-1700 hours, check-out 1100 hours. Late arrivals must be arranged with office.

Season of Operation: Year-round.

Eligibility: AD, NG, Res, Ret and DoD-Civ.

Yurt, A Frame, Cabin, Apt, Spaces:
Cottages (11): One bedroom (3), two
bedroom (8) private bath, fully
furnished with microwave, refrigerator,
coffee maker, utensils, flat screen TV,
SAT TV, Wi-Fi, BBQ pits. Linens
provided. Rates: 1BR $65 daily; 2BR $70
daily.

Support Facilities: Bathhouse, Boat
Launch, Boat Rental, Bowling, Cafeteria,
Commissary, Exchange, Fishing Pier,
Fitness Center, Grills, Ice, Laundry,
Pavilions, Pay Phones, Picnic Area,
Playground, Pool, Rec Center, Rec
Equipment, Restrooms*, RV Storage,
Sewage Dump, Showers*, Snack Bar,
Sports Fields, Tennis Court, Trails. *
Handicap accessible.

Activities: Boating, Fishing*, Hiking.
*License required.

Credit Cards: MasterCard and Visa.

Restrictions: Pets are not permitted.
Water skiing is prohibited.

RV Driving Directions/Location: On
Base. From Tree Road Gate: Continue
straight ahead to check in with ODR,
Bldg 711 ahead on the left.

Area Description: Cottages are along
the shores of Brown Lake, providing a
tranquil and beautiful view.

RV Campground Physical Address: 1 C
Tree Road, Bldg 711, McAlester, OK
74501-5000.

Murphy's Meadow Campground

Reservation/Contact Number Info: C-
918-420-7484.
Recreation Security: C-918-420-6642.
RV Website:
https://mcalester.armymwr.com/progra
ms/murphys-meadow-camp-grounds
GPS Coordinates:
34°50'13.6"N/95°52'37.4"W
Reservations: Call ahead for availability
of campsites; very limited availability
Oct-Nov. All RV and tent sites are first
come, first served. Office hours 0630-
1700 Mon-Thur and 0830-1700 hours
Fri. A self-pay drop box is available for
after-hours arrivals.
Season of Operation: Year round. Oct-
Nov very limited availability.

Eligibility: AD, NG, Res, Ret and DoD-
Civ.

Camper/Trailer Spaces: Cement (17),
back-in, E(110V/30/50A)/S/W hookups.
Overflow, grass (34), back-in, E
(110V/30/50A)/W hookups. Rates: $14
daily.

Tent Spaces: Primitive, no hookups.
Rates: $7.50 daily.

Support Facilities: Bathhouse, Boat
Launch, Boat Rental, Bowling, Cafeteria,
Commissary, Exchange, Fishing Pier,
Fitness Center, Grills, Ice, Laundry,
Pavilions, Pay Phones, Picnic Area,
Playground, Pool, Rec Center, Rec
Equipment, Restrooms*, RV Storage,
Sewage Dump, Showers*, Snack Bar,
Sports Fields, Tennis Court, Trails. *
Handicap accessible.

Activities: Boating, Fishing*, Hiking.
*License required.

Credit Cards: MasterCard and Visa.

Restrictions: Pets must be on a leash.
No swimming. No water skiing.
Maximum stay of 30 days in, may return
after 5 days out.

RV Driving Directions/Location: On
Base. From C Tree Road Gate: Continue
straight ahead to check in with ODR,
Bldg 711 ahead on the left.

Area Description: Located in southeast
Oklahoma on the northwest edge of
Savanna, OK, on the shores of Brown
Lake. Mostly rolling pasture land with
timber-covered hills and creek bottoms.
Great area for vacationing; many lakes
offer fishing, boating and water sports.
A thirty-minute drive to Lake Eufaula,
the third largest artificial lake in the U.S.
Small community of Savanna,
approximately two miles away, provides
essentials not available on post. Limited
support facilities available on post
within walking distance of camp.

RV Campground Physical Address: 1 C
Tree Road, Bldg 711, McAlester, OK
74501-5000.

Tinker Air Force Base

Address: 6001 Arnold Street, Tinker
AFB, OK 73145-9011.

Information Line: Recording, C-405-
732-7321.

Main Base Police: C-405-734-2000/3737. Emergencies dial 911.
Main Installation Website: http://www.tinker.af.mil/
Main Base Location: Located in the "Heart of Oklahoma", just five miles from downtown Oklahoma City.
Directions to Main Gate: From Will Rogers IAP: Exit the airport going north on South Meridian Avenue. Take the I-44 exit, a right turn onto 152 E/Airport Rd to Downtown/Interstate 44. Get into the left hand lane and take I-44E/Interstate 40/Tulsa/Downtown exit and merge onto I-44. After approximately 3 miles, take exit 120B on the right for I-40 East toward Ft Smith. Travel approximately 10 miles and take exit 157B/Air Depot Blvd and turn right for facility ahead. Clearly marked.
NMC: Oklahoma City, 12 miles northwest.
NMI: Fort Sill, 95 miles southwest.
Base Social Media/Facebook: https://www.facebook.com/TinkerAirForceBase
Base Social Media/Twitter: https://twitter.com/Team_Tinker
Chapels: Chaplain, C-405-734-2111.
Dental Clinic: C-405-734-6474.
Medical: Appointment Line, C-405-734-2778.
Veterinary Services: C-405-734-5780.
Beauty/Barber Shop: Main Exchange Barber, C-405-732-5032; Stylique, C-405-737-6509. Express III, C-405-610-3651. Flightline, C-405-734-5969.
Commissary: C-405-734-5965.
Exchange Gas: Express I, C-405-734-7135. Express II, C-405-734-3686. Express III, C-405-733-4679.
Exchange: C-405-733-4561.
Military Clothing: C-405-734-5098.
Financial Institutions: First National Bank of Midwest City, C-405-739-8781. Tinker Federal Credit Union, C-405-732-0324.
Clubs: Tinker Club, C-405-734-3418.
Places to Eat: Cafe 3001, C-405-734-3161; Mulligan's Grill, C-405-734-2909; Pin Deck Snack Bar, C-405-734-3484 and Vanwey DFAC, C-405-734-2918 are on base. Exchange Food Court offers

Charley's, Popeye's, Starbucks, Subway and Taco Bell. Burger King and Domino's Pizza are also on base. Many restaurants within a short drive.
Bowling: Tinker Lanes, C-405-734-3484.
Fitness Center: Annex, C-405-734-2163. Gerrity FC, C-405-734-5607. Tinker FC, C-405-734-4664. Health & Wellness Center, C-405-734-6575.
Golf: Tinker Golf Course, C-405-734-2909.
ITT/ITR: C-405-734-3791.
Library: C-405-734-2626.
Military Museum: Charles B Hall Airpark is on base.
Military Museum Website: http://www.tinker.af.mil/About-Us/Charles-B-Hall-Air-Park/
MWR: C-405-734-2077.
MWR Website: http://tinkerliving.com/
MWR Facebook: https://www.facebook.com/TinkerLiving/
MWR Twitter: https://twitter.com/TinkerLiving
Outdoor Recreation: Outdoor Recreation Services, C-405-734-5875. Offers fishing and camping gear, canoes, kayaks, lawn and garden tools, home improvement tools, sporting equipment, inflatables, party supplies and more.
Swimming: Seasonal Outdoor Pool, C-405-734-9736/5875 offers open and recreational swim.
Things To Do: In Oklahoma City visit Remington Park, Frontier City Amusement Park, the National Cowboy Hall of Fame and Western Heritage Center, the city zoo and tour the mansions of Heritage Hills. Five municipal golf courses, four lakes and many sports events are available.
Walking Trails: Tinker Trails are on base.

RV CAMPING & GETAWAYS
Tinker AFB FamCamp
Reservation/Contact Number Info: C-405-734-2847/5875.
Recreation Security: C-405-734-3737. Emergencies dial 911.
RV Website: https://tinkerliving.com/famcamp/

GPS Coordinates:
35°24'24"N/97°23'58"W

Reservations: No advance reservations. Check-in no later than 2100 hours unless prior arrangements have been made with camp host.

Season of Operation: Year-round.

Eligibility: AD, NG, Res, Ret and DoD-Civ.

Camper/Trailer Spaces: Hardstand (29): Back-in, Maximum 45' in length, E(110/220V/30/50A)/S/W hookups. Rates: $20 daily.

Tent Spaces: Overflow and Tent Sites: No hookups. Rates: $5 daily.

Support Facilities: Chapel, Gas, Golf, Laundry, Picnic Areas, Playgrounds, Restrooms, Sewage Dump, Showers*. * Handicap accessible.

RV Storage: None.

Activities: Fishing*, Golfing. *State and base licenses required for patrons ages sixteen and up. Children younger than sixteen must be accompanied by an adult with a state license.

Credit Cards: MasterCard and Visa.

Restrictions: Pets allowed on leash. Owner must clean up after pet. No firearms allowed. No swimming or boating in ponds.

RV Driving Directions/Location: On Base. From I-240: Take exit 9 to 74th Street and turn right. Travel to Midwest Blvd and turn left to 24/7 Piazza Gate ahead. Please note that the preferred entrance is the Piazza Gate and that other gates may be difficult to maneuver. *Due to construction on the truck gate ALL RV's must enter the installation through the Piazza gate.

Area Description: Located in the midst of Oklahoma City/Midwest City metropolitan area. FAMCAMP is situated in well-developed recreation area offering two fishing ponds. Full range of support facilities available on base.

RV Campground Physical Address: Physical: Patrol Road, Tinker AFB, OK 73145. Mailing Address: Outdoor Recreation, 72nd MSG/SVRO, Bldg 478, Tinker AFB, OK 73145-8101.

OREGON

Camp Rilea Armed Forces Training Center

Address: 33168 Patriot Way, Warrenton, OR 97146.

Information Line: C-503-836-4052.

Main Base Police: Emergencies dial 911.

Main Installation Website: http://www.oregon.gov/OMD/OTC/CampRilea/Pages/home.aspx

Main Base Location: Located off Highway 101 between Astoria and Seaside near the mouth of the Columbia River.

Directions to Main Gate: From Portland: Take US-26 northwest for approximately 65 miles to Oregon Coast. At US-101, proceed north 12 miles. Look for signs off Hwy 101.

NMC: Astoria, 5 miles north.

NMI: Fort Lewis WA, 140 miles NW.

Exchange: C-503-861-3623.

Places to Eat: Many restaurants within a short drive.

Outdoor Recreation: Camp Rilea MWR Services, C-503-836-4052. Offers various rentals including sports equipment, boats, canoes, fishing gear and more.

Things To Do: While here, visit the many National Forests and State Parks that dot the coastline and state. Golf Courses, cheese, wine and food tours, hiking trails, and scenic trips are some of the many activities to enjoy. This is a gorgeous area.

RV CAMPING & GETAWAYS

Camp Rilea Campground & Cabins

Reservation/Contact Number Info: C-503-836-4052.

Recreation Security: Emergencies dial 911.

RV Website: http://www.oregon.gov/OMD/OTC/CampRilea/logistics/Pages/Lodging.aspx

Reservations: Accepted 90 days in advance. Fifteen day maximum stay.

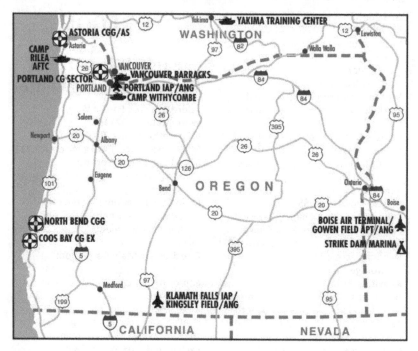

Season of Operation: Year-round.
Eligibility: AD, NG, Res, Ret.
Camper/Trailer Spaces: RV Sites (10), full hookups, CATV. Partial (8), with electric only. Rates: $15 daily.
Tent Spaces: Primitive (3): Fire ring. Rates: $10 daily.
Yurt, A Frame, Cabin, Apt, Spaces: Cabins (2): sleep 4, two-bedroom with one queen bed, two twins, TV/DVD player and VCR. Small kitchen with one full bath. Rates: From $50 per person. Cottages (3): One, two and four-bedrooms with bath, kitchen and living area. Rates: From $50 per person. Linens provided. Huts (13): Ten 1/2 huts and three full; bunks, partial baths, some huts may have microwave and mini-fridge but not guaranteed. Additional bunks and barrack style facilities available. No linens. Rates: $10-$15 daily. Chateau and Hilltop Cottages rate restricted.
Support Facilities: Shoppette.
Activities: Basketball, Beach, Gymnasium, Volleyball, Outdoor Activities, Trails.

Restrictions: Quiet hours 2200-0600. Beach access via Sunset Beach Access, approximately one mile drive away.
RV Driving Directions/Location: On Base. From the Main Gate: Ask for directions.
Area Description: Near the mouth of the Columbia River with great fly fishing, mountain views and outdoor enthusiast activities.
RV Campground Physical Address: Camp Rilea Billeting, Bldg 7400, 91372 Rilea Pacific Road, Warrenton, OR 97146-9711.

Klamath Falls Air National Guard

Address: 211 Arnold Ave, Klamath Falls, OR 97603-0400.
Information Line: C-541-885-6350.
Main Base Police: Emergencies dial 911.
Main Installation Website: http://www.173fw.ang.af.mil/
Main Base Location: Located in Klamath Falls, OR at the southern tip of the Upper Klamath Lake.
Directions to Main Gate: Take I-5 through Medford to OR-140 east. Go 75

miles to Southside Bypass. Go east 4.5 miles to the airport. West of OR-39 and east of US-97, adjacent to Klamath Falls IAP.

NMC: Medford, 80 miles west.

NMI: North Bend CGG, 245 miles northwest.

Base Social Media/Facebook: https://www.facebook.com/173FW

Base Social Media/Twitter: https://twitter.com/173rdfw

Chapels: C-541-885-6239.

Medical: C-541-885-6312.

Beauty/Barber Shop: On base.

Exchange: C-541-885-6371.

Places to Eat: Dining facility on base. Many restaurants within a short drive.

Fitness Center: C-541-885-6141.

Things To Do: Experience top-notch fishing, world class skiing, golf, horseback riding, camping and hunting. Both Crater Lake and Mt. Shasta are nearby.

RV CAMPING & GETAWAYS

Kingsley Campground

Reservation/Contact Number Info: C-541-885-6604, DSN-312-830-6604.

Recreation Security: C-514-885-6663.

RV Website: https://www.armymwr.com/programs-and-services/outdoor-recreation-camping-rv-parks/oregon#Kingsley

GPS Coordinates: 42°9'50"N/121°44'55"W

Reservations: No advance reservations; first come first served. Office hours 0700-1600 Mon-Fri, payment envelopes and rules can be received from the Main Gate. Payment drop box is located in the Main Gate.

Season of Operation: Year-round.

Eligibility: AD, Res, Ret, 100% DAV and DoD-Civ.

Camper/Trailer Spaces: Asphalt (5), Back-in, E/W hookups. Rates: $15 daily, $85 weekly.

Support Facilities: Fitness Center, Picnic Area, Restrooms, Sewage Dump, Showers.

Activities: Volleyball.

Credit Cards: Cash, Check.

Restrictions: Do not park, camp or erect tents on grass. Children under 12 years of age must be supervised at all times. No one under the age of 16 may use the gym facilities without adult supervision. Helmets required when bicycling. Pets must be leashed at all times and not be left unattended. Owners must clean up after pet immediately. No more than two pets allowed. No clotheslines or outside storage. No open fires. Charcoal fires in personal grill only. Picnic table must be cleaned after use. No RV or car washing allowed. Please ensure RV dump station is cleaned after each use. Do not use gym trash cans.

RV Driving Directions/Location: On Base. Take I-5 to OR-140 east, approximately 75 miles to southside bypass. Go east approximately 4.5 miles to the airport.

Area Description: Excellent fishing, skiing, horseback riding and hunting right off post. Both Mt. Shasta and Crater Lake are within an hour's drive. Small BX and clinic located on base.

RV Campground Physical Address: Kingsley Social Club, Attn: Campground, 211 Arnold Ave, Suite 43, Klamath Falls, OR 97603-0400.

PUERTO RICO

Borinquen Coast Guard Air Station

Address: USCG Air Station Borinquen, 260 Guard Road, Aguadilla, PR 00603.

Information Line: C-787-890-8400.

Main Base Police: C-787-890-8472. Emergencies dial 911.

Main Installation Website: http://www.uscg.mil/d7/airstaborinquen/

Main Base Location: This facility is located on the old Ramey Air Force Base, north of Aguadilla.

Directions to Main Gate: Take PR-22 west from San Juan or from Mayaguez to PR-107 north of CGAS. Main Gate is at the end of Wing Road, just past Fifth Street.

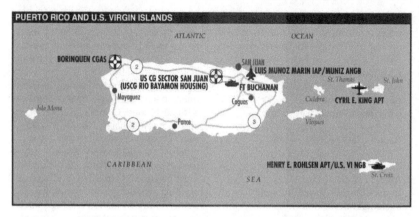

PUERTO RICO AND U.S. VIRGIN ISLANDS

NMC: San Juan, 65 miles east.
NMI: Fort Buchanan, 75 miles east.
Dental Clinic: C-787-890-8477 ext 8482.
Medical: C-787-890-8477.
Exchange Gas: C-787-890-7272.
Exchange: C-787-890-7272.
Clubs: Coast Guard Club W-F with limited hours, C-787-890-8490.
Places to Eat: Ramey Pizza, C-787-890-5544 are within walking distance. The Eclipse, C-787890-0275, Golden Crown, C-787-890-5077, McDonald's and Wendy's are within driving distance.
Fitness Center: Fitness Center is available on base.
Golf: Punta Borinquen Golf Club, C-787-890-2987. Located on military property.
MWR: C-787-890-8400 ext. 8894/8895.
MWR Website:
http://www.uscg.mil/d7/airstaborinquen/MWR/General_Information.asp
Outdoor Recreation: Recreational Gear Locker, C-787-890-8400 ext 8894. Offers various rental equipment. Located in front of the La Plaza complex, the basketball court, and tennis courts are available year round. Tennis courts are lighted and can be used both day and night.
Swimming: An outdoor swimming pool with slides are available on base, C-787-890-8496. Ocean swimming is also available.
Things To Do: There is a theater, swimming pool, picnic areas, several beaches in the surrounding area. Water sports, golf, and horseback riding are nearby.

RV CAMPING & GETAWAYS
Borinquen Recreation Cottages

Reservation/Contact Number Info: C-787-890-8492. Fax C-787-890-8493.
Recreation Security: C-787-890-8472.
RV Website:
https://www.atlanticarea.uscg.mil/Our-Organization/District-7/Units/Air-Station-Borinquen/Departments/MWR/Guest-Housing/
Other Info Website:
https://www.dcms.uscg.mil/Our-Organization/Assistant-Commandant-for-Human-Resources-CG-1/Community-Services-Command-CSC/MWR/Coast-Guard-Lodging/
RV Email Address:
MWRGuestHousing@gmail.com
GPS Coordinates:
18°29'53"N/67°7'57"W
Reservations: Required. Telephone for reservations up to 60 days in advance for AD, up to 45 days in advance for all others. PCS personnel have priority upon receipt of orders. Maximum stay 14 days without orders. Credit card deposit required. Office hours 0930-1600 Mon-Fri.
Season of Operation: Year-round.
Eligibility: AD, NG, Res, Ret, DoD/DHS-Civ and Dep.
Yurt, A Frame, Cabin, Apt, Spaces:
Lighthouse Apartments: Two-bedroom (2), furnished, microwave, A/C, CATV,

housekeeping service. Rates: $155 daily. Guesthouses (33) Three-bedroom standard, furnished, microwave, A/C, CATV, housekeeping service. Rates: $85-$105 daily, maximum of six. Pool Front three bedroom guest house. Rates: $100-$120 daily. Deluxe Guesthouses: Three-bedroom (6), furnished, microwave, A/C, CATV, VCR, housekeeping service. Rates: $110-$130 daily, maximum of six. Three bedroom, two bathroom house. Rates: $139 daily. Four bedroom house, sleeps 8. Rates: $155 daily. Cliff 19 Single Rooms (5): House with five-bedrooms, each with private bath, shared common areas. Rates: $50-$60 daily.

Support Facilities: Beach, Chapel, Convenience Store*, Fitness Center, Golf*, Laundry, Pavilion, Picnic Area, Playground, Pool, Rec Equipment, Tennis courts*. *Off base.

Activities: Fishing, Golfing, Scuba Diving, Sightseeing, Snorkeling, Surfing, Swimming.

Credit Cards: Discover, MasterCard and Visa.

Restrictions: No pets allowed.

RV Driving Directions/Location: On Base. At the Borinquen Coast Guard Station (on the old Ramey Air Force Base), north of Aguadilla. From San Juan: Take PR-22 west to PR-2 west to Aguadilla. Turn right (north) on PR-110. At the end of road turn right, make the second left, then first right again. Turn right in front of Banco Popular. This goes to the Main Gate at the end of Wing Road, just past 5th Street. North From Mayaguez, take PR-2 to left (north) on PR-107. Follow above directions.

Area Description: The recreation area is located in western Puerto Rico on a high cliff overlooking the Caribbean, the perfect setting for beautiful sunsets and whale watching. The converted lighthouse has two apartments which reflect the tropical flavor of the area. Additional recreation cottages are located within the CG housing area. Temperatures range from 70-85°F and humidity is usually low due to a steady easterly breeze. Limited support facilities available on base approximately two miles from the lighthouse.

RV Campground Physical Address: MWR Guesthouse, 260 Guard Road, Aguadilla, PR 00604-5000.

RHODE ISLAND

Carr Point RV Park

Address: Carr Point Cottages & RV Park, Burma Rd/Defense Hwy, Newport, RI 02841.

Information Line: C-401-841-2311, DSN-312-948-2311.

Main Base Police: C-401-841-4041. Emergencies dial 911.

Main Installation Website: http://www.cnic.navy.mil/regions/cnrma/installations/ns_newport.html

Main Base Location: Located on Naragansett Bay approximately four miles north of NNS.

NMC: Newport, adjacent.

NMI: Newport Naval Station, six miles south.

Commissary: Approximately 6 miles to commissary at Newport NS, C-401-841-2111/2112.

Exchange: Approximately 6 miles to Navy Exchange at Newport NS, C-401-841-1399.

ITT/ITR: C-401-841-3116.

MWR: C-401-841-2643/3855, Liberty Ctr: C-401-841-3054; MWR Special Events: C-401-841-3127.

MWR Website: http://www.navymwrnewport.com/

MWR Facebook: https://www.facebook.com/navstanewportmwr/

MWR Twitter: https://twitter.com/NAVSTANPTRIMWR?lang=en

Outdoor Recreation: NS Newport Outdoor Recreation, C-401-841-2568. Offers sporting, camping and party equipment, canoes, kayaks, lawn and garden equipment and winter sport gear.

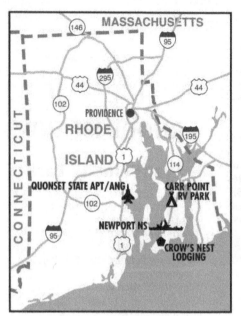

Things To Do: Located on Naragansett Bay approximately four miles from Newport Naval Station. Home of the Newport Jazz Festival, Ben & Jerry's Folk Festival, International Boat Shows and famous Newport mansions. Great public beaches and seafood restaurants nearby. Limited support facilities available on base.

RV CAMPING & GETAWAYS

Carr Point RV Park

Reservation/Contact Number Info: C-401-841-3283.
Recreation Security: C-401-841-4041.
RV Website:
http://get.dodlodging.net/propertys/Carr-Point-RV-Park
Other Info Website:
http://www.navymwrnewport.com/programs/28fabad3-c7f9-4bc1-bdca-467c94a79096
RV Email Address:
NAVSTANewportRIMWR@gmail.com
GPS Coordinates:
41°34'2"N/71°17'41"W
Reservations: Reservations accepted beginning in April. Full payment required at time of reservation. No

refunds for cancellations. Office hours 0930-1530 Tues-Fri. Check-in at campground 1300 hours or later. Check-out 1100. Fourteen day maximum stay. **Season of Operation:** Memorial Day-31 October.
Eligibility: AD, NG, Res, Ret, DoD-Civ, Dep and 100% DAV.
Camper/Trailer Spaces: Gravel (6): Back-in, maximum length 60', E(110V/30A/50A)/W hookups. Picnic table. Rates: $25.50 daily military; $30.50 daily DoD. Water view and partial water view sites.
Support Facilities: Available on base. Auto Shop, Boat Launch, Boat Rental/Storage, Bowling, Cafeteria, Chapel, Commissary, Convenience Store, Equipment Rental, Exchange, Fitness Center, Gasoline, Marina, Mess Hall, Pool, Rec Center, RV Storage, Sports Fields, Tennis Courts. No restroom facilities at park. Restroom/Shower facilities located on base. Private pump station located nearby. $10 dump fee. Note: To reserve pavilion/picnic sites, please call Officers' Club at C-401-841-1442.
RV Storage: Yes. C-401-841-4293.
Activities: Boating, Fishing, Golfing, Picnic, and Swimming available in the area.
Credit Cards: MasterCard and Visa.
Restrictions: Pets must be on leash at all times and must not disturb other campers. Two-week maximum visit.
RV Driving Directions/Location: Off Base. From north and east, take RI-24 to RI-114. After about 1.7 miles take right onto Stringham Road and follow road down the hill. At the foot of the hill, make a sharp left onto Burma Road (or Defense Hwy) and follow 1.5 miles to RV park on the right. From south and west: Take I-95 to RI-138 east, over Jamestown and Newport bridges. Follow signs to Fall River, Cape Cod. Coming off the exit, bear right just before the stop light and go to Rotary. Take right at Rotary and follow the road to the end. Take left onto RI-114 north

to third stop light and turn left onto Access Road. Follow the road for four miles to the facility. Clearly marked.

Area Description: Located on Naragansett Bay approximately four miles from Newport Naval Station. Home of the Newport Jazz Festival, Ben & Jerry's Folk Festival, International Boat Shows and famous Newport mansions. Great public beaches and seafood restaurants nearby. Limited support facilities available on base

RV Campground Physical Address: Mailing Address: GOTickets, Morale, Welfare & Recreation, 656 Whipple Street, Newport, RI 02841.

SOUTH CAROLINA

Charleston Air Force Base

Address: 104 E Simpson Street, Bldg 500, JB Charleston, SC 29404.

Information Line: C-843-963-1110, DSN-312-673-1110.

Main Base Police: C- C-843-963-3600. Emergencies dial 911.

Main Installation Website: http://www.charleston.af.mil/

Main Base Location: Located about 10 miles from downtown Charleston, South Carolina, on approximately 3,400 acres of land within the North Charleston city limits in Charleston County in the heart of the historic Lowcountry in SC.

Directions to Main Gate: From I-95: Take I-26 east to Ashley Phosphate Road/exit 209 A. Turn right onto Ashley Phosphate Road then turn left onto Cross County Road traveling 2.2 miles then turn left onto Dorchester Road. Travel short distance and make a left on W Hill Blvd. Facility ahead.

NMC: Charleston, 10 miles southeast.

NMI: Beaufort MCAS, 70 miles southwest.

Base Social Media/Facebook: https://www.facebook.com/TeamCharleston/

Base Social Media/Twitter: https://twitter.com/TeamCharleston

Chapels: Chaplain, C-843-963-2536.

Dental Clinic: C-843-963-6675.

Medical: Appointment Line, C-843-963-6880.

Veterinary Services: C-843-963-1838.

Beauty/Barber Shop: C-843-552-4880. Stylique, C-843-552-0812.

Commissary: C-843-963-7469.

Exchange Gas: C-843-760-1557.

Exchange: C-843-552-5000.

Financial Institutions: Bank of America Military Branch, C-843-720-4880. Heritage Trust FCU, C-843-832-2600. Wire: Bldg 306, Hours: 0900-1600 Mon-Fri, C-843-963-2370 (Western Union in town).

Clubs: Charleston Club, C-843-963-3914.

Places to Eat: Gaylor DFAC, C-843-963-3590*; Flight Kitchen, C-843-963-3103; Globemaster Grill, C-843-963-1840; Rookie's Sports Grill, C-843-963-3922; Starbucks and Lowcountry Cafe, C-843-963-3921; and Starlifter Grill, C-843-963-3315/3316 are on base. Exchange Food Court offers Burger King, Charley's and Subway. Many restaurants are within a short drive. *Currently closed for 2017 for renovations.

Bowling: Starlifter Bowling Center, C-843-963-3315.

Fitness Center: Air Base Fitness, C-843-963-3347.

Golf: Wrenwoods Golf Course, C-843-963-1833/1834.

ITT/ITR: C-843-963-1732/1672.

Library: AB Main, C-843-963-3320.

MWR: C-843-963-3800/3809.

MWR Website: https://www.jbcharleston.com/

MWR Facebook: https://www.facebook.com/jbcharlestonfss/

MWR Twitter: https://twitter.com/628FSS

Outdoor Recreation: Outdoor Recreation Center, C-843-963-1672/1732. Offers guided tours, sports equipment rentals, outdoor party equipment, bicycles, games, boat rentals and more.

Swimming: Seasonal Outdoor Pool, C-843- 963-3344/1672 offers lap and recreational swim.

Things To Do: Visit stately old mansions along the Battery and Boone Hall. Scenes from "Gone With the Wind" and "North and South" were filmed in this area. Take a water tour and visit historic Fort Sumter in the Charleston Harbor.

Walking Trails: Hiking, walking and jogging trails are available on base.

RV CAMPING & GETAWAYS

JB Charleston Lowcountry FamCamp

Reservation/Contact Number Info: C-843-963-1672/1732.

Recreation Security: C-843-963-6000. Emergencies dial 911.

RV Website:
https://www.jbcharleston.com/
Other Info Website:
https://www.jbcharlestonorc.com/
GPS Coordinates:
32°54'29"N/80°03'45"W

Reservations: Reservations accepted. Office hours 0900-1700 Mon-Fri. Late arrivals check in with Camp Host at Site 5 or 11. Check-in 1500 hours, check-out 1200 hours. Maximum stay for Ashley and Cooper Areas 14 days.

Season of Operation: Year-round.

Eligibility: AD, NG, Res, Ret, Dep and DoD-Civ.

Camper/Trailer Spaces: RV Sites (43): E(120V/50A)/W/S hookups, maximum 50' in length. Handicap accessible. Rates: $23 daily for Ashley and Cooper Area, $540 monthly for Moutrie Area.

Tent Spaces: Overflow Sites: Access to water, electric and dump stations. picnic table. Rates: $18 daily.

Support Facilities: Auto Craft Shop, Auto Repair, Bathhouse, Beach, Boat Rental, Bowling, Chapel, Coin Laundry, Commissary, Equipment Rental, Exchange, Fitness Center, Gasoline, Golf, Grills, Ice, Mess Hall, Pavilions, Picnic Area, Playground, Pool*, Propane (Off Site), Rec Center, Restrooms**, RV Storage, Sewage Dump, Shoppette,

Showers, Snack Bar, Sports Fields, Tennis Courts, Trails. *On base, open May-Aug. **Handicap accessible.

RV Storage: C-843-963-1672/1732.

Activities: Bowling, Golfing, ITT office (tickets for Historic Charleston), Swimming, Walking/Running, Skeet & Trap Range.

Credit Cards: MasterCard and Visa.

Restrictions: Pets allowed on leash. No open fires. Quiet hours 2200-0700. Children under 13 should be escorted to bathhouse.

RV Driving Directions/Location: On Base. From the Back Gate: Turn right immediately after crossing train tracks onto South Aviation Ave. Continue to follow South Aviation Ave which turns into Arthur Ave around the runway. Turn right on Eutaw Circle. Facility ahead.

Area Description: Situated near a wooded picnic area, FAMCAMP is just fifteen minutes away from Charleston, one of the country's most picturesque and historic seaport cities. Full range of support facilities available on base. Formerly called Shady Oaks Family Campground.

RV Campground Physical Address: Outdoor Recreation Center, 101 Scarton Lane, Bldg 647, JB Charleston, SC 29404-5000.

Charleston Naval Weapons Station

Address: 2316 Red Bank Road, Goose Creek, SC 29445.

Information Line: C-843-764-7000, DSN-312-794-7000. JB, C-843-963-1110.

Main Base Police: C-843-794-7777. Emergencies dial 911.

Main Installation Website:
http://www.charleston.af.mil/

Main Base Location: Located about 10 miles from downtown Charleston in North Charleston. The Naval Weapons Station is about 8 miles from the AB in Goose Creek. Both are located in the heart of the Lowcountry.

Directions to Main Gate: From the north or south: Exit I-95 to I-26 east. Travel east for two miles staying left at the fork and traveling another two miles

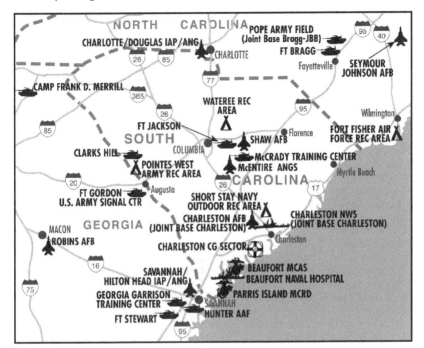

through a traffic light. Turn right onto Redbank Road at the next light. Base is three miles ahead. From Points West: Exit I-26 to Hwy 78/exit 205. Travel east for two miles. Follow remaining directions above.

NMC: Charleston, 10 miles south.
NMI: Beaufort MCAS, 75 miles southwest.
Base Social Media/Facebook:
https://www.facebook.com/TeamCharleston
Base Social Media/Twitter:
https://twitter.com/TeamCharleston
Chapels: Chaplain, C-843-794-7207. All Saints, C-843-794-7222. Good Shephard, C-843-794-7912. Reagan Annex, C-843-794-7919.
Dental Clinic: C-843-794-7944.
Medical: Appointment Line, C-843-794-6221. NHCC Main Line, C-843-794-6000/6001.
Beauty/Barber Shop: C-843-794-7755. NNTCP, C-843-794-7116.
Commissary: C-843-794-2020.
Exchange Gas: Bldg 348, C-775-426-2583.
Exchange: C-843-794-7042.

Financial Institutions: Navy Federal Credit Union, C-888-842-6328. South Carolina Federal Credit Union, C-843-569-8283, Contact Center C-843-797-8300.
Clubs: The Dive Bar and Grill, C-843-794-4238. Redbank Club, C-843-794-7797.
Places to Eat: Red Bank Club Palmetto Grill, C-843-764-7797; Cooper River Cafe, C-843-218-5722. The Dive Bar and Grill, C-843-794-4238; Fairway Grill, C-843-794-7828; Galley, C-843-794-8218 and Marrington Snack Bar, C-843-794-7235 are on base. Many restaurants within a short drive.
Bowling: Marrington Bowling Center, C-843-794-7235.
Fitness Center: Weapons Station FC, C-843-794-4173. Eastside Wellness Center, C-843-794-7012.
Golf: Redbank Plantation Golf Course, C-843-794-7828.
ITT/ITR: C-843-794-2122/2120.
Library: WS Branch Library, C-843-794-7900.
Marina: Short Stay Navy Marina, C-843-743-2608, C-843-761-8353.
MWR: C-843-963-3800/3809.

MWR Website:
https://www.jbcharleston.com/
MWR Facebook:
https://www.facebook.com/jbcharlestonfss/
MWR Twitter:
https://twitter.com/628FSS
Outdoor Recreation: Charleston Weapons Station Outdoor Adventure Center, C-843-794-2120. Offers hunting, fishing, climbing wall, camping equipment, kayaks, sports equipment, riding trails and more.
Swimming: New Wave Aquatic Center Outdoor Pool, C-843-794-4092 offers open swim, recreational swim, slides and swim lessons.
Things To Do: Visit stately old mansions along the Battery and Boone Hall. Scenes from "Gone With the Wind" and "North and South" were filmed in this area. Take a water tour and visit historic Fort Sumter in the Charleston Harbor. Enjoy excellent historical sites and unique shopping and dining experiences.
Walking Trails: Marrington Plantation trails are on base.

RV CAMPING & GETAWAYS
Foster Creek RV Park & Villas

Reservation/Contact Number Info: C-843-794-2120. Camp Host, C-843-200-5596. Fax C-843-764-2116, DSN-312--794-2116.
Recreation Security: C-843-764-7777.
RV Website:
https://www.jbcharleston.com/lodging/foster-creek/
Other Info Website:
https://www.jbcharlestonorc.com/
RV Email Address:
fostercreek@comcast.net
GPS Coordinates:
32°58'38"N/79°58'57"W
Reservations: Reservations accepted up to three months in advance. Full payment required at time of reservation. RV Park: Office hours 1100-1630 Mon-Fri, 0900-1130 Sat. Check-in 1200 hours, check-out 1100 hours. Villas: Office hours 1100-1730 Mon-Fri.

Check-in 1600 hours, check-out 1100 hours.
Season of Operation: Year-round.
Eligibility: AD, NG, Res, Ret, Dep, DoD-Civ, 100% DAV and U.S. Govt Civ Emp.
Camper/Trailer Spaces: Hardstand (54), Back-in, Maximum 70' in length, E(110/220V/20/30/50A)/S/W, picnic table, grill, Wi-Fi. Rates: $22 daily.
Yurt, A Frame, Cabin, Apt, Spaces: Villas (16): Two, Three and Four bedroom villas. Fully furnished. Two bedroom with queen bed and one full, one bath. Rates: $86 daily. Three bedroom with one queen bed, one full and one twin; one full bath and two half baths. Rates: $97 daily. Four bedroom with one queen bed, two full beds and one twin; two full baths. Rates: $110 daily. Three bedroom pet friendly unit $110 daily. Linens provided.
Support Facilities: Auto Craft Shop, Bathhouse, Boat Launch, Bowling, Cafeteria, Chapel, Coin Laundry, Commissary, Convenience Store, Equipment Rental, Exchange, Fishing Pier, Fitness Center, Gas, Golf, Grills, Ice, Mess Hall, Pavilion, Pay Phones, Picnic Area, Playground, Pool, Propane, Restrooms, Sewage Dump, Showers, Sports Fields, Stables, Tennis Courts, Trails.
RV Storage: C-843-794-2120.
Activities: Bicycling, Canoeing, Fishing*, Golf, Hiking, Hunting*, Kayaking, Swimming. Hunting and fishing licenses available at the Outdoor Adventure Center.
Credit Cards: MasterCard and Visa.
Restrictions: Pets allowed on leash at RV park. No firearms allowed. Sponsor must accompany guests. No smoking in Villas. Quiet hours after 2200.
RV Driving Directions/Location: On Base. From the Main Gate: Turn left at Deke Giles St. At the stop sign turn right onto Pulaski St. Drive one mile and the villas and RV park ahead on left.
Area Description: Charleston Naval Weapons Station encompasses more than 17,000 acres of land with 10,000 acres of forest and wetlands, sixteen plus miles of waterfront and four deep water piers. Only 20 minutes from

downtown historic Charleston, Patriot's Pointe and Fort Sumter; and in close proximity to several beautiful area beaches.

RV Campground Physical Address: 500 Pulaski Street, NWS Charleston, Goose Creek, SC 29445. Mailing Address: Outdoor Adventure Center, 1956 Fletcher St, NWS Charleston, Goose Creek, SC 29445.

Clarks Hill Training Site

Address: 212 Kay Waldrop Way, Plum Branch, SC 29845.
Information Line: SCNG, C-803-299-4200.
Main Base Police: Emergencies dial 911.
Main Installation Website: http://www.scguard.com/
Main Base Location: Located in western SC just across the Ga state line along the Savannah River and Clarks Hill Lake, a major recreational area in a rural location.
Directions to Main Gate: From I-20 W and US-221 N: Take exit 200 to a right onto GA 104/River Watch Pkwy. Turn right onto Furys Ferry Road to SC-28W. Turn left onto State Rd S-33-68 in McCormick County. Follow road and take a slight right to Kay Waldrop Way. Facility ahead.
NMC: Appling, GA, 28 miles south and west.
NMI: Fort Gordon, GA, 49 miles south.
Things To Do: J. Strom Thurmond Dam & Lake is a big attraction in the area and is one of the 10 most visited Corps of Engineers lakes in the nation, serving about 5.5 million visitors annually. The lake offers camping, day use areas, boating, fishing, hunting, and trails. Baker Creek State Park and Hickory Knob State Park are located on the shores of the lake. Many seasonal festivals and activities.
Walking Trails: Hiking trails are nearby.

RV CAMPING & GETAWAYS

Clarks Hill RV & Camping

Reservation/Contact Number Info: C-803-299-1957.
RV Website: http://www.scguard.com/resources/billeting/
Reservations: Reservations accepted 30 days in advance if no Military training is scheduled. Reservations may be cancelled if a Military training requirement occurs. Please call ahead for special gate arrangements if arriving after normal duty hours or on a weekend.
Season of Operation: Year-round.
Eligibility: AD, NG, Res, Ret, DoD-Civ, South Carolina Military Dept Civilians.
Camper/Trailer Spaces: Camp pads: E(30A)/W partial hookups. Rates: $10 daily. No Dump Station available.
Tent Spaces: Only allowed on Camp Pads.
Yurt, A Frame, Cabin, Apt, Spaces: Man Huts: Rates: $10 daily. Cabins: Wi-Fi. Rates: $18 daily. Call for details.
Support Facilities: Bathrooms, Dining Hall, Showers.
Activities: Boat Rentals, Boating, Fishing*, Hiking, Picnicking, Swimming, Water Skiing. *South Carolina fishing license required.
Restrictions: No Pets. No ATV's. Campfires only allowed in pre-existing fire sites. No firearms.
RV Driving Directions/Location: Off Base. From I-20 W and US-221 N: Take exit 200 to a right onto GA 104/River Watch Pkwy. Turn right onto Furys Ferry Road to SC-28W.Turn left onto State Rd S-33-68 in McCormick County. Follow road and take a slight right to Kay Waldrop Way. Facility ahead.
Area Description: Clarks Hill is a popular park on J. Strom Thurmond Lake, just off Georgia State Highway 221 near the dam. The 70,000 acre lake and its 1,000+ miles of shoreline provide excellent boating, water skiing, swimming, fishing, hiking and picnicking opportunities.

RV Campground Physical Address: 212 Kay Waldrop Way, Plumb Branch SC 29845

Fort Jackson

Address: 5450 Strom Thurmond Boulevard, Fort Jackson, SC 29207.
Information Line: C-803-751-7511, DSN-312-734-7511.
Main Base Police: C-803-751-3114/3115. Emergencies dial 911.
Main Installation Website: http://jackson.armylive.dodlive.mil/
Main Base Location: Fort Jackson is located in South Carolina, near the state capital of Columbia.
Directions to Main Gate: From I-77 north or south take exit 12 to Strom Thurmond Blvd/Forest Drive to Gate 2. From I-20: Take I-77 toward the base to Gate 2. Watch for signs.
NMC: Columbia, 12 miles southwest.
NMI: Shaw AFB, 35 miles southeast.
Base Social Media/Facebook: https://www.facebook.com/fortjackson/
Base Social Media/Twitter: https://twitter.com/fortjacksonpao
Dental Clinic: C-803-751-2108/2241. Caldwell Dental Clinic, C-803-751-7025/5178. Hagen Dental Clinic, C-803-751-3255/6211. Oliver Dental Clinic, C-803-751-1624/1894.
Medical: Appointment Line, C-803-751-2273. Main Line, C-803-751-2160. McWethy Troop Clinic, C-803-751-6789.
Veterinary Services: C-803-751-7160.
Beauty/Barber Shop: Mini Mall, C-803-787-1274. Gate 1, C-803-743-0402. AIT Troop Store, C-790-4189. Coleman Gym, C-803-786-5495 (appt only). Tank Hill, C-803-782-2582. Perez FC, C-803-782-2052 (appt only). Reception Troop Store, C-803-790-9825. C-803-743-9568. Stylique, C-803-787-3790.
Commissary: C-803-751-5869.
Exchange Gas: Gate 1 Express, C-803-782-2076/5417. Gate 2 Express, C-803-790-4478.
Exchange: C-803-787-1950.
Financial Institutions: All South FCU C-800-272-0695, C-803-736-3110, Wachovia, C-803-790-8345.
Clubs: NCO Club, C-803-782-2218. Officers' Club, C-803-782-8761.

Magruder's Club and Pub, C-803-790-0381.
Places to Eat: Century Lanes Snack Bar, C-803-751-4656; Bogey's Snack Bar, C-803-751-6367 and 512 Trolley, Popeye's and Starbucks are on base. Exchange Food Court offers Arby's, Boston Market, Burger King, Charley's and Taco Bell. Gate 1 Express offers Pizza Hut. Gate 2 Express offers Subway. Many restaurants are within a short drive. Snack Bar is available at the Palmetto Falls Water Park during seasonal operation.
Bowling: Century Lanes, C-803-751-6138. Ivy Lanes, C-803-751-4759 (primarily for Soldiers in Training).
Fitness Center: Andy's FC, C803-751-4177. Coleman Gym, C-803-751-5896. Perez FC, C-803-751-6258. Vanguard Gym, C-803-751-4384/4526. Wellness Programs, C-803-751-3700.
Golf: Fort Jackson Golf Club, C-803-787-4344.
ITT/ITR: Victory Travel Center, C-803-751-5812.
Library: Thomas Lee Hall, C-803-751-5589.
Marina: Weston Lake Marina, C-803-751-5253.
Military Museum: U.S. Army Basic Training Museum. U.S. Army Adjutant General Corps Museum. U.S. Army Chaplain Museum. U.S. Army Finance Corps Museum.
Military Museum Website: https://armyhistory.org/the-fort-jackson-museum-community/
MWR: C-803-751-6990.
MWR Website: https://jackson.armymwr.com/
MWR Facebook: https://www.facebook.com/Fort-Jackson-FMWR-162484245597/
Outdoor Recreation: Marion Street Station Outdoor Recreation, C-803-751-3484. Offers boat rentals, camping gear, party and game activities, bicycles, kayaks and canoes, park and pavilion special event rentals and more.
Swimming: Knight Indoor Pool C-803-751-4796 offers lap swim, open swim, swim lessons. Legion Outdoor Seasonal Pool, C-803-751-4987 offers open swim.

Palmetto Falls Water Park, C-803-751-3475 offers slides, a lazy river, splashdown pool, kiddie pool and snack bar.

Things To Do: Riverbanks Zoological Park, Town Theater amateur productions, carriage rides along historic Broad Street, golf courses, Lake Murray and numerous public recreation areas are popular local activities. Enjoy many on-base activities and recreation areas.

Walking Trails: Fort Jackson Green Zone and Palmetto Trail are on base.

RV CAMPING & GETAWAYS
Legion Landing Cottages

Reservation/Contact Number Info: C-803-751-5812.

RV Website: https://jackson.armymwr.com/programs/jacks-inn

GPS Coordinates: 33°59'58.4"N/80°55'57.8"W

Reservations: Reservations accepted anytime via telephone only. Credit card required to guarantee reservation. Cancellations require a 24-hour notice prior to arrival to avoid fee. Office hours 0730-1600 hours Mon-Fri. Closed weekends and holidays. Two-night reservation generally required. Specific check in information provided at time of reservation. Reservations handled through Victory Travel on base. Check-in 1400 hours, check-out 1200 hours.

Season of Operation: Year-round.

Eligibility: AD, NG, Res, Ret, and their dependents; Widow/ers; DoD-Civ, DoD-Civ Ret and their dependents w/ID; DAVs, eligible guests.

Yurt, A Frame, Cabin, Apt, Spaces: Cottages (6): Two bedroom cottages (4); One bedroom cottages (2), bedding arrangements vary from cottage to cottage, private bath, fully furnished kitchen with microwave, stove top, refrigerator, coffee maker; living area, CATV. Rates: 2BR $119 daily; 1BR $99 daily. Linens provided.

Support Facilities: Full range of support facilities on base.

Activities: Enjoy golfing and many outdoor activities. Outdoor Recreation offers boat rentals, camping gear, party and game activities, bicycles, kayaks and canoes.

Credit Cards: MC, VISA.

Restrictions: Pets are not permitted at this facility.

RV Driving Directions/Location: On base. To Jacks Inn for check in: From Gate 2: Continue on Strom Thurmond Blvd and make right turn at the 3rd traffic signal onto Marion Ave. Go right onto Semmes Road, crossing over Lee Road. Go left onto Knight Road. Facility ahead.

Area Description: Located on base along the Upper Legion Lake in a quiet, peaceful setting.

RV Campground Physical Address: Check in at Jacks Inn on base.

Weston Lake Recreation Area & RV Park

Reservation/Contact Number Info: C-803-751-5253.

Recreation Security: C-803-751-3115.

RV Website: https://jackson.armymwr.com/programs/weston-lake

GPS Coordinates: 34°0'26"N/80°49'42"W

Reservations: Reservations are required. Active Duty may reserve 90 days in advance, all others may make reservations 60 days in advance. Reservations may be made telephone only. Office hours 0900-1700 1 Oct-1 May; 1000-1800 1 May-1 Oct. Check-in at Operations Building begins at 1300, check-out by 1100 hours.

Season of Operation: Year-round.

Eligibility: AD, NG, Res, Ret and DoD-Civ.

Camper/Trailer Spaces: Hardstand (34): Full hookup sites. Rate: $22 daily.

Tent Spaces: Tent pads (10), water hookup. Rates: $10 daily. Sites with no hookups. Rates: $5 daily.

Yurt, A Frame, Cabin, Apt, Spaces: Lakefront Cabins: Two-bedroom (4). Sleeps five. Furnished, private bath, kitchen, microwave, stove, pots/pans, dishes, TV, linens. Rates: $80 daily.

Lakefront Cabins: Two-bedroom with loft (3). Sleeps seven. Furnished, private bath, kitchen, microwave, stove, pots/pans, dishes, TV, linens. Rates: $90 daily. Kamping Kabins: (2) Sleeps two to three. Heat/AC, microwave, refrigerator. Must use communal bathroom. Rates: $20 daily.
Support Facilities: Boat Launch, Boat Rental, Golf, Grills, Group Meeting Facilities, Guarded Swimming Beach, Nature Trail, Picnic Area, Playground, Pontoon Boat, Rec Equipment, Restrooms, Sewage Dump, Showers, Sports Fields, Swing, Trails.
RV Storage: None.
Activities: Boating, Bowling, Fishing*, Golfing, Hunting*, Swimming. *State and base licenses required.
Credit Cards: American Express, MasterCard and Visa.
Restrictions: No pets allowed in cabins; pets allowed on up to 6-foot leash in RV park. No smoking in cabins. No firearms allowed. Hunting and fishing require state and post permits. Nominal fee charged for use of recreation area; campers/lodgers exempt when registered in camping/lodging facilities.
RV Driving Directions/Location: On Base: From I-20 east or west in Columbia: Take exit 76 to I-77 south and exit 9 to SC-262 (Leesburg Road) east. From I-26 east or west: Take exit 155 or exit 116, respectively. Take I-77 north to exit 9. Distance to Weston Lake Recreation Area sign is 9.1 miles. From Sumter on SC-378: Take exit to US-601 north, then turn left onto Leesburg Road after approximately 6 miles. The recreation sign is 7.1 miles on the right.
Area Description: Located adjacent to 240-acre lake with an abundance of wildlife to watch, from deer to black squirrels. Site offers wide range of outdoor activities. Museum and Ernie Pyle Media Center located on post. Columbia, the state capital, offers varied sightseeing, including zoo, Capitol and Coliseum. Full range of support facilities available on post.
RV Campground Physical Address: Weston Lake Recreation Area and RV Park, Recreation Division, 4500 Block of Leesburg Rd, Fort Jackson, SC 29207-5000.

Parris Island Marine Corps Recruit Depot

Address: 283 Blvd De France Avenue, Parris Island, SC 29905.
Information Line: C-843-228-2111.
Main Base Police: C-843-228-3444/3445. Emergencies dial 911.
Main Installation Website: http://www.mcrdpi.marines.mil/
Main Base Location: Located on Parris Island and several smaller islands approximately 4 miles south of the City of Beaufort, South Carolina.
Directions to Main Gate: From the south on I-95 South: Take exit 33. Hwy 21 combines with US 17 North. Follow signs towards Beaufort. At Garden's Corner merge right onto Hwy 21. Take a right on Parris Island Gateway/Hwy 802 at first light after MCAS Beaufort. Follow Hwy 802 until exit for MCRD Parris Island.
NMC: Savannah, GA 43 miles southwest.
NMI: Beaufort BCAS, 14 miles northwest.
Base Social Media/Facebook: https://www.facebook.com/ParrisIsland
Base Social Media/Twitter: https://twitter.com/mcrdpi
Chapels: Chaplain, C-843-228-3533. Depot Chapel, C-843-228-2974. Recruit, C-843-228-3689.
Dental Clinic: C-843-228-3500.
Medical: Beaufort Naval Hospital Appointments, C-843-228-5175/5198. Main Line, C-228-228-5400/5600. Branch Clinic, C-843-228-4237.
Veterinary Services: C-843-228-3317.
Beauty/Barber Shop: C-843-228-3550. Hair Salon, C-843-228-2368.
Commissary: C-843-228-2383.
Exchange Gas: Mini-Mart, C-843-228-1673.
Exchange: C-843-228-1538. Marine Mart, C-843-228-1673.
Military Clothing: C-843-228-1591.
Financial Institutions: Parris Island Armed Services, C-843-228-3818. Navy Federal Credit Union, C-843-521-1157, C-888-842-6328.

Places to Eat: Java Cafe, C-843-228-4685; Subway, C-843-228-3672; The Sand Trap Grill, C-843-228-4578 and Traditions, C-843-228-1566 are on base. Exchange Food Court offers C-Street Bakery, Eddie Peppers, Hot Stuff Pizza and Starbucks. Many restaurants within a short drive.

Bowling: Parris Island Bowling Center, C-843-228-1551.

Fitness Center: Semper Fit Center, C-843-228-1579.

Golf: The Legends at Parris Island, C-843-228-2240.

ITT/ITR: All Points Travel, C-843-228-3557. Tickets, C-843-228-1540.

Library: MCRD Parris Island, C-843-228-1672/1671.

Military Museum: Parris Island Museum, C-843-228-2951.

Military Museum Website: http://parrisislandmuseum.com/

MWR: C-843-228-7675/3302.

MWR Website: http://www.mccs-sc.com

MWR Facebook: https://www.facebook.com/mccs.sc

Outdoor Recreation: MCAS Outdoor Adventure, C-843-228-7472. Offers boating equipment, campers and camping equipment, cookout equipment, bounce houses, water sports equipment, adventure trips, Operation Adrenaline Rush, Parris Island RV Park and more.

Swimming: Parris Island Outdoor Seasonal Pool, C-843-228-1506 offers lap swim, open swim and swim lessons.

Things To Do: There are weekly recruit graduations at 0900 hours on most Fridays. Visit the Beaufort Memorial Museum, Hunting Island State Park, Beaufort County Water Festival, or take in the island's natural beauty riding bikes or experience its splendor from the golf course.

RV CAMPING & GETAWAYS

Parris Island RV Park

Reservation/Contact Number Info: C-843-228-7472.

Recreation Security: C-843-228-3444.

RV Website: http://www.mccs-sc.com/din-lod/rvpark.shtml

GPS Coordinates: 32°19'36.7"N/80°41'48.9"W

Reservations: Reservations accepted at Outdoor Recreation and must be made at least three days in advance. Office hours 0830-1630 Mon-Fri. Full payment at time of reservation. Cancellations accepted with three days of arrival. Check-in 1400 hours, check-out 1200 hours. Maximum stay 30 days.

Season of Operation: Year-round.

Eligibility: AD, Ret, Families and Guests, DOD and Graduating Recruit families.

Camper/Trailer Spaces: RV Sites (18): Full hook up E(20A/30A/50A)/S/W, bathrooms, showers and coin operated laundry available; picnic tables. Rates: $20 daily.

Support Facilities: Full range of support facilities on base.

Activities: Beach, Golfing, Local sightseeing in Beaufort.

Credit Cards: Cash, Check, American Express, Discover, MasterCard and Visa.

Restrictions: Pets are allowed. No firearms or fireworks. Quiet hours 2100-0700.

RV Driving Directions/Location: From the traffic circle: Take the 3rd exit onto Malecon, which becomes Blvd. De France then turn right onto Samoa. Turn left onto Panama and then right onto Cuba. Turn left on St. Mihiel to RV Park. On Family Day Thursdays (0630-0730) and Graduation Day Fridays (0845-1030), please follow detour signs to Alaska and Panama streets.

Area Description: Located near the quaint ocean-side town of Beaufort along the Atlantic Ocean.

RV Campground Physical Address: Parris Island R.V. Park, Building 1018, St. Mihiel Road, MCRD Parris Island, SC 29905.

Shaw Air Force Base

Address: 524 Stuart Avenue, Shaw AFB, SC 29152-5024.

Information Line: C-803-895-1110, DSN-312-965-1110.

Main Base Police: C-803-895-3669/3670, DSN-312-965-3669.

Main Installation Website:
http://www.shaw.af.mil/
Main Base Location: Located west of Sumter, South Carolina, Shaw Air Force Base is about 40 miles east of Columbia, the state capital. The base is centrally located in SC.
Directions to Main Gate: From Augusta: Take I-20 East. At Columbia take I-26 South around the city. Continue on I-77 South around the city then go east onto Highway 76/378. Continue on 378 and the base will be on the left and the exit for Shaw's Main Gate will be on the right. From Charleston: Take I-26 West. Turn onto I-95 North then take Highway 378 west. Main Gate will be on the right. From Savannah: Take I-95 North. Turn West onto Highway 378. Continue on Highway 378. Shaw's Main Gate will be on the right side.
NMC: Columbia, 35 miles west.
NMI: Fort Jackson, 30 miles northwest.
Base Social Media/Facebook:
https://www.facebook.com/20Fighter Wing
Base Social Media/Twitter:
https://twitter.com/20FighterWing
Chapels: Chaplain, C-803-895-1106.
Dental Clinic: C-803-895-6988.
Medical: 20th Medical Group Appoint Line, C-803-895-2273.
Veterinary Services: C-803-895-6155.
Beauty/Barber Shop: Barber, C-803-666-4773. Carolina Skies Barber, C-803-666-2400. Stylique, C-803-666-2390.
Commissary: C-803-895-1281.
Exchange Gas: C-803-666-3231.
Exchange: C-803-666-3050/3051.
Financial Institutions: Wells Fargo Bank, C-803-666-4902/4819. SAFE Federal Credit Union, C-803-469-8600.
Clubs: Top Gun and Main Lounge at Carolina Skies, C-803-666-3651.
Places to Eat: Afterburner Grill, C-803-895-4349; Carolina Skies, C-803-666-3651; Cosmic Grill, C-803-895-2732; Rickenbacker's, C-803-895-6401; Sand-Wich Trap Cafe, C-803-895-1399 and Williams Dining Facility, C-803-895-9791 are on base. Exchange Food Court offers Burger King, Dunkin Donuts, Subway and Taco Bell. Many restaurants are within a short drive.

Bowling: Shaw Lanes Bowling Center, C-803-895-2732.
Fitness Center: Shaw FC, C-803-895-2789. Annex, C-803-895-2789.
Golf: Carolina Lakes Golf Course, C-803-895-1399.
ITT/ITR: C-803-895-4774.
Library: McElveen Library, C-803-895-4518.
MWR: C-803-895-4897.
MWR Website:
http://www.20thfss.com
MWR Facebook:
https://www.facebook.com/20thFSS/
MWR Twitter:
https://twitter.com/20thfss
Outdoor Recreation: Outdoor Recreation, C-803-895-0450. Offers boating equipment, kayaks, trailers, sporting equipment, camping gear, inflatables, party rentals and outdoor household goods.
Swimming: Woodland Seasonal Outdoor Pool, C-803-895-3446 offers lap swim and open swim.
Things To Do: Many outdoor activities in the area including Cypress Trail and Swan Lake Iris Gardens. Visit Sumter County Museum, Palmetto Park, or enjoy the seasonal farmer's market or one of the many festivals throughout the year.
Walking Trails: Running trails available at Shaw Fitness Center.

RV CAMPING & GETAWAYS
Falcon's Nest FamCamp

Reservation/Contact Number Info: C-803-895-0450, DSN-312-965-0450. Fax C-803-895-0453.
RV Website:
https://www.thebestfss.com/
RV Email Address:
outdoorrec@20thfss.com
GPS Coordinates:
33°57′56″N/80°27′17″W
Reservations: Reservations accepted, but not required, 60 days in advance for AD; 30 days in advance for all other authorized users. Pre-payment required. Office hours 0800-1700 Mon-Fri. Check-in time 1200 hours; check-out time 1100 hours. Maximum stay 90

days with space available exceptions. PCS no limit.

Season of Operation: Year-round.

Eligibility: AD, NG, Res, Ret, 100% DAV. Dep, DoD-Civ.

Camper/Trailer Spaces: Back-in (20): E(110/220V/30/50A)/S/W hookups, picnic table, grill. Rates: $20 daily, $120 weekly, $450 monthly. Mail services available.

Tent Spaces: Primitive tent area, picnic table. Rates: $5 daily.

Support Facilities: Boat Rental/Storage, Coin Laundry, Convenience Store, Golf, Grills, Horseshoes, Internet, Playground, Pavilions, Sewage Dump, Showers, Wi-Fi.

RV Storage: None.

Activities: Boating, Camping, Fishing, Golfing, Picnicking.

Credit Cards: MasterCard and Visa.

Restrictions: Pets are allowed in area but must be kept on leash. Quiet hours 2300-0700 daily. All firearms must be registered with security police upon arrival on base.

RV Driving Directions/Location: On Base: From the Main Gate: Go right after shoppette toward the flight line. Signs for FamCamp visible.

Area Description: Situated on east side of Main Base in a peaceful five acre wooded area on perimeter road. Full range of support facilities available on Shaw AFB.

RV Campground Physical Address: Outdoor Recreation, 1 FamCamp Drive, Shaw AFB, SC 29152-5000.

Short Stay Navy Outdoor Recreation Area

Address: Short Stay Recreation, 211 Short Stay Road, Moncks Corner, SC 29461.

Information Line: C-843-764-7000, DSN-312-794-7000.

Main Base Police: Emergencies dial 911.

Main Installation Website: http://www.charleston.af.mil/

Main Base Location: Located on beautiful Lake Moultrie near the town of Moncks Corner in SC.

NMC: Charleston, 40 miles south.

NMI: Charleston Joint Base, 25 miles south.

Base Social Media/Facebook: https://www.facebook.com/shortstayla kelife/

Chapels: Ask front desk for churches in the area.

Medical: JB Charleston Naval Health Clinic/Joint Ambulatory Care Clinic, C-843-794-6000, DSN-312-794-6000.

Commissary: Approximately 25 miles to JB Charleston (Naval Weapon Station) Commissary, C-843-794-7475/2020. Charleston AFB, C-843-963-7469.

Exchange Gas: C-843-764-7573 (NWS Charleston).

Exchange: Approximately 25 miles away from WS Exchange, C-843-764-7042. 30 miles to AF Exchange Charleston, C-843-552-5000.

Places to Eat: Capt'n Roberts Dive, C-843-764-4238. Redbank Club, C-843-764-7797.

Golf: Redbank Plantation Golf Course, C-843-764-7802.

ITT/ITR: C-843-764-2120.

Marina: C-843-743-2608, C-843-761-8353.

Outdoor Recreation: https://www.jbcharlestonorc.com

MWR: C-843-764-7602.

MWR Website: https://www.jbcharleston.com/

Outdoor Recreation: JB Charleston Weapons Station Outdoor Adventure Center, C-843-764-1672/1732. Features an indoor rock wall open to all levels seven days a week. The OAC also has outdoor sports equipment rentals including rock climbing gear, hunting and fishing licenses/permits and camping equipment rentals.

Swimming: New Wave Aquatic Center, C-843-764-7156. Beaches available at nearby Charleston.

Things To Do: Located on Lake Moultrie, a 60,000-acre lake. Enjoy fishing and water sports. Charleston offers beaches, golf, historic sites.

Walking Trails: Palmetto Trails goes all the way from the ocean to the Blue Ridge Mountains.

RV CAMPING & GETAWAYS

Short Stay Recreation Area

Reservation/Contact Number Info: C-843-743-2608.

Recreation Security: C-843-296-7731. Emergencies dial 911.

RV Website: http://www.jbcharleston.com/short-stay-moncks-corner/

Other Info Website: https://www.jbcharlestonorc.com/

GPS Coordinates: 33°15'24"N/79°59'14"W

Reservations: Accepted by telephone only. Reservations accepted 90 days in advance. Full payment due at time of reservation. Office hours 0730-1830 Mon-Sun. Check-in 1500 hours, check-out 1100 hours. Cancellations require 30 days to avoid fee. Office hours 0730-1830 Mon-Sun. Check-in 1500 hours, check-out 1100 hours.

Season of Operation: Year-round.

Eligibility: AD, NG, Res, Ret, DoD-Civ and Guests.

Camper/Trailer Spaces: Waterfront (20): E(110V/50A)/W/CATV hookups, picnic table, grill. Rates: $24-$28 daily, $168-$196 weekly depending on season. Wooded (21), E(110V/30A/50A)/W hookups, picnic table, grill. Rates: $19-$21 daily, $133-$147 weekly depending on season. Wooded (30), E(30A), picnic table, grill. Rates: $16-$18 daily, $112-$126 weekly depending on season, $420 monthly (15 sites).

Tent Spaces: Primitive (15): No hookups, picnic table, grill. Rates: $6 daily, $42 weekly. Seasonal rates apply.

Yurt, A Frame, Cabin, Apt, Spaces: Villas: Three-bedroom (12): Sleeps six, fully furnished, cable, Wi-Fi. Rates: $105-$130 daily. Two-bedroom (26, 2 handicap accessible): Sleeps four, fully furnished, cable, Wi-Fi. Rates: $75-$115 daily depending on cabin. Roundettes (6, one handicap accessible): One and two-bedroom, two queen beds, sleeps four, furnished, private bath, full kitchen, microwave, refrigerator, CATV, cookware and utensils. Rates: $30-$50 depending on size and season. Patrons must provide soap and toiletries.

Support Facilities: Bath House, Beach, Boat Launch, Boat Rental/Storage, Conference Center*, Convenience Store, Fishing License Sales, Fire Rings, Fishing Pier, Gas, Grills, Ice, Laundry/Pay, Marina, Pavilions**, Picnic Areas, Playground, Propane, Rec Equipment, Restrooms, Sewage Dump, Showers, Trails. *Conference Room (1), seats 150. **Pavilions (5), seats 200-375.

RV Storage: None.

Activities: Boating, Canoeing, Fishing*, Hiking (Nearby), Kayaking, Swimming, Volleyball, Water-Skiing. *License required.

Credit Cards: American Express, MasterCard and Visa.

Restrictions: No smoking in villas or cabins. Pets are allowed on leash in campground but are not permitted in villas or cabins. Owners must clean up after pets. Pets may not be left unattended. Campfires in fire rings only. Admission fee for day users. All firearms must be registered with security. Quiet hours 2200-0800. Sponsor of guests must be on-site at all times and is responsible for the actions of their guests. All guests must be registered with office.

RV Driving Directions/Location: Off Base. From US-52 North or South, 5 miles north of Moncks Corner: Exit west and follow signs to Short Stay Navy Outdoor Recreation Area on the shores of Lake Moultrie.

Area Description: Situated on a 55-acre peninsula at southern tip of Lake Moultrie. Excellent freshwater fishing, family programs and activities during summer months. Full range of support facilities at Charleston Naval Weapons Station.

RV Campground Physical Address: Short Stay, Navy Outdoor Recreation Area, 211 Short Stay Road, Moncks Corner, SC 29461-5000.

Wateree Recreation Area

Address: Wateree Recreation, 2030 Baron DeKalb Road, Camden, SC 29020.
Information Line: C-803-895-1110, DSN-312-965-1110.
Main Base Police: Emergencies dial 911.
Main Installation Website: http://www.shaw.af.mil/
Main Base Location: Located in the heart of South Carolina's Olde English District, where the three large river systems, Pee-Dee, Catawba-Wateree and Broad are located, drawing many visitors.
NMC: Columbia, 35 miles southwest.
NMI: Shaw AFB, 35 miles southeast.
Medical: C-803-778-9000, DSN-312-965-6562.
Exchange Gas: C-803-666-3231.
Fitness Center: Annex, C-803-895-0947/0949.
Golf: Carolina Lakes Golf Course, Shaw AFB, C-803-895-1399.
ITT/ITR: C-803-895-4774.
Marina: Wateree Marina, C-803-895-0449/0450
MWR: C-803-432-7976.
MWR Website: https://www.thebestfss.com/
MWR Facebook: https://www.facebook.com/20thFSS/
MWR Twitter: https://twitter.com/20thfss
Outdoor Recreation: Shaw AFB Outdoor Recreation Services, C-803-895-0450. Outdoor Recreation operates the Falcon's Nest FAMCAMP, skeet and trap range, pools, equipment rental, and picnic grounds. Offers guided trips, events, classes and a variety of outdoor activities.
Swimming: Woodland Pool, C-803-895-3446. Pool offers water slide, wading pool and sundeck.
Things To Do: While here, enjoy peaceful surroundings, fishing and boating. Visit the University of South Carolina and Frankie's Fun Park, which is a 14-acre entertainment center with mini golf, go-carts, batting cages and laser tag. This is a great area for family fun and excitement.

Walking Trails: Nature trails available.

RV CAMPING & GETAWAYS

Wateree Recreation Area

Reservation/Contact Number Info: C-1-877-928-8373, C-803-432-7976.
RV Website: https://www.thebestfss.com/lodging/wateree-recreation-area
RV Email Address: wateree@20thfss.com
GPS Coordinates: 34°22'59"N/80°43'44"W
Reservations: Reservations may be made up to 90 days in advance AD, NG and Res. Retirees and all other authorized users up to 60 in advance. Cabins require a 2-night minimum. Tent reservations first come, first serve. Online and telephone reservations accepted. Payment required at time of reservation. Cancellations may be charged $15 fee. Office hours 0800-1700 daily. Closed Thanksgiving, Christmas and New Year's Day. Check-in 1400 hours, check-out 1100 hours. Maximum stay seven days unless space available.
Season of Operation: Year-round.
Eligibility: AD, NG, Res, Ret, DoD-Civ, 100% DAV with DoD ID Card.
Camper/Trailer Spaces: RV Sites (22): E(110V/20A/30A/50A)/W/S, fire ring, grill, picnic table. Rates: $20 daily, $120 weekly, $425 monthly. Seasonal rates apply.
Tent Spaces: Primitive Sites: No hookups, fire ring, grill, picnic table. Rates: $7.50 daily, $18.75 for 3 nights, $35 weekly.
Yurt, A Frame, Cabin, Apt, Spaces: Cabins (16): Two-bedroom (11), three-bedroom (4), one-bedroom (1); each fully equipped with linens, towels, dishes, pots, pans, coffee maker, microwave, TV, HVAC. Seasonal Rates: Three-bedroom, $99 daily; Two-bedroom, $79 daily; One-bedroom, $64 daily. Maximum stay seven days unless space available.
Support Facilities: Bathhouse, Boat Dock/Launch, Boat Rental (Seasonal), Equipment Rental, Grills, Marina,

Pavilions, Picnic Area, Playground, Rec Room, Restrooms, Sewage Dump, Showers.
RV Storage: None.
Activities: Boating, Fishing*, Swimming, Water Sports. *License required.
Credit Cards: MasterCard, Visa, Cash, Check.
Restrictions: Pets are allowed in cabins 4-8, $10 daily fee added. Limit two dogs or two cats or a combination of the two. Pets allowed on leash in camping area. Pets are not permitted on rental boats or on the beach. Firearms allowed only during hunting season, and only with notification of Site Manager at area.
RV Driving Directions/Location: Off Base. Take I-20 west from I-95 (Florence, SC area) to the Camden/Hwy 521 exit. Go north on Hwy 521 through Camden. Take a left onto Hwy 97 (Food Lion on the left). Follow Hwy 97 about 9 miles until signs for Wateree Recreation Area visible. Turn left onto Baron DeKalb Road and follow road around into the park. From the base: Travel north on Hwy 441 to Hwy 521. Take left turn onto Hwy 521 and follow the directions above.
Area Description: Situated in a peaceful, 25-acre wooded area bordering Lake Wateree. Full range of support facilities available at Shaw AFB and Fort Jackson. Roped-off swimming area with sandy beach.
RV Campground Physical Address: Wateree Recreation Area, 2030 Baron DeKalb Rd, Camden, SC 29020.

SOUTH DAKOTA

Ellsworth Air Force Base

Address: 2740 Eaker Drive, Ellsworth AFB, SD 57706.
Information Line: C-605-385-1000.
Main Base Police: C-605-385-4001. Emergencies dial 911.
Main Installation Website: http://www.ellsworth.af.mil/

Main Base Location: Ellsworth AFB is located just outside of Box Elder, South Dakota, just outside Rapid city.
Directions to Main Gate: Ellsworth is located 12 miles east of Rapid City on Interstate 90. Take exit 67B and follow signs to base. Clearly marked.
NMC: Rapid City, 7 miles west.
NMI: Camp Rapid, 14 miles southwest.
Base Social Media/Facebook: https://www.facebook.com/28thBomb Wing
Base Social Media/Twitter: https://twitter.com/28thBombWing
Chapels: Chaplain, C-605-385-1598.
Dental Clinic: C-605-385-3657.
Medical: C-605-385-6700.
Veterinary Services: C-605-385-6091/1589.
Beauty/Barber Shop: Barber, C-605-923-2808. Beauty Salon, C-605-923-4900.
Commissary: C-605-385-4510.
Exchange Gas: C-605-923-5231.
Exchange: C-605-923-4816/4774.
Financial Institutions: Sentinel Federal Credit Union, C-605-923-1405. Wells Fargo Bank, C-605-394-3940.
Clubs: Dakota's Club, C-605-385-1765.
Places to Eat: Dakota's Club, C-605-385-1765; Bandit Lanes Snack Bar, C-605-385-7625 and Raider Cafe and The Fuel Pit are on base. Exchange Food Court offers Burger King and Charley's. Many restaurants within a short drive.
Bowling: Bandit Lanes, C-605-385-2536.
Fitness Center: Bellamy FC, C-605-385-2265.
Golf: Prairie Ridge Golf Course, C-605-923-4999.
ITT/ITR: C-605-385-2997.
Library: Holbrook Library, C-605-385-1688.
Marina: Base lakes offers boating opportunities.
Military Museum: South Dakota Air & Space Museum, C-605-85-5189.
Military Museum Website: http://www.sdairandspacemuseum.com/
MWR: C-605-385-4321.
MWR Website: http://www.ellsworthfss.com/

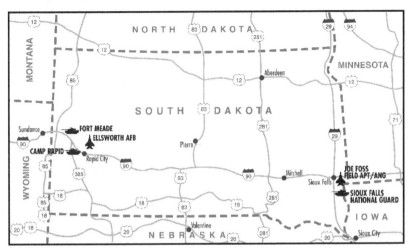

MWR Facebook:
https://www.facebook.com/ellsworthfss/
Outdoor Recreation: Outdoor
Recreation, C-605-385-2997. Offers
campers, trailers, canoes, kayaks,
paddle boards, ice fishing gear, outdoor
adventure gear, archery equipment,
lawn and garden equipment, inflatables
and more.
Swimming: Bellamy Indoor, C-605-385-
2265 offers open swim and lap swim.
Seasonal outdoor pool offers
recreational swim.
Things To Do: Visit the Black Hills Stock
Show, Summer Nights, Hemp Hoe
Down, Central States Fair, Pumpkin
Festival, Festival of Lights Parade,
Dachshund Races, Fat Tire Festival,
Americana Music Festival and many
outdoor recreation areas.

RV CAMPING & GETAWAYS

Ellsworth AFB FamCamp & Cedar Lodge

Reservation/Contact Number Info: C-
605-385-6699/6680. Fax C-605-385-
2998.
Recreation Security: C-605-385-4001.
RV Website:
https://www.ellsworthfss.com/funandf
ood/rec-lodging#famcamp
Other Info Website:
https://www.ellsworthfss.com/funandf
ood/rec-lodging#cedar-lodge

RV Email Address:
ellsworthfamcamp@gmail.com
GPS Coordinates:
44°8'35"N/103°4'10"W
Reservations: Reservations taken one
year in advance. Office hours 0900-1300
Mon-Fri. Check-in 1400 hours. Check-
out at 1200 hours. Cedar Lodge:
Reservations taken 0900-1600 Mon-Fri.
Check in at the Recreational Lodging
office located at FamCamp. Full
payment at time of reservation.
Cancellations require 24-hour notice.
Season of Operation: FamCamp: 15
May-15 Oct; Cedar Lodge: Year-round.
Eligibility: AD, NG, Res, Ret and
DoD/NAF-Civ.
Camper/Trailer Spaces: RV Sites (51):
Full hookup, laundry facilities, showers
and Wi-Fi. Rates: Nov-mid-April $10
daily; mid-April thru June $25 daily;
July-Oct $30 daily. Overflow spaces with
electric $15 daily. Weekly rates
available. for full hookup sites.
Tent Spaces: Tent Spaces: No hookups.
Rates: $5 daily; $30 weekly.
**Yurt, A Frame, Cabin, Apt,
Spaces:** Cedar Lodge: One queen size
bed, sofa, table and chairs, basic cable
TV, Wi-Fi, microwave, safe, linens,
towels, and full size refrigerator. Rates:
July-Aug $125 daily; May-June $90 daily;
Nov-April $40 daily. Check-in: 1400;
check-out: 1100 hours.
Support Facilities: Auto Craft Shop*,
Bath House*, Boat Rental/ Storage,

Bowling, Cafeteria, Camper Rentals, Chapel, Commissary, Exchange, Fitness Center, Gas, Golf, Grills, Laundry, Pavilion, Pay Phones, Picnic Area, Playgrounds, Pools, Rec Center, Rec Equipment, Restrooms, RV Storage ($13/month), Sewage Dump, Shoppette, Sports Fields, Trails, Trap & Skeet. * Handicap accessible.
RV Storage: C-605-385-6699.
Activities: Backpacking, Bicycling, Fishing*, Golfing, Hiking, Hunting*, Sightseeing, Snow Skiing, Swimming, Tours. *State and base licenses required for fishing. Rates: $27 for state license, $2 for base license. State license is required for hunting. There is a raffle for small game hunting, contact recreation area for more information. Cedar Lodge: Free access to outdoor pool located next to the Bellamy Fitness Center (pass included in welcome packet), on-site laundry access, and exercise room.
Credit Cards: MasterCard and Visa.
Restrictions: Pets allowed on leash. Firearms must be checked in with Security Police. No washing vehicles in the FAMCAMP. No open fires. There is a 30 day limit for retirees, DOD, NG, NAF, PCS excluded and can stay as long as needed. Cedar Lodge: Quiet Hours 2200-0700. No pets allowed at Cedar Lodge.
RV Driving Directions/Location: On Base. From I-90 east, Take exit 67 from the east or 67B from the west to the four-way stop. Turn right to go through the Patriot Gate 0600-1800 hours to Lincoln Drive. Turn right on Lincoln and first right into the Fam Camp. Or, go straight to go through the Liberty Gate open 24 hours daily. Take the first right hand turn coming out of the round-about onto Schriever St. Turn right on Arnold Street and onto two-way stop sign. Go straight through stop sign on to Lincoln Drive and turn right at the Fam Camp sign.
Area Description: Located in the southwest corner of South Dakota. Black Hills National Forest, Mount Rushmore National Memorial, Crazy Horse Memorial and Badlands National Park are just a short distance away. Full range of support facilities available on base.
RV Campground Physical Address: Ellsworth AFB FAMCAMP, 8011 Lincoln Ave, Ellsworth AFB, SD 57706-4910.

TENNESSEE

Arnold Air Force Base

Address: AEDC, 100 Kindel Drive, Room B-213 Arnold AFB, TN 37389-2213.
Information Line: C-931-454-3000. DSN-312-340-5011.
Main Base Police: C-931-454-3117, C-931-454-5662.
Main Installation Website: http://www.arnold.af.mil/
Main Base Location: Located in middle Tennessee, nearly equal distance between Nashville and Chattanooga, neighboring Coffee and Franklin counties.
Directions to Main Gate: From US-231 south: Take TN-50/55 east to AEDC Highway in Tullahoma. From I-24: Take AEDC exit 117, 4 miles south of Manchester.
NMC: Chattanooga, 65 miles southeast. Nashville, 65 miles northwest.
NMI: Smyrna ANG Reserve Training Center, 60 miles northwest.
Base Social Media/Facebook: https://www.facebook.com/ArnoldAirForceBase/
Base Social Media/Twitter: https://twitter.com/aedcnews
Chapels: C-931-454-7970.
Medical: C-931-454-5351, DSN-312-340-5351.
Beauty/Barber Shop: C-931- 454-6987.
Commissary: C-931-454-7249.
Exchange: C-931-454-7153.
Military Clothing: C-931-454-7153.
Financial Institutions: Ascend Federal Credit Union, C-931-454-7277.
Clubs: Arnold Lakeside Center, C-931-454-3350.
Places to Eat: Cafe 100, C-931-454-5885 and Mulligan's Grill, C-931-454-3663 are

on base. Many restaurants within a short drive.

Fitness Center: C-931-454-6440. A&E Annex, C-931-454-6584.
Golf: Arnold Golf Course, C-931-454-4653.
ITT/ITR: C-931-454-6804.
Library: C-931-454-7220.
Marina: C-931-454-6084.
MWR: C-931-454-7779.
MWR Website:
http://www.arnold.af.mil/Home/Services
MWR Facebook:
https://www.facebook.com/ArnoldServices/
Outdoor Recreation: Outdoor Recreation, C-931-454-6084. Offers lawn and garden equipment, party rentals, campers, bicycle rentals, pavilions and more.
Swimming: Lakeside swimming area on base.
Things To Do: On this 44,000-acre installation, Woods Reservoir has a 75-mile shoreline for fishing and all water sports. Visit the Grand Ole Opry, Music Row, the Parthenon, the Hermitage in Nashville, Jack Daniel's Distillery, Rock City, Lookout Mountain in Chattanooga and NASA Space Center in Huntsville, AL.
Walking Trails: Running trail and track on base.

RV CAMPING & GETAWAYS

Arnold AFB FamCamp – Crockett Cove – Dogwood Ridge

Reservation/Contact Number Info: C-931-454-6084. Fax C-931-454-3326.
Recreation Security: C-931-454-5662, DSN-312-340-5662.
RV Website:
http://www.arnold.af.mil/Home/Services
GPS Coordinates: 35°19'19"N/86°4'4"W or 4174 Westover Road, Tullahoma, TN, 37388
Reservations: Accepted 90 days in advance for AD; 60 days in advance for Ret; 30 days in advance for DoD and 20 days for all others. Full payment due at time of reservation. Summer Office hours 0800-1800 Tues, Thurs-Sat; 1400-1800 Mon; 1000-1800 Sun; closed Wednesday. Check-in 1400 hours; Check-out 1100 hours.
Season of Operation: Year-round.
Eligibility: AD, NG, Res, Ret, DoD Contract personnel and Arnold AFB-Civ.
Camper/Trailer Spaces: FamCamp Gravel (36), Pull-thru (15), handicap accessible, E(115V/30A/50A)/W hookups, picnic table, grill. Rates: $15-$18 daily depending on season.
Tent Spaces: Primitive (16): No hookups, picnic table, grill. Rates: $6-$8 daily.
Yurt, A Frame, Cabin, Apt, Spaces: Cabins at Crockett Cove (5): Two-bedroom (2), sleeps 6. One-bedroom (3), sleeps 6. Heat/Air, Microwave, Mini-Fridge, Front Porch Swing, Grill, Picnic Table. Bathhouse on site. Linens not provided. Rates: One BR $40-$50 daily; Two BR $50-$60 daily depending on season. Dogwood Ridge Cabins (4): Sleeps 6, fully furnished with kitchen and living area, grill, porch swing, picnic table. Rates: $70-$80 depending on season. Linens not provided.
Support Facilities: Auto Craft Shop, Bathhouse, Beach, Boat Launch/Dock, Boat Rental/Storage, Commissary, Convenience Store, Exchange, Fire Rings, Fishing Pier, Fitness Center, Gas, Golf, Grills, Ice, Laundry, Marina, Pavilion, Picnic Areas, Playground, Rec Center, Rec Equipment, Restrooms, Sewage Dump, Showers, Snack Bar, Sports Fields, Tennis Courts, Trails.
RV Storage: Yes. C-931-454-6084.
Activities: Biking, Boating, Fishing*, Golfing, Hiking, Hunting*, Softball, Swimming, Water Skiing. *State license is required.
Credit Cards: Cash, Check, MasterCard and Visa.
Restrictions: Pets allowed on leash at FamCamp and Crockett Cove. No pets at Dogwood Ridge. No firearms.
RV Driving Directions/Location: On Base. From Gate 2: Turn left onto Pumping Station Road. Go to end and turn right onto Northshore Rd, going through three-way stop. FamCamp is approximately one mile on left.

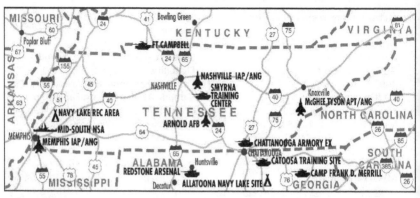

Area Description: Area offers a 4000-acre lake and a variety of recreational and historical sites within a 70-mile radius of the base including Tims Ford State Park, Old Stone Fort State Park, Tennessee Aquarium, Jack Daniel's Distillery in Lynchburg and George Dickle Distillery in Tullahoma. Limited support facilities available on base.

RV Campground Physical Address: Bldg 2915, Northshore Rd, Arnold AFB, TN 37388-5000. Mailing Address: FamCamp, 4174 Westover Road, Arnold AFB, TN 37388-5000.

Mid-South Naval Support Activity

Information Line: C-901-874-5111, DSN-312-882-5111.

Main Base Police: C-901-874-5533. Emergencies dial 911.

Main Installation Website: https://www.cnic.navy.mil/regions/cnrse/installations/nsa_mid_south.html

Main Base Location: NSA Mid-South is located in Millington, TN which lies 21 miles north of downtown Memphis.

Directions to Main Gate: Directions from Memphis International Airport to NSA Mid-South: Head West on Winchester Rd and follow it as it bears left then go right onto Airways Blvd. Turn left onto E Brooks Road for 1.5 miles and then go right onto I-55 North. Travel 1.0 miles and get onto I-240 North. Go 5.4 miles following as road goes into I-240 North/I-40 East. Travel 2.7 miles and take ramp onto Hwy 300

West. Travel 1.0 miles and take ramp for US 51 North. Follow as road goes into US 51 North-East. After 12 miles go right onto Navy Road/Hwy 205. Go 1.9 miles and then turn Left onto 1st Ave. Almost immediately turn right onto Bougainville Street and enter Mid-South NSA.

NMC: Memphis, 20 miles southwest.

NMI: Memphis IA/ANG, 25 miles north.

Base Social Media/Facebook: https://www.facebook.com/NSAMidSouth

Base Social Media/Twitter: https://twitter.com/NSA_MidSouth

Chapels: C-901-874-5341.

Dental Clinic: C-901-874-5351/5361.

Medical: Appointment Line, C-901 874-6100, DSN-312-882-6100.

Veterinary Services: C-901-874-5420.

Beauty/Barber Shop: Hair Care Center, C-901-872-5762.

Commissary: C-901-874-5125.

Exchange Gas: C-901-872-5790.

Exchange: C-901-872-5700.

Financial Institutions: Navy Federal Credit Union, C-1-888-842-6328.

Clubs: John Finn Club, C-901-874-5132. Glen Eagle Golf Club, C-901-874-5415.

Places to Eat: Eagle's Peak Golf Club, C-901-874-5415; Oaks Dining Room, C-901-874-5442; Samuel Adams Brewhouse, C-901-874-5323 and Seven Seas Dining Club, C-901-874-5132 are on base. Exchange Food Court offers Subway. Many restaurants within a short drive.

Fitness Center: Joe Dugger Sports and Fitness Complex, C-901-874-5497.

Golf: Glen Eagle Golf Course, C-901-874-5168.
ITT/ITR: C-901-874-5652/5455.
MWR: C-901-874-5179.
MWR Website:
http://www.navymwrmidsouth.com/
MWR Facebook:
https://www.facebook.com/navymwrmidsouth/
Outdoor Recreation: Outdoor Recreation Center, C-901-874-5675. Offers camping gear, sports equipment, mountain bike rentals, canoes, kayaks, water slides, party rentals, trailers and more.
Swimming: Splash Park, C-901-874-5497 offer outdoor recreation and sunning areas.
Things To Do: Visit Graceland, Beale Street (Home of the Blues) and Shelby Forest State Park, Children's Museum and more. The Memphis area is famous for bird and duck hunting as well as Memphis BBQ and many blues venues.

RV CAMPING & GETAWAYS
Glen Eagle Cottages

Reservation/Contact Number Info: C-901-874-5496.
Recreation Security: C-901-874-5533.
RV Website:
http://get.dodlodging.net/propertys/Mid-South-Cottages-and-RV-Parks
Other Info Website:
http://www.navymwrmidsouth.com/programs/1aa1bac8-2220-488e-8b27-d9688d113268
RV Email Address:
mwrwizard@gmail.com
GPS Coordinates:
35°20'43.5"N/89°51'11.9"W
Reservations: Reservations accepted one year in advance for AD, Res; 6 months in advance for all others. Cancellations must be made 14 days prior to arrival to avoid fee. Front Desk hours 1100-2100 Mon-Fri, 1400-2100 Sat-Sun, 1400-1900 holidays. Office hours 0730-1630 Mon-Fri. Check-in 1500 hours, check-out 1100 hours.
Season of Operation: Year-round.
Eligibility: AD, NG, Res, Ret, and their dependents; Widow/ers; DoD-Civ, DoD-Civ Ret and their dependents w/ID; DAVs.
Yurt, A Frame, Cabin, Apt, Spaces: Cottages at Glen Eagle (8): Three-bedroom (4) sleeps 8, three queen beds, fully furnished, full kitchen, CATV, Wi-Fi. Linens provided. Three bedroom (4), sleeps 8, two queen beds, two twin beds, fully furnished, full kitchen, CATV, Wi-Fi. Linens provided. Rates: $95-$105 for AD, Res. Seasonal and Eligibility rates apply. Confirm category rate at time of reservation. Manor on Attu: Three bedrooms, private baths, fully furnished kitchen, living area, screened porch, outdoor spaces, fenced in yard, ample parking, gas barbecue grill, gazebo and more. Contact facility for rates and information.
Support Facilities: Bathhouse, Chapel, free Laundry, Commissary, Convenience Store, Equipment Rental, Exchange, Fitness Center, Gas, Golf*, Ice, Pavilion, Playground, Rec Center, Restrooms, Shoppette, Splash Park, Sports Fields, Tennis Courts.
Activities: Golfing, Splash Park, Tennis. Paddle boats available at Navy Lake Recreation Area three miles away.
Credit Cards: American Express, Discover, MasterCard and Visa.
Restrictions: Pets are not permitted in cottages.
RV Driving Directions/Location: On Base. North of the Glen Eagle Golf Course on Attu Exd on the left.
Area Description: Located 21 miles north of Memphis and seven miles east of the Mississippi River. Navy Lake Recreation Area three miles away.
RV Campground Physical Address: 8027-8199 Attu Exd, Millington, TN 38053.

Midway RV Park

Reservation/Contact Number Info: C-901-874-5496.
Recreation Security: C-901-874-5533.
RV Website:
http://get.dodlodging.net/propertys/Mid-South-Cottages-and-RV-Parks
Other Info Website:
http://www.navymwrmidsouth.com/programs/55191f3b-36a4-4917-a1e9-62afe9748076

RV Email Address: mwrwizard@gmail.com
GPS Coordinates: 35°19'47"N/89°51'53"W
Reservations: Reservations accepted one year in advance for AD, Res; 6 months in advance for all others. Cancellations must be made 14 days prior to arrival to avoid fee. Front Desk hours 1100-2100 Mon-Fri, 1400-2100 Sat-Sun, 1400-1900 holidays. Office hours 0730-1630 Mon-Fri. Check-in 1500 hours, check-out 1100 hours.
Season of Operation: Year-round.
Eligibility: Midway RV Park: AD, NG, Res, Ret, DoD-Civ, DoD-Ret and 100% DAV. Open to public on space available.
Camper/Trailer Spaces: RV Sites (48): Concrete, E(110V/30/50A)/S/W hookups, back-in with 50' pad, picnic table, Wi-Fi. Rates: $21 daily. Campers (3): 32-34' on-site. Queen bed, 2-4 bunks, sleeps 6, fully furnished with full kitchen, Wi-Fi. Linens provided. Rates: $42 daily.
Support Facilities: Bathhouse, Chapel, free Laundry, Commissary, Convenience Store, Equipment Rental, Exchange, Fitness Center, Gas, Golf*, Ice, Pavilion, Playground, Rec Center, Restrooms, Shoppette, Splash Park, Sports Fields, Tennis Courts.
RV Storage: C-901-874-5440.
Activities: Golfing, Splash Park, Tennis. Paddle boats available at Navy Lake Recreation Area three miles away.
Credit Cards: American Express, Discover, MasterCard and Visa.
Restrictions: Pets must be on leash at RV Park. No firearms. Quiet hours 2200-0600.
RV Driving Directions/Location: On Base. From US-51: Turn East on Navy Road and drive 2 miles to the NSA Mid-South gate and turn right. Once inside the gate, make the first left onto Essex St. and go all the way to the stop sign and turn right onto Singleton Ave. Drive .5 miles to Polaris Drive. and turn left. Drive .2 miles and the RV Park is on the right.
Area Description: Located 21 miles north of Memphis and seven miles east of the Mississippi River. Navy Lake Recreation Area three miles away.
RV Campground Physical Address: Mid-South Cottages and RV Park, Ellison Recreation Center, 430 Essex St, Millington, TN 38054.

TEXAS

Belton Lake Recreation Area (BLORA)

Address: Fort Hood, TX 76544-5056.
Information Line: C-254-287/288-1110, DSN-312-737/738-1110.
Main Base Police: C-254-287-4001. Emergencies dial 911.
Main Installation Website: http://www.hood.army.mil/
Main Base Location: Located 14 miles northeast of main Fort Hood. The outdoor recreation area is primarily range country amidst range cattle along Belton Lake.
NMC: Belton, 11 miles south.
NMI: Fort Hood, adjacent.
Chapels: Ft Hood C-254-288-6545.
Medical: Available on Ft Hood, C-254-288-8000, DSN-312-738-8000.
Commissary: Approximately 14 miles to Warrior Way Commissary at Fort Hood, C-254-287-8025.
Exchange Gas: C-254-532-7200.
Exchange: Approximately 25 miles to Exchange facility at Fort Hood, C-254-532-7200.
Places to Eat: Fort Hood on base dining facilities are within driving distance.
Golf: The Courses of Clear Creek, C-254-287-4130.
ITT/ITR: C-254-287-7310, C-254-532-5292.
Marina: C-254-287-2523.
MWR: C-254-287-4126/1853.
MWR Website: https://hood.armymwr.com/us/hood
MWR Facebook: https://www.facebook.com/forthoodfmwr

Outdoor Recreation: BLORA Recreation, C-254-532-4907. Rental Equipment at Fort Hood, C-254-287-1853/4126. Belton Lake Outdoor Recreational Facility offers horseback riding, boating, swimming, surfing and other water activities including water equipment rentals.

Swimming: Waterslide, C-254-288-2928, Sierra Beach C-254-287-5544.

Things To Do: There is a full range of recreational opportunities offered here. Jet skis, fishing boats, paddle boats and ski boats can all be rented from the facility. There are also plenty of RV and tent campsites and party pavilions available for use by lodging patrons.

Walking Trails: Hiking/nature trails are available at BLORA.

RV CAMPING & GETAWAYS
BLORA

Reservation/Contact Number Info: C-254-287-2523/4907.

Recreation Security: C-254-287-0309.

RV Website: https://hood.armymwr.com/programs/belton-lake-outdoor-recreation-area1

GPS Coordinates: 31°10'3"N/97°34'44"W

Reservations: Required for cottages. Accepted 180 days in advance. Limited reservations for select RV sites but generally first come, first serve. Deposit for half of total reservation fee required when reservation is made. Office hours 24 hours daily. Check-in 1500 hours, check-out 1200 hours.

Season of Operation: Year-round.

Eligibility: AD, NG, Res, Ret, DoD-Civ, Dep and 100% DAV.

Camper/Trailer Spaces: RV Sites: Full hookup sites; single or double pad. Single Rates: $20-$22 daily; $400-$420 monthly. Partial, E/W hookups. Single Rates: $18-$21 daily; $350-$375 monthly.

Tent Spaces: Partial hookups. Rates: $10 daily per tent. Primitive sites, three areas. Rates: $6 daily per tent.

Yurt, A Frame, Cabin, Apt, Spaces: Cottages (15): One bedroom (10), sleeps 4 and Two-bedroom (5), sleeps 6.

Completely furnished with kitchen utensils, towels and linens; full bath, one queen bed(s) and sleeper sofa, screened in porch, BBQ grill, covered picnic table with a bench swing. One BR Rates: $45-$55 daily depending on rank; Two BR Rates: $60-$70, depending on rank. Mobile Homes (2): Three-bedroom, sleeps 8. Fully furnished with kitchen utensils, towels, linens. Full bathroom. Rates: $65-$70 daily.

Support Facilities: Bathhouse, Beach, Boat Launch, Coin Laundry, Equipment Rental, Fire Rings, Fishing Dock, Gas, Grills, Horse Ranch, Ice, Marina, Mountain Bike Trails, Pavilions, Picnic Areas, Playground, Restrooms, RV Storage, Sewage Dump, Showers, Snack Bar, Sports Fields, Telephones**, Trails, Video Rental. *BLORA Gate Fees: I.D. Cardholders: $3, Civilians per car: $10. **Local calls only.

RV Storage: C-254-287-2523/8303.

Activities: Beach, Bicycling, Boating, Fishing*, Golfing, Horseback Riding, Hunting**, Jet Skiing, Jogging, Mountain Biking, Nature Trails, Paddleboat Rides, Paintball, Swimming, Water Skiing, Waterslides (Seasonal). *To fish on Fort Hood, patrons must have a state license. **To hunt on Fort Hood, patrons must have a state license and Area Access Pass obtained through the Sportmen's Center, C-254-532-4552.

Credit Cards: Cash, Check, American Express, MasterCard, and Visa.

Restrictions: Pets are not allowed in cottages and must be on leash at all times. Owner must clean up after pets; owner will be assessed charges for any damage incurred by pets. No firearms or explosive materials. Campfires are only permitted in designated fire rings. Quiet hours 2200-0600 hours. All firearms must be registered with the Provost Marshal's office, C-254-287-2176, before bringing on base. After registering, firearms must be declared at the base gate.

RV Driving Directions/Location: Off Base. From I-35 north or south, near Belton, exit onto US-190 west. Follow .7 miles to Loop 121 north. From Loop 121 north pass stop sign and continue to a traffic light that has a large school on the northwest side of the road. Turn left (west) at light onto Sparta Road and continue for 6 miles to a cattle guard entering Fort Hood. Turn right onto Cottage Road at the Belton Lake Outdoor Recreation Area sign. From Fort Hood Area, take Martin Drive north and exit to Nolan Road, turn left at BLORA entrance.

Area Description: Primarily consisting of range country, with 2,032 acres bordering Belton Lake. Recreational opportunities include hiking and biking in nearby wooded areas and a wide variety of water sports. Belton Lake is known for black and white bass and crappie. Full range of support facilities available on post. Approximately 14 miles northeast of Fort Hood.

RV Campground Physical Address: Belton Lake Outdoor Recreation Area (BLORA), Cottage Rd, Fort Hood, TX 76544-5056.

Camp Mabry

Address: JFTX HQ/Camp Mabry, 2200 W 35th Street, Bldg 10, Austin, TX 78763.
Information Line: C-512-782-5001.
Main Base Police: C-512-782-5004. Emergencies dial 911.
Main Installation Website:
https://tmd.texas.gov/contact-us
Main Base Location: Located in northwestern Austin, in Travis County, Texas with Lake Austin (Colorado River) located approximately one-half mile to the west of the installation.
Directions to Main Gate: From the MOPAC Expressway/Loop 1: Exit the MOPAC Expressway at 35th Street. Drive west .6 miles past the old main gate, which is now barricaded, and go through the light at Exposition, and down a steep hill. At the bottom of the hill, just before a flashing traffic signal, the gated entrance of Camp Mabry is to the right at Maintenance Drive.
NMC: Austin, within city limits.
NMI: Fort Hood, 75 miles north.
Base Social Media/Facebook:
https://www.facebook.com/TexasState Guard

Base Social Media/Twitter:
https://twitter.com/TexasStateGuard
Chapels: C-512-782-5522.
Medical: Troop Clinic, C-512-782-5188.
Beauty/Barber Shop: C-512-371-7077.
Exchange: C-512-467-0050, C-512-459-1872.
Places to Eat: Marlene's Kitchen, C-512-782-6720 is on base. Exchange Food Court offers Subway, C-512-371-7058 and Paradise Smoothie, C-512-419-1007. Many restaurants are within driving distance of the facility.
Military Museum: Texas Military Forces Museum, C-512-782-5659
Military Museum Website:
http://www.texasmilitaryforcesmuseum.org/
Outdoor Recreation: Picnic areas and fishing permits, C-512-782-1062.
Things To Do: Enjoy Austin's Highland Lakes, hill country, Barton Springs, area caverns and wildflowers. There are a number of museums, excellent Tex-Mex food and a lively music scene in town. The Texas Military Forces Museum is across from the lodging facility.

RV CAMPING & GETAWAYS

Camp Mabry Travel Camp

Reservation/Contact Number Info: C-512-782-5500.
Reservations: Only available to NG stationed at Camp Mabry. Not open to AD, retirees or others.

Corpus Christi Naval Air Station

Address: 11001 D Street, Suite 143, Corpus Christi, TX 78419-5021.
Information Line: Quarterdeck/OOD, C-361-961-2384.
Main Base Police: C-361-961-2480/2282.
Main Installation Website:
http://www.cnic.navy.mil/regions/cnrse/installations/nas_corpus_christi.html
Main Base Location: Located in South Texas on the southeast side of the city surrounded on three sides by water: Corpus Christi Bay, Oso Bay and the Laguna Madre.

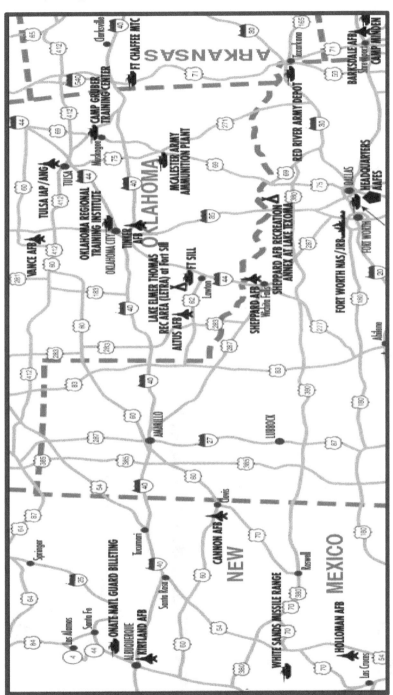

Directions to Main Gate: From San Antonio: On IH 37 merge onto TX-358. Take the South Padre Island Drive/SPID exit. Look for NASCC-CCAD sign.

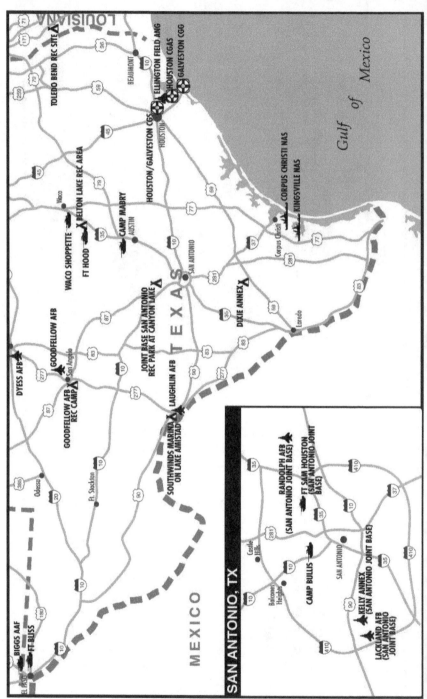

Continue on South Padre Island
Drive/SPID approximately 15 miles and

then exit on NAS Drive to NASCC South
Gate entrance. From the CC Airport:

Take the TX-44 ramp and merge on TX-44. Take the TX-358 exit and merge on TX-358. follow remaining directions above.

NMC: Corpus Christi, 10 miles west.
NMI: Kingsville NAS, 50 miles southwest.
Chapels Phone Numbers: Chaplain, C-361-961- 3751, C-361-533-1394.
Dental Clinic: C-361-961-3838.
Medical: C-361-961-2688/2994, DSN-312-861-2688.
Veterinary Services: C-361-961-3952.
Beauty/Barber Shop: Barber, C-361-961-0309. Beauty Shop, C-361-939-7981.
Commissary: C-361-961-2544/2545.
Exchange Gas: C-361-937-0304.
Exchange: C-361-961-2639/2166.
Financial Institutions: Navy Federal CU, C-361-986-4500, C-800-622-3631.
Clubs: Catalina Club, C-361-961-1155/2541.
Places to Eat: Flight Deck, C-361-961-2249; Gulf Winds Snack Bar, C-361-961-3360; Library Coffee Shop, C-361-961-0368; Subway at Lighthouse Lanes, C-361-361-939-9544 are on base. Many restaurants are within a short drive.
Bowling: Lighthouse Lanes Bowling Center, C-361-961-3805.
Fitness Center: Fitness Express, C-361-961-3164. E Street Gym, C-361-961-2401.
Golf: Gulf Winds Golf Course, C-361-961-3250.
ITT/ITR: C-361-961-3961.
Library: C-361-961-3574.
Marina: Paradise Cove Marina, C-361-961-1293.
MWR: C-361-961-2267/2268.
MWR Website:
http://www.navymwrcorpuschristi.com/
MWR Facebook:
https://www.facebook.com/MWRCorpusChristi
MWR Twitter:
https://twitter.com/NASCC_MWR
Outdoor Recreation: Outdoor Recreation Services, C-361-961-1293/1294. Offers outdoor adventure gear rentals, sports and recreational equipment including volleyballs, softballs, footballs, bats, horseshoes, mountain bikes and safety gear, camping equipment, kayaks, fishing boats and more.
Swimming: Bayside Outdoor Pool, C-361-961-3260 offers open swim and water slides.
Things To Do: Art Museum of South Texas, Corpus Christi Museum of Science and History, Mustang Island Beaches, Padre Island National Seashore, Selena Museum, Texas State Aquarium and USS Lexington.

RV CAMPING & GETAWAYS
Corpus Christi RV Park

Reservation/Contact Number Info: C-1-877-NAVY-BED, C-361-961-1293/1294, DSN-312-861-1293. Fax 361-961-2648.
Recreation Security: C-361-939-2480.
RV Website:
http://get.dodlodging.net/propertys/Navy-Getaways-NAS-Corpus-Christi-RV-Park
Other Info Website:
http://www.navymwrcorpuschristi.com/programs/7227acb2-87e6-48fe-bfb7-56973a9db972
GPS Coordinates:
27°41'44"N/97°15'9"W
Reservations: Accepted via telephone or online. Tent sites must call directly for reservation. Reservations accepted one year in advance for AD; 6 months in advance for Ret; and 3 months in advance for all others. Office hours 0800-1700 Mon-Sat. Closed Sunday. Cancellations must be made 30 day from arrival to avoid fee. Check-in 1400 hours, check-out 1100 hours. Maximum stay 90 days.
Season of Operation: Year-round.
Eligibility: AD, NG, Res, Ret, DoD-Civ, and MWR Guest Card holders.
Camper/Trailer Spaces: Shields RV Park Area (80): Concrete, back-in with 72' accommodation, E(50A)/W/S hookups, picnic table, grill. Rates: $20 daily. Paradise Cove Area (10): Grass/Gravel, with limited pull-thru, E(30A)/S/W hookups, picnic table, grill. Rates: $17 daily. Dry Sites $15 daily.

Tent Spaces: Primitive (10): No hookups, picnic table, grill. Rates: $12 daily.

Support Facilities: Auto Shop, Bath House, Beach, Boat Rental, Bowling, Chapel, Commissary, Convenience Store, Equipment Rental, Exchange, Fishing Pier, Fitness Center, Gas, Golf, Ice, Laundry, Marina, Pavilion, Picnic Area, Playground, Pool, Recreation Center, Restrooms, Sewage Dump, Shoppette, Showers, Sports Fields, Tennis Courts.

RV Storage: None.

Activities: Bicycling, Fishing, Golfing, Kayaking, Sailing, Shell-Collecting, Swimming, Water Skiing, Windsurfing.

Credit Cards: Cash, American Express, MasterCard and Visa.

Restrictions: Pets allowed on leash and must be kept under control at all times. Maximum three pets. Owner must provide shot and rabies vaccination records. No pets left unattended. Owners must clean up after pets. No firearms, campfires or fireworks.

RV Driving Directions/Location: On Base. From the Main Gate: Remain on Lexington Drive and at the second stop sign turn right on Ocean Drive to the RV Park. At the campground entrance, make a right turn to check-in at the marina.

Area Description: Located on beautiful Corpus Christi Bay. Corpus Christi offers a symphony, USS Lexington Museum, historical homes, art museum, the Texas State Aquarium, greyhound racetrack, Harbor Playhouse and the Columbus ships.

RV Campground Physical Address: Outdoor Recreation, Bldg 1757, Corpus Christi NAS, TX 78419.

Dixie Annex

Address: PO Box 1810, CR-401, Freer, TX 78357-1810.

Information Line: C-830-373-4419.

Main Base Police: Emergencies dial 911.

Main Installation Website: https://www.cnic.navy.mil/regions/cnrse/installations/nas_kingsville.html

Main Base Location: Located 23 miles northwest of Freer, TX.

NMC: Corpus Christi, 80 miles east.

NMI: Kingsville NAS, 80 miles northwest.

Base Social Media/Facebook: https://www.facebook.com/nas.kingsville.9/

MWR Website: http://www.navymwrkingsville.com/

RV Camping & Getaways
Dixie Annex

Reservation/Contact Number Info: C-830-373-4419.

Recreation Security: Emergencies dial 911.

RV Website: https://www.cnic.navy.mil/regions/cnrse/installations/nas_kingsville/about/Hunting.html

RV Email Address: kngv-huntmaster@navy.mil

GPS Coordinates: 28°5'9"N/98°44'23"W

Reservations: Reservations required. Children must be age 9 or older. Patrons must pay annual hunting fees only. Closed Thanksgiving weekend (4 days) and two weeks at Christmas. Call for availability and information. No set check-in, check-out time.

Season of Operation: Year-round.

Eligibility: AD, NG, Res, Ret, DoD-Civ, Dep, 100% DAV, DoD-Civ.

Yurt, A Frame, Cabin, Apt, Spaces: Lodge: Rooms (12), Rooms sleep 2-4. One full bed, some with bunks. Kitchen and showers available. Patrons must provide linens. The lodge is adjacent to a cookhouse with four BBQ pits, electric stove, and electric grill. The lodge also has a lounge with tables, big screen satellite TV/VCR/DVD, sofas, 8' pool table, darts, microwave, cooking utensils and pots and pans. Rates: No Charge.

Support Facilities: Grills, Ice, Picnic Area.

RV Storage: None.

Activities: Archery, Bird Watching, Fishing, Hiking, Horseback Riding, Hunting, Shooting Range, Wildlife Photography. Patrons' ATV's and horses are permitted.

Credit Cards: Mastercard and Visa.

Restrictions: Pets must be on leash or kenneled in room. No fully automatic weapons allowed. Alcoholic beverages are allowed but must not be consumed four hours prior to a hunt and/or any activity involving a firearm. ALL hunters must purchase a King's Hunt Club License and Big and Small Game/Bird Hunting Permits at ITT. All Hunters of age are required to possess a valid hunting license from the State of Texas.

RV Driving Directions/Location: Off Base. Escondido Ranch is located in the southwest corner of McMullen County Texas, 25 miles NW of Freer, TX. Take US 59 and SH 44 South from Freer. At 3.2 miles south of Freer turn right on SH 44 West towards Encinal. Travel 8.5 miles to Duval County Road 401. Turn right on Duval CR 401. Travel down 401 for 13 miles, this road dead ends at the ranch. There is only one fork in this road, stay on the right.

Area Description: Located on a hunting ranch in a remote desert area. Check supplies before coming into area, as no support facilities are available. Climate is very dry and hot. Average summer temperature is 105 degrees. All wooded areas are mesquite brush.

RV Campground Physical Address: Mailing Address: Escondido Ranch, P.O. Box 1810, Freer, TX 78357-1810.

Dyess Air Force Base

Address: Arnold Boulevard and S 7th, Dyess AFB, TX 79607.

Information Line: information Line, C-325-696-3113.

Main Base Police: C-325-696-2131. Emergencies dial 911.

Main Installation Website: http://www.dyess.af.mil/

Main Base Location: Located in west-central Texas located in Abilene, it is the center of a 22-county area called "The Big Country," and considered the economic hub of this part of Texas.

Directions to Main Gate: From the North: Take US Highway 277 or 83 south to the South 7th Street exit. Turn right on South 7th to Arnold Blvd. go left onto Arnold Blvd and follow to main gate on the right.

NMC: Abilene, 6 miles northeast.

NMI: Goodfellow AFB, 90 miles southwest.

Base Social Media/Facebook: https://www.facebook.com/DyessAirForceBase

Base Social Media/Twitter: https://twitter.com/DyessAFBase

Chapels: C-325-696-4224.

Dental Clinic: C-325-696-2304.

Medical: Appointments, C-325-696-4677.

Veterinary Services: C-325-696-3366/3367.

Beauty/Barber Shop: C-325-695-2089, C-325-695-0566. Beauty Shop, C-325-691-7233.

Commissary: C-325-696-4802.

Exchange Gas: C-325-692-6721.

Exchange: C-325-692-8996.

Financial Institutions: Bank of America Military Bank, C-325-690-6220. Federal Credit Union, C-325-676-2200, C-1-800-535-2157.

Clubs: Dyess Club, C-325-696-2405.

Places to Eat: Longhorn Dining Facility, C-325-696-2421; The Lift Flightline Kitchen, C-325-696-4861/2421; Deadwood Cafe, C-325-696-4166 and Legends Coffee and Cafe, C-325-696-3927 are on base. Exchange Food Court offers Charlie's, Subway, Smoothie-n-Things, Pinay Kitchen, and Black Box Pizza. Burger King is on base. Many restaurants are within a short drive.

Bowling: Dyess Lanes, C-325-696-4166.

Fitness Center: C-325-696-4306.

Golf: Mesquite Grove Golf Course, C-325-696-4384.

ITT/ITR: C-325-696-5206/5207.

Library: Hangar Center, C-325-696-2618.

MWR: C-325-696-2936.

MWR Website: http://www.dyessfss.com/

MWR Facebook: https://www.facebook.com/pages/DYESS-FORCE-SUPPORT-SQUADRON/277199586654

MWR Twitter: https://twitter.com/DyessFSS

Outdoor Recreation: Outdoor Recreation Center, C-325-696-2402. Offers boats, campers, air castles, grills, dunking booths, garden and camping equipment, base picnic grounds, batting cages and more. It also has the only year-round paintball field in the Abilene area. Adventure, shopping and sightseeing trips available.

Swimming: Outdoor Family Pool, C-325-696-2402 offers open swim. Dyess Fitness Center Indoor Pool, C-325-696-4306 for training and fitness only.

Things To Do: Abilene has an award-winning zoo, a collection of vintage aircraft on display at the base Air Park, boating, fishing and sailing at Lake Fort Phantom Hill and the Buffalo Gap Historic Village to offer.

RV CAMPING & GETAWAYS

Dyess AFB FamCamp

Reservation/Contact Number Info: C-325-696-2444.

Recreation Security: C-325-696-2131. Emergencies dial 911.

RV Website:
http://dyessfss.com/famcamp/

RV Email Address:
7.FSS.Outdoor.Recreation@us.af.mil

GPS Coordinates:
32°26'23.0"N/99°48'50.4"W

Reservations: Reservations accepted 60 days in advance for AD, 30 days for all others. Must submit online reservation form on website for reservations. First night's payment due at time of reservation and is refundable up to the day before check-in. Payment due upon arrival. Office hours 0900-1700 Mon-Tue, Thur-Fri. Closed Wed, Sun. Check-in at Bldg 9220, check-out 1100 hours. Late arrival self-registration located inside laundry room. Check-in with office by 1000 hours next business day. Maximum stay 180 days.

Season of Operation: Year-round.

Eligibility: AD, NG, Res, Ret, DoD-Civ and Eligible Contractors.

Camper/Trailer Spaces: RV Sites (24): Full-hookup, picnic table. grill, CATV, Wi-Fi. Rates: $35 daily, $130 weekly, $350 monthly.

Support Facilities: Auto Hobby, Bathhouse, Bowling, Commissary, Dining, Equipment Rental, Exchange,

Fitness Center, Golf, ITT, Laundry, Showers, Swimming

RV Storage: C-325-696-2444.

Activities: Batting Cages, Bowling, Golfing, Paintball, Swimming.

Credit Cards: MasterCard and Visa.

Restrictions: Pets allowed on leash. No open fires. Do not feed wildlife. Quiet hours 0900-0700.

RV Driving Directions/Location: On Base. From the Main Gate: Ask for directions at gate.

RV Campground Physical Address: 926 Louisiana Drive, Dyess AFB, TX 79607.

Fort Bliss

Address: Robert E. Lee Gate, Bldg 5400 Robert E. Lee, Fort Bliss, TX 79916.

Information Line: C-915-568-2121, DSN-312-978-2121.

Main Base Police: C-915-568-2115.

Main Installation Website:
https://www.bliss.army.mil/

Main Base Location: Fort Bliss is comprised of approximately 1.12 million acres of land in Texas and New México. The Main Cantonment Area of Fort Bliss is located adjacent to El Paso, Texas.

Directions to Main Gate: From I-10: Exit at Joe Battle Blvd/375 loop and travel North to the intersection of the 601 Spur/Liberty Expressway. After exiting follow the loop to the Chaffee exit and arrive at gate. From Airway Blvd: Travel North on Airway Blvd crossing through the intersection of Airport Road. Enter the post from the east side through the Robert E. Lee gate which is a 24-hour gate. From US 54 and enter through the Pershing Gate by following signs for Pershing Road or through the Cassidy Gate by following signs to Cassidy Road.

NMC: El Paso, within city limits.

NMI: Biggs Army Airfield, adjacent.

Base Social Media/Facebook:
https://www.facebook.com/FortBlissGarrison/

Base Social Media/Twitter:
https://twitter.com/armybliss

Chapels: Chaplain, C-915-568-1519. Chaplain Services - SFAC, C-915-568-6879.

Dental Clinic: C-915-569-2511.

Medical: Appointments, C-915-569-2273. C-915-742-2121.
Veterinary Services: C-915-569-2266.
Beauty/Barber Shop: Freedom Crossing, C-915-562-2573. WBAMC, C-915-562-2651. Paul Mitchell, C-915-562-3643.
Commissary: C-915-568-6688.
Exchange Gas: Stuart Express, C-915-564-1810. Luke Express, C-915-566-0418. Purple Heart Express, C-9150581-3204. Logan Heights, C-915-562-4460.
Exchange: C-915-562-7200.
Financial Institutions: Armed Forces Bank, N.A., C-915-562-5454, Wells Fargo Bank, C-915-521-4066.
Clubs: Pershing Pub, C-915-781-6809. Samuel Adams Pub, C-915-744-8427.
Places to Eat: Bullseye Bar & Grill, C-915-568-2983. Java Express, C-915-744-2732. Strike Zone Snack Bar, C-915-568-6272. The Golden Tee, C-915-568-1116. Freedom Crossing Mall offers many restaurant dining options. Exchange Food Court offers Anthony's Pizza, Baskin-Robbins, Charley's. Starbucks, Subway, Taco Bell, Burger King, Arby's, Einstein Bros Bagels and Manchu Wok. Subway, Burger King, Pizza Hut, Smoothie King and other fast food eateries are located throughout the base.
Bowling: Desert Strike Lanes, C-915-568-6272/1685.
Fitness Center: Logan Heights Fitness Center, C-915-568-5198. Stout Fitness Center, C-915-568-3264. Milam Fitness Center, C-915-568-7318. Warrior Gym, C-915-741-5930. Iron Works Gym, C-915-744-5201. Tennis Club & Fitness Zone, C-915-569-5448. Soto Fitness Center, C-915-744-5788. Biggs Fitness Center, C-915-744-8730.
Golf: Underwood Golf Complex, C-915-568-1059.
ITT/ITR: C-915-569-6446.
Library: Mickelson Library, C-915-568-1902. Soldier Activity Center Library, C-915-744-1534.
Military Museum: Fort Bliss and Old Iron Sides Museums. C-915-568-5412,
Military Museum Website: http://www.bliss.army.mil/Museum/
MWR: C-915-568-3500.

MWR Website: https://bliss.armymwr.com
MWR Facebook: https://www.facebook.com/blissmwr
MWR Twitter: https://twitter.com/blissmwr
Outdoor Recreation: Fort Bliss Outdoor Recreation, C-915-744-1532. Offers laser tag, wall climbing, camping equipment, water rentals and backpacking gear.
Swimming: Fort Bliss Aquatic Center, C-915-741-5901 offers three pools for leisure or training activities. Central Fort Bliss Outdoor Pool, C-915-744-1532 offers recreational swim. West Fort Bliss Outdoor Pool, C-915-568-4825 offers water slides and recreational swim. Fort Bliss Splash Park, C-915-744-8087 offers recreational swim for children 10 and under.
Things To Do: Fort Bliss offers many activities on base. Visit Wyler Aerial Tramway, Hueco Tanks State Historic Site, El Paso Museum of Art, El Paso Zoo, El Paso Holocaust Museum, Franklin Mountains State Park or Magoffin Home State Historic Site. Visit old Juarez and the Tiqua Indian Reservation and check out the Scenic Drive that views of all of El Paso and old Mexico.
Walking Trails: Hiking trails available at RV park.

RV CAMPING & GETAWAYS

Fort Bliss RV Park & Family Campground

Reservation/Contact Number Info: C-915-568-0106/4693, DSN-312-978-0106. Fax C-915-568-2028, DSN-312-978-2028.
Recreation Security: C-915-568-2115.
RV Website: https://bliss.armymwr.com/programs/rv-park-and-family-campground
GPS Coordinates: 31°50'26"N/106°26'34"W
Reservations: No advance reservations. Payment must be made in full at time of check-in. Office hours 0800-1600 Mon-Fri, 0800-1500 Sat-Sun and holidays. Check-in at office upon arrival or with

Camp Host if late arrival, check-out 1300 hours. Call for length of stay policy.

Season of Operation: Year-round.
Eligibility: AD, NG, Res, Ret, DoD-Civ (active & retired), Dep, 100% DAV.
Camper/Trailer Spaces: Hardstand/Gravel (133): Pull-thru, maximum length 65', handicap accessible, E(220V/30/50A)/S/W hookups, picnic table, grill. Rates: $18-$19 daily, $108-$114 weekly.
Support Facilities: Auto Craft Shop, Auto Repair, Bath House*, Bowling, Chapel, Coin Laundry, Commissary, Convenience Store, Diesel, Exchange, Family Room w/Wi-Fi Kitchen Area, Fitness Center, Gas, Golf, Grills, Ice, Mess Hall, Pavilion*, Picnic Area*, Playground*, Pool, Propane (Off Base), Rec Center, Restrooms*, RV Storage, Sewage Dump, Shoppette*, Showers, Snack Bar*, Sports Fields, Tennis Courts. *Handicap accessible.
RV Storage: C-915-568-0106.
Activities: Bowling, Golfing, Hiking Trails, Horseback Riding, Swimming, Tennis.
Credit Cards: MasterCard and Visa.
Restrictions: Pets allowed on leash only; owner must clean up after pets. Pets must be walked in designated area, doggie walk. No open fires.
RV Driving Directions/Location: On Base. Located at Logan Heights Annex of Ft. Bliss. From I-10 East or West in El Paso: Take exit 22 north onto US-54 north. Take exit 25 to Ellerthorpe. At Bottom of ramp, stay in left lane and turn left at light, heading west on Ellerthorpe. Go through next signal and campground is on left one block down the road. Follow signs on where to turn. From I-10 east or west of El Paso: Take exit 162 east onto NM-404/Ohar Rd to NM-213 south to US-54. Follow directions above. Check in at the office located in the front of the park entrance.
Area Description: In west Texas near Rio Grande River. Carlsbad Caverns National Park is an easy drive east. White Sands National Monument is a two-hour drive north. Ciudad Juarez, Mexico's largest border city, is a short distance across Rio Grande River. Three museums on post. A full range of support facilities is available on post.
RV Campground Physical Address: 4130 Ellerthorpe Ave, Fort Bliss, TX 79916-5000.

Fort Sam Houston

Address: 2484 Stanley Road, JBSA-Fort Sam Houston, TX 78234.
Information Line: C-210-221-1211.
Main Base Police: C-210-221-2222.
Main Installation Website: http://www.samhouston.army.mil/
Main Base Location: Fort Sam Houston is located on the northeast side of San Antonio, considered Military City USA.
Directions to Main Gate: From the Airport: Follow E Terminal Drive to I-410. Turn left onto I-410 Access Rd/NE I-410 Loop. Take slight left onto I-410 E ramp and merge onto I-410 E. Take exit 24 toward Harry Wurzback Road/Ft. Sam Houston. Continue on road to Post Gate. Continue straight until 4-way stop sign, turn right onto Dickman Road. Destination will be on the left.
NMC: San Antonio, within city limits.
NMI: Randolph AFB/San Antonio JB, 15 miles northeast.
Base Social Media/Facebook: https://www.facebook.com/JointBaseSanAntonio/
Base Social Media/Twitter: https://twitter.com/jbsa_official?lang=en
Chapels: Chaplain, C-210-221-9363. Main Office, C-210-221-5004. AMEDD-Chapel, C-210-221-3231/4210.
Dental Clinic: Budge Clinic, C-210-808-3736/3735. Rhodes Clinic, C- 210-295-4156.
Medical: C-210-916-4141. Moreno Primary Care Clinic, C-210-916-9900.
Veterinary Services: C-210-808-6104.
Beauty/Barber Shop: Mini-Mall, C-210-225-2357. Bldg 2841, C-210-225-1118. SAMMC, C-210-227-7280. C-210-224-4360. Paul Mitchell, C-210-212-8410.
Commissary: C-210-221-4678.
Exchange Gas: C-210-221-3301.
Exchange: C-210-225-5566.

Financial Institutions: Broadway Bank, C-210-227-7131, C-1-888-777-0740. San Antonio Credit Union, C-210-258-1111.
Places to Eat: Backswing Cafe, C-210-221-5863; Sam Houston Lanes Grille, C-210-221-5029; Rocco DFAC, C-210-221-3608; Slagel DFAC, C-210-808-1532/1536 and Sam Houston Community Center are on base. Exchange Food Court offers American Eatery, Anthony's Pizza, Baskin Robbins, Charley's, Subway and Seattle's Best Coffee. Mini-Mall Exchange offers Burger King, Domino's, Subway, Taco Bell and Wing Zone. SAMMC offers Burger King. Einstein Bros Bagels, Popeye's, Starbucks and additional Burger King and Subway locations are on base. Many restaurants are within a short drive.
Bowling: The Bowling Center, C-210-221-4740/3683.
Fitness Center: Jimmy Brought Fitness Center, C-210-2211234. Central Post Fitness Center, C-210-221-3593. Fitness Center on the METC, C-210-808-5709.
Golf: Fort Sam Houston Golf Course, C-210-221-5863.
ITT/ITR: C-210-808-1378/1376.
Library: Campbell Memorial, C-210-221-4387.
Marina: Hancock Cove and Sunnyside Marina at JBSA Canyon Lake, C-830-964-3576.
Military Museum: Fort Sam Houston Museum, C-210-221-6358.
Military Museum Website: http://ameddmuseum.amedd.army.mil/
MWR: C-210-221-2606.
MWR Website: https://jbsatoday.com/
MWR Facebook: https://www.facebook.com/FortSamMWR
MWR Twitter: https://twitter.com/FortSamFMWR
Outdoor Recreation: Outdoor Equipment Center, C-210-221-5225/5224. Outdoor Equipment offers a wide variety of equipment for rent ranging from fishing boats to travel trailers, sporting equipment to camping gear and more.
Swimming: The Aquatic Center C-210-221-4887 offers a 50 meter Olympic size swimming pool, water slides, lap lanes, a kiddy pool. During the summertime, swimming lessons are available, and pool can be reserved for pool parties. Jimmy Brought Fitness Center Indoor Pool, C-210-221-1234 offers lap swim and open swim. Lifeguard Training available.
Things To Do: San Antonio has had a colorful military history. From "Rough Riders" and Teddy Roosevelt to key roles in WWI and WWII, this post continues its legacy today as a medical training center. While you're here, visit the Alamo, Downtown River Walk, Retama Horse Racing Park, Sea World, Six Flags Fiesta Texas and the Medical Museum.
Walking Trails: Available at Salado Park.

RV CAMPING & GETAWAYS

Fort Sam Houston RV Park

Reservation/Contact Number Info: C-210-221-5502.
Recreation Security: C-210-221-2222.
RV Website: https://jbsatoday.com/FSH-RV-Park
Reservations: Accepted up to one year in advance. Office hours 0900-1600 Mon-Fri; 1000-1500 hours Sat-Sun with limited services. Closed all Federal holidays. Cancellation fee of $17 applicable. Check in at campground office upon arrival. Payment due upon arrival. Check-in 1200 hours, check-out 1200 hours.
Season of Operation: Year-round.
Eligibility: AD, NG, Res, Ret, 100% DAV, DoD-Civ (AD/Ret w/ ID card).
Camper/Trailer Spaces: Hardstand (74), Pull-through, Maximum 45' in length with tow car, E(110V/15A/30/50A)/S/W, picnic table and grill. Rates: $20 daily, $120 weekly, $440 monthly.
Support Facilities: Boat/Equipment Rental, Bowling, Chapel, Commissary, PX, Class Six, Shoppette, Gas Station (2), Fitness Center, Golf, Pool, Equestrian Center, Salado Park, Bathhouse/Restrooms, Ice (For Fee), Propane (Fill), Sewage Dump Station located on RV Park grounds.

RV Storage: C-210-221-5224.
Activities: Boating, Golfing, Swimming.
Credit Cards: Cash, Check, MasterCard and Visa.
Restrictions: No personal mail/package delivery service at the RV Park. If having mail or packages forwarded, it must be thru UPS or FEDEX and delivered directly to site number (site numbers are assigned ONLY upon arrival). Please check with the office upon arrival for address to use for UPS and FEDEX. Breed restrictions apply: No Pit Bulls, Rottweiler's, or any dog that shows aggression. Please check with Security Forces for other breed restrictions. No exotic pets. Dogs must be kept on a leash at all times unless in the designated dog run. Owner must pick up after pets immediately. All pets must have current shots.
RV Driving Directions/Location: On Base. Call ahead to confirm directions or verify online at www.fortsammwr.com, construction scheduled for the next 2 years. Winans Gate Hours M-F 0630-2200, Sat, Sun and holidays. From I-35 North or South: Exit 164-A/Rittiman Rd. Proceed west on Rittiman Rd. for approximately 2 miles. Turn left onto Harry Wurzbach, get in the left lane and turn left onto Winans Rd at traffic light. At the three-way stop sign, turn right onto Nursery Rd. The road will split into a "Y" and continue to bear left at the school to remain on Nursery Rd. At the school's fence, take first left on to the new bridge. The RV Park will be the second paved road on the right. If arriving after the Winans Gate hours of operation: From I-35 North or South: Exit 164-A/Rittiman Rd. Proceed west for approximately 2 miles. Turn left onto Harry Wurzbach and continue until reaching gate. From the Gate: Turn Left onto Stanley Rd. Make a left at the first traffic light onto Schofield and continue to the next traffic light. Go left onto Garden. Follow Garden to second stop sign and turn right onto Hardee. Hardee will T-Bone into Williams. Turn left onto Williams. At the stop sign at the school, make a hard right onto Nursery Rd. At the school, make the first left and cross the new bridge. The RV Park will be the second paved road on the right hand side of the road.
Area Description: Surrounded by San Antonio, this historic post has seen much colorful military history, from its namesake to the Rough Riders and Teddy Roosevelt, and played key roles in WWI and WWII. Full range of support facilities on post.
RV Campground Physical Address: Recreational Vehicle Park, Bldg 3514, 3820 Petroleum Dr, Fort Sam Houston, TX 78234-2718. Business Mailing address (not for personal mail): RV Park C/O 502 NAF AO, 2380 Stanley Rd, Ste. 20, JBSA Fort Sam Houston TX, 78234-2718

Goodfellow AFB Recreation Camp

Address: 1950 South Concho Drive, San Angelo, TX 76904-7912.
Information Line: C-325-654-1110, DSN-312-477-1110.
Main Base Police: C-325-654-3504. Emergencies dial 911.
Main Installation Website: http://www.goodfellow.af.mil/
Main Base Location: Located on Lake Nasworthy, a small municipal lake located in San Angelo.
NMC: San Angelo, 3 miles north.
NMI: Goodfellow AFB, 19 miles northeast.
Commissary: Approximately 10 miles to the Commissary at Goodfellow AFB, C-325-653-2441.
Exchange: Approximately 10 miles to the Base Exchange at Goodfellow AFB, C-325-655-5789, C-325-654-3361.
Places to Eat: Snack bar located at Rec Camp.
Marina: Spring Creek Marina, C-325-944-3850.
MWR: C-325-654-3213.
MWR Website: https://www.gogoodfellow.com/
MWR Facebook: https://www.facebook.com/17fssgoodtimes
Outdoor Recreation: Rec Camp, C-325-944-1012. Offers outdoor boating

equipment, waterslide rentals and more.

Swimming: Lake Nasworthy offers a variety of water activities and seasonal pool.

Things To Do: Many outdoor activities including kayaking, sailing, fishing, swimming and more.

JB San Antonio Recreation Park – Canyon Lake

Address: Joint Base San Antonio Recreation Park, 698 Jacobs Creek Park Road, Canyon Lake, TX 78133.

Information Line: C-210-652-1110, DSN-312-487-1110.

Main Base Police: Emergencies dial 911.

Main Installation Website: http://www.jbsa.mil/

Main Base Location: Canyon Lake is a reservoir on the Guadalupe River in the Texas Hill Country.

NMC: San Antonio, 48 miles south of Canyon Lake.

NMI: Randolph AFB, 35 miles southwest of Canyon Lake.

Places to Eat: There are several restaurants within driving distance from Canyon Lake.

Golf: Fort Sam Houston Golf Course, C-210-222-9386.

ITT/ITR: C-210-652-5142 opt. 1.

Marina: 1-888-882-9878, C-830-964-3318.

MWR Phone Number: C-800-280-3466, C-830-226-5357.

MWR Website: https://jbsatoday.com/

MWR Facebook: https://www.facebook.com/502FSS/

MWR Twitter: https://twitter.com/502fss

Outdoor Recreation: Canyon Lake Recreation Park, C-800-280-3466, C-830-226-5357. Offers footballs, soccer balls and horseshoes. For bicycle rental fees, inquire at the Welcome Center located at the Hancock Cove office.

Swimming: Swimming at Canyon Lake Beach area.

Things To Do: Canyon Lake's 80 miles of shoreline simmer with a singular beauty found in central Texas. It is a natural haven for fishing, camping, boating and picnicking. The area includes 300 feet of well-maintained sandy beach and a quarter-acre marina. A full range of support facilities is available at Fort Sam Houston.

RV CAMPING & GETAWAYS

Canyon Lake Recreation Park

Reservation/Contact Number Info: C-800-280-3466, C-830-226-5357. Fax C-830-964-4405.

Recreation Security: Emergencies dial 911.

RV Website: https://jbsatoday.com/JBSA-Canyon-Lake

RV Email Address: jbsalodgingres@gmail.com

GPS Coordinates: 29°53'22"N/98°13'9"W

Reservations: Reservations accepted 6 months in advance for AD; 90 days in advance all others, DOD cardholders. All fees will be charged on the day of arrival. Reservations are confirmed only after payment is processed. Two-night minimum on weekends and holiday stays. Cancellations made 48 hours prior to arrival will be charged a $15 admin fee. Pet fees may apply. RV Sites allow for weekly and monthly rates during winter season only. Summer Office hours 0800-1900 Fri-Sun; 0800 to 1800 Mon-Thur. Winter hours 0800-1500 hours daily. Check-in 1500 hours, check-out 1100 hours. After hours check-in at gate from 1600-2200.

Season of Operation: Year-round.

Eligibility: AD, NG, Res, Ret, 100% DAV, Dep and DoD-Civ AD/Ret

Camper/Trailer Spaces: RV Sites Hancock Cove (26): Full hookup and partial. Includes one vehicle pass. Rates: $18-$20 daily; $110-$120 weekly; $420-$440 monthly depending on site hookups.

Tent Spaces: Camping Area (200): Primitive sites with one vehicle pass. Rates: $15 daily. Sunnyside group camping $85 daily.

Yurt, A Frame, Cabin, Apt, Spaces:
Hancock Cove Cottages (33): Fully
furnished, three bedroom cottages.
Sleeps 8. Linens provided. Rates: $110
daily. Premium cottages $135 daily.
Bunkhouses (10): Two bunkbeds,
refrigerator, microwave, AC and heat.
Rates: $25 daily. Sunnyside Cabins (6):
Fully furnished, full bath, sleeps 7.
Linens provided. Rates: $95 daily. Lofts
(18): Kitchenette and living area, full
bath, sleeps 5. Linens provided. Rates:
$70 daily. Bungalows (15): Refrigerator,
microwave, bath with shower. Sleeps 4.
Rates: $45 daily. Towels are not
provided with units, but bedding is.
Please verify at time of reservation.
Vehicle passes provided.

Support Facilities: Bathhouse, Beach,
Boat Launch, Boat Rental, Boat Slip,
Convenience Store, Fire Rings, Fishing
Pier, Fishing Tackle, Gas (boats only),
Golf, Grills, Group Picnic Area, Ice, Jet
Ski, Laundry, Marina, Nature Trail,
Pavilion, Picnic Areas, Playgrounds,
Propane, Recreation Equipment,
Restrooms, Sewage Dump, Showers,
Trails.

RV Storage: C-830-964-3576.

Activities: Boating, Fishing, Jet Skiing,
Scuba Diving, Swimming, Volleyball,
Water Skiing and more.

Credit Cards: American Express,
MasterCard and Visa.

Restrictions: Pets permitted in pet
friendly areas as designated. No pets in
lodging facilities. Owners responsible
for pet waste. Pets must be on a 6' or
shorter leash at all times. No firearms
are allowed. No smoking in any facility.

RV Driving Directions/Location: Off
Base. Take Interstate 35 through New
Braunfels to the Canyon Lake/Exit 191.
Follow access road to signal lights. Turn
left onto Farm Road 306. Drive
approximately 16 miles to Canyon City.
Continue another 1.5 miles past the
traffic light in Canyon City to Jacobs
Creek Park Road. Turn left on Jacobs
Creek Road and proceed to JBSA
Recreation Park at Canyon Lake.

Area Description: Mild winter
temperatures make this natural haven a
year-round attraction for fishing,

camping, boating and picnicking. There
is a majestic view of the 8,240-acre lake
and its 80-mile shoreline. The recreation
park consists of 250 acres of the most
beautiful lakefront property in the area.
Sandy beaches and marinas make this
an outdoor lovers paradise.

RV Campground Physical Address: JBSA
Recreation Park, 689 Jacobs Creek Park
Road, Canyon Lake, TX 78133-3535.

Kingsville Naval Air Station

Address: 554 McCain Street, Suite 214,
Kingsville, TX 78363.

Information Line: PAO, C-361-516-6146.

Main Base Police: C-361-516-
6217/6200, Emergencies dial 911.

Main Installation Website:
http://www.cnic.navy.mil/regions/cnrse
/installations/nas_kingsville.html

Main Base Location: Located in Kleberg
County, Texas about 2 miles east of
Kingsville in the south gulf coastal
plains.

Directions to Main Gate: Take exit to
Highway 77 at the General Cavazas Blvd
exit and turn east. Main Gate entrance
to the air station is located
approximately one mile ahead.

NMC: Corpus Christi, 50 miles
northeast.

NMI: Corpus Christi, 50 miles northeast.

Base Social Media/Facebook:
https://www.facebook.com/nas.kingsvil
le.9/

Chapels: Chaplain, C-361-516-6331.

Dental Clinic: C-361-516-6332.

Medical: C-361-516-6160/6313, DSN-
312-876-6160.

Beauty/Barber Shop: C-361-516-6447.

Commissary: C-361-516-4242.

Exchange Gas: C-361-516-6361.

Exchange: C-361-516-6362.

Financial Institutions: Federal Credit
Union, C-1-888-842-6328.

Clubs: No-Fly Zone, C-361-516-4701.

Places to Eat: Subway, C-361-592-8900
and Spinz, C-361-516-6506 are on base.
Many restaurants are within a short
drive.

Bowling: Stars & Strikes Bowling Center,
C-361-516-6196.

Fitness Center: Santiago Fitness Center, C-361-516-6171.
ITT/ITR: C-361-516-6449.
Library: C-361-516-6271.
MWR: C-361-516-6232.
MWR Website:
http://www.navymwrkingsville.com/
MWR Facebook:
https://www.facebook.com/NASKMWR
Outdoor Recreation: Community Recreation, C-361-516-6191/6449. Offers boating, camping, fishing, and limited hunting equipment rentals, lawn and garden equipment, bicycles, party rentals and more.
Swimming: Santiago Fitness Center Indoor Pool, C-361-516-6171 offers lap and open swim.
Things To Do: Home of the King Ranch, famous for Santa Gertrudis cattle, beautiful thoroughbred and quarter horses and the historic ranch house. Texas A&M University is also located here.

RV CAMPING & GETAWAYS
Rocking K RV Park

Reservation/Contact Number Info: C-1-877-NAVY-BED, C-360-516-6191, DSN-312-861-6191. Fax C-361-516-6787.
Recreation Security: C-361-516-6217.
RV Website:
http://get.dodlodging.net/propertys/Rocking-K-RV-Park
Other Info Website:
http://www.navymwrkingsville.com/programs/f06d1e88-ec4f-440e-8630-45c93151d24c
GPS Coordinates:
27°29'56"N/97°49'15"W
Reservations: Reservations accepted up to one year in advance for AD, 6 months for all others. Cancellations require 30 day notice prior to arrival to avoid fee. Office hours 0700-1700 Mon; 0800-1700 Tue-Fri. Closed weekends and holidays. Check-out 1200 hours. No maximum stay.
Season of Operation: Year-round.
Eligibility: AD, NG, Res, Ret, DoD-Civ (AD & Ret), Dep and 100% DAV.
Camper/Trailer Spaces: RV Sites (30): Pull-thru, back-in spaces (30' and 60' spaces) with W/E hookups, picnic table. Rates: $18 daily. Camper (1): Permanent trailer with E/W/S hookups, picnic table. Rates: $18.50 daily.
Tent Spaces: Grass Overflow: Primitive, no hookups. Rates: $10 daily.
Support Facilities: Auto Hobby Shop, Bath House, Bicycles, Boat Rentals/Storage, Bowling, Chapel, Coin Laundry, Commissary, Convenience Store, Diesel, Exchange, Fitness Center, Gas, Grills, Laundry, Mechanic/Auto Repair, Mini-Mart, Pavilion, Picnic Areas, Playground, Pool, Propane, Rec Equipment, Restrooms, Sewage Dump, Shoppette, Showers, Snack Bar, Sports Fields & Stables.
RV Storage: C-361-516-6191.
Activities: Birding, Boating, Deep Sea Fishing, Fishing (On Base), Hunting, King Ranch Tours, Swimming, On Base Fishing*. Sports Fields, Tennis Courts, Stables. *Station Permit Required. Available at ITT Office.
Credit Cards: American Express, Discover, MasterCard and Visa.
Restrictions: Pets allowed on leash; owners must have proof of vaccinations for pets. Owners must clean up after pets. No excessive barking. Pets must not be left tied out or unattended. All firearms must be registered with security upon arrival. Quiet hours 2200-0700.
RV Driving Directions/Location: On Base. From the Main Gate: Proceed .2 miles to a "T" and turn left. Proceed .5 miles to water tower and turn left into parking lot to check-in, Bldg 3783, on th left.
Area Description: Park is on the South Texas Birding Trail, 20 minutes from Baffin Bay (trophy trout capital of the world), 45 minutes from beautiful Corpus Christi, and near the world famous King Ranch (the largest working cattle ranch in the continental United States). Full logistical support facilities available on base.
RV Campground Physical Address: 601 Nimitz Ave, Bldg 3765, Kingsville, TX, 78363

Lackland Air Force Base

Address: SW Military Road, Lackland AFB, TX 78236.
Information Line: C-210-671-1110, DSN-312-473-1110.
Main Base Police: C-210-671-2419. Emergencies dial 911.
Main Installation Website:
http://www.jbsa.af.mil/
Main Base Location: Located southwest of San Antonio in Bexar County.
Directions to Main Gate: Arriving from the North on I-35, Highway 281, or I-10: In San Antonio turn right onto Loop 410 West. Take the Valley Hi/Lackland AFB exit and turn left on Valley Hi. Continue ahead to the Airman's Gate.
NMC: San Antonio, 6 miles northeast.
NMI: Fort Sam Houston/San Antonio JB, 18 miles northeast.
Base Social Media/Facebook:
https://www.facebook.com/JointBaseSanAntonio/
Base Social Media/Twitter:
https://twitter.com/jbsalackland
Chapels: Gateway Chapel, C-210-671-2911.
Dental Clinic: AF Dental School and Clinic, C-210-292-0123. Dunn Dental Clinic, C-210-292-8850.
Medical: Wilford Hall, C- 210-292-7412. Urgent Care, C-210-292-7331.
Veterinary Services: C-210-671-3354/3631.
Beauty/Barber Shop: Wilford Hall, C-210-292-4763. BMT, C-210-673-2110. Troop Mall North, C-210-673-4018; Stylique Salon, C-210-670-9956. Security Hill, C-210-923-9405. C-210-673-5252. Paul Mitchell Salon, C-210-674-1341.
Commissary: C-210-671-2837.
Exchange Gas: C-210-674-0848. Troop Mall, C-210-645-1264.
Exchange: C-210-674-6465.
Financial Institutions: Federal Credit Union, Air Force, C-210-673-5610, C-1-800-277-5328. Bank of America Military Bank, C-210-674-6266. Eisenhower National Bank, C-210-673-8420.
Clubs: Gateway Club, C-210-645-7034 offers the Maverick and the Lonestar Lounges. Primo Lounge, C-210-671-1234. Primo Lounge, C-210-671-1224.
Places to Eat: Gateway Club, C-210-645-7034. Greenside Grill, C-210-671-2006. Smoking Joe's BBQ, C-210-671-3784. Susie's Grill, C-210-671-1224. Exchange Food Court offers Arby's. Anthony's Pizza, Baskin Robins, Charley's, Manchu Wok and Starbucks. Express offers Popeye's. Wilford Hall ASC offers Subway and Chocollazo Coffee Shoppe. BMT Mini Mall offers Domino's, Popeye's, Starbucks and Subway. Troop Mall North offers Anthony's Pizza, Baskin Robins, Burger King and Subway. Security Hill Express offers Subway and Tam's Coffee Shop. Amigo Inn Dining Facility, C-210-671-5112/5113. Bldg 5570, C-210- 671-0833/1952. Lackland Training Annex, C-210-671-4818/4819. BMT Training location offers several dining facilities. Additional Burger King location on base and Laziz Mediterranean Food Truck. Many restaurants are within a short drive.
Bowling: Skylark Bowling Center, C-210-671-1234.
Fitness Center: Chaparral Fitness Center, C-210-671-2401/2361. Gateway Fitness Center, C-210- 671-1348/2565. Gillum Fitness Center, C-210-977-2353. Medina Fitness Center, C-210-671-4525/4477. Warhawk Fitness Center, C-210-671-2016/3490.
Golf: Gateway Hills Golf Course, C-210-671-3466/2517.
ITT/ITR: Tickets, C-210-671-3059. Leisure, C-210-671-7111.
Library: C-210-671-3610.
Military Museum: Airman Heritage Museum, C-210-670-0100.
Military Museum Website:
https://myairmanmuseum.org/
MWR: C-210-671-3396.
MWR Website: https://www.myjbsa-fss-mwr.com
MWR Facebook:
https://www.facebook.com/LacklandFSS/
Outdoor Recreation: Lackland Outdoor Adventure Center, C-210-925-5532/5533. Offers boat and camper rentals, party rentals, park and pavilion reservations, home and garden tool

rentals, sporting equipment, trailers, grills and paintball.

Swimming: Skylark Aquatics Center, C-210-671-3780 offers open swim. lap swim and swim lessons. Warhawk Seasonal Outdoor Pool, C-410-671-3445 offers open swim, diving board, kiddie pool and slides.

Things To Do: San Antonio takes its name from Mission San Antonio de Valero. Visiting the local Missions and brushing up on the long history of this gracious city are only a few of the activities for visitors in this part of Texas.

Walking Trails: Scenic trails are available on base.

RV CAMPING & GETAWAYS
Lackland AFB FamCamp

Reservation/Contact Number Info: C-210-671-5179, DSN-312-473-5179. Fax C-210-925-5536.

Recreation Security: C-210-671-2018.

RV Website: https://jbsatoday.com/LAK-FamCampRVPark

GPS Coordinates: 29°23'55"N/98°36'48"W

Reservations: No advance reservations. Office hours 0700-1600 hours Mon-Fri, 1300-1700 hours Sat. Closed Sun. Check-out 1200 hours. Maximum stay 30 days with 24-hour departure before returning. Maximum stay 180 days per year.

Season of Operation: Year-round.

Eligibility: AD, NG, Res, Ret, DoD-Civ (AD and Ret), Dep, 100% DAV.

Camper/Trailer Spaces: RV Sites (41): Full hookup sites, picnic table, grill. Access to showers. Free Wi-Fi. Rates: $20 daily; $120 weekly; $440 monthly. Sponsored guests $22 daily.

Support Facilities: Auto Craft Shop, Boat Rental/Storage, Bowling, Cafeteria, Car Wash, Chapel, Coin Laundry, Commissary, Convenience Store, Exchange, Fitness Center, Gas, Golf, Grills, Ice, ITT, Mess Hall, Parks, Pavilion, Picnic Areas, Playground, Pools, Rec Center, Rec Equipment, Restrooms, RV/Auto Resale Lot, RV Storage, Shoppette, Showers, Shuttle/Bus, Snack Bar, Sports Fields, Stables, Telephones, Tennis Courts.

RV Storage: Yes. C-210-215-0404.

Activities: Biking, Golfing, Hiking, Hunting*, Sightseeing. *State license and base permit are required.

Credit Cards: MasterCard and Visa.

Restrictions: Pets allowed on leashes less than 10' in length. Must have current immunizations. Owner must clean up after pet. Firearms to be checked in to the security police armory. No open fires. Quiet hours 2200-0600 hours.

RV Driving Directions/Location: On Base. From US-90: Exit Acme Road, proceed south on Acme and turn right onto Growden Dr. south to Andrews Rd, turn right on Andrews and go about 1.75 miles. Andrews Rd becomes Kelly Dr. Turn right (north) on Kenly Ave. Turn right on Luke Blvd. Near end of road, turn left on Foster Ave. FAMCAMP is on the right located behind Wilford Hall Medical Center at Bldg 2804.

Area Description: FAMCAMP is located on flat terrain. Pad for RV is 10'x35', for vehicle, 9'x19'. San Antonio offers many and varied opportunities for sightseeing. Conveniently located near to a full range of support facilities available on base. Located near Wilford Hall Medical Center.

RV Campground Physical Address: 2804 Foster Ave, Lackland AFB, TX 78236. Mailing Address: Lackland Outdoor Adventure Center, 37 MSG/SVROF, 309 Westover St, Bldg 871, Lackland AFB, TX 78236-5234

Laughlin Air Force Base

Address: 548 Laughlin Drive, Bldg 468, Laughlin AFB, TX 78843.

Main Base Police: C-830-298-5100. Emergencies dial 911.

Main Installation Website: http://www.laughlin.af.mil/

Main Base Location: Laughlin Air Force Base is located six miles east of Del Rio, Texas, and about nine miles from the international bridge to Ciudad Acuna in

Coahuila, Mexico. It is known as "the best little town on the border".

Directions to Main Gate: From the east/San Antonio: Take Highway 90 west to Del Rio. Laughlin AFB is located on Hwy 90 approximately 6 miles east of Del Rio. From the west in El Paso: Take Interstate Highway 10 east to Van Horn and then follow Hwy 90 east to Del Rio. Or elect to remain on IH 10 east to Sonora and then Hwy 277 south to Del Rio. This is a longer route, but more time spent on the Interstate. Once in Del Rio follow the signs to Highway 90 east directly to Laughlin AFB.

NMC: Del Rio, 6 miles northwest.

NMI: Lackland AFB/San Antonio JB, 140 miles east.

Base Social Media/Facebook: https://www.facebook.com/LaughlinAir ForceBase

Base Social Media/Twitter: https://twitter.com/LaughlinAFB

Chapels: Chaplain, C-830-298-4975/5667. C-830-298-5111.

Dental Clinic: C-830-298-6333/6531.

Medical: C-830-298-6333/6470/6471. DSN-312-732-6333.

Veterinary Services: C-830-298-5500.

Beauty/Barber Shop: C-830-298-0870. Anderson Hall, C-830-298-5344. Stylique Salon, C-830- 298-0390.

Commissary: C-830-298-5822.

Exchange Gas: C-830-298-3867.

Exchange: C-830-298-2111.

Financial Institutions: Border Federal Credit Union, C-830-774-3503/5626, C-830-775-9225. COMPASS Bank, C-830-774-6861.

Clubs: Club XL, C-830-298-5139/5134.

Places to Eat: Stripes, C-830-298-5295; Silver Wings, C-830-298-5661; Cactus Lanes Snack Bar, C-830-298-5526 and The Fit Bar, C-830-298-4640 are on base. Exchange Food Court offers Subway. Many restaurants are within a short drive.

Bowling: Cactus Lanes Bowling Center, C-830-298-5526.

Fitness Center: Losano Fitness Center, C-830-298-5251.

Golf: Leaning Pine Golf Course, C-830-298-5451.

Library: C-830-298-5119.

Marina: Southwinds Marina on Lake Amistad, C-830-775-7800.

MWR: C-830-298-5826.

MWR Website: http://laughlinservices.com/

MWR Facebook: https://www.facebook.com/47FSSLaug hlin

MWR Twitter: https://twitter.com/LAFBServices

Outdoor Recreation: Outdoor Recreation Center, C-830-298-5830. Offers camping, skeet and trap range, paintball, marina, horse stables, picnic grounds and much more. Also offer a wide variety of equipment rentals including camping and outdoor sports equipment.

Swimming: Losano Fitness Center Indoor Pool and Seasonal Outdoor Pool, C-830-298-5251 offers lap swim and open swim.

Things To Do: Visit the historical district in Brown Plaza, Particularly for Cinco de Mayo and Diez y Seis de Septiembre celebrations. The Brinkley Mansion, Val Verde Winery and the visitors center at Lake Amistad, are all worthwhile to visit.

Walking Trails: Outdoor trails are on base.

RV CAMPING & GETAWAYS

Laughlin AFB FamCamp

Reservation/Contact Number Info: C-830-298-5830, DSN-312-732-5830.

Recreation Security: C-830-298-5100.

RV Website: https://www.laughlinfss.com/fun/famc amp/

GPS Coordinates: 29°21'5"N/100°46'54"W

Reservations: Reservations accepted 8 weeks in advance for AD; 6 weeks for Ret; 3 weeks for all others. Reservations may be made by phone with credit card, or in person with first night paid in full upon reservation. Summer Office hours 1000-1700 Mon-Fri, 1000-1400 Sat; Winter hours 1000-1700 Mon-Fri. Check-in with Camp Host at Site 11 or ODR Office, Bldg 540 during business hours. Check-in 1200, check-out 1200. Maximum stay 180 days unless PCS.

Season of Operation: Year-round.

Eligibility: AD, NG, Res, Ret and DoD-Civ.

Camper/Trailer Spaces: Hardstand (20), pull-thru, no maximum length, E(110/220V/30/50A)/W/S hookups, CATV, telephone, picnic table, grill. Rates: $125 daily, $150 weekly, $375 monthly. No overflow available.

Support Facilities: Auto Craft Shop, Bowling, Chapel, Commissary, Exchange, Fitness Center, Gasoline, Golf, Grills, Internet at Library and Lodging, Laundry (Free), Pavilion, Picnic Area, Playground, Pool, Rec Equipment, Restrooms*, RV, Sewage Dump, Sports Fields, Tennis Courts. * Handicap accessible.

RV Storage: Yes. C-830-298-5830.

Activities: Golfing, Swimming, Tennis.

Credit Cards: MasterCard and Visa.

Restrictions: Pets allowed on leash. Firearms are prohibited. To make arrangements for storing of any weapons, contact security forces.

RV Driving Directions/Location: On Base. From the Main Gate: Follow Liberty Drive straight ahead to FamCamp.

Area Description: Situated near Texas/Mexico border and near Presa de la Amistad Reservoir and recreation area. Full range of support facilities on base.

RV Campground Physical Address: Bldg 540 Liberty Ave, Laughlin AFB, TX.

Red River Army Depot

Address: 100 James Carlow Drive, Red River Army Depot, Texarkana, TX 75507.

Information Line: C-903-334-2141, DSN-312-829-2141.

Main Base Police: C-903-334-3911/3333.

Main Installation Website: https://www.redriver.army.mil/

Main Base Location: Located in an area commonly known as the Four States Area. The Depot is situated in Northeast Texas, Bowie County, approximately 18 miles west of Texarkana.

Directions to Main Gate: Driving from Texarkana: Take I-30 West to Exit 206 and go south to Hwy 82 at red light and take a left and proceed approximately 1.3 miles to the Red River Army Depot Main Gate. Driving from Dallas: Take I-30 East to Exit 206 and continue same as above from Texarkana.

NMC: Shreveport, 70 miles southeast.

NMI: Barksdale AFB, 70 miles south.

Base Social Media/Facebook: https://www.facebook.com/RRADTX/

Base Social Media/Twitter: https://twitter.com/RRAD_TX

Medical: C-903-334-2155, DSN-312-829-2155.

Exchange: Shoppette, C-903-832-2687.

Financial Institutions: Credit Union, C-903-334-3156.

Fitness Center: C-903-334-2733.

ITT/ITR: C-903-334-2733.

MWR: C-903-334-4652.

MWR Website: https://redriver.armymwr.com/

MWR Facebook: https://www.facebook.com/RRAD-MWR-Elliott-Lake-718345974955269/

MWR Twitter: https://twitter.com/redrivermwr

Outdoor Recreation: Outdoor Recreation Services, C-903-334-2688. Offers boat rentals, mountain bikes, bounce houses and more.

Swimming: Splashpad on base. Lake Elliott swimming available.

Things To Do: The Country Store has discount tickets to Six Flags over Texas, as well as information on many other attractions in the area.

Walking Trails: Two nature trails on base.

RV CAMPING & GETAWAYS

Elliot Lake Recreation Area

Reservation/Contact Number Info: C-903-334-2688/2254.

Recreation Security: C-903-334-3333.

RV Website: https://redriver.armymwr.com/programs/rentals-lodging

GPS Coordinates: 33°22'55"N/94°16'3"W

Reservations: RV Sites are first come, first serve. Required for cabins and may be made up to six months in advance. Check-in at Elliott Lake Country Store, 1400 hours for cabins. Check-out 1200 hours.

Season of Operation: Year-round.

Eligibility: AD, NG, Res, Ret and DoD-Civ, and all employees of federal, state and local government agencies within the four-state area.

Camper/Trailer Spaces: RV Sites (44): Full hookup sites, back-in. Rates: $15 daily. Other discounts may apply.

Tent Spaces: Remote Primitive (20), no hookups. Rates: $2 daily.

Yurt, A Frame, Cabin, Apt, Spaces: Log Cabins: Two-bedroom/one bath (15), two-bedroom/two bath (2), 3 bedroom/2.5 bath (1), some handicap accessible, furnished, private bath, central heat and air, kitchen, microwave, coffee maker, satellite TV, outdoor patio and grill. Patrons must provide cookware and linens. Rates: 1 BR: $75 daily; 2 BR: $125 daily; 3 BR: $150 daily. Deposit required. Shelters: Electric only. Rates: $6 daily.

Support Facilities: Bait, Beach, Boat Launch, Boat Rental, Canoes, 2 Conference Centers, Country Store, Laundry, Marina, Nature Trails, Pavilion, Picnic Areas, Playground, Rec Equipment, Restrooms, Splashpad, Sewage Dump, Showers*. * Handicap accessible.

RV Storage: None.

Activities: Archery, Boating, Fishing*, Hiking, Hunting*, Swimming. *License is required.

Credit Cards: Cash, Check, American Express, MasterCard and Visa.

Restrictions: Pets are allowed in cabins. Pet deposit required. No firearms. Recreation permit required for all patrons. No lifeguards, swim at own risk. ATVs restricted.

RV Driving Directions/Location: On Base. From the East Gate: Take first left onto Texas Street and follow for two blocks, then turn right onto Avenue K. Follow Avenue K south as it joins East Boundary Patrol Road for 4 miles to a "Y" intersection in the road. Turn left at the "Y" intersection and follow for 3 miles to campground on left. Proceed to second road in campground and turn left for office and registration.

Area Description: Located in a wooded area on 183-acre Elliott Lake in northeast corner of state. Excellent for overnight camping, vacationing, sightseeing and trips into scenic Arkansas mountains. Recreation area is a 210-acre reserve. Wide range of support facilities available on post.

RV Campground Physical Address: Elliot Lake Recreation Facility, Red River Army Depot, Attn: AMSTA-RR-U, Texarkana, TX 75507-5000.

Sheppard AFB Recreation – Lake Texoma

Address: 1030 SAFB Road, Whitesboro, TX 76273.

Information Line: C-940-676-2511, DSN-312-736-2511.

Main Base Police: Emergencies dial 911.

Main Installation Website: http://www.sheppard.af.mil/

Main Base Location: Amidst the beautiful scenery at Lake Texoma lies the Sheppard Annex Lodge.

NMC: Dallas, 100 miles south.

NMI: Fort Worth NAS/JRB, 100 miles south.

Exchange: Convenience store located onsite, C-903-523-4613.

Places to Eat: Steakhouse and lounge located inside of the annex. Catfish Haven, C-903-564-3107, Don's BBQ, C-903-564-5813 and Pelican's Landing, C-903-523-4500 are within driving distance.

Fitness Center: Exercise Room at lodging facility.

Marina: C-903-523-4613.

MWR: C-940-676-3492.

MWR Website: http://www.82fss.com/

MWR Facebook: https://www.facebook.com/SheppardFSS

MWR Twitter: https://twitter.com/SheppardFSS

Outdoor Recreation: Outdoor Recreation C-940-676-4141. Offers camping, fishing and watersports gear, boats, tennis equipment, movies, board games, volleyball, basketball and tennis courts, soccer and softball fields, horseshoes and more.

Swimming: Lake Texoma swimming available.

Things To Do: This facility is located on a very large inland lake. It is the perfect spot for fishing, swimming and other water activities.

Walking Trails: Hiking and nature trails available at facility.

RV CAMPING & GETAWAYS

Lake Texoma Recreation

Reservation/Contact Number Info: C-903-523-4613.

Recreation Security: C-903-893-4388.

RV Website: http://82fss.com/food-fun/sheppard-annex-lake-texoma/

RV Email Address: brenda.riddle@us.af.mil

GPS Coordinates: 33°52'47"N/96°53'55"W

Reservations: Reservations for cabins and RV sites accepted three months in advance for AD beginning on the 1st of each month. Retirees may make reservations from the 6th and DoD-Civ, employees/dependents may make reservations from the 11th of each month. Full payment must be received within 15 days of making reservations to be considered confirmed. Cancellation fee applies. Office hours 0800-1700 daily. Check-in at facility 1500 hours, check-out 1200 hours. Failure to check-out on time will result in charge for extra day. Campsites: Available on first come, first serve basis.

Season of Operation: Year-round.

Eligibility: AD, NG, Res, Ret, Dep, Federal Employees and Guests.

Camper/Trailer Spaces: RV Sites (31): Full E(110V/50A)/S/W hookups. Rates: $25 daily. Partial (16), E(110V/50A)/W hookups. Rates: $20 daily. Weekly and monthly rates available.

Tent Spaces: Primitive sites (30), picnic table, fire ring. Rates: $8 daily.

Yurt, A Frame, Cabin, Apt, Spaces: Cabins: One-bedroom (41), sleeps four

to six, furnished, private bath, microwave, A/C, TV/VCR. Rates: $45-$50 daily. Two-bedroom (4), furnished, private bath, microwave, A/C, TV/VCR. Rates: $60-$65 daily. Three-bedroom (1): Sleeps 8, furnished, private bath, microwave, refrigerator, A/C, TV/VCR. Rates: $95 daily. Linens and towels provided. Treetop Rates: $75 daily. Seasonal rates apply.

Support Facilities: Bait, Basketball Court, Beach, Boat Launch/Slips, Boat Storage, Convenience Store, Crappie House, Fitness Center, Gas, Grills, Laundry, Marina, Movies, Multi-Purpose Court, Pavilions, Picnic Area, Playgrounds, Rec Equipment, Rec Room (With TV), Restrooms, Sewage Dump, Showers, Snack Bar, Steakhouse/Lounge*, Telephone, Trails, Vending Machine, Video Rental. * Open on special occasions.

RV Storage: C-903-523-4613.

Activities: Basketball, Driving Range, Fishing, Hiking, Horseshoes, Softball, Swimming, Volleyball, Water Skiing. Special seasonal holiday activities.

Credit Cards: MasterCard and Visa.

Restrictions: No ATVs or dirt bikes. No firearms. No fireworks. No hunting permitted on the annex.

RV Driving Directions/Location: Off Base. From Dallas/Fort Worth: Take I-35 north to Gainesville, TX then east on Hwy 82. From Oklahoma City: Take I-35 south to Gainesville, then Hwy 82 east. From Wichita Falls: Use Hwy 82. Travel east on Hwy 82 to exit 624, Whitesboro, TX. Travel north on Hwy 377 for 10 miles, you will see a sign for Sheppard Annex. Turn left (north) onto Farm Rd 901, proceed 1.8 miles to Rock Creek Rd. Turn right (east) and follow signs to Sheppard Annex. CAUTION: Road has curves, hills and is narrow. Recreation Area is located on Texas side of Lake Texoma.

Area Description: Located approximately 120 miles east of base at Wichita Falls, near the Texas/Oklahoma line on one of the largest, most popular inland lakes in the area. Some of the best fishing is available as well as a variety of other water sports.

RV Campground Physical Address:
Sheppard AFB Recreation Annex at Lake Texoma, 1030 SAFB Road, Whitesboro, TX 76273-5000.

Southwinds Marina on Lake Amistad

Address: Southwinds Marina, 1522 Marina Access Road, Del Rio, TX 78840-5000.
Information Line: C-830-298-1110.
Main Base Police: C-830-298-5100. Emergencies dial 911.
Main Installation Website:
http://www.laughlin.af.mil/
Main Base Location: Located along the Mexican and American border in the desert with over 850 miles of shoreline and 68,000 acres of lake.
NMC: Del Rio, 12 miles west.
NMI: Laughlin AFB, 22.5 miles west.
Commissary: Approximately 21 miles to the commissary at Laughlin AFB, C-830-298-5822.
Exchange: Approximately 21 miles to the Base Exchange at Laughlin AFB, C-830-298-2111.
Golf: Leaning Pine Golf Course, C-830-298-5451.
Marina: C-830-775-7800.
MWR: C-830-775-7800.
MWR Website:
https://www.laughlinservices.com/
MWR Facebook:
https://www.facebook.com/47FSSLaughlin
MWR Twitter:
https://twitter.com/LAFBServices
Outdoor Recreation: Laughlin AFB Outdoor Recreation, C-830-298-5830.

RV CAMPING & GETAWAYS

Southwinds Marina on Lake Amistad

Reservation/Contact Number Info: C-830-775-7800. Fax C-830-775-5971.
Recreation Security: Emergencies call 911.
RV Website:
https://www.laughlinfss.com/fun/marina/

RV Email Address: lafb.marina@gmail.com
GPS Coordinates: 29°28'17"N/101°2'12"W
Reservations: Reservations required and accepted 8 weeks in advance for AD; 6 weeks in advance for Retirees and all others 3 weeks in advance. Cancellations must be received 24 hours in advance to avoid charge. No refunds after arrival. Check-in at store 0900-1500 Thur-Sun.
Season of Operation: Year-round.
Eligibility: AD, NG, Res, Ret and DoD/NAF-Civ.
Camper/Trailer Spaces: RV Sites (15): E(220V/30/50A)/S/W hookups, picnic table. Rates: $25 daily, $150 weekly, $375 monthly. Partial Hookups (5): W/E only. Rates: $20 daily; $95 weekly; $250 monthly. Trailers (2): On-site with full hookups, fully furnished; sleeps up to eight. Linens are not provided. Rates: $55 daily, $250 weekly, $515 monthly.
Tent Spaces: Tent Spaces: (5): Primitive sites with covered picnic table. Rates: $5 daily.
Yurt, A Frame, Cabin, Apt, Spaces: Cabins (4): sleeps seven, queen bedroom, bunk beds, full-size sofa bed, loft, full bath, full kitchen with microwave, refrigerator, stove, dishes and utensils. Guests must supply own linens, bedding and cleaning supplies. Rates: $55 daily; $215 weekly; $540 monthly.
Support Facilities: Boat Rental, Convenience Store, Grills, Laundry, Pavilion Rental, Picnic Areas, Restrooms, Showers, Sewage Dump, Dry Storage, Wet Slips.
Activities: Boating (ski, fishing and pontoon), Canoeing, Fishing, Kayaking, Natural History, Paddle-boarding, Sailing, Water Skiing. Boat rentals and water activities available on site.
Credit Cards: Cash, Check, MasterCard and Visa.
Restrictions: Pets allowed on leash (RV). No firearms allowed. Generators are permitted.
RV Driving Directions/Location: Off Base. From US-90 west of Del Rio: Take Amistad Dam Road/Spur 349 south

which is the same turn off as Governors Landing. Continue straight down road and stay to the right. Turn right on Marina Access Rd to the end of road. **Area Description:** Situated near Amistad Dam which serves as passageway to Mexico. Ideal freshwater recreation area and outstanding fishing. Many deer in the area. Good base for day trips into Mexico. Convenient to Ciudad Acuna, Mexico. Full range of support facilities at Laughlin AFB 30 miles southeast. **RV Campground Physical Address:** 1522 Marina Access Rd, Del Rio, TX 78840-5000.

UTAH

Carter Creek Camp

Address: CCC, Mill Creek Road, Kamus, UT 84036.
Information Line: C-801-777-1110, DSN-312-777-1110.
Main Base Police: C-801-777-3056, DSN-312-777-3056. Emergencies dial 911.
Main Installation Website: http://www.hill.af.mil/
Main Base Location: Carter Creek Campground is located on the north slope of the beautiful Uinta Mountains primitive area in rural Kamas, UT.
NMC: Salt Lake City, 113 miles southwest.
NMI: Hill AFB, 107 miles west.

RV CAMPING & GETAWAYS
Carter Creek Camp

Reservation/Contact Number Info: C-801-777-9666/3525. Fax C-801-777-3855.
RV Website: https://www.75fss.com/carter-creek/
GPS Coordinates: 40°54'42"N/110°47'31"W
Reservations: Required and accepted 60 days in advance beginning May 1. Payment due at time reservation is made. Cancellations must be made 14

days prior to reservation. Reservation confirmation receipts must be shown at Carter Creek in order to check in with the Camp Host. Note: There are no provisions for drop-in patrons. Office hours 0800-1700 Mon-Fri, 0800-1200 Sat. Check-in 1400-2000 hours with Camp Manager, check-out 1300 hours.
Season of Operation: July 1-Oct 31 (weather permitting).
Eligibility: AD, NG Res, Ret, Dep, DoD-Civ and 100% DAV.
Camper/Trailer Spaces: RV Pads: Gravel (4): E(110/220V/20/30/50A)/W hookups. Rates: $20 daily.
Tent Spaces: Primitive (3): No hookups. Rates: $15 daily.
Yurt, A Frame, Cabin, Apt, Spaces: Cabins (7): One-bedroom (5), sleeps five. Rates: $60 daily. Two-bedroom (1), sleeps seven. Rates: $70 daily. Large Cabin: (1), sleeps six, double bed, single bed, bunk beds, refrigerator, microwave, kitchenette, heater, dining table with chairs. Rates: $100 daily. Patrons must provide own cooking and eating utensils, bed linens, food, towels, soap, warm clothing, fishing gear, ice for personal coolers, and other recreational equipment. Limit five-seven people depending on cabin rented. Trailers: (4): Sleeps four; stove, refrigerator and sink. Rates: $60 daily.
Support Facilities: Bathhouse, Fire Rings, Grills, Picnic Area, Playground, Restrooms, Shower, Swings, Trails.
RV Storage: None.
Activities: Badminton, Fishing*, Hiking, Horseshoes, Hunting*, Volleyball. *License required. UTV Rentals: $90 per day includes one tank of gas. Canoe Rentals: $20 per day includes life jackets and paddles.
Credit Cards: MasterCard and Visa.
Restrictions: Pets allowed on leash; owner must clean up after pet. No shooting in or near camp. Fires permitted in designated areas only. No phone available. No firearms, BB guns, paintball guns, or sling shots allowed in camp. No off-road motorcycles, three wheelers, ATV's or Bicycles allowed in camp. All trash must be taken out of camp when leaving. On weekends

(Friday and Saturday) only two cabins can be rented by each family. The entire camp can be reserved Sunday through Thursday only.

RV Driving Directions/Location: Off Base. Take I-84/I-80 East up Weber Canyon to Evanston, WY exit 5 and Hwy 150 South to the Bear River Service Station at mile mark 49. Go .1 miles and turn left. Proceed approximately 4 miles to Carter Creek Camp, which is on the right side of the road. Look for the sign. The road leading to Carter Creek Camp is gravel.

Area Description: The surroundings of Carter Creek are typical of the Uinta Mountains with Lodgepole Pines and Quaking Aspens; a perfect combination of sight and sound. The rustic campsite is located in mountains at 9000 ft altitude. Fishing lakes and ponds nearby.

RV Campground Physical Address: Mailing Address: Carter Creek Campground, 7526 11th St, Bldg 805, Hill AFB, UT 4056-5000.

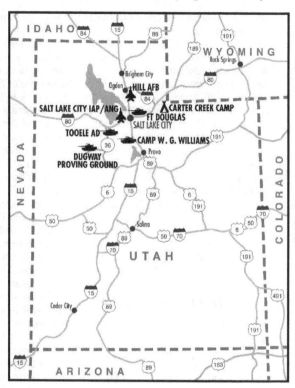

Dugway Proving Ground

Address: Dugway Proving Ground, 5220 Doolittle Ave, Dugway, UT 84022.

Information Line: C-435-831-2116, DSN-314-789-2116.

Main Base Police: C-435-831-2929. Emergencies dial 911.

Main Installation Website: http://www.dugway.army.mil

Main Base Location: Located in rural open range country south of the Great Salt Lake amidst cattle, deer, jack rabbits, antelope and mountain lions.

Directions to Main Gate: From Salt Lake City and the Airport: Take I-80 west to the Tooele/Grantsville/Exit 99. Follow Route 36 South through Erda, Tooele and Stockton (Last gas station is at Stockton, beyond Stockton, the highway will split). Stay right on Route 36. Turn right at the Clover exit onto Route 199. Follow Route 199 to Dugway approximately 25 miles from Clover. Route 199 is a winding mountain road which goes through a pass and on to Dugway. Although the road is well maintained during the winter months, travelers should watch for ice and adhere to all road signs.

NMC: Salt Lake City, 80 miles northeast.

NMI: Tooele Army Depot, 42 miles northeast.

Base Social Media/Facebook: https://www.facebook.com/USArmyDPG

Chapels: C-435-831-2431.

Medical: C-435-831-2211, DSN-312-789-2211.

Veterinary Services: C-801-777-2611.

Commissary: C-435-831-2164.

Exchange Gas: C-435-831-4773.

Exchange: C-435-831-4773.

Financial Institutions: Dugway FCU C-435-831-4572.

Clubs: Community Club, C-435-831-2901.

Places to Eat: Community Club, C-435-831-2901 and Ditto Diner, C-435-831-5193 are on base. Exchange Food Court offers Subway. Limited restaurants within a short drive.

Bowling: Ott Bowling Center, C-435-831-2626 (reservations needed).

Fitness Center: Dugway FC, C-435-831-2705.

ITT/ITR: C-435-831-2318/2705.

Library: C-435-831-2178.

MWR: C-435-831-2028/2093.

MWR Website:
https://dugway.armymwr.com

MWR Facebook:
https://www.facebook.com/dugwaymwr

Outdoor Recreation: Outdoor Recreation, C-435-831-2705. Offers skiing and snowboarding rentals, camping gear, trailers, fishing boats, rafts, mountain bikes, grills, ski/snowboard services and more. Archery range is also available.

Swimming: Seasonal Pool, C-435-831-2784 offers open swim and swim lessons.

Things To Do: With pristine alpine mountains, vast deserts and the mysterious Great Salt Lake, this area offers many outdoor activities and is only minutes away from all the conveniences and excitement of metropolitan Salt Lake City. Visit Temple Square, Big Cottonwood Canyon, The Tabernacle, Liberty Park or the Wheeler Historic Farm.

Walking Trails: Indoor running track at the fitness center.

RV CAMPING & GETAWAYS

Coyote Run RV Park & Campground

Reservation/Contact Number Info: C-435-831-2705.

RV Website:
https://dugway.armymwr.com/programs/coyote-run-rv-park-and-campground

Reservations: Reservations are not accepted. All RV spaces and campsite

are on a first come, first served basis. Contact ODR or Shocklee Fitness Center for details. Office hours 0500-2100 hours Mon-Thurs; 0600-1600 Fri; 0800-1800 Sat-Sun.

Season of Operation: Year-round.

Eligibility: AD, NG, Res, Ret and Dep.

Camper/Trailer Spaces: Dry Sites (33): Dump Station nearby. Rates: $8 nightly; $125 monthly.

Support Facilities: Dump Station, Dog Park. Full range of support facilities available on base.

Area Description: Located in the Great Salt Lake Desert, surrounded on three sides by mountain ranges.

Hill Air Force Base

Address: Hill AFB, 5837 D Avenue, Hill AFB, UT 84056-5720.

Main Base Police: C-801-777-3056. Emergencies dial 911.

Main Installation Website:
http://www.hill.af.mil/

Main Base Location: Located in Davis County in northern Utah, bordered by the Wasatch Mountains on the east and the Great Salt Lake to the west.

Directions to Main Gate: From the East: Follow I-84 West to exit 87 South toward Salt Lake City. Proceed south on US-89 to Hwy 193/Hill Air Force Base. Follow Hwy 193 west for approximately four miles. The South Gate is on the right. From the West: Follow I-80 East to I-215 North toward Ogden. I-215 North merges onto I-15 North. The New Legacy Parkway is also available by taking exit 28 off I-215 onto Legacy Parkway. Follow in until it merges back into I-15. Continue following I-15 North to exit 331/Hill Field Road. Turn right at the ramp exit onto Hill Field Road and proceed straight to the south gate.

NMC: Ogden, 8 miles north.

NMI: Tooele Army Depot, 40 miles southwest.

Base Social Media/Facebook:
https://www.facebook.com/HillAirForceBase

Base Social Media/Twitter:
https://twitter.com/HAFB

Chapels: C-801-777-2106.

Dental Clinic: C-801-777-7011.

Medical: Appointment Line, C-801-728-2600.
Veterinary Services: C-801-777-2611.
Beauty/Barber Shop: Barber, C-801-773-4602. Stylique, C-801-773-4076.
Commissary: C-801-777-2300.
Exchange Gas: West Gate, C-801-774-9072.
Exchange: C-801-773-1207.
Financial Institutions: Wells Fargo Bank, C-801-773-8000. America First Credit Union: East, C-778-8740; West, C-801-778-8775.
Clubs: The Landing, C-801-777-3841.
Places to Eat: 507 Grill, C-801-586-9317 (flightline access only); Break Time Deli, C-801-586-9317; Fast Eddies, C-801-777-1010; Halfway House Snack Bar, C-801-777-3272; Skyward Cafe, C-801-777-4165; Strikes Cafe, C-801-777-6565; Hillcrest DFAC, C-801-777-3428 and The Landing, C-801-777-3841 are on base. Exchange Food Court offers Anthony's Pizza, Arby's, Charley's, Subway and Taco Bell. Burger King, Domino's and Popeye's Chicken are on base. Many restaurants within a short drive.
Bowling: Hill Bowling Center, C-801-777-6565.
Fitness Center: Warrior and Hess Fitness Centers, C-801-777-2762.
Golf: Hubbard Memorial Golf Course, C-801-777-3272.
ITT/ITR: C-801-777-3525/9666.
Library: Gerrity Memorial Library, C-801-777-2533.
Military Museum: Hill Aerospace Museum, C-801-777-6818.
Military Museum Website: http://www.hill.af.mil/Home/Hill-Aerospace-Museum/
MWR: C-801-775-2084.
MWR Website: http://www.75thforcesupport.com/
MWR Facebook: https://www.facebook.com/ForceSupport
MWR Twitter: https://twitter.com/75FSS
Outdoor Recreation: Outdoor Recreation Services, C-801-777-9666/3525. Offers guided trips, hiking, winter equipment rentals and tune-ups, camping gear, canoes, kayaks, stand up paddle boards, ski boats, party barges, lawn and garden equipment, trailers and more.
Swimming: Hess Indoor Pool, C-801-777-2762 offers open and lap swim. Seasonal Outdoor Pool and Splash Pad, C-801-777-9666.
Things To Do: Visit Canyon Falls in the Wasatch Cache National Forest, Great Salt Lake and Lagoon Amusement Park. This area has excellent snow skiing, ice fishing and hiking. Visit Temple Square, Big Cottonwood Canyon, The Tabernacle, Liberty Park or the Wheeler Historic Farm.
Walking Trails: Indoor running track at Warrior FC and The Bubble. Centennial Park and Duck Pond offer 5k running trails.

RV CAMPING & GETAWAYS
Hill AFB FamCamp

Reservation/Contact Number Info: C-801-777-3250, C-801-777-9666.
Recreation Security: Emergencies dial 911.
RV Website: https://75fss.com/famcamp
GPS Coordinates: 41°6'17"N/111°58'35"W
Reservations: Recommended for priority. All others first come, first serve. Office hours 0900-1700 Mon-Tue, 0800-1000 and 1300-1700 Wed-Sun. Payments required in advance with reservations. Cancellation fees may apply. Check in at the back of Centennial Park and the FamCamp Office/Reception Center, Bldg 564. Check-in after 1300. Registration and space assignment 24 hours daily. After hours self-registration box available. Maximum stay 14 days.
Season of Operation: Year-round.
Eligibility: AD, NG, Res, Ret and DoD-Civ, 100% DAV, Sponsored Guests.
Camper/Trailer Spaces: RV sites (45): E(110/220V/20/30/50A)/S/W hookups. Rates: $20 daily. Overflow (4): Rates: $15 daily.
Support Facilities: Boat Rental, Chapel, Gas (No Diesel), Golf, Grills, Gym, Laundry, Pavilions, Picnic Area, Rec

Equipment, Restrooms, Sewage Dump, Showers, Track.

RV Storage: C-801-777-9666.

Activities: Bird Watching, Golfing, Jogging, Sightseeing, Skiing (Snow and Water). The newly renovated FamCamp Reception Center has a pool table, dart board and card games, TV, VCR/DVD player, and access to several hundred movies.

Credit Cards: MasterCard and Visa.

Restrictions: Pets allowed on leash only, must be walked in designated area; owner must clean up after pet. No firearms allowed.

RV Driving Directions/Location: On Base. From the Roy Gate on Wardleigh Road: Stay on Wardleigh Rd for approximately 4 miles until reaching the second stop light which is "E" Ave. Take a right on "E" Ave and go through the next stop light reaching a four-way stop sign which is Balmer St. Take a left on Balmer St and continue to the FamCamp. The entrance into the camp is a right on Park Ave.

Area Description: Located on Hill AFB at the base of the Wasatch Mountains to the east, with the Great Salt Lake to the west, and 20 miles north of downtown Salt Lake City. The FAMCAMP is convenient to several recreation areas located within 30 minutes to three hours of the base and points of interest around Great Salt Lake. Enjoy Pineview Reservoir and Willard Bay for fishing, boating, skiing and swimming. Several ski slopes are within a two hour drive. Museum and Aerospace Park on base. The Family Research Center is located in Salt Lake City and is considered the foremost center in the world for family history. A full range of support facilities are available on base.

RV Campground Physical Address: 5622 Park Lane, Bldg 564, Hill AFB, UT 84056-5000.

Tooele Army Depot

Address: 1 Tooele Army Depot, Tooele, UT 84074-5000.

Information Line: C-435-833-2211, DSN-312-790-2211.

Main Base Police: C-435-833-2314. Emergencies dial 911.

Main Installation Website: http://www.tooele.army.mil/

Main Base Location: Located on the western slopes of the Oquirrh Mountains in the Tooele Valley next to the more popularly known Salt Lake Valley.

Directions to Main Gate: From west I-80: Take exit 99 south to UT-36 south for approximately 15 miles to the main entrance on right side of UT-36.

NMC: Salt Lake City, 40 miles northeast.

NMI: Dugway Proving Ground, 36 miles southwest.

Base Social Media/Facebook: https://www.facebook.com/TooeleArmyDepot

Clubs: Eagle's Nest, C-435-833-5555.

Places to Eat: Ammo Grill, C-435-833-5015 and Eagle's Nest Dining, C-435-833-5555 are on base. Many restaurants within a short drive.

Fitness Center: Tooele FC, C-435-833-2159.

ITT/ITR: C-435-833-3100.

MWR: C-435-833-2005.

MWR Website: https://tooele.armymwr.com/

MWR Facebook: https://www.facebook.com/TEADFMWR/

Outdoor Recreation: Outdoor Recreation, C-435-833-3100. Offers ski boats, fishing boats, kayaks, canoes, wake boards, trailers, camping gear, camping trailers, ATVs, lawn and garden equipment, outdoor sports equipment, party supplies and more.

Swimming: Outdoor Seasonal Pool, C-435-833-2159 offers open, and lap swim. Shallow area, water slide and diving boards for recreational fun.

Things To Do: Visit the Mormon Temple, Temple Square and the Pioneer Memorial Museum. Tooele area has The Miller Motor Sports Park, Deseret Peak Complex, a Train Museum, Pioneer Museum, Benson Grist Mill Historic Site and Pony Express information. Excellent winter sports offering several local ski resorts within driving distance of Tooele as well as great snowmobiling and cross country skiing. Four wheeler riding, hiking, biking, and horseback riding available in summer.

RV CAMPING & GETAWAYS

Deseret Reservoir

Reservation/Contact Number Info: C-435-833-3100.

Recreation Security: Emergencies dial 911.

RV Website: https://tooele.armymwr.com/programs/deseret-reservoir-recreation-area

RV Email Address: Outdoor_Recreation@tooelearmydepot mwr.com

GPS Coordinates: 40°19'32.9"N/112°18'11.3"W

Reservations: Reservations recommended and accepted by phone and in person, Bldg 1011. Limited sites available.

Season of Operation: 1 May-31 Oct.

Eligibility: AD, NG, Res, Ret, Dep.

Camper/Trailer Spaces: RV Sites (4): Full hook-ups available, shade structures, picnic tables. Rates: $20 daily.

Support Facilities: Full range of support activities available on base.

RV Storage: From $15 monthly. C-435-833-3100.

Activities: ATV Rentals, Equipment Rental, Fishing*. Ski Trips, Scenic Nature Trips, Swimming. *License/permits required

Credit Cards: Cash, MasterCard and Visa.

Restrictions: MWR Recreation area is restricted to shore fishing only. MWR post permit required but free of charge.

RV Driving Directions/Location: On Base. Use Stark Road Turn-Off Entrance: Continue on State Road 36 for 8.8 miles, passing the Main Gate entrance, to the Penney's Junction. Turn left/east at the Penney's Junction (Highway 73 toward Lehi/Ophir) and go 3.3 miles to the Tooele Army Depot-South/Stark Road turn off. From the South/Stark Road turn off, turn right and follow road for 3.1 miles. Pull into parking lot on right and check in at Guard Shack, Bldg 5007. After check-in, continue .5 miles to the Rec Area.

Area Description: Home to beautiful scenery, endless outdoor activities and pristine mountainous and wooded areas. Also home to Miller Motorsports Park, state-of-the-art road racing facility for automobiles, motorcycles and karts, only a short drive away. Enjoy great Utah skiing, swimming areas and more.

RV Campground Physical Address: Mailing Address: Outdoor Recreation, TEAD Bldg 1011, Tooele, UT 84074.

VIRGINIA

67th Street Townhomes

Address: 6700 67th Street, Virginia Beach, VA 23459.

Information Line: JEB Quarterdeck, C-757-462-7385.

Main Base Police: C-757-462-4445. Emergencies dial 911.

Main Installation Website: http://www.cnic.navy.mil/regions/cnrm a/installations/jeb_little_creek_fort_sto ry/about.html

Main Base Location: In Virginia Beach on 67th Street along Atlantic Avenue and the oceanfront, near First Landing State Park.

NMC: Virginia Beach, within city limits.

NMI: Fort Story, 3 miles north.

Commissary: JEB Little Creek, C-757-464-3561.

Exchange Gas: Fort Story, C-757-425-0001.

Exchange: Fort Story, C-757-425-0001; JEB Little Creek, C-757-363-3218.

Bowling: Gator Bowl, C-757-462-7952.

Fitness Center: JEB Fort Story, C-757 422-7975; Pierside Gym & Aquatic Center, C-757-462-8280.

Golf: Eagle Haven Golf Course at JEB Little Creek, C757-462-8526.

ITT/ITR: C-757-462-7793.

Marina: Cove Marina at JEB Little Creek, C-757-462-7140.

MWR: MWR JEB-Little Creek-Fort Story, C-757-462-7952/7758/7952/7758.

MWR Website:
http://www.navymwrjblittlecreekfortst
ory.com/
Outdoor Recreation: C-757-462-7516.
Bikes, kayaks, canoes, stand-up paddle
boards, beach umbrellas and chairs are
available for rent.
Swimming: Ocean swimming available.
JEB Little Creek-Fort Story Gator Pool, C-
757462-7173.
Things To Do: Enjoy the Virginia Beach
Boardwalk with plenty of activities,
dining and shopping. Close to JEB Little
Creek, Oceana Naval Air Station and
Dam Neck Annex. Visit Ocean Breeze,
Motor World, the Virginia Aquarium or
take a day trip to Williamsburg,
Jamestown or Yorktown. Busch Gardens
and Water Country a 45 minute drive.
Walking Trails: Biking and hiking trails
available at First Landing State Park and
at Fort Story.

RV CAMPING & GETAWAYS
67th Street Townhomes

Reservation/Contact Number Info: C-1-
877-NAVY-BED, C-757-422-7601.
Recreation Security: Emergencies dial
911.
RV Website:
http://get.dodlodging.net/propertys/Ge
taways-Fort-Story--67th-Street-
Townhouses
Other Info Website:
https://www.navymwrjblittlecreekfortst
ory.com/programs/c53934d3-b6d5-
4f65-9805-a703ead1c978
GPS Coordinates: 36°53'
34''N/75°59'16''W
Reservations: Accepted up to 1 year in
advance for AD; 6 months in advance
for Ret/DoD-Civ. Office hours 0800-
2100 Mon-Sat, 0900-1900 Sun. Online
reservations accepted 24 hours daily.
Cancellations must be made 30 days
prior to arrival to avoid fee. Check-in
1500 hours. Check-out 1100 hours.
Summer reservations require 5-night
minimum. Winter reservations require
2-night minimum. Maximum stay 14
days.
Season of Operation: Year-round.

Eligibility: AD, NG, Res, Ret, Dep, DoD-
Civ.
Yurt, A Frame, Cabin, Apt, Spaces:
Townhomes (20): Two-bedroom
cottages, new modern structures (10):
Sleeps max 5, fully furnished: living
rooms, kitchen, microwave, dishwasher,
dishes, utensils and linens. Weekly
Summer Rates: $190 daily for AD, $215
daily for Ret. Three-bedroom cottages
(10): New modern structures (10):
Sleeps max 7, fully furnished: living
rooms, kitchen, microwave, dishwasher,
dishes, utensils and linens. Weekly
Summer Rates: $215 daily for AD, $240
daily for Ret. Ocean views add $25 daily.
Support Facilities: Limited support
facilities available at Fort Story,
approximately three miles away.
Activities: Beach Swimming, Strolling.
Virginia Beach Boardwalk and
entertainment approximately 30 blocks
south.
Credit Cards: Cash, Check, MasterCard,
Visa.
RV Driving Directions/Location: Off
Base. From Atlantic Blvd of I-264: Travel
north on Atlantic Blvd to 67th Street.
Turn right and cottages are ahead on
left.
Area Description: Located along the
sandy beaches of the Atlantic Ocean in
Virginia Beach. Just north of the
Boardwalk and many exciting festivals
and events throughout the year. Fort
Story is three miles north.
RV Campground Physical Address: 6700
67th Street, Virginia Beach, VA 23459

Bethel Recreation Area

Address: Bethel Park, 123 Saunders
Road, Hampton, VA 23666.
Information Line: C-757-764-
9990/1110.
Main Base Police: C-757-764-5091.
Emergencies dial 911.
**Main Installation
Website:** http://www.jble.af.mil/
Main Base Location: Located in
Hampton along the Big Bethel
Reservoir.
Directions to Main Gate: From I-64
East: Take Exit 258B toward Yorktown.

Continue approximately 1 mile, then turn right onto Harpersville Road. After 1/2 mile, stay straight to continue onto Saunders Road. Bethel Park is 1 mile ahead on left. From I-64 West: Take Exit 261A onto Hampton Roads Center Parkway. Take next right at stop light onto Big Bethel road. Continue 2 miles, then turn left onto Saunders Road. Bethel Park is 1/2 mile ahead on right.

NMC: Hampton, seven miles south.

NMI: Langley AFB 5 miles east.

Commissary: Approximately 5 miles to the commissary at Langley AFB, C-757-764-7604.

Exchange Gas: Gas/Shoppette/Class VI Store: C-757-766-1312 (at Langley AFB, 5 miles away).

Exchange: Approximately 5 miles to the Base Exchange facility at Langley AFB, C-757-766-1282/0373.

MWR Website:
http://new.jbleforcesupport.com/

MWR Facebook:
https://www.facebook.com/jbleforcesupport

RV CAMPING & GETAWAYS
Bethel Recreation Area

Reservation/Contact Number Info: C-757-766-7627. Fax C-757-766-3017.

Recreation Security: C-757-764-5091.

RV Website:
https://jbleforcesupport.com/langley/outdoor-recreation

GPS Coordinates:
37°5'32"N/76°25'51"W.

Reservations: Accepted up to six months in advance. Call for reservations and details. Office hours 0900-1700 Mon-Fri. Check-in 1100 hours, check-out 1300 hours. Maximum stay 90 days; extensions granted per space available.

Season of Operation: Year-round.

Eligibility: AD, NG, Res, Ret, DoD-Civ and Dep.

Camper/Trailer Spaces: RV Sites (25), Back-in, Maximum 25' to 45' in length depending on site, E(220V/50A)/S/W hookups, picnic table, fire ring, grill. Rates: $20 daily, $600 monthly.

Tent Spaces: Primitive (9): No hookups, picnic table, grill. Rates: $10 daily.

Groups sites (2) available. Rates: $25 daily.

Support Facilities: Bathhouse*, Boat Launch, Boat Rental, Coin Laundry, Fire Rings, Fishing Pier, Grills, Ice, Pavilions, Picnic Area, Paintball, Playground, Restrooms*, Sewage Dump, Showers. Full range of support actvities availbe on base three miles away. *Handicap accessible.

RV Storage: None.

Activities: Boating, Canoeing, Fishing, Golfing, Horseshoes, John Boats, Kayaking, Paddle Boats, Volleyball, Paintball.

Credit Cards: MasterCard and Visa.

Restrictions: Pets allowed on leash. No firearms allowed. Park open sunup to sundown. Swimming is not allowed, and gas motors cannot be run in any part of the reservoir. Trolling motors may be used. Reservations are required for pavilions in the park area.

RV Driving Directions/Location: Off Base. From south on I-64: Take VA-134 north approximately five miles then turn left onto Big Bethel Road. Go approximately one mile to the 2nd light, and turn right on Saunders Road, camp is approximately .5 miles on the right. The park is located just before Saunders Road. From I-64: Take exit 261A to a right on Big Bethel Road. Follow Big Bethel Road for 2.5 miles and turn left onto Saunders Road. Proceed for approximately .5 miles then turn right into camp. Entrance for the Park is located just beyond Saunders Road.

Area Description: The recreation area offers the quiet beauty of nature surrounded by the benefits of a large metropolitan locale. The area encompasses 49 acres of land and 187 acres of man-made reservoir with fish and other wildlife in abundance. Busch Gardens, Colonial Williamsburg, and Jamestown are close by, along with many beaches, museums and historical sites.

RV Campground Physical Address: 123 Saunders Rd, Hampton, VA 23665.

Camp Pendleton Army National Guard

Address: 203 Red Horse Drive, Virginia Beach, VA 23451.
Information Line: C-757-493-3122, DSN-312-438-3122.
Main Base Police: C-757-491-5144.
Main Installation Website:
http://vko.va.ngb.army.mil/VirginiaGuard/smr/
Main Base Location: Within the city limits of Virginia Beach, Virginia.
Directions to Main Gate: Camp Pendleton ARNG is located north of Dam Neck Annex, Oceana NAS and approximately 0.25 miles south of Virginia Beach resort area. Take exit 22 off I-264 east onto Birdneck Road and proceed approximately 3 miles until crossing General Booth Blvd. Go to the next left turn lane and enter the Main Gate.
NMC: Virginia Beach, within city limits.
NMI: Dam Neck Annex, Oceana Naval Air Station, adjacent.
Base Social Media/Facebook:
https://www.facebook.com/CampPendletonCTC/
Places to Eat: Many restaurants are within a short driving distance.
Things To Do: Closeness to historic Williamsburg, Jamestown, the resort area and the Eastern Shore makes this place a find for visitors lucky enough to be able to rent one of the apartments, cottages and trailers. Virginia Beach Boardwalk just a few short miles away as well as many other area attractions.

RV CAMPING & GETAWAYS
CPSMR Cottages

Reservation/Contact Number Info: C-757-493-3125.
RV Website:
https://vaguard.dodlive.mil/smrlodging/
GPS Coordinates:
36°49'07.9"N/75°58'52.0"W
Reservations: Reservations accepted anytime in off-season but recommended at least 60 days in advance. Lottery system in place for peak season and is drawn mid-March. Credit card required to guarantee reservation. Cancellations require 14 day notice to avoid fee. Must contact Billeting for reservations. Check in 1300 hours, check out 1000 hours.
Season of Operation: Year-round.
Eligibility: AD, NG, Res, Ret and Dep.
Yurt, A Frame, Cabin, Apt, Spaces: Cottages (10): One, two, three-bedroom cottages (9); five-bedroom (1). Fully furnished with private baths. Linens available for rent $2 per bed. Rates: Vary according to rank and cottage size. From $61-$325 daily. Winter rates discounted. Trailers (3): two and three-bedrooms, fully furnished, private baths. Linens available to rent. Rates: Vary according to rank and trailer size From $90-$112 daily. Trailers not available in winter.
Activities: Beach is nearby.
Credit Cards: Cash, American Express, MasterCard and Visa.
Restrictions: Pets are not permitted in facilities.
RV Driving Directions/Location: On Base. From General Booth Blvd: Continue through Gate to stop sign. Turn left then take the first right onto Headquarters Road. Billeting Office is the 3rd building on the left, next to the Main Post Headquarters.
Area Description: Near Atlantic Ocean off of General Booth Blvd. Close to beaches and the Boardwalk in Virginia Beach.
RV Campground Physical Address: SMRC, 203 Red Horse Drive, Virginia Beach, VA 23451.

Cheatham Annex – Yorktown NWS

Address: 160 Main Rd, Yorktown, VA 23691-0160
Information Line: C-757-887-4000, DSN-312-953-4000.
Main Base Police: C-757-887-4911.
Main Installation Website:
http://cnic.navy.mil/regions/cnrma/installations/nws_yorktown/cheatham_annex.html
Main Base Location: Located near historic Williamsburg, Jamestown and

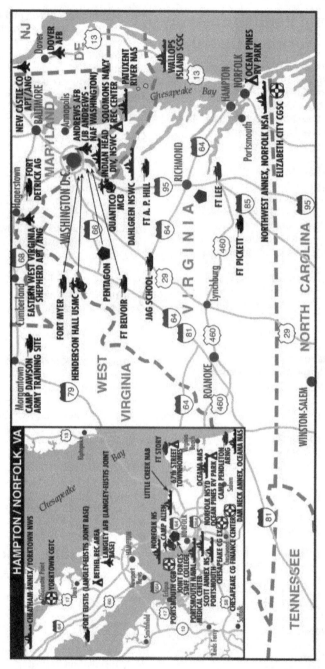

Yorktown off I-64 just 40 miles west of Hampton Roads.
Directions to Main Gate: From I-95: Take I-64 East to exit 242-B/Hwy 199

East to main gate. From Virginia Beach: Take I-64 West to exit 242-B/Hwy 199 East to main gate. From Hwy 17 South:

Take Colonial Parkway toward Williamsburg to Cheatham Annex exit.
NMC: Williamsburg, 6 miles west.
NMI: Fort Eustis/Langley-Eustis JB, 15 miles southeast.
Chapels: C-757-887-4711.
Dental Clinic: Yorktown NWS, C-757-953-8417.
Medical: Yorktown NWS, C-757-953-8432/8454.
Beauty/Barber Shop: Yorktown NWS, C-757-887-0690.
Exchange Gas: C-757-887-3582.
Exchange: C-757-887-3582.
Financial Institutions: Naval Weapons Station Federal Credit Union, C-1-800-469-7328, C-757-887-2452.
Places to Eat: CAX 4th Street Grille, C-757-887-7514. The Cascades, Williamsburg Lodge Bay Room, The Taverns of Colonial Williamsburg (King's Arms Tavern, Shield's Tavern, Chowning's Tavern, Christina Campbell's Tavern), C-757-229-2141 are nearby. Reservations recommended.
Fitness Center: CAX Gym, C-757-887-7453.
Golf: Deer Cove Golf Course, C-757-887-6539.
MWR: C-757-887-7418.
MWR Website:
http://www.navymwryorktown.com/
MWR Facebook:
https://www.facebook.com/nwsycax.mwr/
Outdoor Recreation: CAX Outdoor Rentals, C-757-887-7418. Offers kayaks, canoes, Jon boats, campers and camping gear, bikes, fishing poles and more.
Swimming: Seasonal Outdoor Pool, C-757-887-7453 offers lap swim, open swim and sunbathing pool deck.
Things To Do: Cheatham Annex is an ideal vacation spot with close proximity to Colonial Williamsburg, Yorktown Victory Center, Jamestown, Busch Gardens and Water Country USA. Enjoy the rich historical conflux of the founding, settling, and birth of these United States.
Walking Trails: A nature trail around Cheatham Lake offers an opportunity to explore nature. Travel the 6.2 mile

wooded biking and hiking trail as well. Stop by CAX Outdoors to pick up a trail guide.

RV CAMPING & GETAWAYS

Cheatham Annex Cottages & RV Park

Reservation/Contact Number Info: C-1-877-NAVY-BED, C-757-887-7224. Fax C-757-887-7643.
Recreation Security: C-757-887-4911.
RV Website:
http://get.dodlodging.net/propertys/Cheatham-Annex-Outdoors-and-Cottages
Other Info Website:
http://www.navymwryorktown.com/
GPS Coordinates:
37°17′1″N/76°35′47″W
Reservations: Accepted one year in advance for AD, 6 months in advance for Ret, DoD-Civ. Accepted by phone or online. Office hours 0800-1800 hours Thur-Sun, 0800-2000 Fri-Sat. No deposit required. Cancellations must be made within 30 days of arrival to avoid fee. Payment due upon arrival. Check-in 1500 hours, check-out 1100 hours. Maximum stay 60 days.
Season of Operation: Year-round.
Eligibility: AD, NG, Res, Ret, DoD-Civ, Dep, 100% DAV and DoD-Civ.
Camper/Trailer Spaces: RV Sites (50): Concrete pads, E(220V/30/50A)/S/W, CATV hookups, Wi-Fi; picnic table, grill, select sites with fire rings, off B Street. Rates: $30 daily. Maximum stay 30 days; extensions based on space available.
Tent Spaces: Primitive Sites: Jones Pond and B Street, max 6 people per site, picnic table, fire ring, Rates: $15 daily. Kings Creek Sites 20: Full hookups, picnic table, grill. Rates: $20 daily. Group Camping: Area 284 an KP, max 100 people. Rates: $40 daily.
Yurt, A Frame, Cabin, Apt, Spaces: Five BR Deluxe Cottage (2): sleeps 12-13, water view. Fully furnished with W/D. Rates: $215-$225 daily. Three BR Deluxe Cottage (12): sleeps 6, water view. Fully furnished. Rates: $129-$139 daily. Two BR Deluxe Cottages (30): Sleeps 4-6, water and wooded views. Fully

furnished. Rates: $119-$129 daily. One BR Deluxe Cottage (1): Fully furnished, king size bed; recently renovated with Jacuzzi. Rates: $125-$135 daily; Regular one-bedroom cottages $79-$89 daily. Farmhouse (1): sleeps 6, 3 bedroom with full bath, water view. Newly renovated; boat equipment for fishing included. VIP only; E-7/O-5 above. Rates: $125-$225 daily. All rentals require 6-night stay during peak season.
Support Facilities: Bathhouse, Boat Rental, Bowling, Camping Equipment, Coin Laundry, Diesel**, Exchange, Fire rings, Fishing Pier*, Fitness Center, Gas, Golf, Grills, Pay Phones, Picnic Area, Playground, Pool, Propane, Racquetball Court, Rec Center (newly renovated), Restrooms, Sewage Dump, Showers. * Handicap accessible, **Off-base.
RV Storage: Available at Yorktown; $30 monthly; C-757-887-4233.
Activities: Bicycling, Boating, Crabbing, Fishing*, Golfing, Hiking, Horseshoes, Hunting*, Swimming (Summer Only). *License is required.
Credit Cards: MasterCard and Visa.
Restrictions: No pets allowed in cabins or cabin areas. Pets allowed in campsites but must be on a leash and owner must clean up after pet. No firearms, bow and arrows, pellet guns or BB guns. No campfires unless in designated fire rings. No smoking. Guests responsible for cleanliness of facility upon departure. No refunds for early departure.
RV Driving Directions/Location: On Base. From Norfolk/Virginia Beach: Take I-64 west to exit 242B/Hwy 199 east, which turns into Penniman Rd and leads to Main Gate. From Hwy 17 south: Take Colonial Pkwy toward Williamsburg to Cheatham Annex exit. From I-95: Take I-64 east to exit 242B/Hwy 199 east to Main Gate. Once through gate, stay on Sandra Ave to the campground. Ask at gate for directions to recreation cabins and RV park.
Area Description: Located in historic triangle of Jamestown, Colonial Williamsburg and Yorktown. Convenient to Busch Gardens, Pottery Factory, and College of William and Mary. Limited support facilities on base; full range at Yorktown Naval Weapons Station, eight miles southeast.
RV Campground Physical Address: Cheatham Annex Outdoors & Cottages, Bldg 284 Chase Rd, Williamsburg, VA 23185.

Dam Neck Annex – Oceana NAS

Address: 1912 Regulus Avenue, Bldg 127, Taylor Hall, Virginia Beach, VA 23461.
Information Line: C-757-444-0000.
Main Base Police: Dispatch, C-757-492-6302. Emergency, C-757-433-9111.
Main Installation Website: http://www.cnic.navy.mil/regions/cnrma/installations/nas_oceana/dam_neck_annex.html
Main Base Location: NAS Oceana Dam Neck Annex is located on the Atlantic coast, five miles south of the downtown resort of Virginia Beach.
Directions to Main Gate: From I-64: Take I-264 East toward Va Beach. Take Exit 21A/First Colonial Road/NAS Oceana. Continue past NAS Oceana to the General Booth Intersection and go right. Merge into the left lanes and travel to Dam Neck Road. Go left and follow Dam Neck Road to the main gate.
NMC: Virginia Beach, four miles northwest.
NMI: Oceana NAS, 7 miles northwest.
Chapels: C-757-492-6602.
Dental Clinic: C-757-953-9854/9855.
Medical: Dam Neck Branch Clinic, C-757-953-9915.
Beauty/Barber Shop: C-757-492-7749.
Commissary: Oceana NAS, C-757-428-6401.
Exchange Gas: C-757-492-7794.
Exchange: C-757-492-7780. Beach Package Store, C-757-492-6236.
Financial Institutions: Navy Federal Credit Union (NFCU): Dam Neck MSC C-757-422-6760.
Places to Eat: Seaside Lanes Bar & Grill, C-757-492-6341; Galley, C-757-492-8579; Shifting Sands, C-757-492-6146. Exchange Food Court offers Subway and Panda Express.

Bowling: Seaside Lanes, C-757-492-6341.

Fitness Center: C-757-492-7483.

ITT/ITR: The Dunes, C-757-492-7053.

MWR: C-757-433-2246.

MWR Website:
http://www.navymwroceanadamneck.com/

Outdoor Recreation: The Dunes at Dam Neck, C-757-492-7053. Offers beach activity rentals to include paddle boards, kayaks, boogie boards, and beach umbrellas and chairs.

Swimming: Dam Neck Indoor Pool, C-757-492-7183 offers lap and open swim. Beach area for swimming.

Things To Do: Enjoy the Atlantic Ocean beach, Virginia Beach boardwalk and beach activities.

RV CAMPING & GETAWAYS

Sea Mist RV Campground & Dam Neck Cottages

Reservation/Contact Number Info: Sea Mist RV Park, C-757-492-7545. Cottages, C-757-492-7429, C-1-877-NAVY-BED.

RV Website:
http://get.dodlodging.net/propertys/Sea-Mist-RV-Park

Other Info Website:
http://get.dodlodging.net/propertys/Cottages-at-Dam-Neck

RV Email Address:
seamist@mwrma.com

GPS Coordinates:
36°46'18"N/75°57'20"W.

Reservations: Sea Mist RV Park: Accepted and recommended. Office hours 0900-1600 Mon-Sat, 1230-1600 Sun. Payment due upon arrival. Maximum stay 60 days. Cabins 14-day maximum stay. Check-in 1200 hours, check-out 1100 hours. Dam Neck Cottages: Accepted one year in advance. Office hours 0900-1700 daily. Peak Season requires 7-night stay; Winter Season 2-night minimum. Payment due upon arrival. No refunds after arrival. Peak Season requires 30 day cancellation notice; 14 days for Winter Season to avoid fee. Adjoining units first come, first serve. Check-in at

the Dunes, Bldg 180. Check-in at 1600, check-out 1100 hours.

Season of Operation: Year-round.

Eligibility: AD, NG, Res, Ret, 100% DAV and DoD-Civ. AD have priority.

Camper/Trailer Spaces: Concrete (65), with 2 Pull-thru Spaces, E(20A/30A/50A)/S/W hookups, free Wi-Fi, picnic table and grills. Rates: $25 daily, $154 weekly, $510 monthly. Ask about super double site availability; limited, E(20A/30A/50A)/S/W hookups, free Wi-Fi, picnic table and grills. Rates: $40 daily, $259 weekly, $960 monthly. No tent camping allowed.

Yurt, A Frame, Cabin, Apt, Spaces: Oceanside Beach Cottages (29): Two bedroom (19, 1 handicap accessible). Summer Rates: $142 daily, $819 weekly for AD; Winter: $139 daily, $791 weekly for AD. Three-bedroom (7, 1 handicap accessible) Oceanside Three-bedroom (3): one block away from beach with screened in porches and charcoal grills. Summer Rates: $157 daily, $889 weekly for AD; Winter: $150 daily, $861 weekly for AD. All cottages offer fully furnished with full kitchen, W/D, Wi-Fi. Sea Mist Cabins: (3-1 handicap), Sleeps four, refrigerator, microwave, full bed, bunk beds, A/C, picnic tables, grill. Patrons must provide linens. Rates: $25 daily.

Support Facilities: 2 ADA compliant Bathhouses, Beach, Boat Rental/Storage, Bowling, Chapel, Commissary, Convenience Store, Clubs, Exchange, Fitness Center, Golf, Grills, ITT, Laundry/Dry Cleaners, Mess Hall, Pavilion, Picnic Area, Rec Center, Rec Equipment, ADA compliant Restrooms, Sewage Dump, Shoppette, Showers, Sports Fields, Telephones.

RV Storage: NAS Oceana Skeet and Trap, C-757-433-2875.

Activities: Beaches, Boating, Fishing, Golfing (At NAS Oceana), Hunting (Seasonal), Swimming.

Credit Cards: Cash, Check, MasterCard and Visa. Cottages also accept American Express, Discover.

Restrictions: Firearms must be checked in at security or armory. No pets allowed in cabins or cottages. RV Park: Pets must be tended to, picked up after, and on a leash at all times. No smoking in cabins or cottages. No cooking allowed in cabins. No campfires.

RV Driving Directions/Location: On Base. From the Main Gate to Campground: Take second right (south) onto Regulus Avenue. Campground is .75 miles on the left. From the Main Gate to Cottages: Take first left at blinking light to Cottages.

Area Description: Located along the ocean, Sea Mist offers a beach, seasonal tourist attractions, surf and freshwater fishing (fresh and saltwater licenses required).

RV Campground Physical Address: Sea Mist Campgrounds, 2076 Regulus Ave, Bldg 196, Virginia Beach, VA 23461. Cottages at Dam Neck, 2076 Regulus Ave, Bldg 180, Virginia Beach, VA 23461.

Fort A.P. Hill

Address: Fort A.P. Hill, 18350 1st Street, Fort A.P. Hill, VA 22427.

Main Base Police: C-804-633-8888. Emergencies dial 911.

Main Installation Website:
http://www.aphill.army.mil/

Main Base Location: Located in Caroline County, a largely rural county of great natural beauty, dotted with farms, woodlands and waters.

Directions to Main Gate: From I-95 North: Take exit 104 then turn right onto State Rte 207 East. After about 12 miles State Rte 207 turns into US Rte 301 North. Watch for Fort A.P. Hill signs. Facility on left. From Northern VA/DC using I-95 South: Take exit 126 then turn right onto U.S. Rte 1 South. Travel .6 miles then turn left onto US Rte 17 South. Go about six miles then turn right onto State Rte 2 South. Travel about 13 miles then turn left at the first stoplight in Bowling Green onto E. Broaddus Ave. Travel about 0.5 miles to U.S. Rte 301 and cross U.S. Rte 301 South. Turn left onto U.S. Rte 301 North and watch for signs for facility.

NMC: Richmond, 50 miles southwest.

NMI: Dahlgren Naval Surface Warfare Center, 25 miles northeast.

Base Social Media/Facebook:
https://www.facebook.com/FtAPHill

Base Social Media/Twitter:
https://twitter.com/fort_aphill

RV CAMPING & GETAWAYS

Champ's Campground & Recreational Lodging

Reservation/Contact Number Info: C-804-633-8335/8244, DSN-312-578-8244. Fax C-804-633-8344. Lodging: C-804-633-8335, DSN-312-578-8335, Fax C-804-633-8344.

Recreation Security: C-804-633-8911.

RV Website:
https://aphill.armymwr.com/programs/indexphpcid10242

GPS Coordinates: 38°5'28"N/77°20'3"W

Reservations: RV Park: Reservations not accepted; first come, first serve. No refunds on campsites. Setup in open site then check-in at Outdoor Recreation. Late arrivals must use self check-in, located next to RV Service Center. Office hours 0900-1700 Mon-Fri, 0800-1200 Sat. Maximum stay 60 days. Recreational Lodging: Reservations required with credit card. Accepted 6 months in advance for AD, 5 months all others. Office hours 0800-1630 Mon-Fri; 0900-1500 Sat-Sun. Cabins and Cottages require 48-hour notice. The Lodge requires two week notice to avoid fee. Check-in 1500 hours, check-out 1100. Late arrivals must make prior arrangement with Reservations. Payment due upon arrival. Discounted rates without housekeeping.

Season of Operation: Year-round.

Eligibility: AD, NG, Res, Ret, 100& DAV and DoD-Civ (AD and Ret).

Camper/Trailer Spaces: RV Sites (30): Full hookup sites, picnic table, charcoal grill. 24-hour access to RV Service Center. Rates: $30-$35 daily; $630 monthly. Monthly back-in sites have 60 day max.

Tent Spaces: Archer Group Tent Camping Area, access to showers and restrooms. Rates: $5 daily.

Yurt, A Frame, Cabin, Apt, Spaces: Beaverdam Cottage (1): Two-bedroom, two bath, full kitchen, dining room, living room, fireplace, TV. Linens

provided. Rates: $115 daily.
Farmhouses (2): Five-bedroom (2), 11-13 twin beds in 5BR, full kitchen, 2 baths, living and dining areas, TV, porch. Rates: $185 daily. Lodge at Travis Lake (1): Nine bedrooms, sleeps 19, 5 semi-private bath, furnished, great room with fireplace (2), commercial kitchen, utensils, linens, large screen TV, overlooking lake. Linens provided. Rates: $320 daily with minimum stay 2 nights. Cabins at Travis Lake (7): Four-bedroom (3), 2 bath, kitchen, dining area, TV. Linens provided. Rates: $180 daily. Two-bedroom (3), one bath, kitchenette, dining area, TV. Linens provided. Rates: $90 daily. One-bedroom (1), one bath, kitchenette, dining area, TV. Linens provided. Rates: $75 daily. Cabins at Bullocks Pond (4): Three-bedroom one bath, sleeps six, living room, dining room, kitchen, utensils. Linens provided. Rates: $125 daily. Dolly Hill Guest House (6 Rooms at Bldg 174, 1 Room at Bldg 179): single rooms, queen bed, with private bath, microwave available in backside rooms, kitchenettes and/or refrigerator, TV. Linens provided. Rates: $60 daily.
Support Facilities: Boat Rental, Diesel*, Gas* Laundry/Pay, Long-term RV Storage, Pool, Propane*, Rec Center, Rec Equipment, Restrooms, Sewage Dump, Showers, Wi-Fi. *Off-base
RV Storage: Yes. C-804-633-8244.
Activities: Bicycling, Fishing*, Hunting**. *State and base permits required. Contact Communities Activities Center at C-804-633-8129 for further information. **Requirements are very specific; view details at www.aphill.army.mil/sites/mwr/huntinginfo.asp
Credit Cards: Cash, MasterCard and Visa.
Restrictions: Pets are not allowed in cabins or lodge but are permitted in camping area if on a leash. No firearms allowed except those carried by bona fide hunters during state-regulated hunting season. Hunting and fishing to be done in accordance with the laws of the state of Virginia. No open fires except in designated area.

RV Driving Directions/Location: On Base. From the Main Gate: Follow A P Hill Drive then go left on Campbell Rd. Campground ahead on the left.
Area Description: Located on 77,000 acres of woodlands. With lakes and ponds covering more than 300 acres, it offers abundant hunting and fishing opportunities. Scenic lakeside setting. Limited support facilities on post.
RV Campground Physical Address: Champs: 18616 A P Hill Dr, Bldg 390, Fort A. P. Hill, VA 22247. Lodging: 13956 Tuckers Road, Bldg 172, Fort A.P. Hill, VA 22427.

Fort Belvoir

Address: 9800 Belvoir Road, Bldg 200, Fort Belvoir, VA 22060-5561.
Information Line: C-703-545-6700, DSN-312-227-0101.
Main Base Police: C-703-806-3104/3105/3106. Emergencies dial 911.
Main Installation Website: http://www.belvoir.army.mil/
Main Base Location: Located south of Alexandria, VA in Fairfax County.
Directions to Main Gate: From the Washington DC North: Take I-95 South. Exit the Fairfax County Parkway/Backlick Road (7100) exit 166A. Take the Fairfax County Parkway to its end at Richmond Highway/U.S. Route 1. Turn left onto Route 1. At the first light on the right is the entrance for Tulley Gate on Fort Belvoir. This is the main entrance to the installation and is open 24/7 daily including weekends and holidays.
NMC: Washington D.C., 16 miles.
NMI: Andrews AFB/Andrews-Washington Naval Air Facility Joint Base, MD, 22 miles northeast.
Base Social Media/Facebook: https://www.facebook.com/fortbelvoir
Base Social Media/Twitter: https://twitter.com/Fort_Belvoir
Chapels: Chaplain, C-703-806-3006. C-703-806-4316/4317, C-703-805-2742.
Medical: Information Line, C-571-231-3224. ER, C-571-231-3162. Appointments, C-855-227-6331.
Veterinary Services: C-703-805-4336.

Beauty/Barber Shop: Town Center, C-703-781-3770. Hospital, C-571-231-4150. Beauty Shop, C-703-780-6600. North Post, C-703-799-4975.
Commissary: C-703-806-6674, C-703-781-0536.
Exchange Gas: C-703-806-5263.
Exchange: C-703-806-5416.
Financial Institutions: Belvoir Credit Union C-703-730-1800, SunTrust Bank C-703-781-4706.
Clubs: Officers' Club, C-703-780-0930. Golf Club, C-703-806-5878.
Places to Eat: Vortex Grill, C-703-805-2991. Niblick's Grill, C-703-806-5878. Bozzelli Bros Delicatessen, C-703-781-6861. Exchange Food Court offers Burger King, Charlie's, Pizza Hut, Popeye's, Starbucks, Subway and Taco Bell. Arby's, Dunkin Donuts and Dominos are also on base. Many restaurants within a short drive.
Auto Hobby Shop Phone Numbers: C-703-806-4088.
Bowling: The Bowling Center, C-703-805-2991.
Fitness Center Phone Numbers: Graves Fitness Center, C-703-806-5368. The Body Shop, C-703-806-3100, Kawamura Performance Center, C-703-806-4655. Specker Field House, C-703-806-5368. Wells Field House, C-703-806-5093.
Golf: Fort Belvoir Golf Club, C-703-806-5878.
ITT/ITR: C-703-805-3714.
Library: C-703-806-4244.
Marina: C-703-781-8282.
MWR: C-703-805-4134.
MWR Website:
https://belvoir.armymwr.com/
MWR Facebook:
https://www.facebook.com/fortbelvoirMWR/
MWR Twitter:
https://twitter.com/fortbelvoirmwr
Outdoor Recreation: Outdoor Recreation Services, C-703-805-3081. Offers equipment rental, hunting, fishing, kayaks, a boat launch, skate park, dog park and more.
Swimming: North Post Outdoor Pool, C-703-806-5013, Benyaurd Indoor Pool, C-703-805-2620, Connelly Pool Complex, C-703-780-0193.

Things To Do: While here, see George Washington's Grist Mill and visit nearby Mount Vernon, Woodlawn Plantation and Gunston Hall. Northern Virginia is rich in colonial and Civil War history.

RV CAMPING & GETAWAYS
Fort Belvoir Travel Camp

Reservation/Contact Number Info: C-703-805-3081.
RV Website:
https://belvoir.armymwr.com/programs/recreational-lodging-travel-camp
Reservations: Reservations accepted one year in advance. Credit Card required. Telephone or online reservations accepted. Cancellations or changes must be made 7 days in advance, prior to the day of check-in to receive a full refund. No refunds will be made due to inclement weather. Check-in at the Outdoor Recreation Facility. After hours check-in must be coordinated in advance to obtain gate access code. Check out 1200 hours. Check-out form required.
Season of Operation: Year-round.
Eligibility: AD, Ret, Res, NG, DoD-Civ, Installation Contractors and those listed in AR215-1, paragraph 7-1. Veteran ID is not accepted.
Camper/Trailer Spaces: Concrete (52): Pull-thru and back-in pads with maximum trailer 40', (20A/30A/50A)/S/W, picnic table, fire ring for grilling and campfires. Rates: $50 daily. Waterfront Trailers (6): On-site. Outback Terrain 299 TBH Travel Trailers with full hook ups. Rates: $119 daily. Two-night minimum and $200 deposit required.
Yurt, A Frame, Cabin, Apt, Spaces: Rustic Cabin (1): One-bedroom with queen size bed with bunk above, living room with sleeper sofa, small kitchenette with mini refrigerator, Keurig, microwave and toaster. Bathroom facilities but no showers (guests may use bath house), linens provided, HVAC and Wi-Fi. 2-night minimum stay required. Rates: $79 daily.

Support Facilities: Family Bathhouse, Picnic Area, Playground, Volleyball, Washer/Dryer (coin operated).
RV Storage: C-703-781-8282.
Activities: Biking, Boating, Canoeing, Hiking*, Hunting, Fishing*, Kayaking, Equipment Rental. *C-703-805-3688 for license/permit requirements. Age 16 plus required to obtain fishing license. Two (2) ADA fishing piers.
Credit Cards: Cash, Check, MasterCard and Visa.
Restrictions: Please call for length of stay regulations. Quiet hours 2200-0800. Pets must not be left unattended and must be kept on a leash at all times.
RV Driving Directions/Location: On Base. From Tulley Gate: Turn right on Theote Rd. Turn Right at the fork onto Warren Rd. Take Warren Rd until its end at Johnston Rd and then take a right. Check-in at Outdoor Recreation on the right.
Area Description: Located on the waterfront of Gunston Cove off the Potomac River. Close to Washington D.C. and Quantico, VA.
RV Campground Physical Address: Outdoor Recreation, Bldg 778, 10155 Swift Road, Fort Belvoir, VA 22060.

Fort Eustis

Address: Fort Eustis (Joint Base Langley-Eustis), 2 Washington Boulevard, Fort Eustis, VA 23604.
Information Line: C-757-878-1212.
Main Base Police: C-757-878-4555, DSN-312-826-4555.
Main Installation Website:
http://www.jble.af.mil/
Main Base Location: Fort Eustis is 18 miles west of Hampton, VA on I-64.
Directions to Main Gate: From Newport News/Williamsburg International Airport, Norfolk International Airport and the east: Take Interstate 64 West to exit 250A/Fort Eustis Blvd/Route 105 and proceed west about one mile to enter Fort Eustis. Directions from I-95 and Richmond: Take Interstate 64 East to exit 250A/Fort Eustis Blvd/Route 105 and proceed west about one mile to enter Fort Eustis.
NMC: Newport News, within city limits.

NMI: Yorktown Naval Weapons Station, 7 miles northeast.
Base Social Media/Facebook:
https://www.facebook.com/JointBaseLangleyEustis
Base Social Media/Twitter:
https://twitter.com/JBLEnews
Chapels: C-757-878-1316.
Dental Clinic: C-757-878-3434, C-757-314-7925.
Medical: C-757-314-7500, C-757-314-7939/7766 (BCAC), DSN-312-826-7939/7766.
Veterinary Services: C-757-878-5824.
Beauty/Barber Shop: Barber, C-757-887-1975. Beauty, C-757-812-7582. C-757-878-0293.
Commissary: C-757-878-5966.
Exchange Gas: Fort Eustis Express, C-757-369-3772/3780.
Exchange: C-757-887-0293/0689.
Financial Institutions: 1st Advantage Federal Credit Union, C-1-800-359-7650, C-757-878-2274. Bank of America Military Bank, C-757-887-7840.
Clubs: Fort Eustis Club, C-757-878-5700.
Places to Eat: JuiceFix Juicery, C-757-878-1516. Reggie's, C-757-878-5331. Strike Zone, C-757-878-7138. The Bistro at McDonald Army Health Center, C-757-314-7500. Exchange Food Court, C-757-887-2748 offers Charlie's, Arby's, Taco Bell, Popeye's, and Subway. Starbucks, Burger King and Pizza Hut are on base. Many restaurants are within a short drive.
Bowling: Fort Eustis Bowling Center, C-757-878-5482.
Fitness Center: Anderson Field House, C-757-878-2328. McClellan Fitness Center, C-757-878-5556. Satellite Fitness Center, C-757-878-8080/8081.
Golf: The Pines Golf Course, C-757-878-5331.
ITT/ITR: C-757-878-3694.
Library: Groninger Library, C-757-878-5017.
Military Museum: U.S. Army Transportation Museum, C-757-878-1115.
Military Museum Website:
http://www.transchool.lee.army.mil/Museum/TransportationMuseum/museum.htm

MWR: C-757-878-3694/5031.
MWR Website:
https://jbleforcesupport.com/
MWR Facebook:
https://www.facebook.com/forteustismwr/
MWR Twitter:
https://twitter.com/eustismwr
Outdoor Recreation: Outdoor Recreation Center, C-757-878-2610. Offers hunting, fishing pier, watersports, equipment rentals including boats, camping, sports fields, mini-golf, batting cages, go karts and more.
Swimming: Aquatic Center Adventure Pool, C-757-878-1090 offers whirlpool, mini lazy river, and a mushroom waterfall. Lap pool is available.
Things To Do: Attractions on the Peninsula include Colonial Williamsburg, the Jamestown Settlement, Yorktown Victory Center, Virginia Air and Space Museum, Busch Gardens, Water Country USA, and more.
Walking Trails: Walking trails are available.

RV CAMPING & GETAWAYS

Fort Eustis Outdoor Recreation Area

Reservation/Contact Number Info: C-757-878-2610, DSN-312-826-2610. Fax C-757-878-3916, DSN-312-826-3916.
Recreation Security: C-757-878-4555.
RV Website:
https://jbleforcesupport.com/fort-eustis/outdoor-recreation
GPS Coordinates:
37°9'36"N/76°35'47"W or 828 Kells Drive, Fort Eustis, VA 23604.
Reservations: Accepted up to six months in advance with $20 deposit. Cancellations must be made 72 hours in advance to avoid loss of deposit. Office hours 0800-1700 Mon-Fri. Closed on weekends and holidays. Check in at Outdoor Recreation Office. Check-out no later than 1100. Extra day will be charged for late check-out. Maximum stay 30 days. Cabin check-in 1500 hours, check-out 1100 hours.
Season of Operation: Year-round.

Eligibility: AD, NG, Res, Ret, DoD-Civ (AD and Ret), Dep. And Ft. Eustis Civ-Contractors w/ ID.
Camper/Trailer Spaces: Gravel. Pull-thru (6), Maximum 45' in length; Back-in (3), Maximum 40' in length, E(220V/30A/50A)/S/W, picnic tables, grill. Pavilion on site. Rates: $20 daily. Grass/Dirt: (15), No hookups. Rates: $10 daily.
Yurt, A Frame, Cabin, Apt, Spaces: Cabins: Two-bedroom (5, 1 handicapped accessible), one loft, CATV, cookware/utensils, fireplace, full kitchen, cookware/utensils, housekeeping service, iron/ironing board, linens, microwave, picnic area, refrigerator, telephone, toiletries, TV/VCR. No smoking. Rates: $90 daily.
Support Facilities: Auto Craft Shop, Bathhouse, Bowling, Cafeteria, Commissary, Equipment Rental, Exchange, Fishing Pier, Fitness Center, Gas, Golf, Grills, Laundry/Pay, Mechanic/Auto Repair, Mess Hall, Pavilion, Playground, Pool, Propane, Rec Center, Restrooms, Sewage Dump, Shoppette, Showers, Snack Bar, Sports Fields, Trails.
RV Storage: C-757-878-2610.
Activities: Aquatic Center, Bicycling, Boating, Bowling, Fishing*, Go-Kart Track, Hunting*, Paintball. *License is required.
Credit Cards: MasterCard and Visa.
Restrictions: No smoking in cabins. No pets allowed in cabins. Pets allowed in campsites, owner must clean up after pet and obey leash laws. No firearms permitted. No open fires. VA state fishing and hunting licenses required plus Post Permit. Hunter safety card and Fort Eustis activity pass also required.
RV Driving Directions/Location: On Base. From the Main Gate: Take Washington Blvd through the traffic circle to the light at Jackson. Turn right onto Jackson and proceed to stop sign. Turn right onto Monroe Ave and left onto Kells Dr. Outdoor Recreation is in Bldg 828 at the end of Kells Dr.
Area Description: A prime location for hunting and fishing, the cabins overlook

beautiful Lake Eustis. Within driving distance of Virginia's finest beaches.
RV Campground Physical Address: Fort Eustis Outdoor Recreation Area, 828 Kells Drive, Fort Eustis, VA 23604.

Fort Pickett

Address: Fort Picket HQ, Bldg 472, Military Highway, Blackstone, VA 23824-3034.
Information Line: C-434-292-8621.
Main Base Police: C-434-292-8444. Emergencies dial 911 from on-post phone.
Main Installation Website: http://vko.va.ngb.army.mil/fortpickett/
Main Base Location: The facility is located on US-460, one mile away from the city of Blackstone.
Directions to Main Gate: From I-85: Take exit 27 north on VA-46 to Blackstone. Follow to the main entrance gate. Clearly marked.
NMC: Petersburg, 34 miles northeast.
NMI: Fort Lee, 45 miles northeast.
Base Social Media/Facebook: https://www.facebook.com/FortPickett
Chapels: C-434-298-6106.
Beauty/Barber Shop: C-434-292-5990.
Exchange: C-434-292-8680.
Fitness Center: C-434-292-8626/2613.
Military Museum: Virginia Army National Guard Historical Collection, C-434-298-5321.
MWR: C-434-292-8626.
MWR Website: http://vko.va.ngb.army.mil/fortpickett/mtc/dpca/mwr.htm
Outdoor Recreation: Outdoor Recreation Services, C-434-292-2613. Offers equipment and facilities rental. Call for more information.
Things To Do: Fairfax, Richmond, Charlottesville, Williamsburg and Washington, D.C. are nearby.

RV CAMPING & GETAWAYS

Pickett Park Campground

Reservation/Contact Number Info: C-434-298-0366. Fax C-434-298-0367.
Recreation Security: C-434-292-8444.
RV Email Address: pcktlra@embarqmail.com

Reservations: Reservations required. No restrictions on length of stay. Office hours 0800-1630 Mon-Fri. Closed weekends and holidays.
Season of Operation: Year-round.
Eligibility: Open to all, age 16+ with valid driver's license
Camper/Trailer Spaces: RV Sites (25): Pull-thru (4), back-in (21); 40' maximum length, some sites are shorter. E(110/220V/20/30/50A)/W/S. Rates: $12 daily for 30 days or less. After 30 days, Rates: $9 daily.
Tent Spaces: Grass (12): No hookups. Rates: $5 daily.
Support Facilities: ATM, Barber, Fitness Center, Exchange, Snack Bar. Amenities available off base approximately one mile away.
RV Storage: Rates: $1 daily short and long term.
Activities: Hunting and fishing.
Credit Cards: Cash, Check, Money Order, Discover, MasterCard, and Visa.
Restrictions: Pets allowed on leash. Owners must clean up after pets. Firearms allowed subject to Federal, State and County Laws. Quiet hours 2200-0700.
RV Driving Directions/Location: On Base. From the Main Gate: Follow Military Rd for .9 miles and turn left on 10th St. Almost immediately, turn right on QM Cir W to register with LRA, Bldg 2193 (behind first building on right). Note: West Entrance Gate open 0600-1800 hours Mon-Fri; closed Sat, Sun and holidays. Main Gate open 24/7 daily.
Area Description: Campground is on a quiet, wooded area populated by wildlife. Located within Fort Pickett boundaries on property administered by Nottoway County. Nearby Blackstone is home to the Annual Arts and Crafts Festival held the weekend after Labor Day; Schwartz Tavern, a full-restored Revolutionary War-Era Tavern, now a museum; Bevell's Hardware, from November to January, annually displays a giant 20' by 56' model railroad layout with hundreds of figurines, buildings and scenes; Robert Thomas Carriage Museum, featuring restored antique carriages and buggies; plus antique

mall, restaurants, shopping and churches.

RV Campground Physical Address: 2193 Military Rd, Pickett Park, Blackstone, VA 23824.

Fort Story (JEB Little Creek-Ft Story)

Address: JEB-Fort Story, 300 Guadalcanal Road, Virginia Beach, VA 23459.

Information Line: C-757-422-7305/7311, DSN-312-438-7305/7311.

Main Base Police: Non-emergency, C-757-422-7142/7143, DSN-312-438-7142/7143. Emergency, C-757-422-7141 or dial 911.

Main Installation Website: https://cnic.navy.mil/regions/cnrma/installations/jeb_little_creek_fort_story.html

Main Base Location: Fort Story is located adjacent to the city of Virginia Beach with 1,451 acres of sandy trails, cypress swamps, grassy dunes and soft and hard sand beaches.

Directions to Main Gate: From the south exit of Chesapeake Bay Bridge Tunnel/US-13: Travel east on US-60/Atlantic Avenue to Fort Story. From I-64: Take US-60 east. From I-264: Take exit US-58 and turn left onto North Atlantic Avenue/US-60 to 89th Street to Fort Story.

NMC: Virginia Beach, 3 miles south.

NMI: Little Creek Naval Amphibious Base (Little Creek-Fort Story Joint Expeditionary Base), 10 miles west.

Base Social Media/Facebook: https://www.facebook.com/JEBLCFS

Chapels: C-757-422-7665/7552.

Dental Clinic: C-757-422-7077.

Medical: Boone Clinic - JEB Little Creek, C-757-953-8155, DSN-312-377-8155.

Veterinary Services: C-757-422-7734.

Beauty/Barber Shop: C-757-422-7027.

Commissary: JEB-Little Creek, C-757-464-3561.

Exchange Gas: Fort Story Express, C-757-425-0001.

Exchange: JEB Little Creek, C-757-425-0001.

Places to Eat: Fort Story Express offers deli sandwiches and snacks. Many restaurants are within a short drive.

Fitness Center: Fort Story Gym, C-757-422-7975.

ITT/ITR: JEB Little Creek, C-757-462-7793.

Library: C-757-422-7548

MWR: JEB-Little Creek-Fort Story, C-757-462-7952/7758.

MWR Website: http://www.navymwrjblittlecreekfortstory.com/

Outdoor Recreation: Outdoor Equipment Rental, C-757-422-7472. Fort Story Recreation offers a variety of activities. JEB-Little Creek Cove Marina, C-757-462-7140. MWR JEB-Little Creek-Fort Story, C-757-462-7952/7758.

Swimming: Ocean swimming available.

Things To Do: Visit the Old Cape Henry Lighthouse, Douglas, Virginia Beach Marine Science Museum, Williamsburg Pottery Factory. Busch Gardens. See Military Living's Military RV, Camping and Outdoor Recreation Around the World™ for more information.

Walking Trails: Nature trails available at JEB-Little Creek. First Landing Park is a great place for hiking, biking and nature trails.

RV CAMPING & GETAWAYS

Fort Story Cabins & RV Park

Reservation/Contact Number Info: C-757-422-7601, DSN-312-438-7601.

Recreation Security: Emergencies dial 911.

RV Website: http://www.navymwrjblittlecreekfortstory.com

Other Info Website: http://get.dodlodging.net/propertys/Fort-Story-JEB

GPS Coordinates: 36°55'38"N/76°0'23"W

Reservations: Reservations accepted up to one year in advance for AD, 6 months in advance for Ret, DoD-Civ. Required online or by telephone. Office hours 0800-2100 Mon-Sat, 0900-1730 Sun. Cancellations must be made within 30 days of arrival to avoid fee.

Season of Operation: Year-round.
Eligibility: AD, NG, Res, Ret and DoD-Civ.
Camper/Trailer Spaces: Gravel (16), Back-in, 40' maximum, E(110V/50A)/W hookups, picnic table, fire ring. Rates: $25 daily.
Tent Spaces: Tent Sites (5): E(110V/50A)/W picnic table, fire ring. Rates: $22 daily.
Yurt, A Frame, Cabin, Apt, Spaces: Camping Cabins (3): One 12'x12' room, electricity with hookups, A/C, sleeps 4, one double bed, one set of bunk beds, mini-refrigerator, porch. Linens not provided. Rates: $30 daily.
Support Facilities: Beach, Boat Rentals, Convenience Store, Gas, Laundry, Rec Equipment, Restrooms, Sewage Dump, Showers, Sports Fields, Tennis Courts.
Activities: Lake Fishing, Lighthouse Tour, Lookout Area, Picnic Area, Playground, Swimming.
Credit Cards: MasterCard and Visa.
Restrictions: Pets allowed on leash.
RV Driving Directions/Location: On Base. From Main Gate: Continue straight and campground ahead to the left. directions to other facilities provided at check-in.
Area Description: Fort Story is the site of the first stop of English settlers in the U.S. The Cross at Cape Henry is located here. Old Cape Henry Lighthouse is the first lighthouse built by the federal government. The statue of Admiral Francois Joseph Paul de Grasse, presented to the Virginia Beach Bicentennial Commission in 1976, is also located here. Full range of support facilities available on post.
RV Campground Physical Address: 601 Atlantic Ave, Virginia Beach, VA 23459.

Little Creek Naval Amphibious Base (JEB Little Creek)

Address: 2600 Tawara Court, Bldg 1602, Quarter Deck JEB LCFS, Virginia Beach, VA 23459-3297.
Information Line: C-757-444-0000, Little Creek Base Quarter Deck, C-757-462-7386, DSN-312-253-7386.

Main Base Police: C-757-462-4445. Emergencies dial 911.
Main Installation Website: http://cnic.navy.mil/regions/cnrma/inst allations/jeb_little_creek_fort_story.ht ml
Main Base Location: The base is located at the extreme northwest corner of the city of Virginia Beach and extends to the city of Norfolk.
Directions to Main Gate: From I-64: Take exit 282 to Northampton Blvd/US-13. Continue straight for approximately four miles and take the AMPHIB BASE exit onto Independence Blvd/VA-225. Proceed straight on this road to the Main Gate of the base. From the Chesapeake Bay Bridge/Tunnel: Take US-60 west/Shore Drive to the base.
NMC: Norfolk, 6 miles west.
NMI: Norfolk Naval Station, 12 miles west.
Base Social Media/Facebook: https://www.facebook.com/JEBLCFS
Base Social Media/Twitter: https://twitter.com/JEBLCFS
Chapels: C-757-462-7427/7428.
Dental Clinic: C-757-953-8334/8335/8338.
Medical: Boone Clinic, C-757-953-8351/8354.
Veterinary Services: See Fort Story.
Beauty/Barber Shop: Home Gallery NEX, C-757-363-3265. C-757-363-3252/3253, Barber Shop C-757-363-3315.
Commissary: C-757-464-3561.
Exchange Gas: Westside Mini-Mart, C-757-363-3235. C-757-363-5804. D Street, C-757-363-0145.
Exchange: C-757-363-3276.
Financial Institutions: ABNB Federal Credit Union JEB, C-757-523-5300, C-1-800-443-1141. Bank of America Military Bank JEB Little Creek, C-757-318-7401.
Clubs: McFaul CPO Lounge, C-757-462-2003.
Places to Eat: Eagles Nest, C-757-462-7559. 11th Frame Snack Bar, C-757-462-7758. Galley next to Shields Hall and McDonald's are within walking distance. Many restaurants are within a short drive.
Bowling: Gator Bowl, C-757-462-7952.

Fitness Center: Rockwell Hall Gym, C-757-462-7735. Pierside Gym, C-757-462-8280.
Golf: Eagle Haven Golf Course, C-757-462-8526.
ITT/ITR: Tickets, C-757-462-7793. Travel Agent, C-757-462-3117/7665. Cruise & Travel, C-757-462-2677.
Library: C-757-462-7691.
Marina: Little Creek Cove Marina, C-757-462-7140.
MWR: C-757-462-7952/7758.
MWR Website:
http://www.navymwrjblittlecreekfortstory.com/
Outdoor Recreation: Lake Bradford Outdoor Rentals, C-757-462-7516. Lake Bradford Outdoor Rentals offers pop-up campers, boats and motors, camping equipment, bicycles, hand trucks, industrial cleaning equipment and more. Also offers household items for newcomers.
Swimming: Gator Water Park, C-757-462-7173. Pierside Outdoor Pool, C-757-462-8280 offers lap swim, open swim and swimming lessons. Beach ocean swimming on base.
Things To Do: History is all around Little Creek, with Jamestown and Williamsburg one hour north and Virginia Beach Boardwalk and oceanfront activities a short drive away. First Landing State Park is nearby and the Chesapeake Bay Bridge Tunnel to the Eastern Shore a few short miles to access.
Walking Trails: There are several nature trails on base, near the campground.

RV CAMPING & GETAWAYS

JEB Little Creek Campground & RV Park

Reservation/Contact Number Info: C-757-462-7282, DSN-312-253-7282.
Recreation Security: C-757-462-4445.
RV Website:
http://get.dodlodging.net/propertys/JEB-Little-Creek-Campground-RV-Park
Other Info Website:
http://www.navymwrjblittlecreekfortstory.com/programs/f2afb693-330b-4f87-b3d2-f57906b100e4

GPS Coordinates:
36°54'31"N/76°9'37"W
Reservations: Accepted up to one year in advance for AD; 6 months in advance for Ret, DoD-Civ. Cancellations require 30 day advance notice to avoid fee. Office hours 0800-1600 Mon, Wed, Fri. Check-in 1200 hours, check-out 1200 hours. Late arrivals check-in with Camp Host, Site 39. Maximum stay for RV Park 30 days; extensions space available only.
Season of Operation: Year-round.
Eligibility: AD, NG, Res, Ret and DoD-Civ. AD has priority.
Camper/Trailer Spaces: Concrete (45), E(110V/30/50A)/S/W hookups, CATV, Wi-Fi, picnic table, fire ring; laundry room and bathhouse. Rates: $27 daily.
Tent Spaces: Grass/Sand (9), Primitive, no hookups. Rates: $10 daily. Maximum stay 14 days. Group Site: Primitive, no hookups. Rates: $30 daily.
Support Facilities: RV Park: Beaches (Seasonal), Cable, Change Machine, Grills, Horseshoes, Laundry Room, Modem Hook-Up (In Office), Pavilion, Pay Phones, Picnic Tables, Playground, Restrooms, Sewage Dump (For a Fee), Showers, State-of-the-Art Playground. Nearby: Aerobics, Basketball, Boat Launch, Boat Rental, Boone Clinic, Bowling Center, Car Wash, Camper Rental, Cardio Theater, Change Machine, Chapel, Commissary, Country Store, CPO Club, Driving Range, Exchange, Fishing Pier, Fitness Center, Fitness Trail, Garage, Gas, Golf, Gymnasium, Hobby Shops, Internet, ITT, Jogging Trail, Library, Marina, Pass Office, Post Office, Propane, Racquetball, Rec Center, Rec Equipment, Sports Fields, Sports Gear Issue, Tennis Courts, Theater, Wellness Center.
RV Storage: None.
Activities: Bingo, Boating, Gaming (Seasonal), Golfing, Hiking, Jogging, Monthly Calendar Events, Swimming.
Credit Cards: American Express, Discover, MasterCard and Visa.
Restrictions: Pets must be on leash, tended to and cleaned up after. No fires, firearms, or skateboards allowed.

RV Driving Directions/Location: On Base. From Gate 3: Bear to the right to use the commercial entrance. Ask gate attendant for further directions.

Area Description: The Naval Amphibious Base is nestled among many lakes and other bodies of water in a wooded area near the Chesapeake Bay. Full range of support facilities available on base and conveniently located.

RV Campground Physical Address: JEB Little Creek MWR RV Park, 2112 Amphibious Dr, Bldg 750, Virginia Beach, VA 23459.

Northwest Annex – Norfolk NSA

Address: 1320 Northwest Blvd, Bldg 145, Chesapeake, VA 23322-4102.
Information Line: C-757-421-8000.
Main Base Police: C-757-421-8223. Emergencies dial 911.
Main Installation Website:
https://www.cnic.navy.mil/regions/cnr ma/installations/nsa_hampton_roads/n sa_northwest_annex.html
Main Base Location: The NSA Northwest Annex is located in rural southern Chesapeake, Virginia on the border of North Carolina.
Directions to Main Gate: Driving from I-64 East or West, Around Toll: Take VA-168 South to Hillcrest East exit. Go to second light. Turn right onto Battlefield Blvd. Keep straight until Battlefield ends, approximately 7 miles and the 168 bypass begins. Turn right onto 168 bypass. Turn right on Old Battlefield Blvd which is next light. Immediately turn right onto Ballahack Rd at the 7-11 and travel 3 miles. Turn left onto Relay Road to the base entrance. Turn left into first parking lot.
NMC: Chesapeake, within city limits.
NMI: Norfolk Naval Shipyard, 26 miles northwest.
Chapels: C-757-421-8210.
Dental Clinic: C-757-953-6246.
Medical: C-757-953-6250.
Beauty/Barber Shop: C-757-421-8234.
Exchange Gas: C-757-421-8254.
Exchange: C-757-421-8254.

Places to Eat: The Galley, C-757-421-8328 is within walking distance of the facility. Mariner Snack Bar, C-757-421-8250.
Bowling: Bowling Center, C-757-421-8267.
Fitness Center: Fitness Center, C-757-421-8263.
Golf: Norfolk Naval Station's Sewells Point Golf Course, C-757-444-5572. Eagle Haven Golf Course, JEB Little Creek, C-757-462-8526.
ITT/ITR: C-757-421-8265.
Marina: Norfolk Navy Sailing Center, C-757-444-2918.
MWR: 757-421-8260.
MWR Website:
http://www.navymwrhamptonroads.com/
MWR Facebook:
https://www.facebook.com/NSAMWR/
Outdoor Recreation: Community Recreation, C-757-421-8250. Offers bounce houses, tables, chairs, grills, EZ UP Tents, ice chest coolers, drink coolers, corn hole boards, popcorn and snow cone machine. NAVY MWR picnic and park facilities include barbecue grills, parking, sand volleyball courts, horseshoe pits, picnic tables and more.
Swimming: Outdoor Pool, C-757-421-8268 offers lap swim, open swim and seasonal swim lessons.
Things To Do: Virginia Beach and Norfolk are nearby. Visit the Ocean Breeze Fun Park, Virginia Beach Aquarium, Virginia Beach Oceanfront Beaches and Shops, Nauticus museums and exhibits and The Hampton Roads Naval Museum. Cross the state line into North Carolina and visit the Outer Banks for some dining and entertainment.

RV CAMPING & GETAWAYS
Stewart Campground

Reservation/Contact Number Info: C-757-421-8260/8265.
Recreation Security: C-757-421-8223.
RV Website:
http://get.dodlodging.net/propertys/St ewart-Campgrounds
Other Info Website:
http://www.navymwrhamptonroads.co

m/programs/a6aa35a1-0487-49af-a134-3b5f81bd1e8a

GPS Coordinates:
36°34'12.5"N/76°14'46.8"W

Reservations: Reservations accepted on a first come, first serve basis. Reservations may be made up to 1 year in advance for AD; 6 months in advance for Ret/DoD-Civ. Office hours 1100-2000 Sun-Wed, 1100-1600 Thurs, 1100-2100 Fri-Sat. Late arrivals should find site assignment posted at entrance. Check-in and check-out during normal business hours. Maximum stay 30 days during Summer; maximum stay 60 days during off season.

Season of Operation: Year-round.

Eligibility: AD, NG, Res, Ret, DoD-Civ.

Camper/Trailer Spaces: RV Sites (14): E(30A,50A), back-in with 40' max, picnic table. Two potable water stations with key access, dump station and bathhouse available. Rates: $22-$24 daily. Can accommodate long-term campers and tents.

Support Facilities: Bowling Center, Chapel, Exchange, Galley, Gym, ITT, MWR Office, Pavilion.

RV Storage: C-757-421-8264.

Activities: Volleyball Sand Court.

Credit Cards: American Express, Cash, Discover, MasterCard and Visa.

Restrictions: Pets must be on leash. Quiet hours 2200-0700.

RV Driving Directions/Location: On Base. From the Main Gate: Continue on Relay Rd then go right at Wilderness Rd. Look for sign to camp. Camp is .25 miles ahead on left.

Area Description: Located in southeast Chesapeake and only a short drive to the North Carolina border. The Outer Banks of NC are less than a one-hour drive and Virginia Beach is approximately 30 minutes away.

RV Campground Physical Address: Bldg 237 Relay Rd, Chesapeake, VA 23322.

Ocean Pines RV Park

Address: Ocean Pines RV Park, 4160 Nimitz Drive, Virginia Beach, VA 23454-5311.

Information Line: C-757-433-2366, DSN-312-433-2366.

Main Base Police: C-757-433-9111. Emergencies dial 911.

Main Installation Website:
http://www.cnic.navy.mil/regions/cnrma/installations/nas_oceana.html

Main Base Location: Park is located in the resort town of Virginia Beach, a short drive from the Boardwalk and oceanfront.

Directions to Main Gate: From I-64, take exit I-264 East. Follow I-264 East approximately 10 miles and take exit 20. Follow Oceana Blvd about 1.5 miles and take a right on Harpers Rd. Continue approximately 1 mile, then take right on Nimitz Dr into RV park.

NMC: Virginia Beach, within city limits.

NMI: Oceana Naval Air Station, adjacent.

Commissary: Approximately 2 miles to the Ocean NAS commissary, C-757-428-6401.

Exchange Gas: Approximately 2 miles to the Ocean NAS Gas station. C-757-425-4283, C-757-422-8451.

Exchange: Approximately 2 miles to the Oceana NAS Navy Exchange facility, C-757-425-4260/4261.

Golf: Aeropines Golf Course, C-757-433-2866.

ITT/ITR: C-757-433-3301.

MWR: C-757-433-3215.

MWR Website:
http://www.navymwroceanadamneck.com/

MWR Facebook:
https://www.facebook.com/nasodn.mwr/

Outdoor Recreation: NAS Oceana Outdoor Equipment Rental, C-757-433-3215. Offers beach bike cruisers, bicycling, boating, hiking, kayaking, fishing* and hunting* are available. *State license required.

RV CAMPING & GETAWAYS

Ocean Pines RV Park

Reservation/Contact Number Info: C-1-877-NAVY-BED, C-757-417-7140, C-757-449-2197.

Recreation Security: C-757-433-9111.

RV Website: http://get.dodlodging.net/propertys/Ocean-Pines-RV-Park

Other Info Website:
http://www.navymwroceanadamneck.c
om/programs/d07c58f1-ba1e-4e8c-
acf6-52182791bf87
RV Email Address:
ocpinesrv@mwrma.com
GPS Coordinates:
36°47'42"N/76°1'26"W
Reservations: Reservations
recommended and may be made up to
one year in advance. No deposit
required. Full payment due upon arrival.
Office hours 0900-1600 Mon-Sat, 0800-
1200 Sun. Maximum stay 60 days.
Check-in 1200-1700 hours, check-out
1100 hours.
Season of Operation: Year-round.
Eligibility: AD, NG, Res, Ret, Dep, 100%
DAV and DoD-Civ (local area only).
Camper/Trailer Spaces: Hardstand,
(74), Back-in, maximum 50' in length,
E(110/220V/20/30/50A)/S/W, CATV,
free Wi-Fi, picnic table, grill. Rates: $25
daily. Primitive Sites (2): No hook-ups.
Maximum stay 30 days. No tent
camping allowed at RV sites.
Support Facilities: Auto Craft Shop,
Auto Repair, ADA compliant Bathhouse,
Beach at Dam Neck Annex, Boat
Rental/Storage, Bowling, Chapel, Coin
Laundry, Commissary, Convenience
Store, Equipment Rental, Exchange,
Fitness Center, Gas, Golf, Grills, Mess
Hall, Pavilion, Picnic Area, Playground,
Pool, Propane, Rec Center, Restrooms,
Sewage Dump, Shoppette, Showers,
Sports Fields, Stables, Tennis Courts.
RV Storage: C-757-433-2875 at NAS
Oceana.
Activities: Amphitheater, Antiquing,
Beaches, Bicycling, Boating, Dining,
Fishing*, Hiking, Hunting*, Kayaking,
Museums, Shopping, Swimming at
Aeropalms Waterpark on base. *State
of Virginia requires hunting and fishing
licenses; these can be purchased on
base at ITT Office, or off-base at local
WalMart.
Credit Cards: American Express, Cash,
Discover, MasterCard and Visa.
Restrictions: Pets are allowed on leash
and must not be left unattended.
Owners must immediately clean up
after pet. Firearms must be checked

with armory on base. Quiet hours 2200-
0900.
RV Driving Directions/Location: Off
Base. From I-264 take First
Colonial/Oceana exit. Travel south on
Oceana Blvd/VA-615. Go to the sixth
light and make a right on Harpers Road.
Entrance to park .5 miles down the road
to Nimitz Dr. Signs at street. Check-in at
office.
Area Description: A quiet park, except
for the "Sounds of Freedom" (aka jet
noise from nearby air bases). Close to
the ocean. Throughout the area, the
scenery is enhanced by trees and grass,
as well as a view of the NAS Oceana golf
course.
RV Campground Physical Address: 4160
Nimitz Dr, Virginia Beach, VA 23454-
5311.

Richmond Defense Supply Center

Address: 8000 Jefferson Davis Highway,
Richmond, VA 23237-4474.
Information Line: C-804-279-3861,
DSN-312-695-3861.
Main Base Police: C-804-279-4888.
Emergencies dial 911.
Main Installation Website:
http://www.dla.mil/Distribution/Locatio
ns/Richmond.aspx
Main Base Location: Defense Supply
Center Richmond (DSCR) is located just
south of the city of Richmond and is
accessible from any direction. The
center occupies over 600 acres in
southern Chesterfield County, Virginia.
Directions to Main Gate: From the
North on I-95: Take I-95 south to
Richmond to exit 67. Take Route
150/Chippenham Parkway
approximately one mile to the
Strathmore Road exit. Turn left at the
stop sign. Keep right at the fork in the
road and proceed straight through to
DSCR's North Gate. From the West:
Take I-64 East to Route 288 south to I-
95 north. Take I-95 north to exit 67.
Take Route 150/Chippenham Parkway
approximately one mile to the
Strathmore Road exit. Turn left at the
stop sign. Keep right at the fork in the

road and proceed straight through to DSCR's North Gate.
NMC: Richmond, within city limits.
NMI: Fort Lee, 17 miles southeast.
Base Social Media/Facebook:
https://www.facebook.com/dla.mil
Medical: C-804-279-3821, DSN-312-695-3821.
Exchange: Shoppette, 0900-1700 Mon-Fri.
Financial Institutions: Bellwood Federal Credit Union C-804-271-0181.
Places to Eat: Center Restaurant, Bldg 33 in on base. Arby's is within walking distance of the facility. Halfway House Restaurant, Applebee's, Peking Restaurant, Shoney's, McDonald's, Hardee's and many others are within driving distance.
Fitness Center: Main Fitness Center, C-804-279-3371.
ITT/ITR: C-804-279-1091.
MWR: C-804-279-5235.
MWR Website:
http://www.mwrrichmond.com/
MWR Facebook:
https://www.facebook.com/MWRRichmond
MWR Twitter:
https://twitter.com/thebellwoodclub
Outdoor Recreation: C-804-279-1094. Offers picnic and playground areas, equipment rental and more.
Swimming: Seasonal Pool, C-804-279-4198. Currently closed for 2017 year due to under-staffing.
Things To Do: Richmond is among America's oldest major cities. Patrick Henry, a U.S. Founding Father, famously declared "Give me liberty or give me death" at its St. John's Church in 1775, leading to the Revolutionary War. The White House of the Confederacy, the home of Confederate President Jefferson Davis during the Civil War, is now a museum in Court End, a neighborhood known for Federal-style mansions. Visit Kings Dominion or shopping in the downtown district.
Walking Trails: Outdoor and Indoor walking track. Indoor Track hours 0500-2000 hours Mon- Fri.

RV CAMPING & GETAWAYS

FMWR RV Overnight Camp

Reservation/Contact Number Info: C-804-279-1094.
Recreation Security: Patrolled by DLA Police.
RV Website:
https://www.defensemwr.com/richmond/programs-services/recreation-leisure/rv-camp
Reservations: Reservations may be made via telephone or in person at Bldg 24. Office hours 0800-1600 Mon-Fri.
Season of Operation: Year-round.
Eligibility: Active or retired DoD cardholders and families.
Camper/Trailer Spaces: RV Sites (6): Pull-thru (2); Back-in (4), E(20A,30A,50A)/S/W, fire pits. Rates: $30 daily.
Support Facilities: Dump Station, Gazebos (screened).
RV Storage: C- 804-279-1094.
Credit Cards: MasterCard and Visa.
Restrictions: Pets are allowed.
RV Driving Directions/Location: On Base. From the DSCR's North Gate: Stay Straight for approximately .3 mile and Campground is on left.
Area Description: Located near historic Richmond.
RV Campground Physical Address: FMWR RV Overnight Camp, 6002 Strathmore Road, Richmond, VA 23234.

WASHINGTON

Camp Murray

Address: 1 Militia Drive, Camp Murray, WA 98430-5000.
Information Line: C-253-512-8000.
Main Base Police: C-253-512-7900. Emergencies dial 911.
Main Installation Website:
http://mil.wa.gov/194th-regional-support-wing
Main Base Location: Located adjacent to Joint Base Lewis-McChord near Lakewood, Washington.

Directions to Main Gate: From I-5 south of Tacoma: Take exit 122 west across the railroad tracks and go left through the Camp Murray gate.
NMC: Tacoma,13 miles north.
NMI: Fort Lewis/JB Lewis-McChord, adjacent.
Base Social Media/Facebook: https://www.facebook.com/washingtonguard/
Chapels: C-253-512-8790.
Financial Institutions: American Lake Credit Union, C-253-582-3831.
Military Museum: C-253-512-7834.

RV CAMPING & GETAWAYS

American Lake Beach RV & Campgrounds
Reservation/Contact Number Info: C-253-584-5411, Camp Host, C-253-209-5711. Fax C-253-582-9521.
Recreation Security: C-253-512-8939.
RV Website: https://ngaw-enlisted.org/campground/
GPS Coordinates: 47°7'6"N/122°34'23"W
Reservations: Reservations are accepted up to three days in advance. Telephone reservations require a debit or credit card. Payment due upon arrival. Cancellations must be made 48 hour prior to arrival to avoid fee. Office hours 0900-1600 Mon-Fri. After hours arrivals should contact Camp Host. Check-in 1200 hours, check-out 1100 hours. Maximum stay 30 days; extensions based on space available.
Season of Operation: Year-round for RV Park.
Eligibility: AD, NG, Res and Ret.
Camper/Trailer Spaces: Gravel (28), E(110V/30A/50A)/S/W hookups. Rates: $25 daily for 30A; $32 daily for $50A.
Tent Spaces: Primitive (8): No hookups. Rates: $10 daily. Kitchen use for hourly fee. Tent sites close October 1.
Support Facilities: Beach, Laundromat, Marina, Picnic Area, Playground, Restrooms, Showers.
RV Storage: None.
Activities: Basketball, Boating, Fishing*, Horseshoes, Jogging, Volleyball, Water Skiing. *License is required.
Credit Cards: MasterCard and Visa.
Restrictions: Pets allowed on leash, must be walked in designated areas only. No firearms allowed. Quiet hours 2200-0800 hours. No off-road vehicles. Limit two vehicles per camp or RV site (including RV).

RV Driving Directions/Location: On Base. From the Camp Murray Gate: Follow signs to beach. Register at office.
Area Description: Camp Murray is located on the southern end of Puget Sound in the Olympia Mountain region. Quiet, wooded site along American Lake. Full range available at Fort Lewis, two miles south.
RV Campground Physical Address: Mailing Address: Camp Murray Beach, c/o NGAW, P.O. Box 5144, Camp Murray, Tacoma, WA 98430-5144.

Clear Lake Recreation Area

Address: Clear Lake Recreation, South 14824, Clear Lake Road, Cheney, WA 99004.
Information Line: C-509-247-1212, DSN-312-657-1212.
Main Base Police: C-509-247-5493. Emergencies dial 911.
Main Installation Website:
http://www.fairchild.af.mil/
Main Base Location: Located on the shores of Clear Lake, this 34 acre area is the perfect place for fishing, water skiing, swimming and boating.
NMC: Spokane, 14 miles east.
NMI: Fairchild AFB, 14 miles northeast.
Commissary: Approximately 14 miles to the commissary at Fairchild AFB, C-509-244-5591.
Exchange: Approximately 14 miles to the Base Exchange at Fairchild AFB, C-509-244-2832.
MWR: C-509-247-5484.
MWR Website:
http://www.fairchildfun.com/
MWR Facebook:
https://www.facebook.com/FairchildAirForceBaseFSS/
MWR Twitter:
https://twitter.com/fairchildFSS
Outdoor Recreation: Outdoor Recreation at Fairchild AFB, C-509-247-5920. Offers camping gear, winter sports equipment rental, boats, campers, paintball, lawn care equipment and more.
Swimming: Lake.

RV CAMPING & GETAWAYS

Clear Lake Recreation Area

Reservation/Contact Number
Info: Summer Season, C-509-299-5129, DSN-509-657-5920.
Recreation Security: C-509-247-5493.
RV Website:
http://www.fairchildfun.com/clearlake.html
RV Email Address:
Mike.Johnson01@fairchild.af.mil
GPS Coordinates:
47°31'36"N/117°42'10"W.
Reservations: Reservation accepted beginning 1 April. No deposit required. Payment due upon arrival. No maximum/minimum stay. Summer Season Office hours 0800-2000 daily. Check-in at Main Lodge 1230 hours, check-out 1130 hours.
Season of Operation: Late April-Labor Day.
Eligibility: AD, NG, Res, Ret, DoD-Civ, DoD-Civ Contractors, Dep and 100% DAV. Retired DoD must present valid DoD Retirement card. All others must present valid Military ID Card.
Camper/Trailer Spaces: Hardstand (24), back-in, maximum length 40', E(220V/30/50A)/S/W hookups, picnic table, grill. Rates: $20 daily. Grass/Dirt (3), pull-thru, maximum length 40', E(220V/30A) hookups. Rates: $15 daily.
Tent Spaces: Camp Sites (20): Rates: $10 daily/$60 weekly. Shared water.
Yurt, A Frame, Cabin, Apt, Spaces: Recreational Lodging: Cabins: (7), Sleeps four to six, kitchenette, microwave, refrigerator, heat/AC. Patrons must provide utensils and linens. Rates: $75 daily; $375 weekly. No running water or bathroom in cabin. Water on outside faucet and bathhouse provided. Yurt: (1), 16'. Patrons must provide utensils and linens. Rates: $15 daily; $75 weekly. Note: A yurt is a cabin/tent structure with wooden floor, deck and door, two windows, and stretched-canvas covering with skylight. It is furnished, but has no bathroom or kitchen.

Support Facilities: Bathhouse, Beach, Boat Launch*, Boat Rental, Convenience Store, Diesel**, Equipment Rental, Fire Rings, Fishing Pier, Gas**, Grills, Ice, Internet, Laundry/Pay**, Long-term RV Storage**, Marina, Pavilions, Picnic Areas, Playgrounds, Propane**, Restrooms, Sewage Dump, Showers, Snack Bar, Telephone, Trails. * Handicap accessible. **Off-Site.

RV Storage: Available at Fairchild AFB Outdoor Recreation. Call C-509-247-5920 for more information. Rates $20-$40 monthly.

Activities: Basketball, Boating, Fishing, Golfing*, Horseshoes, Swimming, Volleyball, Water Skiing. *Off-Site.

Credit Cards: MasterCard and Visa.

Restrictions: No smoking in cabins or yurts. Pets allowed on leash; must not be left unattended outside; owner must clean up after pet. No pets on beach. No fireworks. No fires outside of fire rings. Patrons are strongly urged to check on fire bans at the lodge. Quiet hours are 2200-0800. Sponsor must be present to rent any camp area or equipment. Guests without ID's are not allowed to stay without sponsors.

RV Driving Directions/Location: Off Base. From I-90 West Bound: Take exit 264 right onto WA-902/Salnave Road then an immediate right onto Clear Lake Road. From I-90 East Bound: Take exit 264, left onto WA-902/Salnave Road, cross over I-90 and then an immediate right onto Clear Lake Road. Campground is approximately .5 miles ahead on the left.

Area Description: Located on Clear Lake in a state where natural wildlife is a challenge and recreation an adventure. This 34-acre area is the perfect place for camping, water skiing, fishing and boating. Full range of support facilities available on base.

RV Campground Physical Address: 14824 Clear Lake Rd, Cheney WA 99004. Off Season Mailing Address: 92 FSS, 121 North Doolittle Ave, Fairchild AFB, WA 99011-5000.

Fairchild Air Force Base

Address: 92nd ARW, 1 East Bong Street, Suite 103, Fairchild AFB, WA 99011.

Information Line: C-509-247-1212, DSN-312-657-1212.

Main Base Police: C-509-247-5493. Emergencies dial 911.

Main Installation Website: http://www.fairchild.af.mil/

Main Base Location: Fairchild AFB is located in the eastern part of Washington State, in Spokane County, 12 miles west of Spokane.

Directions to Main Gate: Travel west on I-90 continuing through Spokane. Take exit 277 to Highway 2 heading west. Continue on Highway 2 through Airway Heights and Fairchild is approximately three miles from Airway Heights on the left hand side of the road. Signs indicating where to turn into the base are visible.

NMC: Spokane, 13 miles east.

NMI: U.S. Air Force Survival School, 15 miles east.

Base Social Media/Facebook: https://www.facebook.com/FairchildAFB

Base Social Media/Twitter: https://twitter.com/TeamFairchild

Chapels: C-509-247-2264.

Dental Clinic: C-509-247-5829.

Medical: C-509-247-2361, DSN-312-657-2361.

Veterinary Services: C-509-247-2584.

Beauty/Barber Shop: Barber Shop, C-509-244-2848; Beauty, C-509-244-5380.

Commissary: C-509-244-5591.

Exchange Gas: C-509-244-8502/5095.

Exchange: C-509-244-3641.

Financial Institutions: Armed Forces Bank, C-509-244-4391/6289, Global Credit Union, C-509-244-9216, C-1-800-676-4562. Wire: Bldg 2264, Hours: 0900-2100 Mon-Fri, 0900-1600 Sat-Sun, C-509-244-2832 (ask for customer service).

Clubs: The Final Point Club, C-509-244-2865. Ten Pin Cafe, C-509-244-2162.

Places to Eat: Flight Kitchen, C-509-247-2614, Ten Pin Cafe, C-509-244-2162, Ross Dining Facility, C-509-247-5553, Warrior Dining Facility, C-509-247-5348.

Exchange Food Court offers Bravo Burritos, C-509-244-6596. Burger King, Starbucks and Sushi Kyo & Teriyaki are on base. Little Joe's, Rusty Moose Steakhouse, Longhorn BBQ, and popular fast food restaurants are within a short driving distance.

Bowling: FunSpot Bowling Center, C-509-247-2422.

Fitness Center: C-509-247-2791/2792.

ITT/ITR: C-509-247-5649/4797.

Library: C-509-247-5556.

MWR: C-509-247-1800.

MWR Website:
http://www.fairchildfun.com/

MWR Facebook:
https://www.facebook.com/FairchildAir ForceBaseFSS/

MWR Twitter:
https://twitter.com/fairchildFSS

Outdoor Recreation: Outdoor Recreation, C-509-247-5920. Offers trips with the beginner adventurer in mind but plenty of challenges for the most advanced outdoorsman or outdoors woman. Activities include; whitewater rafting, rock climbing and rappelling, horseback riding and more. Costs, times and age-limits vary; contact the center for more information. There are also equipment rentals, a paintball park and a FamCamp.

Swimming: Indoor & Outdoor Pool (seasonal), C-509-247-2242 offers lap swim, open swim and swim lessons.

Things To Do: Be sure to visit Manito Park and the Botanical Gardens, the Cheney Cowles Museum and the historic Campbell House.

RV CAMPING & GETAWAYS

Fairchild AFB FamCamp

Reservation/Contact Number Info: C-509-244-3247, C-509-247-5920.

Recreation Security: C-509-247-5493.

RV Website:
http://www.fairchildfun.com/fcamp.ht ml

GPS Coordinates:
47°37'25"N/117°39'51"W

Reservations: No advance reservations. All spots first come, first serve. Check-in 1000 hours until dark with Camp Host,

site 25. If check-in area is unattended pick a vacant space and Camp host will complete check-in upon return.

Season of Operation: 1 April-31 October.

Eligibility: AD, NG, Res, Ret, DoD-Civ, Dep, 100% DAV, NAF-Civ and their guests must have current DoD ID card; guests must be accompanied by sponsor.

Camper/Trailer Spaces: Gravel (32), Pull-thru, Maximum 45' in length, E(220V/30/50A)/S/W hookups, picnic table, grill. Rates: $20 daily, $120 weekly, $480 monthly based on four weeks.

Support Facilities: Auto Craft Shop, Auto Repair, Bathhouse, Boat Rental/Storage, Bowling, Chapel, Commissary, Convenience Store, Equipment Rental, Exchange, Fitness Center, Grills, Laundry, Mess Hall, Pavilion, Picnic Area, Playground, Pool, Rec Center, Restrooms, RV Storage, Sewage Dump, Shoppette, Showers, Tennis Courts, Trails.

RV Storage: Available. Rates: $20-$35 monthly for spaces 20'-40' in length. Call Outdoor Rec: C-509-247-5920 for more information.

Activities: Archery, Bicycling, Boating, Fishing*, Hiking, Parks, Swimming. *License is required.

Credit Cards: Club Card, MasterCard and Visa.

Restrictions: Pets allowed on leash; owner must clean up after pets and keep them inside at night and when leaving the area. Open fires prohibited. Quiet hours 2200-0700 hours, no generators operated at night. No tent camping. Each site allowed one camping unit and one towing vehicle. Motorcycles allowed only to leave or enter park. No smoking in restrooms or laundry.

RV Driving Directions/Location: On Base. From Gate 2 Rambo Gate 0600-1800 Mon-Fri: Note: Although the sign states "No POV's", this is the gate RV's must take. After clearing the base gate, turn left onto W Eaker Ave. In about .7 miles, turn left on E Arnold St. Go about 1.2 miles and turn right onto S O'Malley

Ave. Take next left turn onto W El Paso Ave. FamCamp is a short distance on the right. Caution: Turn is 130 degree, so get into opposing traffic lane if possible if driving anything with a large turning radius. Driving Directions after 1800 hours and weekends use Gate 1 Main Gate. From the Main Gate: Continue down Mitchell St. the road will bend to the right and turn in to Bong St. Continue until reaching the "T" intersection at Bong St and Seattle Ave. Turn right on Seattle Ave and take an immediate left on Bong St (extension of original Bong St). Continue to stop sign. Proceed forward, road changes to El Paso Ave. Follow directions above.

Area Description: The FAMCAMP is nestled beneath a grove of Spanish Elm trees in a meadow of native grasses. The park is adjacent to a trail that travels the perimeter of the base. Fairchild AFB sits in the hub of the Pacific Northwest with many tourist destinations within driving distance. Additionally, Spokane is host to two of the nation's top hospitals and cardiac treatment centers.

RV Campground Physical Address: 326 El Paso, Fairchild AFB, WA 99011.

Fort Lewis (JB Lewis-McChord)

Address: N 12th Street & Pendleton Avenue, Tacoma, WA 98433.
Information Line: C-253-967-1110, DSN-312-357-1110.
Main Base Police: MP Desk, C-253-967-7112. Emergencies dial 911.
Main Installation Website:
http://www.lewis-mcchord.army.mil/
Main Base Location: Located in the beautiful Pacific Northwest on the Puget Sound, in Washington State, Fort Lewis is located near Olympia, the state capitol.
Directions to Main Gate: Located 45 miles south of Seattle on Interstate 5. Take Interstate 5 south. The highway divides the post. Take exit 120 to the North Fort Lewis exit which will lead to the main gate open 24 hours daily.
NMC: Tacoma, 12 miles north.

NMI: Bremerton Naval Base Kitsap, 45 miles northwest.
Base Social Media/Facebook:
https://www.facebook.com/JBLewisMcChord
Base Social Media/Twitter:
https://twitter.com/jblm_pao
Chapels: C-253-967-4849. Chaplain, C-253-967-3718/1723.
Dental Clinic: C-253-968-1240.
Medical: C-253-968-1110/1145, DSN-312-782-1110.
Veterinary Services: C-253-982-3954.
Beauty/Barber Shop: C-253-964-3252/2778.
Commissary: C-253-966-8456.
Exchange Gas: C-253-964-3587. Madigan Express, C-253-964-2160.
Exchange: C-253-964-3161.
Financial Institutions: Armed Forces Bank, N.A, C-253-964-9266. America's Credit Union, C-253-964-3113.
Clubs: Samuel Adams Brewhouse, C-253-964-2012. The Zone, C-253-477-5756. 10-Pin Bar, C-253-967-4661.
Places to Eat: Samuel Adams Brewhouse, C-253-964-2012. Strike Zone Café, C-253-967-4661. Strike Zone Snack Bar, C-253-982-5372. Battle Bean, C-253-964-8152. Exchange Food Court offers Anthony's, Taco Johns, Subway, Charley's, Manchu Wok and Auntie Anne's. Many restaurants are within a short drive.
Bowling: Bowl Arena Lanes, C-253-967-4661.
Fitness Center: Jensen Family Health & Fitness Center. McVeigh Sports & Fitness Center, C-253-967-5869. Soldiers Fieldhouse, C-253-967-4771, C-253-967-5390. Wilson Sports & Fitness, C-253-967-7471. Sheridan Sports & Fitness, C-253-967-7311 (currently closed for renovations.
Golf: Eagle's Pride Golf Course, C-253-967-6522.
ITT/ITR: C-253-967-3085.
Library: Grandstaff Memorial, C-253-967-5889. Book Patch Children's Library, C-253-967-5533.
Marina: Russell Landing Marina, C-253-967-2510.
Military Museum: Lewis Army Museum, C-253-967-7206.

Military Museum Website:
http://www.fortlewismuseum.com/
MWR: C-253-967-5200.
MWR Website:
http://www.jblmmwr.com/index.html
MWR Facebook:
https://www.facebook.com/JBLMFamil
yMWR
MWR Twitter:
https://twitter.com/JBLMMWR
Outdoor Recreation: NW Adventure
Center, C-253-967-8282/7744. Offers
camping, boating, fishing, aquatic,
sports and party equipment rentals and
paintball.
Swimming: Keeler Pool, C-253-967-
6652. Kimbro Pool, C-253-967-5026.
Soldiers Field House Pool, C-253-967-
5390. Shoreline Park Outdoor Pool, C-
253-967-2510. Summer Cove Beach at
American Lake (seasonal).
Things To Do: From majestic Mount
Rainier to the inland sea waters of
Puget Sound, this is the perfect outdoor
retreat no matter what time of year it
is. Tacoma, Olympia and Seattle are
nearby.

RV CAMPING & GETAWAYS

JB Lewis-McChord Travel Camp

Reservation/Contact Number Info: C-
253-967-7744, DSN-312-357-7744. Fax
C-253-967-3284.
Recreation Security: C-253-967-3107.
RV Website:
https://jblm.armymwr.com/programs/t
ravel-camp-and-cabins
GPS Coordinates:
47°6′32″N/122°35′5″W
Reservations: Recommended and
accepted up to one year in advance
with first night's deposit. Cannot
reserve specific sites. Please inform
campground the size of RV.
Cancellations require 48-hour notice for
refund; less administrative fee. Office
hours 0900-1730 daily. RV/Campsites:
Check-in 1200 hours, check-out 1100
hours. Cabins: Check-in 1530 hours,
check-out 1000 hours. Summer Season
May 1- Sept 30 maximum stay 14 days.
Winter Season Oct 1- April 30 maximum

stay 28 days. All extensions based on
space available. For Chambers and
Lewis Lake sites: No reservations
needed. Check-in with Northwest
Adventure Center
Season of Operation: Year-round.
Eligibility: AD, NG, Res, Ret and
DoD/NAF-Civ.
Camper/Trailer Spaces: RV Sites (48):
E(110V/20/30/50A)/S/W hookups,
picnic table, CATV. Rates: $28-$35 daily
depending on hookup and location.
Tent Spaces: Primitive (5): No hookups,
picnic table, grill. Rates: $12 daily.
Primitive Tent Spaces at Chambers Lake
and Lewis Lake (30): Rates: No Charge.
Yurt, A Frame, Cabin, Apt, Spaces: Log
Cabins (13): One-bedroom (6), sleeps
two to four. Studios (4), sleeps two.
Furnished, bathroom, kitchenette,
utensils, linens, cots, CATV. Rates: One
BR: $105 daily; Studios: $85 daily. Two-
bedroom (2), sleeps six. Rates: $115
daily. Three-bedroom (1), sleeps 8
adults and features a gas fireplace and
outside hot tub. Rates: $160 daily. All
cabins include private bath, standard
kitchen appliances, dishes, TV, DVD, Wi-
Fi. Linens and towel service provided.
Support Facilities: Commissary,
Exchange, Golf, ITT Adventure Center,
Marina. Full range of support facilities
on base.
RV Storage: C-253-967-8282/7744.
Activities: Adventure Trips, Boating,
Golfing, Hunting*, Fishing*, Skeet
Shooting, Swimming. * Permits
required.
Credit Cards: Cash, Check, Visa,
MasterCard.
Restrictions: No pets allowed in cabins.
RV Driving Directions/Location: On
Base. From I-5 north or south: Take exit
120 and go a short distance on 41st
Division Dr to JBLM-Lewis North's Main
Gate. Turn right at the first light onto
San Francisco. Take immediate right
onto NCO Beach Rd. The Northwest
Adventure Center will be on the left in
Bldg 8050 and turn left into
campground.
Area Description: Located in beautiful
western Washington at the base of the
Puget Sound, the area is prime for

sightseeing and recreational opportunities on numerous waterways and lakes in Puget Sound area and nearby national parks: Mount Rainier, Olympic and North Cascades.

RV Campground Physical Address: Northwest Adventure Center, Bldg 8050 NCO Beach Rd., JBLM Lewis North, WA 98433.

Jim Creek Wilderness Recreation Area

Address: Jim Creek Recreation Area, 21027 Jim Creek Road, Arlington, WA 98223.

Information Line: C-425-304-5665.
Main Base Police: C-425-304-3260.
Main Installation Website: http://cnic.navy.mil/regions/cnrnw/inst allations/ns_everett.html

Main Base Location: Just outside of Arlington, WA, about 1 1/2 hours north of Seattle. Nestled in the foothills of the North Cascades.

NMC: Seattle, 45 miles southwest.
NMI: Naval Station Everett, 20 miles southwest.
Medical: C-425-304-4040, DSN-312-727-4040, Emergencies, Dial 911.
Beauty/Barber Shop: C-425-304-4968/4965.
Commissary: About 20 miles to the Smoky Point (Everett NS) Commissary, C-425-304-3379.
Exchange Gas: C-425-304-4926/4962/4927.
Exchange: About 20 miles to the Navy Exchange at Everett NS, C-425-304-4940.
Places to Eat: Many places to eat within walking and driving distance of the facility, ask at front desk for details.
Golf: Cedarcrest Golf Course, Glen Eagle Golf course, Kayak Point Golf course are nearby. Ask for details at Front Desk.
MWR: C-425-304-3690, C-888-463-6697.
MWR Website: http://www.navylifepnw.com/

Outdoor Recreation: Outdoor Adventures at Everett Naval Station, C-425-304-3449. Jim Creek Recreation Area offers fishing*, boating, picnic areas, playgrounds, walking trails,

mountain biking, river rafting*, rock climbing*, snow skiing/XC*, sports fields and much more. *State license required for all patrons ages 15 and up. Contact Everett Naval Station, C-425-304-3449/3909 for more information.

Things To Do: There is a wide variety of outdoor recreational opportunities, including camping, fishing, boating, hiking, biking and team building programs. There are also regular weekend programs from May - September, as well as seasonal events. Nearby Seattle offers great sights such as the Space Needle, Seattle Aquarium and Museum of Flight. Don't forget to visit Mt. Rainier National Park.

Walking Trails: Various trails are available on site.

RV CAMPING & GETAWAYS
Jim Creek Wilderness Rec Area

Reservation/Contact Number Info: C-1-877-NAVY-BED, C-1-888-463-6697 (within WA), C-425-304-5315/5363. Fax C-425-304-5364.

Recreation Security: C-425-304-5314, DSN-312-727-5314.

RV Website: http://get.dodlodging.net/propertys/Ji m-Creek-Recreation-Area

Other Info Website: http://jimcreek.navylifepnw.com/progr ams/7f38068f-b802-4308-9def-12471f9a54c6

GPS Coordinates: 48°12'1"N/121°56'8"W

Reservations: Reservations accepted one year in advance for AD; 6 months in advance for all others. Reservation must be secured with credit card. All group reservations require advance deposit equal to first night's stay payable at time of reservation. Full payment due at check-in. Cancellations must be made within 30 days of arrival to avoid fee. Cancellations within 14 days of arrival result in loss of first night deposit. Summer Season Office hours 0800-1700 Sun-Thur, 0800-2000 Fri-Sat. Limited operating hours during Winter season with stays limited to weekends, holidays and school vacations. Check-in for Bobcat, Bear and the Lodge 1600 hours, check-out 1100 hours. RV Park: Check-in at Recreation Center, Bldg 4, during office hours; check-out 1100 hours. Late arrivals check-in with Camp Host. Late arrival fees apply to all reservations. Lodge: Full lodge reservations taken six months in advance. Individual room reservations taken 90 days in advance. **Season of Operation:** Year-round. **Eligibility:** AD, NG, Res, Ret, DoD-Civ, Dep, 100% DAV, U.S. Govt Civ Emp and Sponsored Groups.

Camper/Trailer Spaces: Concrete (16, with 2 handicap accessible): Back-in (12), pull-thru (4); max 40' and 50' length depending on site; mostly partial hookups with E(110V/30/50A)/W and limited E(110V/30/50A)S/W hookups, limited telephone hookups. All provide portable fireplaces, picnic table, grill. Rates: $35-$40 daily.

Tent Spaces: Gravel/Dirt (18), no hookups; picnic table, fire ring, grill. $15-$23 daily. Limited tent-only sites with picnic table, fire ring and grill. Hike-in sites, limited pre-set tent pads. Group campsites available. Call for current rates.

Yurt, A Frame, Cabin, Apt, Spaces: Log Cabins (25): Cub Camp (4), Cabins 1-4 sleeps six, 2 bunks, 1 futon, electricity, no electric heat. Rates: $75 daily. Coho Camp (1), Cabin 12 sleeps 6, 1 bunk, 1 double bed, no electricity, no heat. Rates: $55 daily. Coyote Camp (5), Cabins 21-25 sleep 6, 1 bunk, 1 double bed, electricity, electric heat, small refrigerator. Rates: $60 daily. Cougar Camp (1), Cabin 26 sleeps six, one bunk, 1 double bed, 1 futon, electricity, electric heat, small refrigerator, dining table w/4 chairs. Rates: $75 daily. Grouse Camp (9), Cabins 27-35; Cougar Camp (3), Cabins 36-38; Doe Camp (2), Cabins 39-40 all equipped with 1 bunk, 1 double bed, electricity, electric heat, small refrigerator. All sleep six. Rates: $75 daily. All cabins offer picnic table, fire ring and grill. Steelhead Camp Deluxe Log Cabins (4): Two bedroom, full bath, full kitchen, loft, living room and dining room, CATV, picnic table, fire

ring with Adirondack chairs. Rates: $150 daily. Minimum 2-night stay. Linens provided. Wilderness Lodge (1): Offers full rental and sleeps up to 50 people or individual suites (11 rooms). Dining room, restaurant style kitchen, common bath and showers, (one for women, one for men). No private baths. Group Reservations: $975-$1,150 depending on season. Individual Rates: $55-$80 daily with no access to kitchen. Apartments: Bear Den (1): One-bedroom apartment, sleeps 5, one queen, one single and one twin hide-a-bed couch. Private kitchen and bath. Rates: $110 daily. Bobcat Den (1): Two-bedroom apartment, sleeps 6, one queen and three singles. Private kitchen with dishwasher and private bath. Rates: $140 daily. Linens provided. Mallard RV Trailers: bedroom with one queen bed, one set of double bunk beds, a full bathroom with shower, and full kitchen. Rates: $95 daily.

Support Facilities: Bathhouse*, Boat Rental, Coin Laundry, Conference Center, Convenience Store, Fire Rings, Fitness Center, Grills, Ice, Lodge, Pavilion, Pay Phones, Picnic Area, Playground, Rec Center, Rec Equipment, Restrooms*, RV Storage, Sewage Dump (For a Fee), Showers*, Sports Fields, Trails. * Handicap accessible.

RV Storage: Monthly storage available for $375 with four dumps or full hook-up.

Activities: Backpacking, Boating, Fishing*, Hiking, Mountain Biking, River Rafting*, Rock Climbing*, Snow Skiing/XC*. Outlet mall and several casinos within 30 miles. *State license required for all patrons ages 15 and up. One-day licenses can be purchased at the Jim Creek Recreation Office. Additionally, all patrons ages 6 and up are required to have a Jim Creek fishing permit. **Nearby.

Credit Cards: American Express, Discover, MasterCard and Visa.

Restrictions: Pets allowed on leash and in cabins. No firearms or fireworks. No open fires or smoking, except in designated areas. No unlicensed off-road vehicles, no private boats, and no swimming allowed. Cameras allowed in unrestricted areas only. Level of radio frequency is considered a potential hazard to people employing electronic life aid/support systems.

RV Driving Directions/Location: Off Base. From I-5 north or south, at Arlington: Take exit 208 east onto WA-530 through Arlington toward Darrington for 7.5 miles. Continue a half mile past mile marker 25, then turn right on Jim Creek Road (266th Street NE). Follow Jim Creek Road for 7 miles to the end.

Area Description: Jim Creek borders the Mt. Baker-Snoqualmie National Forest and the Boulder River Wilderness Area. Located in the foothills of the North Cascades about one hour north of Seattle, Jim Creek has over 5,000 acres.

RV Campground Physical Address: 21027 Jim Creek Rd, Arlington, WA 98223.

McChord Air Force Base (JB Lewis-McChord)

Address: McChord Air Force Base, 530 Barnes Boulevard, McChord Field, WA 98438.

Information Line: C-253-982-1110, DSN-312-382-1110.

Main Base Police: C-253-982-2567. Emergencies dial 911.

Main Installation Website: http://www.lewis-mcchord.army.mil/

Other Info Website: http://www.mcchord.af.mil/

Main Base Location: Located in the beautiful Pacific Northwest on the Puget Sound, in Western Washington, JBLM is near the city of Lakewood.

Directions to Main Gate: Driving from the airport: Access I-5 going South toward Tacoma. Stay on I-5 until reaching exit 125 for McChord Field/Bridgeport Way. Turn left at the end of the on-ramp onto Bridgeport Way SW and proceed approximately .25 miles to the Main Gate.

NMC: Tacoma, 7 miles north.

NMI: Bremerton Naval Base Kitsap, 45 miles northwest.

Base Social Media/Facebook: https://www.facebook.com/JBLewisMcChord/

Base Social Media/Twitter: https://twitter.com/jblm_pao

Chapels: C-253-982-5556.

Dental Clinic: C-253-982-5505.

Medical: Primary Care, C-253-982-5766/5687; Flight Med/Airman's Clinic, C-253-982-8765.

Veterinary Services: C-253-982-3954.

Beauty/Barber Shop: C-253-588-2345.

Commissary: C-253-982-2103/2472/2320/3285.

Exchange Gas: C-253-589-4734.

Exchange: C-253-582-3110.

Financial Institutions: Armed Forces Bank C-253-581-9272, Harborstone Credit Union C-253-584-2260, C-1-800-523-3641.

Clubs: McChord Club, C-253-982-5581.

Places to Eat: Habanero Mexican Grill, C-253-982-4035; Strike Zone Snack Bar, C-253-982-5372; McChord Club, C-253-982-5581 and Battle Bean Cafe, C-253-982-6081 are within walking distance. Exchange Food Court, C-253-581-5145 offers Anthony's Pizza, Sushi Teriyaki, Taco John's, Charley's Grilled Subs, Starbuck's, Manchu Wok, Arby's and Popeye's. Burger King, C-253-582-1188; Subway, C-253-582-1151; and Papa John's, C-253-582-1122 are on base. Denny's, C-253-584-1416 is within a short driving distance.

Bowling: Sounders Lanes, C-253-982-5954.

Fitness Center: McChord Fitness Annex, C-253-982-6700. McChord Main Fitness Center, C-253-982-6707.

Golf: Whispering Firs Golf Course, C-253-982-2124. Pro Shop, C-253-982-4927.

ITT/ITR: New location in Sounders Lanes.

Library: C-253-982-3454.

Military Museum: McChord Air Museum, C-253-982-2485.

Military Museum Website: http://www.mcchordairmuseum.org/

MWR: C-253-967-5200.

MWR Website: http://www.jblmmwr.com

MWR Facebook:
https://www.facebook.com/JBLMFamil yMWR
MWR Twitter:
https://twitter.com/JBLMMWR
Outdoor Recreation: Adventures Unlimited, C-253-982-2206/2303. NW Adventure Center, C-253-967-8282/7744. Adventures Unlimited offers camping, boating, fishing, aquatic, sports and party equipment rentals, and winter ski and gear rental. Northwest Adventure Center at JB Lewis offers trips, outdoor gear, scuba diving, off-road vehicle park, marina and shooting ranges.
Swimming: Outdoor pool is available, C-253-982-2807.
Things To Do: Enjoy many outdoor activities including hiking, biking, canoeing, kayaking, fishing, hunting, mountain climbing and skiing. Visit Seattle attractions such as the Seattle Waterfront & Aquarium, Seattle Center, Pikes Place Market, Woodland Park Zoo, Ballard Locks & Fish Ladder and other national treasures such as Mt. Rainier National Park, Mount St. Helens and Snoqualmie Falls.
Walking Trails: Walking trails are available at nearby parks.

RV CAMPING & GETAWAYS
Holiday Park & FamCamp

Reservation/Contact Number Info: C-235-982-5488, DSN-312-382-5488.
Recreation Security: C-253-982-5624.
RV Website:
https://jblm.armymwr.com/programs/travel-camp-and-cabins
GPS Coordinates:
47°7'13"N/122°28'9"W
Reservations: Reservations accepted one year in advance. Office hours 0830-1700 Tue-Fri, 1230-1530 Sat. Check-in at FamCamp or at 24 hour bulletin board. Check-out 1100 hours. Maximum stay 14 days May-Sep.
Season of Operation: Year-round.
Eligibility: AD, NG, Res, Ret, DoD-Civ, Dep and NAF.
Camper/Trailer Spaces: Asphalt (37): E(110/20/30/50A)/S/W hookups. Some

handicap accessible spaces. Maximum length 40' for most sites. Rates: $25-$28 daily.
Tent Spaces: Primitive (12): no hookups. Rates: $15 daily. Dry Camp: $12 daily. Maximum two tents per site. No sleeping in personal vehicles allowed, truck/canopy/conversion van must be used or dry site.
Yurt, A Frame, Cabin, Apt, Spaces: Yurt (2): Double bed, dining table and chairs, small desk, 16' width. Note: A yurt is a cabin/tent structure with wooden floor, deck and door, two windows, electricity, and stretched-canvas covering with skylight. Rates: $35 daily. Linens not provided.
Support Facilities: Auto Craft Shop, Bath House, Boat Rental/Storage, Book Exchange, Bowling, Chapel, Clubhouse, Coin Laundry, Commissary, Convenience Store, Equipment Rental, Exchange, Fitness Center, Gas, Gazebo, Golf, Grills, Mess Hall, Pavilion, Pay Phones, Picnic Areas, Playground, Pool (Summer), Rec Center, Restrooms*, RV Storage, Sewage Dump, Shoppette, Showers, Snack Bar, Sports Fields, Tennis Courts, Trails, Vending Machine. * Handicap accessible.
RV Storage: Northwest Adventure Center, C-253-967-8282/7744. McChord's Adventures Unlimited, C-253-982-2206/2303.
Activities: Bicycling, Boating, Canoeing, Fishing*, Golfing, Hiking, Horseshoes, Kayaking, Paintball, Sightseeing, Softball, Swimming (Summer), Volleyball. *License is required.
Credit Cards: Cash, MasterCard and Visa.
Restrictions: Two-pet limit. Pets allowed on leash, must have certificate and tag for current rabies vaccination. Owner must clean up after pet. Firearms must be cleared at Security Gate. No open fires. Lit candles must be approved by McChord Fire Department. Quiet hours 2300-0700.
RV Driving Directions/Location: On Base. From the Main Gate (Bridgeport Rd, right off McChord exit, I-5 freeway): Stay in right lane and take first right after entering base onto Fairway Rd.

Stay on this road until reaching the stop sign. Turn left onto Lincoln Blvd, continue to the next stop sign. Turn right onto Outer Drive. Stay on this road until Holiday Park sign visible on the right. Enter and follow one-way road.

Area Description: Located in beautiful western Washington at the base of the Puget Sound, the area is prime for sightseeing and recreational opportunities are numerous on waterways and lakes in the Puget Sound area and nearby national parks: Mount Rainier, Olympic and North Cascades. Camp area is a quiet, wooded area surrounded by giant firs and pines, populated by wildlife. Full range of support facilities on base.

RV Campground Physical Address: Bldg 260, McChord AFB, WA 98438-5000.

Pacific Beach Resort & Conference Center

Address: Pacific Beach Resort, 108 First St N, Pacific Beach, WA 98571.
Information Line: C-425-304-3000, DSN-94-727-3000.
Main Base Police: C-425-304-3260. Emergencies dial 911.
Main Installation Website:
http://www.cnic.navy.mil/regions/cnrnw/installations/ns_everett.html
Main Base Location: Pacific Beach is approximately 150 miles southwest of Seattle, on Washington's scenic Pacific Coast.
NMC: Tacoma, 100 miles east.
NMI: Fort Lewis/JB Lewis-McChord, 95 miles east.
Places to Eat: Full service restaurant and bar, Windjammer Restaurant (0730-2200 hours Mon-Fri and 0730-0100 hours Sat-Sun). And Ocean Crest Resort Restaurant, C-1-800-684-8439 is within driving distance.
Fitness Center: Exercise room at facility.
Golf: Ocean Shores Golf Course. Ask front desk assistant for more information.
Swimming: Pacific ocean swimming is available.
Things To Do: "May be the Navy's best kept vacation secret!" Social room with activities weekends off-season, and

daily in spring, summer and fall. Bowling, exercise room, spa, restaurant and lounge, ball field, horseshoe pits, picnicking and whale watching platform, for what else? Watching whales! Visit Olympic National Forest.

Walking Trails: Hiking and walking trails available at Olympic National Forest.

RV CAMPING & GETAWAYS

Pacific Beach Resort

Reservation/Contact Number Info: C-1-877-NAVY-BED, C-360-276-4414.
Recreation Security: Emergencies dial 911.
RV Website:
http://get.dodlodging.net/propertys/Pacific-Beach--Recreation-Center
Other Info Website:
http://www.navylifepnw.com/programs/c73f010c-1449-4c38-844f-57bb73ccfe3e
RV Email Address:
pacbeach@navylifepnw.com
GPS Coordinates:
47°6'49"N/124°10'34"W
Reservations: Reservations accepted 14 months in advance for AD; 12 months for all others. Reservations require advance deposit equal to the first night's stay. Payment due upon arrival for entire stay. Cottages require a 2-night minimum stay. Holiday reservations may require 4-night minimum. No refund for early departure. Summer Season Office hours 0730-2000 Sat-Thur, 0730-2200 Fri. Winter hours 0730-1800 Sun-Thur, 0730-2200 Fri, 0730-2000 Sat. Cottage and Guest Suites: Check-in 1500 hours, check-out 1100 hours. RV Park and Campsites: Please call for late arrivals; Check-in 1300 hours, check-out 1100 hours.
Season of Operation: Year-round.
Eligibility: AD, Res, Ret, DoD-Civ (AD/Ret), 100% DAV and Federal Emp.
Camper/Trailer Spaces: Hardstand (43), E(220V/30A)/W, CATV hookups, picnic table. Rates: $18-$25 daily depending on season.
Tent Spaces: Tent Sites (19): Gravel, fire ring, showers, restrooms. Rates: $11-

$15 daily depending on season. Group Camp (20): fire ring, showers, restrooms. Rates: $56-$75 depending on season.

Yurt, A Frame, Cabin, Apt, Spaces: Cottages: Five-bedroom, sleeps 8-10. Rates: $142-$220 daily. Four-bedroom (6), sleeps 6-8. Rates: $127-$250 depending on season and location. Three-bedroom (24), sleeps 4-6. Rates: $153-$230 daily depending on season. All units feature kitchen basic cooking and eating utensils, TV/DVD/VCR. Linens provided. Many have ocean views. Hotel Rooms: Standard rooms with one queen bed. Rates: $52-$70 daily. Double rooms with one queen bed, one twin. Rates: $56-$75 daily. Family Units: (4), two queen beds. Rates: $67-$90 daily. All guest rooms feature TV/DVD/VCR, small microwave, refrigerator, coffee maker and hair dryer. Daily housekeeping. King Suites: (6), private wing, gas fireplace, seating area. Pets allowed. Rates: $93-$125 daily. Junior Suites: (4), sleeps 2-4, third floor, king bed, sofa sleeper. Rates: $93-$125 daily. All guest suites feature TV/DVD/VCR, small microwave, refrigerator, coffee maker and hair dryer. Daily housekeeping. Mallard RV Trailers: One queen bed, flat screen TV & DVD player, one set of double bunk beds, 30-amp service, a full bathroom with a shower, and a full kitchen. Rates: $90 daily.

Support Facilities: Bathhouse, Bowling, CATV, Chapel, Convenience Store, Conference Facility, Fitness Center, Game room, Hot Tub/Sauna, Ice, Laundry, Lounge, Meeting Rooms, Pay Phones, Picnic Grounds, Restaurant, Restrooms, Sewage Dump, Showers, Trails. Most restrooms and buildings are handicap accessible.

Activities: Basketball, Beachcombing, Bike Rentals, Clamming, Crabbing, Dancing, Fishing, Golf, Group Activities, Hiking, Hunting, Tennis, Weekly Events. All available at Resort.

Credit Cards: Diners Club, Discover, MasterCard and Visa.

Restrictions: No pets allowed in hotel except for King Suites. Maximum two pets per cottage. Pet fees may apply. Owner must follow leash laws and clean up after pet. No open fires except in pit area, grills and camp stove; must not be left unattended at any time. Quiet hours 2200-0700 hours. No fireworks or other firearms are allowed.

RV Driving Directions/Location: Off Base. From I-5 at Olympia: Take exit 104/Aberdeen/Port Angeles to west on Hwy 101. Hwy 101 becomes WA-8, and then US-12. Take US-12 through Aberdeen to Hoquiam. Follow US-101 north approximately four miles to sign indicating Ocean Beaches, turn left and continue on Ocean Beach Road through Copalis Crossing, Carlisle and Aloha to Pacific Beach. Follow Main Street to entrance to Pacific Beach Resort and Conference Center. Watch for signs to office.

Area Description: Situated on Olympic Peninsula, overlooking Pacific Ocean. A great starting point for exploring the Peninsula with its spectacular rain forest, Quinault Indian Reservation, Olympic National Park and Ocean Shores area. It also offers steel-head and salmon fishing. Full range of support facilities available at Fort Lewis.

RV Campground Physical Address: 108 First St N, Pacific Beach, WA 98571.

Westport Lighthouse Campground & RV Park

Address: Grays Harbor Coast Guard, Ocean Avenue, Westport, WA 98595.

Information Line: C-206-217-6357/6359.

Main Base Police: C-206-217-6408.

Main Installation Website: https://www.pacificarea.uscg.mil/Our-Organization/District-13/

Other Info Website: https://www.dcms.uscg.mil/Our-Organization/Director-of-Operational-Logistics-DOL/Bases/Base-Seattle/

Main Base Location: Located adjacent to the Grays Harbor CG Station in the southeastern section of the Westport Light State Park in Westport, WA.

NMC: Aberdeen, 20 miles north.

NMI: Grays Harbor Coast Guard Station, one mile north.
MWR: C-206-217-6357/6359.
Things To Do: Just minutes away from swimming, fishing, hiking, charter boat fishing, boating, shopping, and bicycle touring.

RV CAMPING & GETAWAYS
Westport Lighthouse Campground & RV Park

Reservation/Contact Number Info: C-206-217-6357/6359. Fax C-206-217-6356.
Recreation Security: Emergencies dial 911.
RV Website:
https://www.dcms.uscg.mil/Our-Organization/Assistant-Commandant-for-Human-Resources-CG-1/Community-Services-Command-CSC/MWR/Coast-Guard-Lodging/
RV Email Address: james.a.graddy@uscg.mil or victor.m.martinez@uscg.mil
GPS Coordinates: 46°53'13"N/124°7'23"W
Reservations: Reservations required. Must be Military ID holder. Reservations accepted starting 5 January for upcoming season. May be made by phone, e-mail or in person. Full payment made at time of reservation by mail-in check, or by payment in office upon check-in. No credit cards. Office hours 0800-1530 hours Mon-Fri. Authorized patrons must check in with the Officer of the Day (OOD) at USCG Station Grays Harbor, 1600 North Nyhus Street, Westport, WA 98595. Must read and sign Patron Rental Agreement to obtain two keys to access the campground, restrooms. Upon departure, the two keys must be returned to the OOD. Check-in 1100 hours, check-out 1100 hours. Maximum stay 14 days.
Season of Operation: 1 May-31 Oct.
Eligibility: AD, NG. Res, Ret, DoD-Civ (AD/Ret), Dep, 100% DAV, Dept of Homeland Security, Military Cadets and their families, Commissioned Corps of Public Health, Commissioned Corps of NOAA on AD, Medal of Honor recipients and un-remarried surviving spouses.
Camper/Trailer Spaces: Grass/Dirt (5), Back-in, Maximum 36' in length, E(110V/30A)/W, firepit, picnic table, grills. Comfort Stations at Park. Rates: $21 daily.
Tent Spaces: Grass/Dirt (7), no hookups, firepits, picnic table, grills, water faucets. Rates: $18 daily.
Support Facilities: Beach, Boat Launch, Boat Rental/Storage, Bowling, Cafeteria, Coin Laundry*, Convenience Store, Fire Rings, Fishing Pier, Gas*, Grills, Ice, Marina, Picnic Area, Propane*, Restrooms, Sewage Dump, Shoppette, Showers, Snack Bar, Trails. *Nearby.
Activities: Bicycle Touring, Boating, Charter Boat Fishing, Fishing, Hiking, Shopping, Swimming.
Credit Cards: None.
Restrictions: There are no sanitary hookups. Open fires are permitted only in the fire and barbecue pits provided. Pets allowed on leash; owner must clean up after pet. No horses. Limit one car per camper, or one vehicle with trailer per camp site. Other vehicles are to be parked at the designated area.
RV Driving Directions/Location: Off Base. From Seattle: Take I-5 southbound towards Portland. Take the US-101 north/exit 104 towards Aberdeen/Port Angeles. Merge onto US-101 north. Take WA-8 west towards Montesano/Aberdeen. WA-8 west becomes US-12 west. US-12 west becomes US 101 north. From Aberdeen, follow the directional signs to Westport and WA-105. From Westport, take a right on South Montesano St and a left at the stoplight on West Ocean Ave. Continue on West Ocean Ave until seeing the sign for "Lighthouse Observation Platform." The entrance to the campground is just before the platform. Check-in at Coast Guard Base Station Greys Harbor, also located in Westport, WA approximately three minutes by car from the campground. Keys to the campground are picked up at this location. Directions to the Coast Guard base: Once in Westport, take a right on Montesano St as above. Follow

until reaching Nyhus St and make a right. CG Station Greys Harbor is located on the right.

Area Description: Located at Grays Harbor Lighthouse, a well-maintained campground boasting a beach atmosphere. Site has RV hookups and is near to many community attractions. A lighthouse on the campground property is available for tours.

RV Campground Physical Address: 1020 W Ocean Ave, Westport, WA 98595. Mailing Address: Commanding Officer, PSSU Seattle MWR, Attn: Campground, 1519 Alaskan Way South, Seattle, WA 98134-1192.

Whidbey Island Naval Air Station

Address: 2853 Langley Boulevard, Oak Harbor, WA 98278.
Information Line: C-360-257-1080.
Main Base Police: C-360-257-3122.
Main Installation Website: http://www.cnic.navy.mil/regions/cnrn w/installations/nas_whidbey_island.ht ml
Main Base Location: Located in Oak Harbor, WA, on beautiful Whidbey Island, part of Island County, which is in the northwest corner of Washington State, 90 miles north of Seattle. Within close proximity to the San Juan Islands and the Cascade and Olympic mountains, Whidbey Island is a haven for outdoor enthusiasts.
Directions to Main Gate: From I-5: Take exit 230. Go southwest on WA-20 to Whidbey Island. The installation is 3 miles west of WA-20 on Ault Field Road.
NMC: Seattle, 80 miles southeast.
NMI: Everett Naval Station, 60 miles southeast.
Chapels: C-360-257-2414.
Dental Clinic: C-360-257-2301.
Medical: C-360-257-9500.
Veterinary Services: C-360-257-2001.
Beauty/Barber Shop: Ault Field, C-360-257-0511. Seaplane, C-360-257-0530. C-360-257-1765.
Commissary: C-360-257-3318.
Exchange Gas: C-360-257-0629. Seaplane, C-360-257-0537.

Exchange: Ault Field, C-360-257-0507. Seaplane Base, C-360-257-0600.
Financial Institutions: Navy Federal Credit Union C-1-888-842-6328, C-1-800-842-NFCU.
Clubs: Officers' Club, C-360-257-2521. Chiefs' Club C-360-257-2505.
Places to Eat: Admiral Nimitz Hall Galley, C-360-257-2469; Bakerview Restaurant, C-360-257-2505; Kegler's Bar & Grill, C-360-257-1567 are on base. Exchange Food Court offers Anchor Grille, C-360-257-0528. Ault Field Exchange offers Subway and Wendy's. Many restaurants are within a short drive.
Bowling: Convergence Zone, C-360-257-2432.
Fitness Center: C-360-257-2420.
Golf: Gallery Golf Course, C-360-257-2178.
ITT/ITR: C-360-257-2432.
Marina: Crescent Harbor Marina, C-360-257-2432.
MWR: C-360-257-6129.
MWR Website: http://www.navylifepnw.com/
MWR Facebook: https://www.facebook.com/WhidbeyFFR
Outdoor Recreation: Convergence Zone, C-360-257-2432. Offers kayak rentals & lessons, sailboat rentals, powerboat rentals, outdoor gear rentals, paintball, and skate park.
Swimming: MWR partners with two local pools in the area, C-360-257-2420 for information and details.
Things To Do: Be sure to visit Deception Pass State Park, Fort Casey State Park, Fort Ebey State Park, City Beach Park, San Juan Islands, Gallery Golf Course, Island County Historical Museum, Whidbey Island Dive Center, Paint Your World, Whale Watching Tours, South Whidbey Island State Park and Whidbey Playhouse while here.
Walking Trails: Many walking trails in the area.

RV CAMPING & GETAWAYS
Cliffside RV Park

Reservation/Contact Number Info: Reservations, C-1-877-NAVY-BED.

Park Office, C-360-257-2649, DSN-312-820-2649. Park Fax, C-360-257-6029, DSN-312-820-6029.
Recreation Security: C-360-257-3893.
RV Website:
http://get.dodlodging.net/propertys/Cliffside-RV-Park
Other Info Website:
http://cliffside.navylifepnw.com/programs/607cfed4-a4c8-4b2e-ae08-c746327cb01a
GPS Coordinates:
48°20'230"N/122°41'227"W
Reservations: Reservations accepted by telephone or online 12 months in advance for AD; 6 months all others. Customer Service Cabin hours 1000-1800 daily. Reservations must be cancelled 14 days prior to arrival date to avoid one-day charge. Two vehicles with maximum 6 people. Maximum stay 30 days. Patrons must vacate for 14 days prior to returning. Check-in 1400 hours, check-out 1200 hours.
Season of Operation: Year-round.
Eligibility: AD, NG, Res, Ret and DoD-Civ.
Camper/Trailer Spaces: RV Spaces (54): Back-in, max length 40', E(110V/30A/50A)/W/S, picnic table, BBQ grill. Rates: $40-$50 depending on location. Mallard RV Trailers: Fully furnished with linens. Rates: $95 daily.
Tent Spaces: Sites (10): Picnic table, fire pit w/grated cook surface, limited BBQ grills available. Rates: $20 daily. Group campsites $70 daily.
Yurt, A Frame, Cabin, Apt, Spaces: Yurts (6): Furnished 16' diameter, wooden floor, beds, futon, tables, chairs, small electrical heater. No linens. Rates: $40 daily.
Support Facilities: BBQ Grills, Laundry (coin operated), Outdoor Gear Rental, Pavilions, Restrooms, Showers. Free Wi-Fi.
RV Storage: Available through RV Park Office.
Activities: Whidbey Fitness Center (nearby), paintball events, snow busses to nearby ski sites (Jan-Mar), Toddler Time activities, bowling (nearby), running and various other outdoor opportunities too numerous to mention.
Credit Cards: American Express, Cash, Discover, MasterCard and Visa.
Restrictions: Eligible personnel may sponsor up to two (2) guest spaces for RV's, campsites and/or yurts on a space available basis. Reservations must be cancelled 14 days prior to arrival date to avoid one-day charge. Two vehicles/6 people/2 pets allowed per site. Maximum stay length is 30 days, at which point you must vacate for 14 days before returning for another 30 day stay. Pets allowed in yurts and trailers (additional charge applies), service animals only allowed in other facilities. No cooking in yurts. Firearms not authorized.
RV Driving Directions/Location: On Base. From the Charles Porter Gate: Turn left onto Midway Street and continue to second stop sign. Turn right onto Saratoga Street. Turn left onto Intruder Street, which is a paved road leading into Cliffside Park. All RVs must enter through the Charles Porter Gate (right at first stoplight on Ault Field road after leaving Hwy 20).
Area Description: Nestled along the shoreline of Whidbey Island, Cliffside overlooks the Strait of Juan de Fuca, Vancouver Island, the San Juan Islands and the Olympic Peninsula. With its awe-inspiring location, Cliffside offers the ambiance of shoreline living, an open window on an ever-changing marine environment and unparalleled sunsets.
RV Campground Physical Address: Cliffside RV Park, 3675 W Lexington, Bldg 2556, Oak Harbor, WA 98278 *Ault Field Location.

WEST VIRGINIA

Camp Dawson Army Training Site

Address: 1001 Army Road, Kingwood, WV 26537.

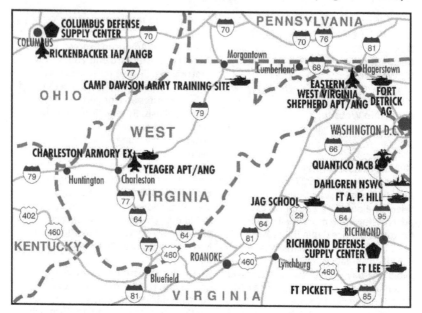

Information Line: C-304-791-4301.
Main Base Police: C-304-791-4140.
Main Installation Website:
http://www.wv.ng.mil/AITEC/
Main Base Location: Nestled in the hills of North Central West Virginia.
Directions to Main Gate: From I-68: Continue on I-68 to exit 23/Bruceton Mills. Follow Route 26 South to the Community of Albright. Signs to Camp Dawson will be visible. Make a left onto St. Joe's Road and go approximately three miles and make a right onto Country Club Road. This leads to the front gate of Camp Dawson.
NMC: Morgantown, 24 miles northwest.
NMI: Sugar Grove NIOC, 100 miles southeast.
Medical: C-304-791-4314.
Beauty/Barber Shop: C-304-791-7341.
Exchange: C-304-791-7009.
Clubs: Liberty Lounge, C-304-791-4383.
Places to Eat: Snack Bar/Joe's Canteen, C-304-791-7008, RTI Cafeteria, C-304-791-7343, Dairy Queen, C-304-329-0177, Hardee's C-304-329-1420, Heldreth Motel Restaurant & Lounge, C-304-329-1145, Mary's Restaurant, C-304-329-1160, Pizza Hut, C-304-329-0455, Preston Country Club, C-304-329-3520, Preston Country Inn, C-304-329-

2220 and McDonald's are within driving distance.
Fitness Center: MPB, C-304-791-4388.
MWR: C-304-791-7002.
MWR Website:
http://www.wv.ngb.army.mil/campdawson/
Outdoor Recreation: MWR, C-304-791-7002. Offers fishing, canoes, paddle boats and more.
Swimming: Heated indoor pool, C-304-791-7001.
Things To Do: Enjoy West Virginia's natural beauty through rafting, hunting and skiing. Camp Dawson lies within driving distance of many of West Virginia's historic sites, numerous resort areas, as well as the Tri State area's many metropolitan centers such as Pittsburgh and Washington D.C.

RV CAMPING & GETAWAYS
Camp Dawson RV Sites

Reservation/Contact Number Info: C-304-791-7001.
Recreation Security: C-304-791-4140.
RV Website:
https://campdawsoneventcenter.org/lodging-options/

Reservations: Contact facility to make reservations or submit request online.
Season of Operation: Year-round.
Eligibility: AD, NG, Res, Ret and DAV.
Camper/Trailer Spaces: RV Sites (6): Electric hookup only, gravel. Rates: $18 daily.
Support Facilities: Dining, Exchange, Pool and Restaurant.
Activities: Enjoy many amenities on base as well as many activities in the surrounding area. Scenic mountain views, hiking and resorts nearby.
Credit Cards: AMEX, Discover, MasterCard and Visa.
Restrictions: Pets allowed.
RV Driving Directions/Location: Ask for directions at the main gate.
Area Description: Located on base and within driving distance of many historical sites and outdoor adventure activities.
RV Campground Physical Address: Camp Dawson, 1001 Army Road, Terra Alta, WV.

WISCONSIN

Fort McCoy

Address: Fort McCoy, 100 East Headquarters Rd, Fort McCoy, WI 54656-5263.
Information Line: C-608-388-2222.
Main Base Police: C-608-388-2000. Emergencies dial 911.
Main Installation Website:
http://www.mccoy.army.mil/
Main Base Location: Located on approximately 60,000 acres between Tomah and Sparta, Wisconsin.
Directions to Main Gate: From LaCrosse/Sparta: Take Interstate 90 East of Sparta and take the first Sparta Exit/Hwy 27 exit 25. Take a left at the stop sign off the exit. Continue on Hwy 27 to the third set of stop lights. Turn on Montgomery Street then turn left on Hwy 21 East and continue for approximately eight miles to Fort McCoy.
NMC: Madison, 100 miles southeast.

NMI: Volk Field ANGB, 25 miles southeast.
Base Social Media/Facebook:
https://www.facebook.com/FtMcCoy/
Base Social Media/Twitter:
https://twitter.com/FortMcCoyWI
Chapels: Chaplain, C-608-388-3528.
Medical: C-608-388-3025.
Beauty/Barber Shop: C-608-269-1710.
Commissary: C-608-388-3542/3543.
Exchange Gas: C-608-269-5604.
Exchange: C-608-269-5604.
Financial Institutions: C-608-372-9277.
Places to Eat: McCoy's Sports Bar, C-608-388-2065; Primo's Express, C-608-388-7673; Dining Facility, C-608-388-4739. Exchange Food Court offers Anthony's Pizza and Robin Hood Sandwiches, C-608-269-5615.
Bowling: C-608-388-7060.
Fitness Center: Rumpel Fitness Center, C-608-388-2290.
ITT/ITR: C-608-388-3011.
Library: C-608-388-3213/3505.
MWR: C-608-388-7400, C-877-864-4969.
MWR Website:
http://mccoy.armymwr.com/us/mccoy/
MWR Facebook:
https://www.facebook.com/mccoymwr
MWR Twitter:
https://twitter.com/FortMcCoyMWR
Outdoor Recreation: Recreation Equipment Checkout, C-608-388-3517, C-1-800-531-4703. Offers camping equipment, boat rentals, canopies, sports equipment and more. Paintball and laser tag courses available.
Swimming: C-608-388-2290. offers swim lessons, lap swim and open swim.
Things To Do: Enjoy a variety of indoor and outdoor activities right on base including paintball, laser tag, fitness activities, skiing, snow tubing, fishing and more. Shopping centers, movie theaters, golfing, bike trails, and snowmobile trails are available within 20 miles of Fort McCoy. There are two casinos and canoeing within 50 miles of Fort McCoy.
Walking Trails: Fit Trail available.

RV CAMPING & GETAWAYS
Pine View Campground

Reservation/Contact Number Info: C-608-388-3517, C-1-800-531-4703, DSN-312-280-3517.

Recreation Security: C-608-388-2222, DSN-312-280-2222.

RV Website:
https://mccoy.armymwr.com/programs/pine-view-campground

GPS Coordinates:
44°1'42"N/90°42'16"W

Reservations: Recommended and accepted up to one year in advance. Online reservations accepted and require payment in full with Credit Card at time of reservation. Cancellations require a 7-day notice. Rainchecks may be issued, but no refunds. Campground Office Hours: Memorial Day-Labor Day: 0800–1800 Sun-Thu, 0800-2100 Fri-Sat; Labor Day - Memorial Day: 0900- 1700 Daily. Please call for Off Season rates. Discounts to holders of Golden Age Passports.

Season of Operation: Year-round.

Eligibility: AD, NG, Res, Ret, DoD Civilians and General Public.

Camper/Trailer Spaces: Hardstand (100), E (110/220V/30/50A)/S/W, CATV. Rates: $20-$50 daily. Hardstand (17), E (110V/15/30A). Rates: $15-$28 daily depending on season.

Tent Spaces: Grass (36), No hook-ups. Rates: $15-$27 daily depending on season.

Yurt, A Frame, Cabin, Apt, Spaces: Duplex: One-bedroom (2), sleeps four, private bath, kitchenette, refrigerator, microwave, coffee maker, toaster, A/C, heat, clock radio, CATV. Linens provided. Rates: $85-$125 daily. Cabins: One-bedroom (2): sleeps six to eight, stove with oven, private bath, living room, loft, kitchen, refrigerator, microwave, coffee maker, toaster, A/C, heat, clock radio, CATV, VCR. Rates: $85-$125 daily. Two-bedroom (6): sleeps six, private bath, living room, kitchen, microwave, refrigerator, clock radio, coffee maker, toaster, CATV, VCR. Linens provided. Rates: $95-$135 daily.

One-room Log Cabin (1): sleeps four, sleeper sofa, private bath, loft, A/C, heat, loft, coffee maker, refrigerator, microwave. Linens provided. Rates: $65-$100 daily. Campers: Aliners, 16', 19' and 29' campers. Sleeps four to nine, A/C, heat, refrigerator, stove. Rates: $85-$115 daily. Yurts: (2), One room, sleeps six, fireplace, refrigerator, microwave, coffee maker, TV, bunk bed/futon (2). Rates: $65-$100 daily.

Support Facilities: Bicycle Rental, Boat Rental, Camp Store, Camper Rental, Grills, Laundry (Nearby), Miniature Golf, Pavilion (For a Fee), Picnic Area, Playground, Propane, Restrooms, RV Storage, Showers, Trails.

RV Storage: C-608-388-7400.

Activities: Bicycling, Disc Golf Course, Fishing*, Hiking, Horseshoes, Hunting*, Laser Tag, Miniature Golf, Paintball, Pedal Boating, Shuffleboard, Skiing**, Swimming, Volleyball, Winter Sports. *License is required. **Whitetail Ridge Recreation Area: Catering to all levels of skiers, Dec-Mar, depending on the weather. Facilities include four lighted and groomed ski slopes with snowmaking capability, downhill and five-mile cross-country skiing, 185' vertical and 1300' long runs, one ski lift, two tubing slopes with handle tow, equipment rental, chalet and snack bar. Groomed snowmobile trail network also passes through the Whitetail Ridge area. For information, call C-608-388-4498, DSN-312-280-4498.

Credit Cards: MasterCard and Visa.

Restrictions: Pets not allowed in rental units. Pets must always be kept on leash. No smoking in rental units.

RV Driving Directions/Location: On Base. From the Main Gate: Follow signs into the recreation area. From I-90/94 west: Drive towards Tomah. At exit 45, I-90 and I-94 will split. Follow I-94 west towards Eau Claire. Take exit 143 to go onto WI-21. Turn left at WI-21 and proceed west for approximately 9 miles to Fort McCoy Gate 19. Follow signs from gate to the recreation area.

Area Description: Beautiful wooded area bounded by Squaw Lake and LaCrosse River. Eleven ponds and small

lakes on post are ideal for fishing activities. Squaw Lake is well stocked with rainbow trout. Wide range of support facilities available on post.

RV Campground Physical Address: Physical Address: West J St, Fort McCoy, WI 54656. Mailing Address: 1668 South J St, Fort McCoy, WI 54656

Rawley Point Cottage

Address: Coast Guard Station, 13 East Street, Two Rivers, WI 54241.
Information Line: C-414-747-7100.
Main Base Police: Emergencies dial 911.
Main Installation Website:
http://www.uscg.mil/d9/sectLakeMichigan/
Main Base Location: Point Beach State Park, WI is Located about 4 miles northeast of Two Rivers, WI.
NMC: Manitowoc, 12 miles south.

NMI: General Mitchell, Air Reserve Station, 6 miles south.

RV CAMPING & GETAWAYS

Rawley Point Cottage

Reservation/Contact Number Info: C-414-747-7185/7100.
Recreation Security: Emergencies call 911.
RV Website:
http://rentals.vacationrentaldesk.com/USCGLighthouses/homepage.html
GPS Coordinates:
44°8'47"N/87°33'50"W (Check-in)
Reservations: Required. Online only. Reservations can be made up to 120 calendar days in advance for AD; 60 calendar days in advance for CG Reservists, Retirees with military pay; 30 calendar days in advance for all

other Reservists; 15 calendar days in advance for CG Auxiliary. Full payment required seven working days prior to check in. Cancellations must be made seven working days prior to check in to avoid having to pay full amount. Office hours 0730-1100 and 1245-1500 Mon-Fri. Check-in between 1300 and 2100 hours, at Coast Guard Station, 13 East Street, Two Rivers, WI to get keys; Check-in 1300-2100 hours, check-out 1200 hours on last day.

Season of Operation: Year-round.

Eligibility: AD, NG, Res, Ret and CG Auxiliary.

Yurt, A Frame, Cabin, Apt, Spaces: Townhouse Units (3), Flat-like units with common door. One large four bedroom unit, two two-bedroom units, furnished, one private bath, one half-bath, kitchen, stove, microwave, pots/pans, dishes, TV/VCR, DVD, W/D. Bed linens are not provided. Rates: $70 daily; 4BR unit $80 daily. Note: Both units may not be rented simultaneously by the same person. Maximum of eight people per unit; strictly enforced.

Support Facilities: Beach, Grills, Picnic Area, Telephones. Nearby park and commercial facilities offer: Camping, Chapel, Golf, Grocery, Laundry, Marina, Rec Center, Tours, Trails.

RV Storage: None.

Activities: Nearby: Cross Country/Snow Skiing, Fishing, Golfing, Hiking, Hunting, Swimming.

Restrictions: Pets allowed on leash; owner responsible for any damages, must clean up after pet daily. Use and possession of firearms must be in accordance with Federal, State, and Local laws. No smoking in house. Two-night to one-week limit. Military member/spouse must be present during the entire reservation. Reservations not transferable, must be cancelled if unable to use. Cabin must be fully cleaned prior to departure.

RV Driving Directions/Location: Off Base. Heading North on I-43: Take exit 42/10 north. Proceed 7 miles and turn right on 17th Street. Cross over draw bridge and turn right on East Street for 4 blocks to CG Station Two Rivers to pick-up keys. From CG Station proceed on East Street to 22nd Street, turn right onto Hwy 42 for 4 blocks. Go straight onto County Road "O." Proceed 4 miles to Point Beach State Park entrance. If a Park Ranger is there, indicate that destination is the CG lighthouse parking lot.

Area Description: Historical 115-year-old lighthouse overlooking Lake Michigan. Cottage is situated within 2800-acre Point Beach State Park. Twin cities of Two Rivers/Manitowoc are rich in festivals, fishing derbies and maritime events. Charter boats provide offshore fishing for lake trout and salmon. Limited support facilities at Two Rivers CG Station.

RV Campground Physical Address: Rawley Point Cottage, CG Sector Lake Michigan Morale Fund, 2420 South Lincoln Memorial Drive, Milwaukee, WI 53207-1997.

Sherwood Point Cottage

Address: Coast Guard Station, 2501 Canal Road, Sturgeon Bay, WI 54235.

Information Line: C-414-747-7100.

Main Base Police: Emergencies dial 911.

Main Installation Website: http://www.uscg.mil/d9/sectLakeMichigan/

Main Base Location: Sherwood Point, WI. Located about 45 miles northeast of Green Bay, WI and 15 miles northwest of Sturgeon Bay, WI.

NMC: Green Bay, 45 miles southwest.

NMI: Fort McCoy, 190 miles southwest.

RV CAMPING & GETAWAYS

Sherwood Point Cottage

Reservation/Contact Number Info: C-414-747-7185/7100.

Recreation Security: Emergencies dial 911.

RV Website: http://rentals.vacationrentaldesk.com/USCGLighthouses/homepage.html

GPS Coordinates: 44°53′29″N/87°25′57″W

Reservations: Required. Online only. Reservations can be made up to 120 calendar days in advance for AD; up to 60 calendar days in advance for CG Reservists and other AD and Retirees receiving retired pay, up to 40 calendar days in advance for other Reservists, and up to 30 calendar days in advance for CG Auxiliary. Full payment required seven working days prior to check in. Cancellations must be made seven working days prior to check in to avoid having to pay full amount. Office hours 0730-1100 and 1245-1500 Mon-Fri. Check-in at Coast Guard Station, 2501 Canal Road, Sturgeon Bay, WI between 1300 and 2100 hours to get keys, check-out by 1200 hours on last day.

Season of Operation: Year-round.

Eligibility: AD, NG, Res, Ret and CG Auxiliary.

Yurt, A Frame, Cabin, Apt, Spaces: Cottage (1): Two-bedroom, sleeps eight, sleeper sofa, stove, refrigerator, microwave, TV/VCR, DVD, washer/dryer, pots/pans, dishes. Linens are not provided. Rates: $80 daily.

Support Facilities: Grill, Picnic Area.

RV Storage: None.

Activities: Fishing, Hiking, Biking and Picnicking, Snow Skiing (Nearby).

Restrictions: Pets allowed on leash; owners responsible for any damages and must clean up after pets daily. Use and possession of firearms must be in accordance with Federal, State, and Local laws. No smoking in house. Two-night to one-week limit. Military member/spouse must be present during the entire reservation. Reservations are not transferrable, must be cancelled if unable to use. Cottage must be fully cleaned prior to departure. Maximum limit of eight (8) persons on grounds at all times is strictly enforced.

RV Driving Directions/Location: Off Base. Check-in at Sturgeon Bay CG Station 2501 Canal Road: From US-41 at Green Bay, take WI-57 north for 44 miles north east to where road crosses the bay. After crossing Sturgeon Bay, proceed .5 miles to Utah St and turn right. Take another right (south) on Cove Rd. Turn left (east) on Canal Rd and follow it as it curves south. Continue south on it for 2.5 miles to Sturgeon Bay CG Station. Cottage directions: From Sturgeon Bay CG Station: Follow Canal Rd north and then west and turn right onto Cove Rd. From there, turn left onto Utah St and after .5 miles turn left onto WI-42/57 south. Follow WI-42 across Sturgeon Bay and then west for 2.5 miles to a right turn (north) onto County S/Duluth Ave. Turn left (west) onto County C. Follow County C for approximately 2 miles to County M. Turn right (north) onto County M. Continue on County M for 4.5 miles to Sherwood Point Road and turn left.

Area Description: Situated on the western shores of Lake Michigan, the cottage overlooks the bay and a wooded area. Cottage is located across the Sawyer Harbor from Potawatomi State Park in Door County. The area is described as a miniature New England and has several small towns within driving distance. These towns abound with shopping, antiques, arts, and maritime themes.

RV Campground Physical Address: Sherwood Point Cottage Commander, Coast Guard Sector Lake Michigan Morale Fund, 2420 South Lincoln Memorial Drive, Milwaukee, WI 53207-1997.

WYOMING

Frances E Warren Air Force Base

Address: 7601 Randall Avenue, Bldg. 207, F.E. Warren AFB, WY 82005-2502.

Information Line: C-307-773-1110, DSN-312-481-1110.

Main Base Police: C-307-773-3501, DSN-312-481-3501.

Main Installation Website: http://www.warren.af.mil/

Main Base Location: F. E. Warren AFB is located in Wyoming's capitol city,

Cheyenne, located within Laramie County.

Directions to Main Gate: The base is immediately adjacent to the West side of the City of Cheyenne and is directly across US Interstate 25 and three miles north of the I-80 and I-25 interchange. Cheyenne can be easily accessed by car, airline, shuttle from Denver International Airport, or bus. Cheyenne is located 100 miles north of Denver, Colorado and is the transportation crossroads in the Southeastern corner of Wyoming. It is eight miles north of the Colorado Border on I-25 and forty miles west of the Nebraska border off I-80. Francis E. Warren AFB Main Entrance and Visitor Center is located at I-25, Exit 11.

NMC: Cheyenne, 1 mile east.

NMI: Cheyenne AP/ANG, 3 miles southwest.

Base Social Media/Facebook:
https://www.facebook.com/warrenAFB

Base Social Media/Twitter:
https://twitter.com/FEWarrenAFB

Chapels: C-307-773-3434.

Dental Clinic: C-307-773-1846.

Medical: C-307-773-3461, DSN-312-481-3461.

Veterinary Services: C-307-773-3354.

Beauty/Barber Shop: C-307-638-3046, C-307-634-7149.

Commissary: C-307-773-3509.

Exchange Gas: C-307-634-7298.

Exchange: C-307-634-1593.

Financial Institutions: Warren Federal Credit Union, C-307-432-5446. Armed Forces Bank, C-307-274-9401.

Clubs: Wrangler Lounge, C-307-773-3048.

Places to Eat: Chadwell's Dining Facility, C-307-773-3838; Birdie's Clubhouse, C-307-773-3556; Game Time Sports Grill, C-307- 773-2210; Awake Coffee Shop, C-307-773-3510. Food Court offers Nipa Hut and Subway., Burger King, C-307-773-2399, and Anthony's Pizza, C-307-773-3402 are within walking distance. San Dong, C-307-634-6613, Chili's, C-307-635-1224 and McDonald's, C-307-632-1222 are within driving distance.

Bowling: Warren Lanes Bowling Center, C-307-773-2210.

Fitness Center: Freedom Hall, C-307-773-6172. Independence Hall, C-307-773-3680.

Golf Name and Phone Numbers: Warren Golf Course, C-307-773-3556.

ITT/ITR: C-307-773-2988.

Military Museum: F.E. Warren AFB Intercontinental Ballistic Missile and Heritage Museum, C-307-773-2980.

Military Museum Website:
http://www.warrenmuseum.com/

MWR: C-307-773-2858.

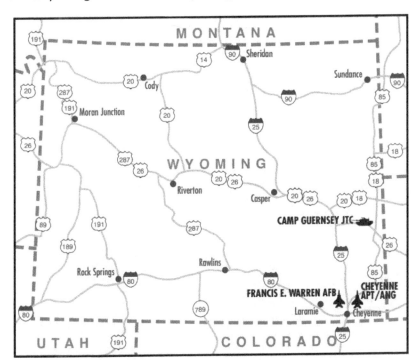

MWR Website:
http://www.funatwarren.com
MWR Facebook:
https://www.facebook.com/FunatWarrenAirForceBase
Ski Area: Outdoor Rec has daily discounted ski lift tickets to Keystone, A-Basin, Winter Park, Copper Mountain, Breckenridge, Vail, Beaver Creek, Loveland, Eldora, Steamboat and more! Season passes available for Copper-Winter Park-Steamboat; Keystone-A-Basin; Loveland. Restrictions apply.
Outdoor Recreation: Outdoor Recreation, C-307-773-2988. Offers equipment rental for parties, tents, tent heaters, sleeping bags, camp stoves, and lanterns. Also offers backcountry adventure equipment including ATVs, snowshoes, and mountain bike rentals.
Swimming: Aquatic Center, C-307-773-3195 offers lap swim, swim lesson, water aerobics and party reservations.
Things To Do: Once a frontier Army post, many of the buildings are on the National Historic Register. Cowboy and Indian lore abound, and nearby

Colorado skiing draws many visitors. Visit Fort Collins, Old Town, Cheyenne Big Boots, Cheyenne Street Railway Trolley, English High Tea and Big Boy Steam Engine.
Walking Trails: Maps of varying measured distances available at the Freedom Hall Fitness Center.

RV CAMPING & GETAWAYS
D.A, Russell FamCamp

Reservation/Contact Number Info: C-307-773-3874/2988, DSN-312-481-3874. Fax C-307-773-4075, DSN-312-481-4075.
Recreation Security: C-307-773-3501.
RV Website:
https://www.funatwarren.com/fam-camp/
RV Email Address:
peter.somontes@warren.af.mil
GPS Coordinates:
41°9'14"N/104°52'20"W.
Reservations: Reservations accepted 30 days in advance. Credit card required. Must check in with office before

selecting site. Reservations for cabin required. Cancellations require minimum 48-hour cancellation notice. Office hours 1000-17000 Mon-Fri, 0900-1300 Sat. Use drop box for overnight camping. Maximum 30-day stay limit when there is a wait list.

Season of Operation: Year-round. No W/S winter season. Showers open daily.

Eligibility: AD, NG, Res, Ret, DoD-Civ and U.S. Govt Civ Emp with access to the base.

Camper/Trailer Spaces: RV sites (40): E(30/50A)/W/S, access to host lounge with bathrooms, showers, lounge area, Wi-Fi. Rates: $25-$30 daily. Special mid-July rates apply. Overflow/Dry Camp (75): No hookups, access to host lounge with amenities. Rates: $10 daily.

Tent Spaces: Tent Sites (10): Primitive, no hookups. Rates: $10 daily.

Yurt, A Frame, Cabin, Apt, Spaces: Cabin (1): One room with double bed, one bunk bed, electricity but no plumbing; porch swing. Patrons must provide own linens. Rates: $25 daily.

Support Facilities: Bathhouse*, Boat Rental, Bowling, Chapel*, Coin Laundry, Commissary, Dining Facility, Exchange, Fitness Center, Golf, Grills, Hot Tub, Ice, Nature Walk Path, Pavilion*, Picnic Area*, Pool*, Rec Equipment, Restrooms*, Sewage Dump (In Summer Only), Shoppette, Shower*, Snack Bar*, Sports Fields*, Tennis Courts, Trails. Exchange and Commissary are on base, about one mile away. *Handicap accessible

RV Storage: C-307-773-2988.

Activities: Fishing*, Swimming, Trips through Outdoor Adventure Program. *State and base licenses are required.

Credit Cards: MasterCard and Visa.

Restrictions: Pets are allowed on leash but may not be left unattended.

RV Driving Directions/Location: On Base. Gate 2 is closed permanently. From Gate 1: Open 24-hours. Go to the second stoplight and turn left on Old Glory Rd. At the next stoplight, go right on Missile Dr. Continue approximately 1.2 miles, following the orange signs to FamCamp. Note: There is a small roundabout just inside Gate 1. If concerned about getting through it, ask the gate guards to hold traffic for a few seconds in order to use both lanes. No problem with accommodating 45' 5th wheels. From Gate 5: Open 0600-1800 Mon-Fri. Go straight at the first intersection and travel approximately 3.2 miles, following the orange signs to FamCamp.

Area Description: Located in open, rolling country in southeast corner of state. Laramie and Medicine Bow National Forest are short driving distance west. Full range of support facilities available on base. Fishing creek located adjacent to FamCamp (Wyoming and Base license required).

RV Campground Physical Address: 7103 Randall Avenue, F.E. Warren AFB, WY 82005.

OVERSEAS RV CAMPING & GETAWAYS

CANADA

14th Wing Greenwood

Address: Greenwood CFB, PO Box 5000, Stn Main, Greenwood, NS B0P 1N0 Canada.

Information Line: C-902-765-1494.

Main Installation Website: http://www.rcaf-arc.forces.gc.ca/en/14-wing/index.page

Main Base Location: Nestled in the heart of Nova Scotia's beautiful Annapolis Valley.

Directions to Main Gate: From NS 101-West: Take 17E for Bishop Mountain Road toward Kingston/Greenwood. Turn left onto Maple Street then right onto Evangeline Trail/Nova Scotia Trunk 1 West looking for sings for Greenwood/Tremont/Kingston/Wilmot/ nova Scotia Trunk W/NS-101W. Turn left on Bridge Street and making a slight left to stay on Bridge Street. Turn left onto Central Avenue seeing signs for CFB Greenwood/Central Avenue. Continue onto Ward Road then Pathfinder Drive to the base.

NMC: Halifax, 150 kilometers southeast.
NMI: 14 Wing Greenwood NS.
Chapels: C-902-765-1494 ext. 5883/5457.
Medical: C-902-765-6340.
Exchange Gas: Commercial gas station within 45 km.
Exchange: C-902-765-6994.
Clubs: Annapolis Mess, C-902-765-1494 ext. 5577.
Bowling: Bowling Centre, C-902-765-1494 ext. 5631.
Fitness Center: Fitness and Sports Centre, C-902-765-1494 ext. 5997.
Golf: Greenwood Golf Club, C-902-765-5800.
Library: C-902-765-1494 ext. 5430.
MWR: C-902-765-5611.
MWR Website:
http://www.cg.cfpsa.ca/cg-pc/greenwood/en/Pages/default.aspx
MWR Facebook:
https://www.facebook.com/GMFRC
Outdoor Recreation: Community Recreation Services, C-902-765-1494 ext. 5337. Coordinator, C-902-765-1494 ext. 5337. Rentals, C-902-765-1494 ext. 5341 for winter and summer equipment rentals including bicycles, canoes, kayaks, snowshoes and more.
Swimming: Aquatics Center, C-902-765-1494 ext. 5341 offers swim lessons, lap swim, mom and tots classes.
Things To Do: The area is host to many festivals and offers a variety of events to take in including the Apple Blossom Festival, the Windsor Pumpkin Festival and Regatta and many farm markets and retail country stores. Also nearby a drive-in theater, parks, winter skiing and summer beach activities.
Walking Trails: Contact Community Recreation Services.

RV CAMPING & GETAWAYS

Lake Pleasant Campers Club

Reservation/Contact Number Info: C-902-547-2882. Fax C-902-547-2822.
RV Website:
https://www.cafconnection.ca/Greenwood/Home.aspx
Other Info Website:
http://www.lakepleasant.ca
RV Email Address:
managerlpcc@ns.sympatico.ca
GPS Coordinates:
44°36'5"N/64°52'30"W
Reservations: Accepted. Confirmed upon receipt of payment. Booking starts in April. Check-in 1300 hours, check-out 1100 hours.
Season of Operation: 15 May-15 Oct.
Eligibility: AD, NG, Res, Ret, DoD-Civ, Dep and 100% DAV.
Camper/Trailer Spaces: Hardstand (4), E(220V/30A)/W hookups. Gravel (1), E(220V/30A)/W hookups. Grass/Dirt (1 Pull-thru), E(220V/30A)/W hookups. Rates: $25 daily.
Tent Spaces: Hardstand (5), E(220V/30A)/W hookups. Gravel (4), E/W, Grass/Dirt (4) E/W Rates: $10 daily.
Yurt, A Frame, Cabin, Apt, Spaces: Cabins: Beaver Retreat Cabins (7), sleep four, two-bedrooms, kitchen, sink, grill, microwave, refrigerator, cots/rollaways, alarm clock. Rates: $55 daily for 14 Wing Recreation Card Holders, $65 daily for all others. Toilets & showers are not available in the cabins but are within short walking distance. Comox Cabins (2), One-bedroom, handicap accessible, sleeps eight, kitchen, sink, grill, microwave, refrigerator, cots/rollaways, alarm clock. Rates: $55 daily for 14 Wing Recreation Card Holders, $65 daily for all others. Toilets & showers are not available in the cabins but are within short walking distance. Old Manager's (or LPCC) Cabin (1), One-bedroom, handicap accessible, sleeps four, kitchen complete with fridge and stove, hot and cold water, electric heat, living room, veranda, outside fire pit and a great view of the lake. The kitchen is set up

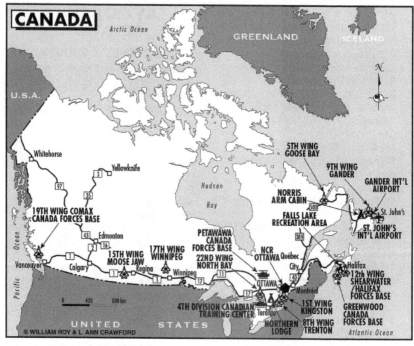

with an electric kettle, toaster, microwave, cutlery, dishes including mugs, glasses, bowls, pots and pans. The only items you must provide include bedding, food and other convenience items to make your stay a pleasant one. Rates: $55 daily for 14 Wing Recreation Card Holders, $65 daily for all others. Toilets & showers are not available in the cabins but are within short walking distance.

Support Facilities: Auto Craft Shop, Bathhouse, Beach, Boat Launch, Boat Rental/Storage, Club House, Coin Laundry, Convenience Store, Fishing Pier, Gas, Golfing*, Grills, Pay Phones, Picnic Area, Playground, Propane, Restrooms, Sewage Dump, Showers, Trails. *Greenwood Golf Course located On Base, approx 50 minute drive.

RV Storage: None.

Activities: Bicycling, Fishing*, Hiking, Swimming. *License is required.

Credit Cards: None.

Restrictions: Pets allowed on leash. Pets not allowed on the beach. No firearms. No smoking.

RV Driving Directions/Location: Off Base. From Halifax: Take Provincial Highway 103 southwest towards Bridgewater (100km). Turn right (northwest) at exit 12 onto Provincial Highway 10 and go approximately 40 kilometers to Springfield. Turn left on Air Force Camp Road, a dirt road, for approximately .6 kilometers to Main Gate. Campground sign is displayed at the end of the road. (A large communications tower is the landmark for the point where two lakes are visible.) From east or west on Provincial Highway 101 (along the west coast of Nova Scotia): Use exit 18 south onto Provincial Highway 10. Go south to Springfield and follow directions above.

Area Description: Located midway between Middleton and Bridgewater, the area is a series of lakes and woodlands.

RV Campground Physical Address: Mailing Address: Lake Pleasant Campers Club, PO Box 1434, Greenwood, NS, B0P 1N0 Canada. Campground Address: Lake Pleasant Campers Club, 240

Airforce Camp Road, Springfield, NS B0R 1H0 Canada.

15th Wing Moose Jaw

Address: 15 Wing Moose Jaw PO Box 5000, Moose Jaw, Saskatchewan S6H 7Z8.
Information Line: PAO, C-306-694-2823.
Main Installation Website:
http://www.rcaf-arc.forces.gc.ca/en/15-wing/index.page
Main Base Location: Located in Moose Jaw, Saskatchewan, west of Regina.
Directions to Main Gate: From Moose Jaw: Travel south on 9 Ave SW to facility entrance.
NMC: Regina, 50 miles east.
Chapels: C-306- 694-2296. Emergency Chaplain, C-306-631-1444.
Exchange: C-306-693-6668.
Clubs: Officers' Mess, Harvard Mess, C-306-694-2299/2298.
Places to Eat: CANEX offers Tim Horton's Express.
Fitness Center: C-306 694-2873.
MWR Website:
https://www.cafconnection.ca/Moose-Jaw/Home.aspx
Outdoor Recreation: PSP Outdoor Recreation, C-306-694-2873 offers a variety of rentals including mountain bikes, golf clubs, baseball equipment, hockey gear, snowshoes and camping gear.
Swimming: PSP Indoor Pool, C-306 694-2873. Kinsmen Sportsplex, C-306 694-4483.
Things To Do: Red Knight Arena and many sports facilities are available on base.
Walking Trails: Bushell Park Walking Trail on base.

RV CAMPING & GETAWAYS

Buffalo Pound Provincial Park

Reservation/Contact Number Info: C-306 694-2222 ext 5521.
Recreation Security: C-306-694-3329. Emergencies dial 911.
RV Website:
https://www.cafconnection.ca/Moose-Jaw/Facilities/Buffalo-Pound-Provincial-Park.aspx
RV Email Address:
scott.osmachenko@forces.gc.ca
Reservations: Reservations accepted via telephone or through the online reservation system. Credit card required to guarantee reservation. Payment due upon arrival. Cancellations must be received 24 hours prior to arrival to avoid fee. Maximum stay 7 days.
Season of Operation: Late May-Late September.
Eligibility: AD, NG, Res, Ret and Dep.
Camper/Trailer Spaces: On-Site RV (2): Sites 15 and 16, furnished campers with essentials. Patrons must bring bedding. Rates: JPSU/IPSC Clients $25 daily plus applicable fees; $45 daily all others.
Activities: Biking, Canoeing, Kayaking, Swimming.
Restrictions: Pets are permitted. Cleaning fee may apply.
RV Driving Directions/Location: Off Base.

19th Wing Comox

Address: 19 Wing Comox, PO Box 1000, Stn Main Lazo, BC Canada V0R 2K0.
Information Line: C-250-339-8211.
Main Installation Website:
http://www.rcaf-arc.forces.gc.ca/en/19-wing/index.page
Main Base Location: Located on Vancouver Island.
Directions to Main Gate: From Victoria on Vancouver Island: Take Trans-Canada Hwy 1 which becomes Provincial Hwy 19 north to Courtenay/Comox. on the east coast of Vancouver Island. Follow signs to 19th Wing Comox Base.
Chapels: C-250-338-8274, C-250-339-8012, C-250-339-8211 ext. 8389.
Medical: Main Desk, C-250-339-8211 ext. 8267.
Exchange: C-250-339-5342.
Clubs: Officer's Mess, C-250-339-8211 ext. 8323, WO and Sgt's Mess, C-250-339-8211 ext. 8326, Jr Ranks, C-250-339-8211 ext. 8452.
Fitness Center: C-250-339-8211 ext. 6690.
Golf: Glacier Greens, C-250-339-6515.

ITT/ITR: MFRC, C-250-339-8290.
Outdoor Recreation: Recreation Services.
MWR: C-250-339-8290, C-1-888-246-0222.
MWR Website:
http://www.familyforce.ca/sites/Comox/EN/Pages/default.aspx
MWR Facebook:
https://www.facebook.com/comoxmfrc
Outdoor Recreation: C-250-339-8211 ext 8781.
Swimming: Aquatics, C-250-339-8211 ext 6989.
Things To Do: The Comox Valley is known as the Recreation Capital of Canada; whose residents live active lifestyles surrounded by the most breathtaking scenery on Vancouver Island. The K'omoks people call this "the land of plenty", so be sure to take advantage its natural beauty. Visit Per Ardua ad Astra, Air Force Beach overlooking the Strait of Georgia, golfing and more.
Walking Trails: Enjoy beach strolling and scenic views of the area's natural beauty.

RV CAMPING & GETAWAYS
TeePee Park Cabins & Campgrounds

Reservation/Contact Number
Info: Regular Season, C-250-339-5271. Fax C-250-339-0638. Off Season, C-250-339-8211 ext. 7173. Fax C-339-250-8203.
Recreation Security: C-250-339-8211 ext 8218.
RV Website:
https://www.cafconnection.ca/Comox/Adults/Recreation.aspx
RV Email Address:
teepeepark@telus.net
GPS Coordinates:
49°43'36"N/124°53'39"W
Reservations: Reservations recommended and accepted 30 days in advance with one month booking at a time. Two first come, first serve sites available. Cancellations must be received at least 48 hours in advance of arrival. Office hours May-Oct: 1000-

2000 Mon-Sun. Check-in 1400 hours, check-out 1100 hours. Note: All rates refer to Canadian currency.
Season of Operation: Campground: April - mid-October. Cabins: Year-round.
Eligibility: AD, NG, Res, Ret, DoD-Civ, Dep, 100% DAV and US Gov't Civ Emp.
Camper/Trailer Spaces: Camper: Grass/Dirt (45,) Back-in, Maximum 60' in length, E(220/30A), picnic table, grill. Basic, water and E/W hookup sites. Rates from $21--$35 daily US military; Weekly: $121-$213; Monthly: $461-$816. Additional guest fees may apply. Call to confirm rates.
Tent Spaces: Tent Spaces: Grass/Dirt (42,) E(220/30A), picnic table, grill. Call for rates.
Yurt, A Frame, Cabin, Apt, Spaces: Cabins: Two-bedrooms (3), furnished with complete kitchen, alarm clock, coin washer/dryer, microwave, cookware/utensils, toiletries, TV/VCR, telephone, picnic grounds. Rates: $81 daily; $499 weekly. Check-in 1400 hours, check-out 1100 hours. Only available to US/Canadian military and retired military. Call to confirm current rates. Linens available for rent.
Support Facilities: Beach*, Coin Laundry, Convenience Store, Fire Rings, Fitness Center, Golf, Grills, Ice, Pavilion*, Picnic Area, Playground, Rec Center, Restrooms*, Sewage Dump, Showers*, Snack Bar, Telephones, Trails. * Handicap accessible.
RV Storage: None.
Activities: Bicycling, Boating, Fishing*, Golfing, Hiking, Scuba Diving, Swimming. *License is required.
Credit Cards: American Express, MasterCard and Visa.
Restrictions: Pets are allowed in the park provided they are on leash. Pet owners are responsible for cleaning up after their pets in all areas. No firearms. Quiet hours: 2300-0700.
RV Driving Directions/Location: On Base. Located just before main gate. Turn left onto Little River road. Take the next right and follow to end of road, bearing right at branch intersection. Turn right into the camp.

Area Description: Tee Pee Park is a modern facility equivalent to BC Provincial parks. Wooded and ocean-view sites overlooking the Straits of Georgia are available. Air Force Beach, adjacent to the campground, is regarded as one of the finest on Vancouver Island. Full support facilities available.

RV Campground Physical Address: Mailing Address: Canadian Forces Base Comox, Attn: FS&R Rec Coordinator, 19 Wing Comox, PO Box 1000, Station Forces, Lazo, BC Canada V0R 2K0.

22nd Wing North Bay

Address: 22 Wing North Bay, Hornell Heights, ON P0H 1P0.
Information Line: C-705-494-2011.
Main Installation Website:
http://www.rcaf-arc.forces.gc.ca/en/22-wing/index.page
Main Base Location: Situated between Lake Nipissing and Trout Lake approximately 3.5 hours from Toronto.
NMC: North Bay, within city limits.
Base Social Media/Facebook:
https://www.facebook.com/RCAF.ARC
Chapels: C-705-494-2011 x 2028.
Exchange: CANEX, C-705-494-2011.
Clubs: Officer, Senior and Junior ranks clubs on base.
Places to Eat: Many restaurants within a short drive.
Fitness Center Phone Numbers: Fitness center on base.
Military Museum: Canadian Forces Museum of Aerospace Defence on base.
MWR Website:
https://www.cafconnection.ca/North-Bay/In-My-Community/22-Wing-Facilities-Hours.aspx
Outdoor Recreation: Equipment Rental services on base.
Swimming: Indoor Swimming Pool, C-705-494-2011 x 2240 offers open swim, swim lessons and training.
Things To Do: North Bay area offers a variety of outdoor activities to include boating, hiking, biking, winter sports activities and ample scenery.

RV CAMPING & GETAWAYS
Cottage Club – North Bay

Reservation/Contact Number Info: C-705-494-2011 x 2613.
RV Website:
https://www.cafconnection.ca/North-Bay/In-My-Community/Recreation-Clubs/Cottage-Club.aspx
RV Email Address:
lindsay.seguin@forces.gc.ca
Reservations: Reservations required. Must be a member of the Cottage Club. Security deposit required at time of reservation.
Season of Operation: Year-round.
Eligibility: Contact facility for membership and eligibility.
Yurt, A Frame, Cabin, Apt, Spaces: Cottages (2): Three-bedroom fully furnished cottages with indoor fireplace. No televisions. Sleeps 8. Must provide own linens and towels. Rates: Varies by season and membership. Rates from $70 daily.
RV Driving Directions/Location: Off Base. From the Tim Horton's on Trout Lake Road travel 16 km to Songis Rd (Trout Lake road turns into Hwy 63). Turn right onto Songis Rd. Travel 6 km and cross a small bridge then another bridge in 8.5 km. For 13.6 km stay straight until passing turnoff for Whitehouse Rd. In 15.7 km there will be a "T" junction with Camp Conewang on the right. Turn left and follow the signs to "22 Wing Cottages".
Area Description: Located approximately 45 minutes east of North Bay along Talon Lake.

4th Division Canadian Training Center – Meaford

Address: 139152 Grey Road 112 RR1 Meaford, Ontario N4L 0A1.
Information Line: C-519-538-1371.
Main Installation Website:
http://www.army-armee.forces.gc.ca/en/4-canadian-division-training-centre/meaford.page

Main Base Location: Located on Nottawasaga Bay, a sub-basin of Georgian Bay and Owen Sound Bay, in southern Ontario.
Directions to Main Gate: From Meaford: Travel on Hwy 26 to Hwy 112 and travel north to facility.
NMC: Meaford, 13 miles southeast.
Base Social Media/Facebook: https://www.facebook.com/4thCanadianDivisionTrainingCentre/
Clubs: Centurion Mess, Sherman Club Jr Rank's Club, C-519-538-1371 ext 6779.
Fitness Center: C-519-538-1371 ext 6769.
MWR: C-519-538-1371 ext 6509.
MWR Website: https://www.cafconnection.ca/Meaford/Home.aspx
Outdoor Recreation: C-519-538-1371 ext 6769 for information on rentals, trails and outdoor activities.
Walking Trails: 5km and 2.5 km trails, cross-country trails and ski trails are available.

RV CAMPING & GETAWAYS
Vail's Point Campground

Reservation/Contact Number Info: C-519-387-7366, C-519-934-0688.
RV Website: http://www.meafordrodandgun.com/index.php/camping/campground-rules
Other Info Website: https://www.cafconnection.ca/Meaford/Facilities/Campground.aspx
Reservations: Reservations can be made in advance or Open Sites are first-come first-served on Fridays. All fees must be paid in advance or upon arrival. Special guest membership fees available. See camp hosts at sites 18 or 32. All arrivals must be before 2200 hours. Check-in between 1200 and 2200 hours, check-out 1200 hours.
Eligibility: Must be active member of either Regular or Reserve components of the CF, a member in good standing of the LFCA TC Rod & Gun Club, or an Authorized employee of CBO and its sub-contractors.
Tent Spaces: Primitive sites. Rates: $5 nightly for members, $10 all others.

Season Rates: $200 for members, $500 for all others.
Support Facilities: Toilets only, no potable water or electricity. Free firewood.
Activities: Beach, boat launch, plenty of open sites and a Children's play area.
RV Driving Directions/Location: Ask for directions at time of reservation.

5th Wing Goose Bay

Address: 5 Wing Goose Bay PO Box 7002, Station A Happy Valley-Goose Bay, Labrador A0P 1S0.
Information Line: Customer Service 24-Hour Line, C-709-896-6900 local 6946.
Main Installation Website: http://www.rcaf-arc.forces.gc.ca/en/5-wing/index.page
Main Base Location: Located in Labrador, on the northeast coast of Canada.
Chapels: Available on base.
Dental Clinic: C-709-896-6900 ext 7222.
Medical: C-709-896-6900 ext 7222.
Exchange: C-709-896-8243.
Clubs: All Rank's Mess - Canuck Club, C-709-896-6900 ext 7831.
Places to Eat: CANEX offers a variety of food as well as a self-service Tim Horton's. A variety of eateries are nearby.
Fitness Center: C-09 896 6900 ext 7708.
Golf: Amaruk Golf Course, C-709-896-2112.
Military Museum: Labrador Military Museum, C-709-896-6900 ext 2177.
MWR: C-709-896-6900.
MWR Website: https://www.cafconnection.ca/Goose-Bay/Home.aspx
Outdoor Recreation: The Base Gym offers a variety of sports equipment to rent including canoes, kayaks, snowshoe gear, bikes, hockey equipment and more.
Swimming: Labrador Training Center located off base.
Things To Do: Whale Watching, Iceberg Viewing, Berry Picking, Hiking, and exploring the great outdoors are just a few of the fun things to do here. In the winter, enjoy snowmobiling, cross-

country and downhill skiing, ice fishing in this culturally rich wonderland.

RV CAMPING & GETAWAYS

Camp Alexander

Reservation/Contact Number Info: C-709-896-6900; local 6610.
RV Website:
https://www.cafconnection.ca/Goose-Bay/Facilities/Camp-Alexander.aspx
RV Email Address:
KIEL.LALONE@forces.gc.ca
GPS Coordinates:
53°18'11.3"N/60°32'06.5"W
Reservations: Contact 5th wing council representative at local 6610.
Season of Operation: Year-round.
Yurt, A Frame, Cabin, Apt, Spaces: Off grid cabin has solar, and generator power, propane stove, BBQ, as well as a wood stove for heat. There are canoes, paddle boats, and a dock for summer water activities. Patrons must bring own water and fuel for generator. Rates: Free.
Support Facilities: Remote cabin.
RV Driving Directions/Location: Ask for directions at time of reservation.
Area Description: Located on Alexander Lake.

Falls Lake Recreation Area

Address: RR #3 Box 6, Falls Lake West, Windsor, NS B0N 2T0 Canada.
Information Line: C-902-721-8325.
Main Base Police: Emergencies dial 911.
Main Installation Website:
https://www.cafconnection.ca/Halifax/Home.aspx
Main Base Location: Located outside Windsor on Falls Lake.
NMC: NMC: Halifax, 100 kilometers southeast
NMI: NMI: CFB Halifax, 70 kilometers northwest.

RV CAMPING & GETAWAYS

Falls Lake Recreation Area

Reservation/Contact Number Info: C-1-877-325-5253.

Recreation Security: Emergencies dial 911.
RV Website:
https://www.cafconnection.ca/Halifax/Facilities/Falls-Lake-Cottages-and-Campground.aspx
RV Email Address:
bookings@fallslake.ca
GPS Coordinates:
44°51'47"N/64°14'59"W
Reservations: Summer reservations accepted up to six months in advance for AD, Ret, Res, NATO, Veterans, DND-Civ, and CFPSA; all other eligible categories three months in advance by phone, email or online. Reservations require credit card at time of reservation. Weekends require Fri-Sat reservations. Chateau and Cabin Cancellation Policy: Cancellations and changes to reservations must be made 14 days prior to the arrival date. Cancellations and changes to reservations within the 14-day cancellation policy will result in full charges. Campground Cancellation Policy: Cancellations and changes to reservations must be made two days prior to the arrival date. Cancellation or changes within two days will result in full charges. Cabins Check-in 1400 hours, check-out 1100 hours. Chateau/Bunkhouse Check-in 1500 hours, check-out 1200 hours. Campground Check-in 1200 hours, check-out 1100 hours. Late check-out fees apply.
Season of Operation: Year-round with seasonal camping May-October.
Eligibility: AD, Res, Ret and Dep.
Camper/Trailer Spaces: RV Spaces (30): Padded gravel, sites (15), E(30A)/W/S, picnic table, fire ring. Rates: From $35 daily; $210 weekly. Grass, primitive sites (15), picnic table, fire ring. Rates: From $22 daily; $130 weekly. Please provide size of trailer at time of reservation.
Yurt, A Frame, Cabin, Apt, Spaces: Cabins (25): Bungalow with two bedrooms with a double bed in each room; full kitchen with fridge, stove, microwave oven, coffee percolator, kettle, toaster, basic pots and pans, dishes and utensils to serve six people.

Additional conveniences include TV (no TV stations are available), DVD player, CD player, AM/FM radio, alarm clock, BBQ and propane tank, outdoor fire pit and picnic table. Cleaning supplies are provided including garbage/recyclable bags, toilet paper, paper towel, dish soap, dish cloth and dish towel. Rates: Prime Season from $125 daily; Off Season from $76 daily. Ranch with 2 floors, one bedroom with two double beds; full kitchen with fridge, stove, microwave oven, coffee percolator, kettle, toaster, basic pots and pans, dishes and utensils to serve six people. Additional conveniences include TV (no TV stations are available), DVD player, CD player, AM/FM radio, alarm clock, BBQ and propane tank, outdoor fire pit and picnic table. Cleaning supplies are provided including garbage/recyclable bags, toilet paper, paper towel, dish soap, dish cloth and dish towel Rates: Prime Season from $110 daily; Off Season from $58 daily. Chateau with three bedrooms, with 2 sets of single bunk beds in each room and a loft upstairs with 8 additional single beds; two full bathrooms. The kitchen has seating for 12 people, but has dishes to serve 20 people, along with the basic pots and pans; microwave oven, coffee maker, toaster, 42" Flat Screen TV, satellite television, and a DVD/CD/AM/FM stereo system. The chateau also has a commercial size BBQ and propane tank. Rates: Prime Season from $270 daily; Off Season from $165 daily. Lines not provided but available for rent for all cabins.
Support Facilities: Bathhouse, Canteen.
RV Storage: C-902-720-3461.
Activities: Badminton, Basketball, Beach, Boat Rentals, Covered Picnic Area, Horseshoes, Laundry, Rental and Sale Items, Showers, Sports Equipment. Volleyball, Washer Toss, Wi-Fi.
Credit Cards: American Express, MasterCard and Visa.
Restrictions: Pets allowed on leash.
RV Driving Directions/Location: Off Base. From Hwy 101: Take exit 5 off Hwy101. From Halifax: Turn left off of the ramp; From the Valley: Turn right

off of the ramp. Travel approximately 1.1 km then turn right by Irving Station. Travel approximately 1.8 km then turn left by Atlantic Radiator onto Hwy 14/Chester Road. Drive approximately 14 km then turn right onto New Ross Road across from the Irving-Lakeside Variety. Drive approximately 3.2 km, ignoring the sign that says Falls Lake Road but rather turn right onto the Falls Lake West/Pioneer Drive which is a dirt road. Travel approximately 4 km then turn right into facility. From Hwy 103: Take exit 8 off Hwy 103. From Halifax: Turn right off of the ramp; From Yarmouth direction: Turn left off of the ramp. Follow Hwy 14 toward Windsor North. Follow directions from Ross road above.
Area Description: Situated on the scenic Falls Lake in Windsor, Nova Scotia. Skiing at Ski Martock is only 14 kilometers from this facility.
RV Campground Physical Address: Mailing Address: Falls Lake Recreational Facility, RR #3 Box 6, Falls Lake West, Windsor, NS B0N 2T0 Canada.

Norris Arm Cabin

Address: Norris Arm Cabin
Information Line: C-709-256-1703.
Main Base Police: Emergencies dial 911.
Main Installation Website: http://www.rcaf-arc.forces.gc.ca/en/9-wing/index.page?
Main Base Location: Located in northeastern locale on the island of Newfoundland.
NMC: Gander Bay, 40 kilometers. south
Base Social Media/Facebook: https://www.facebook.com/rcaf1924
Base Social Media/Twitter: https://twitter.com/RCAF_ARC

RV CAMPING & GETAWAYS
Norris Arm Cabin

Reservation/Contact Number Info: C-709-256-1702 ext 1466.
RV Website: https://www.cafconnection.ca/Gander/Facilities/Norris-Arm-Cabin.aspx

Reservations: Must contact Wing Rec Center to make reservation.

Yurt, A Frame, Cabin, Apt, Spaces: Cabin (1): Primitive 30x30 with two double bunk beds, propane fridge, propane cooker, BBQ and wood stove. There is no running water and the only bathroom facility is an outhouse. Rates: $15 CAN daily.

Support Facilities: No support facilities.

Activities: Remote area.

Restrictions: No running water.

RV Driving Directions/Location: Off Base. Ask for directions at time of reservation.

Area Description: Located next to a large pond and is accessed by a 4km rough road. Very primitive. Near the community of Norris Arms, Canada.

RV Campground Physical Address: Mailing Address: PO Box 6000, Stn Forces Gander NL, A1V 1X1 Canada

Northern Lodge

Address: Lake Shabomeka, Clone, Ontario, CN

Information Line: C-613-392-2811.

Main Base Police: Emergencies dial 911.

Main Installation Website: http://www.rcaf-arc.forces.gc.ca/en/8-wing/index.page

NMC: Kingston, 193 kilometers east; Toronto, 169 kilometers west

NMI: 8th Wing Trenton Canada Forces Base, 115 kilometers south

Exchange Gas: Commercial gas station within 30 km.

RV CAMPING & GETAWAYS

Northern Lodge

Reservation/Contact Number Info: C-613-392-2811 ext 2275.

Recreation Security: C-613-392-2811. Police for lodge: 911.

RV Website: https://www.cafconnection.ca/Trenton/Facilities/Wing-Accommodations/Northern-Lodge.aspx

RV Email Address: reservationsdesk@forces.gc.ca

GPS Coordinates: 44°53'3"N/77°08'43"W

Reservations: Reservations are accepted by phone and e-mail 0830-1630 hours Mon-Fri. Credit card required. Note: Facility users must become members of the Outdoors Pursuit Club to rent cabins if not an active member of CFB Trenton. Membership costs $5 yearly, C-613-392-2811 ext 2627. Peak season and Oct/Nov hunting season all a maximum 7 days. This same restriction will also apply during the deer hunting season in October/November. Check-in 1200 hours at 8th Wing Trenton, check-out 1200 hours.

Season of Operation: Year-round.

Eligibility: AD, NG, Res and Ret.

Camper/Trailer Spaces: Gravel: (2), Back-in, Maximum 25' in length, E(110V/15A)/W. Picnic tables and grills. Rates: $10 daily.

Yurt, A Frame, Cabin, Apt, Spaces: Rustic Cabins: (6). Sleeps 4-8. No potable water on site. Each cabin is equipped with a fridge & stove but no indoor washroom facility. BBQs are provided with each cabin, but members must bring their own tank. There are 2 outdoor privies on site. The Main Lodge is communal in nature and equipped with two full bathrooms, fridge, stove, tables & chairs and a great deck. A limited number of canoes and rowboats are available to use. A playground area is available for the little ones.

Support Facilities: Auto Craft Shop, Auto Repair*, Bath House, Beach, Boat Launch, Boat Rental/Storage, Convenience Store, Gas*, Golf, Grills, Laundry*, Marina, Picnic Area, Playground, Restrooms, Sewage Dump Station*, Showers, Tennis Courts, Trails, Wharf. *These facilities are available off base.

RV Storage: None.

Activities: Boating, Fishing*, Hiking, Swimming. *Nonresident Ontario Province fishing license is required.

Credit Cards: None.

Restrictions: Pets allowed in cabins. Please check with Provincial and Federal websites for regulation in regard to fishing, hunting and firearms.

RV Driving Directions/Location: Off Base. From 8th Wing Trenton: Go east on Provincial Highway 401 to Napanee, then left (north) approximately 45 kilometers on Provincial Highway 41 across Trans-Canada/Provincial Highway 7 just outside the town of Cloyne. (East of Madoc and Tweed on Hwy 7, then North on Hwy 41 at Kaladar). Specific directions given when reservation is made. Check in at 8th Wing Trenton. From Toronto: Take Provincial Highway 401 east approximately 160 kilometers. Take exit 525 south (right) onto Provincial Highway 33, then 2 kilometers to a left (east) on Provincial Highway 2; drive 1 kilometer to Trenton. May also be reached by crossing Canada/USA border on I-81 north to Provincial Highway 401 then west to Provincial Highway 33 and directions as above.

Area Description: Numerous lakes are accessible by walking trails or ATV. A wide variety of fish in the area. Located on Lake Shabomeka, approximately 100 kilometers north of Trenton

Petawawa Canada Forces Base

Address: Petawawa CFB, Menin Rd, Petawawa, ON Canada K8H 2X3.
Information Line: C-613-687-5511.
Main Base Police: C-613-687-4444.
Main Installation Website:
http://www.army-armee.forces.gc.ca/en/cfb-petawawa/index.page
Main Base Location: CFB Petawawa is located 195 kilometers east of Ottawa in the Canadian Province of Ontario.
Directions to Main Gate: From Ottawa: Travel west approximately 195 kilometers on Provincial Hwy 417. Continue past Pembroke. Watch for signs for Canada Forces Base Petawawa. Turn right onto Paquette Road and follow road to the base.
NMC: Ottawa, 195 kilometers east.
Base Social Media/Facebook:
https://www.facebook.com/pages/PSP-Petawawa/128987553852435
Base Social Media/Twitter:
https://twitter.com/psppetawawa

Chapels: C-613-687-5511 ext. 5434.
Dental Clinic: C-613-687-5111 ext. 5619.
Medical: C-613-687-5111 ext. 6457.
Beauty/Barber Shop: C-613-687-5413.
Commissary: Canex Grocery Petawawa, C-613-687-6336.
Exchange: Retail, C-613-687-5595, Grocery, C-613-687-6336.
Clubs: Officer's Mess, C-613-687-5511 ext. 6623, WO and Sgt's Mess, C-613-687-5511 ext. 5781, Jr Ranks' Mess, Coriano, C-613-687-5511 ext. 5756, Kyrenia, C-613-687-5161/5511 ext. 5769.
ITT/ITR: PFMRC, C-613-687-7587 ext. 3222.
Marina: Jubilee Lodge and Marina, C-613-687-5511 ext. 5180.
MWR: C-613-687-7587 ext. 3222.
MWR Website:
https://www.cafconnection.ca/Petawawa/Home.aspx
MWR Facebook:
https://www.facebook.com/pmfrc
MWR Twitter:
https://twitter.com/psppetawawa
Outdoor Recreation: Community Recreation Services, C-613-687-2932. Offers equipment rental, Silver Dart Arena skate park, sports fields, camping, bounce houses and more.
Swimming: Dundonald Hall, C-613-687-5511 ext. 7946 offers 25 meter competitive pool with diving blocks, wading leisure pool with gradual ramp, double-loop waterslide and land sprinkler attached to the wading pool and a 6 person hot tub and sauna.
Things To Do: The area is full of many outdoor adventure sport activities, natural beauty, hiking and biking trails, community events, camping and more.
Walking Trails: Hiking and biking paths plentiful in the area.

RV CAMPING & GETAWAYS

Black Bear Campgrounds

Reservation/Contact Number Info: C-613-687-7268. Fax C-613-588-7909.
Recreation Security: C-613-687-5511 ext 5444.

RV Website:
https://www.cafconnection.ca/Petawawa/Facilities/Black-Bear-Campground.aspx
RV Email Address: blackbear@nrtco.net
GPS Coordinates: 45°55'14"N/77°17'W
Reservations: Reservations accepted beginning 1 January for the following year. Credit card required. Cancellations require 48-hour notice to avoid fee. Camp offers 5 first come, first serve sites. Visit website for application. Check-in 1400 hours, check-out 1100 hours.
Season of Operation: May to Mid-Oct.
Eligibility: AD, NG, Res, Ret and General Public.
Camper/Trailer Spaces: Gravel/Grass (100), Offers serviced sited with basic, water and E(15A/30A)/W hookup sites. Rates from $30-$35 daily US military; Weekly: $180-$210; Summer Seasonal Sites: $1070-$1270. Additional guest fees may apply.
Tent Spaces: Gravel/Grass (20), Rates: $25-$30 daily; Weekly: $150-$180; Summer Seasonal Sites: $700-$845.
Support Facilities: ATM, Beach, Comfort Center with Showers, Firewood, Fishing Pier, Gift Shop, Golf, Laundry, Marina, Museum, Picnic Area, Playground, Rec Center, Rec Equipment, Restrooms, Sewage Dump, Showers, Snack Bar, Telephones, Trails.
RV Storage: C-613-687-7268.
Activities: Bicycling, Curling, Fishing*, Golfing, Hunting*, Shopping, Swimming. *License is required.
Credit Cards: American Express, Discover, MasterCard, Shell and Visa.
Restrictions: Pets allowed on leash. No firearms. Campfires prohibited except in designated areas. Visitors must report to office to get a visitor's pass.
RV Driving Directions/Location: On Base. From Ottawa: Travel west approximately 195 kilometers on Provincial Hwy 417. Continue past Pembroke. Watch for signs for Canada Forces Base Petawawa. Turn right onto Paquette Road and follow road to the base. Once on base, follow sign to the campground and check in at campground office. Both located on the extreme northeastern side of the base along the shore of the Ottawa River.
Area Description: Black Bear Campground is located on the beautiful Ottawa River adjacent to the community beach. Kiska Campground is also available, offering a more open concept style of camping with its own beach located on the Ottawa River as well. Both campgrounds offer great swimming and outstanding views of wildlife and vistas.
RV Campground Physical Address: Black Bear Campground, 154 Lieven Rd, Garrison Petawawa, ON Canada K8H 2X3.

GERMANY

Garmisch Community

Address: USAG Garmisch, Bldg 203, Artillery Kaserne, Unit 24515, APO AE 09053-4515.
Information Line: C-011-49-9662-83-110, C-09662-83-110, DSN 314-475-1110.
Main Base Police: C-08821-750-3801/3827, DSN 314-440-3801/3827. Emergencies dial DSN 114.
Main Installation Website:
https://home.army.mil/bavaria/
Main Base Location: The U.S. Army Garrison (USAG) Garmisch, is located in the German town of Garmisch-Partenkirchen, a beautiful resort area nestled in the Bavarian Alps on the German/Austrian border, southwest of the city of Munich. USAG Garmisch provides community support to the George C. Marshall European Center for Security Studies, the NATO School in nearby Oberammergau, and the Edelweiss Lodge and Resort (ELR), the Armed Forces Recreation Center (AFRC).
Directions to Main Gate: From the direction of Munich to the north: Travel south on the A95/E533 direction of Garmisch-Partenkirchen for approximately 70 KM (42 miles). You will lose the Autobahn (highway) near the town of Eschenlohe. Continue

straight along the B2/E533 from approximately 12 KM (7 miles). Just after the town of Oberau, pass through a tunnel. Take the first exit to the right after leaving the tunnel, B23, direction Garmisch/Grainau. Continue on the B23/Burgstrasse through Garmisch (Promenadenstrasse) and head southwest out of town on Zugspitzstrasse, approximately 5 KM (3 miles). Make a right at the last traffic light before leaving town onto Aussere Maximilianstrasse. Immediately cross the bridge the gate for Artillery Kaserne.

NMC: Munich, approximately 95 km northeast.

NMI: Stuttgart Community, 270 km northwest.

Base Social Media/Facebook:
https://www.facebook.com/USAGBavaria

Base Social Media/Twitter:
https://twitter.com/USAGBavaria

Beauty/Barber Shop: C-011-49-8821-966-7415.

Commissary: C-011-49-8821-90-8997.

Exchange Gas: C-011-49-8821-90-9838.

Exchange: C-011-49-8821-966-7414.

Financial Institutions: Community Bank, C-011-49-8821-750-3619, C-011-49-8821-93430. Service Credit Union, C-011-49-8821-750-3373, C-011-49-8821-7303600.

Places to Eat: Subway and a coffee shop are on base. Marshall Center DFAC is nearby. Many restaurants within a short drive.

Fitness Center: Mueller FC, C-011-49-8821-750-2747.

ITT/ITR: Leisure Travel, C-011-49-8821-750-3370/3005.

Library: Garmisch Library, C-011-49-8821-750-2467.

MWR: C-011-49-8821-750-3702/3005.

MWR Website:
https://garmisch.armymwr.com/

MWR Facebook:
https://www.facebook.com/GarmischFMWR/

Things To Do: Located at the foot of the Zugspitze, Germany's highest mountain. Visit the Partnach Gorge, sign up for the the King's House Hike, explore historic Partenkirchen, head for the hills and take a scenic gondola ride, enjoy the annual Richard Strauss Festival in June or visit the Werdenfels Regional Museum.

Walking Trails: Walking trails are available nearby.

RV CAMPING & GETAWAYS

Edelweiss Village Cabins & Campground

Reservation/Contact Number Info: C-011-49-8821-9440 from USA, C-49-8821-9440 from Europe, C-08821-9440 from Germany, DSN-314-440-2575. Fax C-011-49-8821-3942.

Recreation Security: C-011-49-8821-9440, DSN-314-440-2211. Security Police: 011-49-8821-9440.

RV Website:
https://www.edelweisslodgeandresort.com/accommodations/rooms-suites

RV Email Address:
vacation@edelweisslodgeandresort.com

GPS Coordinates:
47°28'55.8"N/11°03'40.9"E

Reservations: Reservations accepted one year in advance and recommended. All reservations are space-available. Credit card required for reservation. Cancellations require 14 day notice to avoid fee. The Vacation Planning Center office hours 0800-1800 hours Mon-Fri. Campgrounds require adapters and are available at the Edelweiss Lodge and Resort front desk on a first come, first serve basis. A $50 deposit is required to sign out an adapter but is refunded once the adapter is returned. The adapter is a 3-pronged plug that fits into the electrical box and the other connecting end is 220 compatible. The Vacation Planning Center office hours 0800-1800 hours Mon-Fri.

Season of Operation: Year-round.

Eligibility: AD, NG, Res, Ret, and their dependents, DoD-Civ, DoD-Civ Ret, and their dependents, NATO personnel with AE form 600-700 (USAREUR Privilege & Identification Card.

Camper/Trailer Spaces: RV and Tent Sites: Located at Artillery Kaserne. Large campsites with access to private showers, restrooms and laundry facilities. Easy access to Edelweiss Lodge

and Resort for resort-style amenities including the pool, The POiNT Wellness Center and restaurants. Rates: $35 daily; additional adults $5 per person.
Yurt, A Frame, Cabin, Apt, Spaces: Comfy Vacation Cabins: Provide modern conveniences; sleeps 6, private bath and heated shower. Fully equipped kitchenette with microwave and refrigerator; large dining area, Sat TV. Linens provided including towels. Rates: $179 daily with 2-night minimum. Vacation Cabins: Heated cabins, private bath and shower, microwave, refrigerator, Sat TV, BBQ area. Linens provided but do not include towels. Rates: $65 daily with 2-night minimum.
Support Facilities: AAFES Gas Station, Commissary, Community Bank, Convenience Store, Dishwashing, Europe Car Rental, Golf, Laundry, Outdoor Rec Office, Playground, PX, Rec Equipment, Restaurant, Restrooms, Service Credit Union, Sewage Dump, Ski Lodge, Showers. No RV Storage.
Activities: Bicycling, Canoeing, Climbing/Rappelling, Golfing, Ice Skating, Kayaking, Mountain Biking, Paragliding, Skiing, Snowboarding,

Tours, Whitewater Rafting. See website for much more.

Credit Cards: American Express, Discover, MasterCard, Star Card, and Visa.

Restrictions: Pet-friendly cabins available. Pets must be leashed.

RV Driving Directions/Location: On Base. From Munich: Take the Munich-Innsbruck Autobahn 95/E533 south in the direction of Garmisch-Partenkirchen. Continue driving south for approximately 84 km to the new Farchant tunnel. Follow signs for Garmisch-Partenkirchen through the Farchant tunnel and then take Highway 23 to the right, following signs for Garmisch and the Fernpass. Stay on Highway 23 (the "priority road") for just under 4 km and turn right onto Greisgartenstrasse. Drive for approximately .8 km to Loisach River and cross. Follow signs to "U.S. Facilities" and after ID check take a left. The campground is the first right.

Area Description: Located in the Loisach Valley at the foot of Zugspitze, Germany's highest mountain. Several ski areas and mountain recreation opportunities are available, as well as a wide variety of sports and tours and a full range of support facilities. Vacation Village is across the street from the resort, about a 20 minute walk.

RV Campground Physical Address: Edelweiss Vacation Planning Center, Unit 24501, APO AE 09053-5000.

Grafenwoehr Community

Address: Johnson Street, Gebaeude 244, Grafenwoehr, Germany 92655.

Information Line: C-011-49-9641-83-1110.

Main Base Police: C-011-49-9662-83-3398/3397. DSN-314-476-3397. Emergencies dial 114.

Main Installation Website: https://home.army.mil/bavaria/

Main Base Location: United States Army Garrison (USAG) Grafenwoehr consists of Rose Barracks at Vilseck and Main Post at Grafenwoehr, which are located in beautiful Bavaria, about 60 miles northeast of Nuremberg.

Directions to Main Gate: The Nuremberg Airport is located approximately one hour from Grafenwoehr. To get to Grafenwoehr from the airport: Head in the direction of Autobahn A9 toward Berlin. Take exit "Pegnitz/Grafenwoehr" and follow signs to Grafenwoehr (approximately 30-35 KM). Once in the town of Grafenwoehr, turn right at the main intersection and enter main gate 3 on the right. Note: There is not a main gate but rather a gate guard hut. There is no boundary between the town and the post.

NMC: Nuremberg, 91 km southwest.

NMI: Vilseck, 25 km southwest.

Base Social Media/Facebook: https://www.facebook.com/USAGBavaria

Base Social Media/Twitter: https://twitter.com/USAGBavaria

Chapels: Chaplain, C-011-49-9641-83-4129/4130.

Dental Clinic: Grafenwoehr, C-06371-9464-3100.

Medical: Appointment Line, C-06371-9464-3000.

Veterinary Services: C-011-49-9662-83-2370.

Beauty/Barber Shop: Barber, C-011-49-9641-93-1632. Stylique, C-9641-92-68799.

Commissary: C-011-49-9641-83-9402.

Exchange Gas: C-011-49-9641-93-63411.

Exchange: C-011-49-9641-93-6300, DSN 314-475-9705.

Financial Institutions: Community Bank, C-011-49-9641-92240. Service Federal Credit Union, C-011-49-9641-926790. Launderette, C-011-49-9641-1616.

Places to Eat: Java Cafe Bar and Grill and the Grafenwoehr DFAC are on base. Exchange Food Court offers Charley's, Pizza Hut, Popeye's Chicken, Starbucks, Subway and Taco Bell. Burger King and Asian Food & Sushi are also on base. Many restaurants within a short drive.

Bowling: Tower Barracks Bowling & Entertainment Center, C-011-49-9641-83-6177.

Fitness Center: C-011-49-9641-83-9007. Field House, C-011-49-9641-83-9554.

Library: Tower Barracks, C-011-49-9641-83-1740.
MWR: C-011-49-9641-70526-9030.
MWR Website:
https://grafenwoehr.armymwr.com
MWR Facebook:
https://www.facebook.com/BavariaMWR
MWR Twitter:
https://twitter.com/bavariamwr
Outdoor Recreation: Wild B.O.A.R. Outdoor Recreation, C-011-49-9641-83-8529. Offers day and overnight trips to various destinations, rock climbing, hiking and biking, hunting, shooting and fishing, soccer/football fields, tennis courts, basketball courts, cabin rentals and more. Equipment checkout offers a variety of camping gear, party supplies, sports rentals and more.
Things To Do: Visit the Museum for Cultural and Military History, take the Bamberger 6 Huegel-Tour, see the Klosterkirche Speinshart church, visit one of the many castles or enjoy the beautiful scenery.
Walking Trails: Indoor running track available at Fitness Centers.

RV CAMPING & GETAWAYS

Wild B.O.A.R. Recreation Cabins & Campsites

Reservation/Contact Number Info: C-011-49-9641-83-8529, DSN-314-475-8529.
RV Website:
https://grafenwoehr.armymwr.com/programs/outdoor-recreation
Reservations: Reservations are accepted on a first come, first served basis during normal business hours or via email to request information. Office hours 1100-1800 Mon, Tues, Thurs, Fri; 1000-1700 Sat; 1000-1600 Sun. Closed Wednesdays. Check-in 1300 hours; check-out 1100 hours. Contact office for late arrivals or late check-out. All active military, civilian, and retired members with a military ID for base access and their family may utilize these cabins. SOFA restrictions are not applicable at this location.
Season of Operation: Year-round.

Eligibility: AD, NG, Res, Ret, and their dependents; Widow/ers; DoD-Civ, DoD-Civ Ret and their dependents w/ID; DAVs.
Camper/Trailer Spaces: Limited RV sites available at Rose Barracks with water and electric hookup only.
Tent Spaces: Tent sites available at both locations.
Yurt, A Frame, Cabin, Apt, Spaces: Tower Barracks Cabins (6): Two and three bedroom cabins. Sleeps 5-7 depending on cabin. Select units feature stove tops. Rates: 2BR $125 daily, $650 weekly; 3BR $145 daily, $725 weekly. Rose Barracks: Two and three bedroom cabins. Sleeps 4-6 depending on cabin. Rates: 2BR $85 daily, $420 weekly; 3BR $95 daily, $490 weekly.
Support Facilities: Full range of support facilities available on base. Church Service, Laundry Facilities and Wi-Fi available.
Activities: Wild B.O.A.R. Outdoor Recreation complex offers a multitude of opportunities to include a climbing hall, high ropes course, hunting and fishing or skeet and trap shooting, equipment checkout, and multipurpose rooms.
Credit Cards: American Express, Discover, MasterCard and Visa.
Restrictions: Pets are permitted at campsites. Pets are not permitted in cabins.
RV Campground Physical Address: RC600 Tank Road, Tower Barracks, Grafenwoehr, Germany

Rolling Hills RV Park – Baumholder

Information Line: Baumholder, C-011-49-711-680-1110.
Main Base Police: C-011-49-611-143-531-2677. Emergencies dial 112
Main Installation Website:
https://home.army.mil/rheinland-pfalz/
Directions to Main Gate: To Baumholder: From Frankfurt International Airport: Follow signs for A5 towards Basel/Darmstadt. At signs for A67 get in the center/left lane and follow A67. Pass the town of Lorsch and take exit A6 Mannheim, Kaiserslautern

and Saarbruecken. Follow A6 towards Kaiserslautern/Saarbruecken, passing Kaiserslautern, take exit A6 to A62 towards Trier/Kusel. Continue for approximately 20 minutes then take the Freisen exit. Exiting A62 at Freisen, take a right and follow the signs for Baumholder. Once in Baumholder, follow the main road, take a left at the traffic light. Keep going straight through the next traffic light. The main gate is ahead. GPS should enter city: Baumholder, zip: 55774 and street address: Aulenbacher Strasse

Chapels: Baumholder Chaplain, C-011-49-162-270-8348.

Dental Clinic: C-06371-9464-1009, DSN 590-1009.

Medical: Appointment Line, C-011-49-6371-9464-5762, DSN 590-5762.

Beauty/Barber Shop: Bldg 8243, C-06783-9007202. Bldg 8668, C-06783-189405.

Commissary: Approximately 3 km to Baumholder Community Commissary, C-011-49-6783-6-6018. C-06783-6-6018.

Exchange Gas: Approximately 3 km to Baumholder gas station, C-011-49-6783-4754.

Exchange: Approximately 3 km to Baumholder Community Base Exchange facility, C-011-49-6783-99-9900.

Clubs: Tavern on the Rock, C-011-49-611-143-531-2890.

Places to Eat: ava Cafe, C-011-49-611-143-531-2898. Strikers Bowling Center, C-011-49-611-143-531-2830. Dining Facilities (DFAC), Burger King, Popeye's and Subway are on base.

Bowling: Strikers Bowling Center, C-011-49-611-143-531-2830.

Fitness Center: Hall of Champions FC, C-011-49-611-143-531-2838. Mountaineer FC, C-011-49-6783-67418.

Golf: Rolling Hills Golf Course, C-011-49-678-36-7299.

Library: C-011-49-6783-61740.

MWR: Family and MWR One Stop Shop, C-011-49-06783-6-8215

MWR Website: https://baumholder.armymwr.com/

Outdoor Recreation: Outdoor Recreation, C-011-49-06783-6-7182. Offers camping gear, hunting classes, a variety of outdoor adventure trips, party supplies, fishing gear, ski rentals, sports equipment and more.

Things To Do: Visit nearby Idar Oberstein for precious gems and stones, Trier's Roman ruins or the castles and vineyards of the Mosel Valley. The area offers great architecture and scenery.

RV CAMPING & GETAWAYS

Rolling Hills RV Park & Campground

Reservation/Contact Number Info: C-011-49-678-36-7182, DSN-314-485-7182. Fax C-011-49-678-36-6960, DSN-312-485-6960.

Recreation Security: C-112, DSN-112.

RV Website: https://baumholder.armymwr.com/programs/outdoor-recreation

GPS Coordinates: 49°36'25"N/7°18'45"E.

Reservations: Reservations recommended and should be made at least at least two weeks in advance for campsites. Reservations accepted via phone or in person at Smith Barracks ODR, Bldg 8167. Office hours 1000-1800 Mon-Tue, 1000-1800 Thur-Sun. Check-out 1200 hours.

Season of Operation: Year-round.

Eligibility: AD, NG, Res, Ret, DoD-Civ, 100% DAV and Local Nationals.

Camper/Trailer Spaces: Camper Spaces: Hardstand Back-in (40), Maximum length 30'. Handicap accessible, E(220V) hookup. Rates: $10 daily.

Tent Spaces: Camping for groups of 20 or more: Primitive, no hookups. Rates: $35 daily per group.

Support Facilities: Bathhouse, Fire Rings, Fitness Center, Golf, Grills, Ice, Pavilions, Picnic Areas, Playground, Pool (Indoor), Rec Equipment, Restrooms, Showers, Sports Fields, Telephones, Tennis Courts, Trails.

RV Storage: Contact ODR.

Activities: Fishing*, Golfing, Hiking, Indoor Climbing Wall, Kayaking, Rafting, Rock Climbing, Sightseeing, Snow Ski (DH&XC), Windsurfing. * Special permit required from German government for a fishing license. For information, contact C-011-49-6783-66345, DSN-(314-485-6345.

Credit Cards: American Express, Discover, MasterCard and Visa.

Restrictions: Pets allowed on leash. No firearms permitted. No water Nov-Apr.

RV Driving Directions/Location: Off Base. The RV Park is in the Baumholder Pool/Golf Complex. From Kaiserslautern: Take Autobahn 6/E50 west to exit 12. Take Autobahn 62 northwest toward Trier to north at exit 5/Friesen. Continue north Berschweiler Strasse/L348 toward Baumholder for approximately 9 kilometers. Turn left (northwest) on Marconi Road, just south of Baumholder High School. Continue northwest and make first left turn onto Morse Road and then continue southwest. RV Park entrance is on right.

Area Description: Gem city of Idar-Oberstein, famous for its precious stone industry and diamond factory, is nearby. Area has castles, Palatinate Forest, Mosel River and vineyards. Bosen Lake, 11.4 kilometers from post, offers swimming, fishing and windsurfing. Recreation area has most support facilities. Baumholder Lake is one kilometer away and offers swimming during the summer months.

RV Campground Physical Address: Smith Barracks, Avenue C, 55774 Baumholder, Germany. Mailing Address: Outdoor Recreation Baumholder, 222 Base Support Battalion, DCA Box 18, Unit 23746, APO AE 09034-5000.

ITALY

Carney Park Recreation Area

Address: Via Campiglione, 11 Pozzuoli, Italy 80078.

Information Line: C-011-39-081-568-1111, C-011-39-081-568-5547.

Main Base Police: C-011-39-081-568-5638/5639. Emergencies on base dial 911.

Main Installation Website: https://www.cnic.navy.mil/regions/cnreurafswa/installations/nsa_naples.html

Main Base Location: The park is located inside the crater at Carney Park.

NMC: Naples, 18 km southeast.

NMI: Naples, Naval Support Activity, 10 km south.

Commissary: Approximately 20 km away at Naples NSA, C-011-39-081-811-4882.

Exchange Gas: Approximately 20 km away at Capodichino, C-011-39-081-568-4274. Commercial gas station within 20 km.

Exchange: Shoppette approximately 20 km away at NSA Capodichino, C-011-39-081-568-4274. Support Site, C-011-39-081-813-5368.

Places to Eat: Fairways Bar and Grill on site.

Fitness Center: Carney Park Fitness Yurt, C-011-39-081-526-1579.

Golf: Carney Golf Course, C-011-39-081-526-4296.

ITT/ITR: Capodichino, C-081-568-4330. Support Site, C-081-811-7907/7902/7906.

MWR Website: http://www.navymwrnaples.com/

MWR Facebook: https://www.facebook.com/mwrnaples

Outdoor Recreation: Carney Park ODR, C-011-39-081-526-1579. Offers bikes, tents, sports equipment and tables and chairs. See NSA Naples for a full listing of ODR services on base.

Swimming: Olympic-sized pool with water slides and kiddie pool available at Carney Park.

Things To Do: Carney Park is one of the most unique parks in Europe due to its location within an extinct volcanic crater. It is a 96-acre recreation area with a variety of facilities and programs. Founded in 1966, the park has a multi-purpose sport field, numerous men's, women's and youth's softball and baseball fields and a football field. There are tennis courts, outdoor

basketball courts, sand volleyball pits, and children's playground.

Walking Trails: Hiking trails available at Carney Park.

RV CAMPING & GETAWAYS

Carney Park Recreation Area

Reservation/Contact Number Info: C-011-39-081-526-1579. Fax 011-39-081-526-4813.

Recreation Security: C-081-526-3418, DSN-114.

RV Website:
http://get.dodlodging.net/propertys/Carney-Park-Lodging-Naples

Other Info Website:
http://www.navymwrnaples.com/programs/5a552a41-7b5f-4308-af49-c2f368632796

GPS Coordinates: 40°51'4"N/14°6'38"E

Reservations: Highly recommended. Accepted up to six months in advance. Deposit equal to one night's stay required. Cancellations require 72-hour notice to avoid fee. Reservations accepted by phone 0900-1730 hours Mon-Tue, Thu-Fri; 1100-1300 hours Wed; 0900-1630 hours Sat; 1000-1630 hours Sun. Check in 1400 hours, check-out 1030 hours. Maximum stay two weeks. Extensions must be approved.

Season of Operation: Year-round.

Eligibility: AD, NG*, Res*, Ret, DoD-Civ assigned overseas and Dep (under 19 must be accompanied with adult sponsor). *On orders.

Camper/Trailer Spaces: Hardstand (4), Back-in, Maximum 40' in length, E(220V/30A)/W hookups. Rates: $10 daily, $50 weekly. Primitive (2), no electric hookups. Rates: $5 daily, $25 weekly.

Tent Spaces: Grass/Dirt (21), no hookups, 9 spaces with picnic table and grill. Rates: $10 daily, $50 weekly.

Yurt, A Frame, Cabin, Apt, Spaces: Cabin Lofts (3), One-bedroom with loft, (E(110V/220V), double bed, bunk bed and loft, bathrooms, kitchenette, microwave, refrigerator. Linens provided but patrons must supply or rent towels and cooking/eating utensils. Rates: $70 daily, $350 weekly. Cottages (11): E(220V), double bed and sofa, access to common restroom and shower facility, kitchenette, microwave, refrigerator. Linens provided but patrons must supply or rent towels and cooking/eating utensils. Rates: $50 daily, $250 weekly. Cabins (9): E(110V), double bed, single bed or bunk beds, access to common restroom and shower facility, kitchenette, microwave, refrigerator. Linens provided but patrons must supply or rent towels and cooking/eating utensils. Rates: $40 daily, $200 weekly. Yurts: 30 and 20 foot, with or without cot rentals, sleeps 10-15. Rates: Call for rates and information.

Support Facilities: Auto Craft Shop, Bathhouse, Beach, Boat Rental/Storage, Bowling, Cafeteria, Chapel (On Base), Coin Laundry, Commissary, Convenience Store, O'Rays Irish Pub*, Equipment Rental, Exchange*, Fire Rings, Fitness Center, Gas, Golf, Grills, Ice, Paintball, Pavilion, Pay Phones, Picnic Area, Playground, Pool*, Restrooms**, Sewage Dump Station, Shoppette, Showers, Snack Bar, Sports Fields, Sport Store, Ski Equipment, Stables, Tennis. Courts/lighted, Trails. *Summer only. Summer day camp program available for children ages 5-12. Register by day or by week. **Handicapped accessible.

RV Storage: None.

Activities: Aerobics, Archery, Art, Backpacking, Camping, Fishing, Horseback Riding, Kayaking, Mountain Biking, Rubber Stamping, Scrapbook Making, SCUBA, Skiing, Snowboarding, Trekking, Wall Climbing, Yoga.

Credit Cards: American Express, Discover, MasterCard and Visa.

Restrictions: No pets allowed overnight. Horseback riding requires a license. No firearms allowed.

RV Driving Directions/Location: Off Base: From the north on Autostrada 1 (E45), drive south toward Naples. Approximately 2.5 km past the town of Afragola, Autostrada 1 splits; stay to the right to get on Ramo (Ramp) A. Ramo A becomes Ramo Capodichino (both are still technically part of Autostrada 1). Autostrada 1/Ramo Capodichino becomes Autostrada 56/Ramo Capodichino, which becomes Autostrado 56/ Tangenziale (toll road) di Napoli. From the beginning of Ramo A to the beginning of Tangenziale, it is approximately 4 km total. Use the Tangenziale exit to get onto Tangenziale west, drive for about 17.5 km, and take exit 12/Via Campana/Pozzuoli. Drive north 0.5 km to a traffic circle. Complete a three-quarter turn in the circle and take the second exit (the road leading up a hill) onto SP47/ Via Campana. Proceed north on Via Campana for about 0.7 km. Entrance to the park is on the left (west) side of the street. Check-in at Carney Park Sports Store.

Area Description: Active port city of Naples. The Roman cities of Herculanum and Pompeii and active volcano Vesuvius are nearby. The beautiful island of Capri is 13.2 kilometers away by ferry or helicopter. Carney Park, with its large grassy fields and paved roads, is a 96-acre recreation facility located in the crater of an extinct 13th century volcano. The park offers ball fields, a golf course, an Olympic-size swimming pool, campgrounds and a picnic area. The city of Naples offers many fine opportunities for shopping and culture. Patrons can also enjoy ocean kayaking, horse riding, paintball, fishing and skiing. There are five festivals annually. Full range of support facilities available at Naples NSA and Capodichino.

RV Campground Physical Address: Mailing Address: Carney Park Lodging Naples, MWR Naples PSC 817 Box 9, Naples, Italy, FPO AE 09621.

JAPAN

Misawa Air Base

Address: 35 FSS/FSVL Unit 5019, APO, AP 96319. Physical Address: Bldg 670, Misawa-kichi, Aomori-ken, Japan 033-0012.

Information Line: C-011-81-176-77-1110, DSN-315-226-1110.

Main Base Police: DSN-315-226-4358/4359. Emergencies dial 911.

Main Installation Website: http://www.misawa.af.mil

Main Base Location: Misawa Air Base is approximately 400 miles north of Tokyo, on the northeastern part of the main island of Honshu. It is located in

Misawa city on the shores of Lake Ogawara in Aomori Prefecture. As the only combined, joint service installation in the Western Pacific, The Misawa community is made up of Air Force, Navy, and Army active duty members and their families.

Directions to Main Gate: From Narita Airport: Take the Higashi-Kanto Expressway towards Tokyo. As approaching Tokyo, the Higashi-Kanto turns into the Bayshore Route. Take the C2 to the Gaikan Expressway. From the Gaikan Expressway take the Tohoku Expressway, which goes all the way to Aomori. Note: Take the Hachinohe Expressway branch for the last few kilometers to Misawa. Once exiting the Expressway at Misawa, follow the signs to the City Offices and then to the Air Base. Bus service is also available at the Narita Airport.

NMC: Hachinohe City, 28 km southeast.
NMI: Misawa NAF, adjacent.
Base Social Media/Facebook:
https://www.facebook.com/MisawaAir Base/
Base Social Media/Twitter:
https://twitter.com/TeamMisawa
Chapels: C-011-81-176-77-4630, DSN-315-226-4630.
Dental Clinic: C-0176-77-6111 or DSN-315-226-6700.
Medical: Appointment Line, C-0176-77-6111, DSN-315-226-6111.
Veterinary Services: C-011-81-176-77-4502, DSN-315-226-4502.
Beauty/Barber Shop: Bldg 1952 Barber, C-1-469-375-7473. Bldg 325 Barber, C-1-469-375-7474; Stylique, C-1-469-375-7484.
Commissary: C-011-81-176-77-3482.
Exchange Gas: Main Base Gas, C-1-469-375-7428. Bldg 1946 offers 24-hour pumps.
Exchange: C-011-81-176-66-7412.
Financial Institutions: Community Bank: C-011-81-176-77-4070. DSN315-226-4070. Navy Federal Credit Union is on base.
Clubs: Misawa Club, DSN-315-957-1556.
Places to Eat: Bumper's Grill, Cafe Mokuteki, Fire Pit, Lakeview Grille, Nami Grill, the Sports Bar, Tohoku Dining, T's

Burritos, Wild Weasel's Bar and Grill and two dining facilities are on base.
Exchange Food Court offers Baskin-Robbins, Charley's, Dunkin Donuts, Pizza Hut, Subway and Taco Bell. Anthony's Pizza, Burger King and Popeye's are also on base.

Bowling: Walmsley Bowling Center, C-0176-77-8255 then 1-281-657-1554, DSN-315-957-1554.
Fitness Center: Freedom FC, DSN-315-226-9987. Potter FC, DSN-315-226-3982.
Golf: Gosser Memorial Golf Course, C-0176-77-1563, DSN-315-226-1563.
ITT/ITR: C-0176-77-3555, DSN-315-226-3555.
Library: Overstreet Memorial Library, C-0176-77-4083, DSN-315-226-4083.
Marina: Base Beach and Marina, DSN-315-226-9378.
Military Museum: Misawa Aviation and Space Museum.
Military Museum Website: http://www.misawajapan.com/poi/insi de/aviation.asp
MWR: C-011-81-176-77-9272, DSN-315-226-9272.
MWR Website: http://www.35fss.com/
MWR Facebook:
https://www.facebook.com/35FSS
Outdoor Recreation: Outdoor Recreation Center, C-0176-77-9378, DSN-315-226-9378. Offers an indoor activities center which features indoor soccer and a playground. ORC offers camping gear, outdoor sports equipment, winter sport rentals, water sport rentals, lawn and garden equipment, party supplies, park rentals and more.
Swimming: Himberg Indoor Pool, DSN-315-226-3152 offer open swim, lap swim and swim lessons.
Things To Do: Enjoy the excellent eating establishments in downtown Misawa and try a hot bath at Komaki. Explore the Komaki Onsen, Komaki Grand and the Second Grand Hotels. Visit the Misawa Aviation and Space Museum, Hachinohe Fantasy Dome Mall and Hachinohe Pia Do Mall.
Walking Trails: Indoor running track at Weasel's Den.

RV CAMPING & GETAWAYS

Lake Ogawara Beach Cabins

Reservation/Contact Number Info: C-011-81-176-77-9378/3480.
Recreation Security: Using Cell, C-0176-53-1911.
RV Website:
http://www.35fss.com/reservations_rentals.php
Reservations: Reservations accepted in person or via telephone. Summer Office hours 1000-1900 daily. Check-in 1200 hours, check-out 1100 hours.
Season of Operation: Year-round.
Eligibility: AD, Res, Ret.
Tent Spaces: Campsites available. Rates: $15 daily.
Yurt, A Frame, Cabin, Apt, Spaces: Beach Cabins, sleeps 6, one bunk bed, one full size bed and a futon, porch swing. Rates: $30 daily.
Support Facilities: Full range of support facilities on base.
RV Storage: Nearest RVC is at Tama Outdoor Rec Area (off base), operated by Yokota AB, C-011-81-3117-54-6421, DSN-315-224-3421. NOTE: This facility does not provide RV storage.
Activities: Archery, Boating, Jet Skiing, Mini Golf, Paintball, Power Boating, Skeet Shooting, Swimming.
RV Driving Directions/Location: On Base. From the Main Gate: Ask for directions to Outdoor Recreation, Bldg 973 for check-in.
Area Description: Located three miles west of the Pacific and 400 miles north of Tokyo. The area offers coastal beaches and forests with plenty of outdoor recreational activities to include swimming, scuba diving, explorations, hiking and even skiing in the winter months at Land Memorial Ski Lodge.
RV Campground Physical Address: Mailing Address: Outdoor Recreation, 35 FSS/FSCO, Bldg 973, Unit 5019, APO AP 96319.

Okuma Beach

Address: Kunigami-son Kunigami-gun, Okinawa, Japan 905-1412.
Information Line: C-098-962-1990, DSN-315-631-1990. Okuma Main Gate, DSN-315-632-3149.
Main Base Police: Okuma Beach, C-090-9780-2793, DSN-315-632-3109.
Main Installation Website:
http://kadenafss.com/okuma/
Other Info Website:
http://www.kadenafss.com/
Main Base Location: Okuma Beach is approximately 76 km northeast of Kadena Air Base.
Directions to Main Gate: To Okuma Beach: Head north on the expressway towards Nago until the expressway/toll road ends. For a more scenic route: Follow Hwy 58 north. There is also a new tunnel between Kyoda expressway exit and Nago-city. After the expressway ends, continue north on 58 towards Cape Hedo for 36 kilometers. Turn left at the big Okuma beach sign and continue 2 kilometers until seeing Okuma recreation center on the left, passing JAL Okuma, which is a different resort.
NMC: Nago, 45 kilometers south.
NMI: Camp Schwab, 40 kilometers south.
Base Social Media/Facebook:
https://www.facebook.com/theokumabeach/
Commissary: Beach Mart on site.
Exchange Gas: Approximately 38 km to Camp Schwab gas station. Commercial gas station within 3 km.
Exchange: Approximately 38 km away at Camp Schwab, C-011-81-611-625-3846.
Financial Institutions: ATM located on site.
Clubs: Waverunner Lounge is on site.
Places to Eat: Surfside Restaurant, C-098-962-1805, DSN-315-631-1805. Sunset Patio is also on site.
Golf: Habu Links is located at Okuma Beach.
Marina: Water activities located at Okuma Beach.
Outdoor Recreation: Okuma Outdoor Recreation: South Beach, DSN-315-631-1815. North Beach, DSN-315-631-1816. Recreation and boat rentals available (certification by a sanctioned

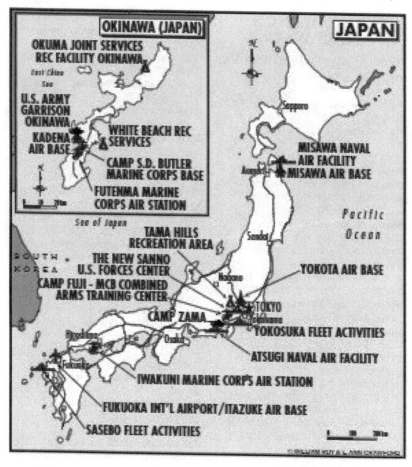

organization or qualification test by instructor required to rent sailboat, wind surfing and diving equipment), Golf Course, Putt-Putt Golf, Bicycle rentals, Camping, Tennis, Basketball, Go-Kart Racetrack, and Outdoor maze available on site.

Swimming: Ocean swimming and water sport activities available.

Things To Do: Retro G Game Room at Okuma Recreational Facility offers a big screen TV, pool table, kiddie korner, air hockey, video games and more. This is a great recreation area with beautiful beaches and plenty of activities.

Walking Trails: Walking trails are available at the recreation area.

RV CAMPING & GETAWAYS
Okuma Beach

Reservation/Contact Number Info: C-011-81-611-734-3102, C-098-962-3102, DSN 315-631-1991/1992.

Recreation Security: From Cell, C-098-934-5911. Emergencies dial 911.

RV Website:
http://kadenafss.com/okuma/

RV Email Address:
okuma.information@18fss.com

GPS Coordinates:
26°44'31"N/128°9'23"E

Reservations: Accepted and recommended. Peak Season allows reservations six months in advance. Off Season reservations accepted 11 months in advance. Deposit equal to one night's stay required at time of reservation. Cancellations must be made 72 hours in advance of check-in to avoid fee. Late arrivals must contact Coral Reef Inn before 1800 hours. All campsites are reserved on a first come, first serve basis. Office hours 1000-1700 hours Mon-Fri. Check-in 1500 hours, check-out 1100 hours.

Season of Operation: Year-round.

Eligibility: AD, NG, Res, Ret and DoD-Civ assigned overseas, including SOFA status personnel, their families and bona fide guests.

Tent Spaces: Beachfront Family Campground (63): Families only; located on South Beach. Rates: $11 daily per tent. Hillside Adult Campground (50): Adults only; located on West Beach. Rates: $11 daily per tent. Both camping site locations provide cooking grills, picnic tables, and access to restroom facilities.

Yurt, A Frame, Cabin, Apt, Spaces: Turtle's Nest Beach House (1): Two bedroom with queen beds, sleeps 10, one bathroom, equipped kitchen with microwave but no stove, refrigerator, TV/DVD, grill. Linens provided. Rates: $185-$215 daily. Ai Beach Cottage (1): Adults Only. One bedroom with queen bed, one bath, sleeps 2, refrigerator, microwave, coffee maker, TV/DVD, grill. Private beach, hot tub, golf cart, gated. Rates: $160-$190 daily. Bayside Cottage (1): Two bedroom with queen beds, sleeps 8, one bathroom, equipped kitchen with microwave but no stove, refrigerator, TV/DVD, grill. Linens provided. Rates: $160-$190 daily. Oasis Bungalow (1): E5+ Only. Five-bedroom with queen beds, three bathrooms, sleeps 10, living room, equipped kitchen with two refrigerators, microwave but no stove, laundry room with W/D, TV/DVD, grill. Linens provided. Rates: $170-$200 daily. Dunes Condo (1): E5+ Only. Seven-bedroom with five master rooms and two regular, all with queen beds, two bathrooms, sleeps 18, equipped kitchen with microwave but no stove, two refrigerators, laundry room with W/D, TV/DVD player in each

room, grill. Linens provided. Rates: $210-$240 daily. Studio Premiere: One room with two queen beds, sleeps 4, one bathroom, refrigerator, microwave, coffee pot, TV/DVD. Linens provided. Rates: $60-$80 daily. Studio: One room with queen bed, sleeps 2, one bathroom, refrigerator, microwave, coffee pot, TV/DVD. Linens provided. Rates: $50-$70 daily. Suite Plus: One-bedroom with two queen beds, sofa sleeper, sleeps 6, one bathroom, living room, refrigerator, microwave, coffee pot, TV/DVD. Linens provided. Rates: $70-$90 daily. Suite: One-bedroom with two queen beds, sofa sleeper, sleeps 6, one bathroom, living room, refrigerator, microwave, coffee pot, TV/DVD. Linens provided. Rates: $65-$85 daily. Sunset Villas: Single rooms with 2 full beds, sleeps 4, living room area, microwave, refrigerator. Picnic table, BBQ grill. Rates: $140-$170 daily.

Support Facilities: Basketball Court, Beaches (2), Bicycle Rental, Boathouse (2), Conference Room, Convenience Store, Dispensary, Game Room, Golf, Laundry, Lounge, Miniature Golf, Picnic Area, Playground, Rec Center, Rec Equipment, Restaurant, Restrooms*, Showers*, Tennis Court, Theater, Trails, Volleyball Sand Pits. * Handicap accessible.

RV Storage: None.

Activities: Aqua Trike, Bicycling, Boating, Fishing, Glass Bottom Boat, Golfing, Go-Kart Track, Hedge Maze, Hiking, Jet Ski, Kayaking, Movies By The Beach, Paddle Boats, Parasailing, Sailing, Scuba Diving, Snorkeling, Swimming, Wake Boarding, Water Skiing, Windsurfing. Glass-bottom boat tours and water instructional classes are available.

Credit Cards: MasterCard and Visa.

Restrictions: No pets and no glass bottles allowed on site. In order to rent sailboat and windsurfing equipment, certification by a sanctioned organization is required. Certification is also required for use of any diving equipment and/or service. No personal watercrafts are allowed within Okuma

operational areas to ensure the safety of all Okuma patrons. No exceptions.
RV Driving Directions/Location: Off Base: Head north on the expressway towards Nago until the expressway/toll road ends. For a more scenic route: Follow Hwy 58 north. There is also a new tunnel between Kyoda expressway exit and Nago-city. After the expressway ends, continue north on 58 towards Cape Hedo for 36 kilometers. Turn left at the big Okuma beach sign and continue 2 kilometers until seeing Okuma recreation center on the left, passing JAL Okuma, which is a different resort.
Area Description: This 120-acre recreational complex is a beautiful, quiet getaway on a peninsula with snow-white beaches on both the Pacific Ocean and East China Sea. Picturesque drive takes you through pineapple fields and acres of sugar cane. Full range of support and outdoor recreational facilities available.
RV Campground Physical Address: Detachment 1, 18th Services Squadron, Unit 5135 Box 10, APO AP 96368-5135.

Tama Hills Recreation Area

Address: 374 FSS/FSFR, Bldg 535, Unit 5123, Yokota AB (Fussa), Japan 197-0001.
Information Line: Yokota Air Base, C-011-81-3117-55-1110, DSN-315-225-1110.
Main Base Police: DSN-315-225-7233.
Main Installation Website:
http://www.yokota.af.mil/
Main Base Location: Yokota Air Base is located on the island of Honshu, Japan, on the Kanto Plain, 28 miles northwest of Tokyo at the foothills of the Okutama Mountains. The base lies within the political boundaries of six municipalities. These are Akishima, Fussa, Hamura, Mizuho, Musashi-Murayama, and Tachikawa.
Directions to Main Gate: If flying into Narita International Airport, Tokyo, it will be necessary to secure transportation to Yokota. The Force Support Squadron (FSS) Vehicle

Operations currently has three buses that travel between Yokota Air Base and Narita International Airport daily.
NMC: Tokyo, 25 miles west.
NMI: Yokota AB, 30 km northwest.
Base Social Media/Facebook:
https://www.facebook.com/yokotaairbase/
Commissary: Approximately 30 km away at Yokota AB Commissary, C-011-81-42-552-2510 ext 58585.
Exchange Gas: Approximately 30 km to Yokota AB gas station. Commercial gas station within 2 km.
Exchange: Approximately 30 km away at Yokota AB Exchange facility, C-469-375-7519.
Clubs: Hillcrest Lounge is on site.
Places to Eat: Tama Lodge Kiji Dining Room and Tee House Restaurant are on site. The Country Store is also on site.
Golf: Tama Hills Golf Course and Par 3 Jr. Course, C-042-374-2811, DSN-315-224-3426.
MWR Website:
http://www.yokotasupport.com/
MWR Facebook:
https://www.facebook.com/YokotaFSS
Outdoor Recreation: Tama Outdoor Recreation, C-011-81-3117-55-5248, DSN-315-227-5248. Offers bike rentals, horseback riding, paintball, archery, miniature golf and more. Also offers a wide variety of outdoor sporting equipment
Things To Do: This is a 500-acre retreat west of Tokyo. It's a quiet getaway offering many facilities, such as a golf course and horse stables. Sanrio Puroland (Hello Kitty) Park, Yomiuriland Amusement Park, Tama Zoological Park, Suntory Brewery Musashino Factory, Ajinomoto Soccer Stadium, shopping, shrines, and the Fuchu Horse Track are all conveniently located outside the gates of Tama. Some are within walking distance others are easily accessible by train.
Walking Trails: Hiking trails available at Tama Hills Recreation Area.

RV CAMPING & GETAWAYS

Tama Hills Recreation Area

Reservation/Contact Number Info: C-011-81-423-77-7009, C-042-377-7009, DSN-315-224-3422. Fax C-011-81-42-378-8446.

Recreation Security: C-011-81-3117-52-1110, DSN-315-225- 1110. Fire: C-119, Medical: C-119, Police: C-110.

RV Website:
http://www.yokotasupport.com/tama-hills/

RV Email Address:
tamahillsjapan.guests@gmail.com

GPS Coordinates:
N 35° 38' 47"/E 139° 28' 59"

Reservations: Reservations accepted for SOFA Status stationed at Yokota 120 days in advance on a first come, first serve basis. SOFA personnel stationed at other bases may secure reservations 120 days in advance for Sun-Thurs, excluding the night before US holidays and 374 AW Family/Down Days; 90 days in advance Fri-Sat. Check-out 1100 hours. Late check-out on space available basis only. Reduced fees applicable. DV Cabins allow for three-day maximum.

Season of Operation: Year-round.

Eligibility: AD, NG, Res, Ret and DoD-Civ.

Tent Spaces: Family Campsites (6), Group Campsites (15): Primitive, shower and bath facilities; kitchen and dining area, picnic table, grill. Rates: $1 daily.

Yurt, A Frame, Cabin, Apt, Spaces: Tama Lodge (15 Rooms, 1 Handicap): Standard, Queen, King and DV Suite Room(s) with bathroom, mini-fridge, microwave, coffee maker, TV/DVD. Linens provided. Rates: $48-$80 daily depending on room. Standard Cabin (7): One bedroom with queen bed, loft with sleeping pad, living room with futon, one bath, TV/DVD. Kitchen area with refrigerator, 2-burner stove, microwave. Picnic table, grill. Linens provided. Rates: $70 daily. DV Cabins (3, Samuri, Shizuka, Shogun): Two-bedrooms with queen beds, full bathroom, TV/DVD. Kitchen with refrigerator, 2-burner stove, microwave. Living rooms and loft areas with futons and entertainment areas. Picnic tables, grills. Hot tubs in two cabins. Rates: $95 daily. Red Horse Lodge (1): Four-bedroom with queen beds, TV/DVD players, separate bathroom. Full size kitchen with microwave, refrigerator, stove w/oven. Living room with fireplace, TV/DVD, dining area and seating. Hot tub, grill. Rates: $195 daily.

Support Facilities: Coin Laundry, Dining, Equipment Rental, Exchange, Lounge, Picnic Area*, Playground, Restrooms, Showers, Sports Fields, Stables, Tennis Courts, Trails.

RV Storage: None.

Activities: Archery, Bicycling, Camping, Golfing, Hiking, Horseback Riding, Jogging, Miniature Golfing, Paint-balling, Softball, Trap Shooting.

Credit Cards: American Express, MasterCard and Visa.

Restrictions: Pets are permitted in select cabins (2).

RV Driving Directions/Location: Off Base: Approximately 45 minutes southeast of Yokota Air Base. From Yokota Air Base; Travel south on Route 16 to Ohnita Intersection. Turn left (east) and continue on Route 16 for approximately 1.5 kilometers to Dogata-Ue Intersection. Continue east onto Okutama Bypass. Route 16 turns right (south) approximately 6.9 kilometers to Hino Intersection. Continue straight ahead (east) onto Route 20 for 4.9 kilometers to Honjuku Ni Intersection. Turn right (south) onto Kamakura Kaido for 2.7 kilometers to Ohkuribashi Intersection and turn left (east) on Kawasaki Kaido/R41 to main entrance to Tama Lodge and Recreation Area on right (south) side of street.

Area Description: A 500-acre retreat west of Tokyo, Tama was originally built by the Japanese Imperial Army in 1938 as a munition's storage area. After extensive repairs and renovations, the center was reopened in 1983. The lodge and cabins all have private baths. Hot tubs are available year-round. It is a quiet, wooded getaway offering a large range of facilities.

RV Campground Physical Address:
Mailing Address: 374 FSS/FSCL, Tama Hills Recreation Area, Unit 5119, Bldg 375, APO AP 96328-5119.

USAG Okinawa – Torii Station

Address: Sobe, Yomitan-son, Okinawa, Japan 904-0304.
Information Line: C-011-81-98-970-5555-644-1110.
Main Installation Website:
https://www.army.mil/okinawa
Main Base Location: U.S. Army Garrison Okinawa (formerly Torii Station) is the main Army installation in Okinawa, Japan. Located in Yomitan-son, Okinawa Prefecture, Japan, it is home to the 10th Area Support Group, 1st Battalion, 1st Special Forces Group, and other units and activities.
Directions to Main Gate: If arriving via the domestic airport, dial 911-5111 to get a base dial tone, and then dial the DSN number you wish to call. You may also be able to get a ride with the Marine Corps or Air Force who pick up personnel from both airports daily. At the International Airport, if your sponsor is not there, look back at the double doors near customs. There is a red sign to the left saying "Welcome to Okinawa U.S. Military Phone". The phone is there specifically for military members and its use is free of charge. There is a list of telephone numbers taped on the counter near the phone.
NMC: Okinawa.
Base Social Media/Facebook:
https://www.facebook.com/USAGOkinawa/
Chapels: DSN-315-644-4454.
Dental Clinic: C-011-81-98-960-4817.
Medical: Kadena Appointment Line, C-098-960-4817, DSN-315-630-4817.
Beauty/Barber Shop: C-036 868-2238, C-1-512-672-7634.
Commissary: Kadena AB, C- 011-81-98-961-3990.
Exchange Gas: C-1-512-672-7637.
Exchange: C-1-512-672-7636.
Places to Eat: CJ's, Havana's, Pirate Republic Coffee Company and Rally Point are on base. Exchange Food Court offers Subway.
Fitness Center: Torri Gym, C-81-98-962-4334, DSN-315-644-4334.
Library: C-81-98-962-5335, DSN-315-644-5647.
MWR: C-81-98-962-4270, DSN-315-644-4270.
MWR Website:
https://torii.armymwr.com/
MWR Facebook:
https://www.facebook.com/toriimwrokinawa/
Outdoor Recreation: Torri Beach Rentals, C-81-98-962-4659, DSN-315-644-4659. Offers kayaks, surfboards, stand-up paddle boards, bounce houses, party supplies and more. Scuba rentals are available as well.
Swimming: Torri Beach offers splash park and beach. Base Pool, C-81-98962-4936 offer unit training only.
Things To Do: Torri Beach offers cabin and campsite rentals for recreational purposes. Visit Ruins of Nagashino Castle and the museum, Ryugashido Cavern, Kawatsu Cherry Blossom Avenue, one of the many historic battlefields or enjoy many beautiful outdoor spaces nearby.

RV CAMPING & GETAWAYS
Torii Beach Campsites

Reservation/Contact Number Info: C-011-81-611-744-4659, DSN-315-644-4659/4698.
RV Website:
https://torii.armymwr.com/programs/torii-beach
GPS Coordinates:
26°22'14.1"N/127°44'08.8"E
Reservations: Accepted via telephone or in person at Outdoor Recreation, Bldg T-301. Office hours 0800-1700 daily.
Season of Operation: Year-round.
Eligibility: AD, NG, Res, Ret, DoD-Civ.
Tent Spaces: Tent Sites, near bathrooms and showers. Contact ODR for current rates.
Yurt, A Frame, Cabin, Apt, Spaces:
Cabins: Beachside, sleeps 6, bathroom, shower, refrigerator, microwave,

CATV/DVD player, outdoor grill. Linens provided. Rates: $45-$75 daily.

Support Facilities: Commissary, Dining, Exchange, Fitness Center, Library, Playground, Pool. Full range of support facilities on base.

Activities: Boating, Kayaks, Paddle Boarding, Splash Park, Swimming, Surfing.

RV Driving Directions/Location: On Base: From the Main Gate: Ask for directions to Torii Beach.

Area Description: Ideally located on base amidst white sandy beaches along the East China Sea. Visitors can enjoy snorkeling, scuba diving or just simple relax on the beach.

RV Campground Physical Address: MWR, Douglas Boulevard, Bldg 5393, 18 FSS Unit 5135 Box 10, APO AP 96368-5135.

White Beach Recreation Area

Address: Commander Fleet Activities Okinawa, PSC 480 Box 1100, FPO AP Okinawa, Japan 96370-1100. Kadena Air Base, Douglas Boulevard, Bldg. 6 (Gate 1), Kadena AB (Okinawa-City), APO, AP 96368.

Information Line: C-011-81-98-938-1111, C-098-938-1111.

Main Base Police: Emergencies dial 911.

Main Installation Website: https://www.cnic.navy.mil/regions/cnrj/installations/cfa_okinawa.html

Main Base Location: Okinawa Fleet Activities is physically located on Kadena AB, and is located in Okinawa City, Okinawa, Japan. Okinawa is a semi-tropical island located between the East China Sea and the Pacific Ocean. Given the extensive tourism, cultural and historical sites, pristine ocean and beaches, live entertainment, parks and restaurants, most people find that Kadena is the best tour of their career!

Directions to Main Gate: Kadena Air Base, located on the west side of Okinawa. Take JP-58 north 25 km from Naha to Kadena's Gate 1 on the right. If your sponsor does not meet you at the AMC terminal, you may call the Shogun Inn registration desk for shuttle service.

Kadena's billeting, the Shogun Inn, provides shuttle service Monday to Friday from 0700-2100 to their guests. If you arrive after hours, you may call DSN: 315-645-8888 or COMM: 098-970-8888 for a taxi on base. Please follow the prompts after dialing the number. Option 8 is for taxi service on Kadena AB.

NMC: Okinawa City, nine miles west.

NMI: Kadena AB, eight miles west.

Base Social Media/Facebook: https://www.facebook.com/COMFLEACTOKI/

Chapels: Kadena AB, C-011-81-611-34-1288, DSN-315-634-1288.

Medical: Kadena AB, C-011-81-611-730-4817, DSN-315-630-4817.

Commissary: Kadena AB, C-011-81-98-961-3990.

Exchange: Kadena AB, C-C-036-868-2280, C-1-512-672-7560.

Clubs: Crow's Nest, C-036-868-2264. Port of Call Club, C-098-954-1888.

Places to Eat: Bama's BBQ, C-Street Cafe, Subway, Wingz@thebeach and Touch-n-Go Diner are on base. See Kadena AB for a full list of additional eateries and Exchange Food Court options.

Fitness Center: Camp Shields FC, C-098-962-4013, DSN-315-632-5091. White Beach FC is open 24-hours daily.

Golf: Banyan Tree Golf Course, C-036-868-2223, DSN-316-966-7321. Chibana Golf Course, C-036-868-2224, DSN-315-966-7327.

ITT/ITR: Kadena AB, C-036-868-2226, DSN-315-966-7333.

MWR: C-81-98-961-6916.

MWR Website: http://www.navymwrokinawa.com/

MWR Facebook: https://www.facebook.com/NavyMWROkinawa/

Outdoor Recreation: See Kadena Air Base.Jungle Raid Paintball, C-080-6485-1680 near White Beach.

Things To Do: Visitors can enjoy many activities, including sunbathing, swimming, surfing and relaxing at the numerous beaches. There are many clubs and other recreational opportunities available to the patrons of the White Beach lodging facility. Also visit the Shurijo Castle, Okinawa Churaumi Aquarium, Okinawa Ocean Expo Park and Okinawa World.

RV CAMPING & GETAWAYS
White Beach Recreation Area

Reservation/Contact Number Info: C-1-877-NAVY-BED, C-011-81-6117-34-6952, DSN-315-634-6952.

Recreation Security: C-011- 81-642-2200/2300.

RV Website:
http://get.dodlodging.net/propertys/Okinawa-Navy-Getaways

Other Info Website:
http://www.navymwrokinawa.com/programs/a48e690f-cf11-46cf-896e-3e649eda1f59

RV Email Address:
MWR-OK.Reservations@fe.navy.mil

GPS Coordinates: 26°18'N/127°49'E

Reservations: Reservation accepted up to one year in advance for AD; 6 months for all others. Credit card is required for all reservations. Office hours 0700-1530 Mon-Fri. Accepted by phone or in person at Navy MWR Office, Kadena AFB, Bldg 3597 or White Beach, Bldg 1096. Check in at White Beach Campground Office, 1400 hours, check-out 1100 hours.

Season of Operation: Year-round.

Eligibility: AD, NG, Res, Ret, DoD-Civ and Dep.

Camper/Trailer Spaces: Deluxe Campers (21): Queen bed, twin sofa bed, bathroom with shower, living room, alarm clock, kitchenette, microwave, small refrigerator, cookware/utensils, dining table/chairs. Rates: $45 daily. Linens provided.

Tent Spaces: Campsites (10): Picnic tables but no grills. Rates: $10 daily.

Yurt, A Frame, Cabin, Apt, Spaces: Cabins: Captain's Cabin (1), prior approval from CFAO; Two-bedroom, master bedroom with queen bed, full-size bunk beds, one full bed; living room, kitchen/dining area, washer and dryer in unit. Rates: $80 daily. One-bedroom (7): Full-Size bunk beds. Rates:

$50 daily. All cabins provide table/chairs, alarm clock, CATV/VCR, cookware/utensils, kitchenette, stove, microwave, small refrigerator. Housekeeping and linens provided. Free Wi-Fi, picnic area. Duplex (3): Queen bed, rollaway bed, twin sofa bed, table/chairs, kitchenette, cookware/utensils, microwave, small refrigerator, TV/DVD. Housekeeping and linens provided. Free Wi-Fi, picnic area, patio furniture. Rates: $55 daily.

Support Facilities: Bathhouse, Beach, Equipment Rental, Fitness Center, Grills, Laundry, Ice, Miniature Golf, Pavilions, Picnic Areas, Playground, Pool, Rec Center, Restrooms*, Shoppette, Showers, Sports Fields, Taxi, Tennis Courts. * Handicap accessible. Food Court, Dinning facility and Barber Shop, Outdoor Rec Center with free WIFI.

RV Storage: None.

Activities: Bathhouse, Beach, Equipment Rental, Fitness Center, Grills, Laundry, Ice, Miniature Golf, Pavilions, Picnic Areas, Playground, Pool, Rec Center, Restrooms*

Credit Cards: American Express, Discover, MasterCard and Visa.

Restrictions: No pets allowed. No fireworks. No firearms allowed.

RV Driving Directions/Location: On Base: On the Pacific Island of Okinawa, south of Japan. On East side of island on Katsuren Peninsula in Buckner Bay. From Hwy 24, north of Okinawa City, turn east on Hwy 329 to Hwy 8 to White Beach.

Area Description: Beautiful beach, many recreational activities, Ocean Cliff and Port of Call Club at White Beach. The clubs are open to all ranks and provide a full-menu dining room, amusement center, ballroom and casual bar.

RV Campground Physical Address: CFAO MWR Marketing, PSC 480 Box 57, FPO AP 96370, OFFICIAL BUSINESS.

Yokosuka Fleet Activities

Address: PSC 473 Box 116, FPO AP 96349-0116.

Information Line: C-011-81-46-816-1110, C-046-816-1110.

Main Base Police: C-046-816-0911. Emergencies dial 911 or 119. Security, DSN-315-243-2300/2301. Ikego, DSN-315-246-8368/8367.

Main Installation Website: http://www.cnic.navy.mil/regions/cnrj/installations/cfa_yokosuka.html

Main Base Location: Yokosuka City is located about 30 miles southwest of Japan's capital city, Tokyo, on the east coast of the main island, Honshu. It is an industrial and residential community, with an area of about 39 square miles, and a population of about 422,441. This 579 acre naval base occupies a small peninsula jutting into Tokyo Bay.

Directions to Main Gate: Transportation to Yokosuka from Yokota is based on flights coming into the AMC terminal. Because the flight schedule changes and is updated frequently there is no online sign-up. However, your Sponsor can sign you up for the bus to Yokosuka once you receive your itinerary by contacting the CFAY bus desk by calling DSN-315-243-7777, the number to call from the USA is C-011-81-46-816-7777. Narita International Airport is located north of Tokyo approximately 120km (80 miles) from Yokosuka, a 1 ½-2 hour bus ride to Yokosuka.

NMC: Tokyo, 38 km north.

Base Social Media/Facebook: https://www.facebook.com/cfayokosuka

Base Social Media/Twitter: https://twitter.com/CFAY_Japan

Chapels: C-011-81-468-16-2010, DSN-315-243-2010.

Dental Clinic: C-011-81-46-816-8808, C-046-816-8808, DSN-315-243-8808.

Medical: Appointment Line, C-011-81-46-816-5352, C-046-816-5352, DSN-315-243-5352. Information, C-011-81-46-816-7144. C-046-816-7144.

Veterinary Services: C-011-81-616-043-6820, DSN-315-243-6820.

Beauty/Barber Shop: Main Store, C-046-816-5384. Fleet Rec Center Barber, C-046-896-4168. Ikego, DSN-315-246-5950.

Commissary: C-011-81-46-816-9904.

Exchange Gas: Ikego, C-046-896-7991.

Exchange: C-011-81-46-816-5577, C-046-816-5577.

Financial Institutions: Community Bank Japan, C-011-81-46-816-4585/4586. Navy Federal Credit Union, C-011-81-46-816-3333.

Clubs: Club Alliance, C-046-816-3000. Cove Bar, Kurofune Lounge, C-046-816-5030. Ikego Club T Lounge, C-046-806-8077.

Places to Eat: Club Alliance offers Italian Gardens Restaurant, C-Street Grille, Sharky's Road House, Sharky's Killer Wings and Craft Beers, and Anchor Lounge. CPO Club and Club Takemiya offer dining, Officers' Club offers Chopsticks Asian To-Go and Kosano Dining Room. Exchange Food Court offers A&W, American Grill, Anthony's Pizza, Baskin Robbins, McDonald's, Manchu Wok, Pizza Hut, Popeye's Chicken, Seattle's Best Coffee, Subway, Taco Bell and two cafeterias. Chili's and Starbucks are also on base. Many restaurants within a short drive.

Bowling: Yokosuka Bowling Center, C-046-816-5158, DSN-315-243-5158.

Fitness Center: Purdy FC, C-046-816-5398, DSN-315-243-5398. Fleet Gym, C-046-816-5304, DSN-315-243-5304. Hawk's Nest Bldg B48, Ikego Gym, C-046-816-5398, DSN-315-243-5398.

ITT/ITR: C-011-81-46-896-5056, C-046-896-5056, DSN-315-241-5056.

Library: C-046-816-5574, DSN-315-243-5574.

Marina: Green Bay Marina, C-046-816-4155, DSN-315-243-4155.

MWR: C-011-81-46-816-7250, DSN-315-243-7250. Ikego, DSN-315-246-8071/5776.

MWR Website: http://www.navymwryokosuka.com/

MWR Facebook: https://www.facebook.com/yokosukamwrhappenings/

Outdoor Recreation: Outdoor Recreation Center, C-011-82-46-816-5732, C-046-816-5732, DSN-315-243-5732. Offers camping gear, bicycle maintenance, outdoor sports equipment and games, party supplies, water sport rentals, winter sports equipment, paintball yard, adventure trips and more.

Swimming: Purdy FC Pool, C-046-896-2945 offers open swim, lap swim and swim lessons.

Things To Do: Located close to Tokyo, near many historic Japanese shrines and beautiful beaches. A 10-minute walk to a shopping mall, and only two hours from Disneyland Tokyo.

RV CAMPING & GETAWAYS

Ikego West Valley Recreation Area

Reservation/Contact Number Info: C-011-81-46-806-8010 (Weekends Only). Outdoor Recreation Center, C-011-81-46-816-5732, DSN-315-243-5732.

RV Website: http://get.dodlodging.net/propertys/Ikego-West-Valley-Campgrounds

Other Info Website: http://www.navymwryokosuka.com/

RV Email Address: ikegocampground@fe.navy.mil

Reservations: Campsite and cabin reservations may be made by phone with a valid credit card. Walk-in reservations are available at the Outdoor Recreation Center Thurs-Tue 1000-1800 hours; the Ikego MWR office Mon-Fri 1000-1800, and the Negishi MWR office Mon-Sat 0900-1800. Payment is required at time of reservation.

Season of Operation: Year-round.

Eligibility: AD, Res, Ret, DoD-Civ, 100% DAV.

Tent Spaces: Campsites: BBQ grill, fire pit and picnic table. Accommodate up to 20 campers per site. Rates: $20 daily.

Yurt, A Frame, Cabin, Apt, Spaces: Cabin (5): Three cabins offer solar powered heat and A/C while two remain in a rustic style. None of the cabins offer running water. All cabins and campsites have a designated BBQ grill. Rates: From $40 daily.

Support Facilities: Basketball Court, Commissary, Exchange, Golf Course, Gymnasium, ITT, Restaurant, Swimming Pool.

Activities: Equipment Rental, Hiking, Paintball, Rec Center.

Credit Cards: Mastercard or Visa.

Restrictions: Cabin rentals for Friday night include transportation provided by Outdoor Recreation Center to the campgrounds due to traffic conditions. Return transportation is not provided, however Jinmuji train station on the Keikyu Line is only a short walk from the paintball field.

RV Driving Directions/Location: On Base. Ask for directions at Gate.

Area Description: Ikego Campgrounds is for outdoors enthusiasts who love nature. Campsites on base, located in the West Valley. The campsite is the perfect place to get away from it all and enjoy Mother Nature at her best, with a beautiful view of the pond.

RV Campground Physical Address: Mailing Address: Ikego West Valley Campgrounds, MWR Outdoor Recreation, PSC 473 Box 60, FPO AP Japan 96349.

NORWAY

Stavanger Sola Air Base

Address: Eikesetveien 29 Stavanger, Norway 4032

Information Line: C-011-47-5195-0500/0581.

Main Installation Website: http://www.jwc.nato.int/

Main Base Location: Stavanger is situated on the Southwestern coast of Norway in the county of Rogaland and lies on a line of latitude level with the Southern tip of Alaska.

Base Social Media/Facebook: https://www.facebook.com/NATO.JWC/

Medical: C-47-5195-0563, DSN-314-224-0563.

Exchange: Shoppette, C-0047-5197-0992.

Places to Eat: Many restaurants within a short drive.

Library: Library on base.

MWR: DSN-314-224-0580.
MWR Website:
https://www.426stavanger.com/
Outdoor Recreation: Outdoor
Recreation, DSN-314-224-05801/0582.
Offers camping gear, outdoor sporting
equipment, party inflatables and games,
stand-up paddle boards, snowboards
and more. Offers adventure trips and
activities.
Things To Do: See and appreciate the
area. Stavanger counts its official
founding year as 1125, the year
Stavanger cathedral was completed.
Stavanger's core is to a large degree
18th- and 19th-century wooden houses
that are protected and considered part
of the city's cultural heritage.

RV CAMPING & GETAWAYS

Stavanger Sola Boat House

**Reservation/Contact Number
Info:** Please see
http://www.426stavanger.com/ for
information request email access.
RV Website:
http://www.426stavanger.com/
GPS Coordinates: 58°54'20.2"N
5°43'17.7"E
Reservations: See
http://www.426stavanger.com/ for
more information on how to contact
this facility.
Season of Operation: Year-round.
Eligibility: Contact for eligibility. See
Reservations.
Yurt, A Frame, Cabin, Apt, Spaces: Boat
House (1): Equipped with a small open
room, tables, chairs, a kitchen,
barbeque, bathroom, and outdoor fire
pit. Rates: Contact facility for rates.
Support Facilities: Small pier into the
fjord looking back towards the Three
Swords Monument and Madla a small
grassy yard and ample parking.
RV Driving Directions/Location: Off
Base. Ask for directions at time of
reservation.
Area Description: Located close to the
Sola Airport on the southern edge of
Hafrsfjord.